THE ROUGH GUIDE TO THE

Blues

by

Nigel Williamson

ROUGH
GUIDES

www.roughguides.com

Credits

The Rough Guide to the Blues

Editor: Greg Ward
Layout: Link Hall
Picture research: Matthew Milton
Proofreading: Amanda Jones
Cover design: Chloe Roberts
Production: Katherine Owers

Rough Guides Reference

Series editor: Mark Ellingham
Editors: Peter Buckley, Duncan Clark,
Tracy Hopkins, Sean Mahoney, Matthew Milton,
Joe Staines, Ruth Tidball
Director: Andrew Lockett

Publishing Information

This first edition published February 2007 by
Rough Guides Ltd, 80 Strand, London WC2R 0RL
345 Hudson St, 4th Floor, New York 10014, USA
Email: mail@roughguides.com

Distributed by the Penguin Group:
Penguin Books Ltd, 80 Strand, London WC2R 0RL
Penguin Putnam, Inc., 375 Hudson Street, NY 10014, USA
Penguin Group (Australia), 250 Camberwell Road, Camberwell, Victoria 3124, Australia
Penguin Books Canada Ltd, 190 Eglington Avenue East, Toronto, Ontario, M4P 2YE, Canada
Penguin Group (New Zealand), 67 Apollo Drive, Mairongi Bay, Auckland 1310, New Zealand

Printed in LegoPrint S.p.A

ISBN 13: 978-1-84353-519-5
ISBN 10: 1-84353-519-X

1 3 5 7 9 8 6 4 2

Contents

Foreword

At the age of fifteen, I first experienced the late curtain calls of the last messengers of the seminal Delta music and its contemporary cousin, reaching out from south side Chicago and Detroit. Son House, Bukka White, John Estes, Skip James, and The Howlin' Wolf appeared before me.

If the scratched ancient imagery from vinyl was not enough, then the sight and sounds of these men – uncomfortable, bemused and fêted – has left a shudder of unknowing and mystery with me that still thrills and inspires today.

Nigel Williamson has transported these angel wraiths into the 21st century – breathing new life into a glorious kaleidoscope of Afro-American music.

Robert Plant, November 2006

Introduction

Like many of my generation, I first became aware of the blues as a teenage English rock fan in the late 1960s, buying records by the likes of Cream and the Doors from my local branch of W.H. Smith's.

When I got home, I would spend hours poring over the small print on the album sleeves. In the songwriting credits, I came across names that as yet meant nothing to me, like Robert Johnson, Skip James and Chester Burnett. I was particularly impressed to find that Burnett was credited with songs that had been recorded by both Eric Clapton and Jim Morrison, and resolved to discover who this secret rock god might be. When he turned out to be a black singer of ferocious

power called Howlin' Wolf, who had been born in the Mississippi Delta way back in 1910, my lifetime's fascination with the blues was born.

My early blues library soon contained Bob Dylan's first album, Robert Johnson's *King Of The Delta Blues Singers*, Fleetwood Mac's *Mr Wonderful*, Chicken Shack's *Forty Blues Fingers Freshly Packed And Ready To Serve*, and a Big Bill Broonzy LP on Folkways that I found in a secondhand bin in the basement of Dobell's in

London's Charing Cross Road. However, only when Giles Oakley unveiled his splendid BBC television series on the history of the blues, *The Devil's Music*, in 1976, along with a superb book of the same title, did I come to appreciate how precious the legacy of the original bluesmen really was, and how essential it was to preserve their stories. I became an amateur student of blues history, and while most of my peers were buying records by the Ramones and Patti Smith, I was tracking down albums by Blind Lemon Jefferson and Tampa Red.

For almost forty years, I have been obsessed not only with the blues, but also with the unique social, cultural and geographical circumstances that produced it. What's more, the older I get, the more potent those early country blues records – many of them now seventy or eighty years old – seem to sound through all the hiss and crackle.

Why the music made by black sharecroppers in the Mississippi Delta came to have such a profound impact on middle-class white teenagers, growing up behind the lace curtains of genteel English suburbia, remains one of life's great unsolved riddles. A major factor must have been the sense of mystery with which the blues is imbued, and the connection it seemed to offer with another world. Steve Winwood once told me that in the gray and drab surroundings of the post-war West Midlands, blues was the world music exotica of its day. I know what he means; the next time I experienced the sensation I felt upon first hearing John Lee Hooker in the 1960s was some twenty years later, when I was introduced to the work of Ali Farka Touré. For me and many others, that in turn awakened a fresh fascination with the musical connections between Mali and Mississippi, and how the blues itself may have crossed the Atlantic in the slave ships centuries ago.

This book is divided into two principal sections – a narrative history of the blues, followed by an A–Z gazetteer of the three hundred or so most significant blues artists, from 1920 to the present day. If the history section seems a lit-

tle shorter than you might at first expect, that's to avoid the danger of pointless and confusing duplication with the A–Z. It's clearly important to provide a chronological overview at the start; even the most comprehensive "Who's Who" cannot hope to discuss how the great blues performers and the various blues styles – not to mention other black American musical forms such as ragtime and jazz – interacted and influenced each other. However, there's little point in giving a blow-by-blow account of the recording career of Muddy Waters in the narrative history, despite his crucial role, when that information most usefully belongs in the substantial biography of Muddy in the A–Z. Maintaining that distinction between the two main sections of the book makes it easier to use them in conjunction with each other, and also enables the history to offer a more concise and accessible account of the origins of the blues, and the social and musical trends that influenced its development.

Compiling the A–Z was hardly a straightforward task. All too frequently, the lives of the great bluesmen are as mysterious as their music. In some instances, we don't know the date or place of their birth. Sometimes we don't even know how or when they died. The standard blues reference works repeat an astonishing number of conflicting stories and much contradictory information. Compare two accounts and you might easily find that one describes the subject as living in Chicago, when the other claims that at the same time he was playing the clubs of Beale Street in Memphis.

This is hardly surprising. When the early blues musicians were recorded in the 1920s and 1930s, no one really cared where they came from or what their stories were. What we know now has been painstakingly pieced together by subsequent generations of researchers and scholars. Often that information is based on oral history, and when you're relying on memories of undocumented events as much as half a century in the past, a certain amount of conflicting evidence and fallible testimony is inevitable. Where we found such contradictions, we could choose to take a decision based on the balance of probability, or to leave the issue unresolved. While we believe this book to hold the most thorough and meticulous consolidation of blues biography yet assembled, we can't promise the unerring accuracy of every detail. We'd be delighted to hear from any readers who have information or corrections that could be incorporated into future editions.

As to the criteria for inclusion, no two authorities define the blues in quite the same way. You can deconstruct the rhythmical arrangement of a twelve-bar motif, or dissect the flattened third and seventh notes of the scale, but most blues musicians will simply tell you that the blues is an emotional feeling rather than an analyzable style. Inevitably, therefore, there's a certain degree of subjectivity about who was selected. We make no apologies for the preponderance of historical names over present-day acts. There are plenty of modern blues bands working the circuit who offer a great night out, and whose fans might reasonably object to their omission here. But with the best will in the world, many of them rely on imitation rather than innovation. While we never drew up a formal checklist of requirements to merit inclusion, a modicum of originality would certainly have been near the top if we had.

Those names we did include are equally open to debate. Was Billie Holiday a blues or jazz singer? Couldn't the space given to blues-rock bands like the Rolling Stones and Led Zeppelin, or to rock'n'rollers such as Chuck Berry and Bo Diddley, be better used to spotlight some of the more obscure but authentic blues performers still plying their trade in tiny bars and roadhouses across the South? However, while no one is claiming that the Stones or Chuck Berry were exclusively or even predominantly blues performers, both played a significant part in blues history. One of the calls we made from the very outset was to accept the blues as a broad church, which runs from Alger "Texas" Alexander singing "Levee Camp Moan" to ZZ Top's reinterpretation of "Dust My Broom".

Finally, a word about the albums recommended for each performer. Many artists are represented by compilations for the simple reason that purpose-made studio albums by blues artists did not become common until the 1960s. Before then, the blues format was always the single, and those albums that did exist were merely compilations of material previously available on 78 or 45. In many cases, particularly where an artist's work has gone out of copyright and entered the public domain, a bewildering number of compilations are now available on all sorts of labels, frequently containing overlapping material. In these instances, compilations have been chosen on a variety of criteria, including comprehensiveness, sound quality, packaging, price and ready availability.

Nigel Williamson

Acknowledgments

Special thanks go to Giles Oakley and Charlie Gillett for their early blues education when I was still a long-haired rock fan who couldn't tell the difference between Peg Leg Howell and "Cripple" Clarence Lofton, and to Mick Linton, who lent me his wonderful collection of old country blues LPs for safekeeping in 1976, while he went backpacking around the world. I looked after them so well that thirty years on I've still got 'em. Thanks also to Nicola Powell and, of course, Robert Plant.

Further thanks go to Mark Ellingham and Andrew Lockett at Rough Guides and, closer to home, to my wife Magali and our two adult sons Adam and Piers, who during the year I spent writing this book were forced to listen to an endless diet of Robert Johnson, Blind Willie McTell and several hundred others. It should have been enough to give anyone those mean and moaning blues, but miraculously they kept smiling throughout.

Part One

The Story

Chapter One

African roots & slavery days

Where did the blues begin? That debate has long exercised academics and ethnomusicologists, and probably generated more heat than light. However, the truth is surely that the blues began several million times over. It was born again and again, every time another African gazed for the last time at the land of his or her birth as the slave ships hauled anchor and began their terrifying journey across the ocean into the unknown, leaving Mother Africa behind forever.

Many never completed the journey and died on the voyage, their bodies unceremoniously thrown overboard into the turbulent waters of the Atlantic. For those who survived the grueling voyage, a cruelly unfathomable life awaited, in which the only certainties were captivity and misery. To look out through the slave gate at La Maison des Esclaves ("Slave House") on Goree Island just off the Atlantic coast of Senegal is to understand where the blues began. There were hundreds of similar slaving posts up and down the coast of West Africa, but Goree is one of the best preserved, and is now maintained by UNESCO as a world heritage site. After the bustle of Dakar, its tranquility is beguiling, with its pastel-colored old buildings and bougainvillea over growing the narrow streets. But it's deceptive, too.

During the 18th and 19th centuries, the island was one of the busiest slave centers in West Africa, and a tour of the Slave House, built by the Dutch in 1776, is a chilling experience. Guides explain how slaves were stuffed into pens measuring ten by six meters, and inspected and priced like animals; how they were chained to the walls, and sea water was piped into the rooms to keep them subdued and in partial submersion; how they were forced to fight for food, to ensure that only the stronger specimens survived; how the weaker ones who died were fed to the sharks; and how the survivors were then branded with the shipping company's insignia before they were packed tightly into the holds of the slave ships for transportation.

When **Nelson Mandela** visited Goree, he dismissed all his aides and flunkies for an hour in order to sit in solitary contemplation in the grim hole, no larger than a dog kennel, where the more obstinate slaves were confined in punishment. Although he had spent long years in captivity on Robben Island, he still felt there was nothing in his experience that enabled him fully to comprehend the enormity of slavery.

No account of the evolution of the blues could be complete without an overview of how millions of people were uprooted and displaced from their African homes and forcibly resettled in the Americas, and of the life of misery and hardship that awaited them there.

The first **slaves** from West Africa arrived in North America in 1619, ironically a year before the Pilgrim Fathers landed at Plymouth, Massachusetts, in search of their own idea of freedom. "About the last of August came a Dutch man-of-war that sold us 20 Negars", wrote Captain John Smith in his *History Of Virginia*. Soon the slave trade was in full swing, as men, women and children from "the slave coast" – comprising what we now know as Benin, Cameroon, the Democratic Republic of Congo, Gabon, Gambia, Ghana, Guinea, Ivory Coast, Liberia, Nigeria, Senegal, Sierra Leone and Togo – were transported thousands of miles across the Atlantic to meet the New World's growing demand for labor. The average life expectancy of a slave once he or she had arrived in the Americas was less than ten years, so the need for a continual supply was almost insatiable.

That demand was supplied by traders from Britain, France, Holland, Spain and Portugal, who transported goods to the west coast of Africa and then exchanged them for cargos of slaves. While it brought enormous prosperity to Europe, the toll on Africa was horrendous. The number of slaves transported over nearly three centuries has been estimated at between 35 and 40 million, although further uncountable numbers were killed in the quest for their capture. Only some fifteen million ever arrived at their intended destination in the New World, for the conditions in which slaves were shipped were appalling. Eighteenth-century diagrams

African culture

It is commonplace today to recognize the influence of African culture on the blues and other aspects of black American life. But it was not always so. Even half a century ago, the myth persisted that Africa was a "dark continent", devoid of any history before the coming of the Europeans and the subsequent colonial era. However, when the traders and slavers arrived in the 17th century, they found sophisticated societies and political systems, organized into kingdoms and empires that were dominated by tribal groupings. Among the most important were the Mandingo, the Ashanti, the Fulani, the Ibo, the Fanti and the Jolof.

The culture, of course, was an oral one, and so the role of the *griot* as the repository of tribal history and mythology was all-important. As they continue to do to this day, the *griots* acted as broadcasters of news and weavers of tales, and were invested with an almost magical aura. Music was one of the key means by which they communicated, so they were also professional musicians. Indeed, music was and remains all-pervasive in African society, an integral part of existence along with drumming and dance. There were songs for every aspect of day-to-day life or social occasion, including hunting, pounding maize, going to war, and religious ceremonies. The characteristic "call and response" style of vocals, was complemented by a wide assortment of musical instruments, many of them of considerable sophistication.

While the slaves were of course unable to transport their instruments, they took their songs and voices, and soon fashioned instruments out of the materials available in the New World. Although they were so far from home, the music they brought with them survived, handed down from generation to generation on the plantations, and it was eventually to have a profound influence on the birth of both jazz and blues. As described on p.69, much academic research has focused on the similarities between contemporary African music and the blues, and a number of collaborations between African and American musicians have attempted to give practical expression to the link.

of the ships' stowage reveal them to have been chained and packed below decks like sardines in a can. Disease, dehydration and suffocation were common, and no one could argue with the conclusion of **John Reader** in his *Africa – A Biography Of A Continent* (1997), that the layouts display "a meticulous concern for mechanical efficiency that ranks with the Holocaust for its callous inhumanity". Voyages could last nine or ten months, and it was not unusual for almost half of a cargo of slaves to die of dysentery en route. The sick were often thrown overboard with the corpses to avoid further contamination. Conditions were so bad that the slaves who died may arguably have even been the lucky ones. The air on the slave decks was so fetid that candles would not burn, and a traveler on one ship reported that the floor was "so covered with blood and mucus … that it resembles a slaughterhouse. It is not in the power of the human imagination to picture to itself a situation more dreadful or disgusting."

Even so, inevitably, those who managed to survive the terrifying journey across the Atlantic brought their African identity with them. As the South African pianist **Abdullah Ibrahim** has pointed out: "People say that slaves were taken from Africa. This is not true. People were taken from Africa, among them healers and priests, and were made into slaves." Their lives may have been stolen. But the spiritual beliefs, tribal customs and traditional music they carried in their heads stayed with them.

The growth of slavery in the South

The first slaves to arrive in Virginia were legally "indentured servants", who in theory could gain their freedom after working for a fixed number of years. By 1661, however – at which point it's estimated that there were still only five thousand slaves in North America – Virginia had legalized slavery, and other American colonies soon followed suit.

The New England colonies in the north had little need of slave labor, as they were already prosperous small farming communities. As early as 1630, Massachusetts passed a law protecting African slaves on the run from their cruel masters. By 1652, Rhode Island had become the first state in the Americas to outlaw slavery, imposing a ten-year limitation that restored the original concept of indentured servitude. An English law of 1686 imposed a death penalty on any master who wilfully killed a slave or servant, and in 1712, Pennsylvania became the first state to prohibit the slave trade.

However in the wide-open spaces of the sparsely-settled but fertile **South**, it was a different story. Labor was in short supply, and the white workforce was both too small and unwilling to put in the back-breaking effort necessary to exploit the land. Slaves provided the answer. By the end of the 17th century, 23,000 of the 28,000 slaves in the American colonies were to be found in the South. After the slave trade was opened up in 1698 to any ship flying the British flag, the first half of the 18th century saw a dramatic increase in the numbers transported from Africa, mostly by traders based in Bristol and Liverpool. By the start of the 19th century, there were one million blacks in America, almost all of them slaves. The demand for a ready supply of able bodies was at first led by the labor-intensive **tobacco** plantations, followed by rice, sugar and – ultimately the most voracious devourer of "field slaves" – **cotton**. The plantation owners also leased their slaves in gangs to construction companies to build houses, docks, bridges, roads, and eventually the railroads. They were cheaper to employ than poor whites, and there was less trouble if they were whipped and beaten and died on the job.

The Abolition struggle

In 1774, **Thomas Jefferson** accused Great Britain of standing in the way of the abolition of the slave trade, which he stated was one of the key goals of the American colonists (though Jefferson himself owned hundreds of slaves over his lifetime and was a plantation owner). Slavery thus became a burning issue in the **War of Independence**, which began the following year and lasted eight years. However, the 1776 Declaration of Independence, with its ringing proclamation that all men had been created equal with an alienable right to "life, liberty and the pursuit of happiness" was simply taken by white landowners in the South as not applying to slaves, who were regarded as property rather than persons. At least when the newly independent United States ultimately agreed its constitution, in 1787, it included a 20-year moratorium on the slave trade. On January 1, 1808, Congress duly banned the importation of slaves into the United States.

While the smuggling of slaves into the US continued for many years, that was only part of the problem. The act that ended the slave trade had said nothing about the plight of the estimated one million slaves already living in the country, and it effectively served to boost their value. As the cotton fields spread across the South, breeding was intensified, and a vigorous trade sprang up in selling slaves between different states.

Meanwhile, the campaign for the **abolition** of slavery itself grew in the North, led by newspapers such as *Freedom's Journal* and *The Liberator*. But the gradual admission of Southern states into the Union, including Mississippi in 1817 and Alabama two years later, created new tensions. Stephen Miller, the governor of South Carolina, notoriously insisted in 1829 that "Slavery is not a national evil; it is a national benefit". Blacks were only suffered to breathe the same air because they were an economic necessity. A dozen years later, the South Carolina legislature even passed a law prohibiting black and white mill workers from

looking out of the same window. And all the time, the black population was growing, reaching 4.4 million by 1860.

Life on the plantations

Plantation life was hard. Contrary to popular misconceptions, however, most plantations were small, family-run affairs. Large plantations, employing a hundred slaves or more, certainly did exist, but they were the exception rather than the rule. At the start of the 19th century, only fifteen percent of slave owners had more than twenty slaves, and many owned just two or three. Those who worked in the "**Big House**" of the plantation owner were considered not so much slaves as "**house servants**". The tough, resourceful but always obliging and cheerful "Mammy", with her range of duties in the Big House, became a legendary figure who was later much sentimentalized. But it was the **field slaves** who made the plantations the engine of the Southern economy. Field slaves were expected to work from "can to can't" – from the moment they could see in the day's first light until darkness mercifully ended their labor. Planting, tending and harvesting were the most obvious chores. But slaves also looked after the livestock and worked as builders, carpenters, mechanics and blacksmiths. In slack times, they were hired out in gangs by their owners to the construction companies building roads, bridges and later railroads. Initially, sugar cane and tobacco were America's principal export to Europe, and source of foreign exchange. Following the invention of the cotton gin, however, and the use of slave labor to clear the Mississippi Delta of its dense hardwood forests from 1835 onwards, the vast alluvial plain was given over to the growth of **cotton**.

Slaves worked in gangs led by a "driver" or overseer, often black himself, who allocated their day's tasks. If they failed to complete them by nightfall, lashings were routine. Those who tried to escape this harsh life by running away were hunted by tracker dogs, brought back and beaten and whipped, sometimes to death.

Apologists for the system talked of the paternalist responsibilities of a plantation master to provide his slaves with protection, food and shelter. Few, if any, slaves saw it like that – particularly as families were commonly and callously split up through the sale of a wife, husband or children considered surplus to requirements. **Sam Chatmon**, born on a plantation in 1899 and one of the family of musicians who formed the **Mississippi Sheiks** in the 1930s, recalled his ex-slave father describing the harsh living conditions before abolition: "He said when he was a child big enough to remember it, they'd go to these barns and get this corn, mixed with this rat stuff, rat waste I'll call it, I won't say the other part. The old ladies would take that on to the children right out there in the pen and mix that stuff up in a big wooden trough and they'd get down and eat it, just like hogs."

Only on a Saturday night and Sunday were the slaves allowed any free time. Inevitably, **music** was at the center of their limited social activities. Sunday meant the compulsory church service, but on Saturday night they got to let their hair down. Drums and horns were forbidden via laws such as the Black Codes of Mississippi, on the grounds that such instruments could be used to communicate and organize revolt. But rudimentary fiddles and banjos and singing and dancing offered vehicles for indigenous forms of expression, still recognizably rooted in Africa.

Out of the frying pan and into the fire: from slavery to segregation

The abolition struggle came to a head with the election of **Abraham Lincoln** as president in November 1860. Although Lincoln was personally opposed to slavery, he did not believe

King Cotton

Celebrated and cursed alike in popular song, cotton was central to the lives of African slaves and their descendants, and unsurprisingly became a powerful motif in the blues. The white, downy fibers of the cotton plant, which flatten as they dry, have been spun and woven since time immemorial. But it was Eli Whitney's invention of the cotton gin in 1793 that revolutionized the farming of cotton and rendered it central to Afro-American folklore. The Southern climate was perfect for growing cotton, and America had exported its first bale to Britain just eight years earlier. Whitney's machine, which separated the cotton fibers from the seeds, enabled huge tracts of the South to be turned into vast plantations. Its impact was immediate upon the length and breadth of the Mississippi Delta and beyond, for cotton devoured labor. Planted in April, the crop required months of constant attention in a process known as "chopping out", as the rows between the plants are weeded and the earth plowed and then banked up around the plants to provide support. During the hottest time in July, the plants needed less attention (hence the line in the song, "summertime and the living is easy"). But it was only a brief respite before the intense labor of the harvest began in August. Picking the cotton was particularly difficult, for the crop clung tenaciously to the boll.

Before the invention of the cotton gin, forty percent of the population of the South were slaves. A quarter of a century later it had shot past fifty percent. The thirty thousand blacks in the state of Mississippi in 1817 had reached 435,000 by the Civil War less than half a century later. The cotton owners grew hugely wealthy. Yet even after the abolition of slavery, their black workers retained the chains of poverty as sharecroppers. The economy of the plantation did not fundamentally alter until 1948 – and it was no liberal piece of legislation in Washington that brought about the change, but the invention of a mechanical picker by the International Harvester company.

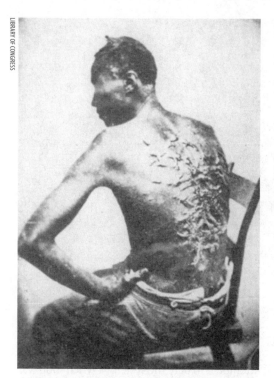

LIBRARY OF CONGRESS

A whipped slave ("Peter"), Baton Rouge, Louisiana, April 2, 1863. His testimony: "Overseer Artayou Carrier whipped me. I was two months in bed sore from the whipping. My master come after I was whipped; he discharged the overseer."

he had the constitutional power to abolish it. Nonetheless, South Carolina was so alarmed at his election that it voted to leave the Union within a month, an action swiftly copied by the slave states of Mississippi, Alabama, Georgia, Florida, Louisiana and Texas. Forming the Confederate States of America, they were swiftly joined by North Carolina, Arkansas, Tennessee and Virginia. The bloody Civil War that followed ostensibly focused on secession rather than slavery. Lincoln came to embrace emancipation as one of his fundamental aims, partly in the hope that it would encourage slaves in the South to revolt. On January 1, 1863, he therefore issued the **Proclamation of Emancipation**. Half a million black slaves duly fled north, and a fair number ended up fighting in the Union army.

Not until January 1865, however, was Lincoln able to persuade Congress to amend the Constitution and outlaw slavery, and that was by

a single vote. By April that year, the Confederate forces had surrendered, and the war was over, though Lincoln himself was assassinated that same month.

After the Civil War, many former slaves moved north and west, particularly to communities already established by freedmen. The vast majority, however, remained in the South, where the economy had been shattered. After the failure of the all-too-brief era known as **Reconstruction**, during which there were genuine attempts to integrate black and white society – in 1875, Congress even passed a Civil Rights bill that made all public racial discrimination illegal, but it was declared unconstitutional eight years later – the North and its politicians effectively washed their hands of the problems of the defeated South. The Southern states were left to their own devices once more; as Giles Oakley put it in his splendid book *The Devil's Music* (1976), the black population of the South "had been abandoned as a ward of the nation".

By 1880, not only were 75 percent of the blacks in the US still living in the Southern states, but the vast majority were still involved in the same kind of agricultural work they had followed before the Civil War, as a feudal system of farm tenancy replaced slavery on the plantations. Under **sharecropping**, a black worker was allocated a plot of land that was his to farm on behalf of the plantation owner, who provided the "furnishings" – housing (inevitably a poorly-constructed, leaking, weather-beaten wood-framed cabin), food, clothing, seed and tools to work the land. After harvest time, when the cotton crop was split fifty–fifty between owner and sharecropper, came the "figurin'" when the landlord calculated what he had provided on credit during the course of the year and deducted it from his tenant's share of the crop. With no way to ensure the fairness of the calculation, the balance sheet was invariably rigged against the sharecropper, who found himself in debt to the landowner. Locked into a cycle of dependence he could not escape, any dreams of making enough money to buy his own land rapidly faded.

The economic repression of the officially emancipated black community was accompanied by a political system of white supremacy known as **segregation**. As the Southern states were readmitted to the Union one by one, and their power to pass their own laws was restored, they ruthlessly set about creating a legal basis for white supremacy. In theory, whites and blacks were "separate but equal". In practice, nothing could have been further from the truth as a system of Segregation Statutes were passed, known as the "**Jim Crow**" laws – the name taken from the blackface minstrel character created by white English migrant Thomas "Daddy" Rice. The laws ostracized blacks and made them second-class citizens. Formal sanctions blocked access to decent housing, jobs, schools, hospitals and public transportation, and ensured that African Americans were kept unskilled, uneducated and living in poverty. Even in death, segregation continued:

LIBRARY OF CONGRESS

Painting depicting Abraham Lincoln (center) at the reading of the Emancipation Proclamation.

many morgues and cemeteries were whites-only. By the end of the 19th century, fourteen states had enacted such laws. For anyone who attempted to defy the system, a lynch mob was waiting to deal out its own terrifying version of summary justice, while those black enterprises, shops and churches that did exist were regularly vandalized or burned to the ground. Several Southern newspapers even backed a crack-brained campaign that urged the US government to seize part of Mexico and turn it into a black homeland.

Chapter Two

African-American music begins

By the end of the Civil War, African-American music had become a highly sophisticated synthesis of the traditions brought by slaves from Africa and the European-derived styles and forms of the white settlers. After the end of forced mass immigration from Africa, when the slave ships had ceased their trade in human suffering, the old traditions were kept alive by oral transmission – just as they had been for generations via the griot tradition back in Africa.

The earliest recorded 17th-century descriptions of the music of the slaves refer to a "loud and shrill" style sung with "strong nasal tones" in African tongues. This African musical heritage remained strong, and was never eradicated. But over time, it was tempered by the vocal style of the hymns and psalms of the rural churches and prayer meetings across the South, attended by European settlers and their black slaves alike. The result was a syncopated kind of religious song that came to be known as the "**negro spiritual**". By 1782, the first black church had been established in Savannah, Georgia. In 1801, a hymnal was published called *A Collection Of Spiritual Songs And Hymns Selected From Various Authors*. Its author – "Richard Allen, African Minister" – went on to become the leader of the African Methodist Episcopal Church and America's first black bishop. Just as significantly, the hymnal was the first codified collection of specifically black music.

The negro spiritual was radically different from the European hymn, as one disapproving Methodist, writing in the late-18th century, made clear: "They sing for hours together, short scraps of disjointed affirmations, pledges or prayers, lengthened out with long repetition choruses. These are all sung in the merry chorus manner of the southern harvest field, or husking frolic method, of the slave blacks. This was hardly the way a God-fearing person should behave." The style was developed further at so-called "camp meetings" – revivalist services held in the woods that attracted thousands, both black and white. Contemporary reports make it clear that the two races sang in contrasting styles: the black congregation being louder, more fervent and free-spirited. Their African roots were also apparent in the dancing at such meetings.

In addition to the influence of the vocal music of the Christian churches, some slaves learned

Spirituals

After the Civil War, **negro spirituals** came to be seen by many whites as the grateful expression of a noble people who had been freed. It was this attitude that led to the formation in 1871 of the **Fisk Jubilee Singers**, who assembled at Fisk University, which was set up in Nashville by Northerners who were keen to provide education for newly freed slaves. Performing sanitized, concert-hall versions of authentic spirituals, as sung by slaves across the South, the Fisk Singers toured America and Europe in order to try and raise funds for the university. Their success ensured that their style was much copied, and songs such as "Swing Low Sweet Chariot", "Nobody Knows The Trouble I Seen", and "Ain't Goin' To Study War No More" all became widely known and popular.

to play European musical instruments, usually the fiddle, but also horns and even the piano. The advertisement columns of early American newspapers show that by the 18th century, the musical skills of slaves were proudly listed to increase their market value when they were sold at auction. Slaves also used home-made stringed instruments, often constructed from **gourds**, to accompany songs about the harsh conditions of slavery. In his journal for 1774, **Nicholas Cresswell** recorded seeing slaves in Maryland dancing to a banjo made out of a gourd: "something in the imitation of a guitar with only four strings". The slaves, he wrote, "would sing in a very satirical manner about the way they were treated, the words and music being rude and uncultivated". We cannot know exactly how that "rude and uncultivated" music sounded, but this could well be the first description of something we might recognize as the forerunner of a blues song.

FISK JUBILEE SINGERS

THE ORIGINAL

Organized Oct. 6th, 1871

UNDER EXCLUSIVE CONTROL OF

THE CENTRAL LYCEUM BUREAU,

Another description of the music of a newly arrived shipload of slaves was published in London in 1816. "They have great amusement in collecting together in groups and singing their favorite African songs; the energy of their action is more remarkable than the harmony of their music", wrote **George Pinckard**. He also described a group of slaves on board a ship in the harbor at Savannah, Georgia, newly arrived from Guinea: "We saw them dance and heard them sing. In dancing they scarcely moved their feet but threw about their arms and twisted and writhed their bodies into a multitude of disgusting and indecent attitudes. Their singing was a wild yell devoid of all softness and harmony, and loudly chanted in harsh harmony."

Such accounts are rare, as most whites at the time still regarded the songs and hollers of slaves as too primitive to be worth documenting. However, in the cities black musicianship was thriving and beginning to be recognized. By the early 19th century Philadelphia boasted an all-black marching band as well as a woodwind band led by the black musician **Frank Johnson**, who even toured England and performed for Queen Victoria in 1838. When **Charles Dickens** visited New York in 1842, he described enjoying the spectacle of "a corpulent black fiddler and his friend who played the tambourine", and he also saw "master **Juba**". Born William Henry Lane in 1825, Juba was the best-known black dancer of jigs and reels, and is today widely regarded as a key link between authentic African dance forms and the blackface minstrel shows that became increasingly popular in the second half of the 19th century.

New Orleans

New Orleans played a critical role in the development and dissemination of the uniquely Afro-American forms of **jazz**, **ragtime** and **blues**. Louisiana enjoyed a remarkable confluence of ethnic groups, the richness and diversity of which was unmatched anywhere else in North America. Its swamplands were first inhabited by Native American **Choctaws**, and then colonized by France just before the 18th century.

Besides the influx of African slaves, many French-Canadians (known as Acadians) poured into Louisiana after they were expelled from Canada by the British in 1755. The Spanish then took over the territory from 1766 until 1801, when it briefly returned to French control before being sold to the United States in 1803. That brought a fresh wave of people to the region, while New Orleans' role as a major seaport introduced Cuban and West Indian influences

into the city. The result was a multi-lingual, multi-cultural population, many of whom strove tenaciously to preserve their different heritages. In the city's free and easy atmosphere, both vice and voodoo flourished, and the different communities inevitably intermingled, not least in the gambling houses, drinking dens and brothels. The clientele in such establishments required entertainment, of course, and music and dancing thrived.

By the early 19th century, one third of the 36,000 population of New Orleans was estimated to be black. The center of their cultural activity became Place Congo – also known as **Congo Square** – where African dancing became a huge attraction. Each group of dancers was accompanied by a band, and the architect **Benjamin Latrobe** described watching one of them in 1820. "The music consists of two drums and a stringed instrument … which no doubt was imported from Africa," he wrote. "On the top fingerboard was the rude figure of a man in a sitting posture, and two pegs behind him to which strings were fastened. It was played upon by a very little old man, apparently 80 or 90 years old."

In due course, brass bands, black orchestras and Creole singers flourished in the Crescent City, creating the crucible from which ragtime and jazz emerged. That rich musical heritage also had a major influence on the birth of the **blues**, as it swiftly spread throughout the Delta via the traveling musicians who performed on the paddle boats that plied the mighty Mississippi River.

This process was dramatically quickened by the upheavals in American society brought about by the Civil War. For the first time, the post war period saw serious attempts to document and collect black music, such as the 1867 publication of *Slave Songs Of The United States*. The music encompassed spirituals, authentic work songs and field hollers, and the "coon songs" of the increasingly popular minstrel companies.

Playlist
"Choo Choo Ch'boogie": Train songs in the blues

The railroad transformed American life in the 19th century – and became a rich subject for song. There were endless stories about legendary engineers, conductors and railroad catastrophes, and the train also became a metaphor for escape and freedom, one with an obvious fascination for itinerant bluesmen.

1 MONKEY & THE ENGINEER Jesse Fuller from **The Lone Cat Sings And Plays Jazz, Folk Songs, Spirituals And Blues**
"The engineer wanted a bite to eat, so he left the monkey sitting on the driver's seat. The monkey pulled the throttle, locomotive jumped the gun, doin' 90 miles an hour down the mainline run…"

2 KASSIE JONES Furry Lewis from **Classic Railroad Songs From Smithsonian Folkways**
One of several songs based on the story of the railroad engineer John Luther Jones, killed in a freight train collision in 1900. The story was first told on record in song by Fiddlin' John Carson in 1923.

3 TRAIN KEPT A-ROLLIN' Tiny Bradshaw from **The Great Composer**
Later a staple for the Yardbirds, but originally recorded by the jump blues pioneer and bandleader Tiny Bradshaw for King Records in 1951.

4 LOVE IN VAIN Robert Johnson from **King Of The Delta Blues Singers**
"When the train left the station it had two lights on behind, the blue light was my baby and the red light was my mind…"

5 FREIGHT TRAIN Elizabeth Cotten from **Freight Train & Other North Carolina Folk Songs & Tunes**
One of the oldest train songs in existence; Elizabeth Cotten, who was born in 1895, recalled singing it as a child. She eventually recorded it in 1957, after Pete Seeger had popularized it.

6 MIDNIGHT SPECIAL Leadbelly from **Classic Railroad Songs From Smithsonian Folkways**
The night train heard by prisoners in jails across the South became a symbol of freedom. In addition to Leadbelly's famous version, the Library of Congress also has renditions from prisons in Texas, Louisiana, Alabama and Mississippi.

7 PRETTIEST TRAIN '22' from **Negro Prison Blues & Songs**
Recorded by Alan Lomax and performed by an unknown prisoner in Parchman Farm penitentiary in 1947–48, and later covered by Odetta among others.

8 ALL ABOARD Muddy Waters from **His Best 1956–64**
Muddy rocking like a train, complete with an unforgettable duel between harmonica players James Cotton and Little Walter.

9 DOWNBOUND TRAIN Chuck Berry from **Chuck Berry: The Anthology**
Backed by a superb Chess house band of Otis Spann on piano, Willie Dixon on bass and Eddie Hardy on drums.

10 BIG RAILROAD BLUES Cannon's Jug Stompers from **The Best Of Cannon's Jug Stompers**
Written by Noah Lewis and later covered by the Grateful Dead, who loved train songs – in fact they began life as a jug band called Mother McCree's Uptown Jug Champions.

Work songs, field hollers and prison songs

Although the spirituals and minstrel shows are better known, the most authentic form of 19th-century black music, in the sense of having the deepest roots in the slaves' African heritage, was the **work song**. On the plantations, field workers would sing or "holler" together while picking cotton. The words were highly repetitious, and the melodies strident and full of blue notes (notes that sound a bit "off" – often bent notes or flattened fifths). The entire performance was frequently interspersed with moaning, humming, whistling and other wordless sounds. The architect **Frederick Olmsted** described the

hollering of a gang of slaves in South Carolina in 1853: "One raised such a sound as I had never heard before, a long, loud, musical shout, rising and falling and breaking into falsetto, his voice ringing through the woods in the clear, frosty night air like a bugle call. As he finished the melody was caught up by another and the another, then by several in chorus."

Freed blacks began to seek employment on the riverboats along the Mississippi, in levee gangs guarding the river banks to control flooding, in saw mills, turpentine camps and in the construction of the rapidly advancing railroads. A culture of folk song developed around each and every one of these occupations. Meanwhile, in the fields, where sharecropping meant that laborers worked in smaller groups or alone, the practice of "hollering" became a more personal expression, although it also allowed for a strident call-and-response communication between workers in adjacent plots, who could hear but not see each other.

Like all folk music, the songs were changed and improvised upon, so no one can claim exclusive authorship. But many of them survive to this day, such as "**John Henry**", the tale of a black rail worker who, depending upon the version sung, either worked himself to death trying to compete with a mechanized steam drill or was crushed in a cave-in while excavating a tunnel. The story's origins are thought to lie in an incident that occurred during the construction of the Big Bend Tunnel on the **C&O Railroad** in the 1870s.

Such songs were often adapted from, or grafted onto, folk ballads that can be traced back to English, Irish and Scottish antecedents. By the late 19th century, a black ballad tradition had developed, characterized by dramatic narrative storytelling in songs that not only recorded the heroic exploits of such unfortunates as John Henry but frequently celebrated "bad" characters and outlaws such as the gambler and murderer **Stagger Lee**, or **Frankie**, who shot and killed her cheating lover **Albert** (or in some versions, Johnny). Many of these songs later became staples of the blues repertoire. Passed

Everybody's walkin' the cake

In addition to their work songs and spirituals, slaves also made music for their own entertainment, especially for **dancing** on a Saturday night. One of the most famous descriptions of such a dance comes from a book called *The Old Plantation And What I Gathered There In An Autumn Month*, written by **James Hungerford**, shortly before abolition in 1859. Hungerford described a pair of singers called Ike and Clotilda and a fiddler called **Uncle Porringer** at a moonlit dance outside their quarters on the edge of the woods: "Upon benches placed against the outside wall of the hut upon each side of the door sat several of the older negroes of both sexes from the neighborhood. Ike was singing the words of a jig in a monotonous tone of voice, beating time meanwhile with his hands alternately against each other and against his body. To this music, about a dozen or so Negro boys and girls were dancing on the hard beaten ground. As soon as she joined the throng, Clotilda without a moment's pause whirled herself among and through the crowd of dancers till, having gained the opposite side to that at which she had entered, she turned and faced them and began to recite verses in a shrill song-song voice, keeping time to the measure, as Ike had done, by beating her hands sometimes against her sides and patting the ground with her feet." The writer goes on to describe Uncle Porringer taking up the fiddle, with the encouragement of a bucket of cider sent down from the "big house", and eventually leaving the multitude dancing into the night to "a lively and rattling jig tune". In the *Curious Listener's Guide To The Blues*, David Evans attributes the origins of the blues riff – a short, repeated, melodic-rhythmic figure that was also later to have a major role in rock music – to such dance tunes, played variously on makeshift banjos, fiddles and washboards, and by fife-and-drum bands.

An anonymous description of a barn dance in Ohio, published in the *Illustrated London News* in 1897, described a similar but more formal affair involving a "graceful and pretty" dance called "The Plantation Quadrille", to which "the older people seated round the room kept rhythmic time … by clapping their hands together, then on one knee, then on the other, stamping the foot the while and singing with great gusto". What this report went on to describe was in fact the **cakewalk**, a form of plantation entertainment in which couples in fancy dress would promenade to the music, and at the end of the evening the best turned-out couple, as voted by a jury of community elders, would "take the cake". This tradition was soon to give birth to the music known as **ragtime**, which in turn had a profound influence on the development of both jazz and the blues.

on by itinerant workers, they also often took on a new and profound symbolism. The train, for example, came to represent a route to freedom, and was soon incorporated into spirituals about trains that were "bound for glory", or about "the gospel train" taking the singers to salvation.

Yet freedom for many remained an impossible dream; for most former slaves, jail was a more likely destination, as blacks were incarcerated on the slightest of pretexts. In prison, they worked in gangs, just as they had under the old system of slavery, with brutal white guards delivering regular beatings to those who slacked. The prisoners sang partly to create a rhythm to work to, but also to let out their emotions and, in the process, perhaps to make their plight a little more bearable.

Minstrel shows

The black vaudeville characters of "**Zip Coon**" and "**Jim Crow**" first emerged in the US during the 1830s – except they weren't

A contemporary cartoon of the blackface minstrel "Zip Coon" (George Dixon)

black at all, but two white performers, their faces blacked-up with burnt cork, who presented the characters as figures of fun and derision. Zip Coon, an "uppity" black dressed in his master's cast-offs who became one of the enduring stereotypes of minstrelsy, was the creation of **George Washington Dixon**. We owe Jim Crow, his poorly dressed Southern relative, to **Thomas "Daddy" Rice**, who based the character on a hobbled black man he had seen dancing and singing on the streets for coins. Such depictions were based on a series of misconceptions, stereotypes and caricatures, and were quite reasonably described by Kevin Phinney, in *Souled America: How Black Music Transformed American Culture*,

as "the antics of those with no taste attempting to please people with bad taste at the expense of those whose tastes were unconsidered". By the 1840s, white American society had developed a liking for black slave songs performed by blacked-up white minstrels. Edwin P. Christy led one of the first and most famous troupes, and his **Christy Minstrels** even toured England to great acclaim. The popularity of such groups grew after the Civil War; other well-known examples included the Virginia Minstrels, the Moore and Burgess Minstrels, and the Ethiopian Serenaders, all of whom sang a similar repertoire that included songs like "Jump Jim Coon" and "Old Zip Crow", as well as the romanticized depictions of black life presented by the white composer **Stephen Foster** in his popular collection, *Plantation Melodies*.

Such black face performers lampooned "darkie" culture with a series of derogatory stereotypes and racist caricatures. As Tony Russell pointed out in *Blacks, Whites And Blues* (1970), theirs was also a ludicrously sentimental view, summoning up "a peaceful picture of woolly-headed slaves strumming their banjos, fishing in the sun and courting little octoroons with improbable names". Furthermore, it was a hopelessly sanitized one too, for "of chain gangs and beatings and slave-drivers we heard not a whisper". Alongside the burnt-cork minstrels, however, genuine black minstrel companies also developed after the Civil War. Four of the best known were Richard and Pringle's **Famous Georgia Minstrels**, the **McCabe & Young Colored Minstrels**, the Hicks and Sawyers Minstrels, and **Haveley's Colored Minstrels**. The latter included the black composer **James Bland**, who wrote some 700 songs, including "Carry Me Back To Old Virginny", which was adopted many years later in the 20th century as the official Virginia state anthem. Both black and white minstrel groups offered a very similar diet of light entertainment and there were even mixed troupes, such as the Primrose and West Minstrels, which featured forty white and thirty black performers. Another popular late 19th-century group, the **Mahara Minstrels**, was led by **W.C. Handy**, the son of a prosperous black Methodist minister in Alabama, who later emerged as a significant figure in the birth of the blues.

Chapter Three

Rags, jazz & the blues

African roots, spirituals, work songs, field hollers, black folk ballads, instrumental jigs and the minstrel shows all played their part as building blocks of the blues. Yet before the blues came to prominence in the early years of the 20th century, another major development in African-American music took place. Known as ragtime, it was the forerunner of jazz.

Ragtime had its roots in the **banjo music** played at rural dances all over the Mississippi Delta in the final couple of decades of the 19th century. So what was a "rag"? The novelist and biographer **Rupert Hughes**, writing in 1899, made clear its origins in the kind of barn dance described in the preceding chapter: "Negroes call their clog dancing 'ragging' and the dance a 'rag', a dance largely shuffling. The dance is a sort of frenzy with frequent yelps of delight from the dancer and spectators and accompanied by the latter with hand clapping and stomping of feet. Banjo figuration is very noticeable in ragtime music and division of one of the beats into two short notes is traceable to the hand clapping."

With the left hand playing a recurring, stride bass figure and the right hand a shifting, syncopated melody, the piano could do the work of several banjos at once. At the same time, the style was also influenced by the New Orleans brass bands, in its shifting of the accent from the strong to the weak beat. And it was as an underground music in the brothels of **New Orleans**, played by black pianists, that

ragtime started out. The first published rag – "Ma Ragtime Baby", written by **Fred Stone** – appeared in 1893. That was swiftly followed by **William Krell**'s "Mississippi Rag" and **Thomas Million Turpin**'s "Harlem Rag", both of which were being widely played by 1897, while **Scott Joplin** published his *Original Rags* in 1899.

From New Orleans, ragtime spread to cities such as **Memphis** and **St Louis**. Soon it was being played in honky-tonks, pool halls, restaurants, saloons, tent shows, carnivals and cabarets – in fact, anywhere there was a piano. In short, it was *the* popular musical style of its day. Adopted by white performers, it became a polite, even prim style, respectable enough to play in the most high-minded drawing room – so much so that many white listeners were unaware of the music's black origins. The idea that ragtime was white music was further spread by the fact that few black composers bothered to publish their rags, content instead to play them in bars for tips. Knowing that they were unlikely to be challenged, more than a few white pianists were all too happy to pass off black-composed rags as their own work.

While ragtime was being enthusiastically embraced by white performers and audiences, black musicians were developing a related piano style with a more powerful and less delicate rhythm. Many years later it came to be known as **boogie-woogie**, but, as with all the musical styles that emerged before the advent of mass recordings, who invented it remains the subject of debate. In 1957, pianist **Roy Carew**, who lived in New Orleans at the turn of the century, reminisced on the boogie-woogie connection with ragtime: "I would say that boogie-woogie was the bad little boy of the rag family who wouldn't study. I heard crude beginnings of it in the back streets of New Orleans in those early years, following 1904, but they were really back streets. Such music never got played in the gilded palaces." In *They All Played Ragtime*, published in 1960, Rudi Blesh and Harriet Janis came up with an even earlier citation when they interviewed the ragtime pianist **Eubie Blake**, who recalled a three-hundred-pound giant of a boogie pianist from Baltimore called **William Turk**: "He had a left-hand like God. He didn't know what key he was playing in, but he played them all. He could play the ragtime stride bass but it bothered him because his stomach got in the way of his arm. So he used a walking bass, instead. I can remember when I was thirteen – this was 1896 – how Turk would play one note with his right hand and at the same time four with his left. We called it 'sixteen'. They call it boogie-woogie now."

Meanwhile, in the **Storyville** district of New Orleans, an extraordinary fusion was taking place between ragtime and a heavier, more emotional style that we have since come to recognize as the precursor of the blues. They called it **jazz**, although nobody has definitively worked out why. Some claim it was a corruption of the name of a New Orleans band called Razz, others that it came from an itinerant Mississippi musician called **Jazbo Brown**, whose name inevitably was shortened to just its first syllable. What is indisputable is that the cultural melting pot that was the Crescent City, and in particular the vast number of black and Creole musicians who played in the brothels and clubs of Basin Street in the heart of Storyville, made it the perfect locus for musical experimentation.

Scott Joplin, the king of ragtime

Although Scott Joplin could hardly be said to have played blues, the music of the "king of ragtime" had a profound influence on its development. Born in Texarkana, on the borders of Texas and Arkansas, in 1868, Joplin learned to play the piano from a German teacher. Moving to St Louis in 1885, he played piano in local saloons and cabarets. In 1894 he moved again to Sedalia, Missouri, where he enrolled in a black academy and learned to read and write music, which gave him a huge advantage as one of the few ragtime pianists able to put his rags down on paper.

Joplin's first published compositions were waltzes and marches, but in 1899 he published his *Original Rags*. These included his famous "Maple Leaf Rag", named after a club in Sedalia, which sold 75,000 copies in its first year. He recorded the song in Minneapolis in 1903, but no copy survives. Further successful rags followed, including "Elite Syncopations" and "The Entertainer" (which enjoyed renewed fame 70 years later as the theme tune of *The Sting*). He moved to New York in 1907, but his career was dogged by the breakdown of his marriage, syphilis and the commercial failure of his extended works, which included a ragtime opera (*Treemonisha*) and a ballet. By 1910, the disease had rendered him almost unable to play. However, in 1916 he managed to record a series of piano rolls of his best known tunes, the master discs of which have survived. He died in a New York hospital the following year.

The first prominent musician in the new "hot jazz" style was **Charles "Buddy" Bolden**. Born in New Orleans in 1877, Bolden learned to play the cornet as a boy. By the 1890s, he was leading a small dance group and creating music that for its time was rhythmically audacious. A riveting, charismatic performer and a famous crowd-pleaser, his tunes had such risqué titles as "All The Whores Like The Way I Ride" and "If You Don't Like My Potatoes Why Do You Dig So Deep?" He went mad in 1906 and spent the last 24 years of his life in a mental institution.

By the time of Bolden's incarceration, jazz was well established – and the blues was also putting down roots. **W.C. Handy**, who was soon to style himself "the father of the blues", claimed to have first heard the blues being sung in 1903, but it's perfectly possible that the music had been in existence in a recognizable if unchronicled form across the South for up to thirty years before then. Bolden was performing a number called "Buddy Bolden's Blues" by the mid-1890s, while Bunk Johnson, who joined his band and

Playlist
Gambling songs

Gamblin', like ramblin', was a way of life for most of the early bluesmen. The throw of the dice, the deal of a card and how a man's fortune could turn on a game of chance also offered a rich source of metaphorical blues philosophy.

1 GEORGIA SKIN BLUES **Memphis Minnie** from **Complete Recorded Works Vol 2**
"I had a man, he gambles all the time, he throw the dice so in vain until he like to lose his mind…"

2 POKER WOMAN BLUES **Blind Blake** from **Blind Blake Vol 3 1928–29**
"Sometime I'm rich, sometime I ain't got a cent, but I've had a good time everywhere I went…"

3 DYIN' CRAPSHOOTER'S BLUES **Blind Willie McTell** from **The Classic Years 1927–40**
"Send poker players to the graveyard, dig my grave with the ace of spades. I want twelve polices in my funeral march, high sheriff playin' blackjack, lead the parade…"

4 SHOOTING HIGH DICE **The Mississippi Sheiks** from **Stop And Listen**
"Now all of your men better take my advice, just hold to your money when shooting them dice…"

5 KING OF SPADES **Peetie Wheatstraw** from **Peetie Wheatstraw Vol 3 1935–36**
"Let me be your dealer, I'm the best dealer in town…"

6 DYING GAMBLER **Blind Willie McTell** from **The Classic Years 1927–40**
"I'll tell you of a poor young man gamblin' night and day. Fell straight down on his death bed, he tried but he could not pray…"

7 LIFE IS LIKE A CARD GAME **Big Joe Turner** from **Classic Hits 1938–52**
"Life is like a card game, I always get a bad deal, I got to play this hand whether I like it, now you know just how I feel…"

8 LITTLE QUEEN OF SPADES **Robert Johnson** from **King Of The Delta Blues Singers Vol 2**
"I'm gon' get me a gamblin' woman, if the last thing that I do…"

9 GAMBLER'S BLUES **Lightnin' Hopkins** from **The Ultimate Texas Bluesman**
"I lost all my money, boys, in a no good gambling game. I was on my bad luck, kept gambling just the same…"

10 YOU'RE MY BEST POKER HAND **T-Bone Walker** from **Midnight Blues**
"The kid spread his hand and then began to blush. But his face turned pale when he saw my queen high flush…"

Day laborers gambling with their cotton money on Saturday afternoon, Mileston Plantation, Mississippi Delta, Mississippi, October 1939.

later taught Louis Armstrong to play trumpet, later claimed: "Bolden was playing blues of all kinds, so when I got with Bolden we helped to make more blues". The great pianist **Jelly Roll Morton**, born in New Orleans in 1885, also offered early recollections of the blues. He recalled hearing a woman named Mamie Desdoumes singing a mournful blues song in New Orleans in 1902. Morton later got into an angry feud with Handy, publicly questioning his reputation as "father of the blues" and accusing him of plagiarism. No shrinking violet himself, he liked to introduce himself at concerts by saying: "I invented jazz". Morton, as much as anyone, illustrates the complex inter relation of blues and jazz. One was primarily a vocal style and the other instrumental. Yet although both were to develop along very different lines, their common roots in black folk culture mean that the two forms remain inextricably linked.

The birth of the blues

The first documented description of what we now recognize as the blues occurred when **W.C. Handy**, who at the time was directing a band called The Knights Of Pythias in Clarksdale, was waiting for a train at Tutwiler, Mississippi, in 1903. There he heard a "lean, loose jointed Negro" playing a guitar by pressing a knife against the strings and singing a song with the repeated line: "Goin' where the Southern cross the Dog". The song was "the weirdest music I had ever heard", Handy later wrote. But the sound – which he dubbed "the blues" – stuck in his mind.

In his autobiography, *Father Of The Blues*, published in 1941, Handy went on to describe his second, equally profound lesson in the blues, which followed a short time after his encounter on the railway platform at Tutwiler. Handy and his orchestra were playing at a dance in Cleveland, when a local group of black musicians asked if they could get up and play. "They were led by a long-legged choco-

late boy and their band consisted of just three pieces, a battered guitar, mandolin and a worn-out bass. The music they made was pretty well in keeping with their looks. They struck up one of these over-and-over strains that seem to have no very clear beginning and certainly no ending at all. The strumming maintained a disturbing monotony, but on and on it went, a kind of stuff that has long been associated with cane rows and levee camps. Thump-thump-thump went their feet on the floor. Their eyes rolled. Their shoulders swayed. And through it all that little agonizing strain persisted. It was not really annoying or unpleasant. Perhaps 'haunting' is a better word, but I commenced to wonder if anybody besides small town rounders and their running mates would go for it." When the trio were showered with coins to a sum far in excess of what Handy's orchestra were being paid for the night, he had his answer. "Then I saw the beauty of primitive music," he recorded. "They had the stuff the people wanted."

Handy decided that he, too, had better give the people "the stuff" they wanted, and began composing and publishing blues tunes, albeit in a somewhat stiff and formal manner. It's also easy to see why the patronizing attitude he displayed in the description above so irritated the likes of **Jelly Roll Morton**. Yet Giles Oakley, author of *The Devil's Music*, is surely right when he credits Handy with being the first person to give the blues a focus: "In formalizing the music that was springing up all over the South in a disparate and incoherent way, he helped to give it an identity."

In 1912, Handy published his famous "Memphis Blues", which Oakley also cites as a seminal moment: "Up to that point the word blues was probably only loosely applied to a wide spectrum of songs – work songs, love songs, devil songs, 'ditties', 'ballits', the over-and-overs, the slow drags, pats, stomps and all kinds of barrelhouse music." In this light Handy deserves his statue in Beale Street in his home town of Memphis and his "father of the blues" tag, despite its strict inaccuracy. Handy's "lean, loose-jointed Negro" at Tutwiler railway station in 1903 was almost certainly not the first blues musician. **Harrison Barnes**, who was a pianist in a New Orleans brothel in the early years of the century, believed that he was playing the blues well before then and that he was not alone. "They were slow tunes; unhappy. They was what they call the blues now, only they called them ditties in them days," he recalled some years later.

In truth, we cannot be any more exact than saying that the blues as we know it emerged some time in the aftermath of the Civil War among a black population struggling to eke out an existence in the face of the open hostility of Southern whites. Apart from one or two pioneering folklorists such as **Howard Odum**, who traveled through the Delta between 1905 and 1908, and collected many songs that were clearly blues, or at least contained lyrics that later recurred in well-known blues songs, few noticed, let alone noted, what was going on in black music at the time. As **Bill Wyman** put it: "It was the contemporary lack of interest in documenting the songs of this beleaguered people that caused our lack of precise knowledge about when the blues began."

W.C. Handy – the man who brought the blues to polite society

Chapter Four

The 1920s: the blues goes crazy

Columbia Records started to produce and sell commercial discs in 1900, and within three years was claiming sales of two million per month. Not until August 10, 1920, however, when Okeh Records took Mamie Smith into a New York studio to cut Perry Bradford's "Crazy Blues", was the first black blues singer recorded.

Although the resultant record was advertised as by "a singer of 'blues' – the music of so new a flavor", itinerant musicians such as **Charley Patton** had for at least a decade before "Crazy Blues" been playing the blues at Delta picnics, juke joints and house parties, while the likes of **Ma Rainey** had been singing them in vaudeville theatres and tent shows. The music had even reached black theaters in northern cities like Chicago, New York and Philadelphia. Thus a ready-made audience for the blues already existed, and Smith became an instant success. The figures claimed by Bradford in his autobiography, *Born With The Blues*, that "Crazy Blues" sold 75,000 copies in the first month and one million in a year, may well have been inflated. But there was certainly more than a grain of truth when he wrote: "There's fourteen million Negroes in our great country and they will buy records if recorded by one of their own, because we are the only folks that can sing and interpret hot jazz songs just off the griddle correctly."

The man Bradford persuaded to record **Mamie Smith** was Okeh's Fred Hagar, who ignored letters threatening that if he recorded "colored girls", a boycott of the company's recordings and phonograph players would ensue. Although few would rate "Crazy Blues" as one of the great blues recordings, and Smith was soon eclipsed by several more talented female singers, it remains of immense symbolic significance. First, it alerted the American record industry to the fact that there was a black audience for gramophone records and spawned the concept of "race records". Secondly, as Giles Oakley noted, Mamie Smith's recording was "the moment the music ceased to be transmitted exclusively through local folk culture with all the transience of 'live' performances".

Thirdly, Smith's recording sent rival record companies scrambling to replicate the success of "Crazy Blues", and thus to discover singers such as **Bessie Smith** and **Ma Rainey**. Both began recording in 1923, for Columbia and

MAMIE SMITH AND HER JAZZ HOUNDS

Sara Martin. Then there was **Lucille Bogan**. While most of her contemporaries were recorded in New York or Chicago, Okeh Records took a portable studio to Atlanta, Georgia, in summer 1923, where they recorded Bogan performing "Pawn Shop Blues" and the lesser-known **Fannie Mae Goosby** singing "Grievous Blues". The first field recording (or "territory recording" as they were initially called) of a blues singer, this marked another significant step in the commercial opening-up of the South as a hotbed of musical talent.

Paramount respectively, and went on to play major roles in the development of the blues, at the apex of a vast sorority of female blues singers. Because theirs was the first style to be recorded, it became known as "**classic blues**". Other practitioners included Lucille Hegamin (on Arto Records), Mary Stafford, Clara Smith and Edith Wilson (Columbia), Ethel Waters and Trixie Smith (both on the briefly flourishing, black-owned Black Swan label) and Ida Cox (Paramount) while Okeh followed its own success with Alberta Hunter, Sippie Wallace, Victoria Spivey and

Most, if not all, of the early blues divas came out of the vaudeville and cabaret circuits. Often backed by jazz bands and frequently dressed in silk or beaded gowns, gold jewelry and even tiaras, many of them sang blues simply because it had become "fashionable". Performers like Ma Rainey and Bessie Smith remained popular into the 1930s, but the blues was about to undergo another sea change as the rougher sound of bottleneck guitars and the guttural voices of the itinerant male blues singers, who were by now proliferating across the Delta, took over.

"The Toby" and the blues circuit

Established in 1909, the **Theater Owners Booking Agency** – variously known as "the Toby" or "Toby Time" – was a network of white-owned theaters that catered for black audiences in cities with sizeable black populations. Among key stops on the circuit were the Monogram Theatre in Chicago, the Pastime and Beale Avenue Palace in Memphis, the Lyric in New Orleans, the Lyceum in Cincinnati, the Dream in Columbus, the Koppin in Detroit, the Bijou in Nashville, the Booker T. Washington in St Louis and the 81 Theatre in Atlanta, owned by the notorious Charles P. Bailey.

The agency booked vaudeville acts and chorus lines of "sepia lovelies", comics and jugglers, often all on the same bill. It was also "on the Toby" that most of the early female blues singers came to prominence. Conditions were generally appalling, with few if any back-stage facilities, and artists were expected to pay their own traveling expenses between engagements. Hence another of the TOBA's nicknames – "Tough On Black Asses".

Of course, there were plenty of other, less formal, places where the early blues singers were guaranteed to find an audience: the juke joints, barrelhouses and fish-fries. And when all else failed, there was always the street corner…

Playlist
Red-hot mamas

Sex sells and it always has. In fact, from the vaudeville of Sophie Tucker to the jazz-blues of Bessie Smith, there were probably more women singing sexually suggestive songs in the early decades of the last century than in our own booty-shaking, permissive times. Here are ten favorite red-hot mamas from the not-so-buttoned up years before World War II.

1 I NEED A LITTLE SUGAR IN MY BOWL Bessie Smith from **The Essential Bessie Smith**
" What's the matter, hard papa, come on and save you mama's soul 'cos I need a little sugar in my bowl…"

2 I WANT A TALL SKINNY PAPA Sister Rosetta Tharpe from **The Gospel Of The Blues**
"He's got to be all right, learn to fight all night, mama will do the rest…"

3 I'M A MIGHTY TIGHT WOMAN Sippie Wallace from **Complete Recorded Works Vol 2**
" If you're a married man you ain't got no business here, 'cos when you're out with me I might make your wife shed a tear…"

4 SHAVE 'EM DRY (#2) Lucille Bogan from **Shave 'Em Dry: Best Of Lucille Bogan**
"I'm going to turn back my mattress, and let you oil my springs, I want you to grind me daddy 'til the bells do ring…"

5 ORGAN GRINDER BLUES Victoria Spivey from **Queen Victoria 1927–37**
"Your sweet music seems to ease my mind, it's not your organ, but it's the way you grind…"

6 IF IT DON'T FIT (DON'T FORCE IT) Barrelhouse Annie from **Sugar In My Bowl (Various Artists)**
"It may stretch, it may not tear at all, but you'll never back that big mule up in my stall…"

7 HOT NUTS (GET 'EM FROM THE PEANUT MAN) Lil Johnson from **Hottest Gal In Town**
" You see that man all dressed in brown, he's got the hottest nuts in town…"

8 HE'S JUST MY SIZE Lillie Mae Kirkham from **Sugar In My Bowl**
"He makes my biscuit rise, he uses the best baking powder and his biscuit's just my size…"

9 NOBODY LOVES A FAT GIRL, BUT OH HOW A FAT GIRL CAN LOVE Sophie Tucker not currently available on CD
" I'm just a truck upon the highway of love, the only game I can get the boys to play is have 'em sit around and guess how much I weigh…"

10 SALTY PAPA BLUES Dinah Washington from **The Essential Dinah Washington**
"I said papa, why you so salty, why do you bring me down, there's no complaint when my other man comes around…"

Tent shows, juke joints, barrelhouses and fish-fries

Most of the **carnival** and **minstrel shows** that toured the South in the early decades of the 20th century employed blues singers. Among the best-known were F.S. Wolcott's **Rabbit Foot Minstrels**, Silas Green's, **Tolliver's Circus and Musical Extravaganza**, the **King And Bush Wide-Mouth Minstrels**, Pete Werley's **Cotton Blossom's Show**, and the **Georgia Smart Set**. They would perform in tents that were transported on trailers, or sometimes on their own railroad cars. To drum up customers when they arrived in a new town, a brass band would tour the streets in a ritual known as "ballyhooing", with individual performers leading the parade – sometimes on

exotic animals such as elephants – while the roustabouts set up the big top, made of boards on a folding frame. In addition to playing small towns across the South, the tent shows would also visit self-contained working communities such as levee camps and the larger plantations.

Even the smallest country town would boast at least one **drinking den**, usually selling bootleg "moonshine" whiskey, where local musicians would play. Such places were in more plentiful supply in the cities, and tended to be concentrated on a specific street. In Atlanta it was Decatur Street, in Dallas the action was on Elm Street, Shreveport had Fannin Street, and in Memphis musical life centered on Beale Street. Known variously as barrelhouses, fish-fries or juke joints, they were tough places – sleazy,

The "Race Record" record labels

OKEH: Founded by German immigrant Otto Heineman, Okeh invented the term "race records" and was the first into the new market with Mamie Smith's "Crazy Blues" in 1920. The label's early excursions into field recordings were organized by Ralph Peer, in centers as far apart as New Orleans, Atlanta, Texas and Kansas City, while Clarence Williams acted as director of race recordings at the label's New York headquarters. Although Okeh merged with Columbia in 1929, records continued to appear on the label until 1934, when it was bought by ARC (American Recording Company).

Okeh artists: Clara Smith, Alberta Hunter, Sippie Wallace, Victoria Spivey, Sara Martin, Lucille Bogan, Blind Boy Fuller, Memphis Minnie, Lonnie Johnson, Bo Carter, Mississippi Sheikhs, Sylvester Weaver, Bo Carter, Memphis Slim, Texas Alexander, Little Hat Jones.

COLUMBIA: Columbia starting selling discs in 1900 and was swift to follow Okeh into the "race" market, signing such female blues singers as Bessie Smith in response to the success of Mamie Smith. An early pioneer of the new electric recording process (which it licensed from Western Electric), the label commenced its extensive field recording program when it cut sides with Peg Leg Howell in Atlanta in 1926. After merging to become part of the British-based EMI in 1931, American Columbia was then sold to the American Recording Company in 1934. ARC was in turn bought by the Columbia Broadcasting System in 1938.

Columbia artists: Bessie Smith, Mary Stafford, Clara Smith, Edith Wilson, Peg Leg Howell, Barbecue Bob, Blind Willie Johnson, Blind Willie McTell, Curley Weaver, Whistlin' Alex Moore.

PARAMOUNT: Founded as a subsidiary of a Wisconsin-based chair company that also made some wooden phonograph cabinets, the Paramount label was launched in 1918. The company initially struggled in the pop market, but blues became its savior after the appointment of black college graduate Mayo Williams as a talent scout in 1922, and its purchase of the black-owned Black Swan label. After signing classic female blues singers like Alberta Hunter, Ida Cox and Ma Rainey, Williams went looking on Chicago's Maxwell Street for a male blues singer to record, and found Papa Charlie Jackson, Blind Lemon Jefferson and Blind Blake. After Mayo left for Okeh in 1927, another scout,

violent and often murderous, with the musical entertainment accompanying not only drinking but gambling and prostitution. "Every modern devilment you can do, the barrelhouse is where it's at," **Big Joe Williams** recalled.

While the imposition of federal **Prohibition** in 1920 closed some venues, rather more went underground and carried on business more or less as normal. Every town had its illegal "speakeasy", and in country areas, where "moonshine" was a way of life, enforcement was lax. In Mississippi, for example, alcohol had been theoretically illegal since 1907, but everybody knew where to go to get a drink.

"We had these little juke joints, little taverns at the time," **Muddy Waters** remembered. "On

a weekend there was this little place in the alley that would stay open all night. We called them **Saturday night fish fries**, they had two or three names, they called 'em juke houses or suppers." There was also a circuit of barrelhouses all over the Piney Woods, the vast tracts of forest across Mississippi, Alabama, Louisiana, Arkansas and Texas where hundreds of lumber camps, logging camps, turpentine camps and saw-mills sprang up, linked by temporary railroads on which hobos, wandering blues musicians and itinerant workers would ride. Each camp or mill would have its own "barrelhouse juke", installed by the company to entertain its workers and sell them cheap liquor. The pianist **Little Brother Montgomery** was a veteran

H.C. Spier, found Charley Patton and Tommy Johnson in Mississippi. Paramount didn't really go in for field recordings, mostly taking its artists to studios in New York (pre-1926), Chicago (1926–29) and then Grafton, Wisconsin (1929–32). The label went out of business in 1932 during the Great Depression, having released some 1100 discs in ten years.

Paramount artists: Alberta Hunter, Ida Cox, Ma Rainey, Papa Charlie Jackson, Blind Lemon Jefferson, Blind Blake, Charley Patton, Tommy Johnson, Son House, Skip James, Son House.

VICTOR/BLUEBIRD: The largest manufacturer of phonographs (including the famous "Victrola") as well as a major record company in the 1920s, Victor entered the "race" market, recording Mamie Smith after she had left Okeh as well as Jelly Roll Morton, the Memphis Jug Band, Cannon's Jug Stompers and Richard "Rabbit" Brown. In 1933, in response to the success of ARC's new cut-price policy of selling "three records for a dollar" in response to the Depression, Victor launched its budget-priced Bluebird line, and transferred most of its blues artists to the new imprint. Central to Bluebird's success was the Chicago-based Lester Melrose, who found most of the acts and recorded them, using in-house musicians to back featured artists and sometimes recording up to forty songs in a day. Victor finally shut Bluebird down in the mid-1940s.

Victor/Bluebird artists: Big Bill Broonzy, Blind John Davis, Roosevelt Sykes, Washboard Sam, Memphis Slim, Big Maceo, Jazz Gillum, Tampa Red, Memphis Minnie, Tommy McClennan, Sonny Boy "John Lee" Williamson, Lonnie Johnson, Leadbelly.

VOCALION: Another evocative name found on certain famous old blues 78s, Vocalion Records was founded in 1916 by the Aeolian Piano Company of New York City. The label had a complex and confusing history. By 1925 it had been acquired by Brunswick Records and six years later was bought up by the American Record Corporation. Eventually it came under the ownership of Columbia. Vocalion took many of its artists, such as Charley Patton, to New York to record, but Brunswick also had one of the most active field-recording units and between 1928 and 1930 recorded bluesmen in Dallas, Memphis, New Orleans and Atlanta.

Vocalion/Brunswick artists: Charley Patton, Ethel Waters, Clarence "Pine Top" Smith, Tampa Red, Cow Cow Davenport, Leroy Carr, Bo Weavil Jackson, Blind Willie McTell, Henry Thomas, Furry Lewis.

of country blues, and he recalled that "it was rough, but they always liked musicians and if you could play they would always take up for you".

Once the migration from the plantations of the Delta to the cities got under way, there was the problem of how to pay the rent. The solution for many was to organize a **rent party**, also known variously as **"Too Tight Parties"**, chitterlin' rags, calico hops, skittles, house shouts, house hops, boogie pitches and Blue Monday parties. The idea was simple: when the rent was due, you'd throw a party, book a blues singer and charge an entrance fee of a quarter and a jug of liquor. **Georgia Tom Dorsey** recalled the rent party scene in Chicago: "I had a place to play

every night. If you got half a dollar or 35 cents a night for playing for three or four hours, you had good money. It wasn't much but you got all that you could drink, all you could eat and a good-looking woman to fan you." Successful rent parties also sometimes became more permanent commercial arrangements known as "good-time flats" or "buffet flats".

The country blues boom

While the early, "classic" women blues singers were performing in the more professional environment of theaters and tent shows, and recording with jazz bands, the itinerant male blues singers, who had abandoned sharecropping to

Blind Lemon Jefferson: first superstar of country blues

Ma Rainey, Williams determined to find a male blues singer and began looking among the itinerant musicians on Chicago's Maxwell Street. There, in August 1924, he found **Papa Charlie Jackson**, a banjo-playing veteran of the medicine and tent show circuit whose repertoire included vaudeville and minstrel songs as well as blues. Williams recorded Jackson singing "Airy Man Blues" and "Papa's Lawdy Lawdy Blues", and he went on to cut early versions of such standards as "I'm Alabama Bound", "Spoonful" and "Shake That Thing".

In fact, Jackson wasn't quite the first bluesman to record. In November 1923, Okeh recorded two solo tracks by the guitarist **Sylvester Weaver** in New York, after he had been employed to accompany Sara Martin, but they were instrumentals. The first country bluesman to sing on a disc was almost certainly the obscure **Ed Andrews**, whom Okeh recorded performing "Barrel House Blues" in April 1924, on one of the label's early field recording trips to Atlanta.

However, Jackson was certainly the first male blues singer to enjoy commercial success, and he recorded a total of around seventy sides. "People like nothing better than to come home after a tiring and busy day and play his records," a Paramount advert claimed at the time. "His hearty voice and gay harmonious strumming of the banjo causes their cares and worries to dwindle away and gives them a carefree frame of mind and makes life one sweet song."

The description emphasizes Jackson's roots as a songster, drawing on folk, minstrel and vaudeville traditions, rather than a bluesman, and several other musicians from the same tradition, such as Daddy Stovepipe, were soon corralled into recording studios. Another such figure, **Leadbelly**, was at this time serving a prison sen-

go on the road, were leading a quite different life, hobo-ing around the South performing on street corners, in barrelhouses, at logging camps and at plantation dances. Initially, their music was regarded by whites as primitive and unworthy of attention, for the blues they were singing was rougher and more spontaneous than that of the great female singers and their jazz accompanists. As bluesman **Johnny Shines** put it "They were singing by arrangements and we were singing by whatever came to us first."

It was inevitable that the recording industry, with its new-found interest in the burgeoning "race" market, would catch on to the popularity of the **country bluesmen**. However, it took time. One of the first to recognize the potential was **Mayo Williams**, a black college graduate who began working for Paramount Records in 1922. After signing a number of female classic blues singers, including **Alberta Hunter**, **Ida Cox** and

Fats Waller dreamt about a reefer "five feet long". Even Ella Fitzgerald reckoned "wacky dust" was "something you can trust". And for the early bluesmen, sniffin' and whiffin' was part of the way of life...

1 A SPOONFUL BLUES Charley Patton from **Founder Of The Delta Blues**
Patton knew plenty of cocaine heads in the late 1920s, although there's a sexual ambiguity to his cocaine spoon, too.

2 DOPE HEAD BLUES Victoria Spivey from **Complete Recorded Works Vol 1**
"Go get my airplane and drive it to my door, I think I'll fly to London. The Prince of Wales is on my trail, I'll take another sniff..."

3 TAKE A WHIFF ON ME Leadbelly from **The Alan Lomax Songbook**
A much-covered track, sometimes it was adapted to "Have A Drink On Me" – alcohol apparently being more acceptable than marijuana or cocaine if you want a hit record.

4 KNOCKIN' MYSELF OUT Lil Green & Big Bill Broonzy from **Dope And Glory (Various Artists)**
"Listen girls and boys, I got a stick. Gimme a match and let me take a whiff quick. I'm going to knock myself out by degrees..."

5 GIMME A PIGFOOT (GIMME A REEFER) Bessie Smith from **Empress Of The Blues**

Bessie took her pleasures indiscriminately, demanding a bottle of beer and a "gang of gin" along with her pigfoot and reefer...

6 COCAINE BLUES Rev Gary Davis from **Rev Gary Davis**
"Cocaine's for horses and not for men, doctor said it kill you, but he don't say when..."

7 COCAINE HABIT BLUES Memphis Jug Band from **Memphis Jug Band**
"Cocaine habit mighty bad, it's the worst old habit that I ever had/hey, hey, honey take a whiff on me..."

8 THE WEED SMOKER'S DREAM The Harlem Hamfats from **Complete Recorded Works Vol 1**
Kansas Joe McCoy's hymn to Madame Marijuana, also known as "Why Don't You Do Right?", in which form it was sung by the improbable figure of Dame Kiri Te Kanawa.

9 JUNKER BLUES Champion Jack Dupree from **Junker Blues**
First recorded by Dupree in the early 1940s, then transmogrified by Fats Domino into "The Fat Man" and also the template for the New Orleans' standard "Junco Partner".

10 JACK I'M MELLOW Trixie Smith from **Complete Recorded Works Vol 2**
"I'm so high and I'm so dry, I'm way up in the sky. The world seems light and I'm so right, Jack I'm mellow..."

tence for murder in a Texas prison, and was not recorded until 1933.

Some time around 1915, Leadbelly had met and briefly worked with **Blind Lemon Jefferson**, who became the first superstar of the country blues after Paramount began recording him in 1926. Jefferson was among the first regularly to record his own material, and his success enabled him to own two cars and employ a chauffeur. While his style may have harked back to earlier forms – Paramount promoted one of his early records as "a real old-fashioned blues by a real old-fashioned blues singer" – his huge record sales meant that men not women now dominated the blues, and led to the flood of male country blues singers who were recorded during the boom years between 1927 and 1930, when blues records were being released at an average rate of ten a week.

Many such singers were never heard of again. Whatever happened to **Big Boy George Owens**, **Talking Billy Anderson**, **Seth Richard**, **Tarter & Gay**, **Jim Towel**, **Billy Bird** and **Papa Egg Shell**? All recorded fewer than four sides apiece, and when those failed to sell in sizeable quantities, they disappeared back into obscurity. Others, like **Blind Blake**, who first recorded for Paramount in Chicago in 1926, went on to enjoy longer recording careers.

Paramount was unique in sticking rigidly to a policy of taking its artists (invariably on the recommendation of local Southern talent scouts) to record in their northern studios. However, by the mid-1920s most of the other labels in the "race" market – Columbia, Okeh, Brunswick, Gennet and Victor – were undertaking frequent trips to the South with mobile units. They recorded bluesmen in makeshift studios in

Playlist
The great lost bluesmen

Despite the huge amount of ongoing research and scholarship, mysteries still abound in blues history. Here are ten classic recordings by artists from the 1920s and early 1930s, who cut a handful of sides and then disappeared.

1 BROWNIE BLUES **Tarter & Gay** from **Ragtime Blues Guitar 1927–30**
This obscure duo recorded just two classic ragtime pieces for Victor in the late 1920s.

2 MIDNIGHT BLUES **Bill Moore** from **Ragtime Blues Guitar 1927–30**
Born in 1894, Moore was a barber from Tappahannock, Virginia, who sang ragtime and gentle blues songs to his own fine guitar accompaniment. This is one of just eight surviving sides, after recording which he presumably went back to being a barber.

3 MILL MAN BLUES **Billy Bird** from **Guitar Wizards 1926–35**
One of four virtuoso guitar sides Bird recorded in 1928 for Columbia, who hoped he was their answer to Paramount's Blind Blake. He never quite made it, and what became of him, nobody knows.

4 BE TRUE BE TRUE BLUES **Henry Sims** from **Mississippi Blues 1927–41**
Sims played fiddle for a while with Charley Patton, which is probably how he came to record this rather fine number under his own name.

5 EAGLES ON A HALF **Geechie Wiley** from **Mississippi Blues 1927–41**
Virtually nothing is known about this obscure blueswoman, who cut three records for Paramount in Grafton,

Wisconsin, in 1930 and 1931. On this track she's accompanied by Elvie Thomas on second guitar.

6 CAIRO BLUES **Henry Spaulding** from **St Louis Town 1929–33**
One of just two sides the St Louis-based Spaulding cut for Brunswick in 1929; nothing to do with Egypt, it's a reference to the town of the same name in Missouri.

7 PENNSYLVANIA WOMAN BLUES **Six Cylinder Smith** from **Tex-Arkana-Louisiana Country 1927–1932**
Great name, great song – but who was he? Some suspect he may have been Blind Joe Taggart, a guitar evangelist who disguised his secular songs under such pseudonyms as Blind Jeremiah Taylor and Blind Joe Amos. But nobody really knows for sure…

8 I'M GOIN' UP THE COUNTRY **Papa Egg Shell** from **Country Blues Collector Items (1928–1933)**
We know his real name was Lawrence Casey and that he recorded four sides for Brunswick in 1929 – but not much else. The song is quite different from the similarly titled Canned Heat number.

9 LONELY BILLY BLUES **Talking Billy Anderson** from **The Great Race Record Labels Vol 2**
A slow piano blues sung in an unusually sweet and refined voice, and one of a mere four sides Anderson recorded for Columbia in 1927.

10 THE COON CRAP GAME **Big Boy George Owens** from **Country Blues Obsurities Vol 1 (1926–1936)**
One of the first male blues singers to record, Owens cut four sides for Gennett in 1926 and was then lost from view.

---

hotel rooms, public halls and even roller-skating rinks. Although the invention of a carbon microphone for electrical recording in 1925 considerably improved recording technology, it was still primitive compared to today. Several decades later, **Mississippi John Hurt** described a 1920s session in a hall in Memphis: "I sat on a chair and they pushed the microphone right up close to my mouth and told me not move after they had found the right position … My neck was sore for days after."

Such terms as "field recording" and "country blues" might seem to suggest singers captured on tape on plantations while taking a snatched break from picking cotton. Certainly, collectors such as Alan and John Lomax did record blues singers in

such circumstances, including Muddy Waters in 1941. However, most of the 1920s blues singers had turned to music in order to escape a life of sharecropping. Although they sometimes visited the old plantations to play at country dances and picnics, those who had not traveled further north to St Louis or Chicago were most likely to be found playing for tips on the street corners and in the barrelhouses of the great Southern cities, such as Jackson, Memphis, Shreveport, New Orleans, Dallas, San Antonio and Atlanta. Each city had its own distinctive musical style. Dallas, for example, developed a strong scene of its own centered on the likes of **Texas Alexander**, **Coley Jones**, the **Dallas String Band** and the young **T-Bone Walker**. But in the country blues of the

1920s, two main rival strands came to dominate – the slashing bottleneck urgency of the **Mississippi Delta** and the lighter, more delicate guitar and vocal styles of the **Piedmont** region to the east of the Appalachians. Musicians of the former school tended to gravitate towards Memphis, and of the latter towards Atlanta.

Memphis and the Delta blues

As the closest big city to the Mississippi Delta, **Memphis**, Tennessee, stood at the heart of the cotton economy. By the 1920s it had also become a magnet for singers and guitarists seeking to escape the economic hardships of the Delta country. They inevitably gravitated to the bars and barrelhouses on Beale Street, a lawless, rowdy and violent environment reminiscent of a wild-west frontier town. Famous for razor fights and stabbings, it was populated by prostitutes, gamblers, hustlers and drifters, as well as blues singers and the occasional bold tourist who wished to see life on what was billed as "the main street of Negro America".

Beale Street became an obvious target for the field-recording units of the "race" record companies, and Victor and Columbia conducted their first sessions in Memphis in 1927. Many of the great Delta bluesmen were recorded in the city over the next three years, including **Mississippi John Hurt**, **Sleepy John Estes**, **Furry Lewis**, **Robert Wilkins**, **Tommy Johnson** and **Memphis Minnie**, one of the few women to emerge from the country blues. **Charley Patton**, an all-pervasive influence on everyone who followed, from Son House to Robert Johnson, did not, however, record in Memphis, as he was signed to **Paramount**, who stuck to their policy of taking their artists to record in their northern studios in Richmond, Indiana, and Grafton, Wisconsin.

The Mississippi Delta

Who first played the blues, and the precise circumstances of its birth, remain shrouded in mystery. But there can be no doubt about where the music emerged – the alluvial plain in the northwest section of the state of Mississippi, created by thousands of years of flooding and known as the **Mississippi Delta**.

In its widest definition, the Delta region begins in southern Illinois and ends in Louisiana, where the Mississippi River empties into the Gulf of Mexico. That vast area consists of 219 counties, and is home to 8.3 million people. However, the Delta is more usually defined as the region that stretches south from Memphis, Tennessee, as far as Vicksburg, some 300 miles from the Gulf. Even more precisely, the writer David Cohn in 1935 defined the Delta as "beginning in the lobby of the Peabody Hotel in Memphis and ending on Catfish Row in Vicksburg". Under this definition, the Delta is about two hundred miles long and seventy miles wide at its broadest point, and constitutes one of the most culturally and geographically distinct regions in the United States.

The regular flooding of the Mississippi River over several millennia, and to a lesser extent that of the Yazoo River to its east, left the land remarkably flat and blessed with some of the most fertile soil on the planet – a perfect and lush location for growing cotton. Until the early 19th century, the plain was covered by hardwood forest. By 1830, settlers had begun to clear the land and plant cotton, and by the Civil War the plantation system had taken over the entire Delta region.

It also created one of the harshest systems of slavery the world has ever seen – an unrelentingly punishing environment that gave birth to the blues. The social and economic problems of the Delta region persist to this day, the product and result of its history of enslavement and the legacies of the cotton plantation era, including the Jim Crow laws, racial segregation of public educational institutions and black disenfranchisement.

Deep Delta blues was not the only music making the clubs on Beale Street hum. In the late 1920s, Memphis also became the center of the **jug band** craze, even if such groups were also recorded in Dallas, Birmingham, Cincinnati and Louisville, Kentucky. In fact, jug bands are thought to have originated in Louisvulle in the early years of the 20th century, becoming a popular attraction at Kentucky race tracks. Utilizing cheap earthenware jugs that gave a low-pitched sound when blown, and thus acted as an alternative to a double bass, the early Louisville jug bands played mainly ragtime and popular dance music, augmented by guitars, banjos, piano, saxophones and cornets. If jugs weren't available, a similar effect could be attained with bottles and cans and any other vessel that resonated when blown across the neck. Other improvised instruments commonly found in jug bands included kazoos, washboards and basses made with a piece of string, a broom handle and a washtub. That tradition of making instruments out of common utensils went back to the earliest days of slavery.

While rougher and bluesier than their Kentucky counterparts, the jug bands that emerged in Memphis during the 1920s were quite different from the solo bluesmen. The emphasis their music placed on ensemble playing and creating a good-time feel was later to find an echo during the skiffle craze in 1950s Britain, and experienced a revival during the American folk boom of the early 1960s, when even pop bands such

Gus Cannon, of Gus Cannon's Jug Stompers, photographed at home in the 1960s

as the Lovin' Spoonful briefly championed the style. The group that spearheaded the craze in the 1920s was the **Memphis Jug Band**. Formed by the guitarist and harmonica player Will Shade, they were first recorded by Victor in the city in 1927. Featuring fiddles, guitars and harmonicas, like most such ensembles they had a fluctuating, haphazard line-up and a repertoire that included not only blues, but jazz, ragtime, comic and novelty songs, and folk tunes. In the wake of the Memphis Jug Band's success, other labels sought to cash in. Paramount was particularly active, recording the Beale Street Sheiks and **Gus Cannon's Jug Stompers**. Other Memphis-based groups included Jed Davenport's Beale Street Jug Band and Jack Kelly's South Memphis Jug Band, while Whistler and His Jug Band from Louisville and the Cincinnati Jug Band from Ohio also enjoyed some popularity. However, the market leaders remained the Memphis bands, who drew not only on an older songster tradition but on the darker sound of the Delta blues to give their music a little more grit.

The decline of the jug bands was partly a result of the growing separation of "country" and "blues" which took place in the mid-1930s, as the fiddle became dominant in the one form and the guitar in the other. By the time the Memphis Jug Band made its last recordings in 1934, the craze was almost over although Shade's group continued to perform around the city until the 1940s. The MJB even briefly reformed in the 1950s, while Gus Cannon came out of retirement in the 1960s after the Rooftop Singers took a cover of his 1929-recorded jug band tune "Walk Right In" to the top of the US pop charts.

Playlist
Jug Band blues

The earliest jug bands played popular dance tunes, but the style that developed in Memphis in the late 1920s was more firmly rooted in country blues and earlier African-American traditions. Gus Cannon's Jug Stompers and Will Shade's Memphis Jug Band were the most popular, but they spawned plenty of imitators and even Big Bill Broonzy and Memphis Minnie cut a few sides backed by jug bands.

1 STEALIN' STEALIN' Memphis Jug Band from **He's In The Jail House Now**
Also known as "Circle Round The Sun", this 1928 recording has since been covered by everyone from reggae singer John Holt to the Grateful Dead.

2 SUN BRIMMERS BLUES Memphis Jug Band from **He's In The Jailhouse Now**
Son Brimmer was a nickname for the band's guitarist Will Shade, who was raised by his grandmother, Annie Brimmer.

3 BEALE STREET BREAKDOWN Jed Davenport's **Beale Street Jug Band** from **Memphis Shakedown: More Jug Band Classics**
Harmonica pyrotechnics from Davenport on a 1930 recording backed by Kansas Joe McCoy and Memphis Minnie.

4 NEW MINGLEWOOD BLUES Noah Lewis's Jug Band from **Memphis Shakedown: More Jug Band Classics**
Recorded in 1930 by Lewis, who was moonlighting from Cannon's Jug Stompers, and an amazing line-up that included "Sleepy" John Estes on guitar and Yank Rachell on mandolin.

5 COLD IRON BED Jack Kelly & His South Memphis **Jug Band** from **Rocking Juice And Chitlins: The Great Jug Bands**

A 1933 recording with a vibrant vocal by Kelly, some great fiddle by Willie Batts, and the guitars of Frank Stokes and Dan Sane.

6 MY DADDY ROCKS ME (WITH ONE STEADY ROLL) Tampa Red And His Hokum Jug Band from **The Essential Tampa Red**
Recorded in 1929, this was reputedly the first song ever to unite the words "rock" and "roll".

7 WALK RIGHT IN Cannon's Jug Stompers from **Cannon's Jug Stompers 1927–30**
First recorded in 1928, the song gave the Rooftop Singers a number one hit some 35 years later, and launched a brief jug band revival.

8 ON THE ROAD AGAIN Memphis Jug Band from **Memphis Jug Band**
A classic 1928 recording of a song later joyously covered by the Grateful Dead, who included more jug band songs in their repertoire than just about any other rock band and also recorded "New Minglewood Blues", "Stealin'" and Noah Lewis's "Viola Lee Blues".

9 BLACK CAT HOOT OWL BLUES Ma Rainey & **Her Tub Jug Washboard Band** from **Don't Fish In My Sea**
Not only tubs, jugs and washboards, but kazoos and banjos, too, make for an odd accompaniment to Rainey's stentorian vocal, but it's strangely appealing.

10 YOU GOTTA HAVE THAT THING Picaninny Jug **Band** from **Memphis Shakedown: More Jug Band Classics**
Unfortunate name, great song. In fact, it was the Memphis Jug Band moonlighting for a rival label in 1932.

Hokum blues

The style known as **hokum blues** was in some ways closely linked to that of the jug bands, and Chicago even boasted a Hokum Jug Band during the early 1930s. While the light, jolly tone once more harked back to an older songster tradition, hokum blues was most specifically characterized by its sexually risqué lyrics, full of clever word play, innuendo and double entendres. Among those who specialized in the style were banjoist Papa Charlie Jackson; the duo Tampa Red and Georgia Tom; Bo Carter; Frankie "Half-Pint" Jaxon; the Harlem Hamfats; and the **Mississippi Sheiks**, whose name even reflected the style, deriving not only from

Rudolph Valentino's popular film *The Sheik* but also from a popular brand of condom. The **Hokum Boys**, whose fluctuating line-up included not only Tampa Red and Georgia Tom but also Big Bill Broonzy and Blind Blake, recorded until 1937.

The archetypal hokum song was probably "It's Tight Like That", recorded by Tampa Red and Georgia Tom in 1928 and much covered thereafter. Other typical titles included "Let's Get Drunk And Truck" and "Let Me Feel It". Many years later, in the 1976 BBC television series *The Devil's Music*, Georgia Tom attempted to explain the hokum blues: "We didn't want to call ourselves blues singers and we didn't want to call ourselves popular singers. I don't know what the word hokum means myself right now, I got to look in the dictionary, if there is such a word in the dictionary. But it was a good word to carry, for nobody knew what it meant and they say. 'Hokum Hokum Boys, we going to see something.' And they did."

Atlanta and the Piedmont blues

The headquarters of the Piedmont blues, **Atlanta**, drew in musicians from the Carolinas, Alabama, Georgia and as far north as Virginia. Much of the area was tobacco rather than cotton country, and the poverty was somewhat less harsh – although as far as black people were concerned, the differences were merely of scale. Musical activity and nightlife centered on the city's Decatur Street, with an audience drawn from the hinterland of dirt-track streets and wooden-framed houses that huddled around it. **Georgia Tom** – then known as Barrelhouse Tom – was a prominent early figure in Atlanta's black musical community before he moved to Chicago in 1916, while **Perry Bradford**, who wrote "Crazy Blues" for Mamie Smith, was another who emerged from the city's vibrant music scene.

By the 1920s, when the mobile recording trucks of Okeh, Columbia, Victor and Brunswick began rolling into town, **Blind Willie McTell** was the most accomplished bluesman around, singing in a clear and melodic light voice and playing a ringing twelve-string guitar with a fluid bottleneck style. With its more resonant tone, the twelve-string instrument became the guitar of choice for many of the other great Atlanta bluesmen of the period, including Barbecue Bob, Charley Lincoln and Peg Leg Howell.

"I know no-one can sing the blues like Blind Willie McTell", sang Bob Dylan

Chapter Five

The 1930s: Depression blues

The Great Depression, which followed in the wake of the Wall Street Crash of October 1929, had a profound effect on the blues and the market for "race" records, as it did on every other walk of American life. At first, the stock market collapse principally hit the rich. But as banks and then small businesses failed in increasing numbers, the effects rapidly trickled down.

Thousands of factories closed, and in three years, economic production fell by 54 per cent. In 1930, there were three million out of work. By 1932 that figure had swelled to more than one in four of the labor force, a figure anywhere between twelve and fifteen million.

Black people may have been systematically excluded from the American dream before the Depression, but that didn't mean that they were immune from the suffering created by its crisis. During the 1920s, 773,000 black workers migrated from the South to the cities of the north, in search of employment and a better life. Inevitably, when employers were forced to lay off their labor force, it was these migrant black workers who were the first to be let go. In rural areas, the poverty and deprivation were even worse. In Mississippi, where only two percent of farm homes had running water and a barely registering half of one percent had electricity, life was already intolerably tough. But although **Georgia Tom** joked that he "didn't feel so depressed for

I didn't have a thing to start with", life for poor rural blacks was about to get even harder.

The Depression plunged the recording industry into crisis. In 1927, record sales had topped 104 million. With disposable income plummeting in every home in the country, annual record sales had shrunk to a paltry six million by 1932. The "race" market was almost wiped out, and Paramount went into liquidation. A few big stars continued to record sporadically in Chicago and other northern cities, but field recording trips to the South all but dried up. The live music circuit also suffered. Many minstrel and tent shows were disbanded, and the TOBA teetered on the brink of extinction. The prime venue for most blues musicians once again became the street corner, where they might play all day for a mere handful of nickels and dimes. Although it wasn't strictly a blues and was recorded by the unlikely figure of Bing Crosby, the 1932 song "Buddy Can You Spare A Dime" perfectly summed up the disillusion and despair:

"They used to tell me I was building a dream
And so I followed the mob.
When there was earth to plow or guns to bear,
I was always there, right on the job.
They used to tell me I was building a dream
With peace and glory ahead –
Why should I be standing in line, just waiting for
*   bread?"*

Initially, the government in Washington was slow to react, hamstrung by the underpinning philosophy of American capitalism which held that anyone could rise to the top – "from log cabin to White House" in the old cliché – by dint of their own hard work. The even more brutal corollary of this ostensibly meritocratic belief was that, therefore, the poor probably deserved their fate due to their own idleness, feckless nature or other inadequacies of character. As a result, President Herbert Hoover offered lit-

tle in terms of federal intervention, and whatever relief was offered initially came from the local authorities. In the South, this meant poor whites received assistance before blacks, who were treated as harshly as ever. Black workers employed in Mississippi state camps in 1932 received just ten cents an hour for working twelve hours per day, seven days per week.

One side effect of the Depression that ultimately helped the blues, however, was the repeal of the **Prohibition** laws. With the entire nation in distress, it became increasingly difficult to deny people the small solace to be found in a drink or two. In 1933, after a thirteen-year ban, the new President Franklin Roosevelt announced that "this would be a good time for a beer", and signed legislation permitting the manufacture and sale of "intoxicating liquors". That led to the opening of a myriad of new bars and drinking clubs where live music was in demand. The

Playlist
Booze and the blues

Whether drowning sorrows or having a high old time, booze and the blues have usually marched together…

1 CORN LIQUOR BLUES Papa Charlie Jackson from **Complete Recorded Works Vol 3**
"I got good corn liquor, I'm the best bootlegger in town, all the other bootleggers get mad when they see me? comin' around…

2 CANNED HEAT BLUES Tommy Johnson from **Complete Recorded Works 1928–29**
The song took its name from the slang term for Sterno, a cooking fuel, made of denatured alcohol and sold in cans, to which Johnson was addicted.

3 WINE O-BABY BOOGIE Big Joe Turner from **Shake, Rattle And Roll**
"I don't mind you spending my money but please don't take it all, well leave me a little so I can have myself a ball…"

4 SLOPPY DRUNK BLUES Leroy Carr from **Whiskey Is My Habit, Women Is All I Crave**
"I love that moonshine whiskey and I'll tell you what I do, the reason why I drink, I'm just trying to get along with you."

5 RUCKUS JUICE AND CHITLIN Memphis Jug Band from **Ruckus Juice & Chitlins, Vol. 1: The Great Jug Bands**
High-spirited juice-in-the-jug recorded by Will Shade's crew in the late 1920s, and also covered by the Hossier Hotshots.

6 BLOODSHOT EYES Wynonie Harris from **Bloodshot Eyes**
"I can tell that you been out on a spree, it's plain that you're lyin', when you say that you've been cryin', don't roll those bloodshot eyes at me…"

7 ONE BOURBON, ONE SCOTCH AND ONE BEER John Lee Hooker from **Best Of John Lee Hooker**
"Hey mister bartender come here, I want another drink and I want it now" – on second thoughts, make that three…

8 JUICE HEAD BABY Eddie Cleanhead Vinson from **Honk For Texas**
"She drinks whiskey like water, drinks gin like lemonade, makes me go to work early while she lies round in the shade…"

9 LET ME GO HOME WHISKEY Amos Milburn from **The Best Of Amos Milburn**
"Let me go home, whiskey, let me walk out the door, well, I'm feelin' so fine, but I just can't take it no more…"

10 DRINKING WINE SPO-DEE-O-DEE Sticks McGhee from **New York Blues**
The original lyric contained the line "drinking wine motherfucker, drinking wine" but when McGhee recorded the song in 1946 for Harlem Records, he changed it to "drinking wine spo-dee-o-dee".

Chicago club scene in particular was invigorated by the renewed flow of alcohol; star performers who benefitted from the new venues included **Leroy Carr**, **Tampa Red** and **Big Bill Broonzy**.

Things only begin to change with the implementation of Roosevelt's **New Deal**, even if it often tended at local level to favor whites over blacks – some joked grimly that one of its key relief institutions, the National Recovery Administration (NRA), stood for "Negroes Ruined Again". Roosevelt officially banned discrimination in federal relief projects and actively appointed African-Americans to positions of authority. Some black leaders complained that he didn't do more at the same time to secure equal constitutional rights or to support anti-lynching measures in the South. Nevertheless, the New Deal represented a sea change in the relationship between the American state and its black citizens, many of whom hailed Roosevelt as a hero, crediting him with saving their jobs, their homes and their dignity. The darkest days

of the Depression had inspired many blues songs, including Tampa Red's "Depression Blues" ("Depression has got me, somebody help me please") and **Sleepy John Estes**' "Down South Blues". Now blues artists began hymning the praises of FDR on songs such as "President Blues" by **Jack Kelly** and the **South Memphis Jug Band**. When Roosevelt eventually died in office in 1945, **Champion Jack Dupree** was merely one of many who penned elegies to him.

The legacy of Charley Patton

By the time the worst of the Depression was over, the focus of the blues had slowly but inexorably begun to shift from the South to cities such as Chicago, St Louis and even New York, where the likes of **Josh White** and **Leadbelly** were at the center of a liberal circle that included folk and blues performers. Down in the Delta, however, the most potent expression of the country blues legacy was still to come.

The Library of Congress

In the world of commercial record labels, the rural blues of the Delta was eventually superseded by new, slicker styles and more sophisticated musical fashions. The field recordings made by folklore collectors such as **John and Alan Lomax** and others for the **Library of Congress** were not constrained by such considerations. Hence, while no record company made any commercial field recordings in Mississippi between 1931 and 1939, the Lomaxes were busy all over the Delta and beyond, looking for singers to record for the Washington DC-based library's **Archive of Folk Song**. In 1933 they traveled sixteen thousand miles through Texas, Louisiana, Mississippi and beyond, with a cumbersome 350-pound recording machine built into the rear of their Ford. Plantations and prisons offered the most fertile ground for finding blues singers, and it was in Angola State Penitentiary that they discovered **Leadbelly** that year. The Mississippi state penitentiary at Parchman Farm, where they recorded in 1933 and again in 1936, 1937 and 1939, was another rich source for song hunters. Two years later, while searching for Robert Johnson in Mississippi – unaware that he was dead – they discovered and recorded an unknown country blues singer called **Muddy Waters** on Stovall's Plantation. On the same trip, they also recorded **Son House** and **Willie Brown**. Their contribution to blues history is doubly invaluable, as the Lomaxes deliberately set out to capture styles and songs that were in danger of dying out, and it's unlikely that many of those they recorded would have been touched by the commercial recording industry. As Alan Lomax put it, the Library of Congress archive "added the voice of the common man to the written history of America". Other collectors who made invaluable field recordings for the library's archive included Charles Seeger, Sidney Robertson, John W. Work, Lewis Jones, Harold Spivacke and two female archivists, Mary Elizabeth Barnicle and Carita Dogget Corse.

Although **Robert Johnson** has since been crowned the king of the Delta bluesmen, many devotees will tell you that **Charley Patton**, who was aged over forty when he first recorded for Paramount in 1929, was the true monarch of Mississippi. A true original whose influence on an entire generation of Delta bluesmen was incalculable, he made the bulk of his recordings in 1929 and 1930, with one final session a few months before his death in 1934. Long before he entered a studio, Patton was a Delta legend, and the list of those who have paid homage to his influence includes Son House, Tommy Johnson, Howlin' Wolf, Muddy Waters, Bukka White, Big Joe Williams and David Honeyboy Edwards.

Patton was also a considerable influence on Robert Johnson himself, which is not to deny that Johnson, who made his first recordings in 1936 and was dead within two years, was also a figure of startling originality. It's ironic that the most profound expression of the pre-war acoustic blues came just as electrification and the urban sounds of Chicago were about to make the form seem anachronistic. It's fascinating to imagine what Johnson, had he lived, might have achieved with an electric guitar. After all, he was of the same generation as John Lee Hooker, Muddy Waters and Howlin' Wolf, and he would surely have torn up the clubs of post-war Chicago had he been afforded the chance to do so. Even Johnson did not quite represent the last stand of the old-style Delta blues; that honor probably belongs to **Bukka White**, who recorded some wonderful sides for Bluebird in 1940, before sinking back into obscurity until he was rediscovered during the 1960s folk-blues revival.

The city blues

Although the Depression helped to shift the focus of the blues from the country to the city, arguably the catastrophe merely speeded up changes that were already underway. Migration from the South to cities like Chicago had started in the 1920s, and many of the great names in the newly urbanized blues had started recording before the Depression. Among them were **Big Bill Broonzy** in 1927; pianist **Leroy Carr**, who cut "How Long How Long Blues" with **Scrapper Blackwell** in 1928; and **Tampa Red**, who recorded "It's Tight Like That" with Georgia Tom the same year. All were to prove hugely influential in the sound that emerged in Chicago during the 1930s.

As we have already seen, the Depression also changed the way the record industry functioned. To counter the disastrous decline in sales, in 1933 Victor introduced its cut-price **Bluebird** imprint, and it was around the Bluebird label and its far-sighted chief talent scout and record producer **Lester Melrose** that the new Chicago sound began to coalesce. The stable of artists Melrose built included Broonzy and Tampa Red, and the sound they created was considerably more sophisticated than the primitive Delta style. Known as the "Bluebird Beat", it came to dominate Chicago blues for the best part of a decade.

Boogie-woogie piano blues

Thanks to its portability and flexibility, the guitar was the obvious first instrument of the traveling blues; you couldn't ride the rails or hobo around with a **piano** on your back. However, a strong tradition of blues piano accompaniment had been established on the theater circuit, and the piano also enjoyed prominence in the barrelhouses and bordellos. **Perry Bradford** played piano on **Mamie Smith**'s "Crazy Blues", Bessie Smith was accompanied by Clarence Williams and Fletcher Henderson, and Ma Rainey by Lovie Austin and later Georgia Tom. But the first blues piano players to enjoy recorded success in their own right were **Leroy Carr** and **Charles "Cow Cow" Davenport**, both of whom were first recorded in 1928.

Carr was later recruited by Lester Melrose, who recorded him in 1935. His piano playing would surely have become another pillar of the "Bluebird Beat" had he not died two months

REDFERNS

Two titans of the boogie joanna: Pete Johnson and
Albert Ammons

Smith shared an apartment in Chicago with two other pianists, **Meade Lux Lewis** and **Albert Ammons**, but did not live to share the success they enjoyed when the boogie-woogie craze swept America in the mid-1930s. Playing in a Chicago club in March 1929, he was shot by a stray bullet in a fight that had nothing to do with him. Other popular blues pianists to emerge from the barrelhouse circuit included **Jimmy Yancey**, "**Cripple**" **Clarence Lofton** and **Roosevelt Sykes**, but boogie-woogie did not hit its peak until after the worst of the Depression had passed. Ammons made his first recordings with his Rhythm Kings in 1936, the same year that Lewis, after one obscure session for Paramount in 1927, got a second chance in a studio with "Honky Tonk Train Blues" (a tune that bore more than a passing similarity to "Pinetop's Boogie-woogie").

The third great pianist in the boogie-woogie trinity was **Pete Johnson**, and all three were booked to play together at **John Hammond**'s From Spirituals To Swing concert at New York's Carnegie Hall in December 1938. Boogie-woogie was already hugely popular with a black audience who, as one contemporary description put it, found that the aggression and tension of ghetto life could "be briefly sublimated by boogie-woogie into the joy of physical release through the pounding excitement of the piano". After Carnegie Hall, boogie-woogie became phenomenally popular with white audiences, too. Ammons hit pay dirt with his signature tune "Boogie-woogie Stomp", as did Johnson with the great "Roll 'Em Pete", and they became huge stars. They frequently played and recorded together as a trio with Lewis, and appeared at such chic nightspots as New York's Café Society, dressed in tuxedos and pounding not out-of-tune old barrelhouse instruments but top-of-the-range Steinway concert grands. The boogie-woogie craze was effectively over by the end of World War II, but it left a lasting impact on blues and jazz, with the likes of **John Lee Hooker** adapting the boogie riff to the electric guitar.

later from acute alcoholism (one of his final recordings for Bluebird was presciently titled "Six Feet Cold In The Ground"). Davenport's "Cow Cow Blues" owed much to a ragtime style, but with its walking bass pattern it was perhaps the first recorded example of the style that came to be known as **boogie-woogie**, an infectious twelve-bar blues characterized by a consistent left-hand bass pattern (sometimes but not always "walking") while the right hand carries the melody, often with extensive use of improvisation. Within months, "Cow Cow Blues" was followed by "Pinetop's Boogie-woogie" by the 24-year old pianist, **Clarence "Pinetop" Smith**. Other records had previously used the word "boogie", but this was the first to use the full term.

Playlist
Ebony and ivory

From the whorehouses of New Orleans to the lumber camps of Alabama, and from the honky tonks of Texas to the juke joints of Mississippi, the piano has always been at the core of the blues. In latter years, it perhaps lost pride of place in many jazz and blues combos to the ubiquitous Hammond organ. But these ten blues and boogie-woogie piano tracks have all left an indelible stamp on musical history.

1 PINETOP'S BOOGIE-WOOGIE Pinetop Smith from **Martin Scorsese Presents The Blues: A Musical Journey**
The first boogie-woogie piano hit, recorded in Chicago in December 1928. Tragically, Smith was murdered before its release.

2 HONKY TONK TRAIN BLUES Meade Lux Lewis from **Boogie-woogie Stomp: Shakin' That Thing**
More classic early boogie-woogie, cut in Chicago in 1927, but not released until after "Pinetop's Boogie-woogie". Intriguingly, Lewis and Smith shared an apartment, together with a third boogie-woogie pioneer, Albert Ammons.

3 HOW LONG HOW LONG BLUES Leroy Carr from **Whiskey Is My Habit, Women Is All I Crave**
Intimate and sophisticated piano blues from 1928 on Carr's greatest composition, accompanied by Scrapper Blackwell on guitar.

4 DIRTY MOTHER FOR YOU (DON'T YOU KNOW) Roosevelt Sykes from **Roosevelt Sykes Vol 4 1934–36**
Known as "the Honeydripper", Sykes evokes the piano blues of the lumber camps, whorehouses and gambling dens where he cut his musical teeth in this ribald 1936 recording.

5 ROLL 'EM PETE Pete Johnson (With Joe Turner) from **Boogie-woogie Stomp: Shakin' That Thing**
Flawless boogie-woogie, recorded following Turner's spectacular appearance at the "Spirituals to Swing" concert at Carnegie Hall in December 1938. Joe Turner's vocal completes the masterpiece.

6 WORRIED LIFE BLUES Big Maceo from **Complete Recorded Works Vol 1 1941–45"**
A shuffling classic recorded in Chicago in 1941 from one of the architects of modern blues piano, with Tampa Red on guitar.

7 HONEYDRIPPER Joe Liggins from **Joe Liggins And The Honeydrippers**
Infectious piano swing from 1944, featuring some equally irresistible sax from Little Willie Jackson and James "Ham" Jackson.

8 DRIFTIN' BLUES Charles Brown from **Driftin' Blues: The Best Of Charles Brown**
Elegant West Coast piano blues, accompanied by his own smooth-as-velvet voice, reveals Brown's classical training on this 1945 classic, released under the name of Johnny Moore's Three Blazers.

9 MOTHER EARTH Memphis Slim from **Mother Earth**
Sweet sophistication and an immaculate arrangement on Slim's signature tune, recorded in Chicago in 1950.

10 GOOD MORNING MR BLUES Otis Spann from **Piano Blues**
Stark but magisterial solo piano blues, recorded in Denmark in the early 1960s after a decade spent playing on some of Chess's greatest recordings by Muddy Waters and others.

St Louis

By the mid-1930s, Chicago had established itself as the main urban center for the blues, but the vibrant scene of **St Louis**, Missouri, was for a while not too far behind. In the early 20th century, St Louis had been the spiritual home of ragtime. It also developed a reputation as a "sinful city", and a haven for gambling, drinking and prostitution. Where such conditions flourished, the blues was not far behind; itinerant musicians and migrant workers arrived fresh from the South whether on Highway 61, by the Illinois Central Railroad or up the mighty Mississippi river. By the 1920s, the city's strategic position on the migratory route north out of the Delta had made it the center of a constant flow of movement. The blues could be heard everywhere around the juke joints, speak-easies and barrelhouses of the city's notorious Morgan Street district, known as "Deep Morgan". Across the river, in the slums of the Valley district of East St Louis, the best-known local bluesman was the great **Peetie Wheatstraw**, also known as "the devil's son-in-law". Other prominent names who worked the rich and diverse St Louis blues scene included **Lonnie Johnson** and the pianist Roosevelt Sykes.

New York

The folk-blues scene that developed in **New York** during the mid 1930s focused on a very different music to that being made in the South, and found black performers playing for a mostly white, middle-class audience. After helping to secure the release of **Leadbelly** from the Louisiana State Penitentiary, folklorist John Lomax employed him as his chauffeur and took him to New York. Leadbelly had made previous recordings for the Library of Congress, but started to record commercially in 1935. His roots in the songster tradition, and repertoire of folk songs and ballads such as "Goodnight Irene", "Cottonfields" and

"The Midnight Special", made his music highly accessible to a white audience. Lionized by East Coast liberal society, he was also befriended by folk singers Woody Guthrie and Pete Seeger, and the circle around Mo Asch's Folkways Records. Also part of the same scene was **Josh White**, who left his home state of South Carolina for New York in 1932. Finding a new middle-class audience interested in radical politics and folk music, he gave many white Americans their first direct contact with the blues. Similarly, **Sonny**

From spirituals to swing

Billed as "an evening of American Negro music", the two **From Spirituals To Swing** concerts, organized by **John Hammond** at New York's Carnegie Hall in 1938 and 1939, represented seminal moments in the march of the blues into the mainstream of white American culture. These were the first major events at which black artists had performed for an integrated audience in such a prestigious venue. Juxtaposing jazz artists, blues masters and gospel singers, Hammond aimed to celebrate the diversity of African-American musical before an audience that had rarely had the opportunity to appreciate such forms. However, he initially encountered huge opposition to his plans, from both sides of the racial divide. The National Association for the Advancement of Colored People (NAACP) were suspicious of a white promoter and refused to sponsor the concerts. Following several other rebuffs in his search for a sponsor, Hammond eventually persuaded *New Masses*, the cultural journal of the American Communist Party, to put up the money.

Hammond also experienced difficulties in putting together his bill. Many of the blues artists on his wish-list were either dead, in prison or otherwise untraceable. Prime among them was **Robert Johnson**; Hammond later claimed that he had signed Johnson, only for him to fail to show up because he had died following a barroom brawl. While Johnson was undoubtedly dead and Hammond had genuinely tried to secure his services, he had not of course signed on, having died four months earlier.

Nevertheless, when Hammond walked on stage to introduce the first concert two days before Christmas 1938, he had managed to assemble an unprecedented line-up. The concert was dedicated to the memory of **Bessie Smith**, who had died following a car crash fifteen months earlier; her niece **Ruby**, accompanied by pianist James P. Johnson, sang in her place. The jazz world was represented by the **Count Basie Orchestra**, gospel by **Sister Rosetta Tharpe** and **Mitchell's Christian Singers**. The blues artists included **Big Bill Broonzy** – whom Hammond romantically but erroneously claimed had left his farm and mule in Arkansas to play – **Sonny Terry**, **Joe Turner**, **Jimmy Rushing** and **Helen Humes**, while the biggest sensation of the evening was probably the **boogie-woogie** piano trio of **Albert Ammons**, **Pete Johnson** and **Meade Lux Lewis**, who together performed a "Cavalcade of Boogie".

That concert having been a sell-out, Hammond organized a second one a year later on Christmas Eve 1939. It featured many of the same artists, as well as the **Benny Goodman Sextet**, featuring guitarist **Charlie Christian**; the gospel voices of the **Golden Gate Quartet**; and blues queen **Ida Cox**. The concerts were recorded and eventually released on the Vanguard label in 1959 as a double album. An expanded three-CD set appeared in 1999, including 23 previously unreleased tracks.

REDFERNS

Mr Huddie Ledbetter, aka Leadbelly

Terry and **Brownie McGhee** moved to the city following their appearance at the From Spiritual To Swing concert at Carnegie Hall in 1938.

The devil's music

In many respects, the development of **gospel music** was quite distinct from that of the blues. The two forms played different social roles and had separate repertoires. However, they were also the opposite sides of the same coin, and the dichotomy between the two was vital to the evolution of each. Many blues singers started out singing in church. However, many of those who sang sacred music regarded secular music as profane, and almost as soon as the blues emerged it was dubbed the "**devil's music**" in some circles. This was hardly surprising, given

that blues performers were to be found performing in gambling clubs, brothels and barrelhouses and that anywhere vice was found, it appeared to be marching to the beat of the blues. In 1941, the black sociologist Charles S. Johnson described the world in which the blues flourished: "It is comprised of individuals who fall outside the recognized and socially sanctioned class categories, that is those persons who are free from the demands of society – the 'wide' people, the vagabonds, the 'worthless' and 'undeserving poor' who are satisfied with their status, the 'outcasts', the 'bad niggers', prostitutes, gamblers, outlaws, renegades and 'free' people. Life in this underworld is hard, but its irresponsible freedom seems to compensate for its disadvantages. These are the people who create the blues and secular songs of the demi-monde."

As the market for blues records grew during the 1920s, a black audience developed in parallel for religious songs and sermons. The first black gospel record, by Madam Hurd Fairfax, was released by Paramount in 1925, while later that year Calvin P. Dixon became the first black preacher to fit a sermon onto a 78 rpm record.

A large number of blues singers, including Charley Patton, Blind Lemon Jefferson, Son House and Blind Willie McTell, sang both blues and spiritual material. Some of those who started out as blues singers, like **Georgia Tom** and **Rev. Gary Davis**, later abandoned the "devil's music" in order exclusively to sing gospel. Others, known as "guitar evangelists", combined the raw earthiness of the Delta blues with gospel sentiments; the most prominent such exponent of the "holy blues" was **Blind Willie Johnson**. By the late 1930s, **Sister Rosetta Tharpe** was also combining the two, singing songs such as "I Want A Small Skinny Papa" alongside her gospel material, and belting out a magnificent and bluesy version of "Rock Me", accompanied by her own guitar and Albert Ammons on piano, at the 1938 Spirituals To Swing concert. Many years later, one critic described Tharpe's per-

Gospel singer-songwriter and pioneer of rock music, Sister Rosetta Tharpe

formance as "essentially a rock song, fifteen-odd years before rock was invented".

Giles Oakley summed up the dialectic between blues and gospel quite brilliantly in the book that accompanied his seminal 1976 BBC television series, *The Devil's Music*: "The blues were antithetical to the standards a preacher was expected to represent in a purely religious sense. The fire-and-brimstone emotionality of the preacher was rich in its own mythology of fate, death, hell and the devil, and in a world as close to the arbitrariness of nature as Mississippi itself where boll-weevils,

floods or simply a bad harvest could devastate a person's livelihood, such symbolism had enormous power. Many blues singers felt torn this way and that, enjoying the good times of the juke joint but still believing they would someday turn their backs on the blues. Belief in the power of faith and the possibility of redemption unto heaven meant that however a brother or sister might stray from the fold, there was always the possibility of a return to the paths of God." In short, blues and gospel became what they were because of each other, not despite each other.

Chapter Six

The 1940s: bright lights, big city

Just as the Depression slowed the development of the record industry in the early 1930s, the entry of America into World War II brought about another hiatus. Although the war effort generated an industrial revival that finally banished the last effects of the earlier economic crash, it also resulted in a shortage of shellac, the raw material used in the manufacture of 78 rpm records. The resultant rationing curtailed record production. At the same time, in 1942, the American Federation of Musicians imposed a recording boycott in protest at the growing trend for jukeboxes and disc jockeys, which it claimed was putting musicians out of work. By the early 1940s there were almost 250,000 jukeboxes in the US, and AFM president James Cesar Petrillo denounced the 78 rpm record as "the number one scab". The strike lasted until 1944, and although few blues musicians were union members, many found their careers brought to an abrupt halt.

Even so, musical entertainment did not stop, and records continued to be manufactured and sold. Most were recordings by white artists – Columbia during this period released nothing but Harry James records – and even Bluebird stopped recording blues artists to concentrate on blander, more mainstream fare, often of a patriotic nature. On the other hand, it was during World War II that *Billboard* introduced the first chart exclusively covering black music – **The Harlem Hit Parade**, based, somewhat haphazardly, on sales in half a dozen "race" record stores around New York. The first "race number one",

in 1942, was "Take It And Git" by Andy Kirk and his Clouds of Joy, a Kansas City big band that included blues and boogie-woogie material in its repertoire. By 1945 the list had been renamed **The Juke Box Race Records Chart**.

Although many blues musicians were called up and sent overseas on military service, some, like Willie Dixon, refused to be drafted and went to prison instead. Others, such as Leadbelly, sang on the radio to support the war effort; one Leadbelly song, "Mr Hitler", specifically talked about Nazi persecution of the Jews. Sonny Boy "John Lee" Williamson, one of the few blues singers to record during the war years, cut a song called "Win The War Blues". This was also the era of the big bands, many of which, such as those led by white band leaders like Artie Shaw and Woody Herman, also played blues – or at least songs with "blues" in their title.

Although on one level the blues was marching into the consciousness of mainstream America, music was still segregated, like almost every other aspect of life. During World War II, **radio** became an increasingly significant force (a growth that the AFM recording boycott had recognized), even if for a long while yet it remained virtually impossible to hear black records on white radio. However, "race" shows presented by black disc jockeys sprung up on radio stations in almost every city where there was a substantial black population. One of the earliest was presented by **Sonny Boy "Rice Miller" Williamson**, who began broadcasting live on the *King Biscuit Time* show on KFFA out of Helena, Arkansas, at the end of 1941. Among the regular listeners inspired by what they heard was a young **B.B. King**. "When we came out of the fields to the house for lunch, we'd get a chance to hear Sonny Boy, 15 minutes daily from 12.15 to 12.30," he recalled many years later. King was to follow Williamson as a radio disc jockey with a show on KWEM, broadcasting out of West Memphis.

The success of the *King Biscuit Time* show – sponsored by a brand of flour – swiftly spawned imitators. In 1942 the Bright Star and Mother's Pride flour companies began their own shows on KFFA, featuring slide guitarist **Robert Nighthawk**. By the late 1940s dozen of stations had entered the fray, including the famous WDIA, which began broadcasting a half-hour black music show in Memphis in 1948. It was so successful that the entire station was soon turned over to black programming, and WDIA became known as the "Mother Station of the Negroes".

Even if music on the radio still tended to be strictly segregated, it was impossi-

ble to legislate who was listening. Before long, adventurous young white listeners were tuning in, and such exposure was to change the course of popular music forever.

The blues goes electric

The emergence of the **electric guitar** began with the popularization of **big bands** during the late 1930s, when it became necessary to amplify the instrument in order to compete with the volume of the large brass sections common to jazz orchestras of the time. Given that jazz and blues were still close cousins, it wasn't long before the trend towards amplification was adopted by blues guitarists. That move was spearheaded by **Aaron Thibeaux "T-Bone" Walker**, who grew up in Texas, but was living in Oklahoma City by the early 1930s. There he was taught to single-pick lines on a guitar by a man named Chuck Richardson. Another of Richardson's pupils, Walker's friend **Charlie Christian**, became the leading pioneer of jazz electric guitar. Walker started to experiment with an electric guitar

T-Bone Walker: godfather of rock'n'roll

REDFERNS

around 1936, and by 1939 it was the centerpiece of his sound, as he picked out complex jazz chords and intricate single-note solos. He also developed an extraordinary stage act, predating such guitar showmen as Chuck Berry and Jimi Hendrix, as amplification liberated him to play his instrument behind his head and between his legs. His biggest hit came in 1948 with "Call It Stormy Monday (But Tuesday's Just As Bad)", and he influenced an entire generation of electric blues guitarists, including B.B. King. "That was the first electric guitar I'd ever heard," King later declared. "And I went crazy. I went completely nutty. I think he had the cleanest touch of anybody I'd ever heard on guitar then."

Walker was also a prime mover in the 1940s West Coast blues scene (see below), where his clean and smooth, jazz-inflected style of electric guitar playing was soon followed by the likes of Lowell Fulson, Pee Wee Crayton and Clarence "Gatemouth" Brown. By then, the electric instrument had become the defining sound in assorted post war blues styles. In Chicago, Arthur "Big Boy" Crudup began using an electric guitar in the early 1940s, while **Muddy Waters** had traded in his acoustic instrument by 1944, and was applying an amplified guitar to his earthy Delta sound. **Memphis Minnie** played an electric guitar as early as 1941 on her biggest hit, "Me And My Chauffeur Blues", while in Texas, **Sam "Lightnin' Hopkins** began recording with an electric guitar in 1946. Around the same time in Detroit, **John Lee Hooker** was also fashioning his own unique electric guitar boogie.

Playlist
West Coast blues

The smooth and sophisticated West Coast style of blues that boomed following the end of World War II borrowed much of its swinging tempo and its rhythms from Texas, where many of its early proponents had originated. Characterized by mellifluous vocals, fluid, jazzy guitar and elegant piano chords, it represented a unique and fascinating development, far from the music's Delta roots.

1 DRIFTIN' BLUES **Johnny Moore & the Three Blazers** from **Driftin' Blues: The Best Of Charles Brown**
Featuring the voice and piano playing of Texas-born Charles Brown, Johnny Moore and the Three Blazers were initially modeled heavily on Nat King Cole's trio, but this introspective, deep-blue ballad from 1946 was a masterpiece.

2 MERRY CHRISTMAS BABY **Charles Brown** from **Driftin' Blues: The Best Of Charles Brown**
After leaving the Three Blazers, Brown enjoyed a string of solo hits, including this 1956 smash which surely ranks as the sultriest Christmas song ever recorded.

3 TIRED BROKE & BUSTED **Floyd Dixon** from **Complete Aladdin Recordings**
Another Texas transplant who replaced Brown in the Blazers, Dixon recorded this for Aladdin in 1950.

4 THREE O'CLOCK BLUES **Lowell Fulson** from **The Best Of Lowell Fulson**
A blues standard from Fulson's pen, which he recorded in 1948 and which was later covered by B.B. King.

5 BABY LET ME HOLD YOUR HAND **Ray Charles** from **Ray Charles 1950–52**
This 1951 solo recording dates from before Charles found fame on Atlantic, when he was still playing with Lowell Fulson and modeling himself on Nat King Cole and Charles Brown.

6 BAD BAD WHISKEY **Amos Milburn** from **The Best Of Amos Milburn**
One of the many blues-in-a-bottle songs by the Texas-born pianist and singer, this gave him a number one in 1950.

7 MEAN OLD WORLD **T-Bone Walker** from **The Complete 1940–54 Recordings**
"Stormy Monday" became Walker's best-known song, but this 1942 recording, backed by Freddie Slack's band, created the template for a generation of West Coast blues guitarists.

8 PLEASE SEND ME SOMEONE TO LOVE **Percy Mayfield** from **The Best Of Percy Mayfield**
The blues as lyric poetry. This rhapsodic, universal lament earned Mayfield an R&B number one in 1950.

9 DOUBLE CROSSING BLUES **Johnny Otis Orchestra** from **The Johnny Otis Rhythm & Blues Caravan: The Complete Savoy Recordings**
A big hit in 1949, featuring the singers Little Esther and Mel Walker.

10 I ALMOST LOST MY MIND **Ivory Joe Hunter** from **I Almost Lost My Mind**
West coast blues at its most laid back and mellow, an R&B number one in 1950.

Playlist
Shouters, screamers and belters

The missing link between the blues and rock'n'roll, the shouters developed their strident vocal style in order to be heard above the uptempo swing and front-line horns of the big bands led by the likes of Lucky Millinder, and the raucous jump combos of the 1940s. Most were male, but a parallel school of big-voiced female divas was also closely related. Here are ten who opened their lungs and turned the volume up to eleven.

1 SHAKE, RATTLE AND ROLL **Big Joe Turner** from **Greatest Hits**
By 1954, Turner was a 43-year-old jazz-blues veteran, but this brought him a new audience and teen adoration, even if Bill Haley's toned-down cover version was a bigger hit.

2 ALL SHE WANTS TO DO IS ROCK **Wynonie Harris** from **Bloodshot Eyes: The Best Of Wynonie Harris**
All the pounding, honking raucousness of Little Richard – but recorded way back in 1949.

3 JUICE HEAD BABY **Eddie "Cleanhead" Vinson** from **Honk For Texas**
Wheezy blues shouter and bebop sax player was an unusual combination, but tracks like this made Vinson a jump-blues giant in the late 1940s.

4 DOWN THE ROAD APIECE **Amos Milburn** from **Chicken Shack Boogie Man**
One of the great unsung post war rockers, Milburn was a smoother-voiced performer than many of the shouters, but he embodied the spirit of good living, booze and fast women on this romping party track, later covered by the Rolling Stones.

5 GOOD ROCKIN' TONITE **Roy Brown** from **Good Rockin' Tonight: The Best Of Roy Brown**
This 1948 R&B hit helped established the language of

"rocking" and "rolling" in popular music, but others were to benefit more than Brown. By the late 1950s, he was reduced to selling encyclopedias door-to-door.

6 'TAINT NOBODY'S BUSINESS IF I DO **Jimmy Witherspoon** from **Jazz Me Blues**
Was Witherspoon a blues singer, an R&B shouter or a jazz crooner? On this rollicking 1949 hit, he straddled the lot…

7 GOIN' TO CHICAGO **Jimmy Rushing** from **The Essential Jimmy Rushing**
Fifteen years shouting with Count Basie's band taught Rushing to pitch his high tenor against a hard-blowing horn section, and it held him in good stead on his exuberant signature tune.

8 HOUND DOG **Big Mama Thornton** from **Hound Dog: The Peacock Recordings**
One of the great female shouters, Thornton will always be remembered for her raucous 1952 version of this Jerry Leiber and Mike Stoller song, recorded by Elvis some four years later.

9 JIM DANDY **La Vern Baker** from **Atlantic R&B Vol 3: 1955–57**
The term "shouter" was for the most part applied to male singers, but Baker's big voice on this 1956 hit was totally in keeping with the style.

10 WHOLE LOTTA SHAKIN' **Big Maybelle** from **The Complete Okeh Sessions**
Another R&B diva in the tradition of the male shouters, Maybelle scored with this storming version in 1955, two years before Jerry Lee Lewis's hit.

West Coast blues

A new wave of migration during and immediately following the war shifted the focus of the blues away from its traditional Southern roots, not only to the cities of the North but also to the **West Coast**. Between 1940 and 1945, an estimated half-million blacks abandoned the South to seek a better life in the promised land of California, while many returning servicemen also joined the great migration westwards, preferring not to resume farming in the segregated South. A disproportionate number of the blues musicians who made California their new home in the 1940s came from **Texas**, and the swinging tempos and rhythms of the Lone Star state

played a major role in shaping the new West Coast blues.

Although a sizeable black community developed around Oakland in the San Francisco Bay area, the main West Coast blues center was **Los Angeles**, and its rapidly expanding ghetto of Watts. Despite the undeniable poverty and deprivation, the spirit on the West Coast was radically different from the more fatalistic attitudes prevalent in the ghettos of cities like Chicago and New York, and went deeper than simply the clement Californian weather. Many of the black migrants in Watts and Oakland were black servicemen who had fought in the war. Even though the US forces still operated segregated units, many soldiers had come to believe that they were fighting for a better and safer world, and had high expectations of sharing in the prosperity and freedom that would supposedly follow. This optimism profoundly affected the West Coast blues. Unlike the deep and dark sound of the Delta, with its evocation of the deprivation and misery of life in the South, the West Coast blues found confident expression in the urbane, sophisticated **jazz-blues** guitar of T-Bone Walker and his ilk; the swinging big-band sound of **jump blues**, described below; and the blues ballads of smooth-voiced **crooners** such as Charles Brown and Jimmy Witherspoon, who were heavily influenced by the success of the so-called "sepia Sinatra", **Nat "King" Cole**. Tellingly, the West Coast sound was also often referred to as **night club blues**, reflecting its new, better heeled location, far removed from the rent parties of the Chicago tenements or the rough-and-tumble juke joints of the Mississippi Delta.

Jump, swing and R&B

The biggest black star of the immediate post war era was **Louis Jordan**. Playing a rowdy fusion of jazz and blues that came to be known as **jump blues**, he had his first hit in 1942, but his great

The new independent record labels

With the end of shellac rationing and the lifting of the AFM's ban on live recording in 1944, previously unexplored markets for black music opened up. New independent record labels started to appear all over the US. The migration to the West Coast had seen **Excelsior** open for business in Los Angeles as early as 1942. That was followed in 1944 by further LA labels Jukebox, which two years later became **Specialty**; Gilt Edge; and Philco, soon to become **Aladdin**. **Modern**, Bronze, Four Star and Super Disc all started up in 1945, and a few years later came **Imperial** (1949) and **Meteor** (1952). In New York, **Apollo** started trading in 1943, followed by **National** in 1944 and **Atlantic** in 1947. The **King** label started in Cincinnati in 1943, **Peacock** in Houston in 1949, and **Bullet** in Nashville in 1946. Meanwhile, the post war boom in Chicago saw the foundation in 1946 of **Miracle**, Hy-Tone and **Mercury**. The same independent spirit also fired Sam Phillips when he started **Sun Records** in Memphis in 1952.

At first, Mercury was the most significant of the bunch, displaying the most comprehensive commitment to the blues. As well as recording the likes of **Big Bill Broonzy**, Sunnyland Slim, Memphis Slim and Robert Lockwood Jr. in Chicago, the label also recorded **Professor Longhair** in New Orleans, **Lightnin' Hopkins** in Houston and **T-Bone Walker** and **Johnny Otis** in Los Angeles. Mercury was joined on the Chicago scene in 1946 by **Aristocrat**, soon to achieve renown as the mighty **Chess Records**.

Most but not all of the new record companies were white owned, and many operated out of back rooms and recorded in garages and basements. Few initially had nationwide distribution, but they were able to flourish on local or regional hits and occasionally leasing "break-out" records to larger record companies for coast-to-coast exposure. Their success was due not only to their own entrepreneurial flair but also to the recurrent failure of major labels like Victor/Bluebird and Columbia to detect or react to changing trends in the "race" market.

Just how swiftly the independents came to dominate the burgeoning market for "race" records can be discerned from an analysis of *Billboard*'s Harlem Hit Parade and Juke Box Race Records charts. Of the 57 records that topped the charts between 1942 and 1947, a total of 49 came on three major labels – Decca, Capitol and Victor/Bluebird. During 1948 and 1949, 26 of the 31 records that topped the charts were released on small, independent labels.

Playlist
Slide guitar

From the primitive "diddley bow" to the sophisticated electric guitars of today, the sound made by sliding a glass bottleneck or metal slide, such as a knife, over the strings has always been associated with the blues.

1 YOU CAN'T KEEP NO BROWN Bo Weavil Jackson from **the Various Artists compilation** Country Blues Bottleneck Guitar Classics 1926–1937
Aggressive and fluent, one of the earliest recorded examples of slide guitar playing, cut in 1927.

2 MOTHERLESS CHILDREN HAVE A HARD TIME Blind Willie Johnson from **The Complete Blind Willie Johnson**
Johnson used a knife rather than a bottleneck to get the shimmering sound on this 1928 recording.

3 TRAVELING RIVERSIDE BLUES Robert Johnson from **King Of The Delta Blues Singers**
Searing slide delta-style played on a steel-bodied National guitar – and unlike so many slide players, Johnson never overplayed.

4 PO' BOY Bukka White from **Fixin' To Die**
His cousin B.B. King never mastered the slide like Bukka did on this recording for the Library of Congress, made in 1939 while he was in Parchman Farm penitentiary.

5 COUNTY FARM Son House from **The Complete Library Of Congress Sessions, 1941–1942**
Playing slashing slide in his trademark open G tuning, Son

House sounds like a man possessed, in a piece based on Blind Lemon Jefferson's "See That My Grave Is Kept Clean".

6 DUST MY BROOM Elmore James from **The Sky Is Crying: The History Of Elmore James**
Arguably the best-known slide guitar riff in the world…

7 WRITE ME A FEW LINES Mississippi Fred McDowell from **Mississippi Delta Blues**
Awesome, driving country blues slide playing from one of the great rediscoveries of the 1950s' revival.

8 CAN'T BE SATISFIED Muddy Waters from **The Anthology**
No one did more than Muddy to transform the acoustic slide guitar style of Son House and Robert Johnson into the modern electric sound of today.

9 STATESBORO BLUES Allman Brothers from **The Allman Brothers At Fillmore East**
Duane Allman used an empty glass Coricidin medicine bottle as a slide – and it made a mighty sound, as can be heard on this thrilling live take on Blind Willie McTell's classic.

10 DARK WAS THE NIGHT Ry Cooder from **The Paris, Texas Soundtrack**
Modeled on Blind Willie Johnson's "Dark Was the Night (Cold Was the Ground)", which Cooder described as "the most soulful, transcendent piece in all American music".

run began in mid-1945. His hits included "Ain't Nobody Here But Us Chickens", "Choo Choo Ch'Boogie" and "Let The Good Times Roll", while his mix of big band style, boogie-woogie, and honking and shouting, represented the last time that the two great forms of early 20th century black music, blues and jazz, truly marched in tandem before going their separate ways. Jordan became the king of the jukeboxes, and his influence on diverse performers from Chuck Berry to B.B. King was profound. As Bill Wyman put it in his excellent *Blues Odyssey*, "Before the war, urban blues seemed like an offshoot or an extension of country blues, but in the hands of Jordan and others like him, it sounded entirely new and a whole lot more exciting."

Jump blues also gave rise to the vocal style known as "**shouting**", as the singers needed to operate at full throttle to be heard over the honk-ing saxophones and general rowdiness. The most successful shouters included **Wynonie Harris** and **Big Joe Turner**, whose respective recordings of "Good Rockin' Tonight" and "Shake, Rattle and Roll" also forged a link between the blues and rock'n'roll. Other jump blues stars included Amos Milburn, Roy Milton and Joe Liggins on the West Coast, Jay "Hootie" McShann in Kansas City, and Roy Brown in New Orleans, a city that had been in on the birth of jazz and, thanks to the likes of Fats Domino, was about to re-establish itself as a major center of musical excellence.

Meanwhile, back in Chicago…

While the West Coast developed its urbane "nightclub blues", and the upbeat sounds of jump blues were dominating the race charts, something of a counter-revolution was taking place in **Chicago**. During the 1940s, blacks from rural Mississippi, Arkansas, Louisiana and Tennessee poured into the city in even greater numbers than they had done pre war. Among them was **Muddy Waters**, who had arrived around 1943, after being recorded on Stovall's Plantation in Mississippi by Alan Lomax two years earlier. This new breed of musicians were all for modernizing the sound of the blues by switching to electric guitars and employing small combos that included both drums and an amplified harmonica, which in effect operated as a pocket brass section. But they were not so interested in "prettying up" the music, along the lines of the mellifluous Chicago style that Lester Melrose had pioneered with his "Bluebird beat" in the late 1930s, remaining instead in thrall to the deep, rough-and-tumble, "downhome" Delta spirit of Charley Patton and Robert Johnson and the bottleneck guitar.

Muddy had switched from acoustic to electric guitar by 1944, and was playing the clubs of Chicago with Jimmy Rogers on harmonica, Eddie Boyd or Sunnyland Slim on piano, and sometimes Claude "Blue Smitty" Smith on second guitar. Then in late 1947 or early 1948 came the Aristocrat Records session that was to change the sound of the blues forever. Singing in a rich and direct Mississippi drawl and playing whining, amplified bottleneck guitar with Big Crawford on rocking bass, Waters cut "I Can't Be Satisfied" and "I Feel Like Going Home". In the control room, label boss Leonard Chess hated the raw, earthy sound, famously demanding: "What the hell's he singing?"

When copies of the record were delivered to stores in April 1948, they are said to have sold out by that same afternoon. Outlets rationed sales to one disc per customer, to forestall the entrepreneurial activities of railroad stewards, who would buy up popular records to re-sell at a profit to the captive audience on their trains. Even Muddy himself claimed he couldn't buy a copy, adding with a twinkle that Leonard Chess swiftly dropped his opposition to the new sound "because I was selling so fast they couldn't press

them fast enough". By September 1948, "I Feel Like Going Home" had translated its Chicago success into national prominence, and reached *Billboard*'s race records chart. The following year Aristocrat started to record Waters with his full club band. As 1949 was also the year that **Willie Dixon** joined the label, making his debut playing on a Robert Nighthawk session, the main elements of the Chess sound that was to dominate and reshape the blues in the early 1950s were now in place.

Around the same time in Detroit, **John Lee Hooker** was updating the country blues to a tough, amplified ghetto sound on such hits as "Boogie Chillen" and "Hobo Blues". However, he remained Detroit's one major commercial success, and the city never rivaled Chicago's domination.

In June 1949, **rhythm and blues** was formally introduced as an all-embracing term to describe black music made for a black audience, when *Billboard* launched the first **R&B** chart to replace its previous "race" chart. Many had never been happy with that word "race", and various attempts had been made to restyle it as "sepia" or "ebony" music, but it was the R&B term that stuck. However, although records by Waters and others began to appear in its chart, *Billboard* took a little longer to notice the shift that was taking place.

Belatedly, the magazine reported in March 1952: "Among the important developments that have been taking place in the rhythm and blues field over the past year, one of the most prominent is the increasing importance of the country or southern style blues and country style singer in this market. At one time there was a wide gulf between the sophisticated big city styles and rocking novelties waxed for the northern market and the country or Delta blues that were popular in the southern regions. Gradually, the two forms intermingled and the country blues tune, now dressed up in arrangements palatable to both northern and southern tastes, have been appearing on all R&B labels."

Chapter Seven

The 1950s: the blues had a baby & they called it rock'n'roll

Of the many seminal dates in blues history, the year 1950, in which the mighty Chess Records name first appeared on a record label, stands among the most crucial of all. And a new and exciting age in rhythm and blues was dawning way beyond the work of Muddy Waters and his cohorts in Chicago.

Checkmate in Chicago: from Muddy Waters to Chuck Berry

John Lee Hooker was making his mark in Detroit. In Memphis, an Alabama disc jockey named Sam Phillips was opening his recording studio on Union Avenue, where he would soon be cutting the first sides by B.B. King and Howlin' Wolf. Down in the Crescent City, Fats Domino was making his recording debut and the idiosyncratic Professor Longhair was strutting his stuff. In suave and sophisticated New York, Ruth Brown was helping to launch the nascent Atlantic Records as an R&B powerhouse with chart-toppers such as "Teardrops In My Eyes", while in laid-back Los Angeles on the West Coast, Percy Mayfield was cutting "Please Send Me Someone To Love" for Specialty. It seemed that every major black city had its own unique style, and the diversity was dazzling.

As Muddy Waters once sang, "I'm the bluest man in this whole Chicago town". The new decade of the 1950s was little more than a month old when Waters cut a song called "Rollin' Stone". By June, the Aristocrat label, owned by the brothers Leonard and Phil Chess, had become the Chess Records Corporation, and "Rollin' Stone" became the second release on the Chess label (the first had been "My Foolish Heart" by saxophonist Gene Ammons).

Waters and Chess went on to dominate the blues scene throughout the first half of the 1950s. In the words of John Collis in his fine book, *The Story Of Chess Records*, the label gave "new life to a blues form that many had thought died out in the war as a commercial force – this was country blues, revived by an alliance of electricity and an ironic urban perspective, capable of combining sophistication and world-weariness with nostalgia and superstition".

REDFERNS

Muddy Waters – Chess Records' very own blues superstar

Over the next few years, Waters became a blues colossus, with a string of R&B hits such as "Hoochie Coochie Man", "I've Got My Mojo Working", "Mannish Boy" and "I'm Ready". In *Souled American – How Black Music Transformed White Culture*, Kevin Phinney described Waters as "the alpha male of the blues, the majestic, supremely self-confident sultan who could entice any woman into his harem", and Marshall Chess confirms the power of Muddy's mojo at the time. "It was sex," he says. "If you'd ever seen Muddy then, the effect he had on women, because blues has always been a women's market. On Saturday night they'd be lined up ten deep."

Playlist
Blowin' the house down

Not for nothing was the humble harmonica known as "the Mississippi saxophone". Even more than the guitar, its pocket-sized proportions perfectly suited the lifestyle of the itinerant pre-war bluesman, although the instrument really came into its own in post-war Chicago, when amplification created a whole new range of sonic possibilities. And when played by these ten, it sounded anything but humble.

1 I BETTER CUT THAT OUT Sonny Boy (John Lee) Williamson from **Right Kind Of Life**
The original Sonny Boy was the most important harmonica player of the pre-war era; this storming rocker, released posthumously in 1948, was later appropriated by Junior Wells.

2 BLOWIN' THE BLUES Sonny Terry from **Blowin' The Blues**
A classic "whoopin'" blues designed to showcase all the technique and trickery available to the inventive harpist, accompanied only by George "Oh Red" Washington's washboard.

3 MOANIN' AT MIDNIGHT Howlin' Wolf from **His Best**
Wolf's extraordinary voice makes it easy to forget that he also blew a mean harp, based almost totally on power rather than technique. Here he conducts a call-and-response duet with himself on this potent 1951 recording.

4 JUKE Little Walter from **His Best**
A magnificent exhibition of amplified harmonica playing from 1952, featuring perhaps the most famous solo of them all. Muddy Waters and Jimmy Rogers are among those in the accompanying band.

5 EASY Walter Horton from **Sun Records Harmonica Classics**
While Horton was not a natural leader – his best work came as a sideman with the likes of Muddy Waters – his deep, heavy tone is heard to brilliant effect on this swaggering instrumental.

6 99 Sonny Boy Williamson II from **The Essential Sonny Boy Williamson**
Sonny Boy number two owed his magnificently sensuous tone and timbre to his virtuosic breath control and the resonating chamber he created by cupping his huge hands around his harp.

7 HOODOO MAN BLUES Junior Wells from **Hoodoo Man Blues**
Junior Wells was another who began his career in Muddy Waters' band; this was his signature tune, here recorded in 1965 with Buddy Guy on guitar.

8 BOOGIE THING James Cotton from **100 Per Cent Cotton**
Cotton makes the harp scream, wail, moan and croon on this opening track from his 1974 classic album.

9 EAST-WEST Paul Butterfield Blues Band from **East-West**
Butterfield stretched the instrument further than it had ever gone before on this 1966 13-minute work-out, which strays into jazz and Indian raga as well as the blues.

10 SAD DREAMS Carey Bell from **Carey Bell's Blues Harp**
Smoking harp playing from the youngster who learned direct from Little Walter, Sonny Boy Williamson II and Big Walter – and who turned seventy himself in 2006.

Charismatic he most certainly was, but part of his success was also down to the stellar group around him, including **Otis Spann** on piano, **Jimmy Rogers** on guitar, harpists **Little Walter**, **Walter "Shakey" Horton** and **James Cotton**, drummer **Fred Below** and the songwriting of the label's "Mr Fix-It", **Willie Dixon**. Apart from Muddy, those who recorded for the label and its subsidiary Checker constitute a Who's Who of post war electric blues. Chess released records by Jimmy Rogers, Eddie Boyd, Willie Mabon, Memphis Slim and John Lee Hooker (moonlighting from Modern under the flimsy disguise of John Lee Booker). Also on Chess was **Howlin' Wolf**, backed by the great Hubert Sumlin on guitar and with Dixon again providing many of

the songs, who became Muddy's main rival as the most glittering jewel in Chess's crown. On **Checker**, which the Chess brothers established as a subsidiary in 1952, came records by **Sonny Boy "Rice Miller" Williamson**, Elmore James and Little Walter among others. Another key to the success of Chess was its smart business acumen in picking up records from smaller independent labels, particularly Sam Phillips's Sun Records in Memphis, from which Chess acquired not only Howlin' Wolf but also a record called "Rocket 88", credited to Jackie Brenston and His Delta Cats (see below).

By 1952 the days of the old guard of Chicago blues were effectively over. Big Bill Broonzy, Washboard Sam and Memphis Minnie all recorded for Chess in the hope of reviving their careers, but Minnie and Sam soon retired while Broonzy astutely reinvented himself as a folk-blues entertainer for a predominantly white audience. However, the dominance of the new breed of electric blues stars who had supplanted them was surprisingly brief. Fired by the records that Sam Phillips was making down in Memphis, Chess was already moving on by 1955, and had found its own black rock'n'roll stars to rival Sun's "million dollar quartet" of Elvis Presley, Carl Perkins, Jerry Lee Lewis and Johnny Cash.

The arrival of **Bo Diddley** and **Chuck Berry**, who dominated the second half of the decade as firmly as Muddy and the rest had the first half, reflected a sea change in black musical tastes that impacted profoundly on the blues. While Chuck and Bo racked up 23 national pop hits between them, and made the Chess brothers rich beyond their dreams, success on the R&B charts for the label's original blues artists was proving increasingly elusive by 1956. Even Waters himself enjoyed no further hits on the R&B chart after 1958. Not surprisingly, the label grew less interested in signing the new blues talent that was still arriving in Chicago every week. That attitude that may have contributed to Willie Dixon's decision in 1956 to quit for the Cobra label, where his first signing was the guitarist **Otis Rush**. However, when Chess entered the LP market in 1957, fittingly *The Best Of Muddy Waters* was the first release in the new format.

While Chess may have dominated the Chicago scene in the 1950s, it was certainly not alone. **Parrot**, **JOB**, **Vee Jay** and **Cobra** were among the rival labels responsible for a healthy rivalry that fostered a golden age of blues in the Windy City. Among other major names recording for Chicago labels in the first half of the decade were J.B. Lenoir, Snooky Prior, Johnny Shines, Billy Boy Arnold, J.B. Hutto, Eddie Taylor and Albert King. Most successful of all was **Jimmy Reed**, who began recording in 1953. His slack, infectious boogie rhythms was still clocking up hit after hit on Vee Jay in the late 1950s and into the early 1960s, long after Muddy Waters had faded from the charts.

Sun rise in Memphis

Memphis was an extraordinary melting pot of musical styles during the early 1950s. **B.B. King** and **Howlin' Wolf** were both playing around town, while singers such as **Bobby Bland**, **Little Milton** and **Little Junior Parker** also adorned a musical scene that for a while rivaled Chicago in its vibrancy.

It was into this dynamic musical vortex that **Samuel Cornelius Phillips** stepped in January 1950, opening his Memphis Recording Studios for business with a motto that promised to record "anything, anytime, anywhere". His earliest clients included local blues artists such as Joe Hill Louis and Lost John Hunter, and by 1951, he had added B.B. King, Howlin' Wolf, Rosco Gordon and Doctor Ross to his roster. In March of that year, he also cut a fast boogie dance track called "Rocket 88" with Ike Turner's Kings of Rhythm, featuring a vocal by saxophonist **Jackie Brenston**. That was subsequently cited by no less an authority than Phillips himself as "**the first rock'n'roll record**" for its revolutionary combination of "blues, country and pop".

Like many of Phillips's early recordings, "Rocket 88" was licensed to Chess, and gave the Chicago label its first number one on the R&B chart. Phillips went on to lease further sides to Chess by Sleepy John Estes, David "Honeyboy" Edwards and others, and also leased material to Modern and RPM. But he swiftly came to realize that he needed his own label, and established **Sun Records** in 1952. He was soon releasing discs by the likes of Rufus Thomas, Little Junior Parker, Little Milton, Mose Vinson, Earl Hooker and James Cotton. The majority of the artists he recorded were black R&B singers, backed by the piano, guitar and saxophone accompaniment popular in the Memphis clubs around Beale Street at the time. As Charlie Gillett noted in his groundbreaking book *The Sound Of The City*: "No particular dominant style linked them all, but common to many of their records was a kind of intimate atmosphere created by the singers and enhanced by the careful documentary recording technique of Phillips."

If Phillips's recording methods were ground-breaking, so was his ability to reach a multi-racial audience. The early Sun recordings started to find an audience beyond the obvious black demographic among hip young white Southern kids, who called themselves "cats", dressed in black fashions and listened to black music. Yet Phillips felt that he could reach an even bigger white audience if he could "find a white man who could sing like a black man". He found just such a voice in **Elvis Presley**; from the moment some time after midnight on July 5, 1954, when the 19-year-old stepped up to the microphone at Sun Studios and recorded Arthur "Big Boy" Crudup's "That's All Right", the world was never quite the same again.

Elvis's early Sun recordings contained a visceral energy and sexuality that, while perhaps not strictly bluesm was mostly definitely influenced by it, and many of his early songs were taken from the repertoire of R&B singers. He cut his final session with Sun in July 1955, recording a version of Junior Parker's "Mystery Train". Phillips recalled that the song was "so embedded in Elvis's mind that when he started to sing it, it was as natural as breathing." The fact that the movement Presley started with "That's All Right Mama" was soon to put many such blues and R&B musicians as its author Crudup out of business, ranks as one of life's crueler ironies.

Way down South: New Orleans, Louisiana and Texas

New Orleans has always marched to a quite different beat to anywhere else in America. After the city's key role in the birth of jazz at the turn of the 20th century, its music scene seemed to

---

Playlist
The blues had a baby

Ten songs the world knows as rock'n'roll classics – and the blues originals they were came from.

1 THAT'S ALL RIGHT Arthur "Big Boy" Crudup from **That's All Right Mamma**
But you'll know it better as Elvis Presley's first single.

2 MYSTERY TRAIN Little Junior Parker from **The Sun Records Story**
Another early Elvis single – but his producer Sam Phillips had actually cut the song a couple of years earlier with a black act.

3 CROSSROADS Robert Johnson from **King Of The Delta Blues Singers**
A staple for Eric Clapton and Cream, whose first album also included songs by Howlin' Wolf and Muddy Waters.

4 GOOD MORNING LITTLE SCHOOL GIRL Sonny Boy Williamson II from **The Best Of Sonny Boy Williamson**
Later covered by the Yardbirds, Van Morrison and countless others.

5 LITTLE RED ROOSTER Howlin' Wolf from **Moanin' In The Moonlight**
A 1964 hit for the Rolling Stones, but originally written by Willie Dixon in Chicago for Chester Burnett (aka Howlin' Wolf).

6 CRAWLING KING SNAKE John Lee Hooker from **The Very Best Of John Lee Hooker**
Hooker learned the song from Big Joe Williams and recorded the definitive version in 1949. Some 22 years later it appeared on the Doors' album *LA Woman*.

7 BABY PLEASE DON'T GO Big Joe Williams from **Best Of Big Joe Williams**
But she did, all the way to Belfast to give Van Morrison and Them one of their early hits.

8 KEY TO THE HIGHWAY Big Bill Broonzy from **The Bill Broonzy Story**
Broonzy played it on an acoustic guitar; then it turned up with Eric Clapton and Duane Allman's twin electric guitars on Derek and the Dominos' *Layla and Other Assorted Love Songs*.

9 I CAN'T QUIT YOU BABY Otis Rush from **The Essential Collection**
Written by Willie Dixon for Otis Rush, this one featured on the debut album by Led Zeppelin.

10 TROUBLE SO HARD Vera Hall from **Natural Blues (Various Artists)**
When Alan and John Lomax recorded Hall singing this in Alabama in the late 1930s, nobody could have guessed it would turn up 60 years later as "Natural Blues" on Moby's multi-platinum album, *Play*.

Lightnin' Hopkins in the studio

retreat into its shell and was largely passed by when the mobile field recording units were touring the South in the 1930s. By the beginning of the 1950s, however, a new musical gumbo was bursting forth from the New Orleans nightclubs. The city's own unique take on jump blues was based on dramatic vocal expression and either an exuberant bouncing beat, epitomized by the phrase *laissez les bons temps rouler*, or an intense, morose shuffle that summoned up unimaginable sadness.

The biggest figure to emerge from the rejuvenated New Orleans scene was **Fats Domino**, whose distinctive boogie-influenced piano style made him first a hit on the R&B charts and then a rock'n'roll star, but he was swiftly followed by the likes of **Smiley Lewis, Lloyd Price** and **Guitar Slim**. The shuffling R&B piano of **Professor Longhair** represented a different strain of New Orleans music, taking in not only traditional blues, jazz and R&B elements but also Afro-Caribbean rhythms and Mardi Gras parade beats. While he was a profound influence on local musicians such as **Dr. John** and

James Booker, he seldom traveled out of the Crescent City, which in many ways remained a self-contained island within American culture. Chess were also active in New Orleans, employing as their agent in the city Paul Gayten, who signed Bobby Charles (one of the first white artists on the label) and Clarence "Frogman" Henry among others.

Elsewhere in Louisiana, a genre known as **swamp blues** emerged around Baton Rouge, thanks largely to producer J.D. Miller and the **Excello** label. Exemplified by the likes of **Lightnin' Slim**, **Slim Harpo**, Lazy Lester and Silas Hogan, its spare mix of electric guitar, harmonica and minimal percussion, given an added edge through the use of reverb, owed something to the influence of the Chicago-based Jimmy Reed, but also added influences drawn from nearby New Orleans and the Texas blues of **Lightnin' Hopkins**. Hopkins himself was based in Houston. After spending the pre-war years playing picnics and dances around the Lone Star state with his cousin Texas Alexander, he had his first R&B hit in 1949 and was a major force for

Playlist
Zydeco

They've always done things differently in Louisiana, the poorest state in the Union, and the region's music is as unique as you'd expect. Cajun is the French-styled music of the state's white population. Zydeco is its black equivalent with deep roots in other African-American forms such as jazz and blues, but with a regional spice all its own.

1 BON TON ROULET Clifton Chenier from **Zydeco Dynamite: The Clifton Chenier Anthology**
Swampy, stomping stuff from the unrivaled king of zydeco and his Red Hot Louisiana Band.

2 ALLONS A LAFAYETTE Joseph and Cleona Falcon from **Harry Smith's Anthology Of American Folk Music**
The first Cajun record, cut in 1928 by this husband-and-wife accordion-and-guitar duo, was an instant hit all over Louisiana.

3 A BLUES DE LA PRISON Amedee Ardoin from **The First Black Zydeco Recording Artist: His Original Recordings 1928–38**
The accordionist Ardoin died in 1941 after being viciously beaten by white racists after he had accepted a white woman's handkerchief to wipe his brow at a concert.

4 HEY NEGRESS Queen Ida from **Caught In The Act**
A typically tough, Louisiana blues ballad from the acknowledged first lady of zydeco, even though these days she lives in San Francisco.

5 BOUGHT A RACOON Buckwheat Zydeco from **Best Of Louisiana Zydeco**
The good times roll on this cracking and humorous piece

from the internationally popular band led by former Clifton Chenier sideman Stanley Dural Jr.

6 PAPER IN MY SHOE Boozoo Chavis from **Paper In My Shoe**
At the end of this session, cut for Eddie Shuler's Goldband Records in 1954, a whiskey-loosened Chavis apparently fell out of his chair but carried on playing. Shuler faded the track out to hide the crash.

7 ZYDECO TWO-STEP Rockin' Dopsie from **Louisiana Music**
From Dopsie's 1991 major label debut album, recorded after his accordion playing on Paul Simon's *Graceland* had introduced the sound of zydeco to millions.

8 GIVE HIM CORNBREAD Beau Jocque from **The Best Of Beau Jocque & The Zydeco Hi-Rollers**
The stonking original version of Beau Jocque's biggest self-composed hit, which has since become a zydeco standard.

9 PERE ET GARCON Zydeco John & Geno Delafose from **Pere Et Garcon**
Two for the price of one as father and son team up on the rocking title track of the 1992 album they recorded together, two years before the death of Delafose Sr.

10 MY TOOT TOOT Rockin' Sidney from **My Toot Toot**
Sidney began as an R&B singer before he discovered zydeco and learned the accordion. The two traditions unite thrillingly on his biggest hit from 1985.

Thanks to Garth Cartwright for several of the tips on this list.

the next five years. He then disappeared until 1959, when he was one of the first blues artists to be rediscovered in the folk-blues revival.

The other principal R&B style to emerge in the region was **zydeco**, which developed in its modern form around 1950 among poor Creoles from rural southern Louisiana. Many of them spoke both English and French, and the term came from a phonetic spelling of "les haricots", the French for green beans, from the song lyric "les haricots sont pas salés" (the beans are not salty).

The genre drew equally on French-based folk songs and dance tunes from the Creole folk tradition played on accordions and washboards, and the rural blues of English-speaking black Americans. The two forms started to mix in

the 1930s, and by 1950, the accordions had become amplified and drums and electric guitars added. The undoubted master of the style, **Clifton Chenier**, was born in Louisiana, and began playing in 1947 after he had relocated to Texas. He swiftly replaced the old-style button accordion played by his father with a more versatile piano keyboard model. Adding influences drawn from the great jump blues shouters and New Orleans R&B, he did not become a full-time professional musician until 1956 but scored major R&B hits on Specialty in the 1950s, and remained zydeco's greatest ambassador until his death in 1987.

Atlantic: the house that Ruth built

In New York, the newly formed **Atlantic Records** gave the blues a metropolitan makeover that would eventually lead all the way to soul music. Formed by Turkish brothers **Ahmet** and **Nesuhi Ertegun** in 1947, the label's first major contribution was to update the image of the "blues mama" of the 1920s. During the early 1950s, **Ruth Brown** sold so many records that Atlantic became known as "the house that Ruth built". Backing her powerful voice with the boogie-based, sax-led band arrangements that were the trademark of the early Atlantic sound, she was followed by **LaVern Baker** (who was billed as "Little Miss Sharecropper"). Both Baker and Brown represented a key link between early-1950s R&B and rock'n'roll. Atlantic also signed **Big Joe Turner**, perhaps the greatest of the blues shouters of the period and another link with the coming rock'n'roll era, via his original version of "Shake, Rattle and Roll", which topped the R&B chart in 1954.

Central to the success of Atlantic was producer **Jerry Wexler**, who had actually coined the term R&B when working as a reporter for *Billboard* and was later to enjoy huge success in the 1960s with the likes of Aretha Franklin. "The R&B I liked best had strong links to jazz and blues," he recalled several decades later. "But the progression of blues and jump blues to R&B happened in almost imperceptible increments." One of the biggest incremental increases came when the label signed **Ray Charles** in 1952. Initially an impersonator of Nat "King" Cole and Charles Brown, Charles cut the groundbreaking "I Got A Woman" in 1954. Combining an arrangement rooted in jazz and blues with a groaning vocal of unbridled passion that was derived from gospel, it has with some justification become known as the first **soul**

Ruth Brown, Atlantic's queen

record. In the late 1940s, Atlantic also dipped a toe in the New Orleans pool of talent, recording sessions with **Professor Longhair**.

The dawn of the folk revival

Little did anyone realize at the start of the 1950s, with the blues apparently going from strength to strength, that by the end of the decade its popularity with a black audience would have lapsed into apparently terminal decline.

Playlist: Ten songs the world learned from Harry Smith

Complete with the highly idiosyncratic précis that Harry Smith offered to every song in the original 1952 booklet:

1 MISSISSIPPI BOWEAVIL BLUES (1929) from **The Masked Marvel (Charley Patton)**
"Bollweavil survives physical attack after cleverly answering farmers' questions…"

2 STACKALEE (1927) from **Frank Hutchinson**
"Theft of stetson hat causes deadly dispute. Victim identifies self as family man…"

3 KASSIE JONES (1928) from **Furry Lewis**
"Crack engineer Jones in fatal collision. Knew Alice Fry. Wife recalls symbolic dream, later consoles children…"

4 FRANKIE (AND ALBERT) (1928) from **Mississippi John Hurt**
"Albert dies preferring Alice Fry, but judge finds Frankie charming at latter's trial".

5 JOHN THE REVELATOR (1930) from **Blind Willie Johnson**
"Daughter of Zion – Judea's lion. Moses to Moses. God redeem. Bought us with blood. Moses saw bush; book of seven seals…"

6 MINGLEWOOD BLUES (1928) from **Cannon's Jug Stompers**
"Never let one woman rule mind, keep you worried trouble all time. Married woman sees me sometimes. Got letter you ought to read, you coming see me knock me on head."

7 SEE THAT MY GRAVE IS KEPT CLEAN (1928) from **Blind Lemon Jefferson**
"Favor I ask you, see my grave kept green. Long lane, no end, bear away with silver chain. Two white horses in line, take me to burying ground. Heart stopped, hands cold. You hear coffin sound? Poor boy in ground. Dig grave with silver spade, lead down with golden chain. You heard church bell? Poor boy dead and gone…"

8 POOR BOY BLUES (1928) from **Ramblin' Thomas**
"Was in Louisiana, doing as please, now in Texas, work or leave. My home ain't Texas , sure don't care. If boat don't land stay on water as long as any man. Boat came rocking like drunken man; home is on water, don't like land…"

9 FISHING BLUES (1928) from **Henry Thomas**
"Went on hill, 12 o'clock; got pole. Went to hardware; got hook, put line on hook. Look down river, one o'clock, spied catfish, got hungry, going to catch catfish. Put on skillet, lid cook shortning bread. You been fishing all time, I'm going fishing, too. Bet life, loving wife, catch more than you…"

10 EXPRESSMAN BLUES (1930) from **Sleepy John Estes and Yank Rachell**
"Expressman you've gone wrong moved girl when I was from home. Woman makes man do things wrong, that's why I sing lonesome song. If you never hear me more, remember morning I walked on your porch. Going to sing this, no more, mandolin under arm, go…"

Eclipsed by new styles such as the black rock'n'roll of Bo Diddley and Chuck Berry and the soulful sounds of Ray Charles, even the great Muddy Waters could no longer make the R&B charts. The championing of the legacy of the original Delta blues passed by default to a handful of white collectors and country-blues enthusiasts who spearheaded a new, predominantly college-based interest in blues music as an adjunct of the folk revival.

The connection between white folk music and acoustic folk-blues had been established in New York from the 1930s onwards, when Leadbelly and Sonny Terry and Brownie McGhee performed regularly with the likes of Woody Guthrie and Pete Seeger, but a pivotal moment came in 1952 with the release of the six-LP *Anthology Of American Folk Music*. The

brainchild of music historian **Harry Smith**, who compiled the set from the archives of Folkways Records, it included white Appalachian folk singers alongside early recordings by such acoustic blues performers as Blind Lemon Jefferson, Sleepy John Estes, the Memphis Jug Band, Charley Patton (credited as "The Masked Marvel"), Furry Lewis and Mississippi John Hurt.

The *Anthology* was hugely influential and much plundered as a source of material by singers in the burgeoning 1950s' folk movement. By the end of the decade collectors and enthusiasts were traveling to the deep South to see which of the original country blues practitioners had survived and whether they could be coaxed back out of retirement. Among the first to be rediscovered were **Lightnin' Hopkins**, who was found and recorded by Sam Charters in 1959. That same year, Charters also published his influential book *The Country Blues*, accompanied by a compilation LP that included tracks not only by Hopkins but Blind Willie McTell, Leroy Carr and Bukka White among others. Also in 1959, during a field trip to the South, **Alan Lomax** found **Fred McDowell** in Como, Mississippi. They would soon be joined by a host of other rediscovered blasts from the past, some of whom – such as **Mississippi John Hurt** – hadn't seen the inside of a recording studio since the 1920s.

REDFERNS

Delta bluesman Furry Lewis, who was rediscovered following the release of *The Anthology Of American Folk Music* in 1952

Chapter Eight

The 1960s: the blues at the crossroads

The blues has been said to be at a crossroads many times in its hundred-year history, but the dawn of the 1960s was a particularly critical juncture. Big social changes were in the air. Five years earlier in 1955, the 43-year-old black seamstress Rosa Parks had refused to give up her seat to a white man on a public bus in Montgomery, Alabama, and the Civil Rights movement had become a moral crusade. Segregation and racial injustice in the deep South were still a fact of daily life, but the march on Washington at the end of August 1963, at which Rev. Martin Luther King Jr. made his famous "I have a dream" speech, proved that the tide could not be halted.

On the centenary of 1863's Emancipation Proclamation, the Civil Rights movement adopted the slogan "Freedom Now". **Martin Luther King Jr.** preached non-violent civil disobedience, but other black leaders such as **Malcolm X** advocated a more militant approach, and the Black Panthers were soon to follow in his wake. With the clamor for "**black power**" came a new pride and confidence that had a profound effect on African-American culture. Young black Americans no longer wanted to be reminded of the "bad old days" of slavery, sharecropping, poverty and humiliation, an aura that hung over the Delta blues like a dark, ominous cloud. They desired music that was self-assertive and said everybody could be part of the American dream, regardless of skin color. The catch-phrase became "say it loud, I'm black and

I'm proud"; as a hit for **Nina Simone** later in the decade put it, "to be young, gifted and black" was where it was at.

The soundtrack to this new black self-confidence was provided by **soul** music, even if you could still hear the pain of the blues in the voices of Southern singers such as Sam Cooke and Otis Redding. In Detroit, a black entrepreneur named Berry Gordy Jr. read the spirit of the changing times and reflected them perfectly on his **Motown** label. Pointedly, his simple but potent slogan "The Sound of Young America" made no mention of being black. With the likes of Diana Ross and the Supremes, Gordy sold records to black and white youth alike as, in a triumph of commerce over race, black music crossed over from the R&B listings to the mainstream pop charts. Motown's sleek and glossy pop anthems carefully avoided any direct mention of the Civil Rights struggle and the message was clear: black Americans were moving uptown and didn't want its new singing stars and musical heroes to remind them of Jim Crow laws, lynchings, cotton picking or any other aspect of the cursed legacy of four hundred years of oppression.

The new attitude effectively finished the blues as a commercial force with a black audience. Even though the records Muddy Waters and Howlin' Wolf made in the 1950s made little or no direct reference to life on the plantation, their background remained an ever-present if unspoken influence on every note they sang and played. As "Mississippi Goddam", another Nina Simone song, made clear, the cotton state was by now virtually a swear word in black society. Even once the blues had left Mississippi, the tough-edged electric urban post-war sound had been born out of the hard times and struggles of migrant life in the ghettos of cities such as Chicago and this, too, seemed to represent a subservient past and an experience that a younger generation of black record-buyers were now happy to forget. In some quarters, the apparent distaste for the blues to the point of virtual denial of its existence as a significant cultural force persists to this day. In 2000, Michael R. Strickland, a black university professor from New Jersey, published an *A-Z Of African American History*. The book was endorsed by the National Association for the Advancement of Colored People (NAACP), whose director penned a foreword. Yet although it contained entries on jazz and soul, the blues did not merit a mention.

The early 1960s were thus hard times for blues performers, many of whom drifted into retirement or were forced to take day jobs away from music. The mighty Chess label also appeared to conclude that the blues had become an anachronism, and sent its stars such as Etta James, Irma Thomas and Laura Lee to make soul records at the Fame studios in Alabama. When the Rolling Stones visited the Chess studios in Chicago in 1964, Keith Richards claims

that they encountered Muddy Waters dressed in overalls and up a ladder with a paintbrush in his hand. This account is disputed by Stones' bassist Bill Wyman and others, but Muddy had not had a hit in six years and when the group returned to record the following day, no one has disputed reports that the great bluesman was employed to help them hump their gear into the studio.

Even as the black audience was turning its back on the blues, however, a new white audience was developing. By the early 1960s, the **folk revival** was in full swing, and Bob Dylan had arrived in its New York epicenter, Greenwich Village. Many of the blues stars who had gone electric in the late 1940s now reinvented themselves once more as acoustic country bluesmen. Thus **John Lee Hooker** played the folk clubs and coffee houses of Greenwich Village, and appeared at the Newport Folk Festival. So too, between 1959 and 1965, did Skip James, Son House, Bukka White, Mississippi Fred McDowell, a solo and acoustic Muddy Waters, Robert Pete Williams, Mance Lipscomb, Jesse Fuller, Rev. Gary Davis, Sonny Terry and Brownie McGhee, Sleepy John Estes, Lightnin' Hopkins, and Memphis Slim. In the book *Baby Let Me Follow You Down*, the white folk singer Eric Von Schmidt described listening to **Mississippi John Hurt** sing "Spike Driver Blues" at Newport: "It was unreal. John Hurt was dead. Had to be. All the guys on that Harry Smith anthology were dead. They'd all recorded back in the 1920s and 1930s. They'd never been seen or heard from since. But there was no denying that the man singing so sweet and playing so beautifully was *the* John Hurt. He had a face – and what a face. He had a hat that he wore like a halo."

Hurt was one of the many bluesmen who were "rediscovered" during the early 1960s, as white academics, enthusiasts and students of the blues such as Chris Strachwitz, Mack McCormick, Harry Oster and the guitarist John Fahey scoured the South in the hope of bringing back to life names that were otherwise only familiar from the fading labels on old 78 rpm records.

Mississippi John Hurt

REDFERNS

and Lipscomb were in their sixties, but had never been recorded. In addition, record labels searched their vaults for material they could re-release for the first time in LP format. The most significant such reissue, Robert Johnson's *King Of The Delta Blues Singers*, appeared on Columbia in 1961.

The British blues boom

By the early 1960s a similar audience for the blues was developing in **Britain**. Big **Bill Broonzy** had first visited the UK in 1951, while **Lonnie Johnson** played London's Royal Festival Hall the following year, helping to inspire the mid-1950s skiffle craze that found **Lonnie Donegan** in the British top ten with a version of Leadbelly's "Rock Island Line". By 1957, **Alexis Korner** and **Cyril Davies** were running the Blues and Barrelhouse Club at London's Roundhouse, where they performed as a British blues duo and also hosted such visiting American performers as Broonzy, Sonny Terry, Memphis Slim, Champion Jack Dupree – and **Muddy Waters**, who on a controversial 1958 tour was booed from some quarters for playing an electric guitar. In 1962, under the name **Blues Incorporated**, Korner and Davies began a Thursday night residency at the Marquee Club. By the end of the year, the band recorded the first British blues album for Decca's Ace of Clubs label.

Two of the greatest, **Skip James** and **Son House**, were coincidentally tracked down on the same day in 1964. House had last been recorded by Alan Lomax in 1941 and was an infirm alcoholic living in Rochester, New York. James, who was found in a Mississippi hospital, had not recorded since 1931. Both had to re learn their old musical skills but recaptured enough of their former power to thrill an audience that had not been born when they started out on the blues road. Others, such as McDowell, Robert Pete Williams

The group of young British musicians that

coalesced around Korner and Davies included future members of the **Rolling Stones** and **Led Zeppelin**. Equally inspired by the rock'n'roll of Chuck Berry and Bo Diddley and the blues of Jimmy Reed, Muddy Waters and Howlin' Wolf, they gave the British blues boom quite a different character from the more scholarly American folk-blues revival. By 1964, such British R&B groups as the Rolling Stones, the Yardbirds, the Animals, Them, the Spencer Davis Group and the Pretty Things were invading the charts with covers of American blues songs. By then **John Mayall** had also moved from Manchester to London. Over the next few years, his **Bluesbreakers** acted as a finishing school for some of the greatest British blues players, including **Eric Clapton**, **Peter Green** and **Mick Taylor**. Within a short time, those guitarists had attained a virtuosity that outstripped almost all of their American counterparts, with the possible exception of **Mike Bloomfield**. According to Summer McStravick and John Roos in their book *Blues-Rock Explosion*, "The British got to be better because back in the late 1950s, having met the blues and fallen in love, they then embellished the music with their own home-grown romantic notions about American blues culture and the bluesman's lifestyle in a big city. Thus Brit bluesmen aggrandized the blues, making the music more popular than in its own homeland."

In such romantic notions, poor blacks from the deep South were imbued with a kind of spiritual purity, and supporting those who sung about the experience became, quite literally, a blues crusade. Neglected at home, visiting American blues musicians were at first shocked and then delighted to find themselves lionized by British audiences and treated as legendary heroes. Happy to swap a seedy Chicago club for the spick-and-span concert setting of Croydon's Fairfield Hall, most of the biggest names in post-war blues, and even those from earlier days who had survived and could still pick out a chord, came on the annual **American Folk Blues Festival** tour, which rolled through Europe every year from 1963 until 1972. Several,

such as Sonny Boy Williamson, Memphis Slim and Champion Jack Dupree, were so pleased both to find an enthusiastic and respectful audience and to leave behind the discrimination of the South that they stayed to make homes in Europe. As Eric Burdon of the Animals later put it, "All these young white kids in England were into this black thing that no longer mattered to anybody else, especially the blacks. These guys were out of work." **Willie Dixon**, who became the tour's unofficial musical director, confirmed this point. "I wouldn't have gone over there in the first place had I been doing all right here," he observed tartly.

The most significant British blues performer to emerge from the 1960s blues scene was **Eric Clapton**, who after spells with the Yardbirds and Mayall (with whom he cut the seminal British blues album, *John Mayall's Bluesbreakers With Eric Clapton*) formed **Cream** in 1966. The group's riff-based blues-rock was louder and heavier than anything that had gone before, and was soon joined by another power trio, the **Jimi Hendrix Experience**, led by a young black American guitarist who had arrived in London in 1966. Together they forged a new "progressive" or "psychedelic" sound that was soon being much imitated on both sides of the Atlantic. In Britain, **Fleetwood Mac**, **Chicken Shack**, **Free**, Rory Gallagher's **Taste** and ultimately **Led Zeppelin**, who arose out of the ashes of the Yardbirds, were among the leading second-wave blues-rock groups. In America, too, white rock'n'roll bands such as **Canned Heat**, **Electric Flag**, **Johnny Winter**, **Santana**, and the **Allman Brothers**, finally began to embrace the blues.

That white rock stars were now reaping rewards for singing the blues on a scale that few of the music's innovators had ever enjoyed led to considerable controversy. The Rolling Stones were accused of "ripping-off" the older bluesmen whose songs they covered, while Led Zeppelin's masterful updating of pre war blues songs brought forth even angrier accusations of plagiarism. Willie Dixon, for one, was forced to resort to legal action to secure royalties on

Playlist
Brit-blues

By the late 1960s, there seemed to be as many blues bands in London as there were in Chicago. What qualified middle-class white boys from the English suburbs to play the music of sharecroppers from the Mississippi Delta has never been fully explained. But there's no doubt that many of them played it with a genuine conviction and passion.

1 I'D RATHER GO BLIND Chicken Shack from **Chicken Shack: The Collection**
Singer Christine Perfect (later McVie) lived up to her then name on the Etta James song.

2 I'M GOING HOME Ten Years After from **Woodstock**
A highlight of the *Woodstock* movie and soundtrack album, which saw Alvin Lee officially crowned the fastest guitarist in the West.

3 NEED YOUR LOVE SO BAD Fleetwood Mac from **The Best Of Fleetwood Mac**
Peter Green's guitar plus strings equals blues heaven.

4 SPOONFUL Cream from **Fresh Cream**
Willie Dixon gets the power trio treatment, on a song copped from Charley Patton in a style copied from Buddy Guy.

5 RAMBLIN' ON MY MIND John Mayall's **Bluesbreakers (with Eric Clapton)** from **John Mayall's Bluesbreakers (with Eric Clapton)**

Robert Johnson cover from the only album that "God" ever made with the Godfather.

6 TRAIN TO NOWHERE Savoy Brown from **Blue Matter**
A train to nowhere arguably carrying coals to Newcastle, from the one British blues band to enjoy more success in America than at home.

7 GOIN' DOWN SLOW Free from **Walk In My Shadow: An Introduction To Free**
Free were all right then, back in the days when their debut album made them the toughest British blues combo of them all.

8 BULLFROG BLUES Rory Gallagher from **The Rory Gallagher Story**
Yes, he came from across the Irish Sea but he sure had those white boy blues.

9 BOYFRIEND BLUES Jo-Ann Kelly from **Blues and Gospel**
The British Bonnie Raitt, who turned down the chance to sing with both Canned Heat and Johnny Winter.

10 DEAR JILL Blodwyn Pig from **A Head Rings Out**
Simple but effective, the best British slide guitar solo ever from ex-Jethro Tull guitarist Mick Abrahams.

the group's "Whole Lotta Love", which had been adapted from his composition, "You Need Love". An ethical debate also raged over whether white men *could* sing the blues with conviction, an argument parodied to witty effect on the Bonzo Dog Doo-Dah Band's 1968 spoof, "Can Blue Men Sing The Whites?". Some purists accused great white British blues singers such as Eric Burdon, Steve Winwood and Van Morrison of representing a new cultural imperialism which they dubbed "black voice" – a parodic echo of the term "blackface", applied to the white minstrels who colored their faces with burnt cork in an earlier era. That "blues are only for blacks" attitude still finds some currency today, in such places as the pages of the American magazine *Living Blues*, established in Chicago in 1970, which continues to pursue a policy of featuring only African-American performers.

Despite the occasional legal action over songwriting royalties, for the most part black American bluesmen were grateful for the renewed attention that the British rockers brought them. Muddy Waters, for one, was always flattered that the Rolling Stones had named themselves after one of his songs, and generously thanked the group for putting blues musicians back on the map in their native America as, in a classic case of taking coals to Newcastle, the "British blues invasion" sold back to the US music that it had begged, borrowed or stolen from America in the first place. As Muddy put it in Nadine Cohodas' book *Spinning Blues Into Gold*, "When that happened, I think to myself how these white kids was sitting down and thinking and playing the blues that my black kids was bypassing. That was a hell of a thing, man, to think about."

A new generation emerges

Although domestic blues performers were enjoying little commercial success in America by the 1960s, it would be misleading to suggest that the blues was in danger of dying out. In Chicago, the once-mighty Chess label may have lost its way, but a new generation of blues musicians was cutting its teeth in the clubs on the West Side, playing not the original music of the Delta sharecroppers but a hard-edged, modern ghetto blues dominated by wailing lead guitar. These like-minded souls included the likes of **Otis Rush**, **Magic Sam**, **Freddie King** and **Buddy Guy**, the latter of whom was cited by Clapton as

the main inspiration for Cream, after he saw him play at London's Marquee Club in 1965. Chicago even had its own premier white blues-rock band, led by **Paul Butterfield** and featuring **Mike Bloomfield** and **Elvin Bishop** on lead guitars, though it has to be said that they lacked the more adventurous creativity of the British bands.

The godfather of the new breed of blues guitarists was **B.B. King**, another who benefitted from the championing of white rock musicians. King had been recording since the late 1940s, but had failed to cross over from the R&B charts to a wider audience. By the mid-1960s, his career seemed to be in decline, while his reputation

Playlist
Blues guitar

The piano and harmonica are key blues instruments, of course – but it was the guitar that defined both the music and the image of the itinerant bluesman playing the juke joints and plantation picnics in the pre-war Delta. In post-war Chicago, the amplified guitar defined the new urban sound that eventually helped to give birth to rock'n'roll. These ten rank as special landmarks.

1 SOUTHERN RAG **Blind Blake** from **The Best Of Blind Blake**
Exemplary picking from the black Django Reinhardt – or was the Gypsy maestro actually the white Blind Blake?

2 MR JOHNSON'S BLUES **Lonnie Johnson** from **The Original Guitar Wizard**
Although he began recording in the 1920s, Johnson was no country blues rustic but a sophisticated, precise blues guitar virtuoso, whose playing led all the way to T-Bone Walker and B.B. King.

3 ATLANTA STRUT **Blind Willie McTell** from **The Best Of Blind Willie McTell**
Nobody could sing the blues like Blind Willie, as Bob Dylan's famous song noted. Very few could play like him either, and his guitar here uncannily echoes the narrative of the lyric.

4 MEAN OLD WORLD **T-Bone Walker** from **The Best Of T-Bone Walker**
Jazz had Charlie Christian and the blues had T-Bone Walker. Between them they invented electric guitar playing, and the single-string improvisations on this 1942 tour de force are still a benchmark for instrumentals more than sixty years on.

5 I CAN'T QUIT YOU BABE **Otis Rush** from **An Introduction To Otis Rush**
The under-recognized Rush was one of the great unsung

heroes of the electric blues guitar. Tracks like this had a huge influence on such white axe heroes as Eric Clapton, Peter Green, Jeff Beck, Jimmy Page and Mick Taylor, as well as American instrumentalists from Mike Bloomfield to Johnny Winter.

6 THREE O'CLOCK BLUES **B.B. King** from **The Best Of B.B. King**
The sweet, crying sound B.B. rings from his guitar on this 1951 cover of a Lowell Fulson song has remained his calling card for more than half a century.

7 FIRST TIME I MET THE BLUES **Buddy Guy** from **First Time I Met The Blues**
After the three Kings came the prince of electric blues guitarists, Buddy Guy. On this, his signature tune, you can hear how he influenced Clapton, Hendrix and Stevie Ray Vaughan.

8 HAVE YOU HEARD **Eric Clapton** from **John Mayall's Bluesbreakers With Eric Clapton**
Everybody has their own favorite Clapton solo, and although it would be wrong to say he never equalled his playing on this 1966 track, it set the bar for the next forty years.

9 LOAN ME A DIME **Duane Allman** from **Boz Scaggs**
Oddly, Duane Allman seemed to keep his best solos for other people's records – Wilson Pickett's "Hey Jude", Derek and The Dominos' "Layla", and this fabulous twelve-minute blues work-out on Boz Scaggs' debut solo album.

10 MAMA TALK TO YOUR DAUGHTER **Magic Sam** from **West Side Soul**
Just when Chicago guitar blues seemed to be running out of steam, along came Samuel Maghett to revitalize it. This cover of a J.B. Lenoir song comes from his classic 1967 set. Sadly, two years later he was dead, aged just 32.

rested on the back catalog of hits he'd record-ed for Modern in the 1950s rather than on his contemporary material. Then in 1968 he played the Fillmore West in San Francisco with Mike Bloomfield and Johnny Winter, who introduced him as "the greatest living blues guitarist", and he finally achieved his pop crossover hit with "The Thrill Is Gone". The next year, he made his first visit to Europe. In subsequent decades, of course, King went on to become the great-est surviving bluesman of them all, but that the 1960s was the least successful and most unsatis-fying decade of his long career is emblematic of the difficulties that the blues faced at the time.

Once some of the blues labels saw white rock bands stealing their thunder, they attempted to make up the lost ground. Buddy Guy had signed to Chess Records in the early 1960s and might conceivably have delivered them an album to compete with the likes of Cream and Hendrix. Instead, Leonard Chess initially dismissed his efforts as "just noise." Later on, when Chess saw that white blues-rock bands were selling records by the truckload with a similar cacophony, the label responded by recording psychedelic blues albums with Muddy Waters and Howlin' Wolf that smacked of such blatant exploitation that they fooled nobody. In any case, by the time the traditional blues industry had caught up to the daylight robbery that had taken place, white blues-rock was already marching off down an even noisier and more bombastic road towards heavy metal.

Chapter Nine

Survival: long live the blues

The last few decades have seen the blues move from being a vital form of expression – giving voice to the concerns of the daily lives of first sharecroppers and then those huddled in the back streets of poor black city neighborhoods – to become a heritage industry. With every year that passes, fewer of the original bluesmen are left standing. Incredibly, at the time of writing, David "Honeyboy Edwards" and Robert Lockwood Jr. both of whom played with Robert Johnson, were still with us, but the connection with the pre-war world of the Mississippi Delta will soon inevitably be lost forever. New stars have emerged, but there has been nobody of sufficient stature to take the place of the pioneers who shaped and molded the blues into the institution it is today. As Giles Oakley put it in a 1997 afterword to a new edition of his 1976 book *The Devil's Music*, "It is still possible to hear plenty of magnificent music, live or on record. But what is far less easy to find is the new-direction innovator."

After the blues-rock explosion of the late 1960s, rock music lost its fascination with the blues during the 1970s. That said, the influence of the blues had permeated deep enough to remain one of the building blocks of modern rock music in perpetuity, and the style of guitar playing forged by the likes of Eric Clapton and Jimi Hendrix is still widely imitated.

As the years have gone by, those authentic bluesmen who have continued to work, such as B.B. King, have became icons, feted by presidents in the White House and marketing men on Madison Avenue alike, and called upon to play on U2 albums.

Muddy Waters became a blues-rock star in the 1970s, playing at The Band's farewell concert, and making a series of fine albums with Johnny Winter prior to his death in 1983. **John Lee Hooker** staged a remarkable comeback in the late 1980s, and probably sold more records in the final ten years of his life than he had in the first four decades of his career. Of the women, **Etta James** and **Koko Taylor** have continued to enjoy success and found a resonance in feminist times with their assertive, self-confident and extrovert style, while the contribution of **Bonnie Raitt** should not be overlooked. With the passing of Hooker in 2001, **B.B. King** became the ultimate grand old man of the blues, a hugely dignified figure who celebrated his eightieth birthday in 2005 with a new album and live dates. In recent years his pre-eminence has only been challenged by **Buddy Guy**, who has continued to grow in stature, playing with the Rolling Stones and Eric Clapton and still making fine albums as he enters his seventies, a decade behind King. The ultimate celebration of the blues as part of an all-American national heritage came in 1994 when the United States Post Office issued a set of six stamps commemorating Bessie Smith, Ma Rainey, Muddy Waters, Howlin' Wolf, Jimmy Rushing and Robert Johnson.

Taj Mahal – pioneering syncretist of global blues   RUF RECORDS

Periodically, the blues shucks off its heritage trappings to become briefly trendy again. That happened in 1980 following the release of *The Blues Brothers* movie, and again a few years later in the wake of the success of the white Texan guitarist **Stevie Ray Vaughan**, who reunited blues and rock audiences more firmly than at any time since the early 1970s, before dying tragically young in 1990 at the age of 35, when his best work was surely still ahead of him. At such moments, major record labels tend hastily to add blues artists to their rosters but, almost invariably, they get dropped again after an album or two.

Among the "younger" bluesmen, **Taj Mahal**, who made his first solo album in 1968, has become a particularly active and dedicated keeper of the blues tradition. Yet even he is now in his mid-60s, and he acknowledged that the blues today is essentially a homage to the past when he noted: "For me it's basically kind of an ancestor worship, in the sense of accessing the great things that ancestors have done." **Albert Collins** started making the best music of his life in the late 1970s, while **Robert Cray** emerged as a bestseller in the 1980s, although his success was then shaded by the mercurial career of Stevie Ray Vaughan.

As the blues has become an institution, a small but active industry has developed alongside it. The level of scholarship has grown enormously, the blues is now studied on academic courses, and the University of Memphis even has an ethnomusicology PhD program specializing in "Southern US folk and popular music." In 1980, the **Blues Foundation** was established in Memphis and was responsible for inaugurating the annual **W.C Handy awards** for excellence in the blues field. Blues museums have sprung up around the South, the graves of many of the old bluesmen have been marked with elaborate headstones – three in the disputed case of

From Mali to Mississippi … and back

One of the few areas where modern blues has found a new challenge and rediscovered a cutting edge has come – ironically – in turning back to its **African** roots. When Duke Ellington was asked if he'd ever heard any African music, the great bandleader replied that he'd been making it all his life. At the time, that was a controversial remark, as ethnomusicologists were still arguing heatedly over whether the roots of American jazz and blues could be traced back to Africa. Today it is widely accepted that the origins of the music developed by black sharecroppers in the Mississippi Delta in the early decades of the 20th century can be traced back to Africa via the slave ships. The cultural trade routes that connect the blues to the music of West Africa in particular have been mapped and explored in noted collaborations between the likes of **Toumani Diabaté** and **Taj Mahal**, and **Ali Farka Touré** with both **Ry Cooder** and **Corey Harris**.

In recent decades, the cross-pollination has grown more complicated as the music has traveled back and forth across the Atlantic. African guitarists such as **Lobi Traoré**, known as the "Bambara bluesman", admit to listening to John Lee Hooker when growing up, and so contemporary African musicians have been influenced by American blues practitioners whose music has its origins in a centuries-old folk memory of Africa.

When Ali Farka Touré was asked how he felt when he first heard Hooker he replied: "I thought 'he's taken our music'. That music comes from history. How did it get here? It was stolen from Africans." Shortly before his death in 2001, I asked Hooker if he had heard Ali Farka Touré and received a remarkably similar answer. "Yeah, I heard him and I said 'he's stealing our music'. Then people started telling me 'no, we stole *his* music because it all comes from Africa.'"

Lobi Traoré also believes that just who influenced whom has become highly confused. "When I was young, before I even knew I would become a musician, I listened to a lot of American blues," he says. "Maybe I was inspired by it. Maybe the blues was inspired by Africa. Maybe it's just a coincidence. But listen. The music I play comes from me and from my place."

The white American blues-rock singer **Bonnie Raitt**, who has played with both Lobi Traoré and Ali Farka Touré, has no doubt about the link. She describes how she felt when she first heard Malian music: "I absolutely could not believe that something as close to the Delta music existed in Africa. The kind of blues that most gets me is Robert Pete Williams, Fred McDowell, Skip James, Son House, John Lee Hooker, the really dark, stark music – and here it was, mirrored back to me."

The black American bluesman Taj Mahal first visited **Mali** in 1979, twenty years before he recorded *Kulanjan* with Toumani Diabaté. He says of their collaboration: "It's a real connection with my ancestors. I've always been searching for American music that still connects with the African tradition. It's been unbroken for 71 generations and the Mande people are responsible for the way guitars and banjos were played in the United States. They're the creators of that specific rhythmic style you hear when someone picks up a blues guitar and starts picking on it and that sad sound, the melancholy, that you hear in the blues and in the older African music."

However, **Corey Harris**, who recorded much of his *Mississippi To Mali* with Ali Farka Touré in Mali, is more circumspect. "I'm not trying to say the blues all came from Mali. It's just one of the strains, the really strong strains that make up black music in America," he says. "The point is you can take that music that we have over here, and it can go over there and be conversant."

Robert Johnson, as nobody can agree exactly where he was interred – and blues tourism is now a thriving business in Mississippi.

New specialist labels such as Alligator, Blind Pig and Silvertone have emerged to take the place of such once famous names as Vocalion, Bluebird, Chess and Vee Jay. Alligator in particular has worked tirelessly at developing and nurturing new talent for the last thirty years and has done much to maintain the blues as more than merely a nostalgic backwater. However, most of the contemporary blues labels cater to a predominantly white audience. One of the few exceptions is **Malaco Records**, based in Jackson, Mississippi. Malaco became a powerhouse of soul-blues in the 1980s with artists like the late **Z.Z. Hill**, and has continued ever since to make records that appeal to black fans of blues, soul and gospel. Other singers who have remained hugely popular with black audiences on what remains of the "chitlin circuit" of the small-town South include **Bobby Bland** and **Bobby Rush**. Meanwhile, a combination of the CD age and the growth of blues scholarship has resulted in thousands of reissues, so blues recordings, both famous and obscure, are now more readily available than ever before.

Recent decades have also seen the blues become an international phenomenon. The blues festival circuit now circles the globe, so that it's perfectly possible to encounter a Japanese band offering a perfect imitation of a traditional Chicago blues combo with only the pronunciation of the lead singer to give the game away. One might have imagined that by the 1990s no authentic bluesmen were still around, waiting to be discovered, but the extraordinary **Fat Possum** label proved everybody wrong by finding **R.L. Burnside** and **Junior Kimbrough** playing a tiny juke joint in the Mississippi hill country and recording them in their seventies. Sadly both have since passed away. The success of Stevie Ray Vaughan inspired several young white blues guitar slingers in the 1990s, such as the teenaged **Jonny Lang** and the almost equally youthful **Kenny**

Wayne Shepherd. Both were preciously gifted guitarists but it was obvious that the blues was never going to be more than a passing fad to them. More significant was the emergence in the 1990s of a new breed of black bluesmen such **as Corey Harris** and **Keb Mo** – playing predominantly acoustically but adventurously – while a new generation of rock-oriented performers such as **Ben Harper** have reinstated the blues as a core element in their sound.

What's left of the blues?

It is constantly asserted that "the blues will never die", and the music's continued existence in some shape or form seems assured. Yet whether it will live on merely as a geriatric pastiche of a once-powerful art form or as a genuinely creative force remains far less certain. Does the blues still carry any meaningful message in the 21st century? And what relevance can music so firmly based in tradition have in a rapidly changing world of digital manipulation?

To those for whom the blues remains a crusade, even to pose such questions represents a heresy. Others, such as Ry Cooder, insist that the commodification of the blues means that it effectively died as a genuine form of emotional expression several decades ago, and has been reduced by modern culture to a soundtrack that can be used to sell denim jeans or cold beer in TV ads. Some, however, remain optimistic that by fusing the blues with other genres such as hip-hop and electronica, a new hybrid blues sound can reclaim contemporary relevance.

In 1999 the New York-based techno artist **Moby** released the album *Play*, which sampled various field recordings made by Alan Lomax and fused them with contemporary beats. The album sold millions around the world, while the single "Natural Blues", featuring the distinctive voice of Vera Hall, became ubiquitous. Its mix of organic emotion from authentic blues recordings and computerized beats and electronic sound effects led to much talk of the emergence of "nu-blues", but in truth that has never really

Playlist
Nu-blues

While much of the modern blues scene has become a heritage industry, the old-skool tradition is still inspiring some highly adventurous and experimental music…

1 MISSISSIPPI KKKROSSROADS **Chris Thomas King** from **Dirty South Hip Hop Blues**
An awesome, hip-hop influenced reworking of blues mythology and the crossroads theme.

2 SOMEDAY BABY **North Mississippi All-Stars** from **Shake Hands With Shorty**
Brothers Luther and Cody Dickinson give a 21st-century reworking to a song previously recorded by Sleepy John Estes and Fred McDowell.

3 SURE NUFF 'N YES I DO **Captain Beefheart & The Magic Band** from **Safe As Milk**
Yes, it's forty years old – but it still sounds startling, fresh and as warped as the day it was minted.

4 RIDE ON (FIGHT ON) **Little Axe** from **The Wolf That House Built**
Skip MacDonald's extraordinary mix of blues guitar, dub and techno-wizardry.

5 ST JAMES **Snakefarm** from **Songs From My Funeral**
A sparse and moody reworking, atmospherically sung by Anna Domino from a superb 1999 album that reworked ten traditional American folk-blues classics in similarly striking fashion.

6 NATURAL BLUES **Moby** from **Play**
A surprise multi-million seller from electro-pioneer Moby, fusing techno-beats with Alan Lomax's field recording of Vera Ward Hall singing "Trouble So Hard".

7 PARCHMAN BLUES **Tangle Eye** from **Alan Lomax's Southern Journey Remixed**
Like Moby, the New Orleans based duo of Scott Billington and Steve Reynolds hit upon the idea of sampling Alan Lomax's field recordings. This track features the voice of Henry Jimson Wallace singing "No More My Lawd" and some funky bass playing by George Porter Jr. of the Meters.

8 IT'S BAD YOU KNOW **R.L. Burnside** from **Come On In**
Contemporary blues from the Fat Possum label, with Burnside's traditional style remixed and reinvented with dance beats. He hated it!

9 DEATH LETTER **Johnny Farmer** from **New Beats From The Delta**
Farmer was born into a sharecropping family in the Delta in 1932; his rendition of Son House's "Death Letter" is here reworked by the Atlanta-based production team Organized Noize.

10 STAGGER LEE **Nick Cave And The Bad Seeds** from **Murder Ballads**
A spooked and ghostly rendition of the familiar folk-blues tune from Cave and his Australian compadres.

Several of these tracks can also be found on a couple of highly recommended compilations, *Balling The Jack: The Birth Of The Nu-Blues* and *Putumayo Presents Blues Lounge*.

happened. Working as **Tangle Eye**, the New Orleans production duo of Scott Billington and Steve Reynolds followed Moby's lead in lending new, electronic arrangements to ancient field recordings made by the Lomaxes, and achieved widespread critical acclaim. Other leading exponents of the "nu-blues" have included Skip Macdonald's **Little Axe** project and the **Fat Possum** label, which has invited some interesting collaborators to rework recordings by R.L. Burnside and Junior Kimbrough. But it would be hard to claim any of this activity genuinely represents a significant new movement. Indeed, to many traditional blues fans, the word "gimmick" more readily comes to mind.

Some claim that rap and hip-hop, with its urban ghetto rage, is a modern manifestation of the core values of earlier African-American forms such as jazz and blues, and one of the most interesting African-American hybrids of recent years has come from the jazz trumpeter and singer **Olu Dara**. Yet sadly, Dara's splendid 1997 album *From Natchez To New York*, on which his more famous son, multi-million selling rapper Nas, guested, went almost unnoticed by most blues-watchers. Others, such as the White Stripes, have clearly incorporated a blues influence into their thoroughly modern rock'n'roll, while the white British rock singer P.J. Harvey has made some astonishing records that owe something to the feral spirit of the blues. However, in terms of steering the blues into previously uncharted waters, frankly none of the white rock exponents of the so-called "nu-blues" has been as remotely bold or as adventurous as Captain Beefheart's still audacious-sounding experiments of forty years ago.

The blues has always been rooted in hardship and suffering, and even in its more up-tempo and hedonistic styles, its motivating force has been to fashion a momentary escape from the pain of life. Yet for many around the world, it remains an uplifting form because, as Giles Oakley puts it, the blues is "one of the great reminders that everybody, even poor, ill-educated people, has a capacity for great creativity". Accordingly, let us end on an optimistic note, for which we turn to the veteran blues academic David Evans, who directs the ethnomusicology program at the University of Memphis. "Blues itself seems to be a music that stays fresh and young, constantly renewing itself," he continues to believe. Even if some of the evidence assembled in this chapter suggests a somewhat different conclusion, let us pray that he's right.

Part Two

A Blues A–Z

Alger "Texas" Alexander

**b Jowett, Texas, Sept 12, 1900;
d April 16, 1954**

Born in the Brazos River area of East Texas in 1900, Alger "Texas" Alexander was one of the earliest male blues singers to be recorded, and was an older cousin of **Lightnin' Hopkins**, who served his apprenticeship accompanying him. He started singing towards the end of World War I, at fish fries, picnics, dances and fairs. He didn't play an instrument, and so was always in need of an accompanist – he's said to have carried a guitar around in the hope of finding someone to play it for him, and it's not known why he never tried to learn.

Recording extensively between 1927 and 1934, Alexander cut some 60 sides in a unique, unpredictable down-home country-blues style that some listeners consider undisciplined and unstructured. Many of his best-known songs were his own compositions, and on numbers such as "Levee Camp Moan" and "Frost Texas Tornado Blues" he chronicled the hardships of black life in rural Texas in a highly personal way. The latter told the story of a vicious storm that killed 41 people in 1930. His first recordings, for Okeh Records, followed in the wake of the phenomenal success of Blind Lemon Jefferson, with whom he may previously have worked. In 1928, when Okeh recorded him both in a New York studio and on field trips to Texas, he cut a memorable version of "The House Of The Rising Sun". His accompanying guitarists included **Dennis "Little Hat" Jones** (one of the great mystery men of the blues, who recorded ten sides for ARC under his own name in 1929 and 1930, and who was never heard of again) **Eddie Lang** and, best of all, the highly sophisticated player **Lonnie Johnson**.

Alexander also cut blues songs with various jazz bands, recording with the legendary **King Oliver** in New York, and working briefly with the **Mississippi Sheiks** on a 1930 session in San Antonio, Texas.

During the Depression, Alexander and Lightnin' Hopkins performed wherever they could, playing on street corners for tips, and taking jobs outside music when times got particularly hard. In the late 1930s, Alexander also worked with **Lowell Fulson** and **Howlin' Wolf**, but he was incarcerated from 1940 until 1945 in the Texas State Penitentiary in Paris, Texas following his conviction for the murder of his wife. One source refers to him being sent to prison for "singing an obscene song", although that may have been a previous jail term. Several of his earlier songs, like "Penitentiary Moan Blues" and "Section Gang Blues", suggest he was already acquainted with prison life. On his release from jail, Alexander teamed up again with Lightnin' Hopkins for live shows in the Houston area, and they recorded together for Aladdin in 1947. He also recorded with pianist **Buster Pickens**, and made his final studio appearance with Benton's Busy Bees in 1950. He died in obscurity from syphilis in 1954, at the age of 53.

Alexander was a small but powerfully built man, and his recordings reveal a primal, booming tenor voice in which it's possible to hear traces of early field hollers. His compositions were often startlingly original and he improvised freely with timing and metre, which could make life difficult for his accompanists. "What he talked about, he lived it", said Lowell Fulson.

⊙ **Texas Alexander Vols 1–3** Matchbox
The collected works from 1927 until 1950, spread across three meticulously researched discs.

⊙ **98 Degrees Blues** Catfish
The best single disc collection, containing a generous 22 tracks, including "Frost Texas Tornado Blues" and "Penitentiary Moan Blues", though sadly not "House Of The Rising Sun".

Luther Allison

b Mayflower, Arkansas, August 17, 1939; d Aug 12, 1997

Considering the intensity of his singing, and the swaggering virtuosity and powerful emotional impact of his guitar playing,

Alligator Records

founded Chicago, 1971 by Bruce Iglauer

Like so many specialist blues labels, Alligator Records owes its existence and success to the passion and vision of one man. Bruce Iglauer fell in love with the blues when he was just 18, after seeing a performance by Mississippi Fred McDowell. Five years later, in 1971, he used his savings to record and produce his favorite band, **Hound Dog Taylor** & the House Rockers. Originally from Cincinnati, Iglauer was working as a clerk at Chicago's Delmark Records, and had discovered Taylor playing at Florence's Lounge on the city's South Side. When his attempts to persuade Delmark to record the band fell on deaf ears, he did the obvious thing and set up his own label. The name came from his habit of clicking out the rhythm of a songs he likes with his teeth.

Iglauer recorded Taylor live in the studio for $900, and used what money was left over to press up 1000 copies. Nine months later, the album had done well enough for him to leave his day job at Delmark and set about running Alligator Records full-time from his apartment. Because the sales of each release had to finance the next, the label made about one record a year. Even so, he managed to put out albums by big-hitters like **Big Walter Horton**, **Son Seals** and **Fenton Robinson**.

In 1975, Alligator signed **Koko Taylor**, who had previously enjoyed great success at Chess Records with "Wang Dang Doodle". She was the label's biggest name yet, and her first Alligator album, *I Got What It Takes*, won a Grammy nomination. That success enabled Alligator to hire its first employee, and to expand to a three-bedroom house on the North Side, where records were warehoused in the basement and kitchen, while Iglauer lived upstairs. In 1978 the label launched its *Living Chicago Blues* series, featuring the best of Chicago's under exposed blues artists, including Jimmy Johnson, Eddie Shaw, Left Hand Frank, Carey Bell, Magic Slim, Pinetop Perkins, Johnny "Big Moose" Walker, A.C. Reed, Scotty & The Rib Tips, Lovie Lee, Lacy Gibson, Billy Branch, Detroit Junior, Luther

"Guitar Jr" Johnson, Queen Sylvia Embry and Lonnie Brooks. Guitarist **Albert Collins** became Alligator's first non-Chicagoan artist in 1978. He went on to make six albums with them, including *Showdown!*, recorded with Johnny Copeland and Robert Cray.

By the mid-1980s, the label boasted a prolific release schedule, and Iglauer continued to produce many of them himself. World-class albums followed by Son Seals, Luther Allison, Charlie Musselwhite, Lonnie Brooks, James Cotton, Buddy Guy, Junior Wells, Carey Bell, Clarence "Gatemouth" Brown, Elvin Bishop, Katie Webster, Billy Boy Arnold, Long John Hunter, John Jackson, and Cephas & Wiggins. Alligator Records featured 125 releases in its catalogue by 1991, and it had become the biggest and most successful independent blues label in the world. To mark its 20th anniversary, Robert Mugge produced the critically acclaimed film *Pride & Joy: The Story Of Alligator Records*.

In recent years, the label has also reissued vintage 1950s material from the Jackson-based Trumpet label, including sides by Sonny Boy Williamson (Rice Miller) and Big Joe Williams, as well as new releases by a younger generation of blues performers including Li'l Ed & the Blues Imperials, C.J. Chenier, Maurice John Vaughn, Sugar Blue, Michael Hill's Blues Mob, Dave Hole, Little Charlie & the Nightcats, Saffire the Uppity Blues Women, William Clarke, Steady Rollin' Bob Margolin, Tinsley Ellis, Kenny Neal and The Kinsey Report. In the 1990s, the label also signed Luther Allison, who recorded three albums for Alligator before his untimely death in 1997. The emergence of Shemekia Copeland, Corey Harris and Coco Montoya has kept Alligator in the forefront of contemporary blues, while the 2004 signing of **Mavis Staples** added another blues/gospel legend to the roster.

⊙ *Various Artists* **Alligator Records 30th Anniversary Collection** Alligator
Thirty songs by all the Alligator stars; one disc features studio recordings, the other live performances.

RUF RECORDS

The late, great Luther Allison

were calling themselves The Four Jivers, and he was making a name for himself jamming in the clubs of Chicago's West Side with the likes of Magic Sam, Otis Rush and Freddie King. During the early 1960s, while King was away on tour, Allison further established his reputation by taking over his band at a weekly residency at Walton's Corner. Briefly relocating to California, he cut sides with fellow Chicagoans Shakey Jake Harris and Sunnyland Slim, before signing to Delmark Records and appearing on the label's classic *Sweet Home Chicago* anthology. His debut solo album, *Love Me Mama*, appeared in 1969. That same year, a storming appearance at the Ann Arbor Blues Festival transformed Allison from a relative unknown (beyond the clubs of Chicago) into a major blues-rock attraction.

Allison signed to Motown in 1972, becoming the soul label's only blues act. However, after three records for Motown's Gordy subsidiary, he moved to Paris, France, convinced that Europe was a more lucrative market for the blues. Over the following two decades, he recorded a dozen albums for a wide variety of labels, building a substantial following for his crossover blues-rock sound, located somewhere between Albert King and Jimi Hendrix.

In the early 1990s, Allison finally returned to Chicago. His first domestic album in 20 years, 1994's *Soul Fixin' Man* on Alligator Records, sparked a career renaissance. The albums *Blue Streak* and *Reckless* followed, combining his fierce, piercing single-note leads with his soul-drenched vocals and a searingly tough rock edge.

Luther Allison should surely have been a far bigger star. Ultimately, perhaps his material was not distinctive enough.

Born in Arkansas in 1939, Allison was the 14th of 15 children. He began to play the blues at the age of ten on a "diddley bow" – a string instrument constructed from wire attached by nails to a wall, with rocks for bridges and a bottle to fret the strings. After his family moved to Chicago in 1951, the twelve-year-old Allison gained a rare introduction into the world of the blues when he found himself classmates with **Muddy Waters'** son. He'd stop by the Waters household after school, and, if he was lucky, catch the great man rehearsing. Not until he was 18, however, did Allison start to play the guitar. He took the name for his first band, The Rolling Stones, from Muddy Waters' song some six years before Mick Jagger and company had the same idea. By that time, Allison's band

Tragically, however, Allison was diagnosed with inoperable lung cancer in July 1997, and died a month later, depriving the blues world of a great guitarist who at 57 was at the peak of his powers.

⊙ **Live In Chicago** Alligator
Recorded at the 1995 Chicago Blues Festival and a sold-out gig at Buddy Guy's Legends club, this captures Allison's white-hot guitar playing, flamboyant showmanship and irresistible energy at their very best.

⊙ **Soul Fixin' Man** Alligator
Allison's 1994 comeback album, produced in Memphis by Jim Gaines, is full of fiery solos and impassioned vocals, and he's backed by a great band.

Mose Allison

b Tippo, Mississippi, Nov 11, 1927

Ask the pianist Mose Allison if he regards himself first and foremost as a blues man or a jazz musician, and he has a stock reply: "It don't matter because to me, they both come from the same place."

Born on a farm on the eastern rim of the Mississippi Delta in 1927, the young Allison taught himself the piano and picked out popular blues and boogie tunes by ear. As a teenager he played trumpet in marching bands and started to write his own songs. He also discovered the jazz sounds of Louis Armstrong, Fats Waller and Duke Ellington, as well as the voice of the man who became his prime inspiration, Nat King Cole. By 1946, he was a member of the army band in Colorado Springs, and he went on to form his own piano-led trio. His playing was influenced by Erroll Garner and Thelonious Monk, while his voice suggested he had been listening not only to Cole, but also to Percy Mayfield and Charles Brown. Yet his world was far removed from that of the uneducated bluesmen whose music he revered. Attending both Mississippi and Louisiana State Universities, he obtained degrees in economics, English and philosophy, while he also cited the composers Bartók, Ives and Hindemith as influences – hardly names familiar to the average Delta musician.

Having moved to New York in 1956, Allison signed the following year to Prestige Records, for whom he recorded *Back Country Suite*, a wonderful collection that fused jazz and blues idioms in a tribute to the Mississippi Delta. He went on to play and record with such jazz greats as Stan Getz, Zoot Sims and Gerry Mulligan as well as with his own Mose Allison Trio, moving from Prestige to Columbia for three years, and then spending a further fifteen years, until 1976, with Atlantic.

During the 1960s, Allison became a major influence on the British R&B scene. Pete Townshend, Georgie Fame, Bill Wyman, Ray Davies, Eric Clapton, Jack Bruce and Van Morrison are among those who have cited him as an influence, while **John Mayall** covered his "Parchman Farm" and The Who recorded his "Young Man's Blues" on the 1970 album *Live At Leeds*. His songs have also been covered by The Clash, Clapton, Bonnie Raitt and Elvis Costello, while Van Morrison went so far as to record an entire album of his material, in collaboration with Ben Sidran and Georgie Fame. Since leaving Atlantic, Allison has recorded for such labels as Elektra and Blue Note, and is still going strong and performing regularly. An excellent biography cemented his reputation in 1995: *One Man's Blues: The Life and Music of Mose Allison* (Quartet Books), by Patti Jones.

His piano style remains notable for its unique mixture of classical and jazz-influenced sophistication with a more earthy, blues-based intimacy, while his intelligent and witty lyrics have a sting in their tail, and are delivered in a nasal but appealingly understated voice that is the epitome of laconic cool. And, talking of epitomes of cool, Allison can be seen performing in the Robert De Niro and Marlon Brando movie of 2001, *The Score*.

⊙ **Best Of Mose Allison** Atlantic
An excellent 20-track compilation of the best of Allison's 1961–76 Atlantic stint, including "Seventh Son", "Your Mind Is On Vacation" and "I Ain't Got Nothing But The Blues".

⊙ **Greatest Hits** OBC
A forty-year-old classic that collects together the best of the material Allison recorded for Prestige in the 1950s.

⊙ *Van Morrison* **Tell Me Something: The Songs Of Mose Allison** Verve
Superb tribute album featuring not only Morrison but fellow Allison disciples Georgie Fame and Ben Sidran. Mose himself appears on two tracks.

The Allman Brothers

formed (the band, that is) in Macon, Georgia, 1969

The Allman Brothers have long straddled the area where blues, rock and southern boogie meet in one extended jam. The band was founded in 1969 by guitarist Duane Allman and his younger brother, singer and keyboardist Greg Allman, who had already played together in the Allman Joys and later the Hour Glass. Much influenced by the likes of **B.B. King**, Duane had made his name at Fame studios in Muscle Shoals, Alabama, contributing memorable licks to tracks by King Curtis, Wilson Pickett and Aretha Franklin. Other founder members of the Allman Brothers Blues Band, as it was initially known, included second guitarist Dickie Betts, bassist Berry Oakley, and the two drummers Butch Trucks and former Otis Redding sideman Jaimoe Johanson.

Signed to Phil Walden's Capricorn Records, the band relocated to Macon, Georgia. Their first album, titled simply *The Allman Brothers Band*, appeared in 1969. Fusing blues roots with rock, Southern boogie and even country elements, its wailing dual lead guitar attack on tracks like "Whipping Post" set them apart from most of their rivals, and was soon much copied. A second album, *Idlewild South*, followed in 1970, but it was the following year's double live set *At Fillmore East* – still ranked among the greatest concert albums of all time – that established them as one of the biggest bands in America. On blues-drenched material like Blind Willie McTell's "Statesboro Blues", Elmore James's "Done Somebody Wrong", T-Bone Walker's "Stormy Monday", and two 29-minute jams around "You Don't Love Me" and "Whipping Post", the interplay between Duane and Dickie reached new dynamic heights, while their guitar duelling was topped by Greg's gritty, blue-eyed soul vocals. Duane Allman's status as one of the finest slide guitarists of his generation was soon reinforced when **Eric Clapton** recruited him to play on the Derek and The Dominos album, *Layla and Other Assorted Love Songs*.

Three months after the *Fillmore East* album was released, however, tragedy struck. On October 29, 1971, Duane Allman was badly injured in a motorcycle accident in Macon when he was hit by a peach truck. He refused hospital treatment and returned home, where he died a couple of hours later, aged 24. The band was already working on its next album when the accident occurred, and named the record *Eat A Peach*, with a cover featuring a drawing of a truck carrying one mammoth-sized peach, in his memory.

Rather than replacing Allman, Betts took sole charge of the lead guitar duties, and a second keyboardist, Chuck Leavell, was added to the line-up. Then, one year and 12 days after Duane's accident, Oakley too was killed in a similar motorcycle collision, just a few blocks from the site of Allman's crash. Despite this second blow, the band vowed to continue, and recruited new bassist Lamar Williams in Oakley's place. The next album,1973's *Brothers And Sisters*, contained their biggest hits in "Ramblin' Man" and "Jessica", but Betts' dominance as both guitarist and songwriter lent a mellower, country influence, and it was clear the group was missing the blues power of Allman's guitar.

Greg Allman and Betts both released solo albums, while most of their colleagues worked on chronic narcotic habits. It was drugs that eventually split the band in 1976. After Allman notoriously testified against a band employee following a drug bust, in order to keep himself out of jail, the rest of the band resolved to have nothing further to do with him. Despite those protestations, a reconstituted line-up featuring Allman, Betts, Johanson and Trucks was back together again by 1978. They split for a second time in 1982, then reassembled once more in 1989, when the brilliant guitarist Warren Hayes joined Betts to reinstate the band's original twin-guitar attack. The resulting *Seven Turns* album was a more than credible effort and they've continued recording and touring ever since, proving a major draw on the nostalgia circuit, and helping to inspire a new generation of so-called jam bands that frankly have little to do with the blues.

The Allmans' saga is a remarkable odyssey of triumph, tragedy, betrayal and redemption, stretching over almost forty years. However, their main interest to blues fans lies in the early albums, on which Duane Allman's explosive guitar playing places him up there with Jeff Beck, Clapton and Stevie Ray Vaughan. Ironically, though, what many regard as his finest blues guitar solo appears not on an Allman Brothers recording at all, but on "Loan

Me A Dime", from Boz Scaggs' Muscle Shoals-recorded, self-titled 1969 debut solo album.

⊙ **Beginnings** Capricorn
On the Allmans' first two albums, reissued on a single CD, their blues roots show through powerfully on material that includes Muddy Waters' "Trouble No More" and "Hoochie Coochie Man" and Greg's own "Whipping Post".

⊙ **At Filmore East – Deluxe Edition** Mercury
This 2003 reissue finds the original 1971 album expanded to more than two hours of music. One of the great, essential live recordings – by anyone.

⊙ **Eat A Peach** Capricorn
Issued in 1972 in the shocked aftermath of Duane's death, this is something of a grab-bag of live and studio tracks, but it features some stellar playing nonetheless.

Albert Ammons

b Chicago, Sept 23, 1907; d Dec 2, 1949

Together with **Pete Johnson** and **Meade Lux Lewis**, Albert Ammons was one of the big three boogie-woogie piano players of the 1930s and 1940s. Arguably, he was the most powerful and versatile of them all, with a style that retained an intense blues feel and a driving rhythmic solidity while also freely crossing over into jazz.

Born in Chicago in 1907, Ammons started to perform in the city's nightclubs as a soloist during the 1920s, while also playing with several different bands and orchestras, including one led by **Louis Banks**. When the Depression first hit and times were hard, he briefly drove a cab, but by 1934 he was leading his own band, the Rhythm Kings, and took up a famous residency at Chicago's Club DeLisa. He made his first recordings for Decca two years later, with a band that included Guy Kelly (trumpet) and Israel Crosby (bass). Greater fame came in the wake of his 1938 Carnegie Hall appearance in **John Hammond**'s first legendary "Spirituals To Swing" concert, when he, Johnson and Lewis performed "A Cavalcade of Boogie" together. That event effectively launched the boogie-woogie craze. Ammons appeared with Johnson and Lewis at New York's chic Café Society, and recorded several sides with them both as duos and as a trio, including the majestic "Boogie-woogie Prayer" Parts One and Two.

Ammons remained popular throughout the 1940s, recording with such musicians as the Port of Harlem Jazzmen, Harry James, and the blues singer **Sippie Wallace**, and even cutting an earthy session with his son, the tenor sax player Gene "Jug" Ammons, who went on to feature in Woody Herman's band. His final sessions for Mercury in 1949 teamed him again with bassist Israel Crosby, while President Harry Truman's inauguration ball that same year was among his last gigs. He died later that year, at the age of 42.

⊙ **Boogie-woogie Man** Topaz
A superb compilation of the best of Albert Ammons. Some 20 piano solos, duos and trios, all recorded between 1936 and 1944, include "Boogie-woogie Prayer", "Bass Goin' Crazy" and a version of "St Louis Blues".

⊙ **Boogie-woogie Stomp** Delmark
These 18 prime slices of boogie-woogie piano, recorded live in 1939 and including additional contributions from Lewis and Johnson, arguably provide a more authentic picture of Ammons' talent than his studio recordings.

Pink Anderson

b Laurens, South Carolina, Feb 12, 1900; d Oct 12, 1974

A "song and dance man" as well as a blues singer, "Pink" Anderson spent much of his performing life with a "medicine show", touting cheap patent medicines and herbal cures of dubious efficacy around the rural Deep South. To lure in the punters, he developed the patter of a stand-up comedian, but he also built up an impressive repertoire that included blues, ballads, rags, and other "songster" material.

Born Pinkney Anderson in South Carolina in 1900, he moved to Greenville with his family when he was very young, and then on to Spartanburg. As a child, he sang and danced for tips on the street as a "buck dancer" and learned the rudiments of guitar. A neighbor, Joe Wicks, taught him to play bottleneck in an open tuning, as well as a repertoire of such well-known songs as "John Henry". He also took further tuition from an old blind singer from Georgia called Simeon Dooley, who had settled in the Spartanburg area and was reportedly a harsh tutor who would beat Anderson on the hands if he played a wrong chord. Pink joined "Doctor" W.R. Kerr's Medicine Show in 1917, but when he wasn't on the road he performed with Dooley on street corners in Spartanburg as Pink and Simmie.

During the mid-1920s, Anderson also began playing with a string band led by **Carl Martin**, which later recorded as the Tennessee Chocolate Drops. Pink and Simmie's reputation as a duo had grown sufficiently by 1928 for them to record four songs, all in the medicine show "songster" tradition, for a Columbia field recording unit in Atlanta. Sadly, these were the only recordings Anderson made until 1950. Although Columbia were keen on further sessions, he refused to record without his partner. Instead, he continued to play in the Spartanburg area, both with Simeon Dooley and with Kerr's medicine show, with whom he stayed for almost 30 years. Along the way he picked up a disciple in the form of harmonica player **Peg Leg Sam**, and he passed his treasure-trove of songs on to him.

As the medicine shows went into decline after World War II and Kerr retired from quackery, Anderson moved on. He was performing with Big Chief Thundercloud's Tent Show at the Virginia State Fair in Charlottesville in 1950 when he was recorded by the blues collector Paul Clayton. The song, "Every Day In The Week", which had featured in his 1928 session, was released on the Riverside label in conjunction with several sides recorded by another Laurens-born musician, **Rev. Gary Davis**.

In 1954, after Dooley had grown increasingly infirm, Anderson teamed up with guitarist Charles "Baby" Tate, harmonica player Keg Shorty Bell and washboard player Charley "Chilly Willy" Williams, and continued to play around Spartanburg. Sam Charters found him there in 1962, and recorded three themed albums, featuring respectively his blues, folk ballads and medicine-show songs. A stroke forced Anderson to stop playing in 1964, and a final attempt to record him in 1970 was a failure. He died four years later.

Anderson is best remembered these days as a quirky footnote in rock history, because Pink Floyd took their name by combining his name with that of the North Carolina blues guitarist, Floyd Council. However, his 1962 recordings prove he deserves better. Although made when he was past his best, they reveal a consummate entertainer, who in his prime must have been an outstanding finger-picking guitarist in the style of **Blind Boy Fuller**.

⊙ **Carolina Bluesman** Prestige-Bluesville
The best of the three LPs recorded by Charters in 1962 showcases Anderson as a blues singer.

⊙ *Various Artists* **Georgia String Bands 1928–1930** Document
This compilation includes the four sides cut by Pink Anderson with Simmie Dooley in Atlanta in 1928.

The Animals

formed in Newcastle, England, 1963; disbanded 1966

For a short period during the 1960s, the Animals ranked second only to the Rolling Stones among British R&B bands. Formed in Newcastle in 1963 by singer Eric Burdon (b Newcastle, May 11, 1941) and pianist Alan Price (b Fairfield, Durham April 19, 1941), along with drummer John Steel, bassist Chas Chandler and guitarist Hilton Valentine, and originally known as the Alan Price Rhythm and Blues Combo, the group released its self-produced debut EP as the Animals in 1963. A limited edition of just 500 copies, it contained versions of **Muddy Waters**' "I Just Wanna Make Love To You", and **John Lee Hooker**'s "Boom Boom". These cuts have a tremendous raw energy. Sean Egan, the band's biographer, suggested in 2001's *Animal Tracks* that "for all their subsequent commercial and artistic success, they may well have peaked on this record".

Despite its minimal pressing, the EP secured the band their first bookings, early in 1964, at London clubs like the Crawdaddy, the Scene and the Ricky Tik. By that time, they had also backed one of their heroes, Sonny Boy Williamson, at Newcastle's Club A-G-Go. Not released until several years later, the tapes reveal a raw and exciting British blues band, with Burdon holding his own with Willamson in duets on "The Night Time Is The Right Time" and "Talkin' Bout You".

The band's early London shows led to their being signed by independent producer Mickie Most, who secured them a contract with EMI's Columbia imprint. Their debut single, "Baby Let Me Take You Home", was adapted from "Baby Let Me Follow You Down", which they had picked up from Bob Dylan's first album. That same record was also the source of the follow-up, the traditional "House of the Rising Sun", in an arrangement Dylan had borrowed from Dave Van Ronk.

Recorded in half an hour at a cost of four pounds and ten shillings, and given a dramatic new guitar riff by Valentine, a soulful organ accompaniment by Price and a tough, bluesy vocal by Burdon, the song topped both the British and American charts by late summer 1964. One of the towering achievements of the

British R&B movement, it was also highly influential, not least on Dylan's own decision to go electric.

An enviable run of gritty, blues-tinged pop singles followed, including the Price/Burdon compositions "I'm Crying", "We've Gotta Get Out of This Place" and "In My Life", and covers of Nina Simone's "Don't Let Me Be Misunderstood" and

Arhoolie Records

founded by Chris Strachwitz in California,1960

When he started Arhoolie Records, Chris Strachwitz's primary intention was to record his idol **Lightnin' Hopkins**, whom he found playing in beer halls during his first field trip to Texas in 1959. However, when he returned the following summer, during a more extensive trip to Texas, Mississippi and Louisiana, Strachwitz realized he didn't have the necessary capital. Instead, he found and recorded **Mance Lipscomb**, who came considerably cheaper. Lipscomb's *Texas Sharecropper and Songster* appeared as the first Arhoolie LP in November 1960, in a pressing of 250 copies packaged and shipped from Strachwitz's kitchen table.

Born in Germany in 1931, Strachwitz first heard swing music as a boy on American Forces Radio. After being sent to college in America in 1947, he swiftly developed a passion for New Orleans jazz as well as blues and gospel. Living on the West Coast, he got to know such San Francisco bluesmen as **Jesse Fuller** and **K.C. Douglas**. Following a spell in the army, and with the arrival of the folk-blues boom, he took the plunge into recording, with generous advice offered by other blues collectors such as Sam Charters and Mack McCormick. His label's name came from a Library of Congress recording made in Mississippi, in which a singer asked what he called the selection he had just sung replied "Arhoolie". The second part of the word was a common name for a field holler among performers of a certain generation.

"My main aim was to document the best authentic down home blues singers and try

to sell the albums to a new, mainly young white 'folk music' audience," Strachwitz later explained. "I also tried to reach our black audiences with this magnificent historic music by releasing 45rpm singles and searching for distributors to reach that market."

After Lipscomb's record came out, Strachwitz's next field trip to the South resulted in his recording with Black Ace, Li'l Son Jackson and Alex Moore. As Arhoolie slowly grew, he made new recordings of **Mississippi Fred McDowell** – including "You Gotta Move", later covered by the Rolling Stones on *Sticky Fingers*, over which Strachwitz had to fight a famous legal battle to get the bluesman his royalties – and discovered **Clifton Chenier**, the king of zydeco. Chenier happened to be a cousin of Lightnin' Hopkins, whom Strachwitz ultimately did manage to record. Other blues artists whose recordings grace Arhoolie's catalogue include Juke Boy Bonner, Guitar Slim, Snooks Eaglin, Lowell Fulson, K.C. Douglas, Elizabeth Cotten (whose album *Live!* won the label a Grammy), Joe Turner, Katie Webster, Big Joe Williams and Robert Pete Williams.

The label has since expanded into other forms of ethnic music. At the time of writing it had recently celebrated its 45th anniversary, with Strachwitz still at the head of its activities as label president.

⊙ *Various Artists* **Arhoolie's 40th Anniversary Collection** Arhoolie
This wonderfully packaged five-CD box set covers not only Arhoolie's blues roster but also its Tejano and world music interests.

Sam Cooke's "Bring It On Home To Me". Price left the band in 1965, taking all of the royalties for "House Of The Rising Sun" with him, and thereby earning considerable bitterness from his former band mates. After he was replaced by Dave Rowberry, The Animals also ended their association with Most, unhappy with his attempts to push them towards pop, and moved to Decca Records. The Rolling Stones were already on the label, so it now boasted the two best R&B bands in Britain. The Animals' first Decca album, *Animalisms*, had an earthier, blues feel – but by the end of 1966, the original group was no more.

Chandler went on to manage Jimi Hendrix, while Burdon re-formed the group as Eric Burdon and the New Animals and enthusiastically embraced psychedelia during 1967's Summer of Love. He went on to the Los Angeles-based funk outfit War, and then embarked on a solo career during which he has from time to time returned to his blues roots.

In many ways, particularly when Mickie Most was calling the shots, The Animals were a pop group rather than a blues band. Yet the visceral power of "House Of The Rising Sun" represented a seminal moment in the development of British blues, while the cover versions on the group's early LPs played an important role in bringing names like John Lee Hooker and Jimmy Reed to a wider audience.

⊙ **The Animals with Sonny Boy Williamson**
Charly
The best of several repackaged versions of a storming night at Newcastle's Club A-Go-Go on December 30, 1963.

⊙ **Animalisms** Repertoire
As well as featuring "Smokestack Lightnin'" and "Going Down Slow", this CD of The Animals' best and grittiest album also includes the four tracks from their 1963 debut EP as a bonus.

Billy "Boy" Arnold

b Chicago, March 16, 1935

One of the first generation of bluesmen to be born in Chicago, rather than migrating there from the South, Billy Arnold was just twelve years old when he knocked on the door of his neighbor, **John Lee "Sonny Boy"**

Williamson and asked for harmonica lessons. Sadly, their relationship was short-lived, as Sonny Boy was murdered in 1948 at the tragically young age of 34. Even so, Arnold learned enough in his three lessons from Williamson to set him on his way as a blues harmonica player.

As an underage boy, hanging around in blues clubs, Arnold saw the likes of **Blind John Davis**, Big Bill Broonzy, Memphis Minnie, Muddy Waters, Johnny Jones, Johnny Shines, Otis Rush, Little Walter, and Earl Hooker. All played a part in his musical education, and he was soon getting up on stage to blow his harp with several of them.

Arnold cut his first 78, featuring "I Ain't Got No Money" and "Hello Stranger", for the obscure Cool label in 1952. Unaware of his nickname, he was surprised when it appeared under the name Billy "Boy" Arnold. "I didn't like it at first," he later recalled. "I was 17 and looked 15 but told people I was 19, so I didn't want to be known as a boy. I wanted to be a man." Even so, the name stuck.

When Arnold *was* 19, he hooked up with a young street musician called Ellis McDaniel – soon to become known to the world as **Bo Diddley**. Using an amplifier Diddley had fashioned out of an orange crate, they auditioned for Chess Records. Arnold's signature "stop-time" keening harp played a major part on Diddley's two-sided debut hit on the subsidiary label Checker, "Bo Diddley" coupled with "I'm a Man". Not content with being a sideman, the ambitious Arnold wanted to make his own records. Diddley apparently told him that he'd never record for Chess because Leonard Chess didn't like him, so he walked across the street to the offices of Vee Jay Records, who were only too delighted to snatch him from under the noses of their great rival.

Arnold's first solo single, "I Wish You Would", borrowed the Bo Diddley beat, and is said to have been the first blues record to feature an electric bass. Both that song and another of his Vee Jay recordings, "I Ain't Got You", were later covered by the Yardbirds. Other fine recordings from the era include "She's Fine, She's Mine" and "Prisoner's Plea". However, he left Vee Jay in 1958 and formed a band that included the guitarist **Mighty Joe Young**. After some obscure recordings for the Mighty H label, the classic *More Blues From The South Side* came out in 1964 on the Prestige label, produced by Sam Charters. Around the same time, Arnold recorded an album with the pianist Johnny Jones, which remained unreleased until 1980.

By the late 1960s, Arnold's popularity in America had faded. For several years he supported his family driving a Chicago bus, and he later became a parole officer for the state of Illinois. However, European audiences did not forget him. He toured with a "Blues Legends" package in 1975, and recorded two albums for the UK-based Red Lightnin' label.

After a long lay-off, Arnold returned to action in 1993 with the Alligator album *Back Where I Belong*. Two years later came *Eldorado Cadillac*, before he switched to the Stony Plain label for 2001's *Boogie'n'Shuffle*, backed by **Duke Robillard**. It was a deserved comeback for an artist who never had the recognition he deserved. Among his many strengths was a fine, individual blues harmonica style that combined the "choking" technique of **Sonny Boy Williamson** with a sound that was often uncannily like that of a wah-wah pedal. He had an urban sophistication that was all his own: a silky but sturdy voice and a repertoire of streetwise, colorful songs.

⊙ **More Blues From The South Side** OBC
Arnold's 1964 Prestige album shows strong traces of Bo Diddley and Junior Wells, but remains a classic, and features strong guitar work from Mighty Joe Young.

⊙ **Back Where I Belong** Alligator
Billy "Boy" Arnold's 1993 comeback album added maturity to his earlier excitement, on an excellent set that opened with a remake of 1955's "I Wish You Would".

James "Kokomo" Arnold

b Lovejoy's Station, Georgia, Feb 15, 1901; d Nov 8, 1968

"Kokomo" Arnold's first career was as a bootlegger, while he ended his working life on a Chicago factory floor. However, for four and a half brief years between 1934 and 1938, he was an outstanding bluesman, with a distinctive, left-handed bottleneck guitar style and a striking, high-pitched wail of a voice, who cut some of the most influential records of the era.

Born to sharecropping parents in Georgia in 1901, James Arnold learned the basics of guitar playing from a cousin whose name has been given variously as James Wigges and John Wiggs. He left the South as a teenager, and found employment first in steel mills in Illinois and Pennsylvania, and then as a farmhand in Buffalo, before he landed up in the early 1920s in New York, where he became a bootlegger. He regarded music as nothing more than a sideline, but made his first recordings, "Paddlin' Madeline Blues" and "Rainy Night Blues" during a brief stay in Memphis in 1930. They were released on the Victor label under the name **Gitfiddle Jim**.

Not until the repeal of Prohibition put him out of the bootlegging business in 1933 did Arnold, by now based in Chicago, decide to try music as a full-time vocation. Between September 1934 and May 1938 he cut 88 sides for Decca, mostly solo but backed on some sides by Peetie Wheatstraw on piano. These included "Old Original Kokomo Blues", a revamp of "Kokomo Blues", which had been recorded by another bootlegging guitarist Scrapper Blackwell in 1928. Named after a popular brand of coffee, the song gave him the name by which he was known ever after.

Arnold's distinctive bottleneck slide style involved playing the guitar flat, often at lightning speed, while he sang in a wailing voice that was so intense it was often unintelligible, despite being punctuated by bursts of great clarity and authority. However, his blues were not only singular but also highly influential. **Robert Johnson** based his "Sweet Home Chicago" on Arnold's version of "Old Original Kokomo Blues", and turned the other song on his first 78rpm Decca release, "Milk Cow Blues", into "Milkcow's Calf Blues". The latter song was subsequently covered by Elvis Presley and Eddie Cochran.

Arnold also played guitar on two tunes cut in July 1936 by Oscar's Chicago Swingers, a dance band led by singer **Sam Theard**, and recorded with **Roosevelt Sykes** and **Mary Johnson**. A popular attraction in the clubs of Chicago, his fame ran as far as New York. Nonetheless, he abruptly quit music in 1938, following a row with Mayo Williams, a black college graduate who had been an influential blues scout for various record labels since the early 1920s, and was then working for Decca Records. No one knows what they argued about, but Arnold apparently took it seriously enough to end his musical career.

Then again, he had always been a reluctant bluesman, once telling his landlady to say he was out when Decca sent a car to pick him up for a recording session. When he was discovered by enthusiastic young blues researchers in Chicago in 1962, he was working in a factory. Although they persuaded him to make a handful of live appearances, he showed no real desire to return to his roots, and he never recorded again. "I was never interested in making records," he told an interviewer. "I always preferred to live a quiet life, just unknown in my basement."

⊙ **Old Original Kokomo Blues** Catfish
Twenty-three of Arnold's classic 1930s sides, including the title track from which he took his name, and "Milk Cow Blues".

⊙ **Complete Recorded Works Vols 1–4** Document
All of Arnold's surviving 94 sides, including the 1930 Gitfiddle Jim tracks as well as no fewer than four versions of "Milk Cow Blues".

B

underworld of pool halls and petty crime, and took up guitar. He swiftly became a virtuoso in both jazz and blues styles, and came under the influence of T-Bone Walker's disciple **Pee Wee Crayton**, whom he met on a trip to the West Coast. Back in the Big Apple, he had become an in-demand session player by the late 1940s, playing on innumerable blues and R&B tracks, mostly for Atlantic, but also for RCA, Decca and Okeh. Classics on which his guitar can be heard include the Drifters' "Money Honey", Big Joe Turner's "Shake, Rattle, and Roll"; Ruth Brown's "Mama, He Treats Your Daughter Mean"; and Big Maybelle's "Whole Lot of Shakin' Going On". He also played with the likes of Ray Charles, Little Willie John, La Vern Baker and **Screamin' Jay Hawkins**.

Baker recorded several singles under his own name during the mid-1950s, and also made a Latin jazz-styled solo album, *Guitar Mambo*. In 1956 he hooked up with the singer Sylvia Vanderpool (originally known as Little Sylvia) to form the duo Mickey and Sylvia, modeled on the success of Les Ford and Mary Paul. Their biggest hit "Love Is Strange", co-written with **Bo Diddley**, featured some fine blues guitar riffs from Baker. He also

Mickey "Guitar" Baker

b Louisville, Kentucky, Oct 15, 1925

Along with the better-known Chuck Berry and Bo Diddley, Mickey Baker was one of the handful of guitarists in the 1950s who drew on blues roots as they helped transform R&B into rock'n'roll.

Born McHouston Baker in Kentucky in 1925, his early life was troubled, and he spent time in a children's home and reform school. He moved to New York at 16, where he drifted into a seedy

Gentleman dandy of the blues, Mickey "Cravate" Baker

REDFERNS

appeared on Tina Turner's first 1962 hit, "It's Gonna Work Out Fine".

An instrumental solo album *The Wildest Guitar*, released on Atlantic in 1959, collected many of Baker's best solo recordings, and remains something of a cult classic. However, he moved to France in the early 1960s. Well positioned for the blues boom in Europe, he joined such visiting American bluesmen as **Champion Jack Dupree** and **Memphis Slim** on tour. He was also responsible for the superb string arrangement on Fleetwood Mac's 1968 version of "Need Your Love So Bad". He made two albums for Stefan Grossman's Kicking Mule label in the late 1970s, and recorded sporadically thereafter, mostly for obscure French labels.

⊙ **The Wildest Guitar** Sepia Tone
Mickey Baker's 1959 collection, which combines rowdy blues playing with smoother jazz stylings, was finally released on CD for the first time in 2003.

Long John Baldry

b Haddon, Derbyshire, Jan 12, 1941; d July 21, 2005

A key figure in the British blues boom of the early 1960s, and a powerful influence on Eric Clapton and the Rolling Stones at the outset of their careers, Long John Baldry ironically enjoyed his greatest success as a middle-of-the-road pop balladeer, when "Let The Heartaches Begin" topped the British charts in 1967.

Although Baldry started out on the London skiffle scene in the late 1950s, folk soon gave way to the blues as his main musical currency. In 1962, he became a founder member and featured vocalist with Blues Incorporated, led by Cyril Davis and Alexis Korner. The band's weekly residency at the Marquee Club in London's Soho became a magnet for an entire generation of upcoming British musicians, who came along to listen and to learn about the blues.

The group recorded what is widely credited as the first British blues album, *R&B From The Marquee*, which came out on Decca's Ace of Clubs imprint in November 1962. By then, Baldry had left for the same lucrative German club circuit that had taken The Beatles to Hamburg. But as the British blues movement and the beat boom gathered pace, his charismatic stage presence and deep, resonant voice was in increasing demand back home. Both Korner and Davies, who by now were leading separate groups, sent telegrams to Germany wooing him to rejoin them. He opted for Davies' R&B All-Stars, because the harmonica player offered to pay his air fare back to Britain.

The All-Stars took over the Marquee residency, and were briefly joined by future Led Zeppelin guitarist **Jimmy Page** as they mixed authentic R&B club performances with slots on pop package tours alongside the likes of Gerry and the Pacemakers and Billy J Kramer and the Dakotas. However, the All-Stars' progress was slowed when Davies developed pleurisy and took to drinking heavily to dull his pain.

Following Davies' death in January 1964, Baldry took over the band, changed the name to the Hoochie Coochie Men, and recruited an unknown young singer, **Rod Stewart**. "Picture this elegant man with a proper English accent, never without a tie, a towering six-foot-seven," Stewart recalled many years later. "I was a huge fan and I was intimidated by his offer but I immediately said yes. In those days the only music we fell in love with was the blues, and John was the first white guy singing it. It was the true blues and everyone looked up to him."

The Hoochie-Coochie Men released one album, 1964's *Long John's Blues*, before Stewart joined Baldry in his next band Steampacket, which also included Julie Driscoll and Brian Auger. Even though all its members were to enjoy individual success, the band struggled. It swiftly disbanded, leaving Baldry to put together another unsuccessful outfit called Bluesology, which included the unknown pianist Reg Dwight, soon to find fame as **Elton John**.

Frustrated by his lack of commercial success, Baldry went solo in 1966, and decided to concentrate on straight pop. "Let The Heartaches Begin" was followed by several minor hits, but he returned to a more blues-rock oriented style with the 1971 album *It Ain't Easy*. Co-produced by Stewart and Elton John, it included the excellent "Don't Try To Lay No Boogie-woogie On The King of Rock'n'Roll".

Baldry moved to Vancouver in 1980, where he lived as a Canadian citizen for the rest of his life.

During the 1990s, he returned to his blues roots with a tribute album to Leadbelly.

⊙ **Long John's Blues/ Looking At Long John** BGO
Although you'll probably want to skip ballads like "You've Lost That Lovin' Feelin'", there's still plenty of fine British blues singing on this, the best Baldry compilation, on numbers such as "Turn On Your Love Light", "Got My Mojo Working" and "Dimples".

⊙ **Remembering Leadbelly** Stony Plain
This 16-track tribute to Leadbelly, recorded in Vancouver in 2002, also includes interviews in which Baldry and Alan Lomax talk about Leadbelly's influence.

Marcia Ball

b Orange, Texas, Mar 20, 1949

Pianist and songwriter Marcia Ball combines Texas blues and Louisiana R&B in invigorating style. A series of acclaimed albums and almost non-stop touring have earned her a loyal following.

Although she was born into a musical family in Texas, Ball grew up just across the state line in the small town of Vinton, Louisiana, in the heart of an area known as "the Texas triangle", which includes portions of both states and also produced such blues names as Janis Joplin, Johnny and Edgar Winter, Queen Ida, Lonnie Brooks and Clifton Chenier. Having taken piano lessons from the age of five, she discovered the power of the blues

at 13, when she saw Irma Thomas perform. "She just blew me away and caught me totally unaware. Once I started my own band, the first stuff I was doing was Irma's," she later recalled of her days in the blues-cum-psychedelic rock outfit Gum, which she helped form while at Louisiana State University in 1966.

Although Ball set out to follow Janis Joplin to San Francisco in 1970, her car broke down in Austin, Texas. While she waited for it to be repaired, she decided the laid-back atmosphere and abundant music bars of the city made it look a fine place for a singer/pianist to live. She's been there ever since.

For a time, Ball sang in a country band called Freda and the Firedogs. Then she discovered the music of the great New Orleans piano player **Professor Longhair**. Its profound impact can be heard on the albums she made for Rounder in the 1980s and 1990s, including *Soulful Dress* (1983), *Hot Tamale Baby* (1985), *Gatorhythms* (1989), *Blue House* (1994) and *Let Me Play With Your Poodle* (1997). In 1990, she collaborated with Angela Strehli and Lou Ann Barton on *Dreams Come True*, which was produced by **Dr. John**. A similar "three divas" project for Rounder with Tracy Nelson and her longtime inspiration, **Irma Thomas**, resulted in 1998's *Sing It!* She left Rounder for Alligator Records in 2001 and released *Presumed Innocent*, followed by *So Many Rivers* two years later.

Mostly performing her own material, although she has also covered songs by the likes of Dr. John and **Clifton Chenier**, Marcia Ball tends to sing in an upper register, but her voice has an appealingly gritty huskiness. Her piano playing, drenched in the traditions of New Orleans, also displays elements of Texan country swing, boogie-woogie, zydeco and Louisiana swamp rock. She is also a spectacular live performer, as can be heard on 2005's *Live! Down The Road*.

⊙ **Sing It!** Rounder
This thrilling 1998 collaboration found Marcia Ball, Tracy Nelson and Irma Thomas backed by a band comprised of funky Memphis-soul stalwarts and New Orleans session stars.

⊙ **Live! Down The Road** Alligator
Marcia Ball is such a legendarily powerful stage performer that it's surprising she took 30 years to get around to making a live album.

Barbecue Bob

b Walton Grove, Georgia, Sept 11, 1902; d Oct 21, 1931

Before every Rolling Stones concert, Keith Richards and Ron Wood retreat to a backstage lair for an acoustic warm-up in which they play their favorite old country blues songs. They call this ritual their "Barbecue Bob session", in recognition of the Atlanta-based twelve-string guitarist and blues pioneer.

The sons of sharecroppers, Robert Hicks and his elder brother Charley – later known as "Charley Lincoln" – were taught guitar by Savannah "Dip" Weaver and her son, Curley Weaver. Both learned to play both the six and the twelve-string guitar, the latter being something of a specialty down Georgia way, where other local practitioners included **Blind Willie McTell**.

By the early 1920s, Robert had followed his brother to Atlanta, and they were performing at parties and dances in a group that included **Curley Weaver** and **Eddie Mapp** on harmonica. 1926 found him working solo at Tidwell's Barbecue Place in the affluent Atlanta suburb of Buckhead, where he cooked and served as well as sang. The following year, Columbia Records decided to base its field recording unit in Atlanta. When their talent scout Don Hornsby recorded Hicks, he posed him in chef's whites for publicity shots. Barbecue Bob was born.

In keeping with his new monicker, Bob's first Columbia release, cut in a downtown Atlanta hotel in March 1927, was called "Barbecue Blues". Backed with "Cloudy Sky Blues", it sold 15,000 copies, making him the label's best-selling male artist. Columbia took him to New York three months later to record its follow-up, "Mississippi Heavy Water Blues", which vividly dealt with that year's devastating Delta floods, also the subject of Charley Patton's "High Water Everywhere". Over the next three years Bob recorded a total of 65 fine sides for Columbia, matching McTell as the biggest name in the Atlanta blues world.

He was joined by his brother on four sides, credited to Barbecue Bob and Laughing Charley, and the pair also recorded as the Georgia Cotton Pickers in 1930, bolstered by old friends Curley Weaver and Eddie. Around the same time, he completed his last solo session as Barbecue Bob for Columbia. He died, less than a year later, of pneumonia at the young age of 29. Charley Lincoln took his death hard; he became an alcoholic, murdered a man on Christmas Day 1955 and died in prison in 1963.

Almost invariably playing a 12-string Stella guitar in open tunings, Barbecue Bob was a consummate stylist, with a heavy, percussive finger-picking style and a deft bottleneck technique. In a rough and expressively warm voice, he sang a repertoire that included blues standards such as "Poor Boy A Long Ways From Home", "Fo' Day Creep" and "Goin' Up The Country". **Canned Heat** had a hit single with a cover of the latter in the 1960s, while Eric Clapton and Steve Miller are among those to have adapted his recording of "Motherless Chile Blues".

⊙ **The Essential Barbecue Bob** Classic Blues
This two-CD compilation collects 36 of Barbecue Bob's Columbia tracks, including "Goin' Up The Country", "Motherless Chile Blues", "Barbecue Blues" and the great "Goodtime Rounder".

⊙ **Complete Recorded Works Vols 1–3** Document
Bob's entire recorded output amounted to 65 tracks – Document have crammed them onto three CDs, each available individually.

Dave Bartholomew

b Edgard, Louisiana, 24 December, 1920

Producer, arranger, songwriter, bandleader, as well as an artist in his own right, Dave Bartholomew helped to shape the sound of New Orleans R&B. The creator of what he called the "Big Beat", he produced and co-wrote most of Fats Domino's major hits during the early 1950s.

Raised in a small town twenty miles west of New Orleans, Bartholomew learned the trumpet as a child, encouraged by his father, who played tuba in a Dixieland jazz band. By 1939, he was working on a Mississippi riverboat, in a band led by Fats Pichon. His career was interrupted by a wartime spell in the army, before he returned to New Orleans in the late 1940s and formed his first band. Members included saxophonists Alvin "Red" Tyler and Lee Allen, pianist Professor Longhair, and drummer Earl Palmer – all of whom went on to become some of the Crescent City's most in-demand sessionmen.

In 1948, Bartholomew stumbled upon a 20-year-old pianist and singer called **Antoine "Fats" Domino** in New Orleans' Hideaway Club. By then, Bartholomew had already worked for several labels, including Specialty, Aladdin and De Luxe. He had a hit for the latter with "Country Boy", in 1949 under his own name. That same year, he took a job with Lew Chudd's newly formed Imperial Records as house producer, arranger and talent scout. One of his first acts was to recommend Domino.

"The Fat Man", released in 1950, was the first of a string of hits produced by Bartholomew and mostly co-written by the pair. Other joint compositions included "Blue Monday", "Let The Four Winds Blow", "I'm In Love Again", "Whole Lotta Loving", "My Girl Josephine" and "I'm Walkin'", although Bartholomew did not have a hand in writing Domino's best-known hit "Blueberry Hill."

Away from Domino, Bartholomew worked prolifically with most of the big names in 1950s' New Orleans. His other credits included Smiley Lewis's "I Hear You Knocking" and "One Night" (later a hit for Elvis Presley in a considerably tamer version); Lloyd Price's "Lawdy Miss Clawdy", also covered by Presley; and recordings by Shirley and Lee, Earl King, Roy Brown, Huey "Piano" Smith, Bobby Mitchell, Chris Kenner, Robert Parker, Frankie Ford and Snooks Eaglin. When Chudd sold Imperial in 1963, Liberty Records relocated the label to Los Angeles. However, Bartholomew declined an invitation to move with them, preferring to stay in New Orleans.

Among the 4000 or so songs Bartholomew claims to have written was 1952's "My Ding-A-Ling", which **Chuck Berry** turned into a number-one hit 20 years later, and "The Monkey". He continued recording under his own name, including a Dixieland album in 1981, and was still leading a big band into the 1990s, with regular appearances at New Orleans' annual Jazz & Heritage Festival. In 1991, he was inducted into the Rock and Roll Hall Of Fame.

Bartholomew remains best known for his influential arranging and production work, rather than for his own records. His trademark sound bridged jump blues, Dixieland jazz and the carnival march-es of Mardi Gras, overloading the lower register with piano, bass, sax and drums to produce the "rumble" of his world-conquering "big beat".

⊙ **The Chronological Dave Bartholomew 1947–50** Classics
This collection of Dave Bartholomew's early tracks serves to chronicle the birth of the modern New Orleans R&B sound.

⊙ **The Big Beat of Dave Bartholomew: 20 of His Milestone Productions 1949–1960** EMI/Capitol
Twenty of Bartholomew's finest sides, including tracks released under his own name as well as songs by Fats Domino, Smiley Lewis, Chris Kenner and others.

Jeff Beck

b Wallington, England, June 24, 1944

Eric Clapton once joked that there must have been something in the water in the English home counties in the 1950s. For a brief moment, the Thames basin came to resemble the Mississippi Delta in its capacity to produce high-class musicians who looked to the blues for their inspiration. The holy trinity of British blues-rock guitarists – Clapton, Jimmy Page and Jeff Beck – all emerged simultaneously from the leafy, middle-class suburbs of outer London. Many claim that, in terms of technique and the sheer range of sounds he coaxed from his guitar, Beck was the most gifted of the lot.

Geoffrey Arnold Beck grew up playing piano and listening to classical music. He was also exposed to jazz and blues on the radio, and what he heard persuaded him to leave the piano behind and pick up a guitar. By the time he went to art college – the customary training-ground for aspiring British rock musicians in the 1960s – he was already an accomplished virtuoso. Beck's stay at college was brief; he soon left to work full-time as a session guitarist. The formidable reputation he acquired playing live with **Screaming Lord Sutch** and the Tridents made him a natural choice as the Yardbirds' lead guitarist in 1965, after Clapton left the group because he wanted to play a purer form of the blues. Beck slotted perfectly into the group's hybrid style that combined pop, rock, blues and psychedelia. Among the first guitarists to experiment with feedback and distortion, notably on the Yardbirds 1966 album *Roger The Engineer*, he anticipated the techniques Jimi Hendrix was about to make his own. Beck played on the band's biggest hits – "For Your Love", "Heart Full Of Soul", "Evil Hearted You", "Shapes Of Things" and "Over Under Sideways Down" – and toured America with them, on the same bill as the Rolling Stones, in 1966. By then **Jimmy Page** had joined the group, which for a brief period had an enviable twin-guitar attack. However, Beck walked out mid-tour due to various personal problems and personality clashes, and the group enjoyed no further top-ten hits after his departure.

Having initially claimed that he was retiring, Beck signed a solo deal with EMI's Columbia subsidiary. After some Mickie Most-produced solo pop hits, the most successful of which was "Hi-Ho Silver Lining", he put together his own band, including the then-unknown Rod Stewart and future Rolling Stones' guitarist Ron Wood on bass. The Jeff Beck Group's 1968 debut album, *Truth*, was a groundbreaking release that rivaled Led Zeppelin's first outing as a seminal influence on the blues-rock and heavy metal bands that emerged in its immediate aftermath. *Beck-Ola*, which followed in 1969, was similar, but by then the group had self-destructed. Beck himself had developed a notorious reputation for unreliability, frequently canceling gigs at short notice. Stewart and Wood quit to form the Faces, and to cap it all, Beck, whose other passion in life was fast cars, suffered a serious accident that resulted in an 18-month lay-off.

He returned in 1971 with a new line-up that produced the album *Rough and Ready*. The self-titled *Jeff Beck Group* was released the following year, but the ever-restless Beck was soon ready to move on again. In 1973 he teamed up with the former rhythm section of the American group **Vanilla Fudge** to form the thunderous power-rock trio Beck, Bogert and Appice. It lasted a year before Beck disappeared, to emerge in 1975 as a solo act with the innovative all-instrumental, jazz-fusion album, *Blow by Blow*. That was followed in 1976 by *Wired*, a collaborative effort with keyboardist Jan Hammer. Beck continued to record sporadically, releasing albums every few years that displayed a disregard verging on contempt for whatever trends were happening in popular music at the time, in between playing with his racing cars and hot rods.

The blues has always remained a potent influence on Jeff Beck's music, and as well as touring with the likes of **Stevie Ray Vaughan** and **B.B. King**, he has covered blues staples like "Rollin' and Tumblin'". While in a sense his contribution to the blues has been relatively slight, he was a major influence on a generation of blues-rock guitarists. His main contribution, however, has been as a sonic innovator and guitar adventurer, constantly seeking to expand the repertoire of sounds associated with the electric instrument. "If I don't break the rules at least ten times in every song then I'm not doing my job properly," he has said. Paradoxically, his playing has always been based on a natural approach that emphasizes manual dexterity over gadgets, and a finger-picking technique that forgoes using picks, in the belief that this allows him greater speed and control. As Clapton once said, asked about Beck's style, "It's all in his hands."

⊙ **Truth** EMI
Featuring Rod Stewart on vocals and Ron Wood on bass, the Jeff Beck Group's 1968 debut stands alongside *Led Zeppelin I* as an influence on a generation of British blues-rockers.

⊙ **Blow By Blow** Epic
The jazz overtones are as strong as the blues influences on this seminal Jeff Beck album, produced by George Martin in 1975.

Carey Bell

b Macon, Mississippi, Nov 14, 1936

Carey Bell learned harmonica from some of the all-time greats of the instrument, including Big Walter Horton, Little Walter Jacobs and Sonny Boy Williamson II. Forging his own style, he went on to play in the bands of both **Muddy Waters** and **Willie Dixon**, and also forged a successful solo career.

The young Carey Bell Harrington's first musical hero was Louis Jordan. Although he originally wanted to be a saxophonist, his family couldn't afford a sax, so his grandfather bought him a harmonica when he was eight. At the age of 13 he began playing professionally with his godfather, pianist Lovie Lee, and the pair eventually decided to try their luck on the Chicago blues scene in 1956.

On their arrival in the Windy City, Bell immediately went to see Little Walter perform at Club

Zanzibar. The two became friends, and the older man was happy to pass on a few tricks. While Bell also met Sonny Boy Williamson II, his biggest influence and mentor was **Big Walter Horton**. "I liked that big tone he had," Bell recalled almost half a century later. "Didn't nobody else have that. Little Walter showed me a lot of things. But Big Walter, he was crazy. He did all kinds of shit other harp players couldn't do."

Even in Chicago, however, the demand for harp players was limited. Bell was forced to take a day job, playing in clubs by night and for tips on Maxwell Street on weekends. As a second string, he decided to take up the electric bass, learning the rudiments from **Hound Dog Taylor**. Once he'd mastered the instrument, he landed gigs with Honeyboy Edwards, Robert Nighthawk, Johnny Young, Eddie Taylor and Earl Hooker. He also got the chance to play bass with Big Walter which, more to the point, enabled him to study the great man's harp technique up close and personal.

By the late 1960s, Bell had reverted full-time to the harp, recording with Earl Hooker for Arhoolie in 1968 and co-leading the house band with guitar-

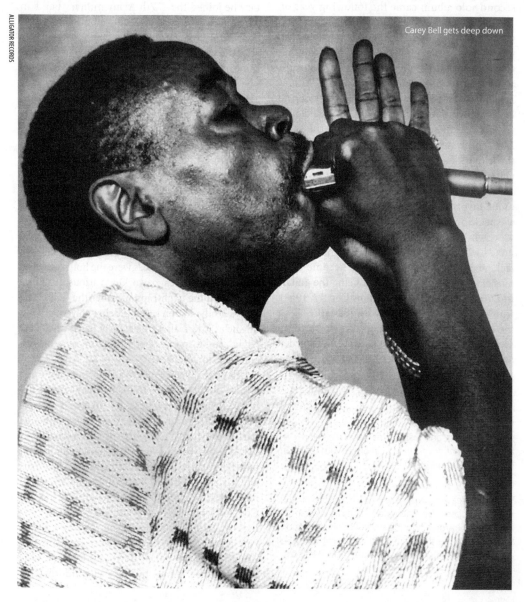

Carey Bell gets deep down

ist Eddie Taylor at Big Duke's Flamingo Club on Chicago's West Side. In 1969, he toured Europe with John Lee Hooker and also recorded his first solo album, *Carey Bell's Blues Harp*, for Delmark Records. Then, in 1970, Muddy Waters offered him a job in his band. He stayed a year and can be heard on the Chess album *The London Sessions*. Shortly after he joined Willie Dixon's Chicago Blues All-Stars, with whom he worked regularly throughout the 1970s.

He also recorded the 1972 album *Big Walter Horton With Carey Bell* for Alligator, while his second solo album came the following year on ABC Bluesway. Bell continued to record for various labels during the 1980s, and teamed up with fellow harmonica players Junior Wells, James Cotton and Billy Branch for the 1990 Alligator album *Harp Attack*. Another solo album, *Mellow Down Easy*, appeared on Blind Pig in 1990, and he returned to Alligator for 1995's *Deep Down*. *Good Luck Man*, which followed for the same label, confirmed Bell's emergence in his sixties as the leader of a heavyweight band that included guitarist Steve Jacobs.

Bell's signature double-reed harmonica technique involves choppy, turbulent phrasing with a "speaking" style, a wide vocabulary and big tone, while his gritty deep-blues vocal attack is mixed with a more urgent, contemporary, funk feel. Several of his children have become blues musicians, the most prominent being the guitarist **Lurrie Bell** (b Chicago, Illinois Dec, 13, 1958), who has toured regularly with his father over the last twenty years. The pair can be heard on *Second Nature*, a live-in-the-studio jam recorded on tour in Scandinavia in 1991 that was released on Alligator in 2004.

⊙ **Carey Bell's Blues Harp** Delmark
Bell's excellent 1969 solo debut featured several other fine musicians, including guitarists Eddie Taylor and Jimmy Dawkins, and pianist Pinetop Perkins. However, it's his harp that drives the proceedings, with total conviction and authority.

⊙ **Deep Down** Alligator
This 1995 release showcases top-notch versions of blues harmonica classics by Little Walter, Sonny Boy Williamson and Walter Horton alongside several original compositions. Among the superb musicians backing Carey Bell are his guitarist son Lurrie and pianist Lucky Peterson.

Fred Below

b Chicago, Illinois, Sept 6, 1926; d Aug 13, 1988

Few drummers merit their own entry in this book, but as the house drummer with Chess Records, who laid down the backbeat on many of the seminal Chicago blues recordings, Fred Below more than deserves a place.

He started playing drums in a high school jazz band and after being conscripted into the US military he joined the 427th Army military band, in which he played with jazz saxophonist and fellow conscript, **Lester Young**. Stationed in Germany after the war, he played the clubs when he was off-duty, booked by Horst Lippman, later to become one of Europe's best-known blues promoters.

On his return to Chicago in 1951, Below found the blues had taken over from jazz as the musical heartbeat of the city. He proved readily adaptable. His friend and fellow drummer Elgin Evans, a member of Muddy Waters' band, found him a gig playing at the Brookmount Hotel with Louis and Dave Myers, in the Four Aces. Initially, the group included **Junior Wells** on harp, but when he went off to join Muddy Waters, the Aces moved in the opposite direction, backing **Little Walter**, who had just left Muddy's group to become a star in his own right. For a while, the Aces were the hottest electric blues band in Chicago, working variously as Little Walter and the Nightcaps and later the Jukes. The Myers brothers soon left, but Below stayed, playing on such Little Walter hits as "My Babe" and "Last Night", and forming a potent rhythm section with **Willie Dixon** on bass.

Below finally left Walter in 1955, but continued to play on his sessions in his new capacity as the house drummer at Chess. By then he'd already played on several Muddy Waters' sessions, as part of the classic 1954 line-up that recorded "I Just Wanna Make Love To You" and included not only Below and Dixon, but Little Walter and pianist Otis Spann. Below went on to play on many more of Waters' finest sides, including "Hoochie Coochie Man" and "I'm Ready", as well as recordings by almost everyone else on the Chess roster. Among those whose records were graced by his drumming were Chuck Berry, Bo Diddley, Otis Rush, Elmore James, Junior Wells, Buddy Guy,

Dinah Washington, John Lee Hooker and Howlin' Wolf. He also went on to work with the Platters, the Moonglows and the Drifters.

With the Aces, Below's crisp, refined and elegant drumming practically invented the trademark Chicago shuffle beat. His style also had a profound impact on the emergence of rock'n'roll, and he remains one of the great unsung heroes of the electric blues. He was also known for his inventive use of the cymbal and wood block, and for his tom-tom fills and other embellishments. Perhaps the finest examples of his work can be heard in the classic drum solo on Little Walter's "Off the Wall". He died in Chicago in 1988, at the age of 61.

Tab Benoit

b Baton Rouge, Louisiana, Nov 17, 1967

One of the most exciting white guitarists on the modern blues scene, Tab Benoit brings a strong Cajun swamp backbeat to his down-and-dirty blues, playing in a dynamic style that reveals the influence of Buddy Guy, Albert Collins and Jimi Hendrix, among others.

Born in Baton Rouge, Benoit was raised in the oil and fishing town of Houma, Louisiana, where he continues to live. He claims he can barely remember a time when he couldn't play the guitar. He was playing covers of rock songs in a local band when hearing a **Buddy Guy** record triggered a love affair with the blues. Much of his blues education came from hanging out at the Blues Box, a ramshackle club run by guitarist Tabby Thomas in Baton Rouge. Benoit's first recorded outing in 1991 found him in stellar company, appearing alongside Dr John, Clarence "Gatemouth" Brown, and Johnny Copeland on Houston-based Justice Records' compilation *Strike A Deep Chord: Blues Guitar For The Homeless*. That came about after he was discovered playing in New Orleans by Barbara Becker, then Dr John's manager. Asked to recommend a hot young guitarist for the project, she nominated Benoit. The label came to hear him play in a blues jam contest at a New Orleans bowling alley; he only came in third, but won the bigger

prize with a place on the compilation and a multi-album solo deal with Justice. His debut album *Nice And Warm*, named after the track he played on *Strike A Deep Chord*, followed in 1993.

Since then he's recorded prolifically, releasing *What I Live For* (1994), *Standing On The Bank* (1995), and *Live: Swampland Jam* (1997) for Justice. After the label went bankrupt, he moved to Vanguard for 1999's *These Blues Are All Mine*, the most roots-based album of his career to date. That same year, he appeared on *Homesick For The Road*, a collaborative album on the Telarc label with guitarists Kenny Neal and Debbie Davies. He next signed to Telarc for the 2002 album *Wetlands*, on which his Cajun background came to the fore, and that same year recorded *Whiskey Store* with fellow Telarc guitarist Jimmy Thackery, harpist **Charlie Musselwhite** and the rhythm section of bassist Tommy Shannon and drummer Chris Layton, who had backed **Stevie Ray Vaughan** in *Double Trouble*. The *Sea Saint Sessions* followed, recorded in New Orleans with various Crescent City luminaries. In 2004 came *Whiskey Store Live*, a feast of dueling guitars recorded once again with Thackery. 2005's *Fever For The Bayou* marked his fifth album for Telarc in just four years.

Coaxing a whirlwind of screaming notes from his Fender Telecaster, Benoit is famous for his high-octane live shows. In recent years, the rock mannerisms of some of his early releases have been set aside, and he has concentrated on creating a signature sound of steamy Cajun-spiced rhythms and east Texas guitar blues, sung in a vocal style influenced by another of his heroes, **Otis Redding**. He's also become something of a favorite of the television industry, with his songs featuring in such shows as *Melrose Place* and *Baywatch*. But don't let that put you off.

⊙ **Wetlands** Telarc
Benoit's wholly satisfying 2002 album mixes original material like the autobiographical "When A Cajun Man Gets The Blues" with such classics as Professor Longhair's "Her Mind Is Gone" and Otis Redding's "These Arms Of Mine".

⊙ **Fever For the Bayou** Telarc
Storming, straight-ahead Louisiana blues was the order of the day on Benoit's 2005 release, combining his own songs with covers of Elmore James and Buddy Guy standards, and featuring a fine, finger-picking acoustic rendition of "My Bucket's Got A Hole In It".

Chuck Berry

b San Jose, Oct 18, 1926

Does the king of rock'n'roll belong in a blues reference book? You shouldn't even need to ask. Chuck Berry's music bursts with blues licks and phrases, while his best recordings found him backed by the cream of Chess's session players. Like his label mate Bo Diddley, Berry created a bridge between the blues and the new rock'n'roll era, and in the twelve sensational bars of guitar with which he opened "Johnny B Goode", he came up with one of the most dramatic motifs in the history of American music.

Born Charles Edward Anderson Berry in California – not St Louis, as he has sometimes claimed – the young Chuck moved with his family to Missouri. He gave his first known performance at fifteen, singing Jay McShann's "Confessin' The Blues" at a high school concert. Having learned to play guitar in the early 1940s, he was soon playing at parties and dances in and around St Louis with Ray Band's Orchestra. At the age of 18, he was convicted for armed robbery and sent to the Algoa reformatory, where he spent the next three years. His time there was not entirely wasted, as he formed a quartet in prison. On his release, he put together the Chuck Berry Combo with drummer **Ebby Harding** and pianist **Johnnie Johnson**, and worked by day as a hairdresser while leading the house band by night at St Louis's Cosmopolitan Club. In 1955 he visited Chicago, where he introduced himself to Elmore James, Howlin' Wolf and Muddy Waters. A demo tape was rejected by both Vee Jay and Mercury, but when Waters recommended him to Chess he had better luck.

At this stage Berry's music combined R&B, swing, jump blues, a guitar style influenced by both **T-Bone Walker** and **Charlie Christian**, the sly wit of Louis Jordan, a vocal style modeled on Nat "King" Cole, and even a touch of black hillbilly country. From that palette, he fashioned his own unique brand of rock'n'roll. The first song he took to Chess, "Ida Red", had a country influence until Leonard Chess suggested he rewrote it. The song re-emerged with new lyrics as a rock'n'roll classic called "Maybelline", with Willie Dixon on bass and Johnson on piano. It topped the R&B charts.

Some of his earliest material, such as "Wee Wee Hours", drew directly on the blues tradition. But it was "Maybelline" that formed the template for a string of charting teen anthems, all characterized by an irresistible backbeat and lyrics that crossed the racial divide to highlight teenage concerns. Highlights included "Roll Over Beethoven", "Rock and Roll Music", "School Days", "Too Much Monkey Business", "Johnny B Goode", "Oh Carol", "Around and Around", "Sweet Little Sixteen" and "Back In The USA". The lyrical preoccupations tended to be a long way removed from the hardship and suffering of the classic Delta blues, even if his coinage of words like "motorvatin'" and "botheration" was very much in the blues tradition. But there was an urgency to the guitar licks that made a lot of early white rock'n'roll sound feeble and insipid in comparison, while Johnson's piano playing was equally forceful. Indeed, many believe Johnson's role in the formation of Berry's trademark sound has never been fully credited.

Berry's triumphant progress was cut short when he was sent to prison for a second time in 1961 for transporting a minor across state lines for immoral purposes. By the time he came out of jail in 1964, pop music had moved on, even if the new wave of the Beatles, the Rolling Stones and the Beach Boys all acknowledged their debt to Berry and covered his songs in their early days. Berry was far from cowed by his jail experience, and several of his best compositions, including "Nadine", "No Particular Place To Go", "Promised Land" and "You Never Can Tell", date from this period. However, after he left Chess in 1965, the songs appeared to dry up, and he seemed careless of his talent, content to be little more than a human jukebox, pumping out his old hits whenever the price was right. When he re-signed to Chess in the early 1970s, albums such as *Back Home* and *San Francisco Dues* indicated a brief return to form, although he went and spoiled things with his appalling novelty take on Dave Bartholomew's "My Ding-A-Ling" in 1972. A travesty of his former genius, it gave him his last big hit. Although he continued touring on the revival/nostalgia circuit, usually with a pick-up band, he appeared forever at odds with himself, and became notorious for short-changing his audiences and selling his own greatness short.

Some of his off-stage activities were equally indefensible, including surrepticiously videotaping women in the bathrooms of his own theme park. Such antics have ensured that, music apart, Chuck Berry is unlikely ever to win a Mr Personality contest. Keith Richards, his self-confessed biggest fan for more than half a century, once famously admitted that he could never warm to his hero, even if he wanted to be "cremated next to him". Yet in terms of his influence on the last fifty years of popular music, Berry remains in a league of his own.

⊙ **Anthology** Chess
An utterly indispensable two-disc collection of the very best of Chuck Berry, featuring 50 of the most memorable rock'n'roll songs ever recorded.

Eric Bibb

b New York, Aug 16, 1951

A leading figure in the acoustic blues revival, Eric Bibb comes from powerful musical stock. His father, Leon Bibb, was well known in the 1960s as a folk singer and a performer in musical theater; his uncle, John Lewis, was the pianist with the Modern Jazz Quartet; and his godfather was **Paul Robeson**.

Eric Bibb grew up in Greenwich Village during the first folk boom, and the likes of Odetta,

Eric Bibb

Pete Seeger, Judy Collins and Bob Dylan were regular visitors to the family home in the early 1960s. Having begun to play guitar at the age of eight, he traveled to Europe as a young man to busk. He lived for several years in both Paris and Stockholm, working as a music and voice teacher and making a series of now hard-to-find albums on local labels. Bibb decided to settle permanently in Sweden in the 1980s. Together with the slide player Goran Wennerbrandt, he built a strong reputation on the European festival and club circuit, but not until 1994's *Spirit And The Blues*, released on the Opus 3 label, did he reach a wider audience. Impressively setting out his stall as a latter-day **Rev. Gary Davis**, the record served as a superb tribute to Bibb's musical roots. Among evocative interpretations of traditional blues and spirituals was the wondrous "Needed Time", the highlight of his warm and intimate live shows.

The follow-up, 1997's *Good Stuff*, was more of a showcase for Bibb's own songwriting, and found his and Wennerbrandt's guitars accompanied by bouzouki, mandolin and harmonium. With the increasing buzz of international media attention came a move to a major label, when he signed with Warner Brothers' Code Blue imprint for his third album *Me To You*. He was not entirely comfortable with the more electric feel of that album, but it did include a fine duet with Taj Mahal, one of his mentors. The next album, *Home To Me*, was a reaction to his unhappy brush with the majors, and saw him returning to an independent label and the more acoustic sound of his earlier work. It was followed by an excellent live recording, *Roadworks*, which successfully captured his remarkable rapport with an audience. Next up was 2001's *Painting Signs*, a deft combination of acoustic blues, folk, jazz and gospel, which was followed in turn by 2003's *Natural Light*. Bibb switched to Telarc Records in 2004 for *Friends*. An ambitious album that included appearances by Taj Mahal, Odetta and Charley Musselwhite, it explored the African roots of the blues via a collaboration with Mali's Mamadou Diabaté and Djelimady Tounkara. In 2005 came *A Ship Called Love* on Telarc and his first retrospective compilation, *Livin', Lovin' And Doin'* on his own label.

Meanwhile, Bibb had also released an album of duets with his father, *Family Affair*, in 2002, while two years later he collaborated with Rory Block

and Maria Muldaur on the Telarc album *Sisters And Brothers*. All of which represents an extraordinarily prolific run of albums over the last decade, which have combined to display the range of his fine guitar playing and his warm voice in a genre-fusing series of shifting musical contexts that has been described as "new world blues". Even so, it's on stage that he seems to be most in his natural element, and a live performance by Bibb can be an enriching and sometimes even a transcendental experience.

⊙ **Spirit & The Blues** Opus 3
Arguably still his best album, Bibb's 1994 debut includes such jaw-dropping tracks as "Needed Time", "In My Father's House" and the impossibly moving "Tell Ol' Bill".

⊙ **Roadworks** Manhaton
This 2003 release showcases Eric Bibb as he is heard best – on stage, with an audience eating out of his hand.

⊙ **Friends** Telarc
A with-special-guests bonanza, the collaborators range from Memphis to Mali and, for once, were picked for artistic reasons rather than just cashing in on a big name.

⊙ **Livin', Lovin' And Doin': A Retrospective** Hat Man
The first compilation of Bibb's career features fifteen tracks recorded between 1998 and 2005, in a variety of different styles.

Big Maceo

b Atlanta, Georgia, March 31, 1905; d Feb 26, 1953

The mere 32 sides that Big Maceo Merriweather recorded in Chicago during the 1940s influenced just about every blues pianist who followed in his wake, including Otis Spann, Little Johnny Jones and Howlin' Wolf's long-time master of the ivories, Henry Gray. With its heavy bass patterns, Maceo's thunderous playing represented a bridge between earlier boogie-woogie players like Albert Ammons and Meade "Lux" Lewis, as well as the more restrained approach of his own favorite, **Leroy Carr**, and the weightier style that came to dominate the Chicago blues of the 1950s.

Born Major Merriweather on a farm on the outskirts of Atlanta in 1905, Maceo grew bigger and taller than any of his ten siblings to stand well over six feet and weigh in at more than 250 pounds. By 1920, he was playing the piano at fish fries and rent parties as well as the cafes and honky-tonks along Atlanta's Harvard Street, although he was over-looked when Columbia set up its field recording unit in Atlanta later in the decade. For a while he lived in Detroit, where he took a job on the Ford production line, but in 1941 he moved again, this time to Chicago. There guitarists **Big Bill Broonzy** and **Tampa Red** recommended him to producer Lester Melrose, who was sufficiently impressed to rush the pianist straight into the studio and record him for the Bluebird label.

That session produced fourteen sides (eight of them with Tampa Red on guitar), including "Worried Life Blues", based on Sleepy John Estes' "Someday Baby". His best-known song, it was later covered by Chuck Berry and Eric Clapton, as well as being adapted by Little Walter as "County Jail Blues" and by Muddy Waters as "Trouble No More".

The group that Maceo formed with Tampa Red, along with a rhythm section of bass and drums, epitomized the early-1940s sound that came to be known as "The Bluebird Beat", and served as the early model for the electrified Chicago blues style that was soon to emerge.

Maceo played regularly around Chicago, and resumed recording at the end of World War II. In 1945, he cut a terrific version of "Chicago Breakdown" with Tampa Red, as well as four sides with Big Bill Broonzy, including "Where The Blues Began". Sadly a stroke then left his right side paralyzed, and cut his career short. Although he attempted several comebacks, his playing had but a shadow of its former strength, and he was reduced to singing or playing with a second pianist alongside him to handle the right-hand duties. Among those who did so was Otis Spann, who modeled his style closely on Maceo. He also recorded with Eddie Boyd beside him on the piano stool for Victor in 1947, and with Johnny Jones for Specialty two years later. That same year a second stroke forced his retirement. After decades of heavy drinking, a heart attack finished him off four years later at the age of 47.

⊙ **King Of The Chicago Blues Piano** Arhoolie All but representing Big Maceo's entire collected works, this 25-track compilation includes some of the greatest piano blues ever recorded – "Chicago Breakdown", "Worried Life Blues", "County Jail Blues" and "Texas Stomp" among them.

Big Maybelle

b Jackson, Tennessee, May 1, 1924; d Jan 23, 1972

Her name serving to honor both her mountainous stature and the power of her blues-shouting voice, Big Maybelle ranked among the finest blues and R&B vocalists of the 1950s.

Having won a talent contest in Memphis at the tender age of eight, Mabel Louise Smith was discovered singing in a Memphis church at the age of twelve, by bandleader **Dave Clark**. As well as singing with his orchestra, she toured with the all-female International Sweethearts of Rhythm before joining Christine Chatman's orchestra. She made her first recordings with Chatman in 1944, while her debut solo sides, backed by trumpeter Hot Lips Page's band, followed three years later on Cincinnati-based King Records. When she signed to Okeh Records in 1952, producer Fred Mendelsohn gave her the name she would be known by for the rest of her career.

Big Maybelle's first Okeh release, "Gabbin' Blues (Don't Run My Business)", hit the R&B charts in 1952, and was followed by "Way Back Home" and "My Country Man". Then in 1955, she cut her earth-trembling version of "Whole Lotta Shakin' Goin' On", a full two years before Jerry Lee Lewis's rendition. The late 1950s saw some of her best sides for the Savoy label, backed by top New York session players, including "Candy", "Ring Dang Dilly", "That's A Pretty Good Love" and "Tell Me Who". It was while she was with Savoy that she made a memorable, belting appearance in Bert Stern's legendary documentary *Jazz on a Summer's Day*, shot at the 1958 Newport Jazz Festival.

Maybelle left Savoy in 1959, and over the next dozen years she recorded for a variety of labels, including Brunswick, Scepter, Chess and Rojac, often in a soul vein. She even recorded covers of songs by the Beatles and Donovan, and her last hit came with a typically barnstorming version of Question Mark and the Mysterians' "96 Tears". But she struggled with a long and serious drug addiction, and slipped into a diabetic coma that led to her death in 1972.

Thanks to her deep, stentorian voice, Big Maybelle was a belter of quite awesome power, sometimes likened to a female Big Joe Turner. She packed a lot of living into her 47 years, and was a hugely influential musical role model: in her autobiography, Aretha Franklin described the phenomenal impression Maybelle made upon her when she saw her in a New Orleans club as she was starting her own career. Big Maybelle was also an inspiration to Janis Joplin, another doomed fast-living blues mama, whom she just managed to outlast.

⊙ **The Complete Okeh Sessions 1952–55** Okeh

The *pièce de résistance* of these 26 early solo recordings by Big Maybelle, is, of course, "Whole Lotta Shakin' Goin' On".

⊙ **Savoy Blues Legends: Candy!** Savoy Jazz

A generous 46 doses of Big Maybelle in her prime, spread across two discs. On many of them she's accompanied by an orchestra, but it takes more than that to drown out the blues power of her colossal voice.

The Bihari Brothers

All four of the Bihari Brothers, who grew up in a large Jewish family of Hungarian descent in Tulsa, Oklahoma, went on to play significant roles in blues history. Between them, they ran an astonishing roster of important record labels, including Modern, Meteor, Flair, Kent, Crown and RMP.

The first brother to venture into the record business was the eldest, Jules (b Philadelphia, Pennsylvania, Sept 8, 1913), who moved to Los Angeles in 1941 and found a job operating jukeboxes in black neighborhoods. Noticing how hard it was to supply the blues and R&B records his customers were demanding, he decided to set up his own record company to fill the gap. Sending for his brothers Joe and Saul, he launched Modern in 1945, and swiftly built it into a major blues label. The first signing – "queen of the boogie" **Hadda Brooks** – was soon followed by Pee Wee Crayton, Johnny Guitar Watson, B.B. King, Elmore James, John Lee Hooker, Etta James, Lightnin' Hopkins, Jimmy Witherspoon, Lowell Fulson and many more. Jules Bihari produced many of the sessions himself and, in a dubious practice common at the time, also claimed composing royalties under the pseudonym Jules Taub, on material he had played no part in writing. Although, as Modern was based in LA, many of its artists were West Coast bluesmen, the brothers were astute enough to employ local producers and talent scouts in the blues urban

heartland centers of Houston, Detroit and Memphis. Among these was Maxwell Davis, who went on to produce many of Modern's most important acts, while youngest sibling Lester Bihari was recruited to run operations in Memphis. He was responsible for bringing **Ike Turner** to the label, and he set up a deal with the Memphis Recording Service, run by Sam Phillips, who soon founded Sun Records. The Phillips connection brought Modern's most successful artist, **B.B. King**, into the fold.

Lester Bihari also set up the Meteor label as a subsidiary outlet for rockabilly acts, while Modern spawned further imprints like RPM, Flair, Riviera, and the budget outlet Crown. After Modern went bankrupt in the mid-1960s, the Biharis launched the Kent imprint, which survived into the 1970s, while Jules Bihari also started his own Big Town label. Around the time Saul Bihari died in 1975, Joe left the company, and so Kent effectively stopped recording new material. When Jules Bihari died in 1984, the family sold their assorted catalog to a consortium that included the British label Ace, which launched an extensive reissue program.

⊙ *Various Artists* **The Original Memphis Blues Brothers** Ace

A 26-track collection of some of the most important artists associated with the Bihari brothers, including B.B. King, Bobby Bland, Rosco Gordon, Junior Parker, and Ike Turner.

Elvin Bishop

b Tulsa, Oklahoma, Oct 21, 1942

White guitarist Elvin Bishop originally made his name playing alongside Mike Bloomfield in the Paul Butterfield Blues Band, in a potent dual-guitar attack that influenced the likes of the Allman Brothers. He later went on to forge a solo career as a bluesman of eclectic tastes and remains a leading exponent of the electric blues to this day.

Bishop first discovered the blues listening to late-night R&B radio in 1950s' Oklahoma, and became an avid record collector. He won a scholarship to read physics at the University of Chicago in 1959, but his real reason for picking the "windy city" was to study the blues; it helped that the campus was located in the middle of the South Side ghetto.

He hooked up for lessons from the guitarist **Little Smokey Smothers**, who played in Howlin' Wolf's band between 1958 and 1961. Bishop was clearly a fast learner; within months he was good enough to jam in South Side blues clubs with the likes of Buddy Guy and Otis Rush. He also teamed up with fellow student and harmonica player Paul Butterfield, and the pair soon recruited **Michael Bloomfield** as a second lead guitarist. By 1963, the Paul Butterfield Blues Band was in place, with Mark Naftalin on keyboards, Jerome Arnold on bass and Sam Lay on drums.

Although in the early days Bishop was somewhat overshadowed by Bloomfield – a monster guitar player – his playing was highly impressive. He recorded four albums with Butterfield: 1965's *Paul Butterfield Blues Band*, the influential *East-West* the following year, and *Resurrection Of Pigboy Crabshaw* (a jokey reference to Bishop's countrified "Okie" persona) and *In My Own Dream*, both of which appeared in 1968. When Bishop left Buttterfield that year, he relocated to San Francisco and he became a regular at jam sessions at the legendary Fillmore auditorium, playing alongside Jimi Hendrix, Eric Clapton and B.B. King among others. Forming his own band, he also signed to Fillmore Records, run by the venue's owner Bill Graham, for whom he recorded three albums.

In 1974, Dicky Betts, the guitarist with the Allman Brothers – whose own twin-guitar attack with Duane Allman had been influenced by the Butterfield Blues Band – helped Bishop get a con-

tract with Capricorn Records, run by the Allmans' manager Phil Walden. Bishop recorded six albums for Capricorn between 1974 and 1978, enjoying chart success with "Travelin' Shoes" and an even bigger hit with "Fooled Around And Fell In Love". The latter, drawn from his 1975 album *Struttin' My Stuff*, and featuring vocals by future Jefferson Starship singer Mickey Thomas, made number three on the US pop chart.

For the decade after Capricorn went bankrupt in 1979, Bishop concentrating on playing clubs. He signed with Alligator in 1988, for whom his first solo album, *Big Fun*, was followed by 1991's *Don't Let The Bossman Get You Down* and 1995's *Ace In The Hole*. *The Skin I'm In* appeared in 1998, *Hometown Boy Makes Good* the following year, and the live *That's My Partner* showcased him alongside his old friend and mentor Little Smokey Smothers in 2000. He returned after a lengthy break in 2005, with *Gettin' My Groove Back* on Blind Pig Records.

Over the years, Bishop has also guested on albums by the likes of **Clifton Chenier** and **John Lee Hooker,** and he toured with **B.B. King** in 1995. His own albums are characterized by entertaining songwriting, fine slide playing and an unpretentious mix of blues roots with contemporary funk, rock and even country flavors.

⊙ **20th Century Masters – The Millennium Collection: The Best of Elvin Bishop** Mercury/ Universal
This compilation of the best tracks from Bishop's Capricorn albums offers a winning blend of blues with funk, soul and rock, and includes – natch – "Fooled Around And Fell in Love".

⊙ **The Skin I'm In** Alligator
This, the most fully realized of Bishop's Alligator releases, dates from 1998, and features searing but disciplined slide guitar on blues that know how to let the good times roll.

Scrapper Blackwell

b Syracuse, North Carolina, Feb 21, 1903; d Oct 7, 1962

Among the most consistently inventive and sophisticated guitarists of the pre-World War II era, "Scrapper" Blackwell is now best remembered for his collaborations with pianist **Leroy Carr.**

One of 16 children in a family of part-Cherokee descent, Francis Hillman Blackwell was inspired by his fiddle-playing father. Totally self-taught, he built his first guitar out of a cigar box, wire and a plank of wood. He also learned to play the piano, and by his teens was working semi-professionally around the bars of Indianapolis, where the family had moved. Occasionally he ventured as far as Chicago for an engagement, but he was reluctant to leave Indianapolis for long, concerned lest his main source of income – a thriving bootlegging business – should suffer in his absence.

It was in a bar in Indianapolis, some time in the mid-1920s, that Blackwell met the Nashville-born Leroy Carr, who introduced himself with a bottle of bootlegged corn liquor. Blackwell was a difficult man, and by all accounts his personal relationship with Carr was often fractious. Musically, however, their rapport made them the most potent and influential guitar-and-piano blues duo of their time. Carr sang in a rich, warm voice, while his piano style was heavy on the bass. That left Blackwell free to explore the treble strings, picking out precise and articulate snapping single-string lines over his chord progressions.

The duo's first recording session in 1928 produced a brace of instant blues standards, in "How Long How Long Blues" and "My Own Lonesome Blues". Further classics, in the shape of "Blues Before Sunrise" and "Sloppy Drunk", soon followed. The pair went on to record more than 100 sides together, first for Vocalion and then for Bluebird, before the heavy-drinking Carr died from nephritis and acute alcohol poisoning in by 1935. Their final recording was the brilliant "When The Sun Goes Down", from which **Robert Johnson** adapted the melody and feel for "Love In Vain".

Blackwell occasionally recorded with other partners, including **Georgia Tom Dorsey**, **Black Bottom McPhail**, and Robinson's Knights of Rest, while throughout his partnership with Carr he regularly recorded on his own for Vocalion and Bluebird. His solo sides are perhaps less dazzling without Carr's stellar contribution. But they still contain some fantastic guitar playing, in a style which, although he only ever played an acoustic instrument, had a marked influence on the electric guitarists who emerged in Chicago after World War II.

By then, however, Blackwell had disappeared from the blues scene. Having cut a tribute to Carr after his death, he turned his back on the music industry. He did not re-emerge until 1958, at the start of the acoustic folk/blues revival, when he was rediscovered living in Indianapolis. The impressive material he subsequently recorded for Prestige/Bluesville suggested he had lost none of his technique or feel. Had he not been shot and killed at the age of 59, when he was the victim of a street robbery in Indianapolis in 1962, he would surely have become a hero to a new generation, alongside the likes of **Rev. Gary Davis** and **Mississippi Fred McDowell**. His killer was never apprehended.

⊙ **The Virtuoso Guitar of Scrapper Blackwell 1925–34** Yazoo
A great Blackwell compilation: despite only holding a meager 14 tracks, it includes solo sides as well as material recorded with Leroy Carr and Black Bottom McPhail, and every one is a classic.

⊙ **Complete Recorded Works in Chronological Order, Vols. 1–2** Document
A collection of all Blackwell's performances released under his own name, with occasional support from Leroy Carr, Josh White and Bumble Bee Slim.

⊙ **Scrapper Blackwell with Brooks Berry** Document
Ten tracks taken from a 1960 studio session, complemented by eleven live recordings from a 1959 comeback concert, offer comprehensive proof that Blackwell still had the chops in his later years.

⊙ **How Long Blues: 1928–1935** EPM
A decent selection of Blackwell's finest duets with Leroy Carr, plus his tribute "My Old Pal", recorded following the pianist's death.

Blind Blake

b Jacksonville, Florida, circa 1895–97; d circa 1933

Considering his importance in the history of American music, remarkably little is known of Blind Blake – we cannot even verify the dates of his birth or death. In his day, as the biggest-selling artist on Paramount Records during the 1920s, he was a major celebrity. Only Blind Lemon Jefferson out-sold him, while the hundred-odd recordings he left, both solo and as an accompanist, virtually invented ragtime guitar.

Playlist
Blind Blake

All from the JSP box set, *All The Published Sides*

1 WEST COAST BLUES (1926)
"Whoop that thing … I'm gonna satisfy you if I can,"
Blake proclaims on a rag-style dance tune that was the flip
of his first Paramount release.

2 TOO TIGHT (1926)
Sheer goodtime hokum with a kazoo, probably played
by Blake himself.

3 HE'S IN THE JAILHOUSE NOW (1927)
This old-time minstrel tune with Gus Cannon on banjo
was later popularized on the *O Brother Where Art Thou?*
movie soundtrack.

4 C.C. PILL BLUES (1928)
As Ry Cooder put it: "That's the whole thing right there.
That's all you need to hear. And then you know: there's a
whole world we've all missed and will never know."

5 HOT POTATOES (1928)
Brilliant ragtime picking, accompanied by some crazy
xylophone from Jimmy Bertrand.

6 NOTORIETY WOMAN BLUES (1928)
"To keep her quiet I knocked her teeth out her mouth…"
Well, they didn't do political correctness in those days.

7 SWEET PAPA LOW DOWN (1928)
Blake joins the Charleston craze, backed by piano, cornet and more xylophone.

8 HASTINGS ST (1929)
Named after a street in Detroit, and featuring Charlie
Spand on boogie-woogie piano. "Everything you wanted
was right there on Hastings Street. Everything you didn't
want was right there," as John Lee Hooker later put it.

9 DIDDIE WAH DIDDIE (1929)
This classic ragtime blues was arguably Blake's ultimate
masterpiece, before the drink got him. Ry Cooder covered
it on *Paradise & Lunch*.

10 DEPRESSION'S GONE FROM ME BLUES (1932)
Blake's final release recycled the riff from "Sitting On
Top Of The World", and was backed by a version of the
Victorian music hall standard "Champagne Charlie Is My
Name", which many doubt was Blake at all.

His mastery of the style was so complete that few, if any, have matched it since.

Despite the best efforts of researchers over more than half a century, however, we still know little more about Blake than what he tells us in his records. The mystery has only added to his legendary status as a guitarist of almost supernatural skill. As Big Bill Broonzy put it, Blake made the guitar "sound like every instrument in the band – saxophone, trombone, clarinets, bass fiddles, drums – everything. I never seed then and I haven't to this day yet seed no one that could take his natural fingers and pick as much guitar as Blind Blake."

Blake certainly had family in the area around Jacksonville, Florida, and was probably born there, some time in the 1890s, although he may have grown up in Georgia. Some reference works claim that his real name was Arthur Phelps, despite his telling Papa Charlie Jackson on a 1929 recording that his name was Arthur Blake. The Georgia theory stems from the fact that in one of his songs, "Southern Rag", he breaks into Geechee, a Creole tongue also known as Gullah. Some researchers therefore believe that he came from Georgia 's Sea Islands, where Geechee was still spoken as a first language well into the 20th century. Others argue that a similar form of plantation Creole was probably widespread at one time across the southern states, and Blake could easily have picked it up anywhere from an old-timer with a long memory.

Whatever his origins, the first confirmed sighting of Blake comes in Chicago in the mid-1920s. The only surviving photo of him, neatly dressed in a three-piece suit and taken in the Windy City at his first Paramount session in 1926, suggests a man of around 30, which leads most blues scholars to presume a date of birth around 1896. Apart from his recordings, virtually the only other known "fact" is that he had a seemingly inexhaustible appetite for booze. Many years later, when Sam Charters asked **Gus Cannon** for his memories of working with Blake, all Cannon could recall was how much whiskey they drank together: "I'm telling you we drank more whiskey than a shop! And that boy would take me out with him at night and get me so turned around I'd be lost if I left his side. He could see more with his blind eyes than I with my two good ones."

Blake was discovered by Paramount Records' scout Mayo Williams, who was looking to repeat the unexpected success the label was enjoying with Blind Lemon Jefferson. Typically, Williams recorded no details about the artist, so we know nothing of where and how Blake learned to play, whether his musical origins lay in blues, guitar instrumentals, or popular ditties, or how he had made his living prior to his contract with Paramount. Yet from his first recordings for the label, backing Leola B. Wilson, it's clear that Blake possessed a highly sophisticated "piano-guitar" technique which made him the master of ragtime blues finger-picking. He also had a warm, relaxed voice that was more marketable than the harsher style of most contemporary country bluesmen.

Starting with "West Coast Blues" – often cited as the first song to feature the word "rock" – Blake recorded 79 known solo sides for Paramount between 1926 and 1932. That made him one of the most frequently recorded artists in the label's "race" catalog. He also partnered banjoist **Gus Cannon**, clarinettist **Johnny Dodds**, **Papa Charlie Jackson**, **Irene Scruggs**, **Ma Rainey** and **Ida Cox**.

His best-known sides include "Early Morning Blues", "Too Tight", "Skeedle Loo Doo Blues", "That Will Never Happen No More", "Southern Rag", "Police Dog Blues", "Playing Policy Blues", "Righteous Blues", and the wonderful novelty song "Diddie Wa Diddie", later covered by Ry Cooder. He sang in a style somewhat reminiscent of Big Bill Broonzy, while the ragtime flavor of tunes like "Southern Rag" and "Blind Arthur's Breakdown" gave his music a spryness and a light, even joyful sound, even when the lyrics dwelled on the familiar blues themes of sex and death, and notwithstanding his devilishly complicated finger-picking.

The guitarist **Stefan Grossman** described Blake's style succinctly: "He was very, very rhythmic and incredibly fast. I don't know anyone who can get to that speed. That's Blake's real claim to fame, because his chord progressions are nothing fancy. But the thumb work is fantastic, and what he's doing with his right hand set him apart from everyone. Rev. Gary Davis said Blake had a 'sportin' right hand'. Davis took that and got into even more complicated modes."

What happened to Blake after his last session for Paramount in June 1932 – an unlikely version of "Champagne Charlie Is My Name" – remains unknown. He disappeared as mysteriously as he had arrived. Broonzy claimed that he died soon after, freezing to death after falling down in a blizzard and being unable to get up again, "him being so fat." If that's true, it's more likely that it was drink rather than his girth that stopped him rising to his feet, for his final recordings contain several hints that booze was getting the better of him. Another story says that he was robbed and murdered in Chicago, a fate that often befell blind men. Rev. Gary Davis reported a rumor that Blake was hit by a streetcar in Atlanta in 1941, while another story holds that he returned to Jacksonville and lived for several more years. "Blind Blake – now, that one's a mystery," admitted another contemporary, Georgia Tom Dorsey, in the 1960s. "How he got out of the

The "inner vision" of Blind Blake

The Paramount Book Of Blues, a promotional booklet published by Paramount Records in 1927, offered the following less-than-enlightening "official" biography of Blind Blake:

"We have all heard expressions of people 'singing in the rain' or 'laughing in the face of adversity', but we never saw such a good example of it, until we came upon the history of Blind Blake. Born in Jacksonville, in sunny Florida, he seemed to absorb some of the sunny atmosphere – disregarding the fact that nature had cruelly denied him a vision of outer things. He could not see the things that others saw – but he had a better gift. A gift of an inner vision, that allowed him to see things more beautiful. The pictures that he alone could see made him long to express them in some way – so he turned to music. He studied long and earnestly – listening to talented pianists and guitar players, and began to gradually draw out harmonious tunes to fit every mood. Now that he is recording exclusively for Paramount, the public has the benefit of his talent, and agrees, as one body, that he has an unexplainable gift of making one laugh or cry as he feels, and sweet chords and tones that come from his talking guitar express a feeling of his mood."

show I don't know. But he was a good worker and a nice fellow to get along with."

⊙ **Complete Recorded Works Vols 1–4**
Document
These four comprehensive discs, sold individually, are presented in Document's usual informative style – or as informative as it's possible to be about the enigmatic Mr Blake.

⊙ **The Master Of Ragtime Guitar: The Essential Recordings Of Blind Blake** Indigo
Of the numerous "best of" compilations that cover Blind Blake's career, this 24-track single disc set does the job better than most, and contains almost all of the key tracks.

⊙ **Ragtime Guitar's Foremost Fingerpicker**
Yazoo
Only 9 of the 23 tracks on this Blind Blake compilation are really twelve-bar blues. However, the likes of "Southern Rag", "Diddie Wah Diddie", and "Blind Arthur's Breakdown" are all irresistible.

Bobby "Blue" Bland

b Rosemark, Tennessee, Jan 27, 1930

Surprisingly few male bluesmen have made it as vocalists alone. Perhaps it's down to the tradition of the blues as music made by itinerant solo performers, but most of the great blues singers have also doubled as guitarists, harmonica players or pianists. There are exceptions, of course, and they don't come much bigger than Bobby "Blue" Bland, and his extraordinary, gospel-tinged voice.

Seeking to escape the prospect of a life picking cotton in the fields of Tennessee, Robert Calvin Brook moved to Memphis during the 1940s, where he began singing in gospel groups, including The Miniatures. Adopting his father's surname of Bland, he found work parking cars at a place called Billy's Garage on Beale Street, and was soon singing with the Beale Streeters, a struggling, short-lived group of future superstars that included B.B. King, Johnny Ace, Junior Parker and Rosco Gordon.

Bland cut his first singles in Memphis in 1951 for Sam Phillips, who licensed the sides to Chess. Ike Turner then produced him for the Modern label, and he also recorded for the Houston-based Duke label, but his career was put on hold when he entered the US army in 1952. Upon his discharge three years later, he resumed recording

for Duke under the direction of trumpeter and arranger **Joe Scott**, who became his mentor, and sculpted virtually every element of his sound. Together they cut some fierce, swaggering slabs of Texas blues, showcasing Bland's unique "crying" vocal style and his so-called "love throat", a trademark gargling sound, atop the guitar of Clarence Hollimon. By the time of his first national hit in 1957, "Farther Up The Road", the guitar duties were in the hands of Auburn "Pat" Hare, who had previously played with **Junior Parker** and **Howlin' Wolf**. (Hare was convicted of murdering his girlfriend and a policeman in 1964, and ultimately died in prison.)

During the late 1950s and the 1960s, Bland consistently turned out classics for Duke, including "Little Boy Blue", "I Pity The Fool", Brook Benton's "I'll Take Care of You", "Two Steps From The Blues", "Yield Not To Temptation", "That's The Way Love Is", "Stormy Monday Blues", "Ain't Nothing You Can Do", and "Ain't Doing Too Bad". Perhaps most memorable of all was 1961's "Turn On Your Love Light", which featured a blistering horn arrangement by Scott, and which subsequently became a highlight of the Grateful Dead's live set.

Bland became a superstar stalwart of the R&B charts, but he was a versatile vocalist whose sophisticated phrasing meant he was equally at home singing soul ballads as injecting a gospel-tinged fervor into a tough-edged blues number. He continued recording for Duke until the label was sold to ABC Records, with Bland being part of the deal. Don't be misled, however, by reference books that tell you this marked the end of his golden period. While his first recordings for ABC, notably 1973's *His California Album* and *Dreamer* from the following year, were perhaps slicker than some of his earlier work, his voice sounded as potent as ever on some well-chosen material, and they sold well in the rock market. In the mid-1970s he teamed up with his old Beale Street friend B.B. King on a brace of sturdy rather than spectacular collaborative albums, but there followed a series of albums for MCA that veered dangerously close to MOR territory, and found him improbably name-checking **Perry Como** as an influence. However, as music writer Greg Ward noted, he might have wanted to be a pop crooner, but "every time he opened his mouth, the emotion just cascaded out" – even a woefully misguided attempt to redefine him for the disco market couldn't disguise the blue quality in his voice. A move to Malaco Records in the mid-1980s offered a more sympathetic musical environment, and he continued touring and recording albums for the label at regular intervals, albeit with an inevitable diminution of some of his primordial vocal power.

Bobby Bland received a lifetime achievement award at the Grammies in 1997, and a similar award from The Blues Foundation the following year, when he also released *Memphis Monday Morning*, the title track of which was his best recording in several years.

⊙ **I Pity The Fool: The Duke Recordings Vol 1** MCA
Here's everything that Bobby recorded for Duke between 1952 and 1960. We're treated to such classics as "Farther Up The Road", "Little Boy Blue", "Cry, Cry, Cry" and "Two Steps From The Blues".

⊙ **Turn On Your Love Light: The Duke** Recordings Vol 2 MCA
This delicious collection of (far-from) Bland gems picks up where Vol 1 left off, and takes the story up to 1964. Highlights include "Turn On Your Love Light", "Yield Not to Temptation", "That's The Way Love Is", and "Stormy Monday Blues", and there are 46 more tracks into the bargain.

⊙ **The Voice** Ace
The finest single-disc anthology of Bobby Bland's output for Duke holds 26 tracks, all abounding in Joe Scott's sublime brass arrangements.

⊙ **His California Album** MCA
A 1973 Bland classic that boasts the best ever version of "If Loving You Is Wrong (I Don't Want To Be Right)".

Rory Block

b Princeton, New Jersey, Nov 6, 1949

Growing up in a Bohemian family in Greenwich Village conveniently ensured that Rory Block was at the epicenter of the early 1960s folk boom, and she could not help but absorb the music that was all around her.

Born Aurora Block, she started to play the guitar at the age of ten. By the age of 14, she was joining Sunday jam sessions in Washington Square Park, in the center of the West Village. After live music in the park was banned, her father hosted the jam sessions in his nearby shop, and she became friends with the likes of **John Sebastian**, **Maria Muldaur** and **Stefan Grossman**. The latter was to prove a particularly significant influence.

In 1964, Rory came across the compilation *Really The Country Blues*. Forty years later she recalled: "From that moment on my life was dedicated to learning how to play blues. I was determined to figure out each and every note and play the great songs with as much accuracy as I could muster, out of a deep reverence for the music." With Grossman, she saw Mississippi John Hurt both in concert and at home in Washington DC; visited Skip James in hos-

Playlist
Bobby "Blue" Bland

All selections are taken from the MCA double album *Bobby Bland: The Anthology*.

1 FARTHER UP THE ROAD (1957) Featuring Pat Hare on guitar, Bland's first national hit was perfect, melodic big band blues.

2 LITTLE BOY BLUE (1958) This one gave Bland his nickname, although there was nothing little about his savage voice.

3 I'LL TAKE CARE OF YOU (1959) A subtle reading of the Brook Benton song, it proved Bland was much more than a shouter.

4 CRY CRY CRY (1961) Bland is here at his devastating, tear-the-house-down peak – one of his most gut-wrenching vocals.

5 I PITY THE FOOL (1961) Blues meets primordial soul.

6 TURN ON YOUR LOVE LIGHT (1961) This is perhaps Bland's best known song, thanks to covers by the Grateful Dead and a hundred other rock bands.

7 YIELD NOT TO TEMPTATION (1962) Bobby at his most frantic, with a blazing Joe Scott horn arrangement.

8 STORMY MONDAY BLUES (1962) An after-hours blues revival of T-Bone Walker's classic, this gave him a surprise pop hit.

9 AIN'T NO LOVE IN THE HEART OF THE CITY (1974) Late-period Bland, convincingly portraying himself as a smooth and sophisticated (but still blues-inflected) soul man.

Blind Pig Records

founded Ann Arbor, Michigan, 1977

For Jerry Del Giudice, who was running a small but thriving blues club in the basement of Ann Arbor's Blind Pig Cafe during the mid-1970s, setting up a record label was the logical next move. Blind Pig records now boasts a catalog of recordings by blues masters such as Muddy Waters, Otis Rush, Johnny Shines and Pinetop Perkins, and a roster of current acts including Tommy Castro, Deborah Coleman, Magic Slim, Elvin Bishop and Coco Montoya. The label has also expanded into other forms of American roots music, including zydeco, R&B and gospel.

The first release appeared in 1974 (three years before the label was formally set up) and featured Boogie-woogie Red, John Lee Hooker's former pianist. He was described by Del Giudice as "pretty much a Blind Pig Cafe staff member, omnipresent at the club, keeping the dust off of the piano with wig-singeing jams night

and day". Distributed privately, *Boogie-woogie Red Live At The Blind Pig* sold several thousand copies, and paved the way for a move to the West Coast in 1977. Blind Pig has grown steadily ever since, and won the Blues Foundation's "Keeping The Blues Alive" award in 2005. The award was particularly appropriate, as the label is especially proud of its role in discovering and exposing the talents of new generations of blues and roots performers like Nick Curran, Renee Austin, and Muddy Waters' son, Big Bill Morganfield.

⊙ *Various Artists* **25th Anniversary Collection** Blind Pig
Thirty-five tracks, spread across two discs, showcase the highlights from Blind Pig's first quarter-century. It comes with a DVD containing footage of younger acts such as Tommy Castro and Deborah Coleman, and an archive interview with Muddy Waters.

---

pital; and traveled to the Bronx to visit Reverend Gary Davis, who gave her lessons. Backstage at the *Village Gate*, she spoke to **Son House**, and he told her he had taught Robert Johnson how to play guitar. Decades later, she attempted to describe why a middle-class white teenage girl from New York felt such a deep affinity with the music of poor rural blacks from a bygone era in the Mississippi Delta: "The music resonated inside me, felt real, beautiful, spoke to what was in my heart, moved my soul ... Inspiration is born in the deepest part of the soul, where boundaries don't exist."

Aged 15, Rory ran away to California, driving across America with Grossman. On their return they made an instructional record called *How To Play Blues Guitar*, on which Block was credited as Sunshine Kate. However, her first solo album did not appear until the mid-1970s by which time she was the mother of two young children. An attempt to write commercial songs, it left her frustrated and unsatisfied, so she went back to blues. She signed to Rounder Records in 1981, and has remained with the label ever since. Her first Rounder release, *High Heeled Blues*, was produced by John Sebastian. In a rave review, *Rolling*

Stone called the collection "some of the most singular and affecting country blues anyone, man or woman, black or white, old or young has cut in recent years".

Block has released a further dozen albums on Rounder, building a solid reputation as a gutsy acoustic country blueswoman, a fine interpreter of the Delta tradition, a potent slide guitarist, a self-possessed singer of great character, and a talented and original songwriter. She also performs upwards of 200 live dates per year, sometimes accompanied by her second son Jordan, who has also recorded with her. Her first child, Thiele, was a highly promising guitarist who died in a road accident in 1986 at the age of 19, and is the subject of Block's affecting tribute album *House Of Hearts*.

⊙ **Best Blues And Originals** Rounder
A fine compilation from Block's first half dozen Rounder albums.

⊙ **Gone Woman Blues: The Country Blues Collection** Rounder
Twenty-two interpretations of classic songs by the likes of Son House, Robert Johnson and Charley Patton, plus a couple of prime Block originals.

⊙ **Sisters And Brothers** Rounder
Rory Block recorded this uplifting folk-blues album in 2004, in a barn in the appropriate location of Unity, Maine, with fellow Greenwich Village veterans Eric Bibb and Maria Muldaur.

Mike Bloomfield

b Chicago, Illinois, July 28, 1943; d Feb 15, 1981

In rock circles, Mike Bloomfield is best remembered as the guitarist on Bob Dylan's "Like A Rolling Stone", and for accompanying Dylan when he appeared with an electric band for the first time, earning the boos of angry folkies at 1965's Newport Folk Festival. Blues enthusiasts remember him as a rival to Eric Clapton for the title of the best white electric blues guitarist of his generation, combining a purist's respect for the music's traditions with the attack of rock'n'roll.

Raised in a prosperous Jewish family on Chicago's North Side, Bloomfield got his first guitar at 13. His earliest inspiration was the sound emerging from Memphis' Sun Studio, and especially Scotty Moore's guitar work on Elvis's early recordings. Living in Chicago, however, it was inevitable that a musically curious young guitarist would gravitate towards the city's vibrant urban blues scene. At fourteen, Bloomfield was checking out the likes of Muddy Waters and **Howling Wolf** in local clubs. Pretty soon he was sitting in with his blues heroes, and while still in his teens he set up an acoustic blues club called the Fickle Pickle, booking appearances by **Sleepy John Estes**, **Yank Rachell** and **Big Joe Williams**. Williams even wrote a song called "Pick A Pickle", with the line "You know Mike Bloomfield ... will always treat you right ... come to the Pickle, every Tuesday night."

Away from the Fickle Pickle, Bloomfield fell in with a bunch of like-minded, blues-loving white musicians including **Paul Butterfield**, whose band he joined. He played on the first two Butterfield Blues Band albums, turning down an invitation in 1965 to join Dylan on a permanent basis to stick with the blues. He eventually left in 1967 to form **The Electric Flag**, which included early Chicago friends Barry Goldberg and Nick Gravenites, as well as Harvey Brooks and Buddy Miles. Despite a successful appearance at the Monterrey Pop Festival and an intriguing debut album, *A Long Time Comin'*, the band lasted barely a year. Bloomfield's next venture, a jam with **Al Kooper** and **Stephen Stills** released as *Super Session*, brilliantly captured the speed, attack and precision of his guitar playing. Surprisingly, it became the best-selling record of his career.

By now, Bloomfield had relocated to San Francisco, and developed both a distaste for fame and a drug habit. Adopting a lower profile, he gigged quietly around the Bay area, toured occasionally as "Bloomfield and Friends" with a group that included Mark Naftalin and Nick Gravenites, taught music, and scored movies like *The Trip* (1967) and *Steelyard Blues* (1973). He joined an Electric Flag reunion in 1974, recorded acoustic blues albums for various labels including Takoma and Kicking Mule, and even made an instructional album for *Guitar Player* magazine called *If You Love Those Blues, Play 'Em As You Please*. Other 1970s projects included Triumvirate and KGB, another short-lived supergroup with Barry Goldberg, Rik Grech and Carmine Appice that recorded an unspectacular album in 1976.

By the end of the 1970s, chronic alcoholism and drug addiction were taking their toll, and Bloomfield became notorious for erratic behavior and missed gigs. He was found dead in his car of a drug overdose in San Francisco in February 1981.

⊙ *Bloomfield, Kooper, Stills* **Super Session** Columbia
In the space of nine hours in 1968, Mike Bloomfield laid down some classic blues with Al Kooper on "Albert's Shuffle", "His Holy Modal Majesty", "Really, Stop", and Curtis Mayfield's "Man's Temptation". Then he packed up his guitar – off to score some heroin it is rumored – and left Stephen Stills to finish the album.

⊙ **If You Love Those Blues, Play 'Em As You Please** Kicking Mule
This 1977 release, enjoyable in its own right, consists of stripped-down acoustic blues with an instructional narrative from Bloomfield before each track.

⊙ **Don't Say That I Ain't Your Man!: Essential Blues 1964–1969** Sony Legacy
A 15-track compilation of the very best of Mike Bloomfield's studio albums with Butterfield and the Electric Flag, as well as his work with Al Kooper and a few rarities.

Blue Horizon Records

founded by Mike Vernon, Surrey 1965

Forever associated with the success of Fleetwood Mac, the Blue Horizon label was the dream of blues enthusiast Mike Vernon. Working as a junior staff producer at Decca Records in 1965, he co-opted his brother Richard and launched Blue Horizon from his Surrey home with a series of a dozen singles. Pressed in limited runs of just 99 copies each, they included material by Hubert Sumlin (recorded in Vernon's living room), Sonny Boy Williamson II, J.B. Lenoir and Eddie Boyd.

Vernon also released material by British blues artists, including John Mayall, Savoy Brown and T.S. (Tony) McPhee. The majors first began to show interest after he signed Peter Green's Fleetwood Mac in 1967, and the band started to attract attention. The next year, Vernon agreed a distribution deal with CBS. When Fleetwood Mac's "Albatross" almost immediately topped the charts, it gave the niche blues label the chance to expand. Vernon signed further British blues acts, including Duster Bennett and Chicken Shack, and it also issued recordings by American bluesmen such as **Otis Rush**, **Lightnin' Slim**, **Champion Jack Dupree**, **Magic Sam** and **Johnny Shines**, and a judicious series of reissues by the likes of **B.B. King, Elmore James**, **Eddie Boyd**, **Furry Lewis** and **Bukka White**.

Once Fleetwood Mac left Blue Horizon, in 1970, CBS lost interest, and dropped the label in the belief that the blues revival was once more on the wane. Vernon diversified, and Blue Horizon enjoyed further success with prog-rock act **Focus**; he even recorded a 1971 album under his own name, with Rory Gallagher as one of the guest guitarists. But the label ceased business in 1972 and, although Vernon reactivated the label in the late 1980s with releases by Lazy Lester, Dana Gillespie, Blues'n'Trouble and the DeLuxe Blues Band, Blue Horizon will always be best remembered for its key contribution to the British blues boom of the 1960s.

⊙ *Various Artists* **The Blue Horizon Story 1965–70** Columbia
All of Blue Horizon's key recordings, spread across three discs in long-box format, and complemented by a superbly produced 60-page booklet that tells the entire story.

⊙ *Various Artists* **History Of British Blues** Sire
A double-CD compilation of British blues from the early 1960s to the early 1970s, assembled by Mike Vernon himself and largely comprising sides that he produced.

The Blues Band

formed London, 1979

At the time former Manfred Mann singer and actor **Paul Jones** put together the Blues Band in 1979, the British blues scene was in the doldrums. It would be an exaggeration to claim that the group was single-handedly responsible for re-energizing the British blues scene, but their spirited approach did, however, certainly enliven things and help to keep the music alive beyond its American heartland, while Jones has remained a tireless ambassador for the blues in a number of other spheres.

Jones is the first to admit that he and former Manfred Mann colleague Tom McGuinness ini-tially put the group together "just for fun", to play the music they loved in pubs and small clubs as a sideline rather than as a serious commercial venture. Having recruited slide player **Dave Kelly** from the John Dummer Blues Band, bassist **Gary Fletcher** from the Wildcats, and **Hughie Flint** on drums (who was later replaced by ex-Family drummer Rob Townsend), their self-released debut *The Official Blues Band Bootleg Album* was sold at gigs and via mail-order. It did well enough to persuade Arista to step in, and issue four albums over the next three years.

The Blues Band split in 1983, but reformed three years later. Although members remain busy with other projects, they continue to gig and release albums regularly. While laying no great claims to originality, the group offers a very British take on the blues and has clearly filled a need. The band's live appearances invariably sell out. Jones has also become the UK's leading blues broadcaster, as well as lending his harmonica skills to recordings by a number of other well-known blues artists.

⊙ **Official Blues Band Bootleg Album/ Ready** BGO
The first two Blues Band albums, from 1979 and 1980, reissued as a twofer. Among the 24 tracks are some splendid covers ranging from Blind Blake's "Diddy Wah Diddy" to Muddy's "I'm Ready", by way of Son House's "Death Letter".

Lucille Bogan

b Amory, Mississippi, April 1, 1897; d Aug 10, 1948

She may never have achieved the same level of artistry or the recognition of her contemporaries Bessie Smith and Ma Rainey, but Lucille Bogan was certainly one of the toughest female blues singers of the pre-war era. Her uncompromising repertoire of songs focused on drinking, gambling, sex and prostitution. Her 1935 rendition of "Shave 'Em Dry" is arguably the bawdiest recorded blues song of them all. "Got nipples on my titties, big as the end of my thumb/I got somethin' between my legs'll make a dead man come" is one of its juiciest couplets. "Now your nuts hang down like a damn bell sapper, and your dick stands up like a steeple/Your goddam ass-hole stands open like a church door, And the crabs walk in like people" is another. Lucille Anderson was born in northeastern Mississippi as the nineteenth century drew to a close. By 1916, she was living in Birmingham, Alabama, having married Nazareth Lee Bogan, a railway fireman who worked the line from Birmingham to Kansas City, which ran through her hometown of Amory.

Bogan first recorded for Okeh Records in New York City in June 1923 with pianist Henry C. Callens, just three years after Mamie Smith had become the first black singer to cut a solo blues record. Her earliest sides were essentially vaudeville songs, but one, "Pawn Shop Blues", cut that summer in Atlanta with Eddie Heywood, Sr., on piano, had a stronger blues flavor. This is claimed to have been the first time a black blues singer had

been recorded outside New York or Chicago; such sessions were quaintly known at the time as "territory" recordings.

Bogan began recording for Paramount in Chicago in 1927. One of her best-known sides from those sessions, "Sweet Petunia", backed by pianist **Alex Channey**, was swiftly copied by **Blind Blake** and **Curley Weaver**. She also recorded with pianist **Will Ezell**, with whom she had an affair. The following year she recorded for Brunswick, backed by Tampa Red and Cow Cow Davenport.

By 1930, Bogan had grown bolder, and her trademark lyrical concerns with drinking and sex were very apparent on songs such as "Sloppy Drunk Blues", "Alley Boogie", "Black Angel Blues" and "Tricks Ain't Walkin' No More" (later covered by Memphis Minnie).

At some point in the early 1930s, she left Chicago to return to Birmingham, where she resumed recording under the nom-de-disc Bessie Jackson. Under the direction of W. R. Calaway, and backed by the pianist Walter Roland, she went on to record her most successful sides for Banner/ American Record Corporation, traveling to New York in 1933 to cut such tracks as "Seaboard Blues", "Troubled Mind", "Groceries On The Shelf" and "Superstitious Blues".

Between 1933 and 1935, as Bessie Jackson, Bogan cut almost a hundred sides with Roland, who had an uncanny ability to bring the best out of her. Her final sessions with the pianist, at which Josh White was also in attendance, took place in New York City in 1935. There they recorded "That's What My Baby Likes", "Man Stealer Blues", and two takes of "Shave 'Em Dry". The unexpurgated version of the latter is a unique document of the kind of sexually explicit song that was sung in after-hours clubs at the time, but usually only recorded with cleaned-up lyrics.

No further recordings of Bogan exist, although her family claimed that she recorded another session in Birmingham in 1937. She spent much of her later years managing her son's jazz group Bogan's Birmingham Busters, before she relocated in 1948 to Los Angeles, where she died from coronary sclerosis at the age of 51.

Although Bogan's powerful voice had clear roots in vaudeville, once she had adopted her Bessie Jackson persona, she became an archetypal blues mama. She was also an excellent songwriter, who sang about subjects nobody else would touch. Her "B.D. Woman's Blues" is a great example, as "B.D." was popular slang at the time for "bull dykes"; she left no one in any doubt as to the song's lesbian intent when she sang, "Comin' a time women ain't gonna need no men". She continued to write songs after she stopped recording. Smokey Hogg recorded her "Gonna Leave Town" for Specialty in 1949, while in recent years Saffire: The Uppity Blues Women have cut several of her compositions.

⊙ **Complete Recorded Works Vols 1–3**
Document
A comprehensive collection on three separately available CDs that includes all of Lucille Bogan's famously innuendo-strewn classics, among them "My Georgia Grind", "B.D. Woman's Blues", and both the unexpurgated and censored versions of "Shave 'Em Dry".

⊙ **Reckless Woman: 1927–1935** EPM
If you're looking for a single-disc overview of Lucille Bogan's career, this 22-tracker more than does her justice.

Graham Bond

b Romford, Essex, October 28, 1937; d May 8, 1974

In terms of the music that he left behind him, Graham Bond was something of an underachiever. Even so, his influence on the development of the British blues and R&B movement during the early 1960s was inestimable.

Classically trained as a pianist from childhood, by his early teens Bond was also playing cello and oboe. He next took up the saxophone after developing an interest in Dixieland jazz, and by 1953 had formed a school jazz band, called the Modernaires.

He stayed in the jazz world until he took his first steps into the burgeoning British blues scene in 1962, playing alongside **Ginger Baker** and **Jack Bruce** in Alexis Korner's Blues Incorporated. The following year, he formed his own band, the Graham Bond Organisation, and the future Cream pair came on board. Guitarist **John McLaughlin** also briefly figured in the line-up, while Dick Heckstall-Smith joined on sax, freeing Bond to concentrate on playing Hammond organ and singing. The combo played hard-edged R&B with a notable jazz flavor, as heard to good effect on *The*

Sound Of '65 and 1966's *There's A Bond Between Us*, which included original material and pile-driving covers of the likes of "Wade In The Water" and "Got My Mojo Working". Reviewing *There's A Bond Between Us*, the *New Musical Express* noted "a restless, wailing rhythmic and sometimes overpowering sound, both vocally and instrumentally from organist Graham Bond, who augments his music with a Mellotron." However, when Baker and Bruce left prior to joining up with Eric Clapton in Cream, the group ran out of steam. It may well have been the absence of a Clapton-style axeman that denied the band greater success Initially Bond added drummer **Jon Hiseman**, but when he too quit to join John Mayall's Bluesbreakers, taking Heckstall-Smith with him, the group effectively collapsed.

Bond had played a major role in popularizing jazz, blues and R&B with British audiences, and been a pioneer on the Hammond, but never again was he a significant force. After a brief stay in America, he formed another band, Graham Bond Initiation, which combined occult and astrological themes with a progressive jazz/R&B sound. By then, few were listening. Bond fell into drug addiction, depression and mental breakdown, and committed suicide by jumping in front of a London Underground train in 1974, at the age of 36.

⊙ **Sound of 65/There's A Bond Between Us**
BGO
The Graham Bond Organisation's first two landmark albums featured the future Cream rhythm section of Jack Bruce and Ginger Baker, and Heckstall-Smith's sax, backing Bond's gruff vocals and Hammond grooves. The lack of a guitarist gives the recordings an unusually "cool" sound.

Juke Boy Bonner

b Bellville, Texas, March 2, 1932; d June 29, 1978

Guitarist, harmonica player and singer, Juke Boy Bonner was a self-sufficient one-man band, a set up that was common enough in the early days of itinerant Delta musicians but had become something of a rarity in the post war urban blues environment in which he operated. Perhaps his main influence was fellow Texan **Lightnin' Hopkins**, though his harmonica style owed much to **Jimmy Reed** and **Sonny Boy Williamson**.

Among his strongest assets was his plain-speaking but poetic songwriting; he left his audience in no doubt that he lived the blues he sang about in songs such as "Struggle Here In Houston", "Life Is A Nightmare", "Life Gave Me A Dirty Deal", and "Going Back To The Country".

Growing up in a poor Texan family at the height of the Depression, Weldon Bonner sang spirituals as a child before taking up the guitar in his teens. He won a talent contest in Houston in 1947, and appeared on local radio. That didn't lead to a recording contract, however, and by the mid-1950s he had made his way to the West Coast. There he cut his debut single for Bob Geddin's Irma label, a version of "Rock With Me Baby", coupled with "Well Baby", with Lafayette "Thing" Thomas on lead guitar. He was credited on the label as Juke Boy Banner, but the record established his trademark sound of driving rhythm guitar and expressive vocals punctuated by fierce bursts of harmonica. Yet it was another four years before he was back in the studio, recording a single for Eddie Shuler's Goldband Records in Lake Charles, Louisiana. It was credited to "The One Man Trio", although it featured **Katie Webster** on piano. The rest of the material from these sessions appeared several years later on Storyville in Europe to some acclaim, and launched a new phase in his career. In the short term, however, it was another dead-end. Bonner returned to Houston where, hospitalized with a stomach illness, he used his enforced bedtime to write some insightful and highly personal lyrics about the bleak life of poor blacks in Texas. He recorded that next batch of songs in the late 1960s, when he signed to Arhoolie.

On his first visit to Europe in 1969, Bonner found a new and appreciative audience. He returned repeatedly during the 1970s. By the end of his life, however, he was working in a chicken processing plant. He died of cirrhosis of the liver in 1978, at the age of 46.

⊙ **Life Gave Me a Dirty Deal** Arhoolie
Twenty-three tracks from Juke Boy Bonner's late 1960s' work for Arhoolie. Many of these hard-livin' songs were based on the poems he wrote while hospitalized in Houston.

James Booker

b New Orleans, Dec 17, 1939; d Nov 8, 1983

A feral and sometimes even crazed character, James Booker enlivened the New Orleans scene with his flamboyant blues and R&B piano and organ playing for thirty years, until his wild lifestyle led to his premature death.

Booker was a contemporary of another famous Crescent City piano player, **Dr. John**, and was classically trained, but at an early age he was also playing organ on a Sunday gospel show on local radio. You couldn't grow up in New Orleans without hearing blues and R&B, and he had soon added them to his repertoire, learning from Isidor "Tuts" Washington and Edward Frank. At fourteen, he'd formed his own band, Booker Boy and the Rhythmaires, and he cut his first sides for Imperial in 1954. Both "Doing The Hambone" and "Thinkin' Bout My Baby" were produced by Dave Bartholomew. That led to sessions with **Fats Domino**, **Lloyd Price** and **Smiley Lewis** among others, and he also recorded singles for Chess and Ace.

In 1959, Booker enrolled at university to study music, although that didn't stop him recording commercially. A year later, he signed for Peacock, and cut the biggest hit of his career with the organ instrumental "Gonzo". However, psychological problems and drug addiction were already taking their toll, and he served a year for heroin possession at Louisiana's Angola State Penitentiary during the late 1960s. That experience prompted his friend Dr. John to write the song "Angola", although he had already sacked him from his band before his arrest. Dr. John also provided the best story about how Booker came to wear his trademark black eyepatch with the silver star – he apparently lost his left eye after being attacked by a bodyguard as he attempted to get paid again for a job for which he'd already cashed three cheques.

On his release from prison, Booker continued working around New Orleans at clubs like Tipitina's and the Maple Leaf. He also played on sessions in the city for Aretha Franklin, Ringo Starr, the Doobie Brothers, B.B. King and many others. When the occasion demanded, he could cut a dramatic figure – at the 1974 New Orleans

REDFERNS

The notorious James Booker

Jazz & Heritage Festival, he arrived stage-side in a rented Rolls Royce, attired in an Indian-style costume with a cape, living up to his nicknames of the "Bayou Maharajah" and the "Piano Prince of New Orleans". Chris Blackwell was impressed enough to sign Booker to Island Records. The album that followed, *Junco Partner*, was excellent in places but inconsistent, as were recordings he made towards the end of his life for Rounder.

Booker's live performances also grew increasingly unpredictable, as he mixed blues with Chopin etudes and often harangued his audiences with rambling monologues about drugs or the CIA. He suffered a fatal heart attack at the age of 43 in 1983, brought on by his drug abuse. He had been taken to a New Orleans charity hospital, where he'd been left in a waiting room. By the time he was attended to, he was already dead.

At its best, Booker's improvisational and frequently inspired gumbo mix of New Orleans jazz, blues, R&B and gospel was as potent as almost anything else the city has produced, his piano playing characterized by a strong left hand that virtually made the bass player redundant and a right hand capable of explosive percussive runs. He also had a soulful, lived-in singing voice that reflected his own inner turmoil and pain – and he certainly seemed to have plenty of that.

⊙ **Junco Partner** Hannibal

James Booker's 1975 solo recording for Island ranged from gutbucket blues and R&B to his take on Chopin's *Minute Waltz* (reworked as "Black Minute Waltz"). At times he sounds too casual for his own good – but then that was always the "Nawlins" way.

⊙ **Resurrection of the Bayou Maharajah** Rounder

Culled from live recordings at the Maple Leaf, this album captures both the genius and the madness of James Booker. At times you'd swear he's playing three pianos at once, and the version of "St James Infirmary" surpasses any you've ever heard.

Eddie Boyd

b Clarksdale, Mississippi, Nov 25, 1914; d July 13, 1994

When asked about producing Eddie Boyd in Chicago during the 1950s, Willie Dixon claimed the only way to get him to record was sit him at a piano with a bottle and wait for the alchemy to start working. But however it was done, it was clearly an effective method – the sides Boyd cut for Chess stand among the label's greatest moments.

Edward Riley Boyd was born on Stovall's Plantation in Mississippi in 1914, a mere six months before **Muddy Waters**, who was raised on the same plantation. A self-taught pianist, influenced by Roosevelt Sykes and Leroy Carr, Boyd worked in the juke joints of the Delta before migrating in 1936 to Memphis, where he and his band the Dixie Rhythm Boys were fixtures on Beale Street. In 1941 he moved again, this time to Chicago, where he worked with **Johnny Shines** and **Sonny Boy Williamson**, and hooked up once more with Muddy Waters, when he turned up a short time later. Boyd also accompanied guitarists Jazz Gillum and Tampa Red on record, and cut some solo sides of his own for RCA Victor.

In 1947 he played piano on a session with Big Maceo, covering for the great pianist's right side, which had been paralyzed by a stroke. The following year he recorded with sax man **J. T. Brown**'s Boogie Band, but it was his 1952 recording of "Five Long Years" that really put him on the map. According to blues legend, he financed the recording himself, and then sold it to JOB Records – a highly unusual practice at the time. The song topped the R&B charts and was later covered by B.B. King, Muddy Waters, Jimmy Reed and Buddy Guy among others. Switching to Chess, Boyd enjoyed further hits with "24 Hours" and "Third Degree", which gave him three major chart busters within a twelve-month span. He stayed with Chess for five years, despite a reportedly stormy relationship with **Leonard Chess**. After a hiatus following a serious car crash in 1957, he returned on Narvel "Cadillac Baby" Eatmon's Bea & Baby imprint, recording several top-class sides with Robert Jr. Lockwood on guitar.

Touring Europe with the American Folk Blues Festival in 1965, Boyd so enjoyed his escape from the discrimination that was still part of day-to-day existence in certain American states that he decided to stay. He settled first in Paris and then, after marrying a Finnish woman in 1970, in Helsinki. Europe offered prolific recording opportunities. He cut his first studio album, *Five Long Years*, in 1965 with **Buddy Guy**. Three years later came *7936 South Rhodes*, which included an appearance by Peter Green. Boyd remained in Finland for the rest of his life, performing regularly until his death there in 1994, at the age of 79.

⊙ **Five Long Years** Evidence
A welcome reissue of Eddie Boyd's album debut from 1965, featuring Buddy Guy on guitar.

⊙ **The Complete Recordings: 1947–1950** EPM
Twenty-one classic early tracks that Boyd recorded for RCA Victor in the late 1940s.

Jackie Brenston

b Clarksdale, Mississippi, Aug 15, 1930; d Dec 15, 1979

The blues had a baby and they called it rock'n'roll – and the man responsible for delivering the bouncing offspring was Jackie Brenston. One day in March 1951, he went into Sam Phillips' studio in Memphis with Ike Turner's Kings of Rhythm, and emerged with a record that would change the world. That was "Rocket 88".

Returning from army service in 1947, the seventeen-year-old Brenston, whose roots lay deep in the Delta, pitched up in Memphis and learned to play tenor saxophone from **Jesse Flowers**. Shortly afterwards, **Ike Turner** recruited him to the Kings of Rhythm. B.B. King, who was working as a disc jockey in Memphis, heard them playing on Beale Street and recommended them to Sam Phillips, who at the time ran Memphis Recording Services studio. Featuring Turner on piano, Willie Kizart on guitar and Raymond Hill on tenor sax, "Rocket 88" flew to the top of the R&B charts. Released under the name Jackie Brenston & His Delta Cats on Chess Records, it was written by Turner, and his name might just as easily have been on the label. Having licensed the track to Chess, Phillips then used the cash to start his own Sun label.

The record clearly came out of the blues tradition. But was "Rocket 88" really the first rock'n'roll record? Or was it just a very good R&B tune with an unusually fast, bottom-heavy eight-to-the-bar boogie rhythm and a great lyric about cars, booze, and women? More than half a century later, that's it's under debate. Phillips himself, however, had no doubt – and as the man who first discovered and recorded Elvis Presley, Carl Perkins and Jerry Lee Lewis, he had some authority in the matter.

Not that the accolade did Brenston much good. None of the follow-ups that appeared under his name on Chess conveyed the same high-octane energy. After a few further singles such as "My Real Gone Rocket" and a duet with Edna McRaney on "Hi-Ho Baby", he joined Lowell Fulson's band, and by 1955 he was back playing sax in Turner's Kings of Rhythm. He did some session work with **Otis Rush** and **Buddy Guy**, and cut a final single, "Want You To Rock Me", with Earl Hooker's band in 1962. Then he quit music and found a job as a truck driver. Sadly, he turned to drink, which contributed to the heart attack that killed him in 1979, at the age of 49.

⊙ *Ike Turner* I *Like Ike! The Best of Ike Turner*
Rhino
In many ways, "Rocket 88" was as much Ike Turner's record as Brenston's, and it's most easily available on this 18-track compilation of Ike's early years with the Kings of Rhythm. The album also includes Brenston's "My Real Gone Rocket", for good measure.

Lonnie Brooks

b. Dubuisson, Louisiana, Dec 18, 1933

L onnie Brooks is best known to millions as the back-porch bluesman who loses his wife in a famous Heineken TV commercial from the 1980s. However, he first forged his bayou-influenced blues in the 1950s and has been playing them with fire and conviction ever since.

Lee Baker, Jr., was discovered in the early 1950s in Port Arthur, Texas, by zydeco legend **Clifton Chenier**, who saw him playing guitar on his porch – suggesting that that beer ad was not so far from the truth. Chenier invited him to join his Red Hot Louisiana Band, and he also began to make a solo name for himself as Guitar Junior, cutting a series of bluesy, swamp-tinged rock'n'roll sides in the late 1950s for the Goldband label, including "Family Rules", "Pick Me Up On Your Way Down" and "The Crawl". By 1960, he was in Chicago (supposedly, he claimed, having hitched a ride there on Sam Cooke's tour bus). There he found himself obliged to change his stage name, as **Luther Johnson** had a prior claim on "Guitar Junior". Becoming "Lonnie Brooks" instead, he set about immersing himself in the Chicago blues scene,

joining Jimmy Reed's touring band and recording solo singles for Mercury and Chess. Confusingly, his first album, *Broke and Hungry*, released on Capitol in 1969, saw him briefly return to the moniker of Guitar Junior.

Brooks spent the next decade playing blues, rock and R&B in the toughest clubs on Chicago's South Side. Then, in 1978, aged 45 and with his career apparently going nowhere, he was invited to contribute four songs to Alligator Records' *Living Chicago Blues* anthology. Mixing rock'n'roll, R&B, Cajun boogie and hard blues in a unique Louisiana/ Chicago hybrid style he dubbed "voodoo blues", the tracks led to a recording deal with the label. Starting with *Bayou Lightning*, a prolific series of albums for Alligator followed, and he continues to tour regularly, sometimes with his son Ronnie Baker Brooks playing rhythm guitar.

⊙ **Bayou Lightning** Alligator
Lonnie Brooks' first widely available album, released in 1979, remains perhaps the finest expression of his thrilling Louisiana-meets-Chicago style of blues.

⊙ **Deluxe Edition** Alligator
Fifteen tracks selected from the best of Lonnie Brooks' eight Alligator albums, including "Like Father Like Son", recorded with his son Ronnie Baker Brooks.

Big Bill Broonzy

b Scott, Mississippi, June 26, 1893 (or possibly 1898); d Aug 15, 1958

C harley Patton's blues may have been deeper and Robert Johnson's more intense, but Big Bill Broonzy was the father figure of the folk blues. The best-selling black male blues singer of the immediate pre war era, Broonzy went on after World War II to become an elder statesman and ambassador, the bluesman who did more than anyone else to make the music of the Mississippi Delta accessible to a new and appreciative white audience.

There's some dispute over the exact date of his birth, but **William Lee Conley Broonzy** first saw the light on the banks of the Mississippi at some point in the 1890s. He grew up in a family of 17 children in Arkansas, where he worked as a field hand and found his singing voice following a mule. He also learned to play the fiddle on a home-made instrument, and by the age of ten he was performing in church. He even briefly considered becoming a preacher before he joined the US army in the latter years of World War I, serving in France. His experience overseas having made him realize "you never be called a man in the South", he had moved north to Chicago by 1920, where he learned guitar from **Papa Charlie Jackson**.

By the time he began his recording career with Paramount in 1927, Broonzy was fluent in both ragtime and blues music. He cut brilliant sides in both styles, working with the likes of pianist **Black Bob**, guitarist **Will Weldon** and **Memphis Minnie**. What was new about his approach was that he articulated the concerns of the many Delta blacks who, like himself, had moved north to Chicago. He did so via music that combined his rural roots with a growing urban sophistication and lyrics that were expressed not with a rustic holler, but with crystal-clear diction.

Broonzy continued to work prodigiously throughout the Depression, recording hundreds of sides for labels including Columbia, Okeh and Bluebird, accompanying the likes of **Bumble Bee Slim** and **Sonny Boy Williamson**, and even acting as a talent scout for various record companies around Chicago. In 1938, he fortuitously appeared in John Hammond's Spirituals To Swing concerts at New York's Carnegie Hall. Hammond had originally been hoping to track down Robert Johnson, not knowing that he was already dead, but when he failed to locate him, Broonzy took his place. He was an immediate success with the white East Coast audience, who liked the combination of his rural roots – he was even introduced as a Mississippi plough hand – and his evident sophistication, and appreciated the precision and clarity of his vocal style which lacked the wilder hollers and whoops of other rural bluesmen. The following year, Broonzy appeared with Benny Goodman and Louis Armstrong in George Seldes's film *Swingin' the Dream*.

Some have criticized Broonzy for adulterating

Playlist
Big Bill Broonzy

1 **DOWN IN THE BASEMENT BLUES** (1928) from **I Can't Be Satisfied**
One of Broonzy's earliest recordings, darker and rougher than most of his later work and bearing the unmistakable influence of Blind Lemon Jefferson.

2 **HOW YOU WANT IT DONE?** (1931) from **I Can't Be Satisfied**
Anyone who says Broonzy was too soft has clearly never heard this rocking guitar boogie…

3 **BIG BILL BLUES** (1932) from Do That Guitar Rag
"Some folks say the Big Bill Blues ain't bad, must not have been the Big Bill Blues they had…"

4 **KEEP YOUR HANDS OFF HER** (1935) from **Where The Blues Began**
This may verge on being a novelty song, but its good-time vibe is irresistibly infectious.

5 **TRUCKING LITTLE WOMAN** (1938) from **I Can't Be Satisfied**
"She's a truckin' mutha for you, don't you know…" Classic Chicago jazz-blues, with Punch Miller on trumpet

6 **IT WAS JUST A DREAM** (1938) from **Big Bill Broonzy Sings Country Blues**
"Dreamed I was in the White House, sittin' in the president's chair/I dreamed he's shaking my hand, said 'Bill, I'm glad you're here".

7 **KEY TO THE HIGHWAY** 1941 from **I Can't Be Satisfied**
Featuring Washboard Sam and Jazz Gillum, and later brilliantly covered by Derek and The Dominos.

8 **CONVERSATION WITH THE BLUES** (1941) from **Big Bill Broonzy 1935–41**
" I believe you've been drinkin' moonshine, blues, cause you don't care what you do…"

9 **ST LOUIS BLUES** (1951) from **Treat Me Right**
Among the finest demonstrations of Broonzy's guitar prowess, this track was recorded in Paris with Sonny Terry on harmonica.

10 **JOHN HENRY** (1956) from **Big Bill Broonzy Sings Folk Songs**
This was one of his Broonzy's last recordings, but there's an undeniable authority to his rendition of the familiar song.

his music to make it more accessible to a white audience. By the early 1940s, however, he was back in the Deep South playing to black audiences, touring with Lil Green's road show, and working in Chicago with Memphis Slim, in addition to his trips east to perform for well-heeled white New Yorkers. Despite his success – and Broonzy was perhaps as close as it got at the time to being a blues superstar – there was a patch during the late 1940s when he worked as a janitor at Iowa State University, where students taught him to write for the first time.

In 1951, Broonzy became the first black bluesman to travel to Europe to perform. He was an instant sensation, with a show that by now was growing increasingly mannered. A polished raconteur, his patter had such hoary lines as "I guess all songs is folk songs – I never heard no horse sing 'em", and he made several return visits. Some saw him as compromised by so directly courting white audiences, a charge which was also leveled at Josh White. Yet all those who followed owed Broonzy a considerable debt, for he effectively opened up a highly lucrative audience for several future generations of American blues artists, many of whom found that fans overseas were sometimes more

appreciative than those at home. Broonzy continued to record prolifically during the 1950s for Mercury, Chess, Columbia and Folkways, among other labels, and he worked with many artists, including white performers like **Pete Seeger**. He published his autobiography *Big Bill Blues* in 1955, retelling his life story to Danish writer Yannick Bruynoghe. After a final British tour in 1957, he died of throat cancer the following year.

Accusations that Broonzy pandered too heavily to white tastes and was therefore somehow less than "authentic" seem silly today. His music indubitably came out of the black experience of his time; he was a direct link with the era of slavery (his mother, who died aged 102 in 1957, was born a slave); he found a way to survive in a harsh world; and he was a key figure in the development of the Chicago blues, influencing the likes of **Muddy Waters**, who recorded an entire tribute album of his songs. During his career, Big Bill recorded more than 350 songs, many of them his own compositions, including such blues standards as "Key To The Highway" and "All By Myself" as well as the socio-political commentary of "Just A Dream" and "Black, Brown and White". In addition, he was a wonderfully inventive guitarist and an accomplished vocalist with a warm and rich timbre. In short, whatever anyone says, there was nothing inauthentic about Broonzy, who always maintained a powerful dignity and remains one of the most important and influential figures in blues history.

⊙ **Young Big Bill Broonzy 1928–1935** Yazoo
"Brownskin Shuffle", "Saturday Night Rub" and a dozen other gems from Broonzy's earliest recordings, way before the white folk crowd discovered him.

⊙ **I Feel So Good** Indigo
This budget-priced collection of 1930s' tracks includes "Key To The Highway", "All By Myself", "I Feel So Good" and "When I Been Drinking" – which make it as good a starting place as any.

⊙ **The Bill Broonzy Story** Polygram
Sixty-five tracks taken from Broonzy's last sessions in 1957. Originally released as a five-LP box set in 1960, they're now available on three CDs.

⊙ **Where The Blues Began** Recall
Forty tracks, spread over two cut-price CDs, that present an overview of Big Bill's career from 1928 until 1946.

⊙ **Complete Recorded Works Vols 1–12** Document
For the true devotee, these 12 CDs only take us up to 1947, with the promise of more to come…

Charles Brown

b Texas City, Texas, Sept 13, 1922; d Jan 21, 1999

The jazz-tinged late-night sound of the pianist and singer Charles Brown epitomized the mellowness of the West Coast blues that emerged in Los Angeles after World War II. Brown's urbane, sophisticated approach – sometimes dubbed "night-club blues" – was also a profound influence on the likes of Ray Charles, Amos Milburn and Floyd Dixon.

The product of a black, middle-class Texan family, classically trained and college-educated with a degree in chemistry, Brown arrived in LA in 1943, ostensibly intending to become a teacher. He swiftly realized he could make more money utilizing his silky piano skills, and he joined guitarist Johnny Moore and bassist Eddie Williams in the **Three Blazers**. Brown stayed three years, cutting some of his best-known sides with the trio, including "Drifting Blues" for Philo Records, which spent almost six months on the R&B chart

and was voted R&B song of the year. Between 1946 and 1948, the Three Blazers were hardly ever out of the charts, recording for labels like Exclusive and Modern and cutting tracks such as "Sunny Road", "So Long", "New Orleans Blues" and "Merry Christmas Baby" – arguably the coolest Yuletide song ever recorded.

Brown enjoyed even greater success when he turned solo, signing to Aladdin and releasing ten suavely elegant R&B top-ten hits between 1949 and 1952. These included the chart-toppers "Trouble Blues" and "Black Night", as well as "Get Yourself Another Fool", "Hard Times" and a cover of **Leroy Carr**'s "In The Evening (When The Sun Goes Down)". Brown called himself a "blue ballad singer" rather than an outright bluesman, and his nightclub mellowness meant that his star began to wane once the brasher, rock'n'roll sounds that emanated from Memphis and New Orleans took over the airwaves in the mid-1950s. He enjoyed another Christmas hit with "Please Come Home For Christmas" on King in 1960, but spent the 1970s and 1980s in obscurity, singing in LA nightspots. He seldom recorded, though an appearance at the 1976 San Francisco Blues Festival reminded blues enthusiasts that he was still around. A 1986 set, *One More For The Road*, heralded a comeback and proved that forty years after "Drifting Blues" he sounded as elegantly hip as ever. **Bonnie Raitt** took up his cause, taking him on tour with her as the opening act and introducing him to a whole new generation of fans. That led to a revival in his recording career, too, as he cut a string of albums in the 1990s for labels like Bullseye and Verve. When he died in 1999, aged 76, pallbearers at his funeral included **Jimmy McCracklin**, **Johnny Otis** and **Little Richard**.

⊙ **Driftin' Blues: The Best Of Charles Brown** EMI
Twenty choice cuts from Brown's early years with the Blazers and solo, including all the big hits.

⊙ **One More For The Road** Alligator
Charles Brown's wonderfully mellow 1986 comeback album, mixing blues and what he called his "blue ballads".

⊙ **All My Life** Bullseye
This fine 1990 example of Brown's mature revival includes cameos from Ruth Brown and Dr. John.

Clarence "Gatemouth" Brown

b Vinton, Louisiana, April 18, 1924; d Sept 8, 2005

Blues, R&B, Texas swing, jazz and Cajun all came together in the music of Clarence "Gatemouth" Brown. Multi-talented on guitar, violin, harmonica, mandolin, viola and drums, he was still performing and recording regularly into his eighties, at the end of a career that started during World War II.

Although Brown was born in Louisiana, he was raised just across the state line in Orange, Texas. He learned guitar and fiddle from his father,and earned the nickname "Gatemouth" from a high school teacher who accused him of having a "voice like a gate". He always said that he took it as a compliment. Initially influenced by the big bands of **Count Basie**, **Lionel Hampton** and **Duke Ellington** – whose "Take The 'A' Train" remained a staple of his live repertoire – his first professional work was as a drummer in the early 1940s. Following a stint in the Army, he made his impromptu debut as a guitarist in 1947. Strolling casually on stage at Don Robey's Bronze Peacock Club in Houston, he picked up an electric Gibson guitar that T-Bone

Walker had put down mid-show, and treated the audience to his own "Gatemouth's Boogie", which opened with the line "My name's Gatemouth and I've just got into your town." Within minutes, he had been showered with six hundred dollars worth of tips, more than Walker's fee for the night. Or, at least, so blues folklore has it.

The astute Robey promptly signed Brown to a management contract and sent him on tour with an orchestra around the South's "chitlin" circuit. Brown was among the first artists signed up when Robey founded Peacock Records, one of the earliest successful black-owned record labels, and went on to cut hits such as "Okie Dokie Stomp", "Boogie Rambler" and "Dirty Work at the Crossroads". His classic Texas-guitar blues style was to influence Albert Collins, Johnny Copeland, Johnny "Guitar" Watson, Lonnie Brooks, Eric Clapton and Joe Louis Walker among others. Around the same time his guitar-playing brother, James "Widemouth" Brown, recorded "Boogie-woogie Nighthawk" for the Jax label.

Gatemouth stayed with Peacock until 1961, and then moved to Nashville. He had already mixed Cajun fiddle into his blues on "Just Before Dawn", his final single for Peacock. Now he added elements of mainstream country music into his repertoire, not always successfully or with the approval of his blues fans. He rebuilt his blues career in the

HIGTONE RECORDS

117

1970s touring Europe, where he found a new audience, and made a diverse series of albums for European labels, including a Louis Jordan tribute and a swamp-rock set as well as collections of deep blues.

Into the 1980s and beyond, Gatemouth recorded prolifically for Rounder, Alligator, Verve and Blue, some of his latter albums displaying his wild fiddle-playing as prominently as his guitar skills. Among featured guests were **Eric Clapton**, Ry Cooder, Maria Muldaur and Leon Russell.

In his final years, Brown battled against lung cancer and heart disease. He died in his hometown of Orange, Texas in September 2005, just days after he'd abandoned New Orleans, where his home was destroyed in the floods that followed Hurricane Katrina.

⊙ **The Original Peacock Recordings** Rounder
All Gatemouth Brown's early hits, including "Dirty Work At The Crossroads", with Jimmy McCracklin's rolling piano complementing his guitar; the horn-laden "Okie Dokie Stomp"; and his final cut for Peacock, 1959's "Just Before Dawn", on which he unleashed his swinging fiddle for the first time.

⊙ **Texas Swing** Rounder
This compilation of Brown's finest work from the early 1980s showcases him in typically genre-jumping fashion, with some breathtaking guitar work on T-Bone Walker's "Rollin' With Bones" and Albert Collins'"Frosty". The stunning horn arrangements feature Alvin "Red" Tyler on tenor sax.

⊙ **Long Way Home** Verve
A fine 1996 album, on which Gatemouth Brown performs fabulous versions of "Blues Power" and "Tobacco Road", aided by sterling contributions from Eric Clapton, Leon Russell and Ry Cooder among others.

Roy Brown

b New Orleans, Louisiana, Sept 10, 1925; d May 25, 1981

The jump blues and swinging boogie style of Roy Brown served as a key link between post war blues and R&B and the new-fangled sound of rock'n'roll. Epitomized by his 1947 release "Good Rockin' Tonight", his pleading, gospel-steeped singing also had a considerable impact on the vocal styles of B.B. King, Bobby Bland and Little Richard.

Brown had an interesting career before he became a bluesman, singing gospel with the Rookie Four and trying his luck as a boxer. By the early 1940s, he was lending his voice to pop ballads in Los Angeles, initially imitating the style of Bing Crosby. Returning to Louisiana in 1945, he formed the Mellodeers. They secured a long-term residency in Galveston, Texas, where Brown also worked for a while with **Clarence Samuels** as a double act, the Blues Twins.

It was in Galveston that he wrote "Good Rockin' Tonight". With the lyrics scribbled on the back of a brown paper bag, he unsuccessfully tried to persuade Wynonie Harris to record it. Brown's own rendition had a soulful, gospel quality to the vocal and became a local hit, whereupon Harris changed his mind. Harris's own version, delivered in his signature "shouting" style, took the song straight to the top of the R&B charts. However, when Elvis Presley came to cover the song in 1954, it was Brown rather than Harris whom he chose to emulate.

After the success of "Good Rockin' Tonight", Brown took to staging "battle of the blues" contests with Harris, and soon had his own string of R&B hits on the Deluxe label, including "Hard Luck Blues", "Boogie At Midnight", "Miss Fanny Brown", "Cadillac Baby" and "Long About Midnight". At one point in 1949, seven of his songs were on the R&B chart simultaneously. He transferred to King Records in 1952, but despite the fact that his music had pointed the way forward to the styles of Little Richard, Jerry Lee Lewis and others, as soon as rock'n'roll hit big, Brown's own popularity went, ironically, into decline.

After Roy Brown moved to Imperial in 1957, producer **Dave Bartholomew** returned him to the charts with a version of Fats Domino's "Let The Four Winds Blow". He continued to record throughout the 1960s on assorted labels, including Summit, Mercury and Bluesway but his albums were solid rather than spectacular and by the end of the decade he was reportedly reduced to selling encyclopedias door-to-door. He staged a brief comeback during the 1970s, playing some European festivals and recording a decent enough album for ABC-Bluesway in 1973, but it never amounted to anything truly significant. Brown succumbed to a heart attack in 1981.

⊙ **Good Rockin' Tonight** Rhino
The best of Roy Brown's early sides for the Deluxe, King and Imperial labels.

Ruth Brown

**b Portsmouth, Virginia, Jan 30 1928;
d Nov 17 2006**

B oasting attitude and technique in equal
measure, Ruth Brown's rich, expressive
voice made her the first major star on
Atlantic Records. The label went on to become the
legendary powerhouse of 1950s' rhythm and blues,
but her success was such that in its early years it
was known as "the house that Ruth built".

The young Ruth Weston started out singing gospel in a church choir led by her father. Inspired by
jazz singers such as Sarah Vaughan, Billie Holiday
and especially Dinah Washington, however, she ran
away from home at the age of 17 to sing with the
trumpeter Jimmy Brown, whom she soon married.
In 1948, disc jockey Willis Conover, who hosted
the *Voice of America* radio show, spotted her performing at a nightclub run by Cab Calloway's sister
Blanche. He recommended her to **Ahmet Ertegun**
and **Herb Abramson**, who were in the process of
establishing a new label called Atlantic. In the face
of strong competition from Capitol Records, she
signed with Atlantic. However her debut recording session for the company was delayed after she
was seriously injured in a car accident in Chester,
Pennsylvania, en route to New York for an appearance at the Apollo.

After nine months in hospital, she re-emerged
in May 1949 to record the lacerating torch ballad "So Long", backed by **Eddie Condon** and his
band. A string of major R&B hits followed, on
which her vocals were complemented by scorching saxophone solos first by **Budd Johnson** and
later **Willis "Gator" Jackson**, who was wrongly
believed by many to be her husband. Between
1949 and 1955, she had five number one R&B hits
and became known as "Miss Rhythm".

Among Brown's biggest sellers were "Teardrops
From My Eyes", "I'll Wait For You", "I Know", "5–
10–15 Hours", "Mama, He Treats Your Daughter
Mean", "Somebody Touched Me", "Mambo Baby",
"I Want To Be Loved" and Chuck Willis' "Oh What
a Dream". Straddling the border between R&B
and rock'n'roll, she also occasionally worked in a
more openly pop vein – one of her hits, Leiber
and Stoller's "Lucky Lips", was even covered by
Cliff Richard.

Brown's final hit for Atlantic came in 1960 with
"Don't Deceive Me". As her hard rocking style
became unfashionable and the hits dried up, she
swiftly faded from view. After leaving Atlantic in
1962, she raised two sons and made her living outside music, even being forced to work as a domestic
help for a time. She returned to recording in the
1970s with releases on DCC and Capitol and also
built a parallel acting career, appearing in the TV
sitcom *Hello, Larry*, in John Waters' 1985 movie
Hairspray (as DJ Motormouth Mabel), and on
Broadway as the star of *Black and Blue*, for which
she won a Tony Award. In addition, she hosted the
radio shows *Harlem Hit Parade* and *Blues Stage*,
and in 1988 signed to Fantasy Records, for whom
she recorded some potent albums, the best of which
was 1991's *Fine And Mellow*.

She also fought a nine-year legal battle to recoup
unpaid royalties from her Atlantic hits. As part of
the settlement that followed her victory, Atlantic
agreed to help fund the formation of the Rhythm &
Blues Foundation, dedicated to helping other blues
and R&B stars of the past who never received their
dues.

⊙ **Miss Rhythm – Greatest Hits and More**
Rhino
An essential two-disc compilation that contains all Ruth
Brown's Atlantic smashes.

⊙ **Blues On Broadway** Fantasy
A fine 1989 set of blues standards, performed to perfection with a good jazz combo.

⊙ **Fine and Mellow** Fantasy
The best of Miss Rhythm's later albums, released in 1991,
demonstrated that while her voice had inevitably lost
some of its power, its emotional expression remained as
strong as ever.

Willie Brown

**b Clarksdale, Mississippi, Aug 6,
1900; d Dec 30, 1952**

W hile his name may be less well known
than some of the musicians he accompanied – notably **Charley Patton, Son
House** and **Robert Johnson** – and only a handful of his solo recordings have survived, the
guitarist Willie Brown was a true pioneer of the
Delta country blues, and a powerful singer in his
own right.

The son of a Mississippi sharecropper, Brown is believed to have been taught guitar by Earl Harris, who also tutored Patton. In his teens, he was partnered by **William Moore** playing plantation picnics, parties and dances, and he also accompanied **Memphis Minnie**. He was backing Patton by 1930, and his second guitar can be heard on many of the seminal sides cut by Patton between 1930 and 1934. He also played with Son House, whom it's believed he backed on "Walking Blues", later adapted by Robert Johnson, as well as the pianist Louise Johnson. After Patton's death, Brown went on to play alongside Robert Johnson, whose guitar style he influenced, and he's almost certainly the character Johnson is referring to in "Cross Road Blues", when he sings: "Tell my friend Willie Brown that I got the cross road blues this mornin'".

Brown probably recorded more solo material than has survived. Some scholars believe that a 1929 side called "Rowdy Blues", credited to Kid Bailey, is in fact Brown under an assumed name. There's no doubt that the solo tracks "M & O Blues" and "Future Blues" are his work; cut for Paramount in 1930, they find him singing two Patton themes in a hoarse, hard-edged voice. Brown's final surviving solo performance, "Make Me A Pallet On The Floor", was recorded by **Alan Lomax** in Mississippi in 1941, on a field trip for the Library of Congress. During the same session, Lomax also recorded Brown backing Son House. He is thought to have done further live work with House during the early 1940s, but subsequently he disappeared from view. Little is known of his activities in the last decade before his death, in 1952.

⊙ *Various Artists* **Masters of the Delta Blues: The Friends of Charley Patton** Yazoo
Alongside work by other "friends" like Tommy Johnson and Bukka White, this fascinating compilation includes Willie Brown's "M & O Blues" and "Future Blues", the mysterious Kid Bailey track that's often credited to him, and material by Son House that features Brown on guitar, including "Walking Blues".

Bob Brozman
b New York, March 8, 1954

The guitarist and ethnomusicologist Bob Brozman began his career as a bluesman, steeped in the heritage of the Delta. However, much like Ry Cooder, he has become a bold musical adventurer, developing an expertise in Hawaiian music and multifarious other slide and picking styles from around the globe.

Brozman's uncle, Barney Josephson, ran Cafe Society, one of the first venues in New York where black musicians played to mostly white audiences. Not surprisingly, Bob started playing guitar at the age of six, and picked up a National steel at thirteen. He went on to study ethnomusicology at Washington University in St Louis, specializing in the history of the Delta blues and its roots, and developing the theory that **Tommy Johnson** and **Charley Patton** must have met at some point. While at university, he made several research trips to the South to find, interview and sometimes play with surviving blues artists from the pre-war era.

His passion for National guitars, of which he now owns over a hundred, also led to a meeting with the instrument's inventor John Dopyera, and the 1993 publication of the learned and definitive tome, *The History And Artistry Of National Resonator Instruments*.

Brozman recorded his first solo album in 1981. Much of his early work for the Kicking Mule and Rounder labels is steeped in vintage country blues and early jazz and ragtime guitar styles. Then in 1988, the Hawaiian slack key guitarist **Tau Moe**, who had begun his recording career in the 1920s, ordered one of his own vintage discs by mail, only to be eagerly contacted by the amazed Brozman. Together they recorded a landmark album, *Remembering The Songs Of Our Youth*, an historic re-creation of the music Moe and his family had been making sixty years earlier. Brozman has since become one of the leading authorities on Hawaiian music, curating a series of historical reissues for Rounder Records. His natural musical curiosity has also resulted in a bewildering number of other collaborative projects with musicians from different cultures around the world. His main interest is

Bob Brozman, with two of his prized guitars

Bumble Bee Slim

b Brunswick, Georgia, May 7, 1905; d Los Angeles 1968

Much influenced by **Leroy Carr** – some would even call him an outright imitator – Bumble Bee Slim was a hugely popular bluesman in the early acoustic Chicago style who recorded prolifically in the 1930s. Many of the almost two hundred sides he cut are now considered classics.

Born Amos Eaton, Slim traveled the South with a circus in his teens before moving to Indianapolis, where he made a living playing rent parties and dances. By the early 1930s he was in Chicago, where he got to know **Big Bill Broonzy, Scrapper Blackwell, Leroy Carr, Casey Bill Weldon** and **Memphis Minnie** among others. Playing a rudimentary version of the guitar style popularized by Blackwell, and singing in a fine, relaxed voice that bore a strong resemblance to Carr's laconic phrasing, he cut his first sides for Bluebird before moving on to Vocalion and then Decca, becoming one of the most recorded bluesmen of the decade.

Among his best-known numbers are "Bricks In My Pillow", "Policy Dream Blues", "Rambling With That Woman", "No Woman No Nickel", "Sail On Little Girl Sail On", and "This Old Life I'm Living", which featured tremendous bottleneck playing from Casey Bill Weldon. He also played on records by Big Bill Broonzy and **Cripple Clarence Lofton**, among others.

By the end of the 1930s Slim had left Chicago, reportedly bored with repeating himself, and was back in Georgia. He was soon on the move again,

the inter-connectedness of modern musical styles around the globe, and thus even on his world music collaborations, much of his playing still displays his mastery of classic Delta blues styles. He is also a noted guitar teacher, running annual International Guitar Seminars, and lectures on ethno musicological subjects.

⊙ **Devil's Slide** Rounder
A fine demonstration of Bob Brozman's total mastery of blues and other vintage guitar styles.

⊙ **Truckload Of Blues** Rounder
This 1992 album concentrates on Brozman's love of country blues, rather than his broader world music interests.

however, relocating to Los Angeles in the early 1940s, and recorded for Specialty and Pacific Jazz during the 1950s in a West Coast blues style that suggested an admirable versatility. Although he continued to play live in small clubs, the blues revival that elevated other pre war stars to the status of celebrities seemed to pass him by.

⊙ **The Essential Bumble Bee Slim** Allegro
The best of Bumble Bee Slim's 1930s' recordings, along with a couple of sides recorded in LA in 1951.

⊙ **Bumble Bee Slim Vols 1–9** Document
We told you Slim was prolific – it takes nine discs to hold all of his 1930s recordings, along with the later sides he recorded in LA in the early 1950s.

R.L. Burnside

b Coldwater, Mississippi, Nov 23, 1926; d Sept 1, 2005

Known as "Rule" to his friends, R.L. Burnside learned his blues from life, and his guitar sound from **John Lee Hooker** and his Mississippi neighbor **Fred McDowell**. However, his career didn't really hit its stride until he was in his sixties, when he emerged as one of the last of the great country blues stylists, playing a modal, rhythm-oriented guitar with a down-and-dirty slide technique perfected over decades of performing in rough-and-tumble juke joints.

Burnside lived much of his life in Holly Springs, in the hill country of northern Mississippi, where he raised fourteen children. He started out sharecropping as a young man, but despairing of its hopelessness, at the end of the 1940s he moved to Chicago, where he worked in a foundry and heard the likes of **Muddy Waters** perform. As later chronicled in the song "R.L.'s Story", he had a hard time in the Windy City, and by the end of the 1950s he was back farming in Mississippi. Inspired by John Lee Hooker, by then he had begun singing the blues and playing guitar in earnest. Further inspiration came from local musicians such as Fred McDowell, **Son Hibler** and **Ranie Burnette**.

For the next thirty years, music was something Burnside did for fun at nights and on weekends, playing in his neighbor **Junior Kimbrough's** juke joint in Holly Springs. There were also

some recordings, starting with an acoustic album for Arhoolie in the late 1960s, when he was discovered by blues folklorists David Evans and George Mitchell. A tour of Europe in the 1970s led to albums for French and Dutch labels, but he returned to north Mississippi and remained virtually unknown beyond the area until he signed to the Oxford-based blues revival label Fat Possum in 1992.

That year, Burnside and Kimbrough featured in the documentary film, *Deep Blues*, based on Robert Palmer's book of the same title. Palmer went on to produce his Fat Possum recording debut, *Bad Luck City*, a successful studio attempt to replicate the sound of the local juke joints. That was followed in 1994 by *Too Bad Jim*, recorded live at Kimbrough's place. Making up for lost time, Fat Possum recorded him prolifically thereafter. *Mr Wizard* appeared in 1997, and *Come On In* the following year. *My Black Name A-Ringin'* was released in 1999, *Wish I Was in Heaven Sitting Down* in 2000, and the live *Burnside On Burnside* in 2001.

Led by Burnside's raw electric guitar playing, most of the albums found him accompanied by his Sound Machine band, including his son Dwayne on bass and son-in-law Calvin Jackson on drums as well, on later recordings, as his grandson Cedric.

He also proved surprisingly adaptable, recording more experimental albums such as 1996's *A Ass Pocket O' Whiskey* for Matador Records, a grunge-laden collaboration with indie-rockers the **Jon Spencer Blues Explosion**. 1998's *Come On In* added elements of electronica and MTV-friendly remixes to his earthy, back-porch blues. Made from his unedited tapes without his active participation, it apparently offended some blues purists so much that Fat Possum received death threats. 2004's *A Bothered Mind* similarly fused more contemporary elements such as rap and hip-hop with Burnside's deep Mississippi roots. Sadly, however, he died in Memphis in 2005 at the age of 78.

⊙ **First Recordings** Fat Possum
The 1967 acoustic field recordings that first brought Burnside to the attention of the world, made by George Mitchell and subsequently remastered and reissued.

⊙ **Bad Luck City** Fat Possum
Burnside's superb Fat Possum debut, from 1992, features lusty vocals, raw guitar work in his classic slide-and-drone modal style, and sterling work from his family band.

⊙ **A Ass Pocket O'Whiskey** Matador
Raw and nasty bad-ass, profane blues-rock chaos from 1996, coupling R.L. Burnside with the Jon Spencer Blues Explosion. With Burnside sounding surprisingly at home, the collaboration works far better than it has any right to.

Paul Butterfield

b Chicago, Dec 17, 1942; d May 3, 1987

The white British blues scene had John Mayall. His equivalent on the other side of the Atlantic was Paul Butterfield, the first white harmonica player to develop a convincingly authentic blues style, and the leader of a storming and groundbreaking racially integrated band, through which many of the best white blues players in America passed.

Butterfield grew up in a middle-class liberal family in Hyde Park, an integrated area on Chicago's South Side. He learned flute as a child, but surrounded by the blues, he took up guitar and harmonica. At fifteen, he was hanging out in clubs, often as the only white kid in the audience, and heard the cream of Chicago's blues musicians, like Muddy Waters, Little Walter and Howlin' Wolf.

Butterfield was soon imitating the music he had heard, playing with fellow fan and future band member, Nick Gravenites. He met another white blues fan at the University of Chicago in guitarist **Elvin Bishop**, and the two soon dropped out of college to pursue music full-time. By 1963, Butterfield had added bassist **Jerome Arnold** and drummer **Sam Lay**, and secured a residency at a Chicago club called Big John's. **Michael Bloomfield** joined soon after, and the Butterfield band signed to Elektra as a quintet in late 1964.

After initial album sessions were scrapped, they added **Mark Naftalin** on keyboards and tried again. However, before the album came out, they were booked to play at the 1965 Newport Folk Festival. Their own set of white electric blues excited as much animosity from traditional blues devotees as did the appearance of Bloomfield, Arnold and Lay backing Bob Dylan for the first electric gig of his career.

The Paul Butterfield Blues Band's self-titled debut album finally appeared at the end of 1965, and caused a considerable stir. Not only was it the first electric Chicago blues release by a white American group, but the combination of Butterfield's wailing harp and sturdy voice with Bloomfield's searing guitar sounded more authentic than just about anything else heard thus far from white blues boys. By the second album, 1966's *East-West*, Billy Davenport had taken over on drums, while the title cut expanded their blues repertoire into a lengthy instrumental suite incorporating jazz, rock, psychedelia and elements of Indian raga.

Bloomfield quit the group in 1967 to form the Electric Flag with **Nick Gravenites**, which allowed Bishop to take a more prominent role on guitar on the band's third album, 1967's *The Resurrection of Pigboy Crabshaw*. The album also featured a horn section, including sax player David Sanborn. *In My Own Dream* followed in 1968 before both Bishop and Naftalin left the band, and Butterfield then recruited nineteen-year-old guitarist **Buzzy Feiten** for the 1969 album, *Keep On Moving*. That same year Butterfield appeared at Woodstock and on Muddy Waters' *Fathers And Sons*.

In 1971, after two further albums including a live set, Butterfield broke up the band and retreated to Woodstock. There he formed the loose collective Better Days, with guitarist Amos Garrett, drummer Chris Parker, white folk-blues singer and guitarist Geoff Muldaur, New Orleans pianist Ronnie Barron and Taj Mahal bassist Billy Rich. Their first album, *Better Days*, released in 1972 on manager Albert Grossman's Bearsville label, is an understated classic. *It All Comes Back* followed in 1973 to positive response, while in 1975 Butterfield backed Muddy Waters again on *The Woodstock Album*, the last ever release on Chess Records.

During the mid-1970s, Butterfield went solo, but his 1976 debut, *Put It In Your Ear*, was a lacklustre affair and he spent the next five years playing sessions. *North–South*, a 1981 solo comeback produced in Memphis by Willie Mitchell, also disappointed. Although still not forty years old, Butterfield was by now in poor health, due to his heavy drinking and growing addiction to heroin. His final album, *The Legendary Paul Butterfield*

Rides Again, appeared in 1986, and he died the following year of a drug overdose.

All Butterfield's best work had been done by the early 1970s, but the impact that the initial *Paul Butterfield Blues Band* album and the group's iconoclastic Newport appearance had on a new generation of white blues players cannot be over-estimated.

⊙ **An Anthology: The Elektra Years** Elektra
Thirty-three tracks spread across two discs, cherry-picking the best of seven Butterfield Blues Band albums released on Elektra between 1966 and 1971.

⊙ **Better Days** Rhino
This 1972 album only holds nine tracks, but it's a laid-back blues classic, featuring knock-out versions of "New Walkin' Blues", "Baby Please Don't Go", and "Nobody's Fault But Mine".

Canned Heat

formed Los Angeles, 1965

Leading lights of the white American blues-rock scene during the 1960s, Canned Heat appeared at both the Monterey Pop and Woodstock festivals, and enjoyed chart success with tracks such as "On The Road Again", "Let's Work Together" and "Going Up The Country".

Founded by blues enthusiasts and collectors **Alan "Blind Owl" Wilson** – a fine harmonica player who had already accompanied **Son House** on his comeback album, *Father Of The Blues* – and **Bob "The Bear" Hite**, they took the name Canned Heat from a 1928 recording by **Tommy Johnson**. The line-up was completed by guitarist Henry "The Sunflower" Vestine from Frank Zappa's Mothers of Invention, Larry "The Mole" Taylor on bass, and Frank Cook, soon to be replaced by Fito de la Parra, on drums. Their self-titled debut album appeared in 1967 and contained somewhat pedestrian takes on twelve-bar standards like "Dust My Broom" and "Rollin' and Tumblin'". The follow-up, however, *Boogie With Canned Heat*, was a major advance, including the twelve-minute "Fried Hockey Boogie", which became a staple of their live sets, and their career-defining "On The Road Again". Written by Wilson and featuring his high spooky vocal, a sitar-like droning intro, insistent beat and hypnotic harmonica, it became a top-ten hit in the UK and also charted strongly in America.

Their third album, *Living The Blues*, included a 19-minute experimental tour de force, "Parthenogenesis", as well as "Goin' Up The Country". Based on Henry Thomas' "Bull Doze

Blues", the latter again made the pop charts, and was a highlight of the *Woodstock* movie.

In 1970, the band teamed up with John Lee Hooker for the spirited *Hooker'n'Heat* album. In their earlier days, they also helped to bring a number of other forgotten bluesmen back into the spotlight, including **Sunnyland Slim**, discovered driving a taxi in Chicago and **Skip James**, whom the band's Henry Vestine found in a hospital in Tunica, Mississippi.

After a third hit single with their cover of Wilbert Harrison's "Let's Work Together", the band was shattered by the 1971 suicide of Wilson, whose body was found in Hite's back yard.

Deprived of their guiding spirit, they nonetheless elected to soldier on, going through regular line-up changes over the coming years until Hite was the only remaining original member. During the 1970s they recorded albums with Memphis Slim and Clarence "Gatemouth" Brown, and were instrumental in promoting the career of **Albert Collins**, even though the band were for a while without a recording contract of their own.

When Hite died after a gig in 1981, Canned Heat regrouped again under the leadership of De La Parra. Larry Taylor also rejoined, as did Vestine, who in 1997 became the third member of the original line-up to die. Although the group were never as hot again as during the late 1960s, a version continues on its boogie-laden quest to this day, while the three original chart hits crop up regularly in TV ads – "On The Road Again" for Miller Beer, "Goin' Up The Country" for Pepsi, Chevrolet and McDonalds, and "Let's Work Together" for Lloyd's Bank.

⊙ **Boogie With Canned Heat** Liberty
Canned Heat's second album, released in 1968, was the one that defined their boogie sound, and included their wonderful remake of "On The Road Again".

⊙ **Hooker'n'Heat** Liberty
At the time this was released, in 1970, it seemed as if Canned Heat were doing John Lee Hooker a favor. Which seems daft now, of course. This album is one of the better collaborations of its kind.

⊙ **Best Of Canned Heat** EMI
To be frank, Canned Heat's three hit singles stand head and shoulders above the rest of their material, and this compilation conveniently collects them all in one place.

Gus Cannon

b Red Banks, Mississippi, Sept 12, 1883; d Oct 15, 1979

Gus Cannon was typical of the earliest generation of bluesmen, whose roots lay in minstrelsy and the traveling medicine shows of the early twentieth century. He went on to form one of the greatest jug bands of them all, and performed around Memphis well into the 1970s, until he died aged 96 – or thereabouts. His tombstone actually claims he was born in 1874, which would have made him an improbable 105.

We do know for sure that Cannon's parents had been slaves and he constructed his first home-made banjo out of kitchen implements at around the age of twelve, learning to play in Clarksdale from a musician called Bud Jackson. In later life, he recalled performing into some kind of primitive early recording device in Mississippi in 1901. If true, that would make him the first recorded bluesman, although no evidence exists other than Cannon's own claim. He was certainly known to **W.C. Handy**, played with the Memphis songster Jim Jackson, and worked with harmonica player Noah Lewis in a lumber camp in Ripley, Tennessee around 1910. Before World War I, touring with the medicine shows, he was billed as "Banjo Joe", and also played guitar, piano and jug. He placed the latter around his neck in an elaborate harness, and played it simultaneously with his banjo. He spent his winters working on a farm, and his summers with medicine shows every year until 1929.

Already in his 40s, Cannon recorded his first solo sessions for Paramount in Chicago in 1927, with **Blind Blake** on guitar. The following year, the Victor label suggested he put a jug band together, modeled on the success of the **Memphis Jug Band**. He summoned Noah Lewis and guitarist Ashley Thompson, who had played with them fifteen years earlier, and the result was Cannon's Jug Stompers. Between 1928 and 1930, with Cannon now playing a metal kerosene can rather than a jug, as well as kazoo and banjo, and Lewis playing a major role, they cut some of the greatest jug band music ever recorded, combining medicine show songs with blues and folk numbers. Among them was the 1929 recording "Walk Right In", which was to become a number one hit in 1963 for the Rooftop Singers.

As musical fashions altered, the Stompers split up and Cannon returned to a solo career. During the tough years of the Depression, he played on street corners in Memphis, while also at times taking jobs outside music to keep body and soul together. However, Cannon was among the first to be rediscovered during the first folk revival of the mid-1950s, and resumed recording in 1956 for Folkways. He also recorded with fellow Memphis survivor Furry Lewis, and even made an album for soul label Stax. He continued to perform in Memphis until shortly before his death, sometimes from a wheelchair. Towards the end of his life, his extreme age made him the object of great interest from blues historians and researchers, and he made a memorable appearance in *The Devil's Music*, BBC TV's fine 1976 documentary series about the blues.

In addition to the 1963 pop hit "Walk Right In", the **Grateful Dead** took numbers such as "New Minglewood Blues" and "Viola Lee Blues" from Cannon's repertoire and Mungo Jerry's 1970 British number one hit "In The Summertime" was another adaptation of one of his tunes.

⊙ *Cannon's Jug Stompers* **The Best of Cannon's Jug Stompers** Yazoo
Twenty-three jug-band classics, recorded between 1928 and 1930 and featuring banjo, harmonica, kerosene can and kazoo.

⊙ **Gus Cannon: Complete Recorded Works Vols 1–2** Document
All Gus Cannon's well-known songs, solo and with the jug band, as well as some fascinating obscurities, such as "Poor Boy Long Ways From Home", on which he plays banjo with a slide.

Captain Beefheart

b Glendale, California, Jan 15, 1941

Delta blues was only one element in the extraordinary musical vision of Captain Beefheart. But it was a vital one, and with his Magic Band he took the blues and warped it into strange, daring and compelling places it had never visited before.

The young Don Vliet – he changed his name to Van Vliet during the early 1960s – was a child prodigy at art, a discipline that ultimately was to replace music in his life. When his family moved to Lancaster in the Mojave Desert, he met and was befriended by the young Frank Zappa. Don taught himself to play free-form saxophone and harmonica, and sang in a deep growl of a voice that was clearly influenced by Howlin' Wolf, and the pair joined together in local R&B groups, the Omens and the Blackouts.

Zappa soon moved to Los Angeles, where he formed the Mothers of Invention. Van Vliet remained in the Mojave area, took the name Captain Beefheart, and formed his first Magic Band in 1964. The initial line-up included guitarists Alex St. Clair and Doug Moon, bassist Jerry Handley and drummer Paul Blakely.

At first Beefheart kept his wilder visions in check, and the Magic Band played what was by his later standards a conventional blues-rock, drawing on the music of the Delta and fusing it with rock'n'roll elements. Their first single, "Diddy Wah Diddy" was based on a Bo Diddley song. However, their label A&M rejected their debut album of Beefheart's own compositions, and forced him to revamp his band, replacing Moon and Blakely with guitarist Jeff Cotton (aka Antennae Jimmy Semens), drummer John "Drumbo" French and, most significantly, the brilliant young slide guitarist **Ry Cooder**. This was the line-up that re-recorded previously scrapped songs such as "Electricity" and "Zig Zag Wanderer", which were released as *Safe As Milk* on Buddha in 1967, one of the most extraordinary debut albums of all time. It was the only Beefheart album on which Cooder appeared.

The follow-up album, 1968's *Strictly Personal*, contained more exploratory psychedelic blues, using then-novel special effects such as phasing, but suffered from ham-fisted mixing, carried out without Beefheart's approval. A rift with his record company followed, but his old friend Zappa rode to the rescue, signing him to his newly formed Straight Records. The double album that resulted, 1969's double *Trout Mask Replica*, was Beefheart's masterpiece. Performed by the definitive line-up of the Magic Band – Semens, Drumbo, guitarist Zoot Horn Rollo (Bill Harkleroad), bassist Rockette Morton (Mark Boston) and bass clarinettist the Mascara Snake (Victor Fleming) – the 28 songs fused Delta blues and free-form jazz into an iconoclastic mesh of conflicting time signatures, harsh slide guitar, clattering, jagged rhythms and avant-garde blowing. Mixed with Beefheart's surreal Beat

lyrics, sung in uncompromising style, it all added up to one of the most innovative and influential – not to say strange and difficult – albums in rock history.

The following year's *Lick My Decals Off, Baby* was similarly uncompromising, although *Clear Spot* and *The Spotlight Kid* in 1972 found him attempting to give his sound a more commercial edge. Different musicians drifted through the Magic Band, and he continued to release innovative albums that combined his roots in the Delta blues with other influences, among them 1974's *Unconditionally Guaranteed*, 1978's *Shiny Beast (Bat Chain Puller)*, and 1980's *Doc At The Radar Station*. After releasing *Ice Cream For Crow* in 1982, he retired from music and returned to the desert to concentrate on his painting. In later years, he was reported to be suffering from multiple sclerosis, which turned him into a virtual recluse.

Beefheart was not a conventional blues artist by any stretch of the term, but he used the blues as a jumping-off point in a unique and audacious way.

⊙ **Safe As Milk** Buddah
Great slide playing from Ry Cooder adorns Beefheart's most conventional blues-rock album, although with the Captain such terms are always relative.

⊙ **Trout Mask Replica** Warner's
At once Captain Beefheart's most difficult but most definitive album. While rooted in blues and jazz, it's warped into another dimension that some have even dubbed "anti-music".

Leroy Carr
b Nashville, Tennessee, March 27, 1905; d April 29, 1935

The writer and blues historian Elijah Wald describes Leroy Carr as "the most influential male blues singer and songwriter of the first half of the twentieth century." An understated pianist with a gentle, expressive voice, his first record, 1928's "How Long How Long Blues", had a revolutionary impact. As Wald points out, previous blues stars, whether vaudevillians like Bessie Smith or street singers like Blind Lemon Jefferson, had needed huge voices to project their music. With the help of new microphone and recording technologies, Carr, who was also noted for his natty suits, sounded like "a cool city dude carrying on a

REDFERNS

Leroy Carr

ism – it was jokingly said that Blackwell bootlegged the liquor and the pianist drank it all up – and he died in 1935 at the age of thirty, leaving a legacy of around two hundred sides. The solid beat of his piano, the biting guitar accompaniment, the light swing of his rhythms, his poetic lyrics and the refined urbanity of his voice all combined to convey a hipness that exerted a profound influence on the bluesmen who followed, from Muddy Waters to T-Bone Walker. As Wald notes, it "signalled a new era in popular music."

Despite Carr's popularity and influence during his own era, his significance was strangely overlooked during the blues revival of the 1960s. After Columbia Records had created a sensation with the release of Robert Johnson's *King of the Delta Blues Singers*, they followed with a Carr compilation called *Blues Before Sunrise*. It made little impact, however. Carr's smooth style was dismissed as a less intense, and therefore somehow less "authentic", version of Johnson's fiercer, more rural blues, even though he predated Johnson and was a considerable influence upon him. Fortunately, later blues enthusiasts and scholars have rescued Carr's reputation, and restored him to his rightful place as a true innovator.

conversation with a few close friends." The recordings he made with the guitarist **Scrapper Blackwell** marked a transition from country to city, and were a pre-electric pointer to the urban blues style that emerged in Chicago after World War II.

Carr moved to Indianapolis as a child, and learned to play piano in his teens. By the early 1920s he was making a living performing at parties and dances around Kentucky. For a time he also traveled with a circus, leading a peripatetic existence across the mid-west and the South. He first met the bootlegging guitarist Scrapper Blackwell in Indianapolis in 1928, and their first recording for Vocalion, "How Long How Long Blues" was an instant hit that proved them to be a perfectly matched, complementary team. Over the next seven years, they recorded dozens of classic songs for the label, including "Hurry Down Sunshine", "Midnight Hour Blues", "Shady Lane Blues" and the classic "Blues Before Sunrise", all penned by Carr. Carr's life was, however, cut short by acute alcohol-

⊙ **Whiskey Is My Habit, Good Women Is All I Crave** Columbia Legacy
This 40-track anthology of the best of Leroy Carr, spread across two discs, including all the classics, among them "How Long How Long Blues" and "Blues Before Sunrise".

⊙ **Complete Recorded Works Vol 1–6**
Document
Everything Leroy Carr recorded between 1928 and 1934, across six chronologically arranged discs.

Playlist
Leroy Carr

All from the Columbia Legacy double album *Whiskey Is My Habit, Good Women Is All I Crave*

1 HOW LONG HOW LONG BLUES (1928)
Carr's first recording ushered in a new style of cool, urbane blues.

2 HUSTLER'S BLUES (1934)
"Whiskey is my habit, good women is all I crave..." Carr may have borrowed the phrase from Lucille Bogan, but he made it all his own.

3 BLUES BEFORE SUNRISE (1932)
John Lee Hooker, Elmore James and Ray Charles were among many who later covered this classic song.

4 MIDNIGHT HOUR BLUES (1932)
Carr was there long before the "wicked Wilson Pickett"...

5 WHEN THE SUN GOES DOWN (1935)
Subtle eloquence and lonesome passion on one of Carr's final recordings.

6 HURRY DOWN SUNSHINE (1932)
Leroy evidently had a thing about the sun...

7 SLOPPY DRUNK (1930)
Pounding piano and stinging guitar that led all the way to Chuck Berry.

8 HARD TIMES DONE DROVE ME TO DRINK (1930)
...and hard times killed him five years later.

Bo Carter

b Bolton, Mississippi, March 21, 1893; d Sept 21, 1964

One of several brothers who performed together in the **Mississippi Sheiks**, Bo Carter was better known on record as a solo artist and fluid guitar picker, many of whose songs specialized in sexual metaphors and ribald imagery.

Young Armenter Chatmon, whose father was allegedly related to Charley Patton, began his musical career playing at "sociables" for white plantation communities, where country dance tunes rather than blues was the musical order of the day. By the mid-1920s, however, he was playing with the Sheiks in Jackson, Mississippi. Discovered by Jackson store owner and talent scout H.C. Spier (who dubbed him "the dirtiest man on record"), he cut 110 sides as a solo artist between 1930 and 1940. These included straight blues numbers as well as the risqué tracks full of sexual innuendo – such as "Banana in Your Fruit Basket", "Pin in Your Cushion", "Please Warm My Weiner" and "Your Biscuits Are Big Enough For Me" – that garnered him considerable popularity. Despite the novelty value of such recordings, he was also an inventive guitarist who deployed different keys and tunings. Among the best-known of his non-ribald songs was his 1928 version of "Corinne Corinne", the first recording of a song that went on to become a blues standard, covered by everyone from Taj Mahal to Bob Dylan. He may even have written it, although it is usually credited as "trad".

Unusually for the time, he's said to have made most of his money from his recordings rather than playing dances. By the 1940s, however, he had gone blind, and changing musical fashions in the blues had reduced him to a marginal figure. He died in poverty and obscurity in Memphis in 1964, aged 71.

⊙ **Greatest: The Essential Bo Carter** Classic Blues
Thirty-six tracks over two CDs, including the standard blues numbers as well as Carter's ribald songs, most of which retain their ability to raise a smile even at this distance.

⊙ **Banana In Your Fruit Basket** Yazoo
A superb compilation of Carter's risqué material from the 1930s, still sounding fresh and spry, and complemented by a quite brilliant set of context-setting liner notes by Steve Calt.

Ray Charles

b Albany, Georgia, Sept 23, 1930; d June 10, 2004

As a singer, pianist and arranger, Ray Charles is acknowledged as "the godfather of soul" and even "the genius of soul". But his music and his career provide the perfect illustration of how the blues and R&B inter mingled with jazz and gospel to create a new form of black popular music that spawned singers like Sam Cooke, James Brown and Jackie Wilson, and led on to Otis Redding, Marvin Gaye, Stevie Wonder and beyond. "I was the first one who started soul. That's true," he told this writer shortly before he died. "I was raised in the church and I knew gospel music. But I knew rhythm and blues, too, because that was the music you heard in the neighborhood. And I thought, 'that's me. That's my sound.' I put those two things together and they called it soul music."

Ray Charles Robinson was born into acute poverty in rural Georgia in 1930, and had a tragic upbringing. He witnessed his brother drown as a young child, was blind from glaucoma by the age of seven, and lost his mother when he was fifteen. As he put it "Music was the only thing that kept me breathing and gave me a way to pick myself up". Having learned to play the piano, clarinet, sax and trumpet, and to read and write music in Braille, at the St. Augustine School for the Deaf and the Blind, he drifted around Florida before moving across the country to Seattle in 1947. There he met and became a mentor to the fourteen-year-old Quincy Jones. Charles began recording for the Downbeat label in 1949 in a smooth, crooning style derivative of **Nat "King" Cole** and **Charles Brown**, and scored his first R&B hit two years later with "Baby, Let Me Hold Your Hand". Yet although these early recordings betray hints of the genius that was to come, at this stage he had still not found his own voice.

During the early 1950s, Charles toured as the pianist in **Lowell Fulson**'s twelve-piece band, worked with Atlantic's big-voiced star turn Ruth Brown, and went to New Orleans to work with Guitar Slim, arranging and playing piano on his unrestrained million-selling R&B hit, "The Things That I Used To Do". Ahmet Ertegun's Atlantic Records acquired his contract in 1952 and he continued to record in a smooth vein on tracks such as "It Should've Been Me" and "Mess Around". Subsequently, with Ertegun's encouragement, he moved away from his "cool" sound towards a more emotional approach that had its roots in blues and gospel. "I started out as an imitator of Nat King Cole," he later admitted. "But then I realized peo-

ple were saying to me, 'hey kid, you sound like Nat,' and they didn't even know my name. Then I remembered that before she died my mother also told me to always be myself, so I thought about applying that to my music." The turning point came on 1954's "I Got A Woman", on which Charles's abandoned vocal style was allowed free reign for the first time. A huge hit, it was also highly controversial for its fusion of gospel moan and secular lyric, the beseeching tones of a preacher in the pulpit given an earthier slant that changed the message from spiritual rapture to sexual longing. It was a combination that even shocked Charles's religious wife when she first heard it, and plenty of bluesmen disapproved, too. "He's mixing the blues with spirituals. I know that's wrong," Big Bill Broonzy observed. "How he takes a spiritual and makes it into a love or sex song, it's a kind of sacrilege," Josh White complained.

The controversy soon subsided and a string of magnificent hits for Atlantic followed including "This Little Girl Of Mine", "Drown In My Own Tears", "Hallelujah I Love Her So", "Lonely Avenue", "Talkin' Bout You", "Drown In My Own Tears", "I Believe To My Soul" and "The Right Time". On these sides Charles's style is virtually beyond categorizing, blending jazz, gospel, swing, R&B, blues and ballads. According to Steve Winwood, Charles was the first person whose records "showed the connection between all these different kinds of music." Van Morrison makes a similar point: " It was all the stuff I was listening to but rolled into one amazing, soulful thing."

Charles's Atlantic years culminated with 1959's "What'd I Say", a magnificent coming together of his many influences with a thrilling call-and-response vocal that crossed over to give him a top-ten pop hit and sold him to a white rock'n'roll audience for the first time. Shortly after, he left Atlantic for ABC and a dream deal that allowed him total artistic control of his recordings, a quite unprecedented concept at the time. It is often said this was the end of his golden period, but his early ABC singles give the lie to such nonsense, as tracks like "Unchain My Heart", "Hit The Road Jack" and "Georgia On My Mind" rank with the greatest of his Atlantic sides. However, a major change was in the wind.

In 1962, Charles released a country album, *The Modern Sounds Of Country And Western*, and topped the pop charts with the extracted "I Can't Stop Loving You". It was doubly shocking to blues and R&B purists; whereas the history of American popular music can be seen as a tale of black performers providing the inspiration and white performers appropriating and popularizing it, here the process was working in reverse. Black music had given white audiences ragtime, jazz, blues, swing, R&B, rock'n'roll and soul. Country was the one popular form that indigenous white culture could call its own, and many were bemused that the "genius of soul" should chose to embrace it.

There were still some fine recordings to come, including "Busted", "Let's Go Get Stoned", "I Don't Need No Doctor" and "Take These Chains From My Heart". But it is an inescapable fact that for the most part from the mid-1960s onwards, as *The Macmillan Encyclopaedia Of Popular Music* puts it, "the edges were blunted, the vibrancy was stilled and the repertoire grew increasingly inoffensive." Although his voice influenced many of the finest singers to emerge in the 1960s, including white rock vocalists such as Joe Cocker, Steve Winwood and Van Morrison, Charles himself moved increasingly into the pop mainstream, singing Beatles covers and standards. He never lost the voice and he continued to tour and record prolifically. But those who longed for him to return to the fire and unbridled soul power of his 1950s recordings were to remain largely disappointed.

Charles told his own story in the powerful 1978 autobiography *Brother Ray* and the tributes on his death in 2004 at the age of 74 were numerous and sincere. His role as one of the seminal figures in the history of modern popular music was acknowledged in the surprisingly honest and moving Hollywood biopic *Ray* in 2005, with Jamie Foxx turning in a brilliant performance in the title role.

⊙ **Pure Genius: The Complete Atlantic Recordings 1952–1959** Rhino
A cornucopia of Charles at his best: Eight discs, nine hours of music and 165 tracks, including 27 previously unreleased or hard-to-find cuts – plus a DVD of his performance at the 1958 Newport Jazz Festival.

⊙ **Ultimate Hits Collection** Rhino
A good one-stop package of 36 of Ray Charles's best-known tracks, covering not only the Atlantic years but including the highlights of his subsequent material for ABC.

⊙ **The Genius Sings The Blues** Atlantic
Ray Charles invented soul, and even made country albums. On this 1961 offering he concentrated on his blues and jazz roots, on tracks such as "Ray's Blues" and "Mr Charles's Blues".

Sam Charters

b Aug 1,1929, Pittsburgh, Pennsylvania

A key architect of the 1950s blues revival, Samuel Charters made a major contribution to enthusing and educating white college-based audiences about the music of the Delta with the simultaneous appearance in 1959 of his book *The Country Blues*, and a companion compilation album of the same name on the Folkways label.

After graduating from Sacramento City College, Charters moved to New Orleans, where he began to study jazz but was soon drawn to the rural blues. He pursued his research by traveling extensively across the south making field recordings and interviewing blues survivors. Among those he discovered was the great Lightnin' Hopkins.

Charters' researches saw the light of day with the publication in 1959 of *The Country Blues*, which predated the works of Paul Oliver and most other blues scholars. It wasn't definitive, and subsequent research has rendered some of it out of date, but as Benjamin Filene noted in his *Romancing The Folk*, "*The Country Blues* was the first full-length treatment of the topic and its evocative style inspired thousands of whites to explore the music." Equally influential was its companion album, which introduced the likes of **Blind Lemon Jefferson**, **Blind Willie McTell** and **Leroy Carr** to many for the first time. Like the more feted *Harry Smith Anthology Of American Folk Music*, the disc was an important resource for other musicians, and Bob Dylan probably took "Fixin' To Die" from **Bukka White**'s version on the album.

As the Lomaxes had done, Charters also traveled outside the United States to collect folk music, visiting the Bahamas to make a series of field recordings that were later issued on Folkways as *The Music Of The Bahamas*. But if he will be remembered for one thing it will surely be for his rediscovery, after a lengthy search, of **Lightnin' Hopkins** in the late 1950s. The story goes later when Charters recorded him for Folkways, Hopkins was unfamiliar with the LP format and tried to leave the studio after just two numbers, believing the job was done. It was with some incredulity that he listened to Charters' explanation of the advances in technology that had created the long-playing format.

A tireless advocate and ambassador for the country blues, Charters recorded numerous blues artists, wrote learned sleeve notes and several other books, including *The Poetry Of The Blues* in 1963. The following year he edited *Sleepy John Estes 1929–1940*. Further publications, often accompanied by photos taken by his wife, Ann, include *The Bluesmen* (1967) and *Sweet As The Showers Of Rain: The Bluesmen Vol 2* (1977); *The Roots Of The Blues: An African Search* (1981); and *The Blues Makers* (1991).

More than just an academic and collector, Charters played in 1964 on the debut album by **Dave Van Ronk's Ragtime Jug Stompers**. Later that same year he and Danny Kalb formed their own band, the New Strangers. In 1967, he helped to launch the career of **Country Joe and The Fish**, producing their first album as they were mutating from a blues-influenced jug and folk act into a full-blown psychedelic rock band.

Charters has kept writing into his seventies, and in recent years has published *The Day Is So Long and The Wages So Small* and 2000's *Blues Faces*. In recognition of a lifetime's devotion to the music, he was inducted into the Blues Hall of Fame.

⊙ *Various Artists* **The Country Blues** Folkways
The original 1959 album, compiled by Samuel Charters, that helped to make songs such as "Walk Right In", "Statesboro Blues", "Stealin'" and "Fixin' To Die" familiar to a new generation.

Sam Chatmon

b Bolton, Mississippi, Jan 10, 1897; d Feb 2, 1983

The son of a slave, Sam Chatmon had several other brothers who were musicians, including Lonnie Chatmon, with whom he performed in the **Mississippi Sheiks**, and **Bo Carter**. He went on to enjoy an Indian summer to his long career during the 1960s folk-blues revival, when he was found to be the only surviving member of the large Chatmon family still to have his musical faculties intact.

Born in the Delta in 1897, Sam played for tips at parties and on street corners throughout Mississippi in the 1920s. His repertoire included rags, ballads and dance tunes as well as blues, and he also worked with **Charley Patton**, who may have been a blood relative. His talents as a sturdy singer and accomplished guitarist who also played mandolin and harmonica were first heard on record in the Mississippi Sheiks, who recorded more than eighty sides between 1930 and 1935 (see separate entry). After the demise of the Sheiks, Sam continued to recorded in a similar style with Lonnie as the Chatmon Brothers. In the early 1940s he moved to Hollandale, Mississippi, where he worked on a plantation.

Rediscovered in the early 1960s after two decades away from music – a blues enthusiast went looking for Bo Carter, whose widow told him instead about Sam – Chatmon once again became a popular performer with white audiences. Performing folk-blues standards as well as the minstrel songs he had learned in his youth, he recorded for Arhoolie and played at folk festivals, almost until his death in 1983 at the age of 86. Among his own compositions he claimed to have written "Cross Cut Saw", made famous first by Tommy McLennan and later Albert King, although his authorship has never been verified. He also had a son, Singin' Sam, who played bass guitar.

⊙ **Sam Chatmon 1970–74** Flyright
Twenty-two tracks and 76 minutes of great country blues, recorded when Sam Chatmon was well into his 70s – there's little or no sign that his powers were failing.

Clifton Chenier

b Opelousas, Louisiana, June 25, 1925; d Dec 12, 1987

The unchallenged King of Zydeco, Clifton Chenier fashioned his flamboyant accordion dance music from a blend of Cajun two-steps, New Orleans R&B, blues from Texas, and big band jazz, sung in a mix of French patois, English and creole. Although the development of any particular style of music can seldom be attributed to one individual, there is not a zydeco player alive who has not to some degree followed the template that Chenier created.

Chenier first learned to play the accordion from his father, a sharecropper and amateur musician. He was also influenced by early rural blues, and the recordings made by Cajun accordionist **Amédé Ardoin** during the 1920s and 1930s. By 1944, Clifton was performing with his brother Cleveland on *frottoir* (rub-board) in the dance halls of Lake Charles, Louisiana, but a year later he was working as a sugar cane cutter in New Iberia, and he spent most of the ensuing decade in Port Arthur, driving a truck and hauling pipe for oil companies. Playing only at weekends, he nevertheless absorbed a wealth of Cajun tunes from other players, and also came under the spell of the recordings of Muddy Waters, Lowell Fulson, Professor Longhair and Fats Domino among others, adding elements of blues and R&B to his sound.

After being discovered by J.R. Fulbright, who recorded him at the Lake Charles radio station KAOK in 1954, Chenier signed to Elko Records, which released such local hits as "Clifton's Blues" and "Louisiana Stomp". His national breakthrough came on Specialty in 1955, with a cover of **Professor Longhair**'s "Ay Tete Fille" ("Hey, Little Girl"), produced by Bumps Blackwell, best known for his work with Little Richard. Only after this success did he gave up his day job, putting together a touring band, the Zydeco Ramblers, which included blues guitarist Philip Walker. Chenier himself played guitar and harmonica as well as accordion, and in1956 signed with Chess Records in Chicago. The label put him on the road with **Etta James**, but his association with Chess was short-lived as by the late 1950s, the popularity of ethnic and regional music styles was in decline.

Chenier moved to Houston in 1958, and continued to record for the Louisiana label Zynn. He was rescued from obscurity in 1965, when the wife of his cousin, **Lightnin' Hopkins**, recommended him to Chris Strachwitz, who had just established the Arhoolie label. The two men differed about Chenier's musical direction, the label owner wanting him to concentrate on traditional Louisiana idioms and the artist wanting

to seek commercial success via a more straightforward R&B style. But they compromised and made some brilliant albums together over the next decade and more. Several of them, such as Chenier's Arhoolie debut, *Louisiana Blues And Zydeco*, featured one side of R&B material and a second side of French two-steps and waltzes.

During the mid-1970s, Chenier seemed to find a new sense of purpose. He embarked on a purple patch, releasing the fine 1976 album *Bogalusa Boogie* and following it three years later with *The Red Hot Louisiana Band*, named after his new combo featuring tenor saxophonist "Blind" John Hart and guitarist Paul Senegal. There are several fine live recordings of the band, and they toured regularly despite the fact that Chenier's health was failing, as a result of diabetes. In 1979, he had part of his foot amputated due to kidney disease, and was required to undergo dialysis treatment every three days, However, that didn't prevent him winning a Grammy for best zydeco album for 1982's *I'm Here!*, recorded for the Alligator label in eight hours flat in Bogalusa, Louisiana. The following year, he performed at the White House for Ronald Reagan, and he continued gigging until one week before his death in 1987, at the age of 62. His son, C.J. Chenier, then took over leadership of his Red Hot Louisiana Band, carrying on the family tradition.

⊙ **Louisiana Blues And Zydeco** Arhoolie
Waltzes, two-steps and fine blues aplenty adorn this collection, recorded between 1964 and 1967. Several of the tracks feature only accordion and percussion, but Chenier makes his instrument sound like an entire orchestra.

⊙ **Bogalusa Boogie** Arhoolie
Clifton Chenier recorded this album in a single day in 1975. Drenched in bayou funk, it features his brother Cleveland on rub-board.

⊙ **I'm Here** Alligator
"I'm the zydeco man", sings Clifton Chenier on the opening track of this 1982 recording with his Red Hot Louisiana Band – and you'd better believe it. He even delivers a blues accordion version of Glen Miller's "In The Mood".

⊙ **Zydeco Dynamite: The Best Of Clifton Chenier** Rhino
A beautifully packaged two-disc overview of Chenier's career, containing forty tracks he recorded for almost a dozen different labels between 1955 and 1984.

Chess Records

formed Chicago, 1950

The pre-eminent blues label of the 1950s and 1960s, at its height Chess Records created a near monopoly of Chicago music, releasing recordings by almost every major blues performer of the era from Muddy Waters and Howlin' Wolf through to black rock'n'rollers like Bo Diddley and Chuck Berry. The label's success was built on a dual strategy, combining an innate understanding of the popular preferences of African-American audiences and then an astute ability to market those tastes to a broader audience.

The name of Chess did not start appearing on records until 1950. By then, however, the Polish-born brothers Leonard and Phil Chess were already well established in the Windy City. They first gained a foothold by operating several night clubs, including the famous Macamba night club on the Southside, and then bought into Aristocrat Records in 1947. Their first releases on Aristocrat were jazz and jump blues, before the arrival of Muddy Waters in 1948 signaled a change of direction. Waters' second release, "I Can't Be Satisfied", was a major hit, prompting the Chess brothers to buy out the third partner in Aristocrat, Evelyn Aron. In 1950 they renamed the label Chess.

Slowly at first, the brothers began to assemble a roster of new urban blues stars. After Waters came Robert Nighthawk, Jimmy Rogers, Eddie Boyd and Howlin' Wolf. Just as significant was the arrival of Willie Dixon as the backroom genius who wrote, produced, arranged and played on many of Chess's greatest tracks. Working out of 2120 South Michigan Avenue – an address later immortalized as a song title by the Rolling Stones, who recorded there in the mid-1960s – the two brothers had well-defined separate roles. Phil handled much of the finance and administration, running the nightclubs and the record company offices, as well as their publishing arm, Arc. Leonard took a more hands-on approach with the artists, acting as talent scout, record producer and even radio plugger.

Before long, Chess was billing itself as "the home of the electric blues" and had added the subsidiary

Checker label, to which the brothers signed Sonny Boy Williamson, Elmore James and Little Walter. They were also smart enough to see the wind of change that was blown by rock'n'roll, and responded to the white stars such as Elvis Presley and Carl Perkins coming out of Sam Phillips' Sun stable in Memphis by signing Chuck Berry and Bo Diddley. Into the 1960s, the label was in the forefront of bringing a second generation of post-war urban bluesmen to prominence, including the likes of Otis Rush and Buddy Guy.

Chess also boasted a number of major female artists including Etta James, Fontella Bass, Koko Taylor and the criminally under rated Sugar Pie De Santo, and made some classic soul sides by the likes of Little Milton, Tommy Tucker, the Dells and Billy Stewart, although this side of Chess's operations has tended to be underplayed by purist-minded blues historians.

Leonard Chess died in 1969. Earlier that year, he and Phil had sold the label to GRT, where producers Ralph Bass and Gene Barge attempted to keep its spirit going. However, the best they could manage hit-wise was Chuck Berry's ghastly "My Ding-A-Ling". With its great reputation eroded, GRT closed down Chess in 1975, selling its back catalog to All Platinum Records. A decade later MCA acquired the rights and began an ambitious long-term reissue campaign. A further repackaging program was launched in 2005.

The role of Chess Records in the history of the post war blues cannot be over estimated. The label would have warranted a far longer entry here, were it not for the fact that all its key artists have their own extensive entries elsewhere in the book.

⊙ *Various Artists* **Chess Blues** (Chess)
More than a hundred prime Chess tracks, on four CDs. Many of the best-known songs and classics are here, but the set is cleverly chosen to present a genuine history of Chicago blues rather than just another rag-bag of greatest hits.

⊙ *Various Artists* **Chess Pieces** (Chess)
This excellent double-album overview of Chess's illustrious history spearheaded the latest 2005/2006 reissue programme.

All available on the box set *Chess Blues*

1 ROLLING STONE Muddy Waters (1950)
It may have been a variation on the old Delta classic "Catfish Blues", but it started a Chicago revolution.

2 ROCKET 88 Jackie Brenston (1951)
The much acclaimed "first rock'n'roll record", cut by Sam Phillips in Memphis, but licensed to Chess as Sun Records had yet to be born.

3 MY BABE Little Walter (1955)
Written by Willie Dixon, this peak in Little Walter's career found him outselling even Muddy Waters.

4 SMOKESTACK LIGHTNIN' Howlin' Wolf (1956)
A vocal of almost supernatural power, complemented by Hubert Sumlin's eerie guitar.

5 DON'T START ME TALKIN' Sonny Boy Williamson II (1956)

Sonny Boy at his sly best, on his first Chess session, backed by Muddy Waters' band.

6 BO DIDDLEY Bo Diddley (1955)
The beat is born.

7 MAYBELLINE Chuck Berry (1955)
Chuck's first record was originally titled "Ida Red". Thankfully he changed it at the last minute

8 FIRST TIME I MET THE BLUES Buddy Guy (1960)
Guy's first single for Chess, with Little Brother Montgomery on piano.

9 WANG DANG DOODLE Koko Taylor (1966)
"As hot as July jam," as the song's composer Willie Dixon put it.

10 I'D RATHER GO BLIND Etta James (1967)
Etta's greatest track was recorded not in Chicago, but at the Fame studios in Muscle Shoals.

Chicken Shack

formed Birmingham, England, 1966

For a brief while during the late 1960s, Chicken Shack were up there with Fleetwood Mac as a cornerstone of the British blues boom, sharing a label with them and a name-check in the Bonzo Dog Doo Dah Band's spoof "Can Blue Men Sing The Whites", via the immortal line "Got those John Mayall, Chicken Shack, Fleetwood Mac can't fail blues". They forged even closer ties when keyboardist and singer Christine Perfect married Fleetwood Mac bassist John McVie, although the driving force behind the group was not so much Perfect as the ebullient and idiosyncratic guitarist Stan Webb.

Having previously played in several obscure Midlands R&B groups, Webb and Perfect formed Chicken Shack in 1967, and immediately took off to Hamburg to work up their chops via a residency at the Star Club. On their return to Britain, the group signed to Mike Vernon's Blue Horizon label. Their debut album, *Forty Blue Fingers Freshly Packed And Ready To Serve*, appeared in 1968 and demonstrated Webb's large debt as a guitarist to Freddie King, Buddy Guy and B.B. King. The fol-

low-up, 1969's *OK Ken?*, featured more of Webb's own compositions and displayed his wacky humor with his impersonations of well-known personalities such as John Peel and Harold Wilson punctuating the tracks.

Chicken Shack tasted chart success in 1969, when Perfect's superb rendition of Etta James' "I'd Rather Go Blind" made the UK top twenty. However, she left soon after, initially to become a housewife but soon joining her new husband in Fleetwood Mac.

Although Webb continued without her, Chicken Shack never really recovered from the loss. Dropped by Blue Horizon, they suffered numerous line-up changes. Webb later joined Savoy Brown for a brief spell in the mid-1970s before forming Broken Glass and then the Stan Webb Band, although he has also repeatedly reformed Chicken Shack with different line-ups. Perfect made an entirely accurate prediction about him in 1968: "He's a blues man and nothing else. If the boom died tomorrow it wouldn't make any difference to Stan. He's only happy blues."

⊙ **Forty Blue Fingers Freshly Packed And Ready To Serve** Blue Horizon)
Packed with covers of songs associated with John Lee Hooker, Buddy Guy, B.B. King and Freddie King, Chicken Shack's 1968 debut album was probably their best, even if it doesn't include the classic "I'd Rather Go Blind".

⊙ **Very Best of Chicken Shack** Columbia
The best way to get hold of "I'd Rather Go Blind", which opens this 20-track selection from Chicken Shack's four Blue Horizon albums.

Eric Clapton

b Ripley, Surrey, May 30, 1945

Eric Clapton was just 21 when he recorded the seminal album of the British blues boom, with **John Mayall's Bluesbreakers**. Graffiti soon started appearing all over London proclaiming that "Clapton is God", and only Jimi Hendrix has ever rivaled his influence on his fellow guitarists. Over a long career he has since ranged over various different musical styles, but the blues has remained at the core of his musical being.

Raised in suburban Surrey in the immediate aftermath of World War II, Clapton fell in love with the blues after hearing **Big Bill Broonzy** in his early teens. From there he graduated to John Lee Hooker and Muddy Waters, and by the age of fifteen he had his first electric guitar. By 1962 he was playing a solo acoustic blues set in

west London pubs, already including much of the material he would reprise thirty years later on the *Unplugged* album.

After working his way through assorted obscure early British R&B bands, including the Roosters and Casey Jones and The Engineers, Clapton rose to prominence as Britain's pre-eminent blues guitarist as a member of the Yardbirds. Although live the band played a potent brand of blues and R&B – heard to good effect on the 1964 album *Five Live Yardbirds*, recorded at the Marquee Club – Clapton was never happy in the studio, as his purist blues instincts clashed with the band's search for commercial pop singles. He left in late 1965 claiming he wanted to play the blues "pure and sincere and uncorrupted" and joined John Mayall's band. Using a Gibson Les Paul to produce a round and mellow tone but at a high volume, he recorded the classic *John Mayall's Bluesbreakers With Eric Clapton*. Their only recording together, it remains arguably the most influential British blues album. Both Clapton's sustained wail and his gritty hard-edged attack were deeply rooted in his admiration for the Chicago blues style, and the album effectively launched the electric guitar sound that

---

Playlist
Eric Clapton

1 HAVE YOU HEARD (1966) from **John Mayall's Bluesbreakers With Eric Clapton**
Eric's solo doesn't come in until 3:25, but then he plays as if his life depends upon it.

2 CROSSROADS (1968) from **Wheels Of Fire**
The power trio at their peak, recorded live in San Francisco.

3 AFTER MIDNIGHT (1970) from **Eric Clapton**
A beautifully understated version of J.J. Cale's sparse, shuffling original.

4 BLUES POWER (1970) from **Eric Clapton**
The title says it all, but it rocks, too.

5 KEY TO THE HIGHWAY (1970) from **Layla And Other Assorted Love Songs**
Eric and Duane Allman take Big Bill Broonzy to places of which he never could have dreamed.

6 HAVE YOU EVER LOVED A WOMAN (1970) from **Layla And Other Assorted Love Songs**
Just when you thought ol' Slowhand's playing couldn't get

any better than "Key To The Highway", three tracks later it did.

7 THE SKY IS CRYING (1975) from **There's One In Every Crowd**
A menacing version of the Elmore James song that features some of Clapton's finest slide work.

8 NOBODY KNOWS YOU WHEN YOU'RE DOWN AND OUT (1992) from **Unplugged**
The steel-stringed acoustic is pulled out of the back of the cupboard for a lovely, unplugged barrelhouse-style version.

9 GROANING THE BLUES (1994) from **From The Cradle**
The Willie Dixon-composed highlight of Eric's first all-blues album since his days with John Mayall.

10 COME ON IN MY KITCHEN (2004) from **Me And Mr Johnson**
An entire album of Robert Johnson songs was a bold enterprise, but this solo acoustic performance proved Eric could sing the blues as well as play them.

was to go on dominating modern rock music long after the 1960s blues boom had faded.

In 1966, Clapton moved on again to form Cream. The band's repertoire included songs by Robert Johnson, **Skip James** and other bluesmen, which were used as the jumping-off point for long, freestyle improvisations that gave Clapton ample scope for extended solos, blasted out at incredible volume through huge banks of Marshall amps. A fuller account of the activities of both Mayall and Cream can be found under separate entries elsewhere in this book.

Clapton passed swiftly through several other groups, including **Blind Faith** and **Derek and the Dominos**, whose repertoire included Broonzy's "Key To The Highway", before embarking on a solo career. All his 1970s solo albums, like *461 Ocean Boulevard*, *There's One In Every Crowd* and *Slowhand*, mixed blues standards such as "Motherless Children" and "Steady Rollin' Man" with his own songs. Following battles with drink and drug problems, his oeuvre took a more middle-of-the-road turn in the 1980s, although he regularly returned to his blues roots on albums such as 1994's *From The Cradle*, and 2004's *Me And Mr Johnson* and *Sessions For Robert J*, both of which contained nothing but **Robert Johnson** covers. That was a project he said he'd always wanted to do, but had never felt mature enough. He described Johnson's music as "an old friend whose influence has driven me all my life".

Over the years Clapton has also guested and collaborated with a lot of his blues heroes, including B.B. King, with whom he recorded 2000's Grammy-winning *Riding With The King*, one of the biggest-selling blues albums of all time.

⊙ **Crossroads** Polydor
This spectacular 4-disc box set covers Clapton's band work with the Yardbirds, John Mayall, Cream et al, as well as his long and varied solo career. It includes all the classics such as "Layla", "Blues Power", "After Midnight", "Further On Up The Road", "Crossroads" and "I Shot the Sheriff".

⊙ **Blues** Polydor
A clever compilation of Eric Clapton's most blues-based tracks, comprising one disc of studio material and a second of live cuts.

⊙ **Martin Scorsese Presents The Blues: Eric Clapton** Polydor
Released in conjunction with Scorsese's 2003 series of blues films, this useful 10-track compilation includes material from Clapton's early days with Mayall, Cream, Blind Faith, and Derek and the Dominos, plus tracks with Howlin' Wolf and Duane Allman.

⊙ **Unplugged** Reprise
A pared-down acoustic gem from 1992, featuring covers of blues standards such as "Walkin' Blues", "San Francisco Bay Blues" and "Alberta", as well as a fine version of "Layla".

⊙ **From The Cradle** Reprise
Surprisingly, Eric Clapton didn't record his first all-blues album until this 1994 offering, featuring songs by Leroy Carr, Lowell Fulson, Elmore James, Freddie King and Muddy Waters.

⊙ **Riding With The King** Reprise
"God" teams up with the King (B.B. that is) on this slick 2000 collection of classic blues guitar duets, including "Ten Long Years", "Three O'Clock Blues" and a great acoustic version of Broonzy's "Key To The Highway".

⊙ **Me And Mr Johnson** Reprise
These tracks started out as jam sessions while Clapton was making another album in 2004 – but they turned out so well they grew into a record in their own right.

Albert Collins

b Leona, Texas, Oct 1, 1932; d Nov 24, 1993

Known variously as "the Iceman" and "the Razor Blade" but above all as "The Master of the Telecaster", Albert Collins was one of the great figures to emerge from the second wave of post war electric bluesmen. His influences included T-Bone Walker, John Lee Hooker and Gatemouth Brown, but he fused Mississippi, Chicago and Texas blues styles into an ice-cool guitar sound that was uniquely his own, characterized by ringing high notes, sustain and echo, a percussive attack that involved plucking the strings with his right hand, and an unusual minor key tuning that he learned from his cousin **Willow Young**. Yes, his singing voice was merely average, and some found the tone of his Telecaster unnecessarily harsh, but he remains among the most individual blues artists to have emerged in the post-1950s era.

The Master of the Telecaster: Mr Albert Collins

A cousin of **Lightnin' Hopkins**, Collins moved with his family to Houston just before World War II, where the likes of Johnny "Guitar" Watson and Johnny Copeland were near neighbors. Surprisingly, however, his early musical hero was the jazz organist Jimmy McGriff, and in his youth he took keyboard lessons, before switching to guitar in 1950. Playing in the same Houston nightclubs as Hopkins, he swiftly developed his own style, courtesy of his use of the capo and minor tunings, and the long guitar lead that allowed him to walk through the audience while still playing.

Collins formed his first band in 1952, which soon grew to become the ten-piece Rhythm Rockers, and he cut his debut single, "The Freeze", for the Houston-based Kangaroo label in 1958. The first of a series of releases with a sub-zero theme, it was followed by "Icy Blue", "Don't Lose Your Cool", "De-Frost" and "Frosty". The latter, the 1962 single that gave him his national breakthrough, was allegedly recorded with young Texan future rock'n'roll heroes **Johnny Winter** and **Janis Joplin** in attendance in the studio. The Arctic theme continued with "Sno-Cone" and "Thaw Out" but despite his success, Collins continued to work day jobs until the late 1960s, when he was lionized by the white blues-rock band, **Canned Heat**, who took him to California. Signing to Imperial Records, with Canned Heat's Bob "The Bear" Hite producing, he immediately achieved the wider exposure that he had previously been denied, opening for acts like the Allman Brothers at the famed Fillmore in San Francisco. His stock also jumped in rock circles when Jimi Hendrix cited his playing as an influence.

In the early 1970s he moved from Imperial to Tumbleweed Records, owned by the Eagles' producer Bill Szymczyk, though it was Joe Walsh who actually produced him. After the label folded in 1973, a lull in his career ensued, coinciding with a similarly quiet period in the popularity of the blues. However, the best was still yet to come. Signing to Alligator Records in 1978, he cut the splendid *Ice Pickin'*, with a superb band known as the Icepickers. A string of impressive albums for the label followed, featuring many songs co-written with his wife Gwen. These included two in-concert sets, 1981's *Frozen Alive!* and 1984's *Live In Japan*, both of which successfully captured the dynamic excitement of his live act. Then in 1985 he teamed up with Johnny Copeland and Robert

Cray (who had decided on a career as a bluesman after seeing Collins play at his high school prom) to record *Showdown!*, which won the ad hoc trio a Grammy award.

In 1990, with the blues enjoying another revival on the back of the success of Stevie Ray Vaughan, Collins signed with Virgin Records' Pointblank subsidiary. With the backing of a major label behind him, he appeared set for even greater success. His Pointblank debut, *Iceman*, appeared in 1991, and was a fine set that led to high-profile appearances at Carnegie Hall and with David Letterman. His final release, *Collins Mix*, was a compilation of his favorite past cuts re-recorded with the likes of **B.B. King** and **Branford Marsalis**. By then, however, he had been diagnosed with liver cancer. He died in 1993 in Las Vegas, where he had moved a decade earlier, at the age of 61.

⊙ **Ice Pickin'** Alligator
The 1978 album that served as Albert Collins' late breakthrough, including some storming guitar instrumentals as well as the superb "When The Welfare Turns Its Back On You".

⊙ **Frozen Alive!** Alligator
A 1981 live recording from the Union Bar in Minneapolis that captures the raw excitement of Collins' powerful concert performances.

⊙ **Showdown!** Alligator
Recorded with fellow guitarists Robert Cray and Johnny "Clyde" Copeland, a blues summit that actually works. Collins seldom gets to sing but he solos beautifully on all nine tracks.

⊙ **The Complete Imperial Recordings** EMI
This two-disc set of Albert Collins' 1969–70 recordings, many of them instrumentals, marks the moment when the "Master of the Telecaster" legend was born.

Ry Cooder

b Santa Monica, California, March 15, 1947

Arguably the most versatile musician of his generation, **Ry Cooder** has during his long career played rock'n'roll, Tex-Mex, Hawaiian, Dixieland, R&B, African guitar duets and Cuban music. This eclecticism has threatened to overshadow his importance as a blues popularizer, via a string of early 1970s' albums that introduced the country blues to a new and youthful rock'n'roll audience.

Having learned to play the guitar at a precociously young age, Cooder was hanging out at local folk clubs by his mid-teens, learning from the likes of Rev. Gary Davis and forging a reputation as something of a musicologist and blues scholar. By 1963 he was in a blues band with Jackie De Shannon, while two years later he formed the short-lived **Rising Sons** with **Taj Mahal**. He was soon in demand as a session musician, playing with the likes of Paul Revere & the Raiders, Randy Newman, Little Feat and countless others. He also briefly joined **Captain Beefheart**'s Magic Band, adding some stunning slide guitar to the 1967 album *Safe As Milk*.

A high-profile session playing slide guitar on **Mick Jagger**'s first solo hit, "Memo From Turner", from the soundtrack to the film *Performance*, led to further sessions with the Rolling Stones, playing on the albums *Let It Bleed* and *Sticky Fingers*. He's never seen fit to confirm or deny the story that he was approached as a potential replacement in the band for Brian Jones. Nonetheless, Keith Richards has freely admitted that he learned the open tuning that gave him the riff for "Honky Tonk Women" from Cooder.

Ry's solo debut came in 1970, with a self-titled album featuring songs by Leadbelly, Blind Willie Johnson, Sleepy John Estes and Woody Guthrie. His status as a cohort of the Stones gave him huge rock'n'roll cred, and provided a platform for him to take obscure country blues songs to an audience that might otherwise never have got to hear them. The follow-up, 1971's *Into The Purple Valley*, drew its repertoire largely from the same sources, but had a fuller sound, with Jim Keltner on drums and Jim Dickinson on bass. *Boomer's Story*, which appeared in 1972, followed a similar pattern, and completed what is often seen a as trilogy of early blues works.

1974's *Paradise And Lunch* expanded his horizons, and included a reggae-fied version of the Valentinos' "It's All Over Now", while *Chicken Skin Music* the following year found him embarking on a bold journey into Tex-Mex and Hawaiian music, and featured contributions from Flaco Jimenez and Gabby Pahinui. From there followed a series of genre albums that Cooder has since all but disowned, including *Jazz, Bop Till You Drop,*

Borderline, The Slide Area and 1987's *Get Rhythm*. After that he abandoned making solo records to concentrate on a lucrative sideline in film soundtracks.

Cooder briefly teamed up with Keltner, John Hiatt and Nick Lowe to form **Little Village** in 1992. However, his heart didn't seem to be in it, and he next embarked on a fascinating series of collaborative world music projects. While most stand outside the scope of this book, mention must be made of *Talking Timbuktu*, an album of guitar duets with the African musician **Ali Farka Touré**, on which the pair explored the connections between the music of Mali and Mississippi in thrilling fashion, and which justifiably won a Grammy award. Cooder then contributed to a sequence of highly successful Cuban albums, starting with 1997's *Buena Vista Social Club*. These may have little to do with his roots as a blues musician, but occasional bursts of his low, moaning slide guitar, often buried deep in the mix, come right out of his early passion for the music of the Delta.

In 2005, Cooder finally resumed his solo recording career, releasing the well-received concept album *Chavez Ravine*. From interviews it is clear that his love of authentic country blues and early R&B remains undimmed, but he has frequently expressed bitter disappointment at the direction modern blues music has taken, acidly suggesting that these days it has been reduced to a marketing tool for selling brands of jeans.

⦿ **Ry Cooder** Reprise
Ry's fine 1970 debut album paid tribute to his roots, with songs by Leadbelly, Sleepy John Estes and Blind Willie Johnson.

⦿ **Into The Purple Valley** Reprise
The second album in Cooder's early-1970s' trilogy, released in 1971, features songs by Leadbelly and Guthrie, alongside some wonderfully antiquated but evocative selections like "FDR In Trinidad" and "Taxes On The Farmer Feeds Us All".

⦿ **Boomer's Story** Reprise
Ry Cooder's third paean to a fast-disappearing America, holds terrific versions of "Dark End Of The Street" and "Comin' In On A Wing And A Prayer".

⦿ **Paradise And Lunch** Reprise
An inspired and unpredictable selection from 1974, including Ry's renditions of numbers by Mississippi Fred McDowell and Bobby Womack, and Earl Hines guesting on a dapper version of Blind Blake's "Diddie Wa Diddie".

Johnny Copeland

b Haynesville, Louisiana, March 27, 1937; d July 4, 1997

Johnny "Clyde" Copeland rivals his great friend Albert Collins to be considered the most significant Texas bluesman of his generation. As well as an intense and distinctive guitar sound, Copeland had the stronger voice, singing in a soulful, gospel-influenced style. However, not until he hit his forties, after decades of struggle, did his hard-edged Texan blues gain the success his talents had long deserved.

Copeland's father, a Louisiana sharecropper, died when his son was still young, and left him his guitar. When his family moved to Houston, Texas, he began singing with his friend Joe "Guitar" Hughes in a band called the Dukes of Rhythm. Performing at Shady's Playhouse, one of the city's leading blues clubs, Copeland attracted immediate attention for his huge, gospel-tinged voice, which was in stark – and noisy – contrast to the smooth, dry vocal style of such Texas blues heroes as T-Bone Walker and Clarence "Gatemouth" Brown.

His early recording career made more of his voice than his guitar-playing, and he recorded some top soul sides for Mercury, All Boy, Golden Eagle and various other labels, mostly in Houston but occasionally in Los Angeles. In 1965, he even cut a soul version of **Bob Dylan**'s "Blowin' In The Wind".

By 1975, Copeland had moved to New York, where he played clubs in Harlem and Greenwich Village by night while working a day job in a burger joint. Then in 1977 he signed to Rounder Records, and released the horn-laden jazz-blues album *Copeland Special*. From that moment he never looked back, touring internationally and recording prodigiously, proving to be not only a generously talented guitarist and vocalist but also a charismatic front man and an excellent songwriter.

Eight albums for Rounder followed, including *Bringin' It All Back Home*, recorded live on a tour of Africa. In 1985 he also made *Showdown!* for the Alligator label with Albert Collins and Robert Cray, which won a Grammy.

The early 1990s found Copeland on Verve Records for the excellent *Catch Up With The Blues*,

but sadly time was running out. In 1994, he was diagnosed with a heart defect inherited from the father he had hardly known, and underwent major surgery. He was fitted with an experimental heart pump and continued to tour when not hospitalized, taking his teenage daughter **Shemekia** on the road with him to open his shows. In January 1997, he underwent a long-awaited heart transplant, and for six months it appeared the operation had been a success. But when complications developed, he died undergoing further surgery in July that year, at the age of 60.

⊙ **Copeland Special** Rounder
The first of Johnny Copeland's seven albums for Rounder, released in 1977, was a sure-fire classic that won him a W.C. Handy award.

⊙ **Honky Tonkin'** Bullseye Blues Classics
An excellent compilation drawn from the five albums Johnny Copeland recorded for Rounder during the 1980s.

⊙ **Houston Roots** Ace
The best available package of Johnny Copeland's early singles.

⊙ **Catch Up With The Blues** Verve
This solid Copeland outing from 1994 features guest appearances by Clarence "Gatemouth" Brown, Lonnie Brooks and Joe "Guitar" Hughes.

Shemekia Copeland

b Harlem, New York, 1979

Since her late-1990s emergence as a teenage singer of rare blues passion, **Shemekia Copeland** has reinvented the tradition of the big-voiced blues diva. Her volcanic delivery and from-the-gut realism has found critics comparing her to a latter-day Etta James, while Robert Plant even dared to suggest she could be "the next Tina Turner".

Born in New York in 1979, she came from sturdy blues stock, as the daughter of Texan bluesman **Johnny Copeland**. He put her on stage at Harlem's famed Cotton Club when she was eight, though she herself recalls mere embarrassment rather than an early desire to sing. By the time she was fifteen, however, her father had been diagnosed with a serious heart disease, and she began to accompany him on tour, not only looking after him in his illness but

MONDAVI ARTS

Shemekia Copeland prepares to fly

also opening for him on stage. "It was like a switch went off in my head," she later recalled, "Suddenly I wanted to sing. It became a want and a need and I had to do it." Though only 16, she already had what one critic described as a "blast-furnace" of a voice. Three years later her ailing father was dead. She has since come to believe that he went on the road during his illness in order to get her career launched before he went. "Dad wanted me to think I was helping him out by opening his shows when he was sick, but really, he was doing it all for me. He would go out and do gigs so I would get known. He went out of his way to get me that exposure," she has said.

Shemekia's debut album, *Turn The Heat Up*, appeared on Alligator Records in 1997, shortly after her father's death. She has since followed it with 2000's *Wicked*, which included a duet with one of her heroines, **Ruth Brown**, 2002's *Talking To Strangers*, produced by **Dr. John**, and 2005's *The Soul Truth*, produced by **Steve Cropper**. All display a powerful fusion of rock, soul and blues, sung with an ever-present sizzling emotional intensity.

Having also developed as an original songwriter, she stands today as one of blues music's brightest hopes for the future, with tradition at its core

but with a thoroughly contemporary attitude. "My music is rooted in blues, but it's different. I'm singing about my era. I'm here and I'm singing about now and not yesterday."

⊙ **Talking To Strangers** Alligator
It took Dr. John in the producer's chair, for her third album in 2002, to get the best out of Shemekia Copeland's full-tilt side and to sidestep the more obvious blues diva clichés.

⊙ **The Soul Truth** Alligator
Shemekia's funkiest, most mature outing, from 2005, is drenched with a strong flavor of Memphis, courtesy of Steve Cropper's production and guitar playing.

Elizabeth Cotten

b Chapel Hill, North Carolina, Jan 5, 1895 (sometimes given as 1893); d June 29, 1987

Although **Elizabeth "Libba" Cotten** was essentially a folk musician, her African-American heritage meant that her style inevitably had a deep connection with the blues. Best-known for "Freight Train", which she wrote when she was twelve, she did not actually record the song until more than a half a century later, after she was discovered by Mike Seeger during the folk-blues revival of the 1950s. She then began her performing career at the age of 68 and continued into her 90s.

Born in North Carolina in the final decade of the 19th century – the exact year is the subject of some debate, although 1895 is most widely accepted – Elizabeth began playing her brother's banjo around the age of eight. She soon moved on to the guitar, developing her own playing method, picking out the chords with her left hand using just two fingers with the instrument laid across her lap.

At the age of twelve she went into domestic service, and saved enough money to buy her own guitar. The timeless "Freight Train" was one of her first compositions, but if she had any thoughts of pursuing a musical career (and there is no evidence that she did), they were shelved when she married Frank Cotten and had her first child, Lillie, at the age of fifteen.

With her family she moved between Washington DC and New York, seeking domestic work. She also joined the church and put her guitar skills on hold for 25 years. After her divorce in 1940, she went to live with Lillie and her five grandchildren in Washington DC, where she worked in a department store. It was there that an extraordinary turn of events took place. One day, she found a lost little girl wondering around the store and returned her to her mother. The girl was Peggy Seeger, the younger sister of Pete Seeger, and Cotten went to work for the family, which was already prominent in folk music circles. When Peggy began learning the guitar, it revived Cotten's interest, and she began to play again, rediscovering an incredibly dextrous finger-picking style.

In 1957, another member of the family, Peggy's brother **Mike Seeger**, produced Cotten's first album for Folkways, *Folk Songs And Instrumentals With Guitar*, which included the memorable "Freight Train". Three years later, Cotten and Seeger performed a concert togeth-

er, and she went on to become a great favorite at folk festivals, mingling her songs with stories about her long life. She also toured with Taj Mahal among others, although she did not leave domestic service until 1970.

Further albums for Folkways followed with *Shake Sugaree* and *When I'm Gone* before 1984's *Elizabeth Cotten, Live!* won her a Grammy award at the age of 89. She gave her last concert at the 1986 Philadelphia Folk Festival, and died the following year.

⊙ Freight Train And Other North Carolina Folk Songs And Tunes Folkways

Elizabeth Cotten's first album, recorded by Mike Seeger in her bedroom in 1957, has been reissued under a different title, but still sounds every bit as wonderful.

⊙ Shake Sugaree Folkways

The 2005 expanded CD reissue contains 26 tracks recorded in 1965 and 1966, ten of them previously unreleased.

Elizabeth Cotten. She could have been a truly great roadie. But became a genius of fingerpicking country-blues guitar instead

REDFERNS

James Cotton

b Tunica, Mississippi, July 1, 1935

Having learned the blues harp from **Sonny Boy "Rice Miller" Williamson, James Cotton** replaced Junior Wells in Muddy Waters' band when he was 19 years old. Over the next five years, he playing on several of Waters' best Chess sides of the late 1950s, including the definitive version of "I've Got My Mojo Working". He then went on to forge a solo career with his tough, high-octane harp playing and dry, roared vocals.

Cotton decided to become a blues harpist as a boy, after hearing Sonny Boy Williamson's *King Biscuit Hour* shows on Radio KFFA, broadcast out of Helena, Arkansas. As an eight-year-old he was already good enough to earn more money in tips playing outside juke joints on a weekend than his father made driving a tractor in a fortnight.

With his parents' blessing, he moved into Williamson's home when he was nine, and learned as an apprentice to the master. At fifteen, he was gigging in Memphis with Joe Willie Wilkins and Willie Nix, and by 1952 had his own fifteen-minute slot on the city's KWEM station. The following year, **Sam Phillips**, who at the time was just setting up his Sun label, recorded him on the single "Straighten Up Baby" – on which Cotton apparently played drums rather than harp – and again in 1954 on "Cotton Crop Blues".

Later that year, **Muddy Waters** and his band played in Memphis, minus a harmonica player, as both Junior Wells and Little Walter were working back in Chicago, and Cotton was asked to deputize. With Phillips and Sun Records now obsessed with the new sound of rock'n'roll rather than blues, Cotton took little persuading to accompany Waters back to Chicago. There he enrolled full-time in Waters' band, Little Walter having embarked on a career as a solo artist with Chess and Wells about to disappear into the army for two years.

Initially, Cotton's role was for touring purposes only, as Chess continued to insist on re-summoning Little Walter on most of Waters' sessions. However, by 1958 Cotton was blowing on such Waters studio recordings as "She's Nineteen Years Old" and "Close To You". It was also Cotton's sug-gestion that Waters added an Ann Cole tune, "Got My Mojo Working", to his repertoire, and although he didn't play on the studio recording (Little Walter again), he did perform on the magnificent live version on the album, *Muddy Waters At Newport 1960*.

Cotton remained with Waters until he began to develop a solo career during the mid-1960s, touring Europe and signing with Verve for the 1967 release of the first of four albums for the label, *Cut You Loose*, recorded with a band that included guitarist Luther Tucker and drummer Sam Lay. Adapting his sound to the changing times, he added rock elements to his blues on 1970's *Taking Care Of Business*, on Capitol, produced by **Todd Rundgren**, and soul flavors on 1974's *100 Per Cent Cotton*, on Buddah Records, produced by New Orleans legend Allen Toussaint. A second Toussaint-produced album followed with 1975's suitably-titled *High Energy*.

In 1984 he signed to Alligator, releasing the excellent *High Compression*, which combined traditional Chicago blues with more funk-driven, horn-inflected material. The same label also teamed him with three other harp players, Junior Wells, Carey Bell and Billy Branch, for *Harp Attack!* Accompanied by Pinetop Perkins on piano, Sammy Lawhorn on guitar and drummer Sam Lay, he also recorded *Take Me Back* for Blind Pig Records, a themed set of blues standards subsequently covered by rock'n'roll bands, conceived as an attempt "to set the record straight."

In later years, throat disease lessened the impact of Cotton's formerly ferocious voice but his harp playing was relatively unaffected, as can be heard on his 1995 return to Verve for *Living The Blues*, which featured guest appearances by Dr. John and Joe Louis Walker.

⊙ **100 Per Cent Cotton** Buddah
Vintage, high-voltage R&B from James Cotton, recorded in 1974 and produced by Allen Toussaint.

⊙ **High Compression** Alligator
Blues-drenched raspy vocals and wailing harp from 1984, the set ranges from the slow burn of "23 Hours Too Long" to the storming "Diggin' My Potatoes".

⊙ **Take Me Back** Blind Pig
Although this 1987 album has divided James Cotton's fans, the choice of material is great and the sidemen exemplary.

Ida Cox

**b Toccoa, Georgia, Feb 25, 1896;
d Nov 10, 1967**

A classic early blues queen, **Ida Cox** began recording in 1923 in a passionate brooding vocal style that was based on emotion rather than prettiness. Her career effectively came to an end in 1944 when she suffered a stroke, although she made a partial comeback and was recorded as late as 1961, and traces of her early power were still evident.

Little is known of the early life of Ida Prather – there are varying accounts of her precise birth date – but it's known she left Georgia as a teenager to sing with traveling vaudeville shows and married fellow minstrel performer Adler Cox. During the early 1920s, she reportedly worked with **Jelly Roll Morton**, while in 1923 she signed to Paramount Records in the rush to sign new blues divas in the wake of the success of Mamie Smith's "Crazy Blues" three years earlier. Over the next six years she cut 78 sides for the label, often accompanied by pianist Lovie Austin, the intense trumpet of Tommy Ladnier and occasionally her piano-playing husband, Jesse Crump. Delivered in a moaning voice that at times turned into a hypnotic drone, many of her best-known recordings were obsessed with mortality, including "Death Letter Blues", "Black Crepe Blues", "Graveyard Bound Blues" and "Coffin Blues". Another memorable title was "Wild Women Don't Have The Blues" and she also cut tracks for assorted other labels, under several different pseudonyms, including Velma Bradley, Kate Lewis and Julia Powers.

For some reason, after 1929 Cox was largely absent from the recording studios, although she toured extensively and was recruited by John Hammond in 1939 for the second of his legendary Spirituals to Swing concerts at New York's Carnegie Hall. Those appearances having restored her profile, she went on to record with jazz artists including Charlie Christian, Lionel Hampton, Fletcher Henderson, Red Allen and Hot Lips Page. A stroke in 1944 forced her into retirement, although she was persuaded back into the studio for some welcome and surprisingly strong final recordings for Riverside in 1961.

⊙ **The Essential Ida Cox** Classic Blues
Two discs that hold three dozen classic Ida Cox tracks from the 1920s, including the splendid "Wild Women Don't Have The Blues".

Robert Cray

b Columbus, Georgia, Aug 1, 1953

R obert Cray emerged in the 1980s as a key figure in the latter-day guitar blues revival then also sweeping the likes of Stevie Ray Vaughan to fame. A fine guitarist in a style clearly influenced by Albert Collins, Peter Green and at times Jimi Hendrix, he's also a sweet soul vocalist. His blues can be pure, but are also eclectically mixed with soul, rock, jazz and R&B influences. Over the last quarter of a century he has matured from a hip young gunslinger to become a senior ambassador for the blues tradition.

Having grown up listening to his parent's Ray Charles and gospel records, Cray formed his first band in Portland at the age of 21. In the early 1980s the band relocated first to Seattle and then to San Francisco, after recording a debut album, *Who's Been Talking*, for Tomato Records. Although the label promptly folded, the band continued to gig prodigiously and played some high-profile support slots for Muddy Waters before his death in 1983. That helped to secure a new record deal with Hightone, whose first fruits, the 1983 album *Bad Influence*, made an immediate impact. That same year, Cray toured with John Lee Hooker and Willie Dixon. In 1985, he enjoyed chart action with *False Accusations*, and also recorded the three-way *Showdown!* for Alligator with Johnny Copeland and Albert Collins. *Strong Persuader* came the following year, by which time Cray had signed to Mercury records. It was among the top-selling blues albums of the decade, won him a Grammy award and crossed over to a white rock audience, with Cray's face appearing on the cover of *Rolling Stone*.

By now, Cray's peers among the ranks of white blues-rock guitarists were mightily impressed with what he was doing, too. Keith Richards invited him to perform in the *Hail! Hail! Rock'n'Roll* concert and film tribute to Chuck Berry, and he also appeared with Tina Turner. Eric Clapton covered

and worked with B.B. King on 1993's *Blues Summit*.

Cray's own fine run of Mercury recordings continued with *Don't Be Afraid Of The Dark* in 1988 and *Midnight Stroll* in 1990, which strayed deep into soul and R&B territory. *I Was Warned* appeared in 1992, while the following year's *Shame And A Sin* featured a guest appearance by Albert Collins. *Some Rainy Morning* in 1995 represented something of a departure, being a soul-drenched vocal album with hardly a trace of his trademark guitar licks, while *Sweet Potato Pie* two years later featured the

his "Bad Influence" in 1986, and subsequently invited Cray both to play on his *Journeyman* album and to appear at his 1991 Royal Albert Hall concert series. The pair also penned a song together, "Old Love", which appeared on Clapton's 1992 *Unplugged* album. It wasn't only white rock musicians who wanted some of what Cray had got. He also featured on **John Lee Hooker**'s late-flowering albums *The Healer*, *Mr Lucky* and *Boom Boom*,

Memphis Horns. That was the last of seven albums in eleven years for Mercury, before Cray moved to Ryko for *Take Your Shoes Off* and *Shoulda Been Home*, both of which further emphasized his sweetly soulful voice. Another move, to Sanctuary, produced 2003's *Time Will Tell*, an even more diverse collection that found him playing an electric sitar on one track, while 2005's *Twenty* took its title from

Playlist
Robert Cray

1 WHEN THE WELFARE TURNS ITS BACK ON YOU (1980) from **Who's Been Talkin'**
A great cover of the Albert Collins song, from Young Bob's precocious debut.

2 BAD INFLUENCE (1983) from **Bad Influence**
This tale of love and lust from Cray's second album was swiftly covered by Eric Clapton.

3 STRONG PERSUADER (1987) from **Strong Persuader**
Stinging urban blues and brassy Southern soul in perfect alignment.

4 SMOKING GUN (1987) from **Strong Persuader**
A top forty hit from a Grammy-winning album.

5 ACROSS THE LINE (1988) from **Don't Be Afraid Of The Dark**
Standout blues shuffle from an album that found Cray moving heavily in a slick soul direction.

6 THE FORECAST (CALLS FOR PAIN) (1990) from **Midnight Stroll**
Edgy, upbeat, soul-blues that sums up why some love Robert Cray, while others think he's a sell-out.

7 I WAS WARNED (1992) from **I Was Warned**
Cray at his most dark and brooding.

8 TRICK OR TREAT (1997) from **Sweet Potato Pie**
He's not just a guitar-slinger. He can sing Otis Redding, too.

9 BACK DOOR SLAM (2004) from **Time Will Tell**
"When I play guitar they all know my name…"

10 TWENTY (2005) from **Twenty**
A gripping, self-penned anti-war ballad about a young GI in Iraq.

one of a growing number of anti-war songs in his repertoire.

Over the years, Cray's approach has come in for a fair amount of criticism from blues purists (or the "bluenatics" as he calls them). More open-minded commentators recognize an important artist with a significant vision to take the blues into a new century as a living and vibrant form, rooted in tradition but not hidebound by it.

⊙ Bad Influence Hightone
The 1983 breakthrough that announced the arrival of Robert Cray as a genuine talent was full of articulate songs, Stax-influenced arrangements and gospelized vocals.

⊙ Strong Persuader Mercury
Cray's 1986 major-label debut was dripping with sting-ing, heartfelt blues, tempered by classic soul and R&B influences, courtesy of the Memphis Horns.

⊙ Sweet Potato Pie Mercury
An addictive combination of blues, rock and soul from 1997. While there's less of Cray's explosive guitar playing than some might prefer, he compensates with some of his finest ever vocals, especially on a brave rendition of Otis Redding's "Trick Or Treat".

Pee Wee Crayton

b Rockdale, Texas, Dec 18, 1914; d June 25, 1985

An imaginative, at times even dazzling elec-tric guitarist, **Pee Wee Crayton** was heavily influenced by **T-Bone Walker**, but tran-scended being a mere imitator with an aggressive and attacking style that was all his own.

The youthful Connie Crayton, born in Texas in 1914, relocated like T-Bone Walker to Los Angeles when he was 21, and subsequently moved north to San Francisco. Not until after World War II did he begin his recording career, signing in 1948 to the LA-based Modern Records, owned by the Bihari Brothers. He enjoyed almost immediate suc-cess when the instrumental "Blues After Hours", based fairly shamelessly on Erskine Hawkins' "After Hours", topped the R&B charts. Although it was followed by the urgent "Texas Hop", "I Love You So", "Pee Wee's Boogie" and "Poppa Stoppa", the hits then dried up, perhaps because he concentrated exclusively on instrumentals. Crayton moved to Aladdin and then in 1954 to Imperial, where he was produced in New Orleans

by **Dave Bartholomew** on such excellent sides as "Every Dog Has His Day", "You Know Yeah" and "Runnin' Wild", on which his stinging guitar was accompanied by characteristic blasts of Crescent City horns.

Crayton next moved to VeeJay in Chicago, releas-ing 1957's brilliant "I Found My Peace Of Mind", and recorded for the Jamie, Guyden and Smash labels during the 1960s. Having re-emerged in 1971 on Vanguard with the album *Things I Used To Do*, he continued touring until his death in 1985.

⊙ Blues After Hours Indigo
This budget-priced compilation of the young Pee Wee Crayton finds him in fine form, churning out shuffling blues tracks during the late 1940s.

Cream

formed in London, 1966

Along with the Jimi Hendrix Experience, **Cream** invented the power-rock trio that became so widely imitated during the early 1970s. Yet **Eric Clapton** originally based the line-up on the trio led by blues guitarist **Buddy Guy**, and their live performances were notable for long blues-rock improvisations around such classic tunes as Skip James's "I'm So Glad", Robert Johnson's "Crossroads" and Albert King's "Born Under A Bad Sign".

The impetus for the band came in the first instance from drummer **Ginger Baker**, formerly of Alexis Korner's Blues Incorporated and the **Graham Bond Organisation**. He approached Clapton shortly after the guitarist had left **John Mayall's Bluesbreakers**, and Clapton in turn sug-gested completing the line-up with bassist **Jack Bruce**, who also became lead singer and principal songwriter. The trio initially saw themselves as a blues-rock combo, playing lengthy blues jams with extended solos. Their debut album, *Fresh Cream*, was released in December 1966, and mixed blues standards with quirky, original psychedelic-fla-vored songs. The follow-up, 1967's *Disraeli Gears*, leaned more towards original compositions by Bruce and his lyricist Pete Brown, and included such enduring rock classics as "Sunshine Of Your Love", "Strange Brew" and "Tales Of Brave Ulysses", on which Clapton played one of the first wah-wah guitar solos. That album established Cream as one of the biggest acts in America, where they toured endlessly. Live they were a quite different proposition from the band heard on *Disraeli Gears*, taking simple blues riffs and constructing around them extravagant, exploratory jams, with "Crossroads" as one of their party pieces. A feel of what their live sets were like was captured on the 1968 double album *Wheels Of Fire*, half of which was an in-concert performance recorded in San Francisco.

However, increasing friction between Bruce and Baker wore the band down, and shortly after the release of *Wheels Of Fire*, Cream announced its intention to disband following two farewell concerts at London's Royal Albert Hall at the end of the year. A posthumous album, *Goodbye*, appeared in 1969 and included a superb cover of "Born Under A Bad Sign", while further live recordings were dredged out of the vaults.

Cream had existed for just two years. Yet in that brief time they transformed the nature of blues-rock, spawned hundreds of copycat bands and helped to promote the legend of such blues greats as Robert Johnson to a white rock audience that might otherwise never have encountered such music. The three original members went on to other projects. Clapton's subsequent exploits were by far the most successful, and are recorded under his individual entry elsewhere in this book. Baker formed the band Air Force and later worked extensively with Nigerian musicians such as Fela Kuti, while Bruce released a string of fine solo albums that became cult classics, before heading off in a more jazz-oriented direction. In 2005, the three original members came together again for triumphant appearances at the Albert Hall, the scene of their farewell 38 years earlier. The storming shows were captured on an excellent CD and DVD.

⊙ **Disraeli Gears** Polydor
Cream's 1967 masterpiece consisted mostly of psyche-delic pop songs, but the stellar playing of all three members showed they were as adept at tight three-minute songs as on long extended jams.

⊙ **Wheels Of Fire** Polydor
This 1968 double album is particularly valuable for its live half, which includes "Crossroads" and "Spoonful".

⊙ **Those Were The Days** Polydor
A magnificent 1997 four-disc box set, repackaging Cream's released work from 1966 to 1969 in its entirety, with additional bonus material.

Arthur "Big Boy" Crudup

**b Forest, Mississippi, Aug 24, 1905;
d March 28, 1974**

Astonishingly, **Arthur Crudup** did not learn to play the guitar until he was in his 30s, but he went on to become a popular bluesman across the South, singing in a high, expressive voice. He also attained immortality by writing "That's All Right", covered by **Elvis Presley** as his first recording in 1954.

Crudup's first musical experience came singing gospel in church choirs. He didn't pick up a guitar until 1937, when he was taught to play by a local bluesman, Papa Harvey, in Clarksdale, Mississippi. He performed at parties, before moving to Chicago in 1939 in the hope of a better life away from the poverty of the South. Supposedly, he lived at first in a packing crate beneath an elevated train track while playing for tips on street corners. Music publisher and producer Lester Melrose discovered him there, and tried him out by inviting him to sing at a party at Tampa Red's house in 1941. Crudup passed the audition, and began recording soon after, releasing the country blues sides "If I Get Lucky" and "Black Pony Blues". Over the next few years he recorded some 80 songs for RCA, working not only in a Delta blues style but also crossing over into Chicago blues and R&B, and recording some of the first blues to feature an electric guitar. Several of his songs became blues standards. They included not only "That's All Right", which he first recorded in 1946, backed by bassist Ransom Knowling and drummer Judge Riley, but also "My Baby Left Me" and "I'm So Glad You're Mine", both of which were also recorded by Presley. Another of his songs, "Mean Old Frisco", was later performed by Brownie McGhee and B.B. King among others, while further notable titles included "Rock Me Mama", "Who's Been Foolin' You", "Keep Your Arms Around Me" and "Ethel Mae".

At some point late in the 1940s, Crudup realized that he was not being paid songwriting royalties, and fell out with Melrose. He angrily returned to Mississippi, where he recorded for the Jackson-based Trumpet label as Elmer James, as well as cutting more sides in Chicago for Checker as Percy Lee Crudup. He also toured with Sonny Boy Williamson (Rice Miller) and the real Elmore

James. However, despite his breach with Melrose, he was still contracted to RCA/Victor, and he continued recording for the label into the early 1950s. By the time Presley recorded "That's All Right" in 1954, Crudup was fading from view, partly due to changing musical tastes but also due to a self-imposed retreat from the music industry due to his continuing anger at being ripped-off. By the late 1950s he was working as a farm laborer in Mississippi. When Bobby Robinson's Harlem-based Fire label attempted to make an album of new versions of his old hits in 1961, recording had to be delayed until the picking season was over

– which suggests that his complaints that he had little or nothing to show for being Elvis Presley's favorite bluesman were entirely justified.

Crudup made a comeback in the 1960s, recording for Delmark – after Big Joe Williams had intervened on his behalf with label owner Bob Koester – and for Liberty. He toured the UK in 1969 and continued to play blues and folk festivals until he died at the age of 68 in 1974.

⊙ **That's All Right Mama** RCA
Twenty tracks that Arthur Crudup recorded for RCA by Lester Melrose between 1941 and 1953, including of course that song.

D

Daddy Stovepipe

b Mobile, Alabama, April 12, 1867;
d Nov 1, 1963

Daddy Stovepipe may well have been the earliest-born blues artist to record, for when he cut his first sides in 1924 he was already 57 years old. Remarkably enough, he was still playing in Chicago almost forty years later. During his long career, he also worked under the names Jimmy Watson and the Rev. Alfred Pitts. (He should not be confused with Stovepipe No 1, who was Sam Jones, a 1920s Cincinnati-based one-man-band, or Sweet Papa Stovepipe, whose real name was McKinley Peebles.)

Johnny Watson took his stage name from the top hat he wore as an itinerant street musician. The first known mention of him comes around the turn of the century, when he was playing 12-string guitar in a mariachi band in Mexico. From there he found employment with the **Rabbit's Foot Minstrels**, a touring tent show that at different times also employed Ma Rainey and Brownie McGhee. By the early 1920s he was working as a one-man band on Maxwell Street in Chicago, while in 1924 he traveled to Richmond, Indiana, to cut two primitive blues sides, including "Sundown Blues", accompanying himself on guitar and rack harmonica. Three years later he was recorded by a mobile unit in Birmingham, Alabama, accompanied by a whistler on sides that were issued under the name Sunny Jim and Whistlin' Joe. 1931 found him back in Chicago, recording twelve sides for Vocalion with the singer and jug player Mississippi Sarah, also known as Mrs Daddy Stovepipe and in real life Sarah Watson. The husband and wife duo recorded four more sides for Bluebird in 1935, including "Greenville Strut",

a reference to the town where they now lived, but Sarah died two years later. Although he was now 70, Daddy Stovepipe took to the road again, playing in a zydeco band in Texas and working once again with Mexican mariachi musicians. By 1948, he was back once more in Chicago, and playing on Maxwell Street. Rediscovered there in 1961, now in his nineties, he recorded the album *Blues From Maxwell Street*, but died two years later.

⊙ *Various Artists* **Alabama Black Country Dance Bands 1924–1949** Document
A compilation that includes Daddy Stovepipe's early recordings, with tracks featuring both Mississippi Sarah and Whistlin' Pete (the name by which Whistlin' Joe was better known).

Rev. Gary Davis

b Laurens, South Carolina, April 30, 1896; d May 5, 1972

Perhaps the greatest finger-picking guitar stylist of them all, with a repertoire that encompassed spirituals, marches, ragtime, jazz, blues, minstrel songs and hokum, **Rev. Gary Davis,** sometimes billed as Blind Gary Davis, made some toweringly fine recordings for ARC in the 1930s but spent long years away from music before his rediscovery in the 1950s. He went on to exert a huge influence on the folk blues revival of the 1960s, inspiring dozens of young guitarists including Jerry Garcia, Ry Cooder, Dave Van Ronk, Jorma Kaukonen, Dave Bromberg and Stefan Grossman. He also left a formidable body of songs, both secular and spiritual, that have been recorded by Bob Dylan, Donovan, Taj Mahal, Jackson Browne, Peter Paul & Mary and the Grateful Dead, among others.

One of eight children, Gary Davis was raised by his grandmother on a farm near Greenville. He was partially blind from childhood, but taught himself to play the guitar by the time he was six, making his first instrument from a pie pan and a broomstick. In an interview with Sam Charters more than half a century later, he recalled: "The first time I ever heard a guitar, I thought it was a brass band coming through. I was a small kid and I asked my mother what it was and she said that was a guitar."

Although he lost his sight completely, he learned to read Braille, and found comfort not only in

REDFERNS

Playlist
Rev. Gary Davis

1 SAMSON & DELILAH (1960) from **Harlem Street Singer**
Also recorded by Blind Willie Johnson, under the title "If I Had My Way, I Would Tear This Building Down".

2 DEATH DON'T HAVE NO MERCY (1960) from **Harlem Street Singer**
This hauntingly bleak song was memorably covered by the Grateful Dead.

3 TWELVE GATES TO THE CITY (1935) from **Meet You At The Station: The Vintage Recordings**
An old Southern spiritual from Davis' first recorded session, inspired by the Book of Revelation.

4 CANDY MAN (1957) from **Pure Religion And Bad Company**
Definitely not the same song that Sammy Davis Jr. sang in *Willy Wonka And The Chocolate Factory*.=

5 BAD COMPANY (BROUGHT ME HERE) (1961) from **Say No To The Devil**
Probably the best version of a song that seemed to turn up on just about every record Davis made after his rediscovery.

6 COCAINE BLUES (1957) from **Pure Religion And Bad Company**
First cut in 1929 by Luke Jordan, who's usually credited as the composer, it was the Rev's version that inspired the likes of Dylan to cover the song.

7 PURE RELIGION (1957) from **Pure Religion And Bad Company**
A call-and-response arrangement in which Davis's ragtime guitar provides the response.

8 I AM THE LIGHT OF THE WORLD (1935) from **Meet You At The Station: The Vintage Recordings**
"I am the light of the world. Whoever follows me will never walk in darkness, but will have the light of life." John 8:12

9 CRUCIFIXION (1957) from **Pure Religion And Bad Company**
It's hard to tell if Davis is singing or preaching. Either way, it's a spellbinding vocal.

10 HESITATION BLUES (1957) from **Pure Religion And Bad Company**
"Lord, if the river was made of whiskey an' I was a duck, I'd just swim to the bottom an' I'd never come up."

music but in a strong religious conviction. By the late 1920s, he was working as a street singer in Durham, North Carolina, and building his formidable repertoire. His exemplary guitar technique may have been aided by an accident in which he slipped on ice and broke his wrist. The bones were set badly, and he was ever after forced to play with an oddly cocked left hand, which many believe assisted him in some unusual chord fingerings. That his street-corner material included spirituals made it harder for the police to move him on, and the demands of the street also helped to foster a singing style that was forceful and clear, with crowd-pleasing melodies augmented by showy guitar work.

Davis was ordained as a Baptist minister in 1933, and took a position at the Free Baptist Connection Church in Washington, North Carolina. But he also toured as a singing gospel preacher, and in 1935 he traveled to New York City to record 16 songs for ARC, covering both spirituals and blues on titles such as "I Saw The Light", "I Am The Light Of The World" and "You Got to Go Down". Among those whose paths he crossed at the time were **Blind Boy Fuller** (a close friend, on whom he became a major influence), and Sonny Terry and Brownie McGhee.

Two years later, Davis and his second wife relocated permanently to New York, where he bought a house on 169th Street in Harlem in 1940. He became a minister at the Missionary Baptist Connection Church, and didn't record again until the 1950s, when he was rediscovered during the first flowering of the folk revival. Working for a number of labels, including Mo Asch's Folkways Records, Stinson, Riverside and Prestige, he found a new, largely white, middle-class, well-educated audience that wasn't overinterested in his preaching but was in awe of his virtuoso guitar playing, with its complex rhythms and counter-melodies, and his rasping, blues-holler of a voice.

By now Davis's material was mostly spiritual in content, although he did still dust down old favorites like "Cocaine", "Candy Man" and "Baby Let Me Follow You Down" for his new fans, all of which have since been heavily covered. His more religious songs such as "Samson and Delilah" and "Death Don't Have No Mercy" have also been much recorded, not least by Bob Dylan and the Grateful Dead.

Davis became a hugely popular fixture at folk festivals during the 1960s, and gave regular guitar tuition at his home in New York. Favoring a large six-string instrument, which he affectionately called "Miss Gibson" in honor of the manufacturer, he described his playing method and teaching style to *Blues Guitar* magazine shortly before he died: "Your forefinger and your thumb, that's the striking hand, and your left hand is your leading hand. Your left hand tells your right hand what strings to touch, what changes to make. That's the greatest help. You see, one hand can't do without the other." It was a finger-picking style that allowed him to maintaining a melodic line while at the same time inserting the most complex harmonies, and both his intonation and phrasing have been much copied by Ry Cooder, Jorma Kaukonen and countless other acoustic guitarists.

He continued performing until his death; in fact it was on the way to a gig in New Jersey when he suffered a fatal heart attack in 1972.

⊙ **Complete Early Recordings** Yazoo
Remastered versions of the old 78s Gary Davis recorded for Arc in the 1930s. Indispensable.

⊙ **Harlem Street Singer** Original Blues Classics
A dozen fine tracks that Rev. Gary Davis recorded in New York in 1960, including such favorites as "Samson And Delilah", "Pure Religion", "Death Don't Have No Mercy", "Twelve Gates To The City", and "I Am The Light Of This World".

⊙ **Blues & Ragtime** Shanachie
A decent collection of Gary Davis's more secular material, including "Cocaine Blues", "Candy Man ", and "Buck Dance", plus an eleven-minute "Hesitation Blues".

⊙ **Pure Religion And Bad Company** Smithsonian/Folkways
This wonderful album, recorded in New York in 1957, features plenty of preaching but even more stellar guitar playing. Several blues songs are delivered as instrumentals so Davis didn't have to utter their profane words.

Jimmy Dawkins

b Tchula, Mississippi, Oct 24, 1936

Although his guitar playing earned **Jimmy Dawkins** the nickname "Fast Fingers", there was always far more to his Chicago style than mere speed, and his style was never flashy.

Dawkins taught himself to play the guitar in Mississippi before he rode a Greyhound bus to Chicago in the mid-1950s. Befriended by harmonica player **Billy Boy Arnold** in the Windy City, he was soon working club dates on the South Side with the likes of Magic Sam, Jimmy Rodgers and Luther Allison.

Besides leading his own band, Dawkins became an in-demand session player. Not until 1969, however, did he record his debut album for Delmark Records, after Magic Sam had recommended him to label boss Bob Koester. Called – inevitably – *Fast Fingers*, it revealed not only an impressive guitar technique but also a sturdy and expressive singing voice. Dawkins went on to record for several other labels, including Black and Blue, MCM, Excello, Isabel, JSP, Rumble, Earwig, Ichiban and Fedora Records, but many believe that his introductory effort remains his best. That said, the Delmark follow-up, 1971's *All For Business*, also contains some fine material, with Otis Rush on second guitar.

A serious student of music, Dawkins became a highly thoughtful figure on the blues scene in later years, who wrote for *Blues Unlimited* magazine and ran his own Leric label to promote new blues artists and keep the tradition alive. Yet he did not abandon his own career, and continued recording and touring into his sixties.

⊙ **Fast Fingers** Delmark
Jimmy Dawkins' 1969 debut, featuring some burnished guitar playing and a bag-load of promise that was never quite fulfilled.

Bo Diddley

b McComb, Mississippi, Dec 30, 1928

The primitive, irresistible beat that **Bo Diddley** invented, and likened to a freight train, was a key component in the transition from blues and R&B to rock'n'roll. Diddley was particularly influential on the British R&B scene of the early 1960s, when his songs were covered by the Rolling Stones, the Animals, the Yardbirds and countless others, and although he never again matched the potency and originality of his early work, he has remained a legendary and much-loved figure for half a century.

Born Otha Elias Bates in Mississippi, he was sent at the age of six to live with his cousin, Guisse McDaniel, in Chicago, and changed his name to Elias McDaniel. He began playing the violin at an early age and after a spell as a teenage boxer – which was when he acquired the name by which he became best known (allegedly a southern slang term meaning "nothing at all" as in "he ain't no bo diddley") – he took to playing on street corners with his friend Jerome Green, while working on construction sites for extra money.

By 1954, Diddley had switched to electric guitar after hearing John Lee Hooker play, and was in Chicago fronting a band that included Green on maracas and Billy Boy Arnold on harmonica. After being turned down by the Vee Jay label, he got a deal at Chess Records where he cut "I'm A Man" and "Bo Diddley", backed by a band that included Otis Spann on piano. Thanks to his distorted guitar and trademark rhythmic excitement, the single became a major, double-sided R&B hit in 1955. Not exactly blues, or even straight R&B – although it owed allegiance to both – this was a new kind of earthy, funky, jive-talking, guitar-based rock'n'roll that was every bit as revolutionary as the sound being forged by his fellow Chess artist and rival **Chuck Berry** around the same time.

Over the next few years, Diddley produced a string of classic singles that included "You Don't Love Me", "Diddley Daddy", "Pretty Thing", "Diddy Wah Diddy", "Who Do You Love?", "Mona", "Road Runner", "Say Man" (his biggest American crossover hit), and "You Can't Judge A Book By Looking At Its Cover". He also developed a reputation as a dynamic live performer, with his trademark rectangular guitars and distorted amplification and unusual inclusion in his band of a female guitarist, first Peggy Jones and then from 1961 Norma Jean Wofford, known as The Duchess, and whom he introduced as his sister, although she was unrelated. Even so, he was a far bigger commercial success in Britain, where he was revered by a generation of aspiring British R&B bands as part of a holy trinity of Chess artists alongside Berry and Muddy Waters. The **Rolling Stones** borrowed heavily from his rhythms, and scored their first hit by adding a full-on Diddley beat to their version of Buddy Holly's "Not Fade Away". The **Pretty Things** took their name from one of his songs, and the Yardbirds, Animals, Manfred Mann and the Kinks all dipped into his songbook. Surprisingly, it took several more years, until the end of the 1960s,

The 21st century Bo Diddley

before American bands such as the Doors and Quicksilver Messenger Service took the hint and joined the plundering of the Diddley oeuvre.

By then, Diddley seemed to be coasting. Little he wrote and recorded from the mid-1960s onwards matched his initial inspired run. Few seemed to care, for his legend was established, and even such ill-conceived notions as marketing him as an ageing soul-funkster on albums such as 1969's *The Black Gladiator* could not tarnish his reputation. He stayed with Chess for twenty years, until the mid-1970s, but was too readily content to sink into

the rock'n'roll revival circuit. Although he toured with the Clash in 1979 and continued to record sporadically, he released little of note until 1995's *A Man Amongst Men*. Released on Mike Vernon's Code Blue label, that included guest appearances by Billy Boy Arnold, Keith Richards and Ronnie Wood, Jimmie Vaughan and Johnny Guitar Watson.

⦿ **The Chess Box** Chess
This 2-disc, 45-track set showcases Diddley's greatest material from 1955 until 1968. The hits are all there, but it's also designed to display his rock-blues versatility.

⊙ **The Essential Bo Diddley** Universal
A single-disc collection, containing 20 Bo Diddley classics, for anyone who wants something more concise than the Chess Box.

Floyd Dixon

b Marshall, Texas, Feb 8, 1929

The cool, jazzy, nightclub-piano blues of **Floyd Dixon** were strongly influenced by **Charles Brown**, whom he met in Los Angeles in the early 1940s and later replaced as pianist in Johnny Moore's Three Blazers. Calling himself Mr Magnificent, Dixon became a superb stylist in his own right, whose significance in the development of the urbane, sophisticated West Coast blues sound was recognized when he was commissioned to write "Olympic Blues" for the 1984 Los Angeles games.

Like Brown, T-Bone Walker, and several others of those who forged the Californian blues style, Dixon, who was also known as J Riggins Jr., hailed originally from Texas. He played piano and sang from an early age, absorbing gospel, blues, jazz and even hillbilly influences, before he moved with his family to Los Angeles in 1942. On the West Coast he soon came under the wing of Charles Brown, then playing with the Three Blazers. When Brown left the group in 1948, Dixon was his natural replacement, and recorded in a remarkably similar style to his mentor with the new Blazers line-up, for both the Aladdin and Combo labels.

He also recorded with his own trio, signing with Modern Records in 1949, and combining his smooth, Brown-derived blues with a more up-tempo, jump blues swing derived from the likes of Louis Jordan and Amos Milburn. Dixon's hits with Modern included "Dallas Blues" and "Mississippi Blues ", before he switched in 1950 to Aladdin. Further hits followed with "Sad Journey Blues", "Telephone Blues" and "Call Operator 210", while his more ribald side was heard on "Red Cherries", "Wine, Wine, Wine", "Too Much Jelly Roll" (penned by a young Jerry Leiber and Mike Stoller), and "Baby, Let's Go Down To The Woods".

By 1953, Dixon was recording for Specialty, while the following year he moved to the Atlantic subsidiary Cat. The constant flitting from label to label did nothing to alter his basic sound, with his

best-known songs from this period including "Hey Bartender" and "Hole In The Wall". He continued to record for various independent West Coast and Texas independent labels throughout the late 1950s and into the 1960s, but by the 1970s he had virtually retired and returned to live quietly in Texas. He made a comeback in 1975, when he toured Europe and his back catalogue was made re-available on Jonas Bernholm's Route 66 label, while during the 1980s he toured as part of the European Blues Caravan with Ruth Brown and Charles Brown.

Dixon signed to Alligator Records in the mid-1990s, recording the *Wake Up And Live* concert album in 1996. A fine and passionate recording, it won him "comeback artist of the year" from *Living Blues* magazine, which praised his "impeccable piano technique, fabulous timing and a voice like a foghorn".

⊙ **Cow Town Blues** Ace
Classic Floyd Dixon recordings from 1948–50, including both his West Coast blues style and some fine jump blues.

⊙ **Marshall Texas Is My Home** Ace
The best of Floyd Dixon's mid-1950s material, including the superb original version of "Hey Bartender".

⊙ **Wake Up And Live** Alligator
Floyd Dixon's strong 1996 comeback album, recorded live with an excellent backing band, delivers stirring versions of his old hits.

Willie Dixon

b Vicksburg, Mississippi, July 1, 1915; d Jan 29, 1992

As the main writer, producer and arranger for **Chess Records** throughout most of its glory years, **Willie Dixon** was the chief architect of the Chicago sound and the backbone of the legendary label's success.

The seventh of fourteen children, Willie James Dixon later recalled that his mother had the unusual habit of turning everything she said into rhymes, a tendency which he copied and believed sowed the seeds of his subsequent songwriting. His earliest musical memory as a child was following a truck that was carrying a band led by Little Brother Montgomery, and he was soon singing bass with the Union Jubilee Singers, a gospel quartet with its own radio program.

Dixon hoboed his way from Vicksburg to Chicago in 1932. He came to the Windy City initially not to play music, but to become a heavyweight boxer. After four fights he was declared Illinois State "Golden Gloves" heavyweight champion, but abandoned his boxing career following a dispute with his manager over money. Dixon's professional musical career began in 1940, when he formed the Five Breezes with Leonard "Baby Doo" Caston, blending jazz, blues and the close vocal harmonies associated with groups like the Mills Brothers and the Ink Spots. The group's progress was abruptly halted when Dixon refused to be called-up for the US Army and was imprisoned for ten months in 1941. On his release, he formed the Four Jumps of Jive, before he reunited in 1945 with Caston and guitarist Bernado Dennis (later replaced by Ollie Crawford) in the **Big Three**.

Playing a mix of blues, boogie-woogie and popular song, the trio's recording debut came with Bullet Records, before they moved to Columbia in 1947. At the same time, Dixon was a regular participant in late-night jam sessions in Chicago's blues clubs, with the likes of Muddy Waters. It was while working in the Big Three that he met the Polish brothers **Phil** and **Leonard Chess**, who had just entered the record business via Aristocrat Records and were about to launch Chess. At first they hired Dixon part-time; his first gig for them was playing bass on a Robert Nighthawk session in 1948. By 1951, however, he was working not only full-time but overtime for Chess as the label's chief scout, A&R man, producer, session musician and songwriter.

Willie Dixon will probably always be best remembered for his productions of his own songs by other artists, including many sides that came to define the Chicago blues. These included "Hoochie Coochie Man" and "I Just Want To Make Love To You" for **Muddy Waters**; "Spoonful", "Little Red Rooster" and "Back Door Man" for **Howlin' Wolf**; "My Babe" for **Little Walter**; "I Can't Quit You Baby" for **Otis Rush**; "You Can't Judge A Book By Looking At The Cover" for **Bo Diddley**; "Wang Dang Doodle" for **Koko Taylor**; and a hundred others. Dixon's songs were also covered or adapted by the likes of the Rolling Stones, Cream, the Doors and Led Zeppelin (who were forced to pay him royalties after not crediting his "You Need Love" as the source of their "Whole Lotta Love").

A proud and self-confident man, Dixon did not always feel that the Chess's brothers appreciated his true worth. At the height of Chess' success in the 1950s, he was being paid a reported hundred dollars per week, and he later resorted to legal action against the label's publishing arm, Arc Music, to regain control of his songwriting copyrights. This growing sense of injustice led to his leaving Chess in 1957 for Cobra Records, although he probably made no more money out of them, as the label collapsed two years later.

Away from Chess, Dixon also recorded the album *Willie's Blues* for Bluesville in 1959 and worked for Duke/Peacock. He returned to Chess in 1960 and stayed until 1971, continuing to be the label's powerhouse, although his double-bass playing, which had driven the Chess sound during the 1950s, was now usually supplanted by a younger, electric bassist.

During the 1960s, Dixon also diversified into booking and managing other artists, teaming up with concert promoter Horst Lippmann to organize the American Folk Blues Festival tours of Europe, and almost certainly earning more from these activities than he did from Chess. He also played as a duo with **Memphis Slim**, releasing an album with him recorded live at the Village Gate.

In the 1970s, Dixon made a major return to live work, touring regularly and finding a particularly appreciative audience in Europe. He also recorded for Ovation, and for Columbia on a collection of his best-known songs called *I Am The Blues*, and established his own Yambo and Spoonful labels. Mindful of his own experience at Chess and in particular the royalties he had never received, in 1982 he set up the Blues Heaven Foundation to help other blues musicians claim their dues and right past wrongs. Despite bypass surgery in 1987 he continued to record, and in 1989 published his autobiography, called, with excusable immodesty, *I Am The Blues*. The same year he produced the music for the film *Ginger Ale Afternoon*, and in later years, although plagued by ill health, he made several cameo film appearances. After having a leg amputated as a result of diabetes, he died in California in 1992.

⊙ **The Willie Dixon Chess Box** (MCA/Universal)
This two-disc set includes five performances by the man himself, plus recordings of his classic tunes by Howlin' Wolf, Muddy Waters, Little Walter, Bo Diddley et al.

Fats Domino

b New Orleans, Louisiana, Feb 26, 1928

Although **Fats Domino** tends to be regarded primarily as a rock'n'roller, he came from a long New Orleans tradition of piano players whose roots lay deep in jazz, boogie-woogie and the blues, and was heavily influenced by the likes of Albert Ammons and Fats Waller.

Antoine Domino has lived in New Orleans all his life. He played piano and sang (in French) as a child, making his first public performance at the age of ten. In his late teens he joined the band led by **Dave Bartholomew**, who would go on to write many of Domino's 1950s hits. After signing to Imperial Records in 1949, his first release, "The Fat Man" – a reworking of Champion Jack Dupree's signature "Junker's Blues" – reached the R&B charts in 1950. Further R&B hits followed with "Every Night About This Time", "Goin' Home", and "Going To The River", all recorded with producer and co-writer Dave Bartholomew and featuring stellar accompaniment from saxophonist Alvin "Red" Tyler and drummer Earl Palmer. In the rock'n'roll era Fats crossed over easily to pop success with "Ain't That A Shame", although it was Pat Boone's cover which was the bigger hit.

A congenial, much-liked figure with a smoky, Creole drawl and a relaxed, bluesy piano style, Domino always rolled as well as rocked, an approach heard to perfection on his 1956 version of "Blueberry Hill", previously recorded by Glenn Miller and Louis Armstrong. By the end of the 1950s he'd notched up almost twenty top-twenty American hits, including "I'm In Love Again", "Blue Monday", "I'm Walkin'", "Whole Lotta Loving", "I Want To Walk You Home" and "Be My Guest". These made him the best-selling black artist of the decade, but his last big hit came with 1960's "Walking To New Orleans".

Domino stayed with Imperial until 1963, when he switched to ABC Paramount. He continued recording without departing signifcantly from his original style, but never recaptured the magic of his sides for Imperial. He also made a few films and toured frequently, becoming a regular both in Las Vegas and at the New Orleans Jazz & Blues Heritage Festival. In 2005, he had to be rescued by boat from his flooded house in New Orleans, following the devastation wreaked by Hurricane Katrina.

⊙ **The Fats Domino Jukebox: 20 Greatest Hits The Way You Originally Heard Them** EMI
Exactly what it says on the tin – twenty of Domino's original, rocking, pounding best sides for Imperial. As Fats never really made the transition from singles to albums, this is pretty much all you need.

Thomas A. Dorsey

b Villa Rica, Georgia, July 1, 1899; d Jan 23, 1993

In the days when he was **Georgia Tom**, **Thomas A. Dorsey** led Ma Rainey's band and recorded some classic blues sides with the bottleneck guitarist **Tampa Red**. He quit the blues in 1932, however, and thereafter worked exclusively in gospel music, composing literally hundreds of songs, many of which remain classics of the genre.

Dorsey originally learned his music from his mother, who was a piano teacher, and his religion from his father, a Baptist minister. The family moved to Atlanta in 1910, where young Tom first encountered the blues working at a theater on Decatur Street. There he heard not only vaudeville acts but also singers like **Ma Rainey** and **Bessie Smith**, whose pianists he studied closely. During World War I, the family moved to Chicago, where he undertook formal training at the Chicago College of Composition and Arranging. He also played in local jazz bands, and was employed as a pianist in one of Al Capone's speakeasies, working under the name Barrelhouse Tommy. After a spell on the road with Will Walker's Whispering Syncopators, he was by 1924 leading Ma Rainey's band, touring with her for the next four years and backing here on recordings such as "Black Eye Blues" and "Sleep Talking Blues". Dorsey also worked as a staff arranger for the Chicago Music Publishing Company, arranged early blues sessions for a number of labels, and was employed as a freelance talent scout by Paramount. His "Riverside Blues" was recorded by King Oliver, while other compositions included "I Want A Daddy To Call My Own" and "Muddy Water Blues".

As Georgia Tom, he teamed up with guitarist Tampa Red in 1928, recording the big-selling and much-covered "It's Tight Like That". Other titles included "All Alone Blues", "Eagle Ridin' Papa", "Pig Meat Blues", "Second-Hand Woman Blues", "Somebody's Been Usin' That Thing", and "Terrible Operation Blues". He also worked as a member of the Hokum Boys, and as a pianist he accompanied artists like Big Bill Broonzy, Scrapper Blackwell, Memphis Minnie and Victoria Spivey.

Dorsey, it seemed, was everywhere on the Chicago "race music" scene during the late 1920s.

Despite his success, however, he became increasingly dissatisfied with the way black artists were treated by white music publishers and record labels. This frustration, coupled with a growing tension between the secular music of the blues and his spiritual beliefs, led to some sort of a breakdown, and in 1932 he renounced the "devil's music". Turning to gospel music, he took the post of director of the choir at the Pilgrim Baptist Church in Chicago's Bronzeville District. Now reverted to his full name, he also became the first independent black publisher of gospel songs, and in 1933 founded the National Convention of Gospel Choirs and Choruses.

A prolific composer of more than four hundred gospel songs, he wrote his best-known number, "Precious Lord", following the death in childbirth of his first wife (who had worked as Ma Rainey's wardrobe mistress). His most famous other gospel song was "Peace in the Valley". Both were recorded by Mahalia Jackson, whom he discovered, and prolifically covered by literally hundreds of other artists.

Dorsey stayed with the Pilgrim Baptist Church until 1970, and continued preaching, touring and singing into his eighties. He died in Chicago at the age of 93 in 1993.

⊙ **Complete Recorded Works Vol 1 1928–30**
Document
The best of Thomas Dorsey's pre-gospel blues material, both solo and with the Hokum Boys.

Champion Jack Dupree

b New Orleans, Louisiana, July 4, 1909; d Jan 21, 1992

One of the great characters of the blues, **Champion Jack Dupree** came out of the barrelhouses of New Orleans to enjoy a long career as a versatile entertainer, playing blues and boogie-woogie piano with a pleasing sideline in amiable storytelling.

William Thomas Dupree's father was a Congolese sailor, while his Creole mother was part Cherokee. Both died in a New Orleans house fire sometime around 1911, leaving him orphaned at the age of two (he later made conflicting claims that the blaze had been set by the Ku Klux Klan and that it was accidental). Whatever the circumstances were, he

Champ Jack at Ronnie Scott's jazz club, London, 1970s

was sent to the New Orleans Home for Colored Waifs, where **Louis Armstrong** was also growing up at much the same time. It was there that he learned to play piano, and when he left the home in the mid-1920s, he eked out a precarious living playing for tips. He continued to perfect his technique by copying local pianists such as Tuts Washington and Willie "Drive 'em Down" Hall, whom he called "father" and from whom he learned his best-known song "Junker's Blues". He also worked with a tribe of Mardi Gras Indians, and when he was old enough began playing in barrelhouses in the city's French Quarter.

In 1930, Dupree moved to Chicago, where he encountered Georgia Tom, before moving on to Detroit and then Indianapolis, where he knew Scrapper Blackwell and Leroy Carr. For a while, music took a back seat as he became a professional boxer with the encouragement of the great Joe Louis, whom he had met in Detroit. By the time he retired from the ring in 1940, he'd clocked up more

than a hundred bouts, and earned the right to add the soubriquet "Champion" to his name.

Boxing behind him, Dupree returned to Chicago and fell in with a group of musicians including Big Bill Broonzy and Tampa Red. They introduced him to the ubiquitous producer Lester Melrose, who recorded him for Okeh Records (and claimed composing and publishing credits on many his songs). His career was interrupted when he was drafted into the US Navy as a cook and he was taken prisoner by the Japanese. After the war, he moved to New York, where he played at the Cotton Club and developed a stage act that involved telling jokes and comic stories between his songs. He recorded for several labels, including Continental, Alert, Apollo and Red Robin, often as a piano-guitar duet with **Brownie McGhee**. He also cut sides for yet more labels under different names, including Brother Blues, Lightnin' Jr. on Empire, Meat Head Johnson and Harelip Jack Dupree, a reference to his comic habit of sometimes mangling his words as if he had a cleft palate (which he certainly did not).

Although the material Dupree recorded around this time was mostly straight blues and boogie-woogie, it displayed a distinctive New Orleans flavor and a rock-solid left-hand. His lyrics were often full of down-home, ribald humor ("Mama, move your false teeth, papa wanna scratch your gums"), but were more usually about jail ("Angola Blues"), gambling, disease ("TB Blues"), drinking, and drug addiction (it was his version of "Junker's Blues" that was adapted by Fats Domino into his first hit "The Fat Man").

Dupree signed with King in 1953, for whom he enjoyed considerable success with titles such as "Tongue Tied Blues", "Harelip Blues ", "Mail Order Woman", "Let the Doorbell Ring" and "Big Leg Emma's". "Walkin' The Blues", recorded as a comic duet with Teddy "Mr. Bear" McRae, gave him his biggest hit, while Jerry Lee Lewis covered his "Shake Baby Shake". From King he moved to RCA's Groove and Vik subsidiaries and then recorded one of his finest albums, *Blues From The Gutter*, for Atlantic in 1958.

The following year he became one of the first blues artists to relocate permanently to Europe. He continued to record and tour prolifically, writing topical songs about subjects like the Vietnam war and the assassination of Martin Luther King. He lived in several countries, including Britain, where he became a familiar fixture on the late 1960s blues scene, recording with John Mayall, Mick Taylor, and Eric Clapton, and releasing several albums on Mike Vernon's Blue Horizon label.

Dupree returned to America temporarily in 1990 to record *Back Home In New Orleans* for Rounder's Bullseye imprint, his first album he'd made in his homeland in over thirty years. The label got two more albums out of him before he died of cancer in Germany in 1992. He was believed to be 82, although nobody could be entirely certain as his exact date of birth was never verified.

⊙ **Champion Jack Dupree Sings The Blues**
King
The best of Dupree's 1950s' material for the King label, although oddly his biggest hit "Walkin' The Blues" isn't here.

⊙ **Blues From The Gutter** Atlantic
Champion Jack Dupree was at his peak for these marvelous 1958 barrelhouse versions of "Stack-O-Lee", "Junker's

Blues" and "Frankie & Johnny", not to mention the risqué "Nasty Boogie".

⊙ **The Complete Blue Horizon Sessions**
Columbia
This double-album compilation, released in 2005, assembles the recordings that Champion Jack Dupree made for Mike Vernon's label in the late 1960s, and incorporates plenty of previously unheard bonus material.

⊙ **Back Home In New Orleans** Bullseye Blues
Back in the city of his birth some eighty years on, in 1980, Champion Jack sounds mighty pleased to be there.

Big Joe Duskin

b Birmingham, Alabama, Feb 10, 1921

The pianist **Big Joe Duskin** was one of the last of the pre-World War II blues musicians to be recorded. Despite being older than the likes of B.B. King, and only half a dozen years younger than Muddy Waters, he didn't make his debut album until 1979.

One of eleven children, Big Joe started out playing piano in church for his preacher father. After the family moved to Cincinnati during the Depression, he discovered a thriving local blues scene, and heard itinerant bluesmen such as Roosevelt Sykes, Memphis Slim and boogie-woogie king Pete Johnson when they passed through town. Whenever his parents weren't around, he put aside the church music and started playing boogie-woogie on the Duskin family upright. When his father caught him, he received a beating and was forced to promise not to play "the devil's music" until after Duskin senior was dead. At the time the Rev. Perry Duskin was close to eighty, and the teenage would-be blues pianist gave his word. In fact, his father lived to an alleged 105. While Joe waited to be released from his promise, he wound up with alternative careers as a Cincinnati policeman and postal worker, although he did play while he was in the army during World War I, when he met Albert Ammons, Pete Johnson and Meade Lux Lewis at forces concerts.

Duskin didn't play again until the early 1970s, when he took up blues piano at the urging of Ohio blues scholar, Steve Tracy. He released his debut album *Cincinnati Stomp* on Arhoolie in 1979, and recorded several albums for European labels in the 1980s and 1990s, supported by festival appearances. He was still recording into the new century when he signed to the American label Yellow Dog Records and released 2004's *Big Joe Jumps Again!*, which featured Peter Frampton on guitar on several tracks.

⊙ **Cincinnati Stomp** Arhoolie
Big Joe Duskin's belated 1979 debut album served up a fine mix of classic blues and boogie-woogie piano, featuring tracks such as "Roll 'em Pete", "Little Red Rooster", "Down The Road Apiece", and "Beat Me Daddy, Eight To The Bar".

⊙ **Big Joe Jumps Again!** Yellow Dog
The classic Cincinnati blues sound lives on even in 2004, with a nicely packaged set complete with extensive liner notes.

Bob Dylan

b Duluth, Minnesota, May 24, 1941

Folk singer, king of protest, voice of his generation, songwriter and rock'n'roll messiah are all epithets likely to be applied to **Bob Dylan** before the term "blues musician" comes to mind. But Dylan's debt to the blues and its unique poetry is significant, profound and recurring, prompting the author Michael Gray to devote an entire 112-page chapter to his connections to the blues in his magisterial study, *Song And Dance Man*.

Dylan was presented with a pile of Leadbelly 78s at his high-school graduation in 1959, and by 1961 his repertoire included songs by Big Bill Broonzy, Blind Willie McTell, Bessie Smith, Big Joe Williams and Muddy Waters. When he arrived in Greenwich Village in 1961, he had the opportunity to see many of the old bluesmen in the flesh, opening for John Lee Hooker, playing harmonica on a Big Joe Williams recording, and meeting the likes of Lonnie Johnson and Blind Boy Fuller. In 1993 he evocatively recalled the experience: "There was a bunch of us, me included, who got to see all these people close up – people like Son House, Rev. Gary Davis and Sleepy John Estes. Just to sit there and be close up and watch them play, you could study what they were doing, plus a bit of their lives rubbed off on you. Those vibes will carry into you forever, really, so it's like those people, they're

still here to me. They're not ghosts of the past or anything. They're continually here."

Dylan's 1962 debut album, *Bob Dylan*, contained only two original songs. For the rest there were covers of classic blues songs such as Blind Lemon Jefferson's "See That My Grave Is Kept Clean", Bukka White's "Fixin' To Die", "Freight Train Blues", "In My Time Of Dyin'" and "House Of The Rising Sun". By the time he recorded his follow-up, he was well on his way to becoming the greatest songwriter in the world, and the album consisted largely of his own compositions. However, thirty years later he returned to the blues songbook for two wonderful acoustic albums, 1992's *Good As I Been To You* and the following year's *World Gone Wrong*, which included songs by the Mississippi Sheiks, Blind Willie McTell, Sleepy John Estes, Blind Blake, Mississippi John Hurt, Rev. Gary Davis and Blind Boy Fuller.

In addition, many of Dylan's own songs have been deeply influenced by the blues, both musically and lyrically. Gray sights dozens of examples, from "Obviously Five Believers" on 1966's *Blonde On Blonde*, which was based on Memphis Minnie's "Me And My Chauffeur Blues", to "Gotta Serve Somebody" from 1979's *Slow Train Coming*, which borrows from Memphis Slim's "Mother Earth".

Some of the words of 1965's "Subterranean Homesick Blues" can be traced back to a 1928 Georgia Tom song, while even on his least blues-like material, Dylan regularly quotes from its poetry. For example, "To Be Alone With You" on his 1969 country album, *Nashville Skyline*, incorporates lines from a song recorded by Roosevelt Sykes in 1937. As Gray put it: "'Dylan inhabits the blues as the best of the old bluesmen did – fusing traditional material into fresh, expressive work of his own."

Dylan has also recorded a brace of magnificent tributes to his blues heroes, in his 1983 "Blind Willie McTell" – whom he probably first heard on Sam Charter's seminal 1959 compilation *Country Blues* – and 2001's "High Water (For Charley Patton)". Should anyone doubt Dylan's reverence for the blues, it's also there in spades in his autobiography *Chronicles Vol 1*, which contains a quite dazzling description of the first time he heard a Robert Johnson record. "He seemed like a guy who could have sprung from the head of Zeus in full armor," Dylan recalled more than forty years after the event.

⊙ **Bob Dylan** Columbia
Although almost all the songs on his 1962 debut are covers, Dylan is not just another white-boy blues singer ripping off the music. He invests familiar blues tunes like "See That My Grave Is Kept Clean" with an emotional intensity that no 20-year-old really had any right to possess.

⊙ **Good As I Been To You** Columbia
Ragged, passionate and timeless versions of songs like "Frankie & Albert", "Sittin' On Top Of The World", "You're Gonna Quit Me", and "Step It Up and Go", recorded solo and acoustic in 1992.

⊙ **World Gone Wrong** Columbia
Dylan so enjoyed getting back in touch with his roots on *Good As I Been to You* that the following year he did it all over again. 1993's selection of folk-blues classics included "Delia", "Blood In My Eyes", "Broke Down Engine", "Stack-o-Lee" and "Ragged and Dirty".

Snooks Eaglin

b New Orleans, Jan 21, 1936

They call **Snooks Eaglin** "the human jukebox" down in New Orleans, on account of a repertoire that supposedly extends to some 2500 songs. That figure has to be an exaggeration, but even if it's only half true, he still deserves the title, after an erratic stop-start recording career. During the 1950s, he cut some superb acoustic country-blues sides. Then, in the early 1960s, he recorded typical Crescent City R&B. While he remained an active live performer and played various sessions, however, it was almost a quarter of a century before he signed another record contract, when he re-emerged on the Black Top label in 1987.

The young Fird Eaglin Jr, whose birth name is sometimes given as "Ferd" or "Ford", lost his sight before he was two, following an operation for glaucoma and a brain tumor. Nicknamed Snooks after a popular radio character, he spent long spells of his childhood in hospital, but his father gave him his first guitar at the age of five, and the two would play together with Eaglin senior on harmonica. Snooks was soon singing and playing in the local Baptist church, and at eleven won a radio talent contest performing "Twelfth Street Rag" on the guitar.

At fifteen, Snooks was a professional musician, joining the R&B combo, the Flamingos, led by a youthful **Allen Toussaint** on piano. On one occasion it's claimed that all the band except Eaglin were too drunk to drive home after a gig, and so the sightless guitarist was put behind the wheel of the group's Studebaker. Eaglin insists to this day that they made it back safely.

After the Flamingos split up, Eaglin recorded as part of Sugar Boy Crawford's backing band, the Cane Cutters, playing on Crawford's Mardi Gras hit, "Jock-A-Mo". He also had a small R&B band of his own, but when times were hard – as they often were – he was to be found playing blues and folk songs on the streets of the French Quarter. There he was discovered in 1958 by the folklorist Dr. Harry Oster, who recorded some brilliant country blues sides with him for Folkways and Folk-Lyric, backed on several tracks by Lucius Bridges on washboard and Percy Randolph on harmonica.

Subsequent albums presented Eaglin as a rustic street singer, but he wasn't happy with the image, feeling there was more to him that that. In the three years after Fats Domino's producer **Dave Bartholomew** signed him to Imperial Records in 1960, he cut nine singles of vintage New Orleans R&B, including "Yours Truly", " Cover Girl", "Don't Slam That Door", and "That Certain Door", backed by fine musicians like pianist **James Booker**, and a full horn section. The sides also betrayed a strong Ray Charles influence in his vocal style, and Eaglin sometimes thereafter even billed himself as "Little Ray Charles".

For most of the 1960s, Snooks adopted a low profile, playing clubs in New Orleans and doing the odd session. Then in 1971 he came out of obscurity to play with **Professor Longhair** at the inaugural New Orleans Jazz & Heritage Festival. That appearance led to his recording an album for the Swedish Sonet label, *The Legacy Of The Blues, Part 2*, and he also recorded some demos with Longhair in Baton Rouge, Woodstock and New York for Albert Grossman's Bearsville label. Oddly, the sessions were not released until 1987, when they appeared on Rounder Records as *Professor Longhair's House Party New Orleans Style: The Lost Sessions 1971–72*. Oddly because on its release, it became clear that Longhair's rolling piano and Eaglin's rollicking electric guitar made an inspired combination.

When Eaglin recorded an album with the **Wild Magnolias** Mardi Gras Indian group in 1974, his funky guitar playing had seldom sounded better. However, although he continued to play around

New Orleans, his recording career remained inactive until 1987, when he signed to Hammond Scott's Black Top Records and released *Baby, You Can Get Your Gun*. Since then, he's released half a dozen more albums on the label, with his guitar playing as crisply funky as ever, and backed by the likes of Anson Funderburgh on guitar, Grady Gaines on sax, Sam Myers on harmonica, keyboardists Ron Levy and Jon Cleary and bassist George Porter Jr.

⊙ **New Orleans Street Singer** Storyville
Great 25-track reissue of Snooks Eaglin's late 1950s' country blues sides, all nimble finger-picking and heartfelt vocals on stunning versions of "I Got A Woman", "Mama, Don't You Tear My Clothes", "Don't You Lie To Me", and the lovely, elegiac "Brown Skin Woman".

⊙ **Baby, You Can Get Your Gun!** Black Top
The great 1987 comeback album. It couldn't be more different from **New Orleans Street Singer**, but in his way Eaglin's just as impressive with an electric guitar in hand as an acoustic one.

⊙ **Live In Japan** Black Top
A 1997 live recording that captures Snooks in all his eclectic – and sometimes eccentric – glory.

David "Honeyboy" Edwards

b Shaw, Mississippi, June 28, 1915

David "Honeyboy" Edwards

REDFERNS

One of the last authentic links with the original Delta blues, **David "Honeyboy" Edwards** is still going strong at the time of writing and about to embark on a tour of Australia. It's extraordinary to realize that he was born only four years after Robert Johnson.

That was in 1915, and by the time he was fourteen he had determined to be a blues guitarist, inspired by **Tommy Johnson**. As he wrote in his autobiography, "I was in 1929 when Tommy Johnson come down from Crystal Springs, Mississippi. He was just a little guy, tan-colored, easy-going, but he drank a whole lot. Listening to Tommy, that's when I really learned something about how to play guitar." While still in his teens, he worked with Tommy McClennan, Robert Petway and Big Joe Williams, making his way around the Delta's juke joints and playing at picnics and house parties. Touring the South during the 1930s, he also played with Robert Johnson, Big Walter Horton, Yank Rachell, Sonny Boy Williamson, Homesick James and Son House, and met Charley Patton. After he had moved to Memphis, he played with such local musicians as the Memphis Jug Band, Will Shade, Memphis Slim and Roosevelt Sykes.

Although Edwards made his first recordings in 1942, cutting fifteen country blues sides for Alan Lomax, for the Library of Congress, at Stovall's Plantation in Clarksdale, Mississippi, he didn't record commercially until 1951. Then, as Mr. Honey, he cut "Who May Your Regular Be" for Arc Records in Houston and "Build A Cave" for Artist.

Moving to Chicago soon after, he played small clubs and street corners with Floyd Jones, Johnny Temple and Kansas City Red. He recorded several songs for Chess in 1953, including the great "Drop Down Mama", although the material remained unreleased for many years, and he also recorded for Sun in Memphis around the same time.

Edwards was rediscovered in the 1970s by Michael Frank, and the pair formed The Honeyboy Edwards Blues Band. Frank went on to found Earwig Records, and in 1979 recorded him with Sunnyland Slim, Kansas City Red, Floyd Jones and Big Walter Horton on the album *Old Friends*. He has continued to record for Earwig ever since, and in 1998 published a fascinating autobiography, *The World Don't Own Me Nothing*. That was bursting with stories about Robert Johnson – whom he claims to have been with on the night he died – Big Joe Williams, Little Walter and many other legendary bluesmen. The book was accompanied by an album of the same name; even in his later years, Edwards was still performing the blues with an astonishing intensity, singing in a dark, throaty shout and ripping notes out of his guitar as if his life depended upon it.

⊙ **Delta Bluesman** Earwig
A fine archive reissue of Edwards' 1941 Library of Congress recordings, complete with interview material.

⊙ **The World Don't Owe Me Nothing** Earwig
David "Honeyboy" Edwards, recorded live in 1997 and featuring harp player Carey Bell. His timing may be eccentric and at times he slips into a different key, but despite the rough edges, he still evokes the Delta tradition in thrilling fashion.

Tinsley Ellis
b Atlanta, Georgia, June 4, 1957

The hard-rocking, blues-soaked guitar playing of **Tinsley Ellis** was initially inspired by British groups such as the Rolling Stones and Cream, before he traced the music back to its source and discovered the three Kings of the blues – Freddie, B.B. and Albert.

Ellis grew up in southern Florida and began playing the guitar at age eight. At fourteen, he went to see **B.B. King** in concert. When the guitarist broke a string, he changed it without missing a note, and handed the broken strand to Ellis.

After the show, King came out and talked with fans, and Ellis knew he was going to become a blues guitarist. Returning to Atlanta in 1975, he joined the Alley Cats. Six years later he teamed up with veteran harpist Chicago Bob Nelson to form the **Heartfixers**, who swiftly became a major attraction around Atlanta, cutting four albums, including *Tore Up*, with vocals by blues shouter **Nappy Brown**. He embarked on a solo career when he signed to Alligator Records in 1988, beginning with *Georgia Blue*, which established him as a modern guitar hero who could marry the power of rock to the emotion of the blues, and found him talked about as a rival to Stevie Ray Vaughan. His third solo album, 1992's *Trouble Time*, featuring Peter Buck of R.E.M. and keyboardist Chuck Leavell, once of the Allman Brothers and these days a Rolling Stones sideman, brought further critical acclaim. *Fire It Up* which appeared in 1997, was helmed by former Atlantic in-house producer Tom Dowd. That was his last release on Alligator before he joined Capricorn Records, for whom he recorded *Kingpin*, an album of southern blues-rock in the Allman Brothers tradition. When the label folded Ellis signed to Telarc for the albums *Hell Or High Water* and *The Hard Way*, before returning to Alligator for 2005's *Live Highwayman*. As an attempt to capture the ferocious power of the 150 performances he averages per year, it's probably his most effective release, causing Alligator president Bruce Iglauer to remark, "'He's great in the studio, but even better live."

⊙ **Live Highwayman** Alligator
High octane stuff with plenty of guitar pyrotechnics; living proof that the stage rather than the studio is Tinsley Ellis' true forte.

Sleepy John Estes
b Ripley, Tennessee, Jan 25, 1899; d June 5, 1977

Sleepy John Estes was a highly influential country blues singer, not once but twice over. During the 1930s, he was a role model to the likes of Big Bill Broonzy and Arthur "Big Boy" Crudup. Then, when he was rediscovered during the folk-blues revival of the early 1960s, he was lionized by Bob Dylan and a new generation of singers.

Born into a sharecropping family at the end of the nineteenth century, Estes lost his sight in one eye as a child when a friend threw a rock at him during a baseball game. He made his first guitar out a cigar box, and began playing at house parties around Brownsville, Tennessee, before moving to Memphis.

Nicknamed "Sleepy" because of his alleged ability to sleep while standing up (another story told that blood pressure problems regularly caused him to pass out), he worked for a while as a gang leader for a railroad maintenance crew. He hooked up in Memphis with harmonica and jug player **Hammie Nixon** and mandolinist **James "Yank" Rachell**, and the three played on Beale Street together for tips. A talent scout from the Victor label heard him, and he cut his first half-dozen sides at the Peabody Hotel in 1929, including "Diving Duck Blues", "Poor John Blues" and "Milk Cow Blues". Estes was a competent guitarist, but his voice was the main attraction, a high, confident instrument of great tonal clarity and emotional depth that immediately earned him another session in early 1930. The Depression then put paid to any further location recordings, so he hopped a freight train to Chicago, where he began recording for the newly established Decca Records. Between 1935 and 1940 he recorded more than thirty classic sides for the label, including "Drop Down Mama", "Airplane Blues" and "Someday Baby Blues", before switching to Bluebird.

Together with Hammie Nixon, Estes toured with the Rabbit Foot Minstrel Show and Dr Grimm's Medicine Show, and he also recorded with Son Bonds and Raymond Thomas as the Delta Boys. However, with wartime Shellac rationing severely limiting the recording of "race" records, he was back in Memphis by 1942, and living in poverty. To make matters worse, he lost the sight in his other eye in 1949. Three years later he recorded half a dozen sides for Sam Phillips at Sun studios, but his style was deemed too old-fashioned and he moved to Brownsville. There his career might have ended, had he not been fortuitously rediscovered a few years later by David Blumenthal, who was making a documentary film. Estes was living in an abandoned sharecropper's shack with his wife and five children, but Blumenthal mentioned his find to Bob Koester of Delmark Records, and the 63-year-old Estes was invited to Chicago.

He still had the sob in his throat – the style that Big Bill Broonzy had called "crying the blues" – and he resumed recording on with appropriately titled *The Legend Of Sleepy John Estes*. Further albums for Delmark followed in a similarly simple but direct style, although 1967's *Electric Sleep*, cut with an amplified Chicago band including Sunnyland Slim and Jimmy Dawkins, was ill-advised. More happily, the label also tracked down his old acoustic colleagues Rachell and Nixon to work with him. They appeared at the Newport Folk Festival together and toured Europe with the American Folk Blues Festival, playing to mostly white audiences, who recognized in Estes a true master of the idiom and a profound lyric poet of the blues. The three old-timers continued performing together into the 1970s, until Estes suffered a stroke in 1976. He died the following year, aged 78.

⊙ I Ain't Gonna Be Worried No More 1929–1941 Yazoo
Twenty-three classic Sleepy John Estes performances, including the sides he recorded in Memphis in 1929 and 1930 as well as the best of his Chicago sessions, including the much-covered "Milk Cow Blues", "Someday Baby Blues" and "Drop Down Mama".

⊙ The Legend of Sleepy John Estes Delmark
Sleepy John's heartwarming 1963 comeback album, recorded with Hammie Nixon but without Yank Rachell.

The Fabulous Thunderbirds

formed Austin, Texas, 1974

Playing straight-ahead and unpretentious blues-rock, the **Fabulous Thunderbirds** were significant players in the 1980s blues revival. They came together when harmonica player **Kim Wilson**, who had been given early encouragement on the instrument by Muddy Waters, met hot young guitar-slinger **Jimmie Vaughan** on the thriving blues scene in the university town of Austin, Texas, during the mid-1970s. Having honed their act as the house band at famed Austin club Antone's, they released their self-titled debut album, a solid, blues-oriented mix of their own songs and covers like Slim Harpo's "Scratch My Back", on Takoma Records in 1979. The following year they signed to Chrysalis, who encouraged them to expand their repertoire. By their third release, 1982's Nick Lowe-produced *T-Bird Rhythm*, they were adding other flavors, including rock'n'roll, soul and Cajun influences.

After Chrysalis abruptly dropped them, the Thunderbirds were left without a record contract for four years, even though they opened shows for the Rolling Stones and Eric Clapton. That exposure eventually led to their signing to Epic in 1986. *Tuff Enuff*, their first album for the label, was recorded with producer Dave Edmunds in London, and represented their commercial peak. The title song, featured in the film *Gung Ho* starring Michael Keaton, went top ten in the US and the album included further American top-forty singles in the Sam and Dave cover "Wrap It Up" and "Look At That". Even so, the next two albums did little business. and alienated blues fans as the band moved further away from their origins in search of mainstream rock success. Vaughan felt alienated, too, and left in 1989 to work with his brother Stevie Ray. Wilson has kept the group going ever since, with various changes of line-up. Among those who have passed through later incarnations of the T-Birds have been guitarists Duke Robillard, Kid Bangham, Nick Curran and Kirk Eli Fletcher. In recent years the T-Birds have moved further in a mainstream rock direction, leading their founder to form **Kim Wilson's Blues Revue** as a side project to play more traditional blues material. The most recent Thunderbirds album was *Painted On*, released on Tone Cool Records in 2005.

⊙ **Tuff Enuff** Epic
The Fabulous Thunderbirds' platinum breakthrough album was still bluesy enough to win them a W.C. Handy award as 1986's best blues band.

⊙ **Best Of The Fabulous Thunderbirds** EMI
A 22-track compilation that's entirely drawn from the Thunderbirds' first four albums.

John Fahey

b Takoma, Maryland, Feb 28, 1939; d Feb 22, 2001

The guitarist **John Fahey** was a blues scholar, whose music drew deeply on the traditions of the Mississippi Delta. But he also applied his extraordinary finger-picking technique to a wide panoply of other styles and influences, to create some of the most innovative and at times idiosyncratic music ever to be coaxed from an acoustic guitar.

By his teens, Fahey was already a collector of rare early blues records and an accomplished guitarist on both six- and twelve-string instruments, inspired by the recordings of Blind Willie Johnson among others. His first album, *The Transfiguration Of Blind Joe Death*, appeared in 1959. Rooted in acoustic blues styles, it also introduced his hugely influential use of open tunings, perplexing harmonics and inventive melody. He went on to release a bewildering number of albums on his own Takoma label, encompassing not only blues themes but jazz, Indian and avant-garde elements, often all at the same time in long, experimental improvisational pieces that defied categorization.

While at college during the early 1960s, Fahey wrote a thesis on **Charley Patton**, which he turned into a book in 1970, and the early bluesman's work remained a lifelong interest. Fahey was also a catalyst in the formation of **Canned Heat**, after Al Wilson had played on one of his albums, and was instrumental in the rediscovery of **Bukka White**. On top of that, via the Takoma label, he encouraged the early careers of other virtuoso guitarists such as Leo Kottke and Robbie Basho. He sold Takoma to Chrysalis in the 1970s, but continued to record prolifically until 1986, when he fell ill with Epstein-Barr syndrome, a long-lasting viral infection that left him in poverty and forced him at one point to sell his guitars and rare record collection. He returned to recording with *City Of Refuge* in 1997, and helped compile Revenant's definitive seven-disc set of Charley Patton's work. The pack-

Fat Possum Records

founded by Matthew Johnson in Oxford, Mississippi, 1990

Based in the heart of Mississippi, **Fat Possum Records** is dedicated to preserving the "dirty blues" that's still being played in a few, dusty, forgotten corners of the Delta. It was founded by **Matthew Johnson**, a history graduate from "Ole Miss" (Oxford's Mississippi State University). He fell in love with the blues as a student, when he frequented the juke joints in the small Delta towns around Greenville. There he came across the veteran **R.L. Burnside**, still making great music but in total obscurity. "I just thought he was great and he didn't have a record out, so I was like, 'Fuck it – I'll put one out myself'," he recalls.

Johnson used a four-thousand-dollar student loan to set up Fat Possum in 1991. After releasing his first Burnside album, he began scouring the Delta for other outposts of the country blues, and soon added **Junior Kimbrough** to the roster. For several years the label struggled; the constant prospect of bankruptcy forced Johnson to pawn or sell just about everything he owned. However, salvation came in 1996 when he signed a deal with the much larger LA-based Epitaph Records, whose roster includes Tom Waits and various heavy metal and punk bands.

With Epitaph's involvement, Fat Possum expanded its original mission statement and began signing new young white acts that drew on the tradition of the Delta blues, such as **Bob Log III** and the **Black Keys**. They also teamed veterans such as Burnside and Kimbrough on a series of experimental, hybrid recordings with the likes of the Beastie Boys and the Jon Spencer Blues Explosion.

Other signings in more traditional blues vein have included Asie Payton, T-Model Ford, Nathaniel Meyer, Robert Belfour and Little Freddie King. The label enjoyed its biggest success in 2002, when it teamed soul veteran **Solomon Burke** with a bunch of contemporary songwriters including Bob Dylan, Van Morrison and Elvis Costello. The result, *Don't Give Up On Me*, although hardly blues, won a Grammy as best blues album.

In 2005, Fat Possum issued a fascinating DVD called *You See Me Laughin' – The Last Of The Hill Country Bluesmen*, featuring Burnside, Kimbrough and others at home and on stage, plus interviews with the likes of Bono and Iggy Pop, paying testimony to the importance of Fat Possum's ongoing work. Burnside's death that same year (Kimbrough having already passed on several years earlier), only served to underline the fact that Johnson had arrived just in time to catch the final flickering of a dying blues tradition in the backwoods of the Mississippi hill country.

What the future holds for the label is uncertain. "I'm sure there's somebody I missed," Johnson says. "But if there is, that's the exception. It used to be that in every little town of four hundred people there'd be two or three that played. Some were just so-so, but there was always somebody who could actually do something. But they're all gone. I'd get there and hear, 'Oh, they just died. You should have been here a month ago.'"

age included exhaustive liner notes by Fahey and a reprint of his 1970 book, but he did not live to see its release, as he died following bypass surgery in 2001.

⊙ The Transfiguration Of Blind Joe Death
Takoma
John Fahey's magical, idiosyncratic, plaintive, resonant takes on the country blues tradition of Mississippi John Hurt, Bukka White and Charley Patton.

⊙ Return Of The Repressed Rhino
An essential 2-disc introduction to a body of work that can be as difficult as it is fascinating.

Fleetwood Mac

formed London, 1967

The multi-platinum pop success of the subsequent *Rumours*-era incarnation of Fleetwood Mac has served to obscure the fact that the original band bearing the name, led by guitarist **Peter Green**, was arguably the finest act to emerge from the British blues boom of the late 1960s.

Formed in 1967 by Green, drummer **Mick Fleetwood** and bass player **John McVie**, all former members of **John Mayall's Bluesbreakers**, the group was swiftly signed by Mike Vernon to his Blue Horizon label. With the addition of **Jeremy Spencer** on second guitar, Fleetwood Mac released their debut album in 1968. A seminal moment in British blues, it confirmed Green as a major guitarist who owed an obvious debt to B.B. King and was, at his best, up there with Clapton.

A working-class Jewish boy from the East End of London, Green delivered sinuous licks with a haunting, sweet-yet-melancholy tone, that had first been heard, to brilliant effect, on the instrumental "The Supernatural", on the only album he cut with the Bluesbreakers after replacing Clapton, *Hard Road*. On the first Fleetwood Mac LP, he sounded even better, combining fluency, speed and technique, while Spencer contributed convincing, copycat Elmore James licks.

On three albums, all released in little more than twelve months between 1968 and 1969 – *Mr. Wonderful*, *English Rose* and *Then Play On* – Green pushed the blues idiom to its limits. In the process, he wrote a series of memorable hit singles

for the band, including the moody instrumental, "Albatross"; the storming "Black Magic Woman", later covered by Santana; a quite superb reading of Little Willie John's "Need Your Love So Bad"; the doom-laden "Oh Well"; the autobiographical "Man of the World"; and "Green Manalishi". All were testament to his bursting and seemingly unstoppable creativity. Even B.B. King was moved to observe that Green was "the only man to ever make me sweat".

However, "Green Manalishi" also seemed to document Green's doomed struggle to halt his escalating descent into madness. That all was not well had first became evident on an American tour in 1969. At the time he was taking copious amounts of LSD, and after one particularly vivid trip in which he claimed to have been visited by an angel holding a starving African child in her arms, he demanded that the band should give all its money away. Needless to say, he got little support from his colleagues. The following year during a tour of Germany, he announced after a three-day acid binge that he couldn't go on. "It was a freedom thing. I wanted to go and live in a commune," he explained to this writer many years later. "In the end I didn't. I had to get away from the group. Acid had a lot to do with it."

Diagnosed as schizophrenic, Green was eventually admitted to a psychiatric hospital in 1973. When he came out, he worked as a grave digger and a hospital porter and when Fleetwood Mac's accountant attempted to deliver him a royalty cheque, he chased him off with an air rifle and was sectioned and given ECT treatment. "I was throwing things around and smashing things up," he recalls. "I smashed a car windscreen and the police came and took me to the station. They asked me if I wanted to go to hospital and I said yes, because I didn't feel safe going back anywhere else."

Green eventually returned to music in 1996 with the **Splinter Group**, but was a shadow of the player he had been. He reported that he had literally had to "relearn" the instrument from basics and had decided from now on to "keep it simple". However, as the Splinter Group released a prolific series of albums, including a 1998 collection of Robert Johnson covers half a dozen years before Clapton's similar outing, you could hear Green's confidence and touch returning, although he never completely regained his former virtuosity.

As for Fleetwood Mac, in 1970, after Green's departure they became a different band and swiftly left their blues roots behind. Green, surprisingly, was not the only guitarist in the band to suffer mental problems. Spencer quit to join the Children of God cult in 1971, while Danny Kirwan, who was recruited in 1968 to give the Mac an unusual three-guitar line-up, also later spent time in a psychiatric hospital.

⊙ **Fleetwood Mac** Blue Horizon
Fleetwood Mac's 1968 debut marked a pivotal moment in the story of British blues, combining covers such as "Shake Your Moneymaker" and "Got To Move" with Green's burgeoning talent as an original songwriter.

⊙ **Mr Wonderful** Blue Horizon
The band's sophomore 1968 effort was even better than their first, full of haunting Green compositions such as "Love That Burns", plus their trademark version of "Dust My Broom". It also features Christine Perfect on several tracks.

⊙ **Then Play On** Reprise
Peter Green's last studio album with Fleetwood Mac, from 1969, was in many ways the most accomplished, including "Oh Well", "Rattlesnake Shake" and the heartfelt "Closing My Eyes".

⊙ **Blues Jam At Chess** Blue Horizon
A dream come true for a bunch of British blues boys: one day in late 1968 Fleetwood Mac found themselves in Chicago at the Chess studios jamming with Buddy Guy, Otis Spann, Willie Dixon, Honeyboy Edwards and Shakey Horton.

Sue Foley

b Ottawa, Canada, March 29, 1968

Despite the trailblazing of **Memphis Minnie**, blues guitar has always been regarded as primarily a male preserve. What little challenge to this orthodoxy there has been has tended in recent years to come from white female players such as Rory Block, Bonnie Raitt and **Sue Foley**.

Foley grew up in Canada listening to her brother's Led Zeppelin and Rolling Stones records. Then one day she read the credits on the labels, and decided she needed to know who W. Dixon and M. Morganfield were. Once she had been enlightened, by the time she was thirteen, she was collecting records by Muddy Waters, Howlin' Wolf, Memphis Minnie and others. Taking up the guitar,

she started jamming around the clubs of Ottawa, before moving to Vancouver, where she bought a Telecaster and began to make a name for herself on the local blues scene, playing in a style that bore the influence of Earl Hooker, Freddie King and Magic Sam. At twenty she made a pilgrimage to Memphis, where one night she got to sit in with Duke Robillard, and was heard by Clifford Antone. He signed her to his eponymous Austin-based label, whereupon she moved to Texas and released four albums, starting with 1992's *Young Girl Blues*.

Despite returning to Canada in the mid-1990s, Foley has continued to record prolifically, including 2000's *Love Comin' Down* for Shanachie – her most commercially successful release to date – and a strong live album, *Change*, which appeared on Ruf in 2004. She's currently researching and writing a book on female guitarists. As her website puts it, "the blues can reach out to a pretty, red-haired teenager living in a downtown working class environment in a quiet orderly town and decide, somehow, that the girl has the heart and soul and toughness to both dig deep and bring the music to another place. The blues is seldom wrong and a lot of people are glad the blues found Sue Foley."

Canadian blueswoman Sue Foley

RUF RECORDS/IVAN OTIS

⊙ **Love Comin' Down** Shanachie
The 2000 album on which Sue Foley finally fulfilled the promise of her days in Texas. The set consists of strong, mostly original songs, with highlights including her ode to a busted marriage, "Two Trains", and a duet with Lucinda Williams on "Empty Cup".

Blind Boy Fuller

b Wadesboro, North Carolina, July 10, 1907; d Feb 13, 1941

An exemplary proponent of the east-coast "Piedmont" style, **Blind Boy Fuller** ranks among the most influential and best-selling singers and guitarists of the pre-World War II era. His impact upon the bluesmen of the Carolinas and down the eastern seaboard into Georgia, who copied his style and covered his songs, was in its way as profound as the influence of Charley Patton or Robert Johnson on the bluesmen of the Mississippi Delta. It's a measure of his popularity that Brownie McGhee began his recording career calling himself Blind Boy Fuller No 2.

Little is known of Fuller's early life, but his original name was Fulton Allen, and when he married his wife Cora Mae Martin in 1926, she was just fourteen, so they had to cross the state line into South Carolina to make their union legal. Within two years he had gone blind and he became highly dependent upon her. The couple moved to Durham (possibly to take advantage of the better aid for the blind available there), where he had the good fortune to meet and become friends with **Rev. Gary Davis**.

Until this point, Fuller does not appear to have been a very serious guitarist. However, he learned swiftly from Davis, and by 1933 was earning a living busking on the streets of Durham with a steel-bodied National guitar. J.B. Long, a local store manager who acted as a talent scout for the American Record Company (ARC), heard him there during the winter of 1934–1935. The following summer, Long, who was responsible for giving him the name Blind Boy Fuller, personally drove him, Bull City Red and Rev. Gary Davis to New York, where all three recorded.

Over the next six years, Fuller recorded 150 sides, mostly for ARC but also including one session for Decca, and backed at times by Bull City Red on washboard, Floyd Council on guitar and harmonica player Sonny Terry. Among his best-known songs were such risqué numbers as "Mama Let Me Lay It On You", "What's That Smells Like Fish?", "Get Yer Ya-Yas Out" (which the Rolling Stones later borrowed as an album title) and "Trucking My Blues Away". He also recorded some deep, mournful blues numbers like "When You Are Gone" and "Lost Lover Blues" as well as a stream of nimble-fingered rags, including "Rag Mama Rag", "Jitterbug Rag" and "Piccolo Rag". He missed out on a high-profile appearance at John Hammond's From Spirituals To Swing concerts at Carnegie Hall in 1938 because he

A record-label publicity photo of Blind Boy Fuller

REDFERNS

was in jail when they came looking for him; Sonny Terry and Brownie McGhee got the gig instead. His health was also declining fast due to his wayward lifestyle, and he contracted both syphilis and serious kidney disease. He recovered sufficiently to record his biggest hit "Step It Up And Go" with Terry in 1940, and made his final recordings a month before he died in February 1941, at the age of 34.

⊙ **East Coast Piedmont Style** Sony
For some reason, this excellent 20-track introduction to Blind Boy Fuller stops at 1939, which means it lacks the great "Step It Up And Go".

⊙ **The Essential** Classic Blues
Three dozen Fuller tracks across two discs, this time including "Step It Up And Go" as well as most of his other best-known songs.

⊙ **The Complete Recordings Vols 1–6**
Document
Everything Blind Boy Fuller ever recorded fits onto six discs, each available individually.

Jesse Fuller

b Jonesboro, Georgia, March 12, 1896; d Jan 29, 1976

Known as "Lone Cat", **Jesse Fuller** was the ultimate one-man blues band, playing twelve-string guitar, harmonica and kazoo on a neck rack, a hi-hat cymbal operated by his right foot, and an upright bass which he worked via foot pedals and levers and called a "fotdella". However, he didn't achieve any recognition as a musician until the 1950s, when his song "San Francisco Bay Blues" became an inescapable anthem of the folk-blues revival.

Jesse Fuller's mother had him adopted at the age of seven, by a family that he later complained beat him, starved him and treated him "worse than a dog". When he was ten, he made himself a crude guitar and began to learn songs from various local musicians. In his teens, he ran away from his hated adoptive family and worked his way around the South. Many years later he gave a fascinating list of his different occupations – grazing cows and working in a buggy factory, laboring in a lumber camp in Alabama and a furniture factory in Brunswick, laying railroad tracks, chopping wood

and toiling as a junkman in Griffin, Georgia. But he was also honing his musical skills, making extra money singing songs he picked up from traveling minstrel shows on street corners.

Shortly after World War I, Fuller moved to Cincinnati and joined the Hagenback Wallace Circus, then some time around 1920 hopped a freight train to California, where he lived for the rest of his life. Ever resourceful, he took a pitch shining shoes outside the gates of the United Artists studio in Hollywood and met Douglas Fairbanks, Sr. and director Raoul Walsh, who got him bit parts in several movies, including *East Of Suez*, *Thief Of Bagdad* and *Heart Of Dixie*.

In 1929, he moved north to Oakland and a job on the Southern Pacific Railroad, while during World War II he worked in the shipyards. Not until the late 1940s did music become his main activity. He secured a residency at a San Francisco club called the Haight Street Barbecue but still kept up his day job, opening a shoeshine stand in Berkeley, doing good business as his musical reputation grew. He appears to have written "San Francisco Bay Blues" around 1954. Assisted by the white folksinger Barbara Dane, he recorded three albums of blues, work songs and spirituals during the 1950s, while a cover of his "San Francisco Bay Blues" by **Ramblin' Jack Elliot** also considerably helped his cause. However, his real breakthrough came via an unofficial appearance at the 1959 Monterey Jazz Festival, where he was heard by the British bandleader **Chris Barber**. That led to an invitation to tour Europe in 1960 – allegedly delivered as he was returning from a day's work picking walnuts for a farm laborer's wages – where he found himself lionized by the emerging generation of British R&B performers, who had never seen anything quite like his "lone cat" style. "I got hearin' about fellers who were making lots of money on records," he explained. "I tried to get some fellers to play with me but they were always busy – drinking wine and gambling. So I said, 'I'm going to make me a one man band' and I did."

Reports of Fuller's European success filtered back home, and he became a regular at American folk and blues festivals and on the college and coffeehouse circuit. Among those who covered "San Francisco Bay Blues" were Peter, Paul and Mary and Donovan, while Eric Clapton and Paul McCartney also recorded versions many years later. Fuller's fellow Bay Area residents the Grateful Dead covered his "Beat It On Down The Line" and "The Monkey And The Engineer". He died in Oakland in 1976 at the age of 79.

⊙ **San Francisco Bay Blues** Original Blues Classics
Considering how influential he was, Jesse Fuller's recordings are not that easy to find. This collection contains a dozen of his best-known songs (including a truly brilliant version of "Stealin'"), but is likely to leave you wanting more.

Lowell Fulson

b Tulsa Oklahoma March 31, 1921; d March 6, 1999

Along with T-Bone Walker, the guitarist Lowell Fulson – not Fulsom as he was billed on some of his recordings – played a crucial role in shaping the post-World War II west coast blues sound, and influenced musicians as diverse as Ray Charles and B.B. King.

Fulson started his career backing **Texas Alexander** around 1939–40. According to some stories, he then hopped a freight train west in search of the promised land. The truth of his arrival on the West coast was actually more prosaic; called up to the US Navy, he was stationed in Oakland during the war. Staying on after his discharge, he was signed to a management deal by the producer Bob Geddins, who recorded him for various labels, including Big Town, Down Beat, Gilt Edge and Trilon. He also put a twelve-piece band together, which for a while included an unknown **Ray Charles** on piano and sax player Stanley Turrentine. Charles later covered Fuslon's "Sinner's Prayer" for Atlantic.

In 1948, Fulson recorded "3 O'Clock Blues", a song that soon gave **B.B. King** his first big hit. He had even greater success when he moved to the Swingtime label in 1950 and released "Lonely Christmas". Other early hits included a version of Memphis Slim's "Nobody Loves Me" that he re-titled "Everyday I Have The Blues"; "Low Society Blues" and "Blue Shadows". After recording briefly for Aladdin he transferred to Chess Records, and enjoyed a huge hit in 1954 on the label's Checker subsidiary label with "Reconsider Baby", cut in Dallas under Stan Lewis's supervision with a sax

section that included David "Fathead" Newman on tenor and Leroy Cooper on baritone. Six years later the song was covered by **Elvis Presley**. In the style of the time, Fulson followed "Reconsider Baby" with the sequel "I'm Glad You Reconsidered". Although he continued to live in California, he stayed with the Chicago-based Chess label until 1963, when he signed to the Kent label, owned by the Bihari brothers. Among the most successful sides he cut for the label was "Tramp", co-written with Jimmy McCracklin and later a hit for Otis Redding and Carla Thomas. He moved to Jewel Records in 1968 and continued recording for assorted small labels before ending up on Rounder's Bullseye imprint, for whom he recorded three albums in the 1990s. He died in 1999, a few weeks short of his 78th birthday.

Backed on his early sides by rollicking piano and a horn section, Fulson forged a potent guitar style that was smooth and strongly jazz-tinged. Although he's often mentioned in the same breath as T-Bone Walker, his guitar playing had more edge and he also proved more adaptable, effortlessly adjusting his style to changing trends to cut some wickedly funk-tinged grooves for Kent in the 1960s.

⊙ **Lowell Fulson 1946–53** JSP
A magnificent 4-disc set that pulls together all Lowell Fulson's earliest material from the late 1940s and early 1950s. Stand-outs include "Trouble Blues", "Three O'Clock Blues", a lovely rendition of "Every Day I Have The Blues", and ace guitar instrumentals "Low Society" and "Juke Box Shuffle".

⊙ **The Complete Chess Masters** MCA
A 45-track, 2-CD collection of Fulson's years with Chess, including "Reconsider Baby" plus "Please Don't Go", "You're Gonna Miss Me" and "Love Grows Cold".

⊙ **The Tramp Years** Ace
Two dozen tracks from Fulson's underrated soul-blues years on Kent in the early 1960s.

Anson Funderburgh

b Dallas, Texas, Nov 15, 1954

Influenced by the likes of Freddie King, Albert Collins and Jimmy Reed, **Anson Funderburgh** is a leading exponent of Texas blues guitar. After playing in various local bands, he recorded with the **Fabulous Thunderbirds** in 1981, then formed his own band the **Rockets**, with whom he's been playing ever since. They signed to the Black Top label in 1984. Two years later, harmonica player **Sam Myers** (b Laurel, Mississippi, Feb 19, 1936; d July 17, 2006) joined the band, doubling as lead singer. A veteran of the Chicago club circuit in the 1950s, Myers had played drums with Elmore James, and he released the great "Sleeping In The Ground" on the Jackson-based Ace label in 1957. "When Sam joined the Rockets we created something that's different and unique," says Anson. "With him, we have both the tradition of blues and the contemporary elements of our sound."

Over a series of fine albums spanning almost twenty years, Funderburgh and Sam Myers wove the separate Texas and Mississippi blues traditions into a highly successful partnership until Myers' death from throat cancer. The group backed Snooks Eaglin, and moved to Rounder's Bullseye Blues imprint in 1999. Their most recent album, *Which Way Is Texas?*, appeared in 2003. Funderburgh is often compared to **Stevie Ray Vaughan**, largely because of their similar age and Texan upbringing, and the fact that both made the Fender Stratocaster their instrument of choice. However, Anson has a quite different sound and style, based on a cleaner and leaner vintage 1950s' tone.

⊙ **Thru The Years: A Retrospective 1981– 1992** Black Top
A decent compilation of the Rockets' first seven albums for Black Top, showcasing both Funderburgh's ace guitar playing and the harp and powerful vocals of Myers.

⊙ **Change In My Pocket** Bullseye
This fine 1999 set from the Rockets ranges from the high-energy title track to the slow-burn of "Little Girl", via the Muddy Waters-influenced "Highway Man" and the Diddley-esque "Willie Jo".

Rory Gallagher

b Ballshannon, Ireland, March 2, 1948; d June 15, 1995

Surely the best bluesman ever to come out of Ireland, **Rory Gallagher** was a guitarist of both power and subtlety. A great ambassador for the blues, he enjoyed success in the rock world without ever compromising his love of the music that originally inspired him.

Born in Donegal but raised in Cork, Gallagher first had his passion for music aroused, like many of his contemporaries, when he saw Elvis Presley on TV. That inspired him both to get his first guitar, and to trace the music back to its blues roots and discover Leadbelly, Muddy Waters and others.

Gallagher started his professional career playing in showbands but, bored by a diet of Irish standards and covers of the latest popular hits, he transformed the Impact Showband into a six-piece R&B outfit and headed for Hamburg's club scene. The band soon slimmed down to a lean threesome, out of which in 1967 he formed **Taste**, a blues-rock power trio who built a healthy following on the British college circuit. Gallagher disbanded the group in 1970 and embarked on a solo career with Polydor. A fine slide player and gutsy singer, he was particularly impressive live, and the excitement of his on-stage performance was well captured on the 1972 album, *Live! In Europe*. It reached the UK top ten, and he dislodged Eric Clapton at the top of the annual Melody Maker "best guitarist" poll.

He followed with a brace of fine studio albums in *Blueprint* and *Tattoo*, both of which appeared in 1973, and that same year guested on **Muddy Waters'** *London Sessions* on Chess. Further collaborations followed, both with **Jerry Lee Lewis**

and with **Albert King** on his *Live In Montreux* album. He was one of several guitarists the Rolling Stones sounded out when they were looking for a replacement for Mick Taylor in 1974, but in the event that year was more memorable for another storming live album, *Irish Tour 1974*, released in conjunction with a Tony Palmer documentary film of the same name.

In 1975, Gallagher left Polydor for Chrysalis, for whom he recorded six albums in seven years. He also continued to gig prolifically, and undertook an estimated thirty US tours in the course of his career. However, he increasingly came to reject the celebrity lifestyle and trappings of rock'n'roll stardom, preferring a more downhome approach in keeping with his blues roots. In 1985, he formed his own label and publishing company, Capo, but his later albums were workmanlike affairs, lacking his earlier fire. He died following a liver transplant in 1995 at the age of 47. His legacy has been well served in recent years by various compilations, remastered and expanded reissues, and a DVD of the 1974 Irish tour film.

⊙ **Live! In Europe** Polydor
Rory Gallagher's classic 1972 live album includes such favorites as Junior Wells' "Messin' With The Kid", Blind Boy Fuller's "Pistol Slapper Blues" and the mandolin stomp "Going To My Hometown", culminating with the great "Bullfrog Blues".

⊙ **The Big Guns: The Very Best of Rory Gallagher** BMG
Two dozen tracks over two discs make this 2005 compilation a decent introduction to Gallagher's work, although hardcore fans have been critical of its somewhat predictable selection.

Larry Garner

b New Orleans, 1952

An inventive songwriter and rootsy guitarist, **Larry Garner** was one of the most interesting names to emerge on the blues scene during the 1990s, after several decades of paying his dues both in and outside music. Born in New Orleans but raised around Baton Rouge, he got his first guitar at eleven, and was taught to play by his uncle George Lather. He was soon performing with a gospel group, the Stars Of Joy, but in his teens he came under the influence of such local bluesmen

RUF RECORDS

The ever patient Larry Garner

as Lonesome Sundown, Silas Hogan, Henry Gray, Clarence Edwards and Guitar Kelly, and he joined his cousin in an R&B group called the Twisters.

A call-up to the US army brought a halt to Garner's nascent career as a blues guitarist. Although he played regularly for his fellow servicemen, when he returned home to Baton Rouge he put ideas of a musical career to one side while he raised a family, and worked for the next two decades at the Dow chemical plant. He played in the evenings when he could, and eventually, in his thirties, he landed a regular slot at Tabby's Blues Box, a famous Baton Rouge club run by the self-styled "king of swamp blues", Tabby Thomas. Even then, his rise was hardly meteoric. He won the B.B. King "Lucille" Award in 1988 for his song "Doghouse Blues" and released a cassette that he sold from the side of the stage at live shows. However, he did not release his debut album proper until 1991, when *Chemical City Shakedown* appeared on Sidetrack Records.

Since then, there's been no stopping him. He's made up for lost time with a prolific run of albums mostly featuring his own material, and has become a regular visitor to Britain and Europe, where he's a popular fixture at blues festivals. In 1993 he signed to the London-based JSP label, for whom he made *Too Blues*, named after the complaint another record company made about his music when turning him down. Two years later he signed to the French label Gitanes Jazz, owned by Verve, which finally found him on a major label and with

some promotional and marketing clout behind him. After two albums, *You Need To Live A Little* and *Baton Rouge*, he then signed to the German Ruf label. He continues to tour prolifically, both in America and Europe.

⊙ **Too Blues** JSP
A fine 10-track showcase for Larry Garner's guitar playing and songwriting talents, from 1993.

⊙ **Once Upon The Blues** Ruf
A winning collection from the year 2000, including the great "Where Blues Turn Black".

Jazz Gillum

b Indianola, Mississippi, Sept 11, 1904; d March 29, 1966

Jazz Gillum was one of the most recorded blues harmonica players of the 1930s and 1940s, often accompanied by **Big Bill Broonzy** on guitar. Born in Mississippi in 1904, he was named William McKinley Gillum in honor of the recently assassinated president. His parents died when he was young, and he was brought up by an uncle who was a church deacon. He made his first music in church, where he learned to play an old pump organ, and he soon picked up the harmonica as well.

Some time around 1915, Gillum and his elder brothers ran away from their sternly religious uncle. By the age of twelve he was in Minter City, working first as a field hand and then in a drug store, supplementing his meager income by playing the harmonica on the streets for tips. At the age of nineteen he joined the musical migration north from Mississippi to Chicago, where he worked a number of day jobs, but found plentiful opportunities to play in the clubs at night. That was how he met Broonzy, who brought him to the attention of Lester Melrose, who recorded a brace of sides by him for Bluebird in 1934. They didn't sell and Gillum returned to obscurity. However, an attempt by the Regal Zonophone label to sign him a couple of years later reignited Bluebird's interest, and he went on to record more than sixty further sides for them before the decade was out. These included "Key To The Highway", a song he's credited with writing and which he recorded both under his own name and accompanying Broonzy. He also cut some sides for Vocalion in 1940, and by World

War II his records were said to be outselling those by every other harmonica player except Sonny Boy "John Lee" Williamson.

Gillum was called up to the US Army in 1942 and served for three years. He resumed his recording career in 1946, cutting another 34 sides for Bluebird, including "Look On Yonder Wall" with Big Maceo on piano, and working regularly with the guitarist Willie Lacey, who proved to be at least as fluent an accompanist as Broonzy. However, while Gillum's playing was highly attractive, characterized by a high, reedy and casual style, it lacked invention. His late 1940s sides showed little or no development from those he cut in the mid-1930s and he proved sadly unable to adapt to changing blues tastes. By the 1950s his star was sinking rapidly, as the new sound of Muddy Waters and co took over the Chicago scene.

Gillum did briefly re-emerge in 1961, when Memphis Slim helped him to record one album for Folkways and another for Candid Records, but they lacked impact and he benefited little from the folk-blues revival, partly because he was not in good shape mentally or physically. The guitarist Mike Bloomfield visited him in 1962, and reported that although the temperature outside was 95 degrees, Gillum was inside his house, in front of his stove, with a coat on. He died in 1966, after being shot in the head in the course of an argument. He was 61.

⊙ **It Sure Had A Kick: The Essential Recordings Of Jazz Gillum** Indigo
Two dozen of Jazz Gillum's prime 1930s tracks, nicely remastered and featuring accompanists including Big Bill Broonzy, Blind John Davis and Washboard Sam.

Rosco Gordon

b Memphis, April 10, 1928; d July 11, 2002

A stalwart of the Memphis blues and R&B scene in the 1940s and 1950s, the pianist Rosco Gordon is perhaps best known for the electrifying sides he cut with Ike Turner at Sam Phillips' Memphis Recording Service.

For many years, blues references books listed Gordon's date of birth as being 1934, but it emerged at the time of his death that he was actually six years older than he had ever let on. The earlier date makes sense, for by the late 1940s he was already a member of the legendary **Beale Streeters**, with **B.B. King** and **Johnny Ace**. A self-taught pianist clearly influenced by the likes of Amos Milburn, he came to the attention of **Ike Turner**, who recorded him at Sam Phillips' studio in 1951. As Phillips had yet to set up his own Sun Records, he sold the masters to Chess, who immediately put out "Booted" as a 78. At the same time, Phillips had also sold the masters to RPM in Los Angeles, and the same record's availability on two different labels helped the track to the top of the R&B charts the following year. The follow-up, "No More Doggin'", was just as successful, and its loping boogie shuffle became known as "Rosco's rhythm". Owing something to the relaxed, rolling piano beats of Fats Domino, the sound was also said to be an influence on the rhythms of **bluebeat** that were to emerge from Jamaica a few years later. When Phillips created Sun Records in 1952, he recorded Gordon on a string of further hits including "The Chicken". The latter launched a brief dance craze, and led to his appearing on stage with a rooster he named "Butch." Gordon also regularly played piano on shows at the famed Memphis radio station, WDIA, where he recorded with the likes of Johnny Ace, Bobby "Blue" Bland and Earl Forest. He left Memphis for New York at the end of the 1950s and recorded "Just A Little Bit" for Vee Jay in 1960. A catchy, sax-inspired tune driven by a riff borrowed from Jimmy McCracklin, it made number two in the R&B charts, but was his last real hit.

In 1970, he formed his own label Bab-Roc with his wife Barbara, with whom he'd recorded a few duets a decade earlier. Little new material appeared, however, and he made his living primarily from running a laundry business. He made something of a comeback in the 1980s, touring the UK and reuniting with B.B. King for a 1982 appearance at London's 100 Club. His final album, *Memphis Tennessee*, was recorded in 2000 with Duke Robillard and his band. He died in 2002 at the age of 74, just days after appearing at a star-studded gala at Memphis' Orpheum Theatre to celebrate the reconstruction of the city's Stax building.

⊙ **Bootin: The Best Of The RPM Years** Ace
Two dozen of Rosco Gordon's finest tracks from the 1950s, including his signature tune "No More Doggin'" as well as "Booted", "Saddled The Cow" and "Dime A Dozen".

Otis Grand

b Beirut, Lebanon, Feb 14, 1950

Billing himself as "the Gentle Giant of the Blues", and eschewing the contemporary rock influences embraced by so many modern bluesmen, the guitarist **Otis Grand** has built a particularly substantial following for his big-band blues in Britain, where he relocated from the US in the late 1980s.

Born Fred Bishti in Beirut in 1950, Grand moved to the West coast of America and began playing blues guitar at the age of thirteen, influenced by the likes of B.B. King, T-Bone Walker and Otis Rush, from whom he took the first part of his name. Playing with local bluesmen around the San Francisco Bay area, he became good friends with **Joe Louis Walker**, who produced his 1988 debut album, *Always Hot*, on the Special Delivery label.

Around the same time, he moved to London, where he formed the ten-piece big band, Otis Grand and The Dance Kings, and toured Europe supporting John Lee Hooker, B.B. King, Albert Collins and Stevie Ray Vaughan among others. A second album, *He Knows The Blues*, featuring Walker again as well as Pee Wee Ellis on horns, came out on the British-based Sequel label in 1992. That was followed by *Nothing Else Matters* in 1994, *Perfume And Grime* in 1996, and a high-energy live album.

By the late 1990s, Grand had started to replicate his European success in America, supported by energetic touring. He has also recorded collaborative albums with Guitar Shorty, Philip Walker, Joe Houston, as well as with his old friend Joe Louis Walker on the album *Guitar Brothers* and with Anson Funderburgh and Debbie Davis on *Grand Union*. A true apostle for the blues, he runs a "Blues in Schools " lecture program aimed at teaching British schoolchildren about the music and prides himself on his purist approach. "For a very long time I never listened to any one but B.B. King and Robert Johnson, and I'm glad I missed out on all the heavy blues-rock acid thing that was going on in the 1960s," he says. "That's the way I've preserved the deep blues roots of my playing."

⊙ **In Grand Style** Sanctuary
A well-packaged 2-disc, 34-track compilation of the best of Otis Grand's studio recordings.

Beirut bluesman Otis Grand

ASHLEY GODWIN

Stefan Grossman

b Brooklyn, New York, April 16, 1945

After studying under none other than the Rev. Gary Davis, Stefan Grossman went on to become one of the most expert young white guitar-pickers of the 1960s folk-blues revival, and has since become a prominent guitar educator and blues historian.

During the early 1960s, Grossman gravitated to the Greenwich Village folk scene, where he saw and met many country blues veterans. In particular, he came under the influence of Rev. Gary Davis, and spent hours at his house in Harlem, absorbing guitar licks and blues lore. He also picked up tips first hand from Mississippi John Hurt, Son House, Skip James, Mance Lipscomb and Fred McDowell.

In 1963, he formed the **Even Dozen Jug Band** with John Sebastian, Maria Muldaur and David Grisman. Three years later he released the instructional Elektra LP, *How To Play Blues Guitar*, on which he attempted to pass on what he had learned. He worked briefly with boho-East Side underground rock/folk group the Fugs, and with keyboarist Barry Goldberg, before he relocated to Europe around 1967. After living in Italy for a short while, he made Britain his base and recorded a string of impressive, if at time slightly academic, blues albums for Transatlantic, such as *Yazoo Basin Boogie* and *Ragtime Cowboy Jew*. He later co-founded the **Kicking Mule** label, not only as a vehicle for his own recordings, but as a showcase for a wide and eclectic range of acoustic blues and folk guitar recordings.

Returning to America in the 1980s, Grossman signed to Shanachie, and has continued to record prolifically ever since. His books include *Ragtime Blues Guitarists* and *The Country Blues Song Book*, and he also runs Vestapol Videos, a company specializing in instructional guitar releases.

⊙ **How To Play Blues Guitar** Shanachie
Everybody's got to start somewhere. For Stefan Grossman, it was this fantastic 1966 primer on fingerpicking techniques: together with Rory Block, he effortlessly demonstrate blues styles from Lonnie Johnson to Charley Patton via Blind Boy Fuller.

⊙ **Yazoo Basin Boogie** Shanachie
Displaying dazzling technique but without the showboating, this 1970 Grossman album includes versions of "I'm So Glad", "Avalon Blues" and "Dallas Rag".

⊙ **Best Of Transatlantic** Castle
Decent 23-track compilation of Stefan Grossman's fingerpickin' early 1970s albums.

The Groundhogs

formed England, 1963

A major British progressive blues-rock band of the late 1960s and early 1970s, who also backed such blues giants as John Lee Hooker and Champion Jack Dupree on their UK visits, the **Groundhogs** were led by the guitarist and blues enthusiast **Tony "T.S." McPhee**. (b

March 22 1942). Part of the first generation of British blues disciples, McPhee developed his interest in American folk-blues during the skiffle craze. In 1962, he was among the many young aspiring blues musicians who were drawn to the Marquee Club in the heart of London's Soho by the weekly residency of **Blues Incorporated**, led by Alexis Korner and Cyril Davis.

McPhee's first group, the Dollarbills, was essentially a pop band, but by 1963 he'd renamed them John Lee's Groundhogs, in recognition of John Lee Hooker and his song "Ground Hog Blues", and added blues pianist **Bob Hall** to the line-up. Musically more adept than most beat groups of the time, the Groundhogs were chosen to back Champion Jack Dupree on his earliest British gigs, while in July 1964, they also got to back their hero, Hooker himself. Hooker was also instrumental in securing their first record release, when he sent an acetate of them performing "Shake It" and "Rock Me Baby" to his label Vee Jay, which released the single on the Interphon label. The group also recorded an album with Hooker, released for some bizarre reason under the title *Live At The A-Go-Go Club, New York*, which was a lie on just about every count for it was actually recorded in a studio in London. The band also recorded several tracks with Mike Vernon, and had a crack at recording an Otis Redding-influenced soul single, before splitting in 1966.

McPhee subsequently busied himself with session work, including playing on Champion Jack Dupree's *From New Orleans To Chicago*, and recorded some blues tracks produced by Jimmy Page on which he was backed by Jo-Ann Kelly and Bob Hall, and which later emerged on the Immediate label. After a brief dalliance in the psychedelic outfit Herbal Mixture, McPhee then formed a new edition of the Groundhogs, with bassist Pete Cruickshank and drummer Ken Pustelnik. Moving into a heavy, prog-rock style but still strongly blues-influenced, the group recorded a string of big-selling albums for Liberty, the most notable of which were *Blues Obituary* (1969), *Thank Christ For The Bomb* (1970), and *Split* (1971). As a power trio they also developed a formidable reputation as a live outfit, playing extended jams built around mutated twelve-bar blues-rock riffs, full of grinding chords. The group split again in 1975, but they have re-formed from time to time for nostalgia tours. McPhee has also recorded and toured as a solo performer.

⊙ **Split** EMI

This re-mastered version of the Groundhogs' 1971 classic features bonus tracks from BBC radio sessions, recorded around the same time. Be warned, though – it's more hard rock than blues.

⊙ **3744 James Road: The HTD Anthology** Castle

A 30-track, 2-disc compilation of the Groundhogs' more blues-oriented material that includes versions of "Smokestack Lightnin'" and "Sittin' On Top Of The World".

Guitar Slim

b Greenwood, Mississippi, Dec 10, 1926; d Feb 7, 1959

Heavily influenced by the Texan guitar style of Clarence "Gatemouth" Brown and T-Bone Walker, **Guitar Slim** brought a new showmanship to the blues, wearing flamboyant costumes in primary colors with his hair dyed to match, performing acrobatics on stage, experimenting with feedback and distortion techniques at high volume long before the days of Jimi Hendrix, and using a 350-foot guitar cable to wander through the audience as he played – and sometimes even out of the door and into the street.

Eddie Jones started out singing in church choirs in Mississippi, before drifting to New Orleans and forming a band with **Huey "Piano" Smith**. It was in the Crescent City that he assumed the persona of Guitar Slim, and began playing one of the first solid-bodied electric guitars. His wild reputation as a live performer soon led to his recording debut with Imperial Records in 1951, who released him under his birth name to little success (the record sold better later when re-credited to Guitar Slim). He then recorded for Bullet Records, before switching to Specialty, for whom he cut "The Things That I Used To Do" in 1954. Featuring **Ray Charles** on piano – it's supposedly him shouting "yeah!" at the end – the songs gave Slim his biggest hit, and its distinctive guitar riff has since been much copied.

In 1956 he signed for Atco, who attempted without much success to market him to the new teenage rock'n'roll audience, in the same way that Chess Records had sold Chuck Berry. After contracting pneumonia while on tour, he died in New York City in 1959, at the tragically young age of 32.

⊙ **The Things That I Used To Do** Ace

Twenty-three Guitar Slim classics, including such prime cuts as "You Give Me Nothing But The Blues" and "Going Down Slow" in addition to the indispensable title track.

Buddy Guy

b Lettsworth, Louisiana, July 30, 1936

Once dubbed by Eric Clapton "by far and without doubt the best guitar player alive," **Buddy Guy** is the best-known name in blues today after the peerless B.B. King, with a track record of uncompromising integrity that stretches back half a century and more.

The Louisiana-born George Guy made his first guitar from household implements, and began copying the "race" records he heard on the radio. By the early 1950s, he was in Baton Rouge, and had already developed a style that was heavily inspired by Texas bluesmen such as T-Bone Walker and Lightnin' Hopkins, as well as a stage presence influenced by the flamboyant Eddie "Guitar Slim" Jones. In 1957 he moved north to Chicago, where he joined the Rufus Foreman Band. He established himself as a name in his own right the following year, when he beat both Magic Sam and Otis Rush in a "Battle of the Blues" contest. Sam, who was already signed to the Cobra label, was gracious enough in defeat to recommend Guy to Eli Toscano, who owned both the Artistic and Cobra labels. Guy cut "Sit And Cry" and "This Is The End" for Artistic, but they didn't sell well enough to prevent Toscano from going bankrupt.

By now, Buddy's obvious talent was in demand, and in 1960 he signed to the market leader Chess Records, serving as a session guitarist for Muddy Waters, Willie Dixon, Howlin' Wolf, Little Walter, Sonny Boy Williamson and Koko Taylor among others. "It keeps me going that I got to play with those guys," he was still saying decades later. "Everyone from Arthur Crudup, Sonny Boy Williamson and even Lonnie Johnson, the day before he died."

Under his own name he recorded such memorable tracks as "First Time I Met The Blues" – written many years earlier by **Little Brother Montgomery**, who played piano on Guy's version – and "Stone Crazy". Sadly, however, Chess was by this time already locked in its own past, and uninterested

REDFERNS

One Guy and his Stratocaster: Buddy back in the 60s

the American expatriate **Jimi Hendrix**, who took such stage antics as playing the guitar with his teeth and behind his back from Guy. One reason the rock'n'roll fraternity took so strongly to Buddy was his age. Guy seemed to represent a new breed of Chicago guitarist, steeped in the traditions of the blues but also capable of speaking to a younger generation. As Tony Russell, the doyen of British blues writers, put it, "He was the first bluesman who didn't come across as soberingly senior, who was youthful enough to jump about and do sexy stuff with his guitar."

While with Vanguard, Guy resumed his partnership with Junior Wells on such collaborative albums as *Hold That Plane!*, and it was this pairing – once described as an electrified version of Sonny Terry and Brownie McGhee – that provided the model for John Belushi and Dan Aykroyd's comic act as the **Blues Brothers**. Their collaboration is perhaps heard to best effect on 1970's *Buddy Guy and Junior Wells Play The Blues*, co-produced by Clapton And Atlantic Records boss Ahmet Ertegun.

Also in 1970, Guy and Wells supported the Rolling Stones on tour; Keith Richards is yet another British guitarist to count among his disciples. A memorable 1974 performance at the Montreux jazz festival by the pair was later released as a live album. However, the remainder of the decade proved lean for Guy. He came back strongly in the 1980s, working again with Wells after the success of the Blues Brothers, and establishing his own blues club, Legends, in Chicago, which has become a famous stop-off for all visiting bluesmen. In 1990 he played with Clapton at London's Royal Albert Hall, and the following year released one of his best-ever albums in *Damn Right I Got The Blues* on Silvertone, which

in the new direction Guy was offering the blues – Leonard Chess reputedly described his playing as "motherfucking noise" – so he moved on. After cutting the superb *Hoodoo Man Blues* album with the harpist **Junior Wells** for Delmark in 1965 (on which he was credited under the pseudonym "Friendly Chap"), he proceeded to record half a dozen superb albums of his own for Vanguard, starting with 1968's *A Man And The Blues*.

Guy had already made his first visit to England with the American Folk Blues Festival, where he become a major influence on a generation of guitarists. These included white Englishmen like **Eric Clapton**, who claimed that seeing Guy playing with a power trio had given him the idea for Cream, **Jeff Beck**, and **Jimmy Page**, as well as

featured Clapton, Beck and Mark Knopfler, and won a Grammy award. The follow-ups, 1993's *Feels Like Rain* and 1994's *Slippin'*, maintained the quality control and during the first half of the 1990s, he was said to have sold five million records, an unprecedented achievement for a blues artist.

Guy has continued to make fine albums for Silvertone ever since, including the brilliant acoustic set *Blues Singer* in 2003 and the most recent, 2005's *Bring 'Em In*, which features guest appearances from Carlos Santana, Keith Richards, Tracy Chapman and Keb Mo among others. He also joined the Rolling Stones once again for several dates on their 2005–2006 world tour, appearing with the band on a version of Ray Charles' "(Night Time Is) The Right Time". He has used his celebrity to found the Buddy Guy Foundation, with a mission to erect tombstones to neglected blues musicians of the past.

⊙ The Complete Chess Studio Recordings Chess

Don't it always seems to go that you don't know what you've got 'til it's gone – Chess may not have rated Buddy Guy in the 1960s, but when he became a blues legend, they put out every track they could find in the vaults. Every note on this 2-disc, 47-track collection is a monument to their misjudgment.

⊙ A Man And The Blues Vanguard

Buddy Guy's dramatic Vanguard debut from 1968, produced by Samuel Charters with a band including Muddy Waters' drummer Fred Below and Otis Spann on piano, and including such great songs as "One Room Country Shack", "Sweet Little Angel" and "Mary Had A Little Lamb", later famously covered by Stevie Ray Vaughan.

⊙ Buddy Guy And Junior Wells Play The Blues Atlantic

A Clapton-produced album of sparkling duets by the original Blues Brothers, recorded in 1970.

⊙ Damn Right I've Got The Blues Silvertone

The 1991 comeback album that deservedly restored Buddy Guy to the spotlight, much as *The Healer* had done for John Lee Hooker.

⊙ Blues Singer Silvertone

Still going strong in the 21st century – 2003, to be precise – Buddy Guy delivers wonderful acoustic versions of such blues classics as "Hard Time Killin' Floor" and "Crawlin' King Snake".

Playlist
Buddy Guy

1 FIRST TIME I MET THE BLUES (1960) from **The Complete Chess Studio Recordings**
A "motherfucking noise" according to Leonard Chess, but a glorious one, with Little Brother Montgomery on piano.

2 STONE CRAZY (1961) from **The Complete Chess Studio Recordings**
Some of Guy's most manic guitar playing, which gave him his one and only chart hit.

3 WEE WEE BABY (1963) from **Folk Festival Of The Blues (Aka Blues From Big Bill's Copacabana)**
A live recording with Muddy Waters and Willie Dixon, on which Guy matches his elders inch for inch.

4 CHITLIN CON CARNE (1965) from **Hoodoo Man Blues**
A superb instrumental workout with harp player Junior Wells.

5 LEAVE MY GIRL ALONE (1966) from **The Complete Chess Studio Recordings**
How did Chess fail to recognize the genius of tracks like this?

6 MARY HAD A LITTLE LAMB (1968) from **A Man And The Blues**
An influence on white blues-rock guitarists from Clapton to Stevie Ray Vaughan.

7 DAMN RIGHT I GOT THE BLUES (1991) from **Damn Right I Got The Blues**
"...from my head down to my shoes..."

8 FEELS LIKE RAIN (1993) from **Feels Like Rain**
A superb version of John Hiatt's song, accompanied by Bonnie Raitt on slide guitar and backing vocals.

9 MY TIME AFTER AWHILE (1995) from **Live! The Real Deal**
A sublime, smoldering, live after-hours version of a song Guy first recorded in the 60s.

10 HARD TIME KILLING FLOOR (2003) from **Blues Singer**
Eric Clapton describes this song as "almost impossible" to play – but Buddy Guy makes it sound easy.

Vera Hall

b Payneville, Alabama, circa 1902; d Jan 29, 1964

Sometimes also credited as Vera Ward Hall, **Vera Hall** recorded one of the finest collections of authentic African-American song for the Library Of Congress, in a voice that the folklorist **John Lomax** described as the loveliest he had ever come across.

Born in Alabama into a poor farming family some time around 1902, Hall worked all her life as a cook and a washerwoman. She was also blessed with an extraordinary voice, although she was not heard on record until the late 1930s. She was originally discovered by the writer and folklorist Ruby Pickens Tartt, who told Lomax about her. Between 1937 and 1940, Lomax and his son Alan recorded her singing some fifty songs solo for the Library of Congress, and as many again duetting with her cousin **Dock Reed**. These included both a cappella spirituals and secular folk-blues on titles such as "Somethin' On My Mind", "Low Down Chariot Let Me Ride", "Wild Ox Moan", "Death Have Mercy", "Trouble So Hard" and "Boll Weevil Blues".

Hall was recorded again in the late 1940s for Folkways' *Negro Folk Music Of Alabama* series, while she traveled to New York City in 1948 at the behest of Alan Lomax to perform at the American Music Festival at Columbia University. Lomax also interviewed her extensively, using the material as the basis for his 1959 book *The Rainbow Sign*. To preserve Hall's privacy he gave her the pseudonym "Nora", but he was clearly describing Vera when he wrote: "Her singing is like a deep-voiced shepherd's flute, mellow and pure in tone, yet always with hints of the lips and the pleasure-loving flesh.

The sound comes from deep within her when she sings, from a source of gold and light, otherwise hidden, and falls directly upon your ear like sunlight. It is a liquid, full contralto, rich in low overtones; but it can leap directly into falsetto and play there as effortlessly as a bird in the wind."

She died in Alabama in 1964, but some 35 years later, the techno-artist Moby introduced her voice to a new generation of listeners when he sampled her singing "Trouble So Hard" on "Natural Blues", the key track from his 1999 multi-platinum album *Play*.

⊙ *Various Artists* **Deep River of Song: Alabama** Rounder Records
No individual disc of Vera Hall's work is available but she features prominently on this collection of recordings made by the Lomaxes for the Library of Congress, which includes "Another Man Done Gone" and "Trouble So Hard".

⊙ *Moby* **Play** Mute
Moby's 1999 masterpiece fluidly mixed ancient voices from the Delta with modern techno elements, although, regrettably, the sleeve notes did not see fit to mention that Vera Hall's was the voice gracing the key track.

John Hammond

b New York, Dec 15, 1910; d July, 1987

John Hammond was arguably the greatest American record producer of the twentieth century. While his first love was jazz, he also discovered and produced a number of key blues artists during the 1930s, and went on to be a mentor to **Bob Dylan** when he was starting out in the early 1960s.

John Henry Hammond II was born into a wealthy New York family and educated at Yale. He studied the piano and violin in his youth, and developed an interest in black music in his teens when he began exploring the streets of Harlem. He wrote in his autobiography many years later that the key moment came in 1927, when he heard **Bessie Smith** singing at her peak at the Alhambra Theatre. The experience determined him to make his career in music and in 1933 he discovered a 17-year-old singer called **Billie Holiday**, produced her first recordings and teamed her with the pianist Teddy Wilson. He also produced Bessie Smith's final sessions, worked with the young **Benny Goodman** (who became his brother-in-law when he married Hammond's sister Alice), and discovered **Count Basie** and **Charlie Christian**. Some of the musicians he worked with found his patrician airs hard to take, but he was a passionate early campaigner against racism, and in 1938 he organized the "Spirituals To Swing" concert at New York's Carnegie Hall, which gave mainstream exposure to several major jazz and blues acts and took black music to a new white, middle-class audience. A second concert followed in 1939.

Following military service in World War II, Hammond lived in Europe for a spell then, back in the US, worked for a number of labels as a staff producer including Vanguard, Keynote, Majestic and Mercury. In 1959 he took a senior post at Columbia Records, where he remained for the next two decades, during which time he supervised the release of Robert Johnson's *King Of The Delta Blues* collection, signed Bob Dylan (who in his early days was referred to at the label as "Hammond's folly") and the youthful Aretha Franklin, and later worked with Bruce Springsteen.

His father's son: John Hammond Jr.

⊙ *Various Artists* **From Spirituals To Swing 1930–1939** Vanguard
Several albums out there document these concerts, but this three-CD set is the most comprehensive. A crucible of black music of the time, there is plenty of the big-band swing of Count Basie, but also spine-tingling blues and gospel contributions from Joe Turner, Pete Johnson, Albert Ammons and Sister Rosetta Tharpe.

John Hammond Jr.

b New York City, Nov 13, 1942

The son of the jazz and blues record producer of the same name, **John Hammond, Jr.** has been playing classic blues since the 1960s, combining potent guitar and harp playing with an expressive vocal style and a burning integrity in his attitude towards his music.

Although young John Hammond didn't grow up with his father – his parents split up when he was a child – he clearly came under his musical influence.

He began playing guitar at school, developing a fascination with the slide technique of the great Delta bluesmen. "I was inspired initially by Chuck Berry and Bo Diddley," he says. "Then I discovered the roots of it all. When I began playing professionally, I incorporated all my passions into what I did solo, so I did Chuck Berry and Bo Diddley songs as well as Muddy Waters and Howlin' Wolf."

No doubt Hammond's name helped, but he clearly had real talent, too. Signing to Vanguard Records in the 1960s, he developed a reputation as a powerful live performer, sharing the bill with blues greats like Muddy Waters and Howlin' Wolf and appearing at the 1963 Newport Folk Festival with the likes of Mississippi John Hurt and Rev. Gary Davis.

Hammond recorded five albums for Vanguard between 1963 and 1967, including *So Many Roads* on which he was backed by the Hawks (later to become the Band) and harpist Charlie Musselwhite. Since then he's continued to record prolifically for a huge number of labels. In the 1970s he was on Atlantic, Columbia and Capricorn, while over the last 25 years he's released albums on Sonet, Rounder, Point Blank and Back Porch Records, working mostly in acoustic vein, and tirelessly touring the world's festivals and blues clubs. His music has seldom deviated from the blues path upon which he embarked during the 1960s, inspired equally by the prewar Delta players such as Robert Johnson and the great Chicago bluesmen of the postwar era. However, in 2001 he released *Wicked Grin*, a collection of songs by **Tom Waits** that was produced by Waits himself, while the follow-up, 2003's *Ready For Love*, his debut for Back Porch Records, was helmed by David Hidalgo of Los Lobos. He also presented the 1992 TV film/DVD release, *The Search For Robert Johnson*.

⊙ **John Hammond Live** Rounder
John Hammond, Jr., in 1992, doing what he probably does best – performing live and solo on a bunch of blues standards that have the audience eating out of his hand.

⊙ **Found True Love** Point Blank
This fine 1995 Hammond release saw him recording with a band that included Duke Robillard on guitar and Charlie Musselwhite on harp.

⊙ **Best Of The Vanguard Years** Vanguard
A good 23-track introduction to John Hammond Jr., featuring strong covers of songs by Robert Johnson and Muddy Waters, and Jimmy Reed's "Big Boss Man".

W.C. Handy

b Muscle Shoals, Alabama, Nov 16, 1873; d March 28, 1958

Due to his self-assumed title of "the father of the blues", **W.C. Handy** has always been a controversial figure, whose true role in the development of the music has been much debated. What is undeniable is that he played a major role in popularizing an already emerging form, and few would begrudge him the statue that stands on Beale Street in Memphis in honor of his part in the history of the blues.

William Christopher Handy was born into a family of ministers in Alabama in 1873, and received his first lessons on the cornet in a barber shop. In 1893 he led a quartet that performed at the Chicago World's Fair, and he spent the next few years traveling the South. After teaching briefly in a music college in Alabama, he joined Mahara's Minstrels as a cornet player and swiftly rose to

become leader of the troupe. In 1902, he formed his own marching band-cum-dance orchestra in Clarksville, Mississippi, and it was the following year that he had his famous first encounter with the blues via an anonymous musician at a railway station in Tutwiler, Mississippi, detailed in the narrative section of this book and widely regarded as the earliest description of a Delta blues singer. Shortly after, his band shared the stage in Cleveland, Mississippi, with a local trio of black folk-blues musicians, and he became fascinated by the way their songs pleased the crowd.

Over the next few years, Handy collected fragments and lyrics from the early blues songs he heard on his travels and in 1912 he famously published the sheet music to "The Memphis Blues". The song is sometimes erroneously referred to as "the first blues", but in fact it was preceded into print both by Artie Matthews' "Seals Blues" and "The Dallas Blues" by Hart A. Wand. That said, it was "The Memphis Blues" that "crystallized the music into a coherent form" as Giles Oakley put it in his 1976 book *The Devil's Music*, and captured the imagination of musicians from the deep South to Broadway.

Handy also penned "Beale Street Blues", inspired by a walk down the famous Memphis thoroughfare one night before World War I. "My attention was caught by the sound of a piano. The insistent Negro rhythms were broken by a tinkle in the treble, then by a rumble in the bass; then they came together," he wrote later in his autobiography. "I entered the cheap cafe and found a colored man at the piano, dog tired. He told me he had to play from seven at night until seven in the morning, and rested himself with alternate hands. He told me of his life, and it seemed to me that this poor, tired, happy-go-lucky musician represented his race. I set it down in notes, keeping faith with all that made the background of that poor piano thumper." "St Louis Blues" was another famous Handy composition, although it remains a matter of conjecture as to how much of his work was original and how much of it collected from itinerant musicians across the South.

Handy took his Memphis Orchestra to New York in 1917, where he stayed and recorded and published further songs. He collected many of them in the 1926 book, *Blues: An Anthology*. He also recorded with **Jelly Roll Morton** (with whom he had a long-running feud), but his career as a performer was ultimately curtailed when an eye disease sent him blind. During the 1930s he wrote and collected spirituals, publishing *W. C. Handy's Collection Of Negro Spirituals* in 1938. That same year, a tribute concert was held for him at New York's Carnegie Hall. Three years later he published his autobiography, *The Father Of The Blues*. He died in New York at the age of 84 in 1958, the same year that Nat King Cole portrayed him on screen in the film *St Louis Blues*.

⊙ **W.C. Handy's Memphis Blues Band** Memphis Archives
Big-band sides recorded in 1917–18 that fuse ragtime, jazz and blues, but beware the crackle and hiss as the original masters were not available to the compilers.

including "Weed Smoker's Dream", later reworked for Lil Green as "Why Don't You Do Right?" They were also in demand as studio sessionmen, backing the singers Johnny Temple, Rosetta Howard and Frankie "Half Pint" Jackson.

They split up when Morand returned to New Orleans in 1939. There was nothing innovative about their style, but they made music that was fun, and they were influential on Louis Jordan and even early Muddy Waters.

⊙ **Let's Get Drunk And Truck** (Fabulous)
While Document Records has done its usual comprehensive job on a 4-disc "collected works" series spanning the Harlem Hamfats' entire career, these fourteen fun tracks will serve most needs.

The Harlem Hamfats

formed Chicago, 1936

The **Harlem Hamfats** were unusual in that they were purely a studio creation put together by **Mayo "Ink" Williams** (b Monmouth, Illinois,1894; d Jan 2, 1980, Chicago). The most successful black record company executive of his day, he was responsible for discovering a host of artists, from Blind Lemon Jefferson to Mahalia Jackson. He conceived the Harlem Hamfats when he was head of black A&R at Decca in Chicago, as a fusion of Delta blues and New Orleans jazz styles and in response to Tampa Red's **Chicago Five**, who had just started recording for the rival Bluebird label. The basic line-up included brothers Joe and Charlie McCoy on guitar and mandolin, both of whom were from Mississippi; the New Orleans trumpet player Herb Morand, who acted as band leader; clarinettist Odell Rand; John Lindsay or Ransom Knowling on bass; Horace Malcolm on piano; and drummers Pearlis Williams and Freddie Flynn. Joe McCoy, who at one time was married to Memphis Minnie, handled most of the vocals and was also a decent songwriter.

The name Harlem Hamfats was Williams's idea of an in-joke, for none of them was from Harlem, while "hamfats" was the name given to unskilled musicians, which they most assuredly were not. Their first release, "Oh Red", was an immediate hit, and they recorded prolifically between 1936 and 1939, cutting some 75 sides. Several boasted risqué lyrics about drinking, sex and drugs,

Corey Harris

b Denver, Colorado, Feb 21, 1969

The very epitome of the post-modern bluesman, Corey Harris learned his chops playing on the streets of New Orleans, but is also a college-educated musician and a blues scholar who has traveled and recorded widely in West Africa while researching the roots of the Delta tradition.

Harris grew up singing in church groups, playing trumpet and tuba in a marching band and in a high school rock group. Yet it was always black music, from R&B and blues to funk and reggae, that most interested him, and he became fascinated by the African roots that lay behind them. His interest was further fueled by a degree course in anthropology, and in the early 1990s he made two extended field trips to Cameroon to study African language and culture. On his return he took a teaching post in Louisiana and began playing on the streets of New Orleans. "Blues was what I understood deepest in myself," he says, "because I grew up with that. My mom was of that generation. She lived in the depression in northeast Texas near Louisiana, so I always heard stories about it. It wasn't a stretch for me to understand what was going on, even though it took me a while to be able to play it."

Harris' debut release, *Between Midnight And Day*, appeared on Alligator in 1995 and made an immediate impact as a modern, rural blues exploration of the songs of Charley Patton, Sleepy John Estes, Fred McDowell and others. *Fish Ain't Bitin'* appeared two years later and was followed by 1999's *Greens From*

Corey Harris, globetrotter of the blues

Turner's Rising Star Fife and Drum Band. Turner himself had died just a week before the sessions, so his twelve-year old granddaughter, Shardé Thomas, played the fife in his place.

Harris followed with 2005's *Daily Bread*, another adventurous collection on which he turned for production assistance to Scott Billington and Steve Reynolds, on the strength of their own impressive album of contemporary remixes of old folk-blues material released as *Alan Lomax's Southern Journey Remixed* under the name Tangleye.

⊙ **Fish Ain't Bitin'** Alligator
Corey Harris' second album, from 1997, consists of near-perfect modern acoustic blues.

⊙ **Greens From The Garden** Alligator
On this eclectic 1999 adventure, Corey Harris expanded his horizons to take in the entire gamut of African-American musical styles.

⊙ **Mississippi To Mali** Rounder
Earthy modern field recordings from 2003, mixing traditional blues and African melodies on songs by Skip James and Blind Willie Johnson with originals by Harris and Ali Farka Touré.

⊙ **Daily Bread** Rounder
West African influences, Delta blues and roots-reggae collide on a 2005 offering that suggests Corey Harris just keeps on getting better.

The Garden, an audacious mix of other black forms such as reggae, ska, hip-hop and ragtime as well as Delta blues. In 2000 came the album *Vu Du Menz*, a collaboration with the New Orleans pianist **Henry Butler**. Harris then moved to Rounder Records to continue his journey on 2002's *Downhome Sophisticate*, which contained his most potent songwriting to date and merged blues, African influences and rock in brilliantly original style.

The following year he visited Mali in West Africa to play with the "king of the African blues", **Ali Farka Touré**, as part of Martin Scorsese's blues film, *Feel Like Going Home*. A few months later he went back without the TV cameras to record tracks for his next album, *Mississippi To Mali*. "I felt like it was important to get with the music from over there, and to bring what little I know from our short tradition here as black people in America, and to put it back together and make a document of it," he said at the time of its release. "I'm not trying to say the blues all came from Mali. It's just one of the strains, one of the really strong strains that make up black music in America. The point is you can take that music that we have over here, and it can go over there and be conversant."

Eight of the album's fifteen tracks were recorded in Africa with musicians including Ali Farka Touré (among them superb versions of Skip James's "Special Rider Blues" and Robert Petway's "Catfish Blues"), and a further four in Mississippi, where collaborators included harmonica player Bobby Rush, veteran blues drummer Sam Carr, and Otha

Wynonie Harris

b Omaha, Nebraska, Aug 21, 1915; d June 14, 1969

Known as "Mr Blues" and heavily influenced by Big Joe Turner, **Wynonie Harris** was, with his big, raucous voice, seldom out of the R&B charts during the late 1940s. Although he rocked with earthy, wanton abandon, and had a storming hit with the classic "Good Rockin' Tonight", he failed to survive the advent of the rock'n'roll era and after the mid-1950s his career went into a tailspin.

Hailing from the unlikely blues wellspring of Nebraska, Harris attended college as a medical student, but by 1938 he was singing blues in Omaha nightclubs. He then relocated to the west coast, where he joined Lucky Millinder's orchestra. Backed by **Johnny Otis** and his band, he cut his first solo release for Philo Records in 1945 on "Around The Clock Blues", which later served as the template for Chuck Berry's "Reeling and Rocking". Next he signed for Apollo Records, for whom he recorded the 1946 jump blues hits "Wynonie's Blues", backed by Illinois Jacquet's combo, and "Playful Baby".

Harris' brash, cocksure style hit a chord, and he enjoyed even greater success when he switched to Cincinnati's King Records, for whom he cut his first number one in 1948 with a cover of Roy Brown's "Good Rockin' Tonight", backed with "Good Morning Mister Blues". Despite its title, Brown's version of the song had not really rocked. With Hal "Cornbread" Singer on tenor sax, Harris's most certainly did. He added gospel hand-claps to the backbeat to create a rollicking rhythm that not only became hugely popular in the blues of the period but also led all the way to the birth of rock'n'roll. Further hits followed, many of them with highly suggestive lyrics including "I Want My Fanny Brown", "I Like My Baby's Pudding", "Good Morning Judge", "Lovin' Machine", "Lollipop Mama", "Sitting On It All The Time", and "All She Wants To Do Is Rock".

For some reason, however, Harris failed to find favor with the new rock'n'roll audience, and by 1955 the hits had dried up. He recorded for Atco and Roulette without success, and in 1963 he moved to LA, where he ran a nightclub and played small club gigs where he could. He recorded a handful of fine blues sides for Chess in 1964, and died of cancer in 1969.

⊙ **Rockin' The Blues** Proper
This exhaustive 4-disc box set contains more than eighty tracks from Wynonie Harris's 1944 to 1950 heyday, and comes with a fine 52-page illustrated booklet.

⊙ **Bloodshot Eyes: The Best Of Wynonie Harris** Rhino
An 18-track, single-disc overview of Wynonie Harris's career, for those who don't want an entire box set's worth.

Alvin Youngblood Hart

b Oakland, California, March 2, 1963

S tanding nearly six foot six and weighing 250 pounds, **Alvin Youngblood Hart** cuts a striking figure. His music is equally memorable, ranging from acoustic rural blues to full-on guitar rock of Hendrix-like intensity.

Hart grew up traveling around the US, the family moving wherever his father could find work. He taught himself to play the guitar at the age of fourteen, by which time he was in Chicago. Although his first band played garage rock, he busily soaked up blues influences, seeking out the city's old blues players and learning as much as he could from them. He was also influenced by frequent trips to his grandmother's home in the hill country of northern Mississippi, where he found a connection with a rural lifestyle and musical culture quite different from the big city. That instilled in him a deep appreciation of the acoustic blues of an earlier generation of performers, including Charley Patton, Leadbelly, Bukka White, Blind Willie McTell and Skip James.

By 1986, and now living in Los Angeles, Hart had totally turned his back on the electric blues scene and was performing exclusively in acoustic "unplugged" style on vintage string instruments he had himself lovingly restored. A spell of military service in the Coast Guard interrupted his musical career, but as luck would have it he ended up stationed in the heart of Mississippi blues country, on a riverboat in Natchez. "There was a saloon in Natchez, a kind of an outlaws-plus-tourists type place, and I'd play music in this bar or even outside in the daytime, playing for tips. Whatever band had the weekend gig, they'd have me sit in with them, playing Muddy Waters, Wilson Pickett, whatever songs we all knew," he recalls.

Hart stayed in the Coast Guard until 1993, by which time he'd been posted to Bolinas, California, where he immersed himself in the Bay Area music scene and befriended local bluesman Joe Louis Walker, who invited him to open for him at a number of gigs. After a series of dates supporting Taj Mahal, he signed to the Sony subsidiary Okeh and his debut album, *Big Mama's Door*, earned him the 1997 W.C. Handy Award for Best New Artist. *Territory* followed in 1998 on Joe Boyd's Hannibal Records and

Alvin Youngblood Hart taking it back to the roots

found him adding rock, reggae and western swing to his Delta blues roots, while 2000's *Start With The Soul* was a crunching electric blues-rock album. On *Down In The Alley*, released in 2002 on the Memphis International label, he returned to his acoustic roots with fine interpretations of tunes by Son House, Charley Patton, Skip James and Leadbelly among others, before switching back to an electric style for 2005's *Motivational Speaker* on Tone Cool.

⊙ **Big Mama's Door** Okeh
Alvin Youngblood Hart's sensational 1997 debut includes cracking versions of such blues standards as "Gallow's Pole" and "Pony Blues".

⊙ **Territory** Hannibal
On this 1998 release, Alvin Youngblood Hart was less blues-centric than on his debut, but the sounds of the Delta still underpin his more eclectic approach.

⊙ **Down In The Alley** Memphis International
Alvin Youngblood Hart's fourth release marked a welcome return to acoustic country blues, with an inspired selection including Patton's "Tom Rushen Blues", Leadbelly's "Alberta", and a great take on "Motherless Child".

Screamin' Jay Hawkins

b Cleveland, Ohio, July 18, 1929; d Feb 12, 2000

The outrageous stage performances of **Screamin' Jay Hawkins** sometimes obscured the fact that he was also an amazing singer with an untamed blues power and an enviable ability to scat and ad-lib, who will always be remembered for his feral rendition of "I Put A Spell On You".

According to one story, Jalacy Hawkins was raised by Blackfoot Indians. He certainly learned to play piano and saxophone as a youth, and was sufficiently inspired by the voice of Paul Robeson that he's said to have considered a career as an operatic baritone. Instead, he became a boxer, winning an amateur Golden Gloves contest at the age of fourteen and becoming middleweight champion of Alaska when he was twenty.

Hawkins then retired from the ring to play piano, working with Illinois Jacquet, Gene

188

Ammons and others. He joined Tiny Grimes' Rocking Highlanders in 1951, and recorded "Why Did You Waste My Time" with the band as well as some solo sides on both Mercury's Wing subsidiary and Grand Records. His big break came when his friend **Wynonie Harris** brought him to New York in 1956, and he recorded the extraordinary "I Put A Spell On You" for Columbia's Okeh imprint, backed by an ace band including guitarist Mickey Baker and saxophonist Sam "The Man" Taylor. Seldom can any record ever have been blessed with a vocal of such total abandon, and the track raised howls of protest. Some accused Hawkins of being drunk, which he apparently was, while one critic even complained that he sounded "cannibalistic".

He had now found a unique style, and further tracks followed in similarly untamed vein, including "Hong Kong", "Alligator Wine", "Person To Person", "Feast Of The Mau Mau", "I Hear Voices" and "There's Something Wrong With You", even if none of them quite captured the same manic spontaneity of "I Put A Spell On You". He also developed an extraordinary live show, in which he appeared on stage leaping out of a coffin, and which involved such stage props as a flaming skull on a stick, which he named Henry.

By the 1960s, Hawkins' style had begun to seem both histrionic and old-fashioned, although he enjoyed a certain renewed notoriety with his lavatorial "Constipation Blues", recorded for Phillips in 1969. Yet he continued to tour and record steadily, appeared in the 1978 film, *American Hot Wax*, and he opened for the Rolling Stones in 1980. Keith Richards later helped him to record a remake of "I Put A Spell On You". He also made memorable movie appearances in *Mystery Train* and *A Rage in Harlem*.

When Hawkins died in 2000 following emergency surgery to treat an aneurysm, he left an enduring legacy, not only via "I Put A Spell On You" and the long list of those who covered it from Van Morrison to Nina Simone, but on an entire school of rock performers specializing in stage outrage, from Arthur Brown and Alice Cooper to Black Sabbath. He also left a large number of children by different mothers, who managed to find each other via a much-publicized website, www.jayskids.com, which asked "Are You Screaming Jay Hawkins' child?".

⊙ **Voodoo Jive: The Best Of Screamin' Jay Hawkins** Rhino
Seventeen tracks upon which Hawkins does indeed scream some jive of a distinctly voodoo variety.

Jimi Hendrix

b Seattle, Washington, Nov 27, 1942; d Sept 18, 1970

Had he been born a few decades earlier, **Jimi Hendrix** would surely have been a bluesman to rank alongside the likes of Charley Patton, Robert Johnson and Muddy Waters. Instead, he came of age in the rock'n'roll era, and although the blues was a cornerstone of his music, he went on to make some of the most revolutionary rock music ever heard, and played the electric guitar with a virtuosity and invention that still has not been matched more than 35 years after his death.

James Marshal Hendrix taught himself to play the guitar, which explains how he came to play left-handed and upside down on a right-handed instrument. By the age of twelve, he had graduated to an electric guitar and spent long hours listening to blues records and learning the licks of Robert Johnson, Hubert Sumlin, Elmore James and B.B. King. After playing in local rock'n'roll bands, he joined the US Army at the age of seventeen, enlisting as a paratrooper in the 101st Airbourne Division.

On his discharge in 1962, Hendrix began working as a guitar for hire, playing back-up for Little Richard, Ike and Tina Turner, Wilson Pickett, Sam Cooke, the Isley Brothers and King Curtis among others. By late 1965 he was living in Greenwich Village, New York, where he formed his first band, Jimmy James and the Blue Flames. He was discovered working the Village clubs by former Animals bassist **Chas Chandler**, who offered to become his manager and bring him to England.

On his arrival in 1966, he formed the **Jimi Hendrix Experience** with **Noel Redding** on bass and **Mitch Mitchell** on drums. The combination of his instrumental virtuosity and his showmanship had a huge and immediate impact, particularly on fellow guitarists like Pete Townshend, Eric Clapton and Jeff Beck, who flocked to see his early London club appearances. After signing to Track Records, over the next four years he set about changing the face of popular music with the intensity of his art. A discussion of the psychedelic and heavy rock elements of his music isn't particularly relevant here, other than to stress how deeply rooted in the blues much of his playing was.

Hendrix's three studio albums with the Experience, 1967's *Are You Experienced?* and *Axis: Bold As Love*, and 1968's *Electric Ladyland*, were essentially rock albums filledwith songs characterized by hippy, trippy lyrics. However, his blues roots were fully exposed on tracks such as "Red House", while the likes of "Voodoo Chile (Slight Return)" could also trace a lineage back to the Delta bluesmen. Even his infamously distorted version of "Star Spangled Banner" at the Woodstock festival in 1969 was drenched in the spirit of the blues, albeit warped and twisted into weird shapes it had never previously assumed.

Apparently influenced by criticisms that he had become an "Uncle Tom" figure, playing for primarily white audiences, Hendrix dissolved the Experience and formed the all-black **Band of Gypsies**, with drummer Buddy Miles and bassist Billy Cox, whom he'd known in the US Army. They recorded just one album before he died on Sept 18,1970, choking on his own vomit after taking several sleeping pills.

Since his death, numerous albums have repackaged Hendrix's work and raided the vaults for every last note of his guitar playing ever recorded, whether in a studio or in concert. One source calculates that more than 300 recordings not released during his lifetime have appeared since his death. The quality and motivation of many of these releases has been questionable, but the two albums that have compiled the tracks showing his debt to the Delta, and his prowess as a bluesman, can be unreservedly recommended.

⊙ **Blues** Polydor
A 1994 compilation that includes Jimi Hendrix's versions of Muddy Waters'"Mannish Boy" and Albert King's "Born Under A Bad Sign", brilliantly book-ended by acoustic and electric versions of"Hear My Train A-Comin".

⊙ **Martin Scorsese Presents The Blues: Jimi Hendrix** Polydor
An intriguing set released in conjunction with Scorsese's 2003 series of PBS blues films, which as well as "Red House", "Hear My Train A-Comin'", and "Voodoo Chile" includes the previously unreleased "Georgia Blues" and "Blue Window".

Z.Z. Hill

b Naples, Texas, Sept 30, 1935; d April 27, 1984

A soul-blues singer with a classic style influenced by Bobby Bland and Johnnie Taylor, Z.Z. Hill enjoyed one of the biggest blues hits of the 1980s with "Down Home Blues" at a time when appearances by blues songs in the charts had become exceedingly rare.

Arzell Hill started out in the 1950s singing in the Spiritual Five gospel group. All the while, however, he was collecting secular records by the likes of not only Bland and Taylor but B.B. King, Freddie King, Sam Cooke and Wilson Pickett. In 1964 he moved to California and recorded "You Were Wrong" for his brother's M.H. label. Later that year he signed to Kent, recording such sophisticated soul-blues sides as "Hey Little Girl" and "I Found Love", before he moved to United Artists, for the hit "Love Is So Good When You're Stealing It".

In 1980, Hill signed to **Malaco Records**, where in his mid-forties he enjoyed the most successful phase of his career, both commercially and artistically. During the late 1970s he had got sidetracked into disco but, starting with the single "I'm Gonna Stop You From Givin' Me The Blues", Malaco took him back to his blues roots with a strong appeal to a black female audience and a rich vein of cheatin' songs about adultery. He went on to cut four albums for the label, including 1982's *Down Home Blues*. The title track was still on the R&B chart two years later when Hill died of a heart attack in 1984, at the age of 48.

⊙ **Greatest Hits** Malaco
In the absence of career retrospective that includes Z.Z. Hill's earlier singles, this 11-track compilation of his 1980s' work for Malaco offers a fine showcase for his Bobby Bland-influenced vocals.

Silas Hogan

b Westover, Louisiana, Sept 15, 1911; d Jan 9, 1994

A mainstay of the blues scene in Baton Rouge, Louisiana, for half a century, **Silas Hogan** was already in his 50s by the time he made his first recordings in a style he always described as the "low down blues".

Hogan learned his blues from a guitar-playing uncle as well as the recordings of Blind Lemon Jefferson and Kokomo Arnold. As a young man, he played at house parties on guitar and kazoo. "A dollar and a half was all you got. Start early and play all night," as he later put it. By the end of the 1930s he was in Baton Rouge, working in an oil refinery and playing in the city's blues clubs by night. Yet it was 1959 before he entered a recording studio, and even then the tracks appeared under the name of drummer Jimmy Dotson. In 1962, he was finally signed to **Excello Records**. Backed by a tight trio that included former Guitar Slim sideman Guitar Kelly and bassist Gene Douzier, he cut both Louisiana swamp blues and R&B sides at Jay Miller's Crowley studio in a powerful style that betrayed the influence of Jimmy Reed and Lightnin' Slim. He made further recordings for Arhoolie and Blue Horizon and continued playing around Baton Rouge for the remainder of his life. As late as the end of the 1980s, he was playing a Saturday night residency at top local nightclub Tabby Thomas' Blues Box, and he recorded a 1988 album for the UK label, Blues South West, with a band that included his son Sam on drums. He died in 1994, at the age of 83.

⊙ **Trouble: The Excello Masters** Excello
A generous 26 sides, culled from Silas Hogan's early 1960s recordings produced by Jay Miller.

Smokey Hogg

b Westconnie, Texas, Jan 27, 1914; d May 1, 1960

Influenced by Big Bill Broonzy and Peetie Wheatstraw, the work of **Smokey Hogg** divides blues enthusiasts into two camps. Some find the intimate style of his country blues and unique rhythmic approach highly endearing; others believe his eccentric sense of timing ruined everything he ever recorded.

Raised on a farm in East Texas, Andrew Hogg was taught to play guitar by his father, Frank Hogg, and teamed up in his teens with slide guitarist and vocalist B.K. Turner (aka Black Ace). With Hogg sometimes billed as **Little Peetie Wheatstraw**, the pair played dances, juke joints and the turpentine and logging camps around East Texas, and traveled to Chicago in 1937 to record two sides for

Decca Records, "Family Trouble Blues" and "Kind Hearted Blues".

After army service, the postwar years found Hogg busking around the Deep Ellum area of Dallas, where he was heard by Herb Ritter, who ran the local label Bluebonnet Records. Ritter recorded several sides with Hogg and leased them to Modern Records in Los Angeles. A version of Big Bill Broonzy's "Too Many Drivers" did well enough for Modern to bring him to LA for further sessions, which produced his two biggest hits, "Long Tall Mama" in 1949 and "Little School Girl" the following year. On his Modern sides he was accompanied by a trio that usually included the pianist **Hadda Brooks** (b Los Angeles, Oct 29, 1916; d Nov 21, 2002), who seemed to have little trouble with Hogg's unique and ramshackle sense of timing.

Hogg went on to record more than hundred sides for Modern, and further material for a huge number of other labels, including Combo, Recorded In Hollywood, Specialty, Imperial, Federal and Mercury. He died of cancer in 1960, at the age of 46; a blues singer who turned up in New York around 1970 claiming to be Hogg was proved to be an imposter.

⊙ **Deep Ellum Rambler** Ace
A well-researched compilation with 17 tracks Smokey Hogg recorded for Modern plus ten previously un-issued recordings from the 1940s. His idiosyncratic approach will either charm or infuriate – or sometimes both at the same time.

Billie Holiday

b Philadelphia, Pennsylvania, April 7, 1915; d July 17, 1959

There are those who will tell you that **Billie Holiday** was not a blues singer, but strictly jazz. Frankly, it's a pointless argument. True, she recorded primarily in a jazz context. But as the official website to her memory declares, "Her singing expressed an incredible depth of emotion that spoke of hard times and injustice as well as triumph" – which has to be about as good a definition of blues singing as you can get.

Eleanora Fagan spent much of her early life in Baltimore, Maryland, where she was raised in extreme poverty by a mother who had been just thirteen when she was born. At the age of twelve, she moved to Harlem, and was at one point arrested for prostitution. She also auditioned as a dancer at a local speakeasy. Instead she landed a job as a singer, and was eighteen when she was discovered by record producer **John Hammond**. Impressed by the rough, bluesy quality she brought to her repertoire of standards, he was convinced she had created a new style of jazz singing, and over the next few years teamed her in the studio with a range of great musicians, including Benny Goodman, Teddy Wilson, Duke Ellington, Ben Webster, and saxophonist **Lester Young**, who gave her the name "Lady Day". She also toured with the bands of Count Basie and Artie Shaw, before becoming a solo singer in 1939.

With Young in particular she created some of the greatest jazz recordings of all time. Most potent

of all was "Strange Fruit", a chilling song about a lynching which she recorded in 1939. Among her other memorable sides from the era were "God Bless The Child" and "Gloomy Sunday", both of which seemed to express an incredible pain at the center of her life. By the mid-1940s, she had become addicted to heroin and cut an increasingly tragic figure. The 1950s were a period of steady decline into addiction and alcoholism, with a concomitant decline in the control of her voice. She died in 1959 at the age of 44, and was even arrested for possession of narcotics on her deathbed. The world's greatest jazz singer? For sure. But not for nothing did she call her autobiography *Lady Sings The Blues*. She lived them, and you can hear it in almost every note she ever recorded.

⊙ **Lady Day: The Complete Billie Holiday On Columbia 1933–1944** Sony

A magnificent ten-disc box set that holds everything Holiday recorded before she went into decline.

⊙ **Lady Day: The Best Of Billie Holiday** Sony

Anyone looking for a more compact collection of Billie Holiday's classic Columbia sides need look further than this 2-disc set, which compiles 36 of the key tracks from the massive box set.

⊙ **The Commodore Master Takes** Polygram

You won't find "Strange Fruit" on the above sets, for the simple reason that Columbia deemed the song too controversial to record. Instead, Billie cut it for Milt Gabler's Commodore Records, and it appears on this compilation of the sixteen tracks she recorded for the independent label between 1939 and 1944, along with such other classics as "Billie's Blues" and "I Gotta Right To Sing The Blues".

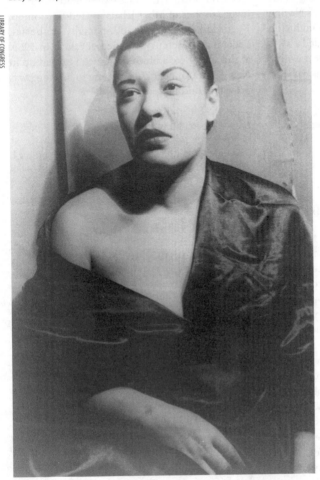

Lady Day – epitome of the blues

LIBRARY OF CONGRESS

Homesick James

b Somerville, Tennessee, May 3, 1914

The guitar and bass playing of **Homesick James** can be heard on many recordings by his better-known cousin **Elmore James**. But over a long career he's also made numerous solo recordings, while after his cousin's death in 1963, he became the keeper of the flame for the slashing Elmore James style of bottleneck playing.

Born James Williamson in Tennessee, he has sometimes claimed his date of birth as 1905, although 1914 is widely accepted. His early years remain surrounded in confusion, and he has made various conflicting claims over the years about his activities, but it seems likely that by his late teens he was playing guitar at house parties, dances and fish fries. On his musical travels around the South in the 1920s, he came across the likes of Yank Rachell, Sleepy John Estes, Blind Boy Fuller and Big Joe Williams, and developed his characteristic slide guitar style, running a pen-knife over the strings.

Settling in Chicago in 1932, James formed a band that included **Snooky Pryor** and **Babyface Leroy Foster**. He claims to have cut a few sides for RCA Victor in 1937, but his first recordings to reach an audience were made for Art Sheridan's Chance Records in 1952 and 1953, when he cut "Lonesome Ole Train" and "Homesick", the song that gave him his name.

During the 1950s he also worked as a sideman, backing Sonny Boy "Rice Miller" Williamson and his younger cousin, Elmore James, whose style he emulated and in whose band, the **Broomdusters**, he played. However, although he was four years older than Elmore, his claim to have taught him the riff to "Dust My Broom" should probably be taken with a pinch of salt. In the 1960s, he recorded a crashing, electrified version of Robert Johnson's "Crossroads" for Colt, and further tracks for Prestige and Vanguard. He visited Europe several times with the American Folk Blues Festival and in the early 1970s recorded several albums for the British-based Big Bear label, including one with his old friend Snooky Pryor. During the 1990s he was recorded by several labels keen to document the work of one of the last links with the prewar blues, including Appaloosa, Earwig and Icehouse. He was still playing into the new century and traveled to New Orleans in 2004, to record the album *My Home Ain't Here* for Fedora Records. At the time of writing he was believed to be the oldest surviving bluesman, a year ahead of David "Honeyboy" Edwards.

⊙ **Blues On The South Side** Original Blues Classics
Blistering bottleneck guitar and gruff, emotional vocals on a 1964 recording that Homesick James made with pianist Lafayette Leake, bassist Eddie Taylor, and drummer Clifton James.

⊙ **The Big Bear Sessions** Castle
This 39-track, 2-disc compilation comprises the albums *Home Sweet Homesick James* from 1973, the following year's *Shake Your Boogie*, and 1975's collaborative *Homesick James & Snooky Pryor*.

Earl Hooker

b Clarksdale, Mississippi, Jan 15, 1930; d April 21, 1970

Earl Hooker was a brilliant but under-appreciated blues guitarist of shimmering clarity, whose talent has seldom received the recognition it deserved. Overshadowed by his second cousin John Lee, he suffered ill-health during his lifetime, and did not record his first full-length album until shortly before his death at forty years old.

Earl Zebedee Hooker moved with his family to Chicago when he was a boy. He started playing guitar in his mid-teens after meeting **Robert Nighthawk**, who was a major influence on his playing. Known to his friends as "Zeb", he was by the early 1950s playing in the band led by **Ike Turner**, who recommended him to the King label for whom he cut a few sides in 1952. He also recorded for Sun Records in Memphis, again following a recommendation from Turner, but spent most of the decade on the road before returning to Chicago in the early 1960s. There he recorded a number of powerful instrumentals including "Blue Guitar", "Tanya", "Blues in D Natural" and "Universal Rock", for labels including Chess, Chief and Age. He found employment as a sideman on recordings by **Muddy Waters** (it's his slide playing that can be heard on "You Shook Me"), Junior Wells, Sleepy John Estes, Brownie McGhee and A.C. Reed, and played the searing solo on Lillian Offitt's "Will My Man be Home Tonight", later copied by **Otis Rush** on his instrumental "I Wonder Why".

In 1968 he signed to Chris Strachwitz's **Arhoolie Records**, after being recommended by Buddy Guy. Several of his Arhoolie sides featured backing from well-known Chicago sidemen like Louis and Dave Myers, Carey Bell, Andrew Odom and Eddie Taylor. The following year he traveled to Europe as part of the American Folk Blues Festival. His appeal to the new blues-rock audience was potentially enormous, for he was more than ready to adapt to the tastes of the times, using a wah-wah pedal on several recordings and playing a double-necked guitar in the style of Jimmy Page. But he was already ill with advancing tuberculosis, and died in Chicago in 1970 at the age of forty.

After Hooker's death, B.B. King cited him as one of his favorite guitarists, offering the unusual but flattering analogy: "If Earl Hooker was a truck driver, he'd be able to back his rig into any space, no matter how tight."

⊙ **Two Bugs And A Roach** Arhoolie
Earl Hooker wasn't much of a singer, but this 1969 recording displays his guitar virtuosity, and finds him playing slide guitar through a wah-wah pedal.

⊙ **Simply The Best** MCA
Some blistering guitar solos over nineteen tracks, including sides issued under Earl Hooker's own name as well as recordings made with Muddy Waters, Johnny "Big Moose" Walker, Charles Brown, and Sonny Terry and Brownie McGhee, as well as a duet with cousin John Lee.

John Lee Hooker

b Clarksdale, Mississippi, Aug 22, 1917; d June 21, 2001

A true original, **John Lee Hooker** was a colossus whose compelling, mysterious sound dominated the blues scene for more than half a century.

One of at least eleven children, he was born in Mississippi to a sharecropping family around 1917 – there has always been some dispute about the exact year – and learned guitar from his stepfather, **Will Moore**. At fourteen he ran away to Detroit and enlisted in the army. He was thrown out after three months when they discovered he had lied about his age, which explains the later confusion about the year of his birth. Sent back to Mississippi, he had no intention of wasting his life working on a farm. By the mid-1930s he was in Memphis, where he was befriended by **Robert Lockwood**. Hooker keenly soaked up as much blues lore as he could from Lockwood and oth-

ers, before moving to Cincinnati, where he played in juke joints as well as singing gospel with the Fairfield Four and the Big Six.

By the early 1940s Hooker had made his way to Detroit. Working in a car factory by day and singing at house parties and in the clubs around Hastings Street by night, he honed his distinctive boogie style. He was discovered by Bernard Besman, the owner of Sensation Records, who recorded him for the first time in 1948. The results, which Besman immediately leased to Modern Records, included "Boogie Chillen" with its hypnotic drone, which gave Hooker a million-seller. Developed from the sounds he had picked up in the blues and jazz clubs on Hastings Street, the sparse arrangement, twangy electric guitar, deep stuttering voice and tapping foot keeping the beat were to become his trademark for the next half century. Further hits followed with "Crawling King Snake" and "Hobo Blues".

At the time, Hooker mostly recorded solo, his rich baritone voice and electric guitar accompanied only by the constant tapping of his foot. It has often been said that he was recorded solo because of his idiosyncratic timing, which meant that his songs were as likely to have eleven and a half or thirteen bars as the standard twelve, and which made it difficult to accompany him, but he did record several sides with **Eddie Kirkland** on second guitar. Whatever the truth of this, the sound he made was groundbreaking, combining an earthy, downhome feel with a hip urbanity and primal sexuality that was irresistible.

He went on to record for Joe Van Battle's JVB label, which also leased his recordings to Modern, which remained the main outlet for Hooker's releases until 1955. But he also recorded for a vast array of other labels, under a bewildering array of different names to confuse the copyright lawyers. For Regent, he was Delta John. On Savoy, he became Birmingham Sam and His Magic Guitar. When he recorded for Acorn, they called him The Boogie Man. On Staff, he was Johnny Williams; he was Texas Slim or John Lee Cooker on King; and he was Johnny Lee on DeLuxe. He even recorded for Chess in 1950 and 1951 as John Lee Booker.

Under his real name, Hooker started a relationship with Vee Jay after leaving Modern that continued until the mid-1960s, and produced hits like "Dimples" and "Boom Boom". As the solo, one-man-band format came to be regarded as increasingly old-fashioned, he began to record more regularly

Hooker in the studio, in the 50s

with a group that included Eddie Taylor on guitar. In truth, however, little development is discernible across any of these recordings, with or without a band. Once Hooker had found his style, it was so unique that he saw no reason to change it.

The folk-blues revival of the early 1960s found him back in solo mode, playing in Greenwich Village (with an unknown Bob Dylan as his support act) and at the Newport Folk Festival. After he toured Europe for the first time in 1962, with the American Folk Blues Festival, he was also lionized by the young, white R&B bands emerging in Britain. The Rolling Stones name-checked him as a hero, while the Animals, the Yardbirds and Them – fronted by **Van Morrison**, who was to become a major figure in the late resurgence in Hooker's career – all covered his songs.

American bands were slower to take up Hooker's cause, but by the early 1970s the Doors had covered "Crawling King Snake", while **Canned Heat** recorded the 1971 album *Hooker'n' Heat* with him, after he had relocated to Los Angeles. As the rock world's interest in the blues declined, Hooker's profile fell away again, but he continued

to tour regularly and to record for assorted labels throughout the 1970s and 1980s. Then came one of the most spectacular comebacks, not just in the history of the blues, but in all of popular music. After years of decidedly average recordings that failed to recapture the excitement of his sides for Modern and Vee Jay, 1989's *The Healer* teamed him with a glittering bunch of guests including Carlos Santana, Keith Richards, Bonnie Raitt, Los Lobos and Robert Cray. Produced by Roy Rogers, the results were simply brilliant, and the record flew out of the stores, to the point where it was declared to be the best selling blues album ever. It also led to a tribute concert to him at Madison Square Garden in 1990, appearances with the Rolling Stones and Eric Clapton, and his induction into the Rock'n'Roll Hall of Fame in 1991.

That same year, *Mr Lucky*, the follow-up to *The Healer*, appeared, and paired him with Van Morrison, Ry Cooder, Albert Collins and others to repeat the success of its predecessor. Although the voice may have been a little deeper, in essence, Hooker was still delivering up exactly the same old glorious boogie he had been peddling all his life, his incessant riffs played with an open-tuned guitar and a timeless stomp of his foot. As Keith Richards put it, "You're not going to mistake John Lee Hooker for anyone else."

Invigorated by recording with younger performers and thoroughly enjoying his status as the blues' elder statesman, he was also in demand for film appearances and TV advertisements. A new version of "Boom Boom" was used for a Lee Jeans commercial in 1992, and gave its name to his next album. Once again produced by Rogers, it featured yet more stellar collaborations, although this time the guest list was made up not of rock stars but Hooker's fellow bluesmen, such as Jimmie Vaughan, Albert Collins and Charlie Musselwhite. A fourth album in similar vein followed in 1995 with *Chill Out*, once again produced by Roy Rogers, whereupon Hooker announced he was retiring. He wasn't, of course; he was back on stage the following year. He also returned to the studio with Van Morrison for 1997's superb *Don't Look Back*, which included splendid versions of Morrison's "Healing Game" and Jimi Hendrix's "Red House", and won two Grammy awards.

It was calculated that Hooker sold more records in the final dozen years of his career than in the

Playlist
John Lee Hooker

1 DIMPLES (1956) from **The Complete Blues Compilation: John Lee Hooker**
"You got dimples in your jaw, you my babe, I got my eyes on you…"

2 BOOM BOOM (1961) from **John Lee Hooker The Definitive Collection**
"Boom boom boom boom, A-haw haw haw haw, hmmm…"

3 BOOGIE CHILLUN (1948) from **The Legendary Modern Recordings**
"I heard papa tell mama, let that boy boogie-woogie, it's in him and it got to come out…"

4 CRAWLIN' KING SNAKE (1959) from **John Lee Hooker The Definitive Collection**
"You know I'm gon' crawl up to your window baby, wanna crawl up to your door, you got anything I want baby, wanna crawl up on your floor…"

5 I'M IN THE MOOD (1959) from **John Lee Hooker The Definitive Collection**
"My mother told me to leave that girl alone, but my mother didn't know what that little girl was puttin' down…"

6 THIS IS HIP (1963) from **The Complete Blues Compilation: John Lee Hooker**
"Will you come to my house and you dance with me, you hold me tight and you kiss me too? This is hip pretty baby…"

7 HOBO BLUES (1949) from **The Legendary Modern Recordings**
"You know I hoboed, hoboed, hoboed, hoboed, hoboed a long, long way from home, oh lord…"

8 I DON'T WANNA GO TO VIETNAM (1968) from **Tantalising The Blues**
"There's a whole lot of trouble right here at home, don't need to go to Vietnam. We oughta stay at home, stay out of trouble…"

9 BIG LEGS TIGHT SKIRT (1964) from **The Complete Blues Compilation: John Lee Hooker**
"I'm talkin''bout, mini skirt and tight skirt and big legs, strollin' down the avenue. I can't stand it!"

10 THE HEALER (1989) from **The Healer**
"My woman had left me, blues came along and healed me. Heal! Heal!"

first forty years combined. His final recordings with another bunch of celebrity guests, including Morrison, Elvin Bishop, Johnny Winter and Dickie Betts of the Allman Brothers, appeared posthumously on *Face To Face*.

John Lee Hooker's death in 2001, at the age of 83, marked the end of an era. More than almost any other bluesman, his sound seemed to hark back to something deep and primal in the very soul of African-American experience. Bonnie Raitt reckoned that his music was "the most erotic thing I ever heard" and if it's a cliché to say that we shall never see his like again, that doesn't make it any less true.

⊙ **The Legendary Modern Recordings 1948–1954** Virgin
Two dozen recordings from where it all started, including the hits that were the foundation of Hooker's career. Totally essential.

⊙ **Don't Look Back** Complete Blues
A superb 20-track selection of the best of John Lee Hooker's Vee Jay recordings between 1955 and 1964, not to be confused with his 1997 release of the same name.

⊙ **The Healer** Point Blank
Released in 1989, this has to be the comeback album of all time, from the title track with Carlos Santana to the sensational version of "I'm In The Mood" with Bonnie Raitt.

⊙ **Don't Look Back** Virgin
Produced by Van Morrison, and including four duets with him as well as contributions from Los Lobos and Charles Brown, this late John Lee Hooker album came out in 1997.

⊙ **Very Best Of John Lee Hooker** Rhino
A bold 16-song attempt at a career overview spanning many different labels and all eras of John Lee's career, from 1948's "Boogie Chillen", by way of "Boom Boom" and "One Bourbon, One Scotch, One Beer", to a 1987 version of Robert Johnson's "Terraplane Blues".

Lightnin' Hopkins

b Centreville, Texas, March 15, 1912; d Jan 30, 1982

A poet among country bluesmen, **Lightnin' Hopkins** enjoyed two distinct careers – one singing for a black audience in the late 1940s and early 1950s, and another playing for the white college crowd during the folk-blues revival of the 1960s.

Sam Hopkins' father having died when he was three, he was taught to play the guitar by his older brother, Joel. He made his first instrument, a cigar-box guitar with chicken-wire strings, when he was eight, and was soon playing with his older cousin, **Texas Alexander**. At some point during the early 1920s, he met **Blind Lemon Jefferson**, who encouraged him with guitar tips. While still in his mid-teens, he embarked upon the life of a hobo, jumping trains, gambling and playing the blues on street corners, sometimes with Alexander. It was a lifestyle that soon got him into trouble; in the mid-1930s he served time at the Houston County Prison Farm for an unknown offence.

On his release, Hopkins resumed playing with Alexander, but times were hard and they were also forced to take various day jobs as well. His big break came in 1946, when he and Alexander were offered a recording contract by the Los Angeles-based Aladdin Records. Yet for some reason, Hopkins alone turned up at the studio to cut "Katie Mae", accompanied by piano player **Wilson "Thunder" Smith**. Inevitably, the pair were billed as "Thunder and Lightnin'", and the name stuck with Hopkins from then on. He was invited back for a second session in 1947, and went on to cut almost fifty sides for the label. He also recorded for other companies, including Gold Star Records in Houston, where he settled from 1950 onwards. His recordings from this period are uniformly majestic, and several were hits on the R&B charts, including "Shotgun Express", "Tom Moore's Farm", "Big Mama Jump", "Fast Mail Rambler", "Fast Life Woman" and "Short Haired Woman". Although he toured and recorded prolifically until the mid-1950s, his fame remained confined almost entirely to a black audience, and as the electric blues coming out of Chicago made his acoustic style seem increasingly old-fashioned, he dropped out of view.

Little could he have known that an entire new career awaited. When the young blues enthusiast **Sam Charters** tracked him down in 1959, Hopkins recorded a comeback album in his apartment using a borrowed guitar. When *The Roots Of Lightnin' Hopkins* was released on Folkway Records, he suddenly found himself up there with Muddy Waters and John Lee Hooker among the new heroes of the folk-blues revival. His new recordings showed that he had lost none of his intensity; tracks such as "Mojo Hand" and "Penitentiary Blues" are among the finest he ever made. Hopkins was also extraordinarily prolific, recording something like

Playlist
Lightnin' Hopkins

1 KATIE MAE (1946) from **The Complete Aladdin Recordings**
"She walks like she got oil wells in her back yard…"

2 TIM MOORE'S FARM (1949) from **The Complete Aladdin Recordings**
This rare protest song from Hopkins' rural past was a big R&B chart hit.

3 LET ME PLAY WITH YOUR POODLE (1947) from **The Complete Aladdin Recordings**
Lightnin' was a friendly man, always kind to animals.

4 SHORT HAIRED WOMAN (1947) from **The Complete Aladdin Recordings"**
"You know rats and wigs'll get ya killed…"

5 BIG MAMA JUMP (1947) from **The Complete Aladdin Recordings**
"Don't stop for nothin', don't even stop at a red light"

6 FEEL SO BAD (1946) from **The Complete Aladdin Recordings**
"…like a ball game on a rainy day"

7 LIGHTNIN'S BOOGIE (1948) from **The Complete Aladdin Recordings**
Beating out the rhythm on the body of his guitar, Lightnin' proves that Hooker wasn't the only one who could boogie.

8 AUTOMOBILE BLUES (1949) from **The Complete Aladdin Recordings**
One of several Hopkins songs from which Bob Dylan borrowed liberally; this one became "Leopard-Skin Pill Box Hat".

9 PENITENTIARY BLUES (1959) from **The Very Best Of Lightnin' Hopkins**
Played on a borrowed guitar, this was one of Hopkins' first and finest recordings for Folkways after his rediscovery.

10 MOJO HAND (1960) from **Mojo Hand: The Lightnin' Hopkins Anthology**
"I'm goin' to Louisiana, and get me a mojo hand/I'm gonna fix my woman so she can't have no other man…"

35 albums in the 1960s for any label that would pay him up-front with a decent cash advance. Given his astonishing capacity to improvise lyrics – many of the compositions he called "air songs" were made up more or less on the spot – there was never a shortage of material.

Hopkins played at New York's Carnegie Hall with Pete Seeger and Joan Baez, and toured Europe with the American Folk Blues Festival in 1964, on one of the only two occasions that he overcame his fear of flying to cross the Atlantic. By the end of the decade he was opening for the Grateful Dead and Jefferson Airplane, and was the subject of a fine film, *The Blues According To Lightnin' Hopkins*, which won a prize at the Chicago Film Festival as best documentary. Age and a car crash in 1970 slowed him down over his final years, and he died of cancer in 1982, aged 79.

⊙ **Complete Aladdin Recordings** EMI
A double album containing 43 of Lightnin' Hopkins' masterful late-1940s' sides, including "Katie Mae", "Short Haired Woman" and "Big Mama Jump".

⊙ **Gold Star Sessions Vols One & Two** Arhoolie
Fabulous, stellar Texas blues from Hopkins' days in Houston in the 1950s.

⊙ **The Roots Of Lightnin' Hopkins** Smithsonian Folkways
The 1959 set that put Lightnin' Hopkins back on the map, including "Penitentiary Blues", "Bad Luck" and "Trouble", as well as his "Reminiscences of Blind Lemon".

⊙ **Mojo Hand** Rhino
For newcomers to Lightnin' Hopkins, this 40-track career overview, ranging from 1947 to 1969, makes as good a place as any to start.

Walter "Shakey" Horton

b Horn Lake, Mississippi, Dec 8, 1918; d Dec 8, 1981

Hailed by Willie Dixon as "the best harmonica player I ever heard", **Walter Horton** claimed to have played with Robert Johnson in the 1930s, and went on to accompany Muddy Waters in the 1950s. Variously known as Big Walter, Shakey or just "Mumbles", he also recorded some powerful sides under his own name.

Horton was given his first harmonica by his father at the age of five. During the late 1920s, he moved to Memphis with his mother, where he won a local talent contest. He later told Samuel Charters that he had recorded with the **Memphis Jug Band** as "Shakey Walter" in 1927, but since he would have been just nine at the time, blues historians are divided as to his veracity. At the very least he seems to have known and learned from Will Shade, the Jug Band's main harmonica player, and from Hammie Nixon. In turn, he claimed to have given harmonica instruction to Little Walter and Sonny Boy "Rice Miller" Williamson, even though the latter was almost twenty years his senior.

It seems probable that Horton cut his first sides in Memphis in 1939, accompanying Charlie "Little Buddy" Doyle, but like so much of his early life, confirmation is hard to come by. By now he had begun to amplify his harmonica, making him one of the first to do so. During the 1940s he shifted back and forth between Chicago and Memphis, working day jobs and playing wherever he could. Some sessions he recorded for Sam Phillips in 1951 were leased to Modern under the name **Mumbles**. Two years later, he cut his first hit for Sun, the instrumental "Easy", a classic harmonica blues based on Ivory Joe Hunter's "I Almost Lost My Mind", accompanied by Jimmy DeBerry on guitar.

Back in Chicago, Horton played on some superb sides with the guitarist **Johnny Shines**, including "Evening Sun" and "Brutal Hearted Woman", and teamed up with Jimmy Reed's sideman Eddie Taylor. In the mid-1950s he joined **Muddy Waters'** band as a replacement for Junior Wells, who had been called up to the army. After backing Waters on sides such as "Forty Days And Forty Nights" and "Mad Love (I Want You To Love Me)", he was unceremoniously fired when he turned up drunk one day (although another story holds Walters was piqued because he was playing too many side gigs). Among the other artists he accompanied during this period, many of them for Chess, were Otis Rush ("I Can't Quit You Baby"), Koko Taylor, Jimmy Rogers ("Walking By Myself"), Johnny Young, J.B. Hutto, Big Mama Thornton, Robert Nighthawk and Sunnyland Slim. He was also a massive influence on a younger generation of harp players, including Charlie Musselwhite and Carey Bell.

Horton's first solo album, *The Soul Of Blues Harmonica*, produced by Willie Dixon and featuring Buddy Guy, appeared on Argo in 1965. During the 1970s, he joined Dixon's Chicago Blues All Stars package tours, and in 1972 recorded an album of duets with his protégé Carey Bell for Alligator. He reunited with Muddy Waters on his 1977 album *I'm Ready*, recorded a couple of solo albums for Blind Pig Records, and had a cameo role in *The Blues Brothers* in 1980, accompanying John Lee Hooker. He died the following year, on his 63rd birthday.

⊙ **Mouth Harp Maestro** Ace
Sixteen tracks from Walter Horton's 1950s' recordings, many of them produced by Sam Phillips. Sadly, however, the classic "Easy" is not among them.

⊙ **Big Walter Horton With Carey Bell** Alligator
Although Walter Horton was never particularly comfortable as a bandleader, he sounded great here in 1972 with Bell to bolster his confidence, singing on eight tracks with three blistering instrumentals.

Son House

b Riverton, Mississippi, March 21, 1902; d Oct 19, 1988

An intense singer, guitarist and performer, **Son House** helped with his early recordings to invent the modern blues, and his fierce sound was an influence on almost everyone who came after him, from Robert Johnson to Muddy Waters.

Although some, not least House himself, were to claim an earlier date, it's generally thought that Eddie James House Jr. was born near Clarksdale in 1902. His father played in a brass band, but after his parents separated when he was seven or eight years old, he moved with his mother to Tallulah, Louisiana. Brought up in a religious home, he become a Baptist preacher at a young age, and didn't pick up the guitar until around 1927, under the influence of slide player **Willie Wilson**. By now he was back in Mississippi, where the following year he was sentenced to a year on Parchman State Farm for manslaughter, after pleading self-defense. On his release, House left the ministry and fully embraced the "devil's music", although it was the ongoing tension between his spiritual and secular sides that probably gave his singing and playing its intensity.

Having played with **Charley Patton** and **Willie Brown** at juke joints, parties, levee camps and plantation dances, House was spotted by a Paramount talent scout in 1930, and traveled north to Grafton, Wisconsin, to make his first recordings. There he cut "My Black Mama (parts 1 & 2)", "Preachin' The Blues (parts 1 & 2)", "Dry Spell Blues (parts 1 & 2)" and a test recording of "Walkin Blues", not intended for release at the time and rediscovered in a cache of old Paramount recordings in 1985. A recording of "Clarksdale Moan" made at the same time was also lost. Long regarded as the Holy Grail of blues collecting. In September 2005 an anonymous collector announced he had obtained a 78 of the song in good condition. It was released commercially in April 2006 on the Yazoo Records collection, *The Stuff That Dreams Are Made Of*.

Despite the fact that all are today recognized as masterpieces – indeed, there are those who claim them as the absolute high water mark of the country blues – these early sides failed to sell, and House and Brown spent the remainder of the decade traveling the South as itinerant musicians. During this time, House met both **Robert Johnson** and **Muddy Waters**, and taught both men several guitar riffs, including "Walking Blues".

House didn't record again until 1941, when on a tip from Waters, **Alan Lomax** tracked him down at Lake Cormorant and made some field recordings for the Library of Congress. He was so pleased with the results he sought out House for another session the following year. Several cuts, like "Levee Camp Blues" and "Government Fleet Blues", featured House backed by a small band, including his old friend Willie Brown. Others, like "Shetland Pony Blues" and "The Jinx Blues", were entirely solo. In either style, the sides possess a remarkable power and dignity, and Lomax rated these as the best sessions he ever recorded. House later recalled : "All I got was a bottle of Coke, but it was cold and good."

In 1943, House moved to Rochester in upstate New York. By 1948 Brown was dead, and House had apparently given up music, taking a job with the New York Central Railroad. He was only rediscovered by Dick Waterman in 1964, by which time he was not a well man, and had a serious drink problem. **Al Wilson**, soon to find fame with Canned Heat, had to help him relearn his old songs. Yet when he had got his chops back, his sound had lost virtually none of its old intensity. Waterman later

Playlist
Son House

All are taken from *Martin Scorsese Presents Son House*

1 MY BLACK MAMA (1930)
Son's first release; his snapping single strings and ringing slide defined the Delta blues guitar style.

2 PREACHIN' THE BLUES (1930)
"I wish I had religion this very day, but the women and the whiskey they would not let me pray".

3 DRY SPELL BLUES (1930)
A song about the Mississippi drought for once, rather than the great Delta flood.

4 LEVEE CAMP BLUES (1941)
After an eleven-year break from recording, Son returned with a more modern twelve-bar blues sound backed by Willie Brown on second guitar and Leroy Williams on harp.

5 WALKIN' BLUES (1941)
Robert Johnson based his "Walkin' Blues" on House's "My Black Mama", but Son's "Walkin'" was quite different.

6 SPECIAL RIDER BLUES (1942)
What House could do with just one chord was truly amazing.

7 THE PONY BLUES (1942)
A solo version of the Charley Patton song Son learned from Willie Brown. House, by the way, thought Patton was "a jerk".

8 DEATH LETTER (1965)
A chilling song given a mature and confident delivery in the wake of his comeback concerts at Newport and Carnegie Hall.

9 JOHN THE REVELATOR (1965)
The unaccompanied voice of the preacher man in full-on religious fervor.

10 LEVEE CAMP MOAN (1965)
A great vocal, with Canned Heat's Al Wilson on harp.

---

described the Son House he had found. "When he played, his eyes rolled back in his head and he went somewhere else … He transported himself back without any trickery and became the essence of the Delta. He would then finish the song, blink his eyes, and re-accustom himself to where he was at the time."

After his rediscovery, House continued working for a decade until his second retirement in 1974. Far from diminishing his greatness, his comeback cemented his reputation as one of the founding fathers of the blues, and thrilled everyone who heard him. He played all the major American folk and blues festivals, visited Europe to appear at the Montreux Jazz Festival, and recorded several albums, including the aptly titled *Father Of Folk Blues* for Columbia, which included quite staggering versions of "Death Letter", "Grinnin' in Your Face" and "John The Revelator". He died of cancer of the larynx in 1988 at the age of 86.

⊙ **Preachin' The Blues** Catfish
Son House's original recordings from 1930, including the fantastic version of "Walkin, Blues" that was discovered in 1985 (though not the long-lost "Clarksdale Moan") are supplemented by tracks from the 1941-42 Lomax sessions.

⊙ **Father Of The Delta Blues: The Complete 1965 Sessions** Columbia

An expanded version of Son House's great 1965 comeback album, reissued with leftover tracks.

⊙ **Delta Blues & Spirituals by Son House** EMI
A live recording, made in England in 1970, that features some of House's most famous songs, plus snippets of him in conversation.

Peg Leg Howell

b Eatonton, Georgia, March 5, 1888; d Aug 11, 1966

The singer and guitarist **Peg Leg Howell** recorded some fascinating blues and rags in the 1920s, both solo and with a string band. Often in a style that was by then already dying out, they represented a bridge between the old plantation work songs and early twentieth-century blues music.

The young Joshua Barnes Howell worked on his parents' farm, and did not take up the guitar until he was twenty. Even then, it was at first only a hobby. He only turned to music seriously after he was shot in the right leg during an altercation with his brother-in-law, and the limb had subsequently to be amputated. No longer able to work in the fields, he looked for other sources of income.

In 1923 he moved to Atlanta, where he took up bootlegging and playing on street corners for tips in a group known as "Peg Leg" Howell and His Gang, backed by Henry Williams on guitar, Eddie Anthony on fiddle and Eugene Pedin on mandolin. Howell's musical activities were briefly interrupted when the police caught up with his bootlegging sideline in 1925 and he was sentenced to twelve months in prison but he was back playing on the streets of Atlanta the following year when a scout from Columbia Records heard him. He recorded an initial four sides for the label, including "New Prison Blues", a product of his time in River Camp jail. The following year they recorded him again, this time with Williams and Anthony, and he cut further sessions for Columbia on the twice-yearly visits to Atlanta by the label's field recording unit in 1928 and 1929. The solo sides and the band recordings were quite different in character, the former introspective and doomy, and the latter in a rowdier, dance style.

After Columbia stopped recording him, Howell returned to bootlegging, but he continued to play around Atlanta with Anthony until the fiddler's death in 1934. After that, Howell appears to have given up music. He was rediscovered by Testament Records in 1963. By then he was 75 years old, extremely ill and confined to a wheelchair, having had his other leg removed in 1952 as a result of diabetes. Disappointingly, the material the label recorded displayed little of the magic of his early recordings. He died three years later.

⊙ **Peg Leg Howell & Eddie Anthony Vols One & Two** (Document)
A mix of blues, ballads, rags and songster stuff all recorded during the late 1920s. Anthony's fiddle is prominent on many of the sides.

Howlin' Wolf

b West Point, Mississippi, June 10, 1910; d Jan 10, 1976

Standing more than six feet tall and weighing three hundred pounds, **Howlin' Wolf** dominated the postwar Chicago blues scene in every way. An electrifying live performer who used his physical stature to enhance the emotional intensity of his singing, his presence was every bit as commanding on record.

One of six children, Chester Arthur Burnett acquired the name Howlin' Wolf as a child. "I got that from my grandfather, he used to tell me stories about the wolves in that part of the country," he later explained, although the nickname evidently also referred to his appetite for creating mischief and mayhem. He began singing in church as a child and worked as a boy on plantations in Mississippi and Arkansas, learning the blues from hearing itinerant musicians like **Charley Patton**, **Tommy Johnson** and **Willie Brown**. During his teens, when not working in the fields, he began to spend his weekends playing that same circuit of plantation picnics and juke joints, and testing out the parameters of his already mighty voice. His threatening physical presence also earned him such nicknames as Big Foot Chester and Bull Cow. By the early 1930s, he was playing alongside the likes of **Robert Johnson**, **Robert Lockwood Jr.**, and **Sonny Boy "Rice Miller" Williamson**, as well as his original heroes. From each of his fellow bluesmen he seemed to learn something, molding a set of diverse influences into his own unique style. From Willie Brown and others he picked up the rudiments of guitar playing. Patton instilled an understanding of the importance of showmanship, while from Tommy Johnson came the moans which he added to his gruff voice. Finally, he learned to play harmonica from Williamson, who married Wolf's half-sister.

Discharged after three years in the army in 1944, he returned to Mississippi and resumed singing, while still earning his basic living from farming. That situation only changed in 1948, when he moved to West Memphis and put together his first band. Among those who backed him at different times were harmonica players James Cotton and Little Junior Parker, and guitarists Pat Hare, Matt "Guitar" Murphy, and Willie Johnson. He also landed a job as a disc jockey on the radio station KWEM, which brought him to the attention of **Sam Phillips** and his talent scout, **Ike Turner**. He cut his first sides, "Moanin' at Midnight" and "How Many More Years", for Phillips' Memphis Recording Service in 1951. Phillips leased the tunes to Chess Records in Chicago and sold further material to RPM/Modern. But the battle to secure his services on a permanent basis was won by Chess, and in 1953 Wolf moved to Chicago, which would be his home for the rest of his life.

The wolf sure blew a mean harp

Working with **Willie Dixon**, who provided a ready supply of great songs, Wolf had an immediate impact with classic electric blues sides such as "Spoonful", "Evil", "Little Red Rooster", "Back Door Man", and "I Ain't Superstitious" (all written by Dixon), as well as his own "Smokestack Lightning" and "Killing Floor". Although he could play guitar, he left that first to Jody Williams and then to the great **Hubert Sumlin**, and concentrated on his voice. And what a voice it was, a gripping, primal sound full of deep unfathomable mystery and an almost overwhelming intensity and yet with a surprising subtlety in his phrasing. On stage he was an equally irresistible force, jumping up and down one minute and writhing on the floor the next. That he didn't start recording until he was in his forties made him appear as though he had sprung fully formed like an elemental force from the Delta ground, a sense that his raw, earth-shaking voice somehow seemed to embody.

Between Wolf and Chess's other main attraction, **Muddy Waters**, there developed a deep and perfectly healthy rivalry. Both competed for Dixon's best songs, and each seemed to drive the other on to fresh heights, as they came between them to define the sound of the postwar electric Chicago blues. A 1962 LP (popularly known as "the rocking chair album" on account of the cover art) rounded up songs such as "Shake For Me", "Little Red Rooster", "Wang Dang Doodle", "Spoonful", "Going Down Slow", "Back Door Man" and another half dozen titles, and became a classic, earning him new, adoring audience among the new wave of R&B groups emerging in Britain. Wolf traveled to Europe with the American Blues Festival, and footage of a 1965 TV appearance with the **Rolling Stones** shows a

Playlist
Howlin' Wolf

All are taken from *His Best* and *His Best Vol Two*

1 MOANIN' AT MIDNIGHT (1951)
Recorded in Memphis, with Wolf on harmonica and Willie Johnson playing the belligerent, striding guitar riff.

2 HOW MANY MORE YEARS (1951)
The stomping B-side of Wolf's first single, later covered by Led Zeppelin as "How Many More Times".

3 THE RED ROOSTER (1961)
Covered by both Sam Cooke and the Rolling Stones, but Wolf's original version is still definitive.

4 SPOONFUL (1960)
The song dates back to Wolf's early mentor Charley Patton, but is best known in rock circles as an elongated jam by Cream.

5 EVIL (1954)
"Another mule is kickin' in your stall"

6 BACK DOOR MAN (1961)
The Doors covered this one – but like Jagger and Robert Plant, Jim Morrison couldn't capture the Wolf's intensity.

7 I AIN'T SUPERSTITIOUS (1962)
"But when my left eye jumps, somebody's got to go…"

8 SMOKESTACK LIGHTNING (1956)
"Ah, whoo-hoo-ooh…" the signature howl from Wolf's signature song.

9 KILLING FLOOR (1964)
An awesome vocal performance, backed by both Hubert Sumlin and Buddy Guy on dueling guitars.

10 (MEET ME) DOWN IN THE BOTTOM (1961)
The Wolf at his swaggering, forceful best with Jimmy Rogers on magnificent Delta slide guitar.

youthful Mick Jagger sitting almost worshipfully at his feet. A few years later, successful covers of his songs by white rock groups such as Cream and the Doors led to a 1969 attempt to update some of his old material on a rock album of which the cover announced, "This is Howlin' Wolf's new album. He doesn't like it much." Titled simply *The Howlin' Wolf Album*, it was long unavailable: some have tried to reclaim it as an overlooked classic, but it still sounds more like a trend-chasing oddity than anything else. In 1970, Chess sent him to Britain to record *The London Howlin' Wolf Sessions*, with Eric Clapton, Steve Winwood, the Rolling Stones rhythm section of Bill Wyman and Charlie Watts, and other British rockers.

By then, however, Wolf was in poor health following a heart attack, and a car accident in 1971 left him needing kidney dialysis treatment. Despite his illness, he continued working, releasing a live album in 1972 and *Back Door Wolf* two years later, which included the topical "Coon On The Moon" and "Watergate Blues", both written by sax player Eddie Shaw. Bizarrely, it also featured blues harpsichord, played by Detroit Jr. He gave his final live performance in Chicago with B.B. King in November 1975 and died two months later of kidney failure, at the age of 65. Yet his spirit lives on through the extraordinary recordings he left behind. As Sam Phillips once noted, "When I heard Howlin' Wolf, I said, 'This is where the soul of man never dies.'"

⊙ **His Best** Chess
This twenty-song compilation ranges from 1951's "Moanin' at Midnight" to 1964's "Killing Floor", which features Buddy Guy on guitar.

⊙ **Howlin' Wolf/Moanin' In The Moonlight** MCA/Chess
The Wolf's first two, stunning Chess LPs, *Moanin' At Midnight* and the "rocking chair album", re-released on one value-for-money CD, and bursting with gems.

⊙ **Howlin' Wolf: The Chess Box** Chess
75 tracks sequenced chronologically over three CDs, including Wolf's early Memphis recordings as well as most of his classic Chicago sides.

⊙ **Howlin' Wolf Rides Again** Ace
These early-1950s sides were cut under the direction of Ike Turner in Memphis; including "House Rockin' Boogie" and "Riding In The Moonlight", they feature great guitar solos by Willie Johnson.

⊙ **The London Howlin' Wolf Sessions** Chess
The British rock aristocracy help out on a 1970 recording,

but although his voice is not quite as strong as it was a decade earlier, it's still Wolf and his longtime Chicago guitarist Hubert Sumlin that steal the show.

Helen Humes

b Louisville, Kentucky, June 23, 1913; d Sept 13, 1981

The singer **Helen Humes** represented the link between big band music and the blues, leaving an impressive legacy that spanned blues shouting, R&B, jazz phrasing and the sentimental popular song.

Humes learned to play trumpet and piano as well as singing with her local Sunday school band, and began her recording career when she was just fourteen, cutting the country blues "Cross Eyed Blues" for Okeh Records in St Louis in 1927. A few years later she moved to New York, where she worked with various bandleaders including **Harry James**, with whom she recorded "Jubilee", "I Can Dream Can't I", "That's The Dreamer In Me" and "Song Of The Wanderer". Then she replaced Billie Holiday in **Count Basie**'s band in 1938 at the second time of asking, having initially turned the gig down because the pay was too low. She stayed with Basie until 1941, singing alongside **Jimmy Rushing**. Among her best-known performances with Basie were "Dark Rapture", "Blame It On My Last Affair", "And The Angels Sing", "It's Torture" and "Between The Devil And The Deep Blue Sea".

After leaving Basie, Humes relocated to Los Angeles for a solo career, adopting a blues-ier style on sides such as "Fortune Tellin' Man", "Be-Baba-Leba", "Keep Your Mind On Me" and "Suspicious Blues", all recorded for Savoy in 1944. She cut further sessions for Black & White Records, but her biggest success came when she signed in 1947 to Philo, for whom she recorded the hits "Blue Prelude" and "Every Now And Then", as well as "Unlucky Woman" and "McShann's Boogie Blues" with **Jay McShann**. She also recorded for Aladdin and Mercury, cutting such fine sides as "See See Rider", "Jet Propelled Papa", "I Refuse To Sing The Blues", "They Raided The Joint" and "Today I Sing The Blues". During the 1950s she recorded for both Discovery and Modern, enjoying a big R&B hit on the latter with a live version of "Million Dollar Secret". She also had four tracks on the Aladdin album *Blues After Hours*, one of the very first R&B releases in the then-new LP format.

Humes made several albums for Contemporary in the 1960s, before emigrating to Australia. She came out of retirement in 1973 to sing with Basie at the Newport Jazz Festival, and cut several more albums before her death in 1981, at the age of 68.

⊙ **Blue Prelude 1927-47** (Topaz)
An excellent survey of Helen Humes' early career, from the country blues of "Cross Eyed Blues" to her big band recordings with Harry James, Basie and Buck Clayton.

⊙ **Today I Sing The Blues** EPM
This anthology includes many of Humes' best solo recordings for Philo/ Aladdin from the late 1940s, including several of the sides she cut with Jay McShann.

Alberta Hunter

b Memphis, Tennessee, April 1, 1895; d Oct 17, 1984

Among the very first blues singers to be recorded in the early 1920s, **Alberta Hunter** came from the same generation as Ma Rainey and Bessie Smith, but remarkably enough she was still singing with her rich contralto voice intact and her spirit undimmed some

sixty years later. Hunter ran away from Memphis to Chicago at twelve to become a singer. By 1911, was singing in a bordello on the South Side called Dago Frank's, before moving on to more salubrious nightspots. She got married in 1919 for a mere two months, but had a more successful lesbian relationship with Lottie Taylor, the niece of the black entertainer Burt Williams, that lasted many years.

For a while Hunter performed as a duet with New Orleans ragtime pianist **Tony Jackson**, who was openly gay. She became a popular figure in the speakeasies of Chicago at the height of the city's gangster era, and sang at the Dreamland Cafe with **King Oliver**'s band, billed as "The Sweetheart of Dreamland". But if it was a tough schooling, she was equal to it. "I'd sing softly, and if the people at the next table would want to hear what I was doing, they'd have to call me over and give me a tip," she recalled many years later. However, after her pianist was shot dead on stage one night in 1921, she decided to move to New York. There she made her first recordings with **Fletcher Henderson** and his orchestra for Black Swan, and then moved to Paramount. In 1922, she cut her own composition "Down Hearted Blues", which was memorably covered by **Bessie Smith** the following year.

When the Original Memphis Five supported her in 1923 on several sides including "Tain't Nobody's Biz-ness If I Do", "If You Want To Keep Your Daddy Home" and "Bleeding Heart Blues" she made history as the first African-American singer to be backed by a white band. The following year she sang on the Red Onion Jazz Babies sessions that brought **Louis Armstrong** and **Sidney Bechet** together for the first time. Recording prolifically throughout the 1920s, she cut sides under her own name for Okeh, Victor and Columbia, and worked for several other labels under various pseudonyms, including Alberta Prime, May Alix and Josephine Beatty.

Hunter also developed a lucrative sideline appearing in musical revues, taking over from Bessie Smith in *How Come?* in New York, and traveling to Europe in 1927 to sing in *Showboat* with **Paul Robeson**. She returned to Europe regularly throughout the 1930s, appearing in London at the Drury Lane Theatre and in cabaret at the Dorchester Hotel, and during World War II entertained the American troops in Asia and the South Pacific.

After the war she continued singing in New

Blues belter and feminist icon: Alberta Hunter   REDFERNS

York until she retired from music in 1954, and at the age of 59, enrolled in a nursing course. Nurse Hunter worked in a New York hospital for the next 23 years, until her employers insisted that at 82, it was time for her to retire. Astonishingly, she then resumed her singing career. She had cut a couple of albums in the early 1960s, but otherwise had not performed professionally since 1954. Yet she began singing again in clubs and on concert platforms, recorded the title song of the 1978 movie *Remember My Name*, and cut a couple of albums that revealed her vibrato-laden voice had lost little of its former conviction. She died in 1984 at the age of 89.

⊙ **Young Alberta Hunter** Jass
A decent overview of Hunter's early work, including sides she cut with Louis Armstrong.

⊙ **Amtrak Blues** Columbia
Alberta Hunter, as produced by John Hammond Sr. in 1978, not long before she died. She really had no right to sound this good in her eighties.

Ivory Joe Hunter

b Kirbyville, Texas, Oct 11, 1914; d Nov 8, 1974

Over his varied career, the singer and pianist **Ivory Joe Hunter** straddled blues, jump blues, boogie-woogie, R&B and even country. He was also a prolific songwriter, who penned Elvis Presley two top-twenty hits.

Hunter was raised in southeast Texas, where his mother sung gospel and his father played guitar. Having learned to play the piano in his teens, he made his first recording in 1933 for the Library of Congress. Pounding out blues and ballads, he played around the Gulf Coast region, and had his own radio show on KFDM in Beaumont, Texas, until he migrated to California during World War II. There he made his first commercial recordings, with **Johnny Moore's Three Blazers**, singing in a velvet-smooth style reminiscent of Nat King Cole and Charles Brown, and clearly influenced as a pianist by Fats Waller. For a while he released records on his own labels, Pacific and Ivory, including his own composition, "Blues At Sunrise", which became a hit after he leased it for national distribution to Exclusive Records, and the equally successful "Pretty Mama Blues". Further R&B hits followed in 1949 on the Cincinnati-

based King Records with "Waiting In Vain" and "Guess Who", recorded with sidemen from Duke Ellington's orchestra. The following year, he topped the R&B chart with "I Almost Lost My Mind" on MGM, which later became a number one for the aseptic Pat Boone.

Ivory Joe was now a hot commodity. Further hits followed, and by the time he signed to Atlantic in 1954 he already had more than 100 sides to his name. Atlantic successfully crossed him over to the pop charts with "Since I Met You Baby" in 1956, but by the end of the decade his popularity as an R&B performer was in decline. He continued to score prolifically as a songwriter, however; **Elvis Presley** had major hits with Hunter's "My Wish Came True" and "Ain't That Loving You Baby".

He re-emerged in the 1960s as a country singer, and made regular appearances in Nashville at the Grand Ole Opry. He re-embraced his R&B roots in 1971 with *The Return Of Ivory Joe Hunter* on Epic, backed by a simmering Memphis band including Isaac Hayes on keyboards, trumpeter Gene "Bowlegs" Miller and saxist Charles Chalmers, but it didn't lead to the revival of interest in his career that the label had hoped for. He died of lung cancer in Memphis in 1974.

⊙ **Since I Met You Baby – The Best Of Ivory Joe Hunter** Razor and Tie
A generous 24-track overview of Ivory Joe's sides for labels such as MGM and Atlantic in the 1950s, including both R&B and pop hits.

⊙ **The King Sides Vol One** King
A boogie-oriented collection of material cut by Ivory Joe Hunter for King during the late 1940s, including several swinging jump blues tunes backed by members of Duke Ellington's orchestra.

Mississippi John Hurt

b Teoc, Mississippi, March 8, 1892; d Nov 2, 1966

Of all the acoustic bluesmen whose work came to light as a result of the folk-blues revival of the 1960s, the rediscovery of **John Hurt** ranks among the most spectacular.

Born in Mississippi in either 1892 or 1893, John Smith Hurt was the eighth of ten children, and began to play the guitar when he was around nine years old. Living in Avalon in the remote Carroll

County in the southern part of the state, he seldom got to see the itinerant bluesmen who were becoming a familiar sight in more populous parts of Mississippi, and learned his songs instead from older field hands. Hurt himself spent much of his life working in the fields, but earned small change playing at local dances and parties, often accompanied by two white musicians, fiddler Willie Narmour and guitarist Shell Smith.

It was Narmour who led to Hurt's recording debut for Okeh Records in 1928, after record company scout Tommy Rockwell heard him win a fiddle contest. Rockwell wasn't too interested in the fiddler but asked him if he knew any other good local musicians. Narmour told him about Hurt, whom he located and took to Memphis, where he recorded "Frankie" and "Nobody's Dirty Business". Released as a single – it was Okeh who added the "Mississippi' to his name – the sides didn't sell well. However, Rockwell was convinced that he had found a major talent, and took Hurt to New York for another session. The handful of sides he recorded there, including "Candy Man Blues", "Avalon Blues" and "Ain't No Tellin'" (sometimes known as "Make Me A Pallet On The Floor"), were rooted in the ragtime and songster traditions as much as the blues, and Hurt delivered them brilliantly in his typical relaxed manner and soft voice. Yet his style was too sweet for tastes that at the time preferred the grittier sounds of Charley Patton and Blind Lemon Jefferson. Hurt was dismissed as sounding old-fashioned and that, together with the onset of the Depression, conspired to send him straight back to the fields and obscurity.

There he remained for three decades, until blues collector **Tom Hoskins** found him in 1963. Several folklorists had already gone looking for him a few years earlier, after interest in Hurt had been revived when the inclusion of two of his recordings, "Frankie" and "Spike Driver Blues", on Harry Smith's 1952 *Anthology Of American Folk Music*. Hoskins tracked him down in his hometown when he realized that Hurt's song "Avalon Blues", recorded in New York in 1928, referred to Avalon, Mississippi. As a piece of detective work it was simple enough. "Avalon's my home-town, always on my mind", Hurt had sung. Although modern maps of Mississippi didn't indicate anywhere called Avalon, Hoskins scoured older sources until he found Avalon on an ancient 1878 map. When he arrived there, he asked at the local store if they'd ever heard of Mississippi John Hurt, and was told he could be found "a mile down that road, third mailbox up the hill." Following these instructions, he found the seventy-year-old Hurt down the road and up the hill, where he was driving a tractor.

Hoskins persuaded Hurt to travel with him to Washington DC where he recorded him for the

Playlist
Mississippi John Hurt

1 AVALON BLUES (1928) from **Avalon Blues: The Complete 1928 Okeh Recordings**
Recorded in New York during a freezing December, this features the homesick lyric that eventually led to Hurt's rediscovery more than thirty years later.

2 SPIKE DRIVER BLUES (1928) from **Avalon Blues: The Complete 1928 Okeh Recordings**
Hurt's variation on the folk song "John Henry", which he learned when working for the Illinois Central railroad.

3 FRANKIE (AND ALBERT) (1928) from **Avalon Blues: The Complete 1928 Okeh Recordings**
"The same thing as Frankie and Johnnie", as he says in the spoken introduction. Along with "Spike Driver Blues", one of the two tracks included on the Harry Smith anthology.

4 CANDY MAN (1966) from **The Complete Studio Recordings**
"His stick candy don't melt away, it just gets better, so the ladies say"

5 CORRINA CORRINA (1966) from **The Complete Studio Recordings**
No wonder Hurt sings and picks it with such finesse – although it wasn't one of the songs he cut in 1928, by the time of this recording he'd been playing it for more than forty years.

6 MAKE ME A PALLET ON YOUR FLOOR (1966) from **The Complete Studio Recordings**
Just in case you didn't know, a pallet is "a straw-filled tick or mattress or a small, hard, or temporary bed".

7 COFFEE BLUES (1966) from **The Complete Studio Recordings**
Hurt may have name-checked Maxwell House in his intro to the song but he insisted on whiskey in the mug from which he drank on stage.

Piedmont label. He also booked a series of live appearances, including a triumphant performance at the 1963 Newport Folk Festival. Hurt repeated the success the following year, and signed to Vanguard Records, where he recorded some masterful sessions under the watchful eye of folksinger Patrick Sky for what proved to be his final albums. His brief but glorious Indian summer ended in 1966 when he died following a heart attack. He left a lasting legacy on a new generation of folk-blues performers, including Bob Dylan and Donovan who recorded his songs, and he was still exerting a powerful influence decades after his death on modern acoustic bluesmen such as Kelly Joe Phelps and Keb Mo.

⊙ **Avalon Blues** Columbia
Mississippi John Hurt's early recordings may have seemed old-fashioned to blues fans in the late 1920s; today they simply sound timeless.

⊙ **The Complete Studio Recordings** Vanguard
A magnificent 3-disc box set containing 42 tracks that Hurt recorded at the end of his life for Vanguard, full of a gentle grace, charm and dignity.

J.B. Hutto

b Blackwell, South Carolina, April 26, 1926; d June 12 1983

While his electric slide guitar playing owed much to Elmore James, **J.B. Hutto** stamped his own powerful and distinctive mark on the Chicago blues, and after his mentor's death, took on his mantle.

Joseph Benjamin Hutto's family moved from South Carolina to Augusta, Georgia, when he was young. There he formed a vocal group with his brothers and sisters known as The Golden Crown Gospel Singers. However, not until he moved to Chicago after the death of his father in the late 1940s did he take up music seriously, playing piano and drumming with local bluesman Johnny Ferguson and his band, The Twisters. Backstage between sets he began playing around on Ferguson's guitar, and was soon performing on weekends on Maxwell Street, often with the one-man band **Eddie Hines**, sometimes known as "Porkchop". But it was hearing **Elmore James** in 1950 that was to change his life. Fascinated by

the guitarist's bottleneck style, Hutto followed him around, studying and copying his technique.

By the time he formed his first band **The Hawks**, featuring Porkchop on washboard and George Mayweather on harmonica, Hutto was playing exclusively on slide, with Joe Custom on second guitar. The Hawks made their first recordings for the Chess subsidiary label, Chance, in 1954, and although the sides made little impact at the time, they have subsequently come to be regarded as classics of their kind.

A disillusioned Hutto quit music soon afterwards, and took a job as a janitor in a funeral home. He wasn't heard of again until 1964. Elmore James had died the previous year and Hutto decided it was his duty to pick up his baton – or rather his bottleneck slide. A new version of The Hawks, including drummer Frank Kirkland and bass player Herman Hassell, became the house band at Turner's Blues Lounge on the South Side, and Hutto turned into a dynamic live performer and a showman in the style of Guitar Slim, dressing in flamboyantly colored outfits and outrageous hats and using a long guitar lead to wander through the audience.

In 1966 Hutto appeared on the album *Masters Of Modern Blues* on Testament Records, which also featured Johnny Young, Walter "Shakey" Horton, bassist Lee Jackson and drummer Fred Below. The following year Hutto and the Hawks contributed five tracks to the Delmark Records compilation, *Chicago/The Blues/Today!* His first full-length solo disc followed in 1967 with *Hawk Squat*. In 1973 came *Slidewinder*, showcasing his big voice and slashing slide work, which some consider to be his finest work. He continued recording in a fierce, driving style for various labels including JSP, Varrick and Wolf. His final album *Slippin' & Slidin'* appeared in 1983, the year he died of cancer aged 57. His legacy lives on through the playing of his nephew, **Lil' Ed Williams**, whom Hutto taught.

⊙ **Masters Of The Modern Blues** Testament
J.B. Hutto's all-star 1966 band in fine spontaneous takes of songs such as Big Joe Williams's "Sloppy Drunk", "Dust My Broom", "Going Down Slow" and Roosevelt Sykes'"Mistake In Life".

⊙ **Slidewinder** Delmark
Rough-hewn but vivid slide playing and tough boogie rhythms characterize J.B. Hutto's 1972 classic, recorded with The Hawks.

J

Bo Weavil Jackson

date and place of birth and death unknown

Although the identity and history of many of the early bluesmen long remained unknown, blues scholars have over the years tracked down most of their details. One of the handful that still eludes them is **Bo Weavil Jackson**, who remains a romantic character about whom we know little other than the handful of recordings that survive. His real name is thought to have been Sam Butler, and on the basis of several references in his lyrics, he is believed to have hailed from Birmingham, Alabama, even if Paramount Records, for whom he recorded, promoted him as having "come down from the Carolinas". Equally unclear is how he arrived in Chicago in 1926, to cut thirteen great sides of country blues and spirituals characterized by high-pitched singing and brilliant slide guitar. There seem to have been at least two sessions, recorded just weeks apart for Paramount and Vocalion. A record salesman of the time named Harry Charles recalled him as a street bum, playing on the street corner for small change after his sessions were done, but believed his real name was James Butler. Whatever his name, his sides reveal a fast-fingered guitarist with a highly original technique on such blues numbers as "Some Scream High Yellow" and "You Can't Keep No Brown".

⊙ *Various Artists* Backwoods Blues
Document
This entertaining if uneven compilation includes the complete recordings of Bo Weavil Jackson, plus sides by such other early blues figures as Bobby Grant, Lane Hardin and King Solomon Hill.

Bullmoose Jackson

b Cleveland, Ohio, Jan 1, 1919; d July 31, 1989

The saxophonist **Bullmoose Jackson** was also a notable singer whose R&B hits often had a strongly suggestive quality. He took up the saxophone in his youth, and started his first band at school. By 1939, the trumpeter Freddie Webster had recruited him to play in the **Harlem Hotshots**, and Jackson moved to Buffalo, New York. In 1943 he was back in Cleveland replacing tenor sax player Lucky Thompson in the **Lucky Millinder** band, where he acquired the name "Bullmoose". He also acquired an unexpected reputation as a singer, when one night at a gig in Texas, the scheduled singer Wynonie Harris failed to show. Jackson stepped up to the microphone in his place to croon the song "Hurry, Hurry", and a whole new career was born.

Jackson stayed with Millinder until 1948, appearing that same year with the band in the film *Boarding House Blues*. By that time he had already launched a solo career, recording for Syd Nathan's King label. In 1947, his "I Love You, Yes I Do" outsold anything he recorded with Millinder, and became the first million-selling R&B single. Accompanied by his band, the Buffalo Bearcats, he followed with a string of smoothly crooned hits including "All My Love Belongs To You" and "Little Girls Don't Cry". He also scored in a different market with a series of belting jump blues songs full of sexual innuendo, including "I Want A Bowlegged Woman", "Nosey Joe", "Oh John" and his notorious "Big Ten Inch (Record)".

In 1955, Jackson signed to the Chess subsidiary Marterry, while the following year he switched to Encino. By the 1960s, however, he had been reduced to re-recording his old hits, and took a job with a catering firm at Washington DC's Howard University. He made a comeback in 1983 after he was tracked down by Carl Grefenstette from the Pittsburgh-based band **The Flashcats**, who included several of his songs in their act. They invited him to join them on stage and he sold out a series of Pittsburgh concerts, becoming a cult hero. Jackson was elated. "I'm very proud that people still remember me," he said. "They've resurrected an old man. I had one foot in the grave and the other on a banana peel. They dug me out and here I am."

That success also led to his first new recordings in two decades, on the 1985 album *Moosemania!* on the Bogus label. Also that year, he appeared at New York's Carnegie Hall, and toured Europe with the Johnny Otis Show. He continued to perform until 1987, when his health began to fail. He gave his last performance with The Flashcats in Pittsburgh in 1988, and died of cancer the following year at the age of seventy. In another nice twist to his renaissance, during the last year of his life he was cared for by an old girlfriend, who had lost touch but got back in contact with him after reading about his newfound success in a newspaper.

⊙ **Greatest Hits: I Want A Bowlegged Woman** King
Classic jump blues and risqué lyrics from Bullmoose Jackson's heyday during the 1940s and 1950s.

Jim Jackson

b Hernando, Mississippi, c 1884; d 1937

For many years, **Jim Jackson** remained one of the more mysterious figures of the early Delta blues, although his "Jim Jackson's Kansas City Blues Parts 1 & 2" was one of the biggest "race" records of the 1920s. Although he wasn't heard of again after 1930, assiduous research has recently pieced together a reliable account of the life and career of a performer whose recorded repertoire offers a fascinating insight into nineteenth-century black song styles.

Jackson was born to a sharecropping family in a small town twenty miles south of Memphis, and he was raised on a farm. His father played the guitar and passed on his skills, while local guitarist **Frank Stokes** was another early influence. By around 1905, Jackson was working as a dancer, guitarist and singer with the medicine and minstrel shows, and he was still traveling with troupes such as the Silas Green Minstrels and the Rabbit Foot Minstrels, as late as 1930. He also played local dances, plantation picnics and fish fries, sometimes alongside **Gus Cannon** and fellow Hernando native **Robert Wilkins**. By the end of World War I, Jackson was playing the clubs on Beale Street in Memphis, teaming up with the likes of **Furry Lewis** and future Memphis Jug Band guitarist **Will Shade**. In 1919 he is even recorded as having performed for guests at Memphis's upmarket Peabody Hotel.

All that experience gave Jackson a repertoire of hundreds of songs, covering rags, ballads, vaudeville numbers and folk tunes as well as blues. That brought him to the attention of Paramount talent scout **H.C. Speir**, who in 1927 was looking for blues performers to emulate the success of Blind Lemon Jefferson. After signing him, however, Speir decided that Jackson was a "cocaine head" and sold his contract to Loren Watson at Vocalion Records. Watson took him to Chicago in October 1927, where he recorded "Jim Jackson's Kansas City Blues, Parts 1 & 2". Among the biggest-selling records of its time, it was soon adapted by **Charley Patton** as "Going To Move To Alabama". Jackson was swiftly rushed back into the studio to cut "Kansas City Blues, Parts 3 & 4" and eight other titles. Later in 1928, a field recording team from Victor Records cut Jackson singing "I'm Wild About My Lovin'" and the comic, hymn-like parody "I Heard the Voice of a Pork Chop", both of which were songs he must have sung with the medicine shows. His popularity was such that he even appeared in King Vidor's all-black 1929 film *Hallelujah!* He made his last recordings in 1930, but then as the Depression set in, left Memphis to return to Hernando, where he was reported to have died in 1937.

⊙ **Complete Recorded Works Vol 1 & Vol 2** Document
The ever-reliable Document Records do their usual comprehensive job, compiling 47 recordings that Jim Jackson made between 1927 and 1930. The two discs are available separately, so if you're only planning to buy one, it's worth knowing that all four parts of his famous "Kansas City Blues" are on volume one.

John Jackson

b Woodville, Virginia, Feb 25, 1924; d Jan 20, 2002

Sometimes known as "the king of the Piedmont blues", **John Jackson** had a huge repertoire of songs and kept alive the tradition of the prewar acoustic blues into the twenty-first century.

Raised on a farm in Virginia, Jackson was one of fourteen children. His father played a battered old guitar, while his mother was proficient on accordion and harmonica. Jackson started picking on his father's guitar at the age of four, and his own mail-order instrument followed soon after. He learned slide and open tunings from a young convict called Happy on a chain gang during the Depression. Happy lived with the family after his release, while Jackson further developed his chops listening to 78s on the family Victrola and copying the recordings of Blind Lemon Jefferson, Mississippi John Hurt, and Blind Boy Fuller, as well as country artists like Uncle Dave Macon and the Carter Family.

He began playing at local parties and juke joints, but gave up the guitar in the 1940s, appalled at the violent fights that often broke out in the kind of venues he was playing. By 1948 he had taken a job on a dairy farm, and he later worked as a caretaker and a gravedigger.

Around 1960, Jackson resumed playing the guitar when he bought a second-hand Gibson acoustic. "Chuck" Perdue, founder of the Folklore Society of Greater Washington, heard him playing Mississippi John Hurt's "Candy Man". After much coaxing, Jackson was persuaded on stage at a Mance Lipscomb show, where he was heard in turn by **Chris Strachwitz** of **Arhoolie Records**. As the record label boss later wrote, he instantly knew that he had to record "this sweet and gentle guy that history had almost passed by." Jackson made his first recordings for Arhoolie in Fairfax in 1965, and eventually released three albums on the label, the third being cut in Europe while on tour with the American Folk Blues Festival in 1969.

A fixture in his trademark felt fedora at folk and blues festivals for more than thirty years, Jackson was a songster as well as a bluesman, with a vast repertoire that included rags, ballads and hillbilly tunes as well as classic acoustic blues, all delivered with an easy, swinging style and a strongly accented voice. Later albums included 1978's *Step It Up And Go* and *Deep In The Bottom* four years later, both for Rounder Records, while he released his final album, *Front Porch Blues*, on Alligator in 1999, three years before he died of cancer.

⊙ **Don't Let Your Deal Go Down** Arhoolie
Twenty-six fine tracks culled from John Jackson's three original Arhoolie releases, all characterized by their honesty and unpretentiousness.

⊙ **Front Porch Blues** Alligator
John Jackson's final album from 1999. Each of the songs is accompanied in the liner notes by his personal remi-

nisces, and they include a great version of Reverend Gary Davis's "Death Don't Have No Mercy".

Lil Son Jackson

b Barry, Texas, Aug 16, 1915; d May 30, 1976

A Texas contemporary of Lightnin' Hopkins with an appealingly rustic approach, **Lil Son Jackson** recoded in the 1940s for Gold Star, in the 1950s for Imperial, and then again during the 1960s folk-blues revival for Arhoolie. He thereby left a legacy of earthy Texas country blues of the highest order, covering three decades.

Melvin Jackson grew up in a sharecropping family in Texas. His was a musical environment, for his father loved blues and taught him guitar, and his mother sang gospel songs. Initially, the latter's influence won out, and Melvin left home in the 1930s to work with the gospel group the Blue Eagle Four. He also served an apprenticeship as a mechanic, serving in Europe with the US army during World War II. Following his discharge in 1946, and encouraged by the praise of the army buddies he entertained with his songs and guitar, he sent a demo to Bill Quinn, owner of the Houston-based Gold Star Records, which already had fellow Texan bluesman **Lightnin' Hopkins** on its books. Quinn was sufficiently impressed to sign Jackson, and his "Freedom Train Blues" became a jukebox hit and made the national R&B chart in 1948. Two years later, he moved to Imperial Records, for whom he recorded prolifically until 1954, both solo in a style that reflected his rural roots and with a small band on several sessions in a more contemporary R&B vein. His best sides included "Rockin' And Rollin'", which he cut in 1950, and became better known as "Rock Me Baby", as later recorded by B.B. King. He also toured extensively, but gave up playing in the mid-1950s, partly due to changing musical tastes brought about by the arrival of rock'n'roll, and partly due to a serious road accident. When he recovered, he went back to a job as a mechanic and working for his local church in Texas. He was persuaded to resume recording in 1960 after he was tracked down by Arhoolie Records boss **Chris Strachwitz**, who cut almost two dozen songs with him and released the best of them on an excellent self-titled album.

⊙ **Complete Imperial Recordings** EMI
A 2-disc set of Jackson's 1950s' recordings, including the classic "Rockin' And Rollin'".

⊙ **Blues Come To Texas** Arhoolie
An expanded version of Lil Son Jackson's 1960 comeback album, featuring twenty tracks, including such Texan titles as "Blues Came To Texas", "I Walked From Dallas" and "West Dallas Blues".

Papa Charlie Jackson

b New Orleans, c 1885; d 1938

Papa Charlie Jackson is regularly cited as the first bluesman to record, although he was an interesting figure rather than the major blues pioneer that such an accolade might suggest. In fact, strictly speaking he wasn't the first at all, for Sylvester Weaver had already been recorded when Jackson cut his first sides for the Paramount label in 1924, playing his trademark hybrid banjo-guitar. However, his mystique has been enhanced by the fact that we know little about him, other than the dates of his recording sessions, and even the details of his death in Chicago in 1938 are unverified.

William Henry Jackson was born some time during the mid-1880s, probably in New Orleans, where it is presumed that he began playing a six-string banjo tuned like a guitar. Although we know nothing of his early life, the likelihood is that he traveled with medicine and minstrel shows, developing a repertoire of bawdy ballads, vaudeville, hokum, novelty and rag songs as well as early blues. By the early 1920s he had settled in Chicago and was busking on Maxwell Street and playing at house parties. Then in August 1924, Paramount recorded him singing "Papa's Lawdy Lawdy Blues" and "Airy Man Blues", tunes that combined both jazz and songster elements and banjo chording that found melody and rhythm tumbling over each other. A month later they recorded a follow-up, cutting "Salt Lake City Blues" and "Salty Dog Blues". The following year he cut one of his most enduring numbers, "Shake That Thing", as well as a duet with **Ida Cox** on "Mister Man, Parts 1 and 2". Another famous duet came in 1928 when he recorded two sides including "Ma And Pa Poorhouse Blues" with **Ma Rainey**, which were the last recordings she ever made. He also recorded further duets with Hattie McDaniels and Lucille Bogan.

Jackson's banjo playing was also in demand with jazz bands. In 1926 he recorded with Freddie Keppard and his Jazz Cardinals, cutting "Stockyard Strut" and a second version of "Salty Dog", and he also recorded with Tiny Parham's band, which featured **Kid Ory**. One of his most fascinating recordings was made with **Blind Blake** in 1929, when they cut "Papa Charlie And Blind Blake Talk About It Parts One And Two", a wonderful and unusual hybrid of blues jam, hokum, ragtime and sly humor between two old rounders.

Although Jackson occasionally switched to guitar or ukelele, the majority of his recordings feature his customized six-stringed banjo-guitar, on which he was a virtuoso performer, combining chordal solos and jazzy single-note runs with a plectrum with the finger-picking styles of a rural blues guitarist. His last recordings for Paramount came in 1930 when he cut "You Got That Wrong" and "Self Experience". He then disappeared for four years, returning to the studio for one final session for the Okeh label in November 1934, including three songs accompanied by his friend **Big Bill Broonzy** on guitar. He died in 1938 in circumstances that remain unknown.

⊙ **Complete Recorded Works Vols 1–3** Document)
Once again, Document comes to the rescue of an overlooked musical legacy with their usual impeccably researched and comprehensively annotated approach, although they had less success in cleaning up the sound of some ancient tapes. Historically, the first volume is probably the most interesting collection.

Elmore James

b Richland, Mississippi, Jan 27, 1918; d May 23, 1963

With the dramatic slide guitar motif that opens "Dust My Broom", **Elmore James** created perhaps the most recognizable and widely imitated blues riff of all time, and electrified the country blues legacy of Robert Johnson.

James grew up on several different farms in Mississippi, and his first instrument was the "diddley bow", in effect little more than a strand of wire nailed to the front porch. By the age of fourteen, he had graduated to a twenty-dollar National guitar and was playing at parties, dances and juke joints in the Durant area of Mississippi under the names Cleanhead James or Joe Willie James.

During the mid-1930s, James moved to Greenville, where he befriended bluesmen like **Sonny Boy (Rice Miller) Williamson**, **Robert Johnson**, Arthur "Big Boy" Crudup, Luther Hoff and Johnny Temple. Although he accompanied Williamson for several years, it was Johnson's guitar playing, and in particular his slide technique, that proved to be the biggest influence on James. Some time around 1939, he put together his own band and became one of the earliest bluesmen to switch to an electric guitar.

James was called up to the US Navy in 1943, and took part in the invasion of Guam before he was discharged in 1945. Returning to Belzoni, he roomed with Sonny Boy Williamson, and they resumed their musical partnership. As a trio, with James' cousin **"Homesick" James Williamson**, they were regularly to be found playing on Beale Street in Memphis, while James also backed Sonny Boy on the *King Biscuit Hour* radio show, broadcast out of Helena, Arkansas.

Elmore James made his first recording for Lillian McMurry's Trumpet label in 1951, cutting his landmark version of Robert Johnson's "Dust My Broom". A seminal moment in blues history, it reached number nine on the R&B charts. Success encouraged James to move to Chicago the following year, where he formed the first of several bands known as the **Broomdusters**. He recorded for sev-

The Diddley Bow

"What a diddley bow is... there's one string of wire – way back then, when you buy a broom, a special kind of wire was wrapped around the bottom to hold the straw on the broom. That's the kind of wire we would use. Because it was smaller than hay-baling wire, it sound better. You'd nail it up against a wall. You got one nail here, you wrapped the wire around it real tight, twist it so it won't come loose and then you drive it into the wall, tight as you can get it. Pull the wire stretched tight as you can, do the same thing the other end. You get you a glass snuff bottle and put that in between the string and the wall and press it down and that's what get you the sound. Then you find you a cake flavor bottle and that's what you pick it with, slide it up and down and it changed the tuning."

Guitarist and Fat Possum recording artist **CeDell Davis** describes playing a diddley bow when growing up in the 1930s in Helena, Arkansas. From *Portrait Of The Blues* by Paul Trynka (Da Capo Press, 1997).

eral labels throughout the 1950s, including Chess, Flair, Meteor, Chief and Fire. Recording with a band that usually included Homesick James on bass, pianist Little Johnny Jones, drummer Odie Payne and tenor sax player J.T. Brown – several of whom had played in Tampa Red's band – he came up with such great sides as "The Sky Is Crying", Tampa Red's "It Hurts Me Too" (a posthumous hit on the R&B chart in 1965), "I Believe", "Dust My Blues", "Bleeding Heart", "Done Somebody Wrong" and "Shake Your Moneymaker". He recorded slow blues and boogies and sang in a powerful, passionate voice, but his trademarks were always his blistering riffs and his fiercely intense slide playing.

James died in Chicago in 1963, after suffering a heart attack at the home of Homesick James. Illness made him look much older than his 45 years, and he didn't live long enough to observe the powerful influence he exerted on the British blues boom. The Rolling Stones' Brian Jones was a disciple, and for a time called himself Elmo' Lewis in honor of his hero. John Mayall recorded "Mr James" as a tribute, while Fleetwood Mac's Jeremy Spencer successfully copied every last nuance of James' slide guitar style.

⊙ **The Sky Is Crying: The History Of Elmore James** Rhino
Among the classic Elmore James sides included on this single-disc collection are "Dust My Broom", "The Sky Is Crying" and "It Hurts Me Too".

⊙ **The Classic Early Recordings** Ace
A triple-disc set that includes all of Elmore James' obvious hits, and considerably more besides.

Etta James

b Los Angeles, Jan 25, 1938

The early years of the blues were dominated by female singers like Mamie Smith, Bessie Smith and Ma Rainey. By the time **Etta James** came to prominence in the 1950s, however, with her R&B-tinged style, the blues was almost totally a male preserve. Etta became known as "the matriarch of the blues", a title for which she has few rivals, and the way she belted, screamed, growled, purred and cried made her the biggest female artist ever to record for Chess Records.

Born in Los Angeles in 1938 to an Italian father and a black mother who had her fostered,

Jamesetta Hawkins was taught to sing aged five by James Earle Hines, musical director of the Echoes of Eden gospel choir. When she was twelve, she was reunited with her birth mother in San Francisco, and soon after began singing in a female trio called the **Creolettes**. At sixteen, she was discovered when bandleader **Johnny Otis** auditioned her backstage at the Fillmore Auditorium. He started to record her, and, by simply reversing the syllables of her birth name, he was also responsible for the name by which she was known from then on.

Although Etta wrote in her autobiography many years later that her mother had always told her "don't listen to that gutbucket blues", her first recording suggested she'd ignored the advice. 1954's self-composed "Roll With Me Henry" was a direct answer to Hank Ballard's hit "Work With Me, Annie", albeit re-titled "The Wallflower" in a bid to disguise its risqué lyric. Backed by Otis's band, with **Richard Berry** singing the second vocal, it became an R&B number one in 1955. Soon afterwards, a cover version by Georgia Gibbs, with the original title restored, topped the pop charts.

James followed with another R&B hit in "Good Rockin' Daddy", and also recorded several sides in the late 1950s as Etta James & the Peaches (to this day, she's sometimes referred to as "Miss Peaches"). However, her career didn't truly take off until 1960, when Harvey Fuqua signed her to the Chess subsidiary **Argo**, for whom she racked up ten R&B hits in her first three years. These included "All I Could Do Was Cry"; "At Last", a bluesy cover of a Glenn Miller song that ranks among her finest-ever performances; "Trust In Me", a cover of Mildred Bailey's 1937 hit; "Don't Cry Baby"; "Something's Got A Hold On Me"; "Stop The Wedding"; and "Pushover". She also cut several duets with Fuqua, including the Jimmy Reed-influenced "If I Can't Have You". Her greatest records of the decade didn't come until 1967, when she recorded "Tell Mama" and "I'd Rather Go Blind", a stunningly moody, almost despairing song that was later a hit for Christine Perfect and Chicken Shack. Tellingly, both tracks were recorded not in Chicago but at the Fame studios in **Muscle Shoals**, Alabama, where the celebrated house band provided the perfect deep soul accompaniment to her abrasive, big-voiced approach.

She later revealed how label owner Leonard Chess got her to sing with such intensity. "When I

Peroxide R&B diva Etta James

bravura version of Muddy Waters' "I Just Want To Make Love To You" in not one but two major TV advertising campaigns in the late 1990s carried her back into the charts. *Rage To Survive*, an autobiography of almost brutal honesty, was published in 1995. Her most recent album, *Let's Roll*, won her another Grammy for best contemporary blues album in 2004, a year after she had received a Grammy Lifetime Achievement award. It was a just recognition of one of the greatest female blues vocalists of them all.

⊙ **Her Best: The Chess 50th Anniversary Collection** Chess
A near-perfect single-disc compilation of the best of Etta James's Chess material, recorded between 1960 and 1973.

⊙ **The Very Best Of Etta James: The Chess Singles** Chess
A magnificent 53-track collection of potent blues, R&B and deep soul, spread over three generous discs.

⊙ **Mystery Lady: Songs Of Billie Holiday** Private Music
It takes something special to bring something new to Lady Day's back catalogue, but Etta James manages it on this Grammy-winning 1994 collection.

⊙ **Let's Roll** Private Music
"The blues is my business and business is good," James sings – and you'd better believe it on this Grammy-winning collection, recorded in 2003, that marks a return to the tough R&B style of her Chess sides.

got to a part where he thought I should squawl or scream, he'd punch me in the side. I mean literally *punch* me," she reported. However, her progress was checked by a turbulent private life and drug addiction, and although she continued recording for Chess until 1977, the 1970s were a lean decade. She then moved to Warner Brothers and recorded the fine 1978 album *Deep In The Night*, and eventually overcame her heroin addiction as her career took on a new lease of life, supporting the Rolling Stones on tour and singing at the opening ceremony of the Los Angeles Olympics in 1984. Keith Richards is a particular fan. "She's a voice from heaven and hell," he once remarked. "When you listen to the sister, you are stroked and ravaged at the same time."

Still touring and recording for assorted labels, James has made a specialty of bluesy covers of songs about love and loss, such as "Need Your Love So Bad" and "The Night Time Is The Right Time". She won a Grammy in 1994 for *Mystery Lady*, her Private Music tribute album to Billie Holliday, while the use of her voice singing a

Skip James

b Bentonia, Yazoo City, Mississippi, June 21, 1902; d Oct 3, 1969

S kip James was quite simply one of the very greatest Delta bluesmen of them all. There are those among his fans who claim that had he disappeared in the 1930s, rather than living on to be rediscovered as an old man in the 1960s, his deep, dark blues would today be as revered as those of Robert Johnson.

Nehemiah Curtis James heard local fiddle-based dance musicians during his Mississippi-plantation childhood, and acquired the nickname "Skippy" on account of his dancing style. He picked up the guitar early, his mother buying him his first instrument in 1912, but he also had piano lessons.

By the early 1920s he was an itinerant laborer hobo-ing around Mississippi, working with road construction and levee-building gangs as well as in lumber and saw-mill camps, an experience which he described in one of his earliest songs, "Illinois Blues". By the mid-1920s he was back in the Bentonia area, where he sharecropped, and made "white lightnin'" bootleg whiskey. He also began to play with local musicians such as **Henry Stuckey** and the brothers Charlie and Jesse Sims. From Stuckey he learned to play guitar in the open E-minor tuning that became his trademark, and developed the three-finger picking technique that so dazzled on his early recordings. The two men worked together at picnics, parties and juke joints around the Delta, and their association has generated much talk of a "Bentonia school" of the blues, although most scholars now regard the term as something of an exaggeration.

After being recommended by the Jackson-based record store owner and talent scout H.C. Speir, James auditioned for Paramount Records and traveled to Grafton, Wisconsin in February 1931 for the only recording sessions of his prewar career. A total of at least eighteen and possibly 26 sides were recorded, including the stunning "Devil Got My Woman", on which James sings in a haunting, high tenor "I'd rather be the devil than be that woman's man" with an intensity surely inspired by personal circumstance after his sixteen-year-old wife had left him. The writer Greg Ward has described the track as "a clear prefiguration of Robert Johnson's doom-laden 'Hellhound On My Trail'".

Other stand-outs include "I'm So Glad", featuring a guitar part of almost impossible complexity that was based on Art Sizemore and George A. Little's 1927 song "So Tired"; "Special Rider Blues"; the bleak "Hard Time Killing Floor Blues"; "Cypress Grove Blues"; and the frenzied "22-20 Blues", which Robert Johnson adapted as "32-20

Blues". The latter piece was one of several James played on the piano, in a stabbing, staccato style that he had learned from a pianist/pimp called Will Crabtree in Memphis, where he worked briefly as a pianist in a brothel.

The eighteen sides that were issued at the time, on nine 78s, are among the rarest and most sought-after early discs among blues collectors, and the sessions represent one of the most remarkable legacies of early Delta blues. Yet James didn't record again for more than thirty years. Paramount went broke owing him money, which persuaded him that the music business was "a barrel of crabs", and the Depression also dented the sales of "race" recordings. In addition James had "gotten religion". One of the titles he had recorded in 1931 was called "Jesus Is A Mighty Good Leader", and following his own advice he became a Baptist minister, later switching to the Methodists during the 1940s.

Not until 1964 did the researches of blues enthusiasts **John Fahey** and **Henry Vestine**, later of Canned Heat, find him in a hospital in Tunica, Mississippi. James was understandably bitter about

Nehemiah Curtis James – a guitar player of almost impossible complexity

215

the way his earlier career had led to nothing. In an interview shortly after his rediscovery, he complained: "I was so disappointed. Wouldn't you be disappointed, man? I cut 26 sides for Paramount. I didn't get paid but forty dollars. That's not doing very good. Wouldn't you be disappointed?"

He took little persuading to pick up his guitar again, appeared at the 1964 Newport Folk Festival, and resumed his recording career with albums for the Takoma, Melodeon and Vanguard labels. Many of his songs were covered by the new generation of blues bands, most notably Cream, who recorded a version of "I'm So Glad", basing their version on his simpler 1960s re-recording, rather than the complexities of the 1931 original. The royalties gave him his first significant income from his music in his life, but sadly came too late, and were used to cover his funeral expenses, when he died in Philadelphia in 1969 at the age of 67, after a prolonged struggle with cancer.

⊙ **The Vanguard Sessions: Blues From The Delta** Vanguard
Twenty tracks from sessions that Skip James recorded for Vanguard between 1966 and 1968, including remakes of "Devil Got My Woman", "I'm So Glad" and "Hard Time Killing Floor Blues", plus "Crow Jane", and even James's rendition of "Careless Love".

Blind Lemon Jefferson

b Worthman, Texas, circa Sept 1893; d Dec 1929

A seminal figure in blues history, **Blind Lemon Jefferson** was not the first male blues singer to be recorded. But he was the first to enjoy major commercial success, influencing all who followed him and starting the rush to record bluesmen across the South.

For many years it was believed that Jefferson was born in July 1897, but recent research has suggested the true date was probably four years earlier, in September 1893. That's thought to have happened in Couchman, near Worthman, East Texas, some sixty miles south of Dallas. No one knows whether Lemon was his real name. One of seven children, he was blind or near-blind either from birth or from a very young age. As that prevented him from working as a farm hand, he turned instead to music.

Despite his sightlessness, Jefferson seems to have been possessed of a fiercely independent spirit. By 1912 he was wandering East Texas, playing at house parties and plantation picnics, and in brothels and on street corners, combining blues songs with spirituals and folk tunes. Living on his wits and his intuition, he was also said to carry a gun for protection and even to have used it on several occasions. He appears to have spent the next few years traveling extensively around Texas and possibly beyond, but by 1917 he was settled in the Deep Ellum district of Dallas. There he met and played with **Leadbelly**, who claimed to have acted as his "eyes" by leading him around town, and later recorded "Blind Lemon Blues" in his honor. **T-Bone Walker**, then still a young boy, also recalled performing a similar service as Jefferson's "lead boy".

He must have been very good even at this early stage, if the stories that his singing could earn up to 150 dollars a day are true. He reportedly used the money to support a wife and child, although they have never been traced or identified. Towards the end of 1925, a Dallas record store owner named R.T. Ashford, who realized he could make money selling Jefferson's records to his sizeable number of local fans, recommended him to Art Laibily at Paramount Records. In December 1925 or January 1926, he traveled to Chicago to make his first recordings.

Lemon Jefferson's recording career lasted less than four years, but between 1926 and 1929 he went on to cut almost a hundred sides, all for Paramount Records bar two sides for Okeh. His first two songs were religious in nature, and were released under the pseudonym **Deacon L.J. Bates**. But soon he was recording pure blues material, beginning with "Long Lonesome Blues" and followed by "Booster Blues", which gave him his first hit in March 1926, backed with "Dry Southern Blues". That release changed the face of recorded blues, and the direction of popular music. From then on, his records sold in what were for the time unprecedented quantities, sparking record companies to send their scouts scouring the South in search of further bluesmen. Jefferson himself soon had enough money to buy two cars, and to employ a chauffeur to drive them.

His classic and much-covered songs – most of which he wrote himself, with unusually vivid lyrics – included "See That My Grave Is Kept Clean"; "Match Box Blues"; "Black Snake Moan", which Paramount advertised as "weird, slimy and creepy"; "Rabbit Foot Blues"; and "Jack O'Diamond Blues". Singing in a high-pitched voice of great penetration and range that was the product of years of performing outdoors without amplification, he accompanied himself on guitar in a dense, unorthodox style that has proved surprisingly hard to imitate. As former Rolling Stone **Bill Wyman** has suggested, he was in many ways the first male pop star, for his records presented a *sound* rather than just a song, which meant that for the first time the artist and not the material was the main selling-point. That Jefferson was being marketed as a personality is reinforced by the profile of him that was included in his record label's promotional Paramount's *Book Of The Blues*: "Can anyone imagine a fate more horrible than to find that one is blind? Such was the fate of Blind Lemon Jefferson … He learned to play a guitar and for years he entertained his friends freely – moaning his weird songs as a means of forgetting his affliction."

Despite his status, just one photograph of Blind Lemon Jefferson exists, which was used on a record label. It shows a bulky, well-dressed man with a soft, almost babyish face wearing small round glasses and with his eyes closed. He died in mysterious circumstances in the winter of 1929 on the streets of Chicago. One popular account holds that he froze to death in a December snow blizzard, although his producer **Mayo Williams** believed that he had died in the back of his car, possibly of a heart attack, and had been abandoned by his driver.

On his death, the Rev. Emmett Dickinson preached a sermon in which he opined Jefferson's life was "in many respects like that of our Lord Jesus Christ. Like Him, unto the age of thirty he was unknown. And also like Him, in a short space of little over three years, his name and his works were known in every home."

Williams, on behalf of Paramount Records, paid for the return of Jefferson's body to Texas by train, accompanied by pianist **Will Ezell**, and he was buried at Wortham Negro Cemetery (now renamed Wortham Black Cemetery). Yet despite his status as the first male star of the blues, he was laid to rest in an unmarked grave. In 1967 a Texas historical monument marker was erected in the vicinity of his plot, the precise location of which is unknown. Eventually, a new granite headstone was erected in 1997. Underneath his name, the words on the stone simply declared: "One Of America's Outstanding Original Musicians".

Playlist
Blind Lemon Jefferson

All are taken from *Black Snake Moan*

1 PRISON CELL BLUES (1928)
"I wrote to the governor, please turn me a-loose, since I don't get no answer, I know it ain't no use…"

2 BLACK SNAKE MOAN (1927)
According to Paramount's advertising campaign, this was "weird, slimy and creepy". They meant it as a compliment.

3 MATCHBOX BLUES (1927)
"I'm sittin' here wonderin' would a matchbox hold my clothes, I ain't got so many matches but I got so far to go…"

4 RISING HIGH WATER BLUES (1927)
Inspired by the great Mississippi flood of 1927; see also Charley Patton.

5 RABBIT FOOT BLUES (1926)
"I wanna stop these mad-looking women from worrying me…"

6 HE AROSE FROM THE DEAD (1927)
Jefferson in upbeat gospel mode; particularly fascinating because it hardly sounds like him at all.

7 THAT CRAWLING BABY BLUES (1929)
"Married man rocks some other man's babe, fool thinks he is rockin' his own"

8 JACK O'DIAMOND BLUES (1926)
Well it's a hard card to play.

9 SEE THAT MY GRAVE IS KEPT CLEAN (1927)
A song that 35 years later provided one of the highlights of Bob Dylan's debut album.

10 HANGMAN'S BLUES (1928)
"Lord, I'm almost dyin', gasping for my breath and a triflin' woman waiting to celebrate my death…"

⊙ **Classic Sides** JSP

This comprehensive 4-disc box set, containing a total of 94 sides, holds most but not quite all of Blind Lemon Jefferson's recorded output.

⊙ **Black Snake Moan** Complete Blues

If you want a single disc collecting the best of Jefferson's work, these twenty tracks do the job well, although the sound has not been cleaned up and transferred as well as it could have been.

⊙ **Squeeze My Lemon** Catfish

Another well-compiled 23-track compilation of Blind Lemon Jefferson's best-known songs, at a budget price.

Little Willie John

b Cullendale, Arkansas, Nov 15, 1937; d May 26, 1968

There's a group of 1950s R&B stars who never quite made the transition to either rock'n'roll or soul, and consequently inhabit an almost lost musical world in which they've all too easily been overlooked, neglected and forgotten. Take **Little Willie John**; under different circumstances, his fabulous voice could easily have seen him emulate the crossover success of contemporaries like Sam Cooke and James Brown. He ranks unquestionably among the finest singers of blues ballads of his generation, and however far he strayed from the basic territory, as Greg Ward has written, "everything he touched remained imbued with the blues".

One of ten children, John moved to Detroit as a child, and became a singing prodigy, recording for Savoy Records at the age sixteen. He signed for Syd Nathan's King Records in 1955, making his debut for the label with a potent version of "All Around The World", which was later revived by **Little Milton** as "Grits Ain't Groceries". That was followed over the next five years by the magnificent tear-jerker "Need Your Love So Bad", written by his brother Meris John and later regally covered by Fleetwood Mac; "Suffering With The Blues"; "Talk To Me Talk To Me"; "Let Them Talk"; "Leave My Kitten Alone"; and "Sleep". Then, of course, there was 1958's "Fever", written by Otis Blackwell and Eddie Cooley but sometimes co-credited to John, which gave him a hit but was an even bigger one in note-for-note copies by **Peggy Lee** and **Elvis Presley**.

Standing just five foot four inches tall, Little Willie had an unstable temper and a taste for liquor, and he always carried a gun and a knife. In 1964, he stabbed a man during an argument in Seattle. Convicted of manslaughter, he was sent to the Washington State penitentiary. He died in prison in 1968, in confused circumstances; some say he suffered a heart attack when already ill with pneumonia, others claim he was asphyxiated. He was just thirty, and James Brown immediately recorded a tribute album to him. His older sister **Mable John** (b Bastrop, Louisiana, Nov 3, 1930), who wrote "Leave My Kitten Alone", went on to record for Stax during the 1960s, and later joined Ray Charles as a member of the Raelettes.

⊙ **All Fifteen Of His Chart Hits** King

A terrible title, but great music – and from "Need Your Love So Bad" to "Fever" nobody can accuse this collection of failing to do Little Willie John justice.

Blind Willie Johnson

b Temple, Texas, circa 1902; d 1949 (or 1950)

Nowhere did the "devil's music" of the blues come together with sanctified gospel singing more potently than in the work of **Blind Willie Johnson**. His "Dark Was The Night, Cold Was The Ground" was once called "the most transcendent piece in all American music" by **Ry Cooder**, who adapted it as the theme for his soundtrack to *Paris, Texas*.

Johnson's date of birth is usually given as 1902, but nobody really knows, and it could have been as early as the mid-1890s. Marlin, Texas, was long believed to be his place of birth, and certainly he grew up there, but modern research now suggests he was born near Temple. He went blind at the age of seven in equally shadowy circumstances. His mother had died when he was a baby, and Johnson's father remarried. One story holds that when his father caught his stepmother cheating on him, he beat her up, and her revenge was to throw lye-water into the boy's face to blind him.

By then, he had already announced his intention of become a preacher, and fashioned his first guitar out of a cigar box, using the blade of a pocket knife as a slide. His father would take him as a boy to nearby towns on the weekend and leave him to play on street corners with a tin cup tied around his neck to collect the tips, but he also played at Baptist Association meetings. He began recording for Columbia Records in 1927, by which time he was living in Dallas. Over the next three years, he recorded some thirty sides of remarkable and consistent quality. Singing in a gravel-toned, rasping bass voice and playing haunting bottleneck guitar, he performed songs that were mostly spiritual in nature. But it was said he had the power to make a religious song sound like the blues, and a blues song sound holy.

Many of Johnson's best-known sides were adapted from old hymns, including "Let Your Light Shine On Me", "Jesus Make Up My Dying Bed", "Motherless Children Have A Hard Time", "Nobody's Fault But Mine", "God Don't Never Change", "Bye And Bye I'm Going To See The King", "God Moves On The Water" and "I Know His Blood Can Make Me Whole". He was allegedly arrested for singing "If I Had My Way I'd Tear The Building Down" outside a courthouse, and charged with inciting a riot. However, his absolute masterpiece was "Dark Was The Night, Cold Was The Ground". A raw, tortured and terrifying mainly instrumental song about the crucifixion, the recording became decades later one of the tracks launched into space with the *Voyager* spacecraft in 1977 to represent twentieth-century culture.

It seems likely that Johnson also recorded a brace of un-issued blues sides under the name **Blind Texas Marlin**. On several sides he was accompanied by a female singer, long assumed to be his wife Angeline Robinson, the sister of Texan guitarist L.C. "Good Rockin'" Robinson, whom Johnson is said to have taught to play. However, it is now believed the singer was an earlier girlfriend or wife named Willie B. Harris. His last sessions took place in Atlanta around Easter 1930 and he spent his final years in Beaumont, Texas, where he continued to play on street corners and is remembered as a neat, dignified and gentle man. Late in the 1940s, a fire burned down his home. Although he survived that mishap, he returned to the burnt-out ruin and slept on a mattress covered in newspapers, to soak up the water from the fire hoses. Unsurprisingly, he contracted pneumonia, and died in 1949 or possibly early 1950. The exact date is unclear, because he was apparently refused admittance to hospital because of his blindness. He died alone.

Although there are considerable holes in our knowledge of Johnson's life, much of what we do know comes from the researches of Sam Charters, who in the late 1950s tracked down and interviewed Johnson's wife Angeline. Charters also documented the influence on Johnson's distinctive vocal style of an obscure, older singer named Madkin Butler.

Playlist
Blind Willie Johnson

All are taken from from *The Complete Blind Willie Johnson*

1 I KNOW HIS BLOOD CAN MAKE ME WHOLE (1927)
Johnson's first recording outsold even Bessie Smith, and had to be immediately re-pressed.

2 KEEP YOUR LAMPS TRIMMED AND BURNING (1928)
"… for this old world is almost done…"

3 "IT'S NOBODY'S FAULT BUT MINE" (1927)
"If I don't read it my soul be lost, I have a bible in my home."

4 DARK WAS THE NIGHT, COLD WAS THE GROUND (1927)
Used by Ry Cooder as the inspiration for his *Paris Texas* soundtrack.

5 IF I HAD MY WAY I'D TEAR THIS BUILDING DOWN (1927)
Blind Willie's version of the Samson and Delilah epic.

6 JESUS IS COMING SOON (1928)
"Bible plainly says, said the people in the cities dyin', account of they wicked ways"

7 JOHN THE REVELATOR (1930)
"God walked down in the cool of the day, and called Adam by his name, but he refused to answer, 'cause he was naked and ashamed…"

8 YOU'RE GOING TO NEED SOMEBODY ON YOUR BOND (1930)
From Johnson's last session in Atlanta. After that, he sang only in the Mt Olive Baptist Church church and on street corners in Beaumont, Texas.

⊙ **The Complete Blind Willie Johnson**
Columbia
A sublime collection of thirty spine-tingling tracks – all Johnson ever recorded – spread across a two-disc set.

Lil Johnson

dates of birth and death unknown

Just about all we know about **Lil Johnson** is that she cut some seriously sexy blues sides during the 1930s, and she always sounded like she was having a good time. She began recording in 1929, accompanied by pianists Montana Taylor and Charles Avery. Over the next seven years she recorded more than fifty sides, mostly for Vocalion, and often accompanied by pianist **Black Bob**. Her song titles tell you all you need to know. Among her more suggestive favorites were "Press My Button"; "Ring My Bell"; "Get 'Em From The Peanut Man" (also known as "Hot Nuts"); "You'll Never Miss Your Jelly Till Your Jelly Roller Is Gone"; "Anybody Want To Buy My Cabbage?"; and "My Stove's In Good Condition", which features **Big Bill Broonzy** on guitar. When she didn't have sex on the brain, she took brief detours into the world of hard-drinking songs, with sides like "Was I Drunk".

All were sung in an abrasive, blues-drenched voice, and her songs these days regularly turn up on themed compilations. Johnson was just one of many similar singers at the time; anyone wishing to investigate this fascinating sub-genre further should try the *Sugar In my Bowl* compilation listed below.

Just as no one knows where she came from, we remain equally in the dark as to what became of her after her recording career ended. We don't even have an idea of what she looked like, for no photos have survived.

⊙ **Complete Recorded Works Vol 1–3**
Document
All the Lil Johnson you need – and probably considerably more. Volume three is rounded out by several tracks featuring the similarly rude but obscure singer, Barrelhouse Annie.

⊙ *Various Artists* **Sugar In My Bowl, Hard Drivin' Mamas: Vintage Sex Songs 1923–52**
Buzzola
Risqué favorites not only from Lil Johnson, but also Bessie Smith, Sippie Wallace, Victoria Spivey and Lucille Bogan's notorious uncensored version of "Shave 'Em Dry".

Lonnie Johnson

b New Orleans, Feb 8, 1899; d June 16, 1970

A pioneer of blues guitar, Lonnie Johnson was a virtuoso performer who is often credited with having invented the guitar solo. As such, he influenced almost every bluesman who subsequently picked up the instrument, from Robert Johnson to B.B. King, as well as jazz players such as the great Django Reinhardt.

Born into a family of musicians in the last year of the nineteenth century, Johnson played the violin as a child. Before he reached his teens, he was entertaining in the saloons and bordellos of New Orleans' red-light district, Storyville. He spent several years in Europe during World War I, and on his return to the Crescent City in 1919, he took to the road, playing guitar, banjo and violin in various bands, often with his older brother James "Steady Roll" Johnson. He eventually settled in St Louis, where he won a talent contest in 1925 that led to a recording contract with Okeh Records and a further move to Chicago.

Installed as guitarist in Okeh's house band, Johnson recorded at an astonishing rate, both under his own name and as an accompanist. During one two-year period, the label issued a record by Johnson on average every two weeks, while between 1925 and 1932 he cut almost two hundred sides, singing in a mellow and sophisticated style, playing lithe, swinging guitar, and even bowing some mournful violin. He also cut some red-hot duets, like "Two Tone Stomp" and "Guitar Blues", with white guitarist **Eddie Lang**, who was forced to masquerade as Blind Willie Dunn to disguise the inter-racial nature of their collaboration. Johnson also recorded with **Louis Armstrong's Hot Five** ("Savoy Blues"), **King Oliver, Duke Ellington** ("Hot and Bothered"), and a group called Blind Willie Dunn's Gin Bottle Four, that also included songwriter-pianist **Hoagy Carmichael**. Among the female blues singers he accompanied in the studio were Victoria Spivey, Helen Humes and Clara Smith, as well as his wife Mary Johnson.

RUF RECORDS

Okeh records stalwart Lonnie Johnson, 1940s

Playlist
Lonnie Johnson

1 MR JOHNSON'S BLUES (1925) from **Steppin' On The Blues**
His first recording, with a brief vocal, long guitar instrumental and piano accompaniment.

2 ROCKS IN MY BED (NO 2) (1941) from **Playing With The Strings**
A superb version recorded with a trio in Chicago.

3 LIFE SAVER BLUES (1927) from **Playing With The Strings**
One of the tracks that induced Robert Johnson falsely to claim Lonnie as his brother.

4 TOMORROW NIGHT (1947) from **The Best Of Lonnie Johnson: Tomorrow Night**
To the surprise of everyone – most of all Lonnie, who was in his fiftieth year – this topped the R&B chart for seven weeks in 1948.

5 BULL FROG MOAN (1929) from **Playing With The Strings**
A dazzling instrumental guitar duet with Eddie Lang.

6 CARELESS LOVE (1927) from **Lonnie Johnson, Volume 2: 1927–32**
Like "Tomorrow Night", this was later covered by a young man called Elvis Presley.

7 UNCLE NED DON'T USE YOUR HEAD (1931) from **Playing With The Strings**
Hardly a blues song, but masterful picking and a wonderfully bawdy lyric.

8 ROAMIN' RAMBLER BLUES (1927) from **Playing With The Strings**
A fine example of Johnson's mellow vocal style, even if his claim to have started his peripatetic ways at the age of two should be taken with a pinch of salt.

9 SHE'S MAKING WHOOPIE IN HELL TONIGHT (1930) from **Steppin' On The Blues**
"Devil got 90,000 women, he just needs one more; you're just the type of woman for him, mama, you're booked out and bound to go…"

10 TOOTHACHE BLUES (1928) from **Steppin' On The Blues**
An irresistibly risqué vocal duet with Victoria Spivey, accompanied by Clarence Williams on piano.

Johnson stopped recording for a while during the Depression years and moved to Cleveland, Ohio. However, he returned to Chicago before the end of the decade, and in 1939 was signed by Lester Melrose to Bluebird Records, where he adapted readily to the electric guitar and recorded with the pianist **Blind John Davis**. In 1947, he transferred to the Cincinnati-based King Records, and enjoyed a huge R&B number one when the mellow ballad "Tomorrow Night" topped the R&B charts for seven weeks in 1948. Further hits followed, with "Pleasing You (As Long As I Live)", "So Tired" and "Confused".

Then he disappeared again for most of the 1950s, until he was rediscovered by disc jockey Chris Albertson in 1959, by which time he was working as a janitor at a hotel in Philadelphia. Delighted to get the chance of another comeback, he recorded several albums for the Bluesville label and toured Europe with the American Folk Blues Festival in 1963, although much of his later work was heavily jazz-tinged. Two years later he moved to Toronto where he opened a club. He was badly injured in a car accident in the city in 1969, and died a year later as a result.

⊙ **Blues In My Fingers** Indigo
A great introduction to Lonnie Johnson's work from the 1920s and early 1930s, including some fine guitar solos and his duets with Eddie Lang.

⊙ **Steppin' On The Blues** Columbia
A satisfying compilation of Johnson's finest blues and jazz sides from his prolific 1925–32 period.

⊙ **The Original Guitar Wizard** Proper
This 4-disc box set contains almost hundred recordings from 1928–52.

⊙ **Blues By Lonnie Johnson** Original Blues Classics
Probably the best of Lonnie Johnson's Bluesville comeback albums, this 1960 recording found him in sharp and compelling form.

⊙ **Blues And Ballads** Original Blues Classics
On his second Bluesville album of 1960, Lonnie Johnson is joined by veteran guitar and banjo player Elmer Snowdon, in whose band Duke Ellington played during the 1920s, and who was making his first recordings since 1934.

Luther "Guitar Junior" Johnson

b Itta Bena, Mississippi, April 11, 1939

Not to be confused with Luther "Georgia Boy" Johnson, who was also part of the Chess stable and played with Muddy Waters, or for that matter with Atlanta's Luther "Houserocker" Johnson, **Luther "Guitar Junior" Johnson** played in bands led by Magic Sam and Muddy Waters, and has recorded prolifically as a solo artist.

After teaching himself guitar in his early teens, Johnson moved north with his family to Chicago in 1955. He was just sixteen, and it was an exciting time for an aspiring blues guitar player to arrive in the city. Hanging around the clubs on the West Side, he was befriended by **Magic Sam**, with whom he played for several years.

In 1972 he joined **Muddy Waters**' band, replacing another guitarist of the same name, Luther "Georgia Boy" Johnson, who was also sometimes known as "Snake". He stayed with Waters until 1979, touring the world with him, and was given his own chance to front the band for a few of his tunes during each show. During his time with Muddy, he shared stages with the Rolling Stones, Eric Clapton, the Allman Brothers and Johnny Winter, and made a guest appearance in the movie *The Blues Brothers* as well.

A dynamic live performer, Johnson tours with relentless energy these days with his own band the **Magic Rockers**, and has recorded a string of solidly impressive modern blues albums, beginning with *Luther's Blues* on the French label Black & Blue in 1976. He also made three albums with the **Nighthawks**, and has recorded for Alligator, Rooster Blues, Bullseye and Telarc.

⊙ **Slammin' On The West Side** (Telarc)
On this diverse 1996 album, Luther Johnson ranges from classic Chicago electric blues, to acoustic numbers, jump blues and blues-funk.

Merline Johnson

b Mississippi, circa 1912; d unknown

The life of **Merline Johnson** – known as "the Yas Yas Girl", in an unusual American example of rhyming slang for the word "ass" best known for its use in Blind Boy Fuller's song "Get Yer Yas Yas Out" and later borrowed by the Rolling Stones as a title for a live album – is almost as shadowy as that of her contemporary Lil Johnson, although at least some photographs of her do exist.

Johnson started recording in Chicago in 1937 with the powerful "Sold It To The Devil". Over the next four years she cut some seventy sides, including the deliciously suggestive "Don't You Make Me High", singing in a tough and confident voice, and backed by such top Chicago blues musicians as **Big Bill Broonzy**, **Lonnie Johnson** and **Blind John Davis**, sometimes credited as Her Rhythm Rascals. After 1942, she dropped out of sight, re-emerging to record one final four-side session for Okeh Records in Chicago in 1947 before she disappeared again.

⊙ **The Yas Yas Girl** (Best Of Blues 1988)
While Document Records have done their usual scholarly job of compiling Merline Johnson's complete recordings over three CDs, this single-disc collection will satisfy most needs.

Pete Johnson

**b Kansas City, March 25, 1904;
d March 23, 1967**

Along with **Albert Ammons** and **Meade Lux Lewis**, **Pete Johnson** was one of the three great pianists who spearheaded the boogie-woogie craze in the 1930s.

Johnson in fact started out as a drummer, and didn't make the switch to the piano until 1926. He took to the keyboard immediately, and was soon backing **Big Joe Turner**, a working relationship that was to last on and off for forty years. He also worked solo around the clubs, developing a sparkling technique allied to enormous melodic invention. In 1936, John Hammond Jr. invited both Johnson and Turner to New York City to record, and two years later they appeared at his famous Spirituals To Swing concerts at the Carnegie Hall. Within two weeks of the gig, Johnson and Turner had gone into the Columbia studio and cut the classic "Roll 'Em Pete", and opened the city's new Café Society club, with Meade Lux Lewis and Albert Ammons also in attendance. The three pianists worked together as the **Boogie-woogie Trio**, while Johnson and Ammons also appeared

with Lena Horne in the 1941 movie *Boogie-woogie Dream*, sitting at separate baby grands and playing a four-handed boogie of quite awesome power.

Johnson continued to work with Turner on albums such as 1956's *Boss Of The Blues*, and he also recorded with **Jimmy Rushing**, but by the arrival of the rock'n'roll era his star was on the wane. He reappeared at the 1958 Newport Jazz Festival, but later that year suffered a stroke that left him partly paralyzed on his left side. He wasn't seen on a stage again until John Hammond persuaded him to appear at his 1967 Spirituals to Swing thirtieth anniversary concert. Pianist Ray Bryant sat alongside him at the piano and took the left hand part, leaving Johnson to play with his good right hand. With Big Joe Turner on stage as well, he then performed "Roll 'Em Pete" for one last emotional time. He died two months later at the age of 62.

⊙ **Roll 'Em Pete** Topaz
An excellent compilation of 25 of Pete Johnson's classic blues and boogie-woogie piano tracks.

⊙ **The Boogie-woogie Boys: The Complete Library** Document
The trinity of Pete Johnson, Meade Lux Lewis and Albert Ammons, all on one disc that serves as the perfect introduction to the style.

Robert Johnson

**b Hazlehurst, Mississippi, May 8, 1911;
d Aug 16, 1938**

"He seemed like a guy who could have sprung from the head of Zeus in full armor," Bob Dylan recalled of the moment he first heard the voice of the most exotic and mysterious bluesman of them all. In his lifetime, **Robert Johnson** released just eleven 78rpm records. They were enough to make him perhaps the most influential of all the Delta musicians within the blues community. Then in the 1960s, the reissue of his recordings meant the rest of the world got to hear him as well, and his impact on a new generation brought up in the rock'n'roll era was even more dramatic.

Dylan was one of the first of his generation to hear Johnson, after he was given an acetate of the soon-to-be-released compilation album *King Of The Delta Blues Singers* by Columbia staff producer John Hammond on the day he signed to the label in 1961. His reaction to what he heard was fairly typical of the impact Johnson had on almost everybody at the time. Yet no one has articulated those feelings more eloquently than Dylan, when he described the moment of epiphany in his acclaimed 2004 autobiography, *Chronicles Vol One*. "The songs weren't customary blues songs. They were perfected pieces," he wrote. "They jumped all over the place in range and subject matter, short punchy verses that resulted in some panoramic story – fires of mankind blasting off the surface of this spinning piece of plastic. It felt like a ghost had come into the room, a fearsome apparition. I just couldn't imagine how Johnson's mind could go in and out of so many places. He seems to know about everything."

It's as thrilling a description as you're ever likely to read of the genius of Robert Johnson – and it took another great itinerant genius of American music to express it. Quite simply, Johnson was the most influential bluesman of all time, and stands alongside Dylan and Elvis Presley among the architects of popular music in the modern era.

Although he was long a shadowy and mysterious figure, no Delta bluesman has had his life and background researched more thoroughly than Robert Johnson, and we can now thread together a reasonably comprehensive picture of his life. Johnson's grandparents were slaves, and his mother Julia Ann Majors married Charles Dodds in Hazlehurst, Mississippi, in February 1889. Dodds left Mississippi around 1907 and moved to Memphis, where he assumed the name of Spencer. In her husband's absence, Julia Dodds took up with Noah Johnson and gave birth to Robert Johnson on or around May 8, 1911, in Hazlehurst. Their liaison did not last, and in 1914 mother and son moved to Memphis, where she was reunited with Charles.

However, by this time, her husband had another "wife" and family, and Julia soon moved on, leaving Robert behind. He stayed with the Spencers until around 1918, when the couple decided they could no longer cope with his increasingly wilful behavior. He was packed off back to his mother, who by now was living in Robinsonville, a small cotton town twenty miles south of Memphis. There he lived with his mother and new stepfather, Willie "Dusty" Willis, until adulthood, and was sometimes known as Little Robert Dusty.

By the mid-1920s, by which time the Willis fam-

ily was living on the Abbay and Leatherman plantation in nearby Commerce, Mississippi, the teenage Robert Spencer, as he preferred to be known, had begun playing first the jew's harp and then the harmonica. Within a few years, he had graduated to the guitar, which he played with the harmonica fixed around his neck on a rack made with baling wire. He had also started listening in earnest to early "race records"; **Leroy Carr**'s 1928 "How Long How Long Blues" was said to be a particular favorite.

Local musician **Willie Brown** gave Robert tuition and he derived further inspiration from visiting bluesmen such as **Charley Patton**. He also learned from other local musicans Myles Robson and Ernest "Whiskey Red" Brown, while reluctantly making his living sharecropping. In early 1929, when he was still only seventeen, he married fifteen-year-old Virginia Travis in Penton, Mississippi, and the couple went to live with Robert's older half-sister Bessie and her husband on the Kline plantation east of Robinsonville. Virginia died in childbirth the following year.

During the summer of 1930, **Son House** came to live in Robinsonville, and Johnson became a disciple of his intense Delta blues style, following him around the juke joints. Tired of sharecropping, in late 1930 he hobo-ed his way two hundred miles south to Hazlehurst, in search of his real father. It's unclear whether he found him, but he discovered a new mentor in bluesman **Ike Zinnerman**, who was playing for local construction gangs and in the lumber camps. He also took a new wife, Calletta "Callie" Craft, more than ten years his senior and with three children from previous marriages. Some of the mythology that later attached itself to Johnson seems to have come from Zinnerman, who claimed he had learned to play guitar in a graveyard at midnight while sitting on a tombstone. Johnson began keeping a little book in which he wrote the songs he learned from Zinnerman. The two played together at local juke joints and country suppers and dances on weekends, but as Johnson's confidence and ability grew, he increasingly took the path of the solo bluesman. He became known locally as R.L., which he claimed stood for Robert Lonnie, after Lonnie Johnson whom he much admired, although it also stood for Robert Leroy, the names his mother had given him at birth.

Johnson and his wife moved to Clarksdale in the mid-1930s, but he soon deserted her. By the time he made a brief return to Robinsonville to see his mother, it was obvious to his old colleagues Son House and Willie Brown that he had become a superlative bluesman. House may have inadvertently started the diabolic rumors about him by joking that he must have signed a pact with the devil. Next he relocated to Helena, Arkansas, where he met and played with such bluesmen as **Sonny Boy Williamson**, Robert Nighthawk, Elmore James, David "Honeyboy" Edwards, Howlin' Wolf and Johnny Shines. He also moved in with another woman, Estella Coleman, and taught her son **Robert Lockwood, Jr.** to play the blues. Not that he was around Helena too much, as he traveled far and wide across the Delta, chasing other women and playing juke joints with a repertoire that included not only blues but anything his audiences requested, from pop songs and sentimental ballads to hillbilly dances and polkas. He even apparently did a decent version of "Yes, Sir, That's My Baby".

During his travels around the Delta in 1936, Johnson approached **H.C. Speir**, who ran a music store in Jackson, Mississippi, and acted as a talent scout for several blues labels. Speir auditioned Johnson and passed on his details to ARC's Ernie Oertle, who took Johnson to San Antonio, Texas, to record his first sessions in November 1936. They produced "Terraplane Blues", which was to remain Johnson's best-selling release in his lifetime. He recorded again a few months later, this time with Don Law in Dallas, Texas, in June 1937. Between them, the two sessions produced 29 songs, with alternate versions of nearly half of them; the full legacy therefore comprises a total of 42 recordings.

Some time after what was to prove his final session, the restless Johnson took to the road again, traveling to Chicago, St Louis, Detroit, Canada, New York and New Jersey, sometimes performing with a pianist and drummer during his travels. "If you'd wake him up in the middle of the night and tell him there was a freight train coming through he'd say 'let's catch it', and he'd take hold of his guitar and off he'd go," according to **Johnny Shines**, who traveled with him.

In July 1938, Johnson was back in Mississippi, playing at a juke joint in Greenwood at the intersection of Highways 82 and 49, known as Three Forks. One Saturday night he was sharing the bill there with Honeyboy Edwards and Sonny Boy Williamson when he was poisoned, probably with strychnine in an open bottle of whiskey sent over by the club's jealous owner, whose wife Johnson had been seeing. He might have survived the poisoning but probably contracted pneumonia which proved fatal. According to his death certificate, which was not tracked down until thirty years later, he died in Greenwood on August 16, 1938.

Not long afterwards, unaware that Johnson was dead, John Hammond tried to contact him to book him for that December's From Spirituals to Swing concert at New York's Carnegie Hall. He could not be found and **Big Bill Broonzy** took his place. For a long time, mystery surrounded Johnson's disappearance, but the details of his death eventually trickled out. Subsequent research revealed that he had been buried in an unmarked grave, probably in the graveyard of the Little Zion Church near Greenwood, although dedicated fans have since placed gravestones in three separate rural cemeteries outside the town.

It's endlessly fascinating to speculate what might have happened if Johnson had lived and played at Carnegie Hall. Hammond himself joined in the game several years later, saying: "I wanted black music to make an impression on a white audience and so we got the finest exponents of blues, jazz and gospel music that we could find. Can you imagine how famous Robert Johnson would be today had he been able to make it?"

One also wonders what music Johnson might have made if he'd lived on into the 1940s, moved to Chicago and gone electric as Muddy Waters and many others from the Delta tradition did. On the other hand, it's possible that his mysterious death in the long run only served to enhance his fame. Just two photographs of him survive, and wild stories and rumors about him have proliferated. Based partly on the lyrics of songs such as "Hellhound On My Trail", "Me And The Devil Blues", and "Crossroad Blues", fans eagerly related how he had sold his soul to the devil in return for his musical skill. He was also said to have the "evil eye", a story that probably had more prosaic origins in the fact that he had a small cataract.

Following the release of the *King Of The Delta Blues Singers* LP in 1961, the Johnson cult went into overdrive. Researchers visited his old haunts in Mississippi to piece together his story, several books appeared, and his songs were recorded by the Rolling Stones, Led Zeppelin and Eric Clapton among others. Among his most covered titles are "Crossroad Blues", "Terraplane Blues", "Come On In My Kitchen", "Walkin' Blues", "Preachin' Blues (Up

Playlist
Robert Johnson

All are taken from *Complete Recordings*

1 TRAVELING RIVERSIDE BLUES (1937)
"You can squeeze my lemon 'til the juice run down my leg..."

2 STOP BREAKING DOWN BLUES (1937)
" The stuff I got'll bust your brains out, baby, ooh, it'll make you lose your mind..."

3 COME ON IN MY KITCHEN (1936)
"The woman I love, took from my best friend, some joker got lucky, stole her back again..."

4 TERRAPLANE BLUES (1936)
"I even flash my lights mama, this horn won't even blow, got a short in this connection, well, babe, it's way down below..."

5 CROSS ROAD BLUES (1936)
"Standin' at the crossroad, risin' sun goin down, I believe to my soul now, poor Bob is sinkin' down..."

6 WALKIN' BLUES (1936)
"Some people tell me that the worried blues ain't bad, worse old feeling I most ever had..."

7 PREACHIN' BLUES (UP JUMPED THE DEVIL) (1937)
"The blues is a low-down achin' heart disease, like consumption killing me by degrees..."

8 IF I HAD POSSESSION OVER JUDGEMENT DAY (1936)
"... Lord, the little woman I'm lovin' wouldn't have no right to pray ..."

9 HELLHOUND ON MY TRAIL (1937)
"You sprinkled hot foot powder all around your daddy's door..."

10 ME AND THE DEVIL BLUES (1937)
"Hello, Satan, I believe it's time to go..."

Jumped The Devil)", "Ramblin' On My Mind", "Me And The Devil Blues", "Hellhound On My Trail", "I Believe I'll Dust My Broom" and "Love In Vain".

Some critics have complained that Johnson was derivative and copied from the likes of Lonnie Johnson (no relation), Skip James, Son House, Peetie Wheatstraw, Scrapper Blackwell and Kokomo Arnold, among others. Such borrowing is part and parcel of the blues tradition, of course. But to accuse Johnson of imitating anyone is also a brain-dead piece of nonsense. The Rolling Stones began by ripping off Chuck Berry, but ended up sounding nothing like him. And in Johnson's case, wherever he derived his influences and whatever his many and various sources, he sounded like no one but himself, a true original who has been much imitated but never matched.

His precise, intense guitar playing was a dazzling juxtaposition of shuffling rhythms and slide guitar lead lines that left almost everyone else trailing in his wake. Although working in a pre-electric era, his music points the way to the electric boogie sound that was to emerge in postwar Chicago. He sang like a man possessed or haunted, and quite probably both. Giles Oakley in *The Devil's Music* described Johnson's voice on his most spooked sides as sounding "as if on the edge of an abyss of complete psychic disintegration".

Then there were his songs, which tellingly is

the aspect that Bob Dylan concentrated on when he wrote about Johnson in *Chronicles*, recognizing an approach that bypassed "tedious descriptions that other blues writers would have written whole songs about". Instead, Johnson dealt with themes of loss, alienation, paranoia, demonic possession and despair in an elemental way. Even when he adapted from earlier songs, as he often did, Johnson fashioned his material into something utterly unique and original.

⊙ **King Of The Delta Blues Singers** Sony
A remastered version of the original 1961 album release that introduced Robert Johnson to the world at large, with an iconic cover and 17 of the most powerful blues sides ever recorded. Arguably the most influential album in the history of not just the blues but rock music, too.

⊙ **King Of The Delta Blues Singers Vol Two** Sony
A further 17 tracks from Robert Johnson, on a companion volume that belatedly appeared in 1970, with another stunningly evocative cover.

⊙ **Complete Recordings** Sony
This CD box set, containing all 41 known sides that Robert Johnson recorded, first appeared in 1990. In many ways it supersedes the two volumes above, although the packaging lacks the historical resonance of the vinyl reissues, and listening to it straight through requires you to hear successive alternate takes of the same songs.

Tommy Johnson

b Terry, Mississippi, circa 1896;
d Nov 1, 1956

Singing in what the blues historian Tony Russell memorably described as "the gentle, unflustered air of a man fishing on a summer's evening," **Tommy Johnson** left us just a handful of sides, recorded over four sessions in 1928, to show why he had such a high reputation among other Delta bluesmen.

Although Johnson's exact date of birth is not known, he was born some time during the mid-1890s on George Miller's Plantation near Terry, Mississippi, twenty miles south of Jackson. He was one of thirteen children, and his family moved to Crystal Springs, Mississippi, around 1910. He learned guitar from an older brother called LeDell, and the pair were soon playing at local parties, picnics and fish fries. When Johnson married – he later immortalized his wife in the song "Maggie Campbell Blues" – the newlyweds took a sharecropper's plot on Webb Jennings's Plantation in the Yazoo region, close to Dockery's Plantation where **Muddy Waters** was growing up, and **Charley Patton** and **Willie Brown** were based. Despite his recent marriage, he picked up the itinerant lifestyle of a Delta bluesmen from them, and was soon hobo-ing around the South, playing wherever he could to finance his drinking and womanizing.

After sowing these wild oats, Johnson returned to Crystal Springs, and a life as a sharecropper, in 1920. He also resumed his musical partnership with LeDell, with whom he played on the streets of Jackson for tips at weekends. He cut his first records, along with second guitarist **Charlie McCoy**, for Victor Records in Memphis in February 1928, under the direction of Ralph Peer. These included his most enduring songs, the much-covered "Big Road Blues" and "Cool Drink Of Water Blues", with its memorable line "I asked her for water and she brought me gasoline", as later adapted by **Howlin' Wolf**.

When Johnson recorded again in August 1928, he cut several tracks about alcoholism, including the chilling "Canned Heat Blues" – in which he described how when he couldn't get whiskey he would drink Sterno, a cooking fuel based on denatured alcohol that was similar to methylated spirits – and "Alcohol And Jake Blues". His last session found him traveling to Grafton, Wisconsin,

in December 1929 to record for Paramount. He was allegedly so drunk most of the time that it took him two weeks to record six sides. Although he lived on for another 27 years, he never entered a studio again.

Although the Depression put an end to Johnson's recording career, he worked on a medicine show with **Ishmon Bracey** during the 1930s, and continued to perform around the Jackson area for the rest of his life. He died of a heart attack after playing a party in Crystal Springs on Nov 1, 1956.

Johnson's eerie falsetto voice could adapt to a quasi-yodel or transform to a growl anticipatory of Howlin' Wolf, and was accompanied by exquisitely rhythmic guitar playing with a walking bass style. His influence was widespread, and Robert Johnson (no relation) was prominent among his disciples. Like his namesake, he was said to have made a pact with the devil at the crossroads and he also carried a large rabbit's foot with him wherever he played. He was also a powerful showman, noted for playing for hours on end and much given to antics such as playing the guitar between his legs and behind his head, a trick that he copied from Charley Patton.

⊙ **Complete Recorded Works** Document
The full fifteen songs that Tommy Johnson cut between 1928 and 1929, but seventeen tracks in total, as "Black Mare Blues" and "Lonesome Home Blues" are both heard in two alternative takes.

⊙ **Tommy Johnson & Associates** Catfish
The eight most important sides recorded in Johnson's career, coupled with fourteen context-setting tracks by such contemporaries as the Mississippi Sheiks, Kokomo Arnold, Bumble Bee Slim and Ishmon Bracey.

Curtis Jones

b Naples, Texas, Aug 18, 1906;
d Sept 11, 1971

Briefly one of the best-selling blues artists of the late 1930s, although his career continued into the 1960s, **Curtis Jones** was known for songs such as "Lonesome Bedroom Blues" and "Tin Pan Alley".

Having started out as a guitarist, Jones started playing the piano some time in his early twenties, when he was based in Dallas. He arrived in Chicago around 1936, where he was befriended by **Big Bill Broonzy**, who later declared: "He had a way of playing piano I haven't never heard nobody play, or even try to. Nobody could learn his style." He made his first recording the following year for Vocalion with "Lonesome Bedroom Blues", inspired by a break-up with his wife. Over the next four years he also recorded for Bluebird and Okeh, but his career was brought to a halt in 1941 by America's entry into World War II. Jones didn't record again until 1953, when the disc jockey Al Benson issued the one-off single "Wrong Blues" and "Cool Playing Blues" on his Parrot label, with L.C. McKinley on guitar.

During the blues revival of the 1960s, Jones recorded for Prestige's Bluesville with Johnny "Big Moose" Walker on guitar, and for Delmark on an album called *Lonesome Bedroom Blues*, which included a remake of his best known song plus a new version of "Tin Pan Alley". He left Chicago in early 1962 and moved to Europe, where he remained for the rest of his life. He recorded further albums, including for Mike Vernon's Blue Horizon label, and toured in 1968 with the American Folk Blues Festival. He died in Munich, Germany, in 1971, aged 65, by which time he was apparently living in considerable poverty. In a sad coda to his life, his grave site was sold off at the end of the 1970s because nobody had paid for its upkeep.

⊙ **Lonesome Bedroom Blues 1937–41** EPM
A generous 25 sides from Curtis Jones's early recordings in Chicago for various labels.

⊙ **Lonesome Bedroom Blues** Delmark
Not to be confused with the album above, Curtis Jones's rather good 1962 album for Delmark was the last he ever recorded in America.

Janis Joplin

b Port Arthur, Texas, Jan 19, 1943; d Oct 4, 1970

O f all the white rock'n'roll musicans who adopted the blues in the 1960s, few sang it with more emotional commitment and sheer ball-breaking power than **Janis Joplin**.

Raised in Port Arthur, Texas – a petroleum town with a strong blues tradition – Janis was from her youth offended by the racial segregation she saw all around her. She soon developed an interest in black music, and began to sing in local coffee houses, copying the songs and styles of Bessie Smith, Odetta and Leadbelly. By the early 1960s,

she had enrolled as a student at the University of Texas in Austin, where, influenced by Beat culture, she developed a taste for wild living, drink and drugs. In 1966, she was invited by an old friend Chet Helms to audition for an up-and-coming group in San Francisco, where he was now living. Joplin arrived just as hippie-dom and flower power were taking off in the city's Haight-Ashbury district, and landed the job, fronting **Big Brother and the Holding Company**.

Under Joplin's influence the group's psychedelic rock took on a blues-ier aspect. After a poorly produced debut album for Mainstream Records, the band made a major impact in June 1967 at the Monterey International Pop Festival, where Janis roared her way through a bravura performance of Big Mama Thornton's "Ball and Chain" in typical full-throated style. Bob Dylan's manager Albert Grossman was impressed enough to add the group to his management stable, and negotiated a recording contract with Columbia. From the cover drawing by Robert Crumb, which depicted her as an old-fashioned blues mama, to the explosive music inside, their label debut, 1968's *Cheap Thrills*, was a masterpiece. Highlights included "Turtle Blues", on which Joplin's earthy vocal was accompanied by blues piano and juke joint sound effects; a dynamic "Ball and Chain"; a ripping take on Irma Franklin's "Piece Of My Heart"; and her extraordinary redefinition of Gershwin's "Summertime".

By the end of the year, Joplin had been persuaded by Grossman to branch out on her own, and her solo debut *I Got Dem 'Ol Kozmic Blues Again, Mama!* appeared in 1969. She then formed the Full Tilt Boogie Band, but died of a heroin overdose in Los Angeles in 1970, while putting the finishing touches to her next album. Released posthumously as *Pearl*, it is widely regarded as her finest testament as a white blues singer. At the time of her death she was just 27. She has since become a legendary figure, an example of rock'n'roll's "live fast die young" fixation, along with Jimi Hendrix and Jim Morrison, both of whom died in the same twelve-month period.

Some critics have claimed Janis's voice lacked subtlety and nuance. Listen to her extraordinary reading of "Summertime", and it's obvious that's untrue, although the criticism also misses the point, for much of her expressiveness lay in her raw power. Had she lived, she would surely have moved on from her rock-chick leanings and matured into an even more significant blues and jazz singer.

⊙ **Big Brother and the Holding Company**
Cheap Thrills **Columbia**
This 1968 album remains a masterpiece of psychedelic blues-rock, and a highlight not just of Janis Joplin's career but of the entire San Francisco scene of the late 1960s.

⊙ **I Got Dem 'Ol Kozmic Blues Again, Mama!** Columbia
While not as strong as *Pearl*, this is still a fine record, with "Try (Just A Little Bit Harder)", "One Good Man", "Little Girl Blue" and "Work Me Lord" among the stand-outs.

⊙ **Pearl** Columbia
"Me and Bobby McGhee" and "Mercedes Benz" are the best-known songs, but "A Woman Left Lonely", "Buried Alive In The Blues", "Cry Baby" and "Move Over" all display Janis's blues power to even better effect.

⊙ **Box Of Pearls: The Janis Joplin Collection** Columbia
A 4-disc set that includes all Janis's official releases with Big Brother and solo, plus plenty of previously unreleased material.

Louis Jordan

b Brinkley, Arkansas, July 8, 1908; d Feb 4, 1975

Louis Jordan pioneered the style that became known as "jump blues", a rowdy, honking and shouting mix of blues, jazz and R&B that briefly dominated African-American music immediately after World War II, and epitomized the shift in the blues audience from the rural south to the urban centers of the north and west. His music was also a direct precursor of rock'n'roll.

Jordan started playing the saxophone at the age of seven, and was also proficient on clarinet and piano. At fifteen, he was playing professionally, and had followed his father into the **Rabbit Foot Minstrels**, supporting such singers as Ida Cox, Ma Rainey and Bessie Smith. He's believed to have made his first studio recordings with The Jungle Band in 1929, and over the next few years played in the bands of **Louis Armstrong**, Clarence Williams and Ella Fitzgerald before he joined **Chick Webb**'s orchestra, staying until 1938, shortly before the bandleader's death. His first record as a leader, "Honey In The Bee Ball", appeared on Decca as The Elks Rendezvous Band. That name was soon changed to the **The Tympani Five**, despite the fact that it numbered considerably more members than that, including Bill Jennings

and Carl Hogan on guitar, Wild Bill Davis and Bill Doggett on piano, Chris Columbus on drums and Dallas Bartley on bass. Jordan enjoyed his first R&B hit in 1942 with "I'm Gonna Leave You On The Outskirts Of Town". Developing a fine comic line in jive-talking lyrics, which were subsequently a major influence on the songwriting of **Chuck Berry**, over the next eight years he racked up a staggering 57 R&B chart hits. Eighteen were number ones, earning him the title "King of the Juke Boxes".

"Is You Is Or Is You Ain't Ma Baby?", Jordan's first million-seller, came in 1944, the same year that "G.I. Jive" topped both R&B and pop charts. "Caldonia" was another million-seller, and then in 1946, a year that represented the peak of the jump blues craze, "Buzz Me", "Stone Cold Dead In The Market", the immortal "Choo Choo Ch'Boogie" and "Ain't Nobody Here But Us Chickens" all hit number one. Further hits followed, including "Saturday Night Fish Fry" in 1949. But by the early 1950s, the era of jump blues was on its way out and rock'n'roll – which owed much to Jordan's shuffling boogie rhythms – was just around the corner.

By 1954, Jordan had left Decca, but he went on to record for Aladdin, RCA and Mercury. Adapting readily enough to the new rock'n'roll style, he cut songs like "Let The Good Times Roll" and "Salt Pork, West Virginia". Even so, he could not compete with the likes of Bill Haley, who covered his songs. He failed to trouble the charts again, and later noted with some bitterness that rock'n'roll was simply rhythm & blues music played by white people.

Jordan seldom recorded after the early 1960s, although he cut one last album in 1972. He died in Los Angeles following a heart attack in 1975 at the age of 66. His music enjoyed a major revival in popularity in the 1990s, however, after the musical *Five Guys Named Moe*, named after one of his hits and featuring several more, ran to great success and acclaim on Broadway and London's West End.

⊙ **The Best Of Louis Jordan** MCA
Twenty of Louis Jordan's classic hits from the 1940s and early 1950s.

⊙ **Louis Jordan And His Tympani Five** JSP
A single-disc volume of Louis Jordan's greatest hits should suffice for most people. But for those who want more, this 5-disc box set contains more than 130 sides from his Decca years.

Keb Mo

b Los Angeles, Oct 3, 1951

Although **Keb Mo** helped to spearhead the acoustic folk-blues revival of the 1990s, he is a highly versatile guitarist, who is equally at home playing soul and R&B styles on an electric instrument with a full-on band.

Kevin Moore's parents migrated west from the deep South before he was born. His first musical exposure was to gospel music, but he learned guitar at an early age and got his first professional engagement in a band backing the veteran electric fiddle player **Papa John Creach**, who was a member of Jefferson Airplane in the early 1970s. He went on to play on three of Creach's albums before

Kevin Moore, aka Keb Mo

WOLF TRAP FOUNDATION

he cut an R&B tinged solo album, *Rainmaker*, in 1980 for Casablanca Records. The label folded soon after, stalling Moore's solo career, and he joined the **Whodunit Band** led by sax player Monk Higgins.

A career breakthrough finally came about in an unexpected fashion in 1990, after Moore had portrayed a Delta bluesman in the play *Rabbit Foot* staged by the LA Theatre Centre. He also performed in *Spunk*, a production based on the writings of Zora Neale Hurston, and acted the part of Robert Johnson in *Can't You Hear The Wind Howl?*, a documentary drama narrated by Danny Glover. His theatrical excursions led to a recording contract with Okeh Records, and the Grammy-winning album *Keb Mo* – a name given him by drummer Quentin Dunnard – appeared in 1994, combining Robert Johnson covers with his own songs. *Just Like You* followed in 1996, and ranged from raw acoustic blues to soul with guest appearances by celebrity fans Bonnie Raitt and Jackson Browne. *Slow Down* arrived in 1998, and *Door* two years later. 2001 saw the release of *Big Wide Grin*, while there were two more in 2004, *Keep It Simple* and *Peace: Back By Popular Demand*, a covers album of protest songs by Buffalo Springfield, John Lennon, Bob Dylan, Marvin Gaye and others that tellingly appeared during the US presidential election campaign.

⊙ **Keb Mo** Okeh
Great original songs as well as a couple of Robert Johnson covers on Keb Mo's 1994 blues debut, mixing acoustic blues with funkier work-outs.

⊙ **Martin Scorsese Presents The Blues: Keb Mo** Sony
A 16-track collection ranging across his entire career, issued in conjunction with Scorsese's 2003 American TV series on the blues, in which Keb Mo was showcased.

⊙ **Peace: Back By Popular Demand** Sony
This 2004 album introduced a slicker, jazz-based sound, but Keb Mo delivers a wonderful selection of protest songs with soulful conviction.

Jo Ann Kelly

b Streatham, London, Jan 5, 1944; d Oct 21, 1990

With a fine voice and style much influenced by Memphis Minnie, blues purist **Jo Ann Kelly** was the queen of British blues singers. Had she displayed greater ambition, there seems little doubt that she could have been a major blues-rock star.

Born in south London, Jo Ann and her younger brother **Dave Kelly** – later a founder member of the Blues Band – came to the blues like many of their generation via the skiffle craze. She started playing guitar at the age of thirteen, and in 1962 formed an acoustic duo with blues pianist **Bob Hall**. Her recording debut came on a limited edition EP cut with Groundhogs guitarist **Tony McPhee** in 1964. As the blues explosion took off, she stepped up from the clubs to the college circuit, with a repertoire that included songs by Bessie Smith and Sister Rosetta Tharpe as well as Charley Patton and Robert Johnson, sung in a voice of convincing authenticity and accompanied by her own expert acoustic blues guitar on both six- and twelve-string instruments.

After singing on the debut album by the **John Dummer Band**, which also included her brother Dave, and appearing on various compilations, Kelly released her first full-length solo album on Columbia in 1969. That same year, she sang a duet with **Mississippi Fred McDowell** in London on "When I Lay My Burden Down", and turned down an opportunity to join Canned Heat, with whom she jammed at Britain's second National Blues Federation Convention. She later refused a similar invitation to play in Johnny Winter's band on similar grounds – she preferred to stick to the acoustic blues. For a short while in the early 1970s she had a small band called **Spare Rib**, and she also guested on various albums by British blues alumni, often credited as "Memphis Lil". She continued to tour and record throughout the 1980s, occasionally guesting alongside her brother in the Blues Band, who also backed her in a show called *Ladies and the Blues*, in which she paid tribute to her female role models.

In 1988, Kelly was diagnosed with a brain tumor. She returned to the stage after an apparently successful operation, but collapsed and died in 1990 at the age of 46. As one obituarist put it : "To many American performers, Jo Ann Kelly was the only British singer to earn their respect for her development of what they would be justified in thinking of as 'their' genre."

⊙ **Jo Ann Kelly** Beat Goes On
A reissue of Kelly's debut 1969 Columbia album. She might look like a spinster librarian on the cover, but inside lurks a feisty blues mama.

Junior Kimbrough

b Hudsonville, Mississippi, July 28, 1930; d Jan 17, 1998

Junior Kimbrough didn't release his debut album until 1992, by which time he was 62 years old. But by then, he had been playing his mesmerizing, minimal blues around the juke joints and bars of Mississippi's hill country for more than forty years.

David Kimbrough learned to play his father's guitar as a small boy in North Mississippi, while his parents were working in the fields. By his late teens he was playing in local juke joints, often with his friend and contemporary **R.L. Burnside**. In due course, his family home in Holly Springs became in effect a local blues club known as Junior's Place, where everyone gathered on a weekend to play and drink. Achieving considerable fame locally, he played with near neighbor **Mississippi Fred McDowell** and taught the guitar to a white boy called **Charlie Feathers**, who would later play a significant part in the Sun Records story.

Kimbrough's quiet life continued, playing music with his family and friends – or perhaps not so quiet, as he claimed to have fathered more than thirty children – until 1992, when he was discovered by **Fat Possum Records** and appeared in Robert Mugge's film *Deep Blues*. His first album, *All Night Long*, was produced by critic **Robert Palmer**, and for the first time the world took notice of Junior Kimbrough's elemental music, sung in a voice that was a cross between a mountain holler and a strangled cry. Sadly, by this time he was physically unable to tour, although there were a few famous live dates with Iggy Pop, during which he sat on a chair and played for forty-five minutes. So hypnotic were his performances that many in the audience thought he was playing the same song for the entire set, but the sound was so extraordinary that nobody complained. For the most part, in order to hear Kimbrough, you had to go to Mississippi – and once the word was out, many did. Members of the Rolling Stones, Sonic Youth and U2 were among those who made the pilgrimage to Holly Springs to experience Kimbrough playing at home in his own environment.

The follow-up, *Sad Days, Lonely Nights*, was as good, if less startling. Kimbrough's third album, the splendidly titled *Most Things Haven't Worked Out*, appeared in 1997 shortly before his death from heart failure in early 1998 at the age of 67. A further album, *God Knows I Tried*, was released posthumously.

⊙ **All Night Long** Fat Possum

Stark and original ancient blues on Junior Kimbrough's belated 1995 debut, sounding like a stripped-down, more elemental John Lee Hooker.

⊙ **God Knows I Tried** Fat Possum

A posthumous collection of previously unreleased tracks that Junior Kimbrough recorded between 1992 and 1997.

Albert King

b Indianola, Mississippi, April 23, 1923; d Dec 21, 1992

The reason that **Albert King** isn't regarded as the greatest blues guitarist of them all is down to his namesake B.B., who grabbed the title "King of the Blues" before him. A regal player with a soulful tone that was unique (perhaps because like Jimi Hendrix he played left-handed on a right-hand guitar strung "upside-down"), King was a key influence not only on black guitarists like Otis Rush and Robert Cray, but also on several generations of white blues-rock performers, from Eric Clapton to Stevie Ray Vaughan.

Albert Nelson was born in 1923 in Indianola, Mississippi, which by pure coincidence was the same town as **B.B. King**. One of thirteen children of an itinerant preacher, he was raised in Forrest City, Arkansas, and taught himself how to play guitar as a child on an instrument he constructed out of a cigar box. Although he began playing with various gospel groups, he was something of a late starter as a professional bluesman. In 1950, he moved to Osceola, Arkansas, where he drove a bulldozer by day and played by night with the In The Groove Boys, the house band at the T-99 nightclub, owned by M.C. Reeder. Three years later he moved again to Gary, Indiana, where in 1953 he joined a band that also featured guitarists **Jimmy Reed** and **John Brim**. That meant King – the name he adopted after B.B. King's "Three O'Clock Blues" had become a big hit – was reduced to playing drums. Shortly afterwards, however, he met Chess Records main man Willie Dixon, who arranged an

audition at Parrot Records. Back on guitar, he cut his first five sides for Parrot in late 1953, including "Be On Your Merry Way" and "Bad Luck Blues", which were coupled as his first single. The record failed to sell, and by 1954 he was back in Osceola, playing with the In The Groove Boys.

King wasn't satisfied with that for long, and in 1956, he and "Lucy" – his trademark Gibson Flying V, named once again in honor of B.B.'s guitar "Lucille" – moved to St Louis. It took three more years of paying his dues in local blues clubs before he landed another recording contract with Bobbin Records. Eventually, the single "Don't Throw Your Love On Me So Strong" did well enough locally for the larger Cincinnati-based King Records to lease the track for nationwide distribution in 1961. That gave him his first hit on the national R&B chart, and King Records leased further material from Bobbin, much of it produced by **Ike Turner**, including an album, *Big Blues*, which appeared in 1963. King's old friend Willie Dixon also got in on the act, and bought in further sides from Bobbin for Chess.

Once his contract with Bobbin was up, King recorded briefly for the St Louis label Coun-Tree. Then he made the best move of his career, by signing to Memphis' **Stax Records** in 1966. Teamed with the label's exemplary house band, **Booker T. & the MG's**, King's blues took on a tight, soul-influenced groove on R&B hits such as "Laundromat Blues", "Cross Cut Saw", "The Hunter" and "Born Under A Bad Sign". Thanks to his rhythmic lead lines, razor-sharp tone and extravagant note-bending, such tracks had an immediate impact, both with black record buyers and in white rock circles, influencing both Jimi Hendrix and Eric Clapton, while Cream and Free were among the British blues-rock bands who covered his songs. Back home, he also became a regular favorite at such hippie venues as San Francisco's Fillmore West.

King's Stax singles were collected on the 1967 release *Born Under A Bad Sign*, which the writer Robert Palmer called "the most stirring hard blues LP of the 1960s". *King Of The Blues Guitar* appeared in 1968, followed in 1969 by the in-concert album *Live Wire/Blues Power* and *Years Gone By*, and a 1970 tribute to Memphis' own **Elvis Presley** called *Blues For Elvis: King Does The King's Things*. In the 1970s, he strayed further into soul and funk on albums such as *Lovejoy*, *I'll Play The Blues For You* and *I Wanna Get Funky*, while "That's What The Blues Is All About" gave him a hit single. By the

RUF RECORDS

Blues king of the flying V

time Stax went bankrupt in the mid-1970s, King had already left to sign for the RCA subsidiary Utopia, for whom he made the albums *Truckload*

Of Loving and *Albert Live*, which returned him to a more overtly blues sound. In 1978 he signed to Tomato, and then moved on to Fantasy Records in 1983. He announced his retirement in the mid-'80s, but didn't mean it and was soon back on stage, continuing to tour until 1992, when he suffered a fatal heart attack, at the age of 69.

⊙ Born Under A Bad Sign Stax
Some of the best blues singles ever recorded, including "Crosscut Saw", "Born Under A Bad Sign" and "Laundromat Blues", all drawn from Albert King's 1960s Stax pomp.

⊙ Live Wire/Blues Power Stax
The other side to King's classic three-minute singles – extended blues work-outs, recorded live at the Fillmore in 1968.

⊙ In Session Stax
The only recordings made by King with his disciple Stevie Ray Vaughan, recorded for a TV show in 1983.

⊙ Years Gone By Stax
King's first proper album (as opposed to a collection of singles), recorded in 1969 and including both straight blues and soul arrangements. Highlights include a reworking of the standard ""Blues at Sunrise", a brilliant "Killing Floor" and material from Stax's own in-house team, including the witty "If The Washing Don't Get You The Rinsing Will".

⊙ Very Best Of Albert King Rhino
A fine single-disc career retrospective, spanning early material for King Records such as "Let's Have A Natural Ball", on through his Stax years, and ending with "Cadillac Assembly Line", released on the Tomato label.

Playlist
Albert King

1 DON'T THROW YOUR LOVE ON ME SO STRONG (1961) from **The Complete King & Bobbin Recordings**
King's first major hit is surprisingly hard to find in the original version, although a number of compilations feature a live rendition from 1968.

2 LAUNDROMAT BLUES (1966) from **Born Under A Bad Sign**
King's first Stax single was a great favorite with Rory Gallagher.

3 CROSS CUT SAW (1967) from **Born Under A Bad Sign**
Eric Clapton's guitar solo on Cream's "Strange Brew" is virtually a note-for-note copy of King's solo on this Stax hit.

4 THE HUNTER (1967) from **Born Under A Bad Sign**
What made British blues-rockers love Albert King so? This Stax track was covered by Paul Rodgers and Free.

5 BORN UNDER A BAD SIGN (1967) from **Born Under A Bad Sign**
Written by Booker T. Jones and William Bell and covered by Cream, but King's remains the definitive version.

6 AS THE YEARS GO PASSING BY (1967) from **Born Under A Bad Sign**
Eric Clapton admits the riff for "Layla" owes much to this King classic.

7 THAT'S WHAT THE BLUES IS ALL ABOUT (1973) from **The Best Of Albert King**
The definitive statement from the definitive bluesman.

8 STORMY MONDAY (1983) from **Albert King With Stevie Ray Vaughan In Session**
A great version of the T-Bone Walker classic, recorded live with Stevie Ray Vaughan for a TV special.

B.B. King

b Indianola, Mississippi, Sept 16, 1925

" I don't want to go fishing every day," said **B.B. King**, when he was asked what kept him playing the blues on the occasion of his eightieth birthday in September 2005. "So what else is there for me to do?"

Born on a Mississippi cotton plantation in 1925, Riley B. King was sent off to be raised by his share-cropping grandmother in Kilmichael at an early age. His first musical experiences came in church, and by the age of twelve he'd formed a gospel vocal group and learned to play guitar from a local preacher. After his grandmother died in 1940, King continued sharecropping on her land, but soon he moved to Lexington to be reunited with his father. He stayed a couple of years before returning to the area where he had grown up to work on a farm run by the Cartledge family, who also loaned King the money to buy his first guitar. He then moved back to Indianola, working as a sharecropper and a trac-tor driver, and accompanying the Famous St John's

B.B. King: his bowtie may be wonky, but his blues are straight-up

Gospel Singers on guitar. More significantly, he was also playing the blues on the corner of Church and Second Streets in Indianola on Saturday nights, and traveling to other Delta towns to busk for tips – and dong very well, by all accounts. King had the blues in his veins, but his decision to play them full-time was also based on a hard-headed realization that he could make far money playing the blues than making gospel music with the St John's Singers. In 1946, he left Indianola with nothing more than his guitar and two and a half dollars in his pocket, and hitchhiked north to Memphis, Tennessee. There he roomed with his cousin, **Bukka White**, who gave him lessons in the life of a bluesman. After ten months of struggle in Memphis, however, King decided that his career was heading nowhere and retreated back to driving a tractor in Indianola to pay off his sharecropping debts.

Towards the end of 1948, King returned to Memphis for a second time, this time with his wife in tow. He was soon busking on Beale Street, where he teamed up with other unknown hope-fuls such as **Rosco Gordon** and **Bobby Bland** in the suitably named **Beale Streeters**. His first big break came in 1948, when he performed on Sonny Boy "Rice Miller" Williamson's *King Biscuit Hour* radio program across the river in West Memphis. He soon had his own slot on the black radio sta-tion WDIA, called *King's Spo*t, sponsored by the health tonic Pepticon and evoking shades of the old traveling medicine shows as he was obliged to sing "Pepticon, Pepticon, sure is good – you can get it anywhere in your neighborhood". That led to a bigger show called the *Sepia Swing Club*, and it was as a radio disc jockey that he got his name. As a Memphis street musician he had been known as Beale Street Blues Boy. On air it was shortened to **Blues Boy King**, and eventually B.B. King.

King's radio fame assisted his musical career no end, and he cut his first record for the Bullet Recording and Transcription Company in 1949. He soon moved on to sing for the **Bihari** brothers, who ran the Modern, RPM and Kent labels, having been recommended to them by the ubiquitous **Ike Turner**. King stayed with the Biharis for the next decade. His first R&B hit came in 1951 with a ver-sion of Lowell Fulson's "Three O'Clock Blues". That was followed by a purple patch which produced the likes of "You Don't Know Me", "Please Love Me", "You Upset Me Baby", "Whole Lotta Love" (not the Led Zeppelin song), "Every Day I Have

Playlist
B.B. King

1 THREE O'CLOCK BLUES (1951) from the box set **B.B. King: King Of The Blues**
B.B.'s cover of Lowell Fulson's 1948 hit gave him his first number one on the R&B chart.

2 ROCK ME BABY (1958) from the box set **B.B. King: King Of The Blues**
Among the finest of King's pre-ABC singles for the Bihari brothers.

3 SWEET LITTLE ANGEL (1964) from the box set **B.B. King: King Of The Blues**
Recorded in concert in Chicago, and originally included on the classic *Live At The Regal* album.

4 PAYING THE COST TO BE THE BOSS (1968) from the box set **B.B. King: King Of The Blues**
"You must be crazy woman, you just gotta be out of your mind . As long as I'm footin' the bills, I'm paying the cost to be the boss": B.B.'s less-than-enlightened comment on women's lib.

5 THE THRILL IS GONE (1969) from the box set **B.B. King: King Of The Blues**
First recorded by Roy Hawkins in 1951, this mighty, string-laden cover, produced by Bill Szymczyk, changed King's career eighteen years later.

6 HUMMINGBIRD (1970) from the box set **B.B. King: King Of The Blues**
Written by Leon Russell and included on the Indianola *Mississippi Seeds* album, aimed firmly at the white rock audience.

7 DON'T MAKE ME PAY FOR HIS MISTAKES (1975) from the box set **B.B. King: King Of The Blues**
After a series of sleek, soul-tinged albums, King returned to hardcore blues on *Lucille Talks Back*, which included this stellar version of Z.Z. Hill's 1971 hit.

8 LET THE GOOD TIMES ROLL (1976) from the box set **B.B. King: King Of The Blues**
The sparks fly on a live duet with Bobby Bland.

9 WHEN LOVES COMES TO TOWN (1988) from the box set **B.B. King: King Of The Blues**
Recorded with U2, after KIng asked Bono to write him a song, and subsequently released as a single.

10 HELP THE POOR (2000) from **Riding with the King**
King first recorded the song in 1964 with Latin percussion and a female chorus, then revived it 36 years later as a duet with Eric Clapton.

The Blues", "Sneakin' Around", "Ten Long Years", "Bad Luck" and "Sweet Little Angel", in a style that was sweeter and less tough-sounding than much of his later work.

Despite his presence in the R&B charts, most of King's income was still coming from playing live. During the 1950s he was playing more than three hundred one-night stands a year on the "chitlin circuit" of small town cafes, ghetto theaters, country dance halls, road houses and juke joints. It was an incident at a dance in Twist, Arkansas, in the mid-1950s that famously gave his guitar its name. When a fight broke out and an overturned stove set fire to the hall, King fled to safety. Realizing that he had abandoned his guitar, he rushed back in to retrieve it, risking his life. When he later found out that the fight had been over a woman named **Lucille**, he bestowed the name on his instrument. All his favorite instruments ever since have been called "Lucille", and Gibson has even marketed a B.B.-approved guitar model under the name.

By the end of the 1950s, King's playing had gained a much harder attack, and he began the next decade with a revival of Joe Turner's "Sweet Sixteen". In 1962 he moved to ABC-Paramount, in the footsteps of Fats Domino and Ray Charles, and two years later the label released the seminal *Live At The Regal* album. More R&B hits followed, with the singles "How Blue Can You Get" and "Paying The Cost To Be tThe Boss". Then, in 1969, came his *annus mirabilis*, which saw "Why I Sing The Blues" as well as his biggest crossover pop hit, "The Thrill Is Gone", recorded after his divorce from his second wife, on which the emotion of his vocal matches the passion of his guitar playing. Oddly, throughout the blues folk-revival of the 1960s, when so many old Delta blues performers were being rediscovered, King had remained firmly trapped in the chitlin circuit. However, the success of "The Thrill Is Gone" brought him to the attention of a wider audience, and he finally made his debut on network TV, eighteen years after his first R&B hit. His first visit to Europe also had to wait until 1969, and that same year he further raised his profile with a white rock audience when he toured with the Rolling Stones.

With King's belated emergence onto a broader stage came recognition as one of the all-time great guitar virtuosos. His style drew on the likes of **Charlie Christian** and T-Bone Walker – he once said Walker's "Stormy Monday" was the record that set him on the path to being a bluesman and was "the prettiest sound I ever heard in my life" – but he also borrowed from **Lonnie Johnson** and **Blind Lemon Jefferson** to create a unique synthesis that was entirely his own. It was rooted in fluid single-string runs punctuated by loud chords, subtle vibrato rather than slide, and plenty of bent or sustained notes to create an almost vocal style. "The minute I stop singing orally, I start to sing by playing Lucille," he once said.

While the popularity of the blues went into decline during the 1970s, King was one of the few whose stature continued to grow. He recorded the albums *To Know You Is To Love You* and *I Like To Live The Love* in Philadelphia with the same smooth soul team that had powered the hits of the Spinners and the O'Jays. There were also collaborative albums with **Bobby Bland** and the **Crusaders**, while he maintained a ridiculously busy concert schedule, keeping up a punishing three hundred dates a year. It was a pattern he maintained throughout the 1980s, during which time he also found himself in increasing demand for commercials, film soundtracks and TV themes, and celebrity guest appearances, the most memorable of which was "When Love Comes To Town" on the 1988 **U2** album *Rattle And Hum*. He's also recorded with the Rolling Stones, Willie Nelson, Dr. John, Joe Cocker, Pink Floyd's David Gilmour, Grover Washington, the Dave Brubeck Quartet, Pat Metheny and even with The Simpsons.

His relentless touring meant he spent less time in the studio than he might have done, but in the 1990s as he approached seventy, he announced he was cutting down his live work to a more modest two hundred dates a year. His 1993 album *Blues Summit* was a gem, featuring duets with John Lee Hooker, Buddy Guy, Albert Collins, Etta James, Lowell Fulson and Koko Taylor, and in 2000 he scored the biggest-selling album of his career with *Riding With The King*, a collaboration with **Eric Clapton**. He celebrated his eightieth birthday in 2005 with the star-studded *B.B. King And Friends: 80* album, this time including duets with Van Morrison, Eric Clapton, Mark Knopfler, Sheryl Crow, Gloria Estefan, Bobby Bland and Elton John among others.

He also pledged that despite turning eighty, he had no intention of retiring. "Blues music doesn't get exposed on radio like other types of music, so if I don't take it to the people, they don't know I'm out here," he told *Billboard*. "I go around the country or out of the country – and I've played ninety

different countries – and I noticed a long time ago when I go to some city, the record sales go up."

⊙ **Live At The Regal** Universal
This classic B.B. King recording, made in Chicago on Nov 21, 1964, remains one of the most powerful live blues albums ever released.

⊙ **The RPM Hits 1951–57** Ace
A generous single-disc 26-tracker that offers the best from B.B. King's early recordings, from "Three O'Clock Blues" to "Did You Ever Love A Woman".

⊙ **Indianola Mississippi Seeds** BGO
The first album after B.B. King finally achieved crossover success in 1969 featured contributions from such rock luminaries as Joe Walsh, Carole King and Leon Russell. While still blues, it had a rock inflection not all of his fans enjoyed.

⊙ **Blues Summit** Universal
A 1993 convention with not a pop collaboration in sight, just solid blues and R&B duets all night long, with old friends such as Buddy Guy and John Lee Hooker.

⊙ **Riding With The King** Reprise
A dozen duets with Eric Clapton on a set of blues standards, including a shuffling acoustic version of "Key To The Highway" and a great "Three O'Clock Blues".

⊙ **B.B.King and Friends : 80** Universal
B.B. King's rather good 2005 birthday celebration features a dozen star guests, mostly from the pop world but also including Bobby Bland. The surprise package is Latin diva Gloria Estefan, who sounds unexpectedly, um, glorious on "There Must Be A Better World Somewhere".

⊙ **King Of The Blues** Universal
Splendid 4-disc box set, beautifully presented in a long box and covering everything from B.B.'s debut 1949 recordings for Bullet to his collaboration with U2 some forty years later.

⊙ **B.B. King Anthology** Universal
There are various "best of B.B. King" and greatest hits collections out there, but other than the box set above, the best is probably this 2-disc, 34-track collection, which includes all of his hits as well as a few choice collaborations such as "When Love Comes To Town".

Chris Thomas King

b Baton Rouge, Louisiana, Oct 14, 1962

Chris **Thomas King** came to the attention of a mass audience playing a bluesman modeled on Tommy Johnson in the Coen brothers' 2000 movie *O Brother, Where Art Thou?* By then, however, he already had half a dozen diverse albums

Multi-instrumentalist Chris Thomas King

ing off in a fresh direction, for 1998's *Red Mud* on Black Top Records was a return to the blues' acoustic roots. Then he moved to Blind Pig Records for *Me, My Guitar And The Blues*, a hybrid of acoustic blues, New Orleans-flavored R&B, funk and hip-hop.

King's eerie performance of Skip James' "Hard Time Killing Floor Blues" on the Grammy-winning, million-selling sound-track to *O Brother* should have opened up a new audience, and he also appeared on *Down From The Mountain: O Brother, Where Art Thou?*, a live album featuring many of the artists from the movie.

to his credit, on which he forged a bold fusion of blues tradition and contemporary influences.

Born in Louisiana in 1964, the son of **Tabby Thomas**, who owns the famed Baton Rouge blues club Tabby's Blues Box, Chris grew up knowing bluesmen like Henry Gray, Slim Harpo and Silas Hogan. Initially, however, he was more interested in rock and soul music. His passion for blues guitar didn't develop until his late teens, when he began touring with his father and got to jam with the likes of **Lowell Fulson** and **Buddy Guy**. He signed to Arhoolie in 1986 and his debut album, *The Beginning*, released under the name Chris Thomas, found him playing all the instruments himself. Moving to Austin, Texas, he next signed to Hightone, for whom he made 1990's *Cry Of The Prophets* and *Simple* in 1992, both of which attempted to drag the blues towards the twenty-first century.

Believing that his futuristic nu-blues might find a more receptive audience in Europe, Thomas relocated to Denmark where he record-ed the iconoclastic *21st Century Blues: From Da Hood*, an audacious and controversial mix of rap and blues that appeared on the BMG subsidiary Private Music in 1995. Back in Louisiana, his fifth album appeared on Scotti Brothers Records the following year. Titled *Chris Thomas King* – the first album to feature the addition of "King" in his name – it found him harking back to the clas-sic Stax R&B sound of the 1970s. In fact, virtually every disc he makes seems to find him march-

However, the success of *O Brother* proved to be something of a freakish one-off, and King's subse-quent solo albums have sold in similar quantities to those released before the film. After 2001's *The Legend Of Tommy Johnson Act I*, an attempt at an overview of different traditional blues styles, he started his own label, 21st Century Blues, to release 2002's *Dirty South Hip-Hop Blues*. The funk-tinged *Why My Guitar Screams And Moans* came two years later. He also portrayed Lowell Fulson alongside Jamie Foxx's brilliant depiction of Ray Charles in the 2005 biopic *Ray*.

⊙ **Me, My Guitar And The Blues** Blind Pig
This 2000 release is possibly the best of Chris Thomas King's hybrid albums, and includes intriguing covers of Albert King's "Born Under A Bad Sign" and Robert Johnson's "Stones In My Passway".

⊙ **The Legend Of Tommy Johnson Act I** Valley
A brave 2001 attempt to chronicle the twentieth-cen-tury development of the blues, with none of the hip-hop elements and scratching that characterize so much of King's work.

Earl King

b New Orleans, Louisiana, Feb 7, 1934; d April 17, 2003

A mainstay of the New Orleans blues scene for half a century, the singer and guitarist **Earl King** was also a potent songwriter, whose compositions were covered by Fats Domino, Dr. John and Jimi Hendrix among others.

Earl Silas Johnson IV was said to be the seventh son of a seventh son. His father, a blues pianist who played in local bars and speakeasies, died when he was a small boy. King might have followed in his musical footsteps, but he was raised instead by his mother, a large woman known affectionately as Big Chief – a title he later gave to one of his best-known songs. His first musical experiences came singing gospel in church, and it was as a vocalist that he was hired by **Huey "Piano" Smith**. While singing in Smith's band, he was also persuaded to take up the guitar. Working regularly at such famous New Orleans clubs as the Tijuana and the Dew Drop Inn, he met and became close friends with the flamboyant **Guitar Slim**. He began to model his own playing on that of his friend, and his mimicry was so good that when he played a series of dates under Slim's name, while Slim was briefly hospitalized, the deception went undetected.

King made his first recording, "Have You Gone Crazy", as Earl Johnson for Savoy in 1953, backed by Huey Smith on piano and Lee Allen on saxophone. When he recorded again for Specialty in 1954, he was billed for the first time as Earl King, although that was actually a printing error, as label boss Art Rupe had planned to market him as "King Earl". He next turned up on Johnny Vincent's Ace Records, where he became house guitarist and recorded some of his own best sides, including "Those Lonely, Lonely Nights", backed as so often by Huey Smith.

Also recording as Handsome Earl, King stayed with Ace until 1960, cutting some rollicking sides in classic New Orleans style, before he moved to Imperial to work with Fats Domino's arranger and producer **Dave Bartholomew**. One of their first sides together was "Come On (Let The Good Times Roll)", which was later covered by **Jimi Hendrix**. Other hits included "Trick Bag", as covered by the Meters and Robert Palmer, and "Always A First Time". King also became an in-demand songwriter, penning "Do Re Mi" for Lee Dorsey, "He's Mine" for Bernardine Washington, and "Teasin' You" for Willie Tee. On "Big Chief", which he wrote for **Professor Longhair**, King's guide vocal and whistling part were intended for demo purposes but ended up on the record. Others for whom he wrote material included Fats Domino, Johnny Adams and Jimmy Clanton. During the 1960s King also

recorded for Motown, but the tracks remained unissued. In addition, he cut sessions for Amy and Wand and some Allen Toussaint-produced sides for Atlantic, which didn't see the light of day until 1981. He also played numerous sessions for most of the leading names on the New Orleans scene.

Changing musical tastes sidelined King somewhat in the 1970s while his former protégé **Dr. John** became the main standard-bearer for the New Orleans sound. However, he re-emerged in 1986 on the Black Top label, backed by **Roomful of Blues** on the album *Glazed*. *Sexual Telepathy* in 1990 and *Hard River To Cross* three years later followed on the same label. In the last years of his life, he suffered with diabetes, and he died of complications arising from the disease in New Orleans in 2003.

⊙ **Pearls: The Very Best Of Earl King 1955–1960** Westside
A cracking compilation of 25 of Earl King's finest tracks for Ace Records, including many making their first appearance on CD.

⊙ **Come On: The Complete Imperial Recordings** Okra Tone
Seventeen King tracks produced by Dave Bartholomew in the early 1960s, among them such well-known hits as "Come On (Let The Good Times Roll)", "Trick Bag" and "Always A First Time."

⊙ **Glazed** Black Top
On this atmospheric 1986 release, Earl King is backed by Roomful Of Blues, who effectively re-create the steamy feel of a New Orleans bar-room.

Freddie King

b Gilmer, Texas, Sept 3, 1934; d Dec 28, 1976

No relation to any of the other blues guitarists sharing the same name – like so many of his confrères, his was a stage name – **Freddie King** was a leading light on the Chicago blues in the 1960s, and his aggressive playing proved a major influence on the emergence of blues-rock.

Freddie Christian took his performing name from an uncle, Leon King, who taught him to play the guitar at the age of six. He grew up absorbing the country blues of Blind Lemon Jefferson, Lightnin' Hopkins, and Arthur "Big Boy" Crudup, but in 1950 he moved with his family to Chicago. There he switched to electric guitar, and was able to see at first hand the likes of B. B. King and Muddy Waters, and take instruction from Eddie Taylor and Jimmie Rodgers. Over the next few years he played sessions with the likes of Little Sonny Cooper, Earlee Payton and Smokey Smothers, formed a band called the Every Hour Blues Boys, and made his solo recording debut in 1957 when "Country Boy" on the obscure El-Bee label.

King failed to attract national attention until 1960, when he signed to Federal, a subsidiary of the Cincinnati-based King Records. Under the guidance of King/Federal's A&R man and pianist **Sonny Thompson**, the guitarist recorded such numbers as "Lonesome Whistle Blues", "I'm Tore Down", and a potent rendition of "Have You Ever Loved A Woman". The writing credit on the latter, which was covered by **Eric Clapton** in 1971with Derek and the Dominos, is given as Billy Myles. At least one major blues reference work and a number of websites have made the assumption that King and Myles were one and the same, but there's no evidence for that, and it appears that Myles was actually an in-house songwriter for Ember/Herald Records in New York.

It was with a series of instrumentals that King made his biggest impact, however. The best known, "Hide Away", adapted from a Hound Dog Taylor tune and named after the Chicago blues club Mel's Hideaway Lounge, made the American pop charts in 1961. This was the era of twangy guitar hits, and King also recorded novelty tracks such as "Bossa Nova Watusi Twist", "Monkey Donkey" and "Surf Monkey". But there were also substantial blues songs such as "The Welfare (Turns Its Back On You)".

King left Federal in the late 1960s, by which time he'd returned to Texas and taken up residence in Dallas. By then, he'd also become a hero to English blues-rock guitarists such as Clapton, Fleetwood Mac's Peter Green and Chicken Shack's Stan Webb. His new status as a rock hero led to a recording contract with Atlantic subsidiary Cotillon in 1968. He then moved to Shelter Records, run by Leon Russell and Denny Cordell and in 1974 switched to RSO Records, owned by Clapton's then-manager Robert Stigwood. Unsurprisingly, much of the material he recorded in this period had a strong rock influence, but his guitar work remained exemplary. Highlights from his 1970s' output include the original version of the much-covered "Going Down", which appeared on the Leon Russell-produced album

Getting Ready in 1971 and "Sugar Sweet", a duet with Clapton on his 1974 debut for RSO, *Burglar*. After supporting Clapton on tour in 1976, King died in Dallas later that year from heart failure, three days after playing his last gig. He was 42.

⊙ **Freddie King Ultimate Collection** Hip-O
A great retrospective of Freddie King's career, ranging from "Have You Ever Loved A Woman" through the hit instrumentals to 1970's "Going Down" and his duet with Clapton.

⊙ **Getting Ready** EMI
Produced by Leon Russell in 1971, despite the rock posturing this is a fine album on which Chicago, Texas and Memphis styles all come together in thrilling fashion.

Big Daddy Kinsey

b Pleasant Grove, Mississippi, March 18, 1927; d April 3, 2001

A devoted disciple of Muddy Waters, **Big Daddy Kinsey** sang the blues and played slide guitar with a raw Delta emotion, and also presided over a famous blues dynasty.

Lester Kinsey was the son of a minister, whose father bought him his first guitar at the age of six and encouraged him to play gospel music. Much to his parent's disgust – his father did all he could to discourage his interest in the "devil's music" – young Lester was soon sneaking off to see the likes of local bluesmen like **Muddy Waters** and **Pinetop Perkins** play in juke joints. At seventeen, he moved to Gary, Indiana, and took a job in a steel mill. Settling down to raise a family, Kinsey put his musical career on hold for several years. However, his interest revived when his son **Donald** started playing guitar at four and another son Ralph took up the drums at six. He joined a local group called the Soul Brothers, and then went on to play slide guitar and harmonica with Fred "Baby Boy" Robertson. By the late 1960s, when his sons reached their teens, they began playing with their father as Big Daddy Kinsey and His Fabulous Sons, and made their first recording backing Eddie Silvers. During the 1970s, with Kinsey still working in the steel mill, the sons went off to see the world, and play with other musicians, including **Albert King** and **Bob Marley**. By 1984 they were back in Indiana, and Big Daddy finally quit his day job to work full time as the **Kinsey Report**, with Ralph, Donald, a third son Kenneth on bass, and family friend Ron Prince on guitar. Their first album, *Bad Situation*, appeared on Rooster Records in 1985, and included Kinsey's "Tribute To Muddy". Four years later, Big Daddy signed to Blind Pig for the album *Can't Let Go*, and his most successful album came in 1993 with *I Am The Blues*, which featured contributions from Buddy Guy, James Cotton and Pinetop Perkins. The Kinsey Report also made albums for Alligator and Point Blank, which featured not only blues but elements of funk and reggae, courtesy of the influence of son Donald, who had played guitar on Bob Marley's *Rastaman Vibration* and *Kaya* albums. Big Daddy died of prostate cancer in 2001.

⊙ **Can't Let Go** Blind Pig
Solid Delta stylings from 1990, backed by the family and including Big Daddy's eight-and-a-half-minute tribute song, "Howlin' Wolf".

⊙ **I Am The Blues** Verve
This 1993 tribute to Kinsey's role model Muddy Waters re-creates the atmosphere of a Saturday night fish fry. Kicking off with "Ode To Muddy Waters" and following with versions of "Mannish Boy" and "Got My Mojo Workin'", Kinsey is backed by the likes of Buddy Guy and Pinetop Perkins as well as his own sons.

Koerner, Ray & Glover

formed Minneapolis, Minnesota, 1962

Performing as the trio **Koerner, Ray & Glover**, guitarists **"Spider" John Koerner** and **Dave "Snaker" Ray**, and harmonica player **Tony "Little Sun" Glover** were among the first musicians in the early 1960s to prove that white, college-educated artists could play an authentic version of the country blues.

The trio pitched up on the Minneapolis folk and student scene in the early 1960s, at much the same time as Bob Dylan, before he took himself off to Greenwich Village. Sharing a love of Delta blues, they played in local coffee houses as an acoustic trio before making their first album, *Blues, Rags & Hollers*, in a single twelve-hour session for Audiophile Records in Milwaukee in 1963. When a copy reached Jac Holzman, head of Elektra Records, he not only signed them but bought the rights to the album and reissued it. Koerner, Ray

& Glover went on to cut six albums for Elektra, and became folk festival favorites. Their interpretations of old jug, folk and blues standards were highly influential, and introduced many listeners to the classic repertoire of American vernacular song.

By the end of the 1960s, Koerner had launched a solo career with the 1969 Elektra album *Running, Jumping, Standing Still*, while Ray had set up his own Minnesota-based label Sweet Jane Records, and released albums by the likes of Bonnie Raitt, Junior Wells and Koerner himself, when he returned from an extended stay in Europe.

Glover has written several harmonica instruction books and worked as a music journalist, becoming an authority on Bob Dylan – he appeared in Martin Scorsese's Dylan documentary *No Direction Home* – and writing a biography of Little Walter. The trio got back together in 1984 to make the performance/documentary film, *Blues, Rags & Hollers: The Koerner, Ray & Glover Story*, and supported it with various festival performances.

Ray and Glover have also performed and recorded on and off as a duo over the years. In 1996, the full trio once again reunited for a series of concerts, which were captured on the live album *One Foot In The Groove*, their first recording in thirty years. The three continued to tour sporadically ever since, until Dave Ray's death in 2002. They were much-loved performers who played a small but proud part in the re-popularization of the blues at a critical moment in the music's history when its light was most in danger of being snuffed out.

⊙ **Blues, Rags & Hollers** Red House
True, you can tell that Koerner, Ray & Glover are a bunch of over-earnest white boys rather than Mississippi sharecroppers, especially on covers such as Robert Johnson's "Dust My Broom". But their original 1963 record still possesses an undeniable period charm.

⊙ **One Foot In The Groove** Tim Kerr Records
Back together again in 1996, after thirty years, Koerner, Ray & Glover take a perfectly picked acoustic journey through American roots music.

Alexis Korner

**b Paris, France, April 19, 1928;
d Jan 1, 1984**

Although John Mayall is widely known as "the father of British blues", in many ways the title more fairly belongs to **Alexis Korner**. Born in Paris of Greek, Turkish and Austrian extraction, Korner fled with his family to Britain in 1940 after the Nazi invasion of France. He later remembered the war years in London as a heady mix of "bombing, the blitz, and boogie-woogie", and fondly recalled stealing records from a Shepherd's Bush market stall, including Jimmy Yancy's "Slow And Easy Blues", which he claimed totally changed his life.

Korner started playing boogie-woogie on the family piano, and records by Albert Ammons and Pete Johnson also found their way into his possession, probably by equally nefarious means. When his father objected to his piano being used to play boogie-woogie, Alexia switched to guitar. Around the end of the war he heard Leadbelly and Woody Guthrie records for the first time, and in the early 1950s he joined **Chris Barber**'s band, which was probably Britain's first skiffle group. Their repertoire consisted of songs like "Midnight Special" but as Korner went on to discover records by Leroy Carr, Blind Willie Johnson and Robert Johnson, he came to realize that there was a much deeper blues to be explored than Leadbelly's folk tunes.

After a spell working at the BBC as a studio manager, Alexis turned to professional music. He played regularly at the London Skiffle Club, run by harmonica player **Cyril Davies**, and soon persuaded him to close the joint down and re-open it as The London Blues and Barrelhouse Club. Among the visiting blues musicians who played there were Muddy Waters, Memphis Slim, Speckled Red, Roosevelt Sykes, Sonny Terry and Brownie McGhee, Jack Dupree and Little Brother Montgomery. It was the perfect opportunity to learn the blues at first hand, particularly as Korner got to accompany many of them.

With Davis, he formed **Blues Incorporated**, and the group's weekly residency at London's Marquee Club became a magnet for a generation of young blues enthusiasts, including most of the future members of the **Rolling Stones** and **Eric Clapton**, who claims he didn't even know an electric guitar existed in Britain until he saw Korner playing one. The 1962 album *R&B From The Marquee* was the first British blues record, but Davies left the group around the time of its release and died in early 1964. Korner kept the Blues Incorporated name, but over the next few years took the band in a more jazz-oriented direction. By 1967, he had embarked on a solo career, although he also led a number of short-lived outfits such as Free At Last, New Church and Snape, and worked briefly as duo with **Robert Plant**, before the singer joined Led Zeppelin.

Korner's only commercial success came with another of his ad hoc bands, **CCS**, who hit the charts in 1970 with an instrumental version of Led Zeppelin's "Whole Lotta Love", which became the theme of the BBC's *Top of the Pops* chart round-up. He was also a noted broadcaster, promoting blues music via his shows on both BBC Radio One and the BBC World Service in deep, gravelly tones which also made him popular as a provider of TV voice-overs. He put together his final group, **Rocket 88**, in 1981. A typically loose and informal conglomeration, it played swing blues, and featured the likes of Charlie Watts, Jack Bruce and Ian Stewart when they were available.

Korner died of throat cancer in London in 1984, at the age of 55. A vibrant personality, he left a legacy of a couple of dozen albums, although ultimately he was more important as a catalyst than a performer.

⊙ *Blues Incorporated* **R&B From The Marquee** Radioactive
Dating from 1962, this is considered the first British blues album, although the historical interest is slightly stronger than the musical content.

⊙ **Kornerstoned** Castle
A decent 2-disc introduction to Alexis Korner's varied output, from early skiffle tracks through Blues Incorporated to his brief hit-making period with CCS, via the only recording he made with Robert Plant.

2000 he signed to Sugar Hill for *Levee Town*, followed by *The Road We're On* three years later. *Grant Street*, a live album recorded with a stripped down power trio, appeared in 2005. With his unique guitar style – using a bottleneck slide, fingered chords and palm and thumb-picking techniques all at the same time – he is also in huge demand as a session musician, and has recorded with Leslie West, Junior Wells, Mark Knopfler, Dolly Parton, Beausoleil, John Mayall, John Hiatt, Kenny Loggins and Marshall Crenshaw to name but a few.

⊙ **Levee Town** Sugar Hill
Blues and zydeco and scintillating Landreth slide guitar work – what more could you want?

⊙ **The Road We're On** Sugar Hill
There's less zydeco and more straight-ahead blues on this 2003 album, including opener "True Blue", which may just be the best thing Sonny Landreth has ever recorded.

Sonny Landreth

b Canton, Mississippi, Feb 1, 1951

A contemporary master of slide guitar, **Sonny Landreth** is a musician's musician whose virtuoso skills are spoken of in awed tones by other guitarists. **Eric Clapton**, for example, has described him as "probably the most underestimated musician on the planet and also probably one of the most advanced."

Born into a white Mississippi family in 1951, a stone's throw from the home of slide guitar genius **Elmore James**, Landreth grew up in Lafayette, Louisiana. His first instrument was trumpet, but he took up the guitar at thirteen. Following a 1971 move to Colorado, where he formed the rock band Brer Rabbit, he was back in Louisiana by the mid-1970s. There he joined **Clifton Chenier** as the only white musician in his Red Hot Louisiana Band, and earned the title "the king of slydeco" for his slide guitar playing.

Landreth's debut album, *Blues Attack*, appeared in 1981, the first of two releases on Jay Miller's Blues Unlimited label. Further solo releases followed with *Outward Bound* in 1992 and *South Of I-10* in 1995. In

Sonny Landreth ponders a tricky new palm-and-thumb picking technique

WOLFTRAP.ORG

Jonny Lang

b Fargo, North Dakota, Jan 29, 1981

Like so many child prodigies, **Jonny Lang**, who emerged as a teenage blues guitarist of precocious talent during the 1990s, has subsequently found it hard to maintain momentum.

Born in North Dakota in 1981, he attended a show by the Bad Medicine Blues Band when he was twelve, joined the group soon after, and within months was leading the line-up, which he renamed Kid Jonny Lang and the Big Bang. By 1996, Lang and his group had moved from Fargo to Minneapolis, and his debut album *Smokin'* appeared in 1996. The phenomenon of a fifteen-year-old blues guitar hero created a wave of publicity which launched a bidding war among major labels. A&M won the race to sign him later that year, and his first A&M album, *Lie to Me*, appeared in 1997. Produced by David Z (who had previously worked with Janet Jackson and Fine Young Cannibals), it excited further attention. Soon he was sharing a stage and duetting with such veteran blues guitarists as Luther Allison, Lonnie Brooks and Buddy Guy. His third album, *Wander This World*, was another fiery blues-rock set, and appeared in 1998.

Then Lang disappeared for five years, before finally resurfacing as a 22-year-old with *Long Time Coming* in 2003. "It's been a long time coming, never thought it'd take so long," he sang on the stark, acoustic title track. However, the rest of the album veered into arena rock territory with a bunch of melodic, mainstream mid-tempo songs that owed more to Prince and Michael McDonald than to Muddy Waters and Howlin' Wolf.

⊙ **Lie To Me** A&M
Fast and flashy guitar playing, and a mix of Jonny Lang's own precocious compositions and blues standards. Hearing a fifteen-year-old singing Sonny Boy Williamson's "Good Morning Little School Girl" certainly gives the song a new meaning.

Lazy Lester

b Torras, Louisiana, June 20, 1933

Thanks to his crisp, high-pitched harmonica playing, and the languid vocal style to which he owed his name, **Lazy Lester** was a key mover in the development of the Louisiana **swamp blues** sound in the 1950s.

Raised near Baton Rouge, Louisiana, Leslie Johnson was initially influenced by Jimmy Reed and Little Walter. He got his professional start as a sideman with **Lightnin' Slim**, a lifelong friend whom he first met riding on a bus in 1954. Slim recruited the 21-year-old harpist to his band, and habitually introduced Lester's solos with the words "Play your harmonica, son." Slim was at the time recording with **Jay Miller** for the Feature label. When he took Johnson into the studio, the producer found that the harpist was just as talented on guitar and drums (he also played mandolin, piano and accordion). Soon afterwards, Miller began working for Nashville-based **Excello Records**, and signed Johnson to the label, giving him the name Lazy Lester, on account of his laid-back demeanor and relaxed singing style. Miller also used him on many Excello sessions, for artists including **Slim Harpo**, Katie Webster, Lonesome Sundown and others, as well as of course as Lightnin' Slim.

Lester's early solo hits included "Sugar Coated Love" and "I'm A Lover Not A Fighter", which was later covered by the Kinks. He continued recording until the mid-1960s, but by then younger R&B and soul audiences saw swamp blues as old-fashioned, and he sank into obscurity. Lester moved around the country, and in 1975 relocated to Pontiac, Michigan, where he married Slim Harpo's sister. He did not record again until 1987, when his career was resurrected after a group of British fans persuaded him to come out of retirement. He toured Britain that year, and recorded *Lazy Lester Rides Again* for London's Blue Horizon label, while the Flyright label began an extensive reissue program of his Excello recordings.

Back in America, Lester was signed by Alligator Records, who released *Harp And Soul* in 1988, and he has since recorded further albums for Antone's and Texas Music.

⊙ **I Hear You Knockin': The Excello Singles**
Excello
A superb single-disc collection of thirty tracks that Lazy Lester recorded between 1956 and 1965.

⊙ **Harp And Soul** Alligator
This 1991 album demonstrated that Lazy Lester could still blow a mean harp despite his long lay-off, and included a terrific version of James Carr's "Dark End Of The Street".

Leadbelly

b Mooringsport, Louisiana, Jan 29, 1885; d Dec 6, 1949

With his huge repertoire of blues, ballads, minstrel tunes, dance numbers, gospel and even children's songs, and a larger-than-life personality, **Leadbelly** did more than anyone else in the twentieth century to define the black American folk tradition.

Huddie William Ledbetter was born on January 29, 1885, into a family of sharecroppers that lived on the Jeter Plantation near Mooringsport, Louisiana. Unusually for the time, he was an only child. He moved with his parents Wesley and Sally to Leigh, Texas, when he was five, and was taught to play the accordion by his uncle Terrel Ledbetter, before he later picked up the guitar. By around 1905, Huddie had become an itinerant musician, traveling around Texas and Louisiana playing on street corners and at "sukey-jumps" (based on an early nineteenth-century word for a slave, the phrase originally meant a party in slave quarters but came to mean any get-together with music and dancing) and working as a laborer when times were hard. Shreveport's notorious red-light district Fannin Street was a particularly favored hangout, and in the song "Follow Me Down" he later recalled how his mother had begged him to stay away from the locality.

During the course of his hobo-ing, he met and played with **Blind Lemon Jefferson**, to whom he later paid tribute to in the song "(My Friend) Blind Lemon". Jefferson was also a strong influence on Leadbelly's rural-blues repertoire, although he picked up a vast number of songs from every imaginable source, and supplemented them with his own compositions. He learned many in jail, which is where he also acquired the name Leadbelly on account of his physical toughness. A rough and frequently violent character in his youth, he bust out of prison in 1917 while serving time for assault (his parents allegedly sold their land to pay for his defense). He spent the next two years on the run, using the alias Walter Boyd to avoid recapture. However, his inability to stop womanizing and brawling did not lend itself to laying low. In 1918 or 1919, he got in a fight with a relative called Will Stafford over a woman, during the course of which Stafford was fatally shot in the head. Leadbelly maintained it was an accident, but was convicted

of "murder and assault to kill", and sentenced to thirty years' hard labor under the name of Boyd. He worked on a chain gang and it was probably during this prison spell that he learned or conceivably wrote one of his best-known songs, "The Midnight Special". His musical gifts served him well, making him popular with other prisoners and guards alike. By 1925, he was out again, after pleading for a pardon from the state governor by writing him a song. Or so Leadbelly claimed. The truth of this has never been verified, and he had a famous ability to mythologize and romanticize his own life.

Leadbelly remained free for five years and returned to Louisiana, where oddly enough he escaped the attention of the record scouts who were now scouring the South for blues singers. In 1930 he was arrested again, convicted of attempted homicide and sent to the Louisiana State Penitentiary for ten years. Although he later claimed that he had assaulted six men who had tried to steal his supply of whiskey, court records reveal that he was tried for assaulting a white Salvation Army Officer, after he had been told to stop dancing while they played "Onward Christian Soldiers", and he had pulled a knife.

It was in the state penitentiary in Angola, Louisiana, that Leadbelly was found in 1933 by the folklorists **John Lomax** and his son **Alan**, who were touring the South collecting and recording songs for the Library of Congress. Amazed by his enormous repertoire (he claimed to know some five hundred songs), intense vocal style and commanding physical presence, they recorded more than hundred songs with him in the course of a few days. Knowing they had only recorded a fraction of the material he knew, they returned for more the following year. When they did, Leadbelly suggested that he remake the song pleading for a pardon that had worked in Texas, and see if it would have the desired effect a second time on Louisiana Governor OK Allen. "We agreed to make a record of his petition on the other side of one of his favorite ballads, "Goodnight Irene," Alan Lomax wrote. "I took the record to Governor Allen on July 1. On August 1 Leadbelly got his pardon. On September 1 I was sitting in a hotel in Texas when I felt a tap on my shoulder. I looked up and there was Leadbelly with his guitar, his knife, and a sugar bag packed with all his earthly belongings. He said, 'Boss, you got me out of jail and now I've come to be your man.'" In fact, he had not been pardoned, but released under a "double good time" clause to save costs, and there is no evidence that the song played any part in his release.

Lomax took Leadbelly as his chauffeur and recording assistant to New York, where he arrived on December 31, 1934. He was immediately lionized in liberal circles as a link with an era and lifestyle that seemed to belong to an another world. The first article about him appeared in the *New York Herald Tribune* in January 1935 beneath the headline: "Lomax Arrives with Leadbelly, Negro Minstrel: Sweet singer of the swamplands here to do a few tunes between homicides." Not everybody appreciated the way he was presented, and some felt he was being patronized. "The legend tended to make white audiences see Leadbelly as somewhat less than human, as they might see an animal in a zoo," one critic has subsequently complained. To be fair, the Lomaxes were also appalled by some of the more sensationalist newspaper articles.

Certainly, while Leadbelly's expressive voice and twelve-string guitar accompaniment were certainly thrilling, there's no doubt that the mystique of his convict past, his commanding physical presence, and the horrific scars on his neck earned in one of his many fights, added to his allure. He even acted out parts of his story for a contemporary newsreel. Despite his life of hardship and incarceration, his spirit had not been broken or his self-confidence dimmed. When he was taken to hear Cab Calloway in a Harlem club shortly after his arrival in New York, he bragged to John Lomax that he could "beat that man singin' every time". Yet he could also be subservient when it suited him, and Lomax wrote that when the hat was being passed for tips, "he always became the smiling cajoling Southern darky minstrel extracting nickels from his 'white folks.' He would bow and thank each visitor with amusing comments, 'Bless Gawd, dat's a dime! Where is all de quarters? Thank you, boss! Thank you, missy, thank you! Wait back dere, don' you see me comin'?"

John Lomax negotiated a contract with Macmillan to write *Negro Folk Songs As Sung By Leadbelly*. Published in 1936, the book detailed his personal history and discovery in prison, with transcriptions of his songs and notes about their place in American folklore. He also made better recordings of many of the songs Leadbelly had recorded in Louisiana for the Library of Congress, and arranged a recording contract with ARC. However, Leadbelly had not lost his old habit of settling disagreements with violence, and Lomax severed his links with him after the singer had threatened him with a knife, probably in a dispute

Playlist
Leadbelly

1 MIDNIGHT SPECIAL (1934) from **The Library Of Congress Recordings**
"Ain't no food upon the table and no fork up in the pan, but you better not complain, boy, you get in trouble with the man…"

2 IRENE (1933) from **The Library Of Congress Recordings**
Leadbelly recorded the song dozens of times, sometimes as "Goodnight Irene", but this was the first, in Angola penitentiary.

3 FRANKIE AND ALBERT (1933) from **The Library Of Congress Recordings**
Another song from his first prison session with the Lomaxes which he subsequently re-recorded many times.

4 BLIND LEMON BLUES (1934) from **The Library Of Congress Recordings**
Fine slide playing on a track recorded by the Lomaxes in Angola penitentiary.

5 PICK A BALE OF COTTON (1935) from **The Library Of Congress Recordings**
Such a standard even Abba felt compelled to cover it.

6 BOURGEOIS BLUES (1938) from **The Library Of Congress Recordings**
"Home of the brave, land of the free, I don't wanna be mistreated by no bourgeoisie…"

7 FANNIN' STREET (1941) from **Bourgeois Blues: Leadbelly Legacy, Vol. 2**
Named after the street in Shreveport, Louisiana where he learned to be wild.

8 GALLIS POLE (1941) from **Bourgeois Blues: Leadbelly Legacy, Vol. 2**
A hanging tale, remade by Page and Plant on *Led Zeppelin III*.

9 ROCK ISLAND LINE (1948) from **Leadbelly's Last Sessions**
First recorded in 1937, but this version comes from Leadbelly's final session for Folkways, a year before he died.

10 HOW LONG BLUES (1942) from **The Alan Lomax Blues Songbook**
Backed by Sonny Terry and Brownie McGhee.

over payments relating to the book. Yet it was this very air of unpredictable danger that made Leadbelly so interesting to many of his listeners. "Without his violent past, white audiences never would have noticed him," the young Lomax later wrote, and unlike his father, he remained close to the singer for the rest of his life. True to form, Leadbelly was arrested again in 1939 for assaulting a man whom he stabbed sixteen times with a knife. Perhaps because his victim this time was black, he was sentenced to less than a year in Riker's Island prison and eventually only served eight months.

During the 1940s, Leadbelly became part of a circle of musicians that included Woody Guthrie, Josh White, Sonny Terry and Brownie McGhee, adding topical songs to his repertoire such as "Bourgeois Blues", which described the racial prejudice he encountered in Washington, DC, and touring with the radical group, People's Songs Inc. He also recorded prolifically for different labels, cutting both "race records" for the black market and folk records for his white audience. Apart from his solo sides for Alan Lomax and Moe Asch's Folkways label, he recorded for RCA with the Golden Gate Quartet and also for Capitol during an eighteen-month stay in Los Angeles between 1944 and 1945.

Leadbelly made his only visit to Europe in 1949 for the Paris Jazz Fair, where he fell ill. On his return home, tests revealed that he had amyotrophic lateral sclerosis, and he died in New York in December, 1949, at the age of 64. Six months later the Weavers took his "Goodnight Irene", a song he had learned from his uncle, to number one in the charts. The songs he sang informed the early 1960s' folk revival and have continued to exert a wide influence, covered by everyone from the Beach Boys ("Cottonfields") to Led Zeppelin ("Gallows Pole"), while Pearl Jam wrote the song "Yellow Ledbetter" about him.

Musicologists point out that as a musician Leadbelly was no technical virtuoso – his tempo varied according to his feelings, and he stuck to simple chords. But his treasury of songs was unparalleled and his singing style unforgettable in its intensity; seldom have genuine folk artist and genius been combined with such potency.

⊙ **King Of The Twelve String Guitar** Sony
Recorded in New York in 1935, this album is rare indeed for Leadbelly in consisting entirely of blues songs, and includes versions of "Death Letter Blues" and "Roberta".

⊙ **Complete Library Of Congress Recordings** Rounder
Leadbelly sure knew a lot of songs – all of the recordings Lomax made for the Library of Congress spread colossally across twelve discs.

⊙ **Leadbelly's Legacy Vols 1–4** Smithsonian/ Folkways
The pick of the recordings made by Mo Asch for his Folkways label between 1941 and 1948. Each disc is arranged thematically, and available individually.

⊙ **Very Best Of Leadbelly** Music Club
A great value single-disc selection from Leadbelly's Library of Congress and Folkways recordings, including the obvious favorites such as "Midnight Special", "Rock Island Line" and "Goodnight Irene".

⊙ **Last Sessions** Smithsonian Folkways
Almost hundred songs and stories that Leadbelly recorded in 1948, spread across another marathon box set – this time over four discs.

⊙ **Definitive Leadbelly** Catfish
Another competitively priced box set of 75 songs over three discs, marred by an irritating lack of information about where and when the recordings were made.

Led Zeppelin

formed London, 1968

L ed Zeppelin were not a blues band. They were arguably the mightiest and heaviest rock band of them all, who created some of the most epically memorable riffs ever committed to disc. Their domination of the rock world is outside the scope of this book, although it is a fascinating story in its own right. However, they drew heavily on the blues – not always without controversy – and used such influences to forge some of the most potent music of the last 40 years, the reverberations of which continue to resound loudly in both rock and blues today.

Formed in 1968 out of the ashes of London-based R&B outfit the Yardbirds, the band was initially going to be called the New Yardbirds, before The Who's drummer **Keith Moon** suggested Led Zeppelin. Both of the band's main songwriters, guitarist **Jimmy Page** (b Heston, Middlesex, Jan 9, 1944), and singer **Robert Plant** (b West Bromwich, Aug 20, 1948), were obsessive blues fans who bonded over their reverence for the Delta masters. They were joined by **John Bonham** on drums (b Birmingham, May

Playlist
Led Zeppelin

1 YOU SHOOK ME (1969) from **Led Zeppelin**
A Willie Dixon song that had already been covered by the Jeff Beck Group.

2 I CAN'T QUIT YOU BABY (1969) from **Led Zeppelin**
Another Willie Dixon tune from their debut album, before Page and Plant got into their writing stride.

3 WHOLE LOTTA LOVE (1969) from **Led Zeppelin II**
This time Dixon wasn't credited, but the song borrowed liberally from his "You Need Love".

4 THE LEMON SONG (1969) from **Led Zeppelin II**
The influences of Robert Johnson, Albert King and Howlin' Wolf among others all bled onto this notorious track.

5 BRING IT ON HOME (1969) from **Led Zeppelin II**
Opens with a nod to Sonny Boy Williamson.

6 GALLOWS POLE (1970) from **Led Zeppelin III**
A great version of the Leadbelly classic.

7 HATS OFF TO HARPER (1970) from **Led Zeppelin III**
Based on Bukka White's "Shake 'Em On Down".

8 WHEN THE LEVEE BREAKS (1971) from **Led Zeppelin IV**
Memphis Minnie's song as it had never been heard before.

9 IN MY TIME OF DYING (1975) from **Physical Graffiti**
Led Zep knew this Blind Willie Johnson song from the version on Bob Dylan's first album.

10 NOBODY'S FAULT BUT MINE (1976) from **Presence**
Another Blind Willie Johnson classic.

11 WE'RE GONNA GROOVE (1982) from **Coda**
Recorded in 1969, this B.B. King song was not released until after the band had split up.

31, 1948; d Sept 25, 1980) and **John Paul Jones** on bass (b Sidcup, Kent, June 3, 1946).

The band's debut album was a blues-drenched affair that included two **Willie Dixon** songs and the traditional "Babe I'm Gonna Leave You", which they had actually found on a Joan Baez record. Plant's vocals on another track, "How Many More Times", also found him borrowing lines from Albert King's "The Hunter". Recorded in just 30 hours, it was a magnificent set that was clearly steeped in the blues but used such influences to forge a sound that at the time was fresh and unique: blues-rock at its most exciting, dynamic and visceral.

The follow-up, *Led Zeppelin II*, was if anything even better and included the majestic "Whole Lotta Love", which became their signature tune. It also provoked controversy. The song borrowed liberally from Willie Dixon's "You Need Love", but, unlike their first album, Dixon wasn't credited. He sued, and Led Zeppelin settled out of court. Similarly, "The Lemon Song" drew on "Killin' Floor" by **Howlin' Wolf** and on Albert King's "Cross-Cut Saw" and borrowed lyrically from **Robert Johnson** with its infamous "squeeze my lemon" sequence. The songwriting credit was given to Plant, Page, Jones and Bonham, provoking a protest from Jewel Music, the publishers of "Killin' Floor"; it resulted in another settlement, and a change in the songwriting credit on future

copies of the album.

Ever since, the band's detractors have argued that they stole from the blues without giving credit. In truth, they made some of the most original and exciting rock music the world has ever heard and to accuse them of plagiarism shows a total lack of understanding of what they achieved. The band themselves responded to the criticisms by pointing out that much of the blues derived from uncredited, traditional sources and that the Delta's musicians had always borrowed copiously from each other. They also asserted, quite rightly, that Led Zeppelin crafted the blues idioms that they were influenced by into something that was both totally unique and entirely their own. On any objective judgment, the worst criticism that can be leveled is that in their early days they were on a couple of occasions careless about citing the source of their inspiration.

By 1970, Zeppelin were probably the biggest and loudest rock band in the world. But they were still looking to the blues for inspiration on *Led Zeppelin III*, which included "Gallows Pole", a trad folk tune that was popularized by **Leadbelly**, although Page apparently based the group's take on it on a version by Fred Gerlach. Another song on the same album, "Hats Off To Harper", a tribute to the maverick English folk singer **Roy Harper**, borrowed from the **Bukka White** tune "Shake 'Em On

Down". *Led Zeppelin IV*, which appeared in 1971, included "When The Levee Breaks", based on the 1929 recording by Memphis Minnie and Kansas Joe McCoy. Given a monster riff of quite awesome power, and a drum beat that has become iconic, it appeared with the entirely justifiable writing credit, "Page, Plant, Jones, Bonham, Minnie."
Even in the middle of their rock'n'roll excess, the blues remained a source for much of Led Zeppelin's work. 1975's *Physical Graffiti* featured a version of "In My Time Of Dyin'", while *Presence*, released the year after, included a dynamite version of **Blind Willie Johnson**'s "Nobody's Fault But Mine". Led Zeppelin broke up in 1980, following the death of drummer John Bonham, but the posthumously released *Coda* featured further blues songs, carefully credited – critics please note – to B.B. King and Willie Dixon. The remaining three members pursued solo careers. Robert Plant, in particular, has remained a staunch advocate of the blues, and is an enthusiastic collector with an encyclopedic knowledge of the most obscure recordings and artists.

⊙ **The Early Blues Roots Of Led Zeppelin**
Catfish
The first three Led Zep albums are stone cold rock classics – you should own them. But, from a pure blues perspective, this collection of the material from which they derived inspiration makes for fascinating listening. It includes tracks by Memphis Minnie, Sonny Boy Williamson, Blind Willie Johnson, Robert Johnson, Bukka White, Leadbelly and Big Bill Broonzy.

J.B. Lenoir

b Monticello, Mississippi, May 5, 1929; d April 29, 1967

Listening today to the power of his recorded work, both solo and with a rocking band, it's hard to understand why **J.B. Lenoir** never quite achieved the status and recognition he deserved during his lifetime.

Allegedly only ever given initials rather than a full name, J.B. learned guitar from his father Dewitt, and was influenced early on by Blind Lemon Jefferson, Arthur "Big Boy" Crudup and, in particular, Lightnin' Hopkins. He spent some time in New Orleans during the late 1940s, where he may have played with Sonny Boy "Rice Miller" Williamson and Elmore James, but by 1949 he

was in Chicago, where **Big Bill Broonzy** became his patron and he was also befriended by Memphis Minnie and Big Maceo.

Singing in an unusual, high-pitched voice, and with a strong boogie style reminiscent of John Lee Hooker or Jimmy Reed, Lenoir was also a talented songwriter with a political awareness that was as bold as it was rare. His first single, recorded for JOB but leased to Chess, was 1951's "Korea Blues". Three years later he came out with another piece of outspoken topical commentary in "Eisenhower Blues", a track controversial enough in its attack on the president for his record label of the time, Parrot, to force him to re-cut it as "Tax Paying Blues".

On JOB with his own band – the **Bayou Boys**, whose members included Sunnyland Slim on piano and Alfred Wallace on drums – Lenoir's releases included "Let's Roll" and the romping "The Mojo", featuring sax player J.T. Brown. In 1954 for Al Benson's Parrot label, he recorded his best-known song, the much covered "Mama Talk To Your Daughter". The success of the latter led to Willie Dixon recruiting Lenoir to Chess. He recorded for the Checker label from 1955 to 1958, cutting sides such as the humorous "Don't Touch My Head" and "Natural Man", featuring sax players Alex Atkins and Ernest Cotton, and drummer Al Galvin. He was a flamboyant character, described by Dixon in his autobiography as "a helluva showman, cause he had this long tiger-striped coat with tails". After his association with Checker ended, he moved first to Shad and then in 1960 to Vee Jay. In 1963 he hooked up with USA Records, recording as **J.B. Lenoir and his African Hunch Rhythm**, and developing an interest in African-style percussion.

By now Lenoir was struggling to make ends meet as a professional musician, and was forced to take a day job. Yet his best was still to come. While working in the kitchens at the University of Illinois in Champaign, he teamed up again with his old friend Willie Dixon, who produced some superb acoustic demos with him, including such topical songs as "Vietnam Blues", "Alabama March" and "Shot On James Meredith", tellingly released not in America but in Europe by the German blues promoter Horst Lippmann on the albums *Alabama Blues* and *Down In Mississippi*. With his acoustic guitar accompanied only by the drums of **Fred Below**, the albums marked him out as an articulate spokesman for social justice and signaled what could have been a bold new direction in modern acoustic blues. Sadly it was not to be, for Lenoir died in April 1967 from injuries sustained three weeks earlier in a car crash.

⊙ His JOB Recordings Paula
J.B. Lenoir's early, boogie-style recordings with a red-hot band, augmented by a handful of tracks on which he accompanied Sunnyland Slim and Johnny Shines.

⊙ Martin Scorsese Presents The Blues: J.B. Lenoir Chess
The Scorsese billing is gratuitous, for the only link is that the album was released to coincide with his 2003 TV series on the blues. However, this is the best place to find Lenoir's 1950s Chess and Parrot material, including "Korea Blues", "Eisenhower Blues", and "Mama Talk To Your Daughter".

⊙ Vietnam Blues Evidence
The two acoustic albums that J.B. Lenoir recorded with Willie Dixon in 1965 and 1966, reissued on a single CD. Lines such as "Every black child born in Mississippi, you know the poor child is born dead," are delivered with an intensity that has to be heard to be believed.

Furry Lewis

b Greenwood, Mississippi, March 6, 1893; d Sept 14, 1981

While postwar bluesmen like John Lee Hooker and B.B. King were still going strong half a century later, **Furry Lewis** was one of the few from the first pioneering generation of country bluesmen to show a similar longevity.

Even though the date was for a long time given as 1899, Walter Lewis was actually born in Mississippi in 1893. He acquired the nickname "Furry" as a child. Around the turn of the century, his family moved to Memphis, where he learned to play the guitar from an old man from Arkansas he only ever knew as "Blind Joe". Many of the songs Joe taught Lewis predated the blues as we know it, and went back to nineteenth-century stories about working-class folk heroes like Casey Jones and John Henry. By around 1908, he was playing in brothels and bars around Memphis as well as in the street, and he even performed several dates with **W.C. Handy**'s Orchestra.

During World War I, Lewis hobo-ed around the South. By the time he returned to Memphis

in 1917, he had lost a leg in a railroad accident. That didn't prevent him touring with Dr. Willie Lewis's Medicine Show, and while on the road he met Memphis Minnie, Bessie Smith, Blind Lemon Jefferson and Texas Alexander. When in town, he also worked up and down Beale Street with the likes of Jim Jackson, Gus Cannon and Will Shade, and occasionally appeared with the Memphis Jug Band.

In 1927, Lewis traveled to Chicago and cut his first sides for Vocalion, accompanied by fellow guitarist Landers Walton and mandolin player Charles Jackson. The following year he recorded for Victor in Memphis, but by 1929, he was back with Vocalion, displaying a nimble finger-picking style and proficient slide technique. The Great Depression ended his recording career, however, and he took a day job as a street sweeper for the City of Memphis, which he held until 1966, by which time he was 73. When not sweeping the streets, he continued to play on them throughout the 1930s and 1940s. After that, his style was deemed to be so outdated that he seldom played again until the folk-blues revival of the 1960s, when he was among the first of the prewar bluesman to be "rediscovered" by **Sam Charters**. It was no easy matter to persuade Lewis to resume his musical career, but Charters eventually cajoled him into the studio to cut albums for Prestige Bluesville, when he struggled to capture his former command.

Further albums followed, as did a film cameo with Burt Reynolds in *W.W. And The Dixie Dance Kings*. He was also much championed by the rock world, playing college venues at which he talked the talk, telling a new audience that had no reason to disbelieve him that he had "invented" bottleneck guitar. Lewis' renewed celebrity was crowned when **Joni Mitchell** wrote and recorded the song "Furry Sings The Blues" about him on her 1976 album, *Hejira*. He died in Memphis in 1981, at the age of 88.

⊙ In His Prime 1927-28 Yazoo
A collection of fourteen of the 23 songs that Furry Lewis recorded during the 1920s, including "Kassie Jones", parts one and two, and "Rock Island Blues".

⊙ Shake 'Em On Down Fantasy
Twenty spirited tracks from the Sam Charters-supervised sessions made on Furry Lewis' 1961 rediscovery, including great versions of "John Henry", "Casey Jones" and "Frankie and Johnny".

Smiley Lewis

b DeQuincey, Louisiana, July 5, 1913; d Oct 7, 1966

After Fats Domino, **Smiley Lewis** was perhaps the greatest singer to emerge from New Orleans during the 1950s. However, he could have been forgiven for ruefully feeling that there are no prizes for coming second best, after Domino covered his "Blue Monday" with considerably more success, and then a fellow from Memphis called Presley did the same thing with his "One Night".

Overton Amos Lemons moved to the Crescent City towards the end of the 1920s. There he played cafes and clubs in the French Quarter, often with pianist **"Tuts" Washington**, and sometimes billed as "Smiling" Lewis. Not until 1947 did he made his recording debut on DeLuxe Records, with "Here Comes Smiley", and success didn't arrive until 1950, when he moved to Imperial and debuted for the label with "Tee-Nah-Nah".

Lewis was right in on the start of the new rocking R&B sound that emerged from New Orleans in the early 1950s, and scored several local hits before his first major national R&B hit, 1952's "The Bells Are Ringing". His 1955 recording of the self-penned "I Hear You Knocking", a seminal slice of New Orleans blues with **Dave Bartholomew** leading the band and some joyous work from **Huey Smith** on piano, was an even bigger smash. Lewis also enjoyed success with "Bumpity Bump", "Down The Road", "Lost Weekend", "Real Gone Lover", "She's Got Me Hook, Line and Sinker", and "Rootin' And Tootin'", usually backed up by the roaring horns of Lee Allen, Clarence Hall and Herb Hardesty.

However, Lewis's own work was all too often eclipsed by covers of his songs. It didn't help that Lewis was already in his forties; **Fats Domino**, who was some fifteen years younger, stole all the glory when he covered Lewis's "Blue Monday", while **Elvis Presley** also had a hit with a cleaned-up version of his risqué "One Night". Even Bartholomew, who produced both Lewis and Domino, admitted the older man was a "bad luck singer", whose talent was not rewarded with the sales his records deserved. Lewis did have one last blast left in his locker before he left Imperial – the brilliant "Shame, Shame, Shame", the success of which was helped by its appearance on the soundtrack of the film *Baby Doll* in 1957.

Lewis briefly moved to Okeh in 1961, but his last few years were a struggle, as record companies deemed his style anachronistic. He bowed out with an **Allen Toussaint**-helmed remake of "The Bells Are Ringing" in 1965 and died from stomach cancer the following year in New Orleans, an almost forgotten man, at the age of 53. His reputation enjoyed something of a revival after the British roots-rocker **Dave Edmunds** had a number one hit in the UK in 1970 with a remake of Lewis's "I Hear You Knocking", and he has arguably been better appreciated since his passing than he was in his lifetime.

⊙ **Shame Shame Shame** Bear Family
An exhaustive 100-track, 4-disc retrospective that firmly establishes Smiley Lewis's credentials as the main rival to Fats Domino as the greatest hit-maker to emerge from the Crescent City in the second half of the twentieth century.

⊙ **The Best Of Smiley Lewis: I Hear You Knocking** Collectables
If the box set above seems too much of a good thing, this single disc, 25-track compilation contains all Lewis's best-known songs, and will serve most purposes.

Meade "Lux" Lewis

b Louisville, Kentucky, Sept 4, 1905; d June 7, 1964

One of the trio of pianists, along with **Pete Johnson** and **Albert Ammons**, who spearheaded the boogie-woogie craze in the 1930s, **Meade "Lux" Lewis** practically defined the style with his "Honky Tonk Train Blues".

The Kentucky-born Lewis gravitated to Chicago by the 1920s, where he played piano by night in speakeasies and worked by day with his friend Albert Ammons in a taxi firm. The apartment he shared with Ammons and a third piano player, **Pine Top Smith**, provided the perfect environment for the emergence of a new, rollicking style of blues piano. Heavily influenced by the work of Jimmy Yancey as well as Smith's own "Pine Top's Boogie-woogie", Lewis recorded "Honky Tonk Train Blues" for Paramount in 1927. It became not only his signature piece but a cornerstone of the boogie-woogie repertoire, although no one took much notice of the record until several years later, when record company executive and talent scout **John Hammond** heard it and tracked Lewis down in Chicago. Hammond re-recorded him playing

"Honky Tonk Train Blues" in 1935, and three years later recruited Lewis and Ammons to play at his 1938 Spirituals to Swing concert at New York's Carnegie Hall, along with Pete Johnson. Their fast-flowing rhythms caused a sensation. New York went boogie-woogie crazy, and Lewis and his colleagues were booked to open Café Society, a new Manhattan nightclub which became *the* place for white audiences to hear black musicians.

Lewis recorded prodigiously, both solo and with Ammons and Johnson. Unusually, he also recorded on harpsichord and celeste, which he played in a Blue Note quartet with **Edmond Hall** and **Charlie Christian**, and he cut further sides with the Port of Harlem Seven. When the boogie-woogie craze began to fade on the East coast, he left for Los Angeles, where he was recorded in 1944 by Mo Asch of Folkways. He remained a celebrity, appearing in several films and playing in upmarket supper clubs and lounges, and made his final recordings in 1962. He died in a car crash in Minneapolis in 1964, at the age of 58.

⊙ **Meade Lux Lewis Vol 1: 1927–39; Vol 2: 1939–41; Vol 3: 1941–44** Classics
Three discs arranged chronologically, including several versions of Lewis's "Honky Tonk Train Blues", his five-part tour de force "The Blues", recorded in 1939, and even examples of his harpsichord and celeste playing.

⊙ **Boogie And Blues** Topaz
The best single-disc introduction to Meade "Lux" Lewis's work, recorded between 1936 and 1941.

Meade "Lux" Lewis REDFERNS

Joe Liggins

b Guthrie, Oklahoma, July 9, 1916; d July 26, 1987

Along with his band the **Honeydrippers**, pianist **Joe Liggins** was a major figure in the jump blues scene immediately after World War II. Born in rural Oklahoma in 1916, Liggins started out playing brass instruments, but by his mid-teens was an accomplished piano player and arranger. Like many from the dust bowl state, he fled with his family during the early 1930s for the promised land of California, and arrived in San Diego in 1932. Seven years later, he moved up the coast to Los Angeles, where he found employment with bands led by **Illinois Jacquet**, **Cee Pee Johnson** and finally **Sammy Franklin**'s California Rhythm Rascals. In 1945, Liggins came up with a shuffling boogie tune he called "The Honeydripper". When Franklin foolishly declined to record it, Liggins put together his own combo, which he named the Honeydrippers and featured sax player **Little Willie Jackson**, and recorded the tune for Leon Rene's Exclusive label. A huge hit, it topped the R&B chart and sold an estimated two million copies.

Over the next five years, Liggins enjoyed further hits such as "I've Got A Right To Cry", "Harlemesque", "Caravan", "Dripper's Boogie", "Think Of Me", "Dripper's Blues", "Tan And Roll 'Em", and even a version of the old standard "Sweet Georgia Brown", all for Exclusive. When the label went bust at the end of 1949, Liggins and his Honeydrippers signed to Art Rupe's Specialty Records. The change gave his career fresh impetus, and 1950's "Pink Champagne" was almost as big a hit as "The Honeydripper", which he also re-recorded for Specialty.

Just how big Liggins was at this time can be gauged by the fact that when he traveled to New York in 1950, he was booked to play an entire week at Harlem's Apollo Theatre. His only rival in the jump blues field was his label-mate **Roy Milton**, as accentuated when Specialty released their competing versions of the song "That's The One For Me" as a stunt – and had hits with both.

However, in the face of the rock'n'roll onslaught, Specialty had dropped Liggins by the mid-1950s. He moved to Mercury and then Wing, Aladdin and Vita Records in rapid succession, but with no further success. Even when Dot Records purchased the original Exclusive masters and reissued "The Honeydripper", it seemed there was no longer any interest. Liggins continued playing in obscurity, before enjoying some renewed recognition on the blues circuit in the 1970s, still playing with a band that included Little Willie Jackson. He died in Los Angeles in 1987 at the age of 71.

During his most successful years in the late 1940s, Liggins engaged his younger brother **Jimmy** (b Newby, Oklahoma, Oct 14, 1922; d July 18, 1983) as his driver. While so employed, Jimmy Liggins also learned to play the guitar and formed the **Drops Of Joy**. He signed for Specialty Records in 1947 and enjoyed a number of hits in a jazz-blues style, most notably "Teardrop Blues" and "Cadillac Boogie".

⊙ **Joe Liggins And The Honeydrippers** Ace
An indispensable 25-track compilation that includes "The Honeydripper" and "Pink Champagne".

⊙ *Various Artists* **Specialty Legends Of Jump Blues Vol One** Ace
For the wider context of Joe Liggins' work, check out this excellent compilation, which includes sides not only by Liggins himself, but also by his brother Jimmy, Roy Milton and Percy Mayfield.

Lightnin' Slim

b St Louis, Missouri, March 13, 1913; d July 27, 1974

The Louisiana swamp blues of **Lightnin' Slim** drew on the down-home style of Lightnin' Hopkins and the Chicago boogie of Jimmy Reed to create a dark and somber sound that was entirely Slim's own.

Although Otis Hicks was born on a farm just outside St Louis, his family made the unusual move of heading down to St Francisville, Louisiana, in 1926, just as the great migration from the South to the cities of the north was gathering pace. He learned to play guitar in an open E natural tuning from his father and an older brother, Layfield. His rudimentary, even crude style, served him well enough, and by the late 1930s he was playing on the rural circuit of plantation picnics and

He's evil: Lightnin' Slim   REDFERNS

dances. He moved to Baton Rouge in 1946, and performed in local juke joints, sometimes as a solo guitarist, and at other times with a band led by a figure known as Big Poppa, or with harmonica player Schoolboy Cleve. After appearing on local radio, Slim was recommended in 1954 by disc jockey Ray "Diggy Do" Meaders to the Crowley-based impresario Jay Miller, who recorded him for the Feature label. His debut release was "Bad Luck Blues", which included the immortal blues line "If it wasn't for bad luck, I'd have no luck at all", and his early sides had a tough, unadorned, home-made feel that was almost anarchic. His grainy, world-weary vocals and raw, electric guitar playing were supported only by harmonica and drums, or rather what the writer Greg Ward describes as "largely random percussive thumps on whatever happened to be lying around in the studio." Ward also reckoned he was the only guitarist who could play a solo with no notes. Nevertheless, the overall sound was strangely irresistible and made him the first real blues star in Miller's stable, who soon transferred him to the bigger Excello label.

Slim's recordings with Lazy Lester on harmonica from this period, such as "Hoodoo Blues", "Mean Old Lonesome Train", and his biggest hit, 1959's "Rooster Blues", are particularly outstanding. Many of his songs were such blatant rip-offs that all you can do is admire his cheek. His "Just Made Twenty-One", for example, is so obviously based on **John Lee Hooker**'s "Boogie Chillen" that you wonder how he was able to get away with it. Others whose songs were reworked and then brazenly claimed as his own included **Jimmy Reed** and **Muddy Waters**, while his guitar solos – at least those that had any notes – were mostly borrowed from **Lightnin' Hopkins**, along with his name. Yet somehow the results were utterly charismatic.

Slim recorded for Excello for twelve years, but the relationship came to an end in 1966 after he crashed Miller's truck. Rather than stay and face his wrath, he lit out for Detroit and found a fresh impetus to his career, working the American festival and college circuit as a double act with his brother-in-law **Slim Harpo**. He also found an enthusiastic new audience in Europe, where he toured with the American Folk Blues Festival. After Harpo's death in 1970, he continued to perform solo until his death from cancer in Detroit in 1974, at the age of 61.

⊙ **I'm Evil** Excello

A generous 27 tracks on a single disc drawn from Lightnin' Slim's Feature/Excello recordings, featuring more bad women, bad whiskey and bad luck than even the lowest-down swamp bluesman should be expected to bear.

⊙ **Rooster Blues** Hip-O

Fifteen of Lightnin' Slim's best Excello singles, many of them recorded with Lazy Lester.

Mance Lipscomb

b Navasota, Texas, April 9, 1895; d Jan 30, 1976

Although **Mance Lipscomb** didn't record until he was 65 years old, he went on to become a much respected figure in the 1960s folk-blues revival, as one of the last links with the nineteenth-century songster tradition. By then he had honed his pleasing and muscular style over half of century spent playing around Texas on weekends, when not working on his tenanted farm.

Mance's father had been a slave in Alabama called Bowdie Glenn, who acquired the name Lipscomb when he was sold to a family of that name. He was also a noted fiddle player, and his son soon picked up the violin, although he moved on when his mother bought him a guitar when he was eleven, and was soon accompanying his father at suppers and Saturday-night dances. Life was hard for the family, as they sharecropped for various local landowners, including one notorious bully called Tom Moore, the subject of a local ballad, "Tom Moore's Farm", which Lipscomb recorded in 1960. While working on Moore's farm, he struck a foreman for abusing his mother, and was forced to go into hiding. Even when he recorded the song many years later, he still feared reprisals and insisted it was released anonymously.

During the 1920s, Lipscomb met and heard fellow Texan bluesmen **Blind Lemon Jefferson** and **Blind Willie Johnson**. However, the offer to record never arose, perhaps because although he certainly played some country blues, much of the rest of his material, which included ballads, spirituals, rags, reels, breakdowns, polkas, waltzes and dance tunes that encompassed such forgotten steps as the buzzard lope and hop scop, was already considered old-fashioned. Even after his discovery in the 1960s, Lipscomb still insisted that he was a "songster" rather than a bluesman, and proudly boasted that he had some 350 pieces in his repertoire, spanning two centuries.

In 1956, he moved to Houston, working for a lumber company during the day and playing at night in bars with **Lightnin' Hopkins**, whom he had first met in Galveston in 1938. After an accident in the lumber yard in 1958, he used the injury money he received to return to Navasota, where he was finally able to buy some land of his own and build a house. He was working as a foreman on a highway-mowing crew when he was discovered by Chris Strachwitz of Arhoolie Records and Texas blues historian Mack McCormick in 1960.

Lipscomb went on to record seven albums for Arhoolie, and became a popular performer on the folk and blues festival circuit, intermingling his songs with lengthy reminiscences about his past. His stories were subsequently taped and are now archived in the oral history department at the University of Texas in Austin. His story was also the subject of Les Blank's 1970 film, *A Well-Spent Life*. Bad health meant he spent the last couple of years of his life in a nursing home and he died in Navasota in early 1976, aged eighty.

⊙ **Texas Songster** Arhoolie
A 22-track compilation that offers a cross-section of the diversity of Mance Lipscomb's 1960s' material.

⊙ **Texas Blues Guitar** Arhoolie
A decent collection of Mance Lipscomb's more blues-based material.

⊙ **Trouble In Mind** Rhino
This nicely repackaged reissue of a 1964 recording includes thirteen previously unreleased tracks, including "Hey Lawdy Mama" and Memphis Minnie's "Bumble Bee Blues", and, illustrating Lipscomb's eclectic songster side, the old vaudeville song "Shine On Harvest Moon".

Little Milton

b Inverness, Mississippi, Sept 7, 1934; d Aug 4, 2005

Having spent more than half a century playing the blues, **Little Milton** was still going strong right up to the day he died at the age of seventy, while this book was being compiled.

James Milton Campbell Jr. was born to sharecropper parents on a Mississippi farm in 1934. His father, known as Big Milton, worked in the fields by day, and played the blues by night in local juke joints and barrelhouses. Little Milton followed in his footsteps, and was playing the guitar before he was in his teens. Determined not to spend his life picking cotton, he moved in the late 1940s to Helena, Arkansas, the home of **Sonny Boy Williamson**, who became an early mentor. By the early 1950s, he was accompanying the pianist Willie Love in Greenville, Mississippi, where he came to the attention of **Ike Turner**, then working for Sam Phillips's **Sun** label in Memphis.

With Turner in the producer's chair, Little Milton recorded a series of singles for Sun in 1953 and 1954, including "Beggin' My Baby", "If You Love Me" and "Lookin' For My Baby". He made further recordings for Meteor, but his first hit on the R&B chart came on the Bobbin label in 1958 with "I'm A Lonely Man", by which time he'd moved to St Louis. Three years later, he was on the move again, this time to Chicago, where he signed to the Chess subsidiary **Checker**. He stayed with the label for the next decade, recording such hits as "Grits Ain't Groceries", "Who's Cheating Who?", "Baby I Love You", "If Walls Could Talk", "Feel So Bad", "Hey, Hey, The Blues Is Alright" and "We're Gonna Make It", which became something of an anthem during the civil rights struggle.

While Milton's guitar style owed much to **B.B. King**, his horn-driven sound rarely stuck to the classic twelve-bar blues structure. In 1971 he switched to the Stax label, where his soul-tinged R&B hits included "Tin Pan Alley", "Walking The Back Streets And Crying" and "That's What Love Will Make You Do".

After Stax went bankrupt in 1976, Milton seemed to lose his way, cutting a series of funk-influenced records that failed to do full justice to his talent. However, he enjoyed a renaissance when he signed to **Malaco** Records in 1984, returning to his blues roots with tracks such as "The Blues Is Alright", which became his signature tune. Around the same time he left Chicago and moved to Las Vegas, although he also kept a home in Memphis.

Milton's last album, *Think Of Me*, was released on Telarc in May 2005, just three months before his death, and combined his classic blues-soul sound with a more contemporary approach. Around the time of its release, he was asked his definition of the blues. "Really it's about everyday life and that's what makes it meaningful," he replied. "The blues has been here forever and it's staying here forever. When we're all gone there'll always be someone to step in and keep it warm."

⊙ **Anthology 1953–61** Varese
Twenty-seven tracks on a single disc from Little Milton's early years on Sun, Meteor and Bobbin.

⊙ **Welcome To The Club: The Essential Chess Recordings** Chess
A brilliant double-CD compilation of gut-wrenching soul blues from the 1950s and 1960s, including such all-time greats as "Grits Ain't Groceries".

⊙ **The Complete Stax Singles** Ace
Twenty soulful Little Milton sides from the 1970s, produced by Don Davis and Al Jackson, including such classic blues as "Walking The Back Streets And Crying", soul ballads like "That's What Love Will Make You Do", and even the country-soul of "Behind Closed Doors".

⊙ **Greatest Hits** Malaco
These fourteen groove-laden tracks representing the best of Little Milton's horn-driven work for Malaco in the 1980s and 1990s.

⊙ **Think Of Me** Telarc
To the delight of his more purist blues fans, Little Milton's 2005 swansong found him in more stripped-down vein, without the strings, horns and big production.

Little Walter

b Marksville, Louisiana, May 1, 1930; d Feb 15, 1968

With his peerless playing with Muddy Waters, **Little Walter** defined the sound of the Chicago blues harp. However, he was far more than just a sideman, and as a gifted singer, composer and bandleader, he stands as one of the giants of the postwar urban blues movement.

Walter Marion Jacobs had taught himself to play the harmonica by the age of eight, and ran away from home at twelve to become a street musician in New Orleans. From there he worked his way north, and by 1943 he was in Helena, Arkansas, home of his first harmonica hero **Sonny Boy "Rice Miller" Williamson**. He stayed there for three years, and performed on the famous *King Biscuit Hour* radio show with Houston Stackhouse. By 1946 he was in Chicago, playing on Maxwell Street and astonishing the likes of Tampa Red, Big Bill Broonzy and Memphis Slim with his precocious sixteen-year-old talent. Jacobs made his first recordings the following year for the Ora Nelle label, but his big break came two years later when **Muddy Waters** added him to his band, alongside Ernest "Big" Crawford on bass, Jimmy Rodgers on second guitar and Leroy Foster on drums.

The band set about rewriting blues history, becoming one of the classic Chicago line-ups both live and in the studio. Little Walter stayed for four years, his amplified harmonica creating an almost saxophone-like sound (around Chicago, the harp was sometimes called "the Mississippi saxophone"), and making a major contribution to what came to be regarded as Waters' trademark style. His inventive lines, created by his technique of holding the harmonica and a small amplifier in the cup of his hands and effectively playing them both together, proved to be the perfect foil as he underscored and answered Muddy's powerful vocals with a killer combination of fluency and power on sides such as "Country Boy", "Louisiana Blues", "Long Distance Call", "Honey Bee", "They Call Me Muddy Waters", "Too Young To Know", "She Moves Me" and "Still A Fool".

"He was wild and he had to play fast," as Waters later put it, and it was obvious that the aggressively ambitious Walter was not going to remain content with being a sideman for long. In 1952, he enjoyed his first solo hit with the harmonica instrumental "Juke". Based on a tune called "Your Cat Will Play" and credited to Little Walter and the Night Caps, it was recorded as an afterthought at the end of a Waters session, and topped the R&B chart for eight weeks. Although Walter remained with Muddy for recording purposes, and even continued to live in his basement, he immediately exploited the surprise success of "Juke" by pulling out halfway through a Waters tour in order to launch his own band.

Playlist
Little Walter

1 LONG DISTANCE CALL (1950) from **Muddy Waters: His Best 1947–55**
On this Muddy Waters track, Walter became the first blues harp player to record amplified harmonica.

2 JUKE (1952) from **His Best: The Chess 50th Anniversary Collection**
The instrumental that gave Walter his first hit under his own name.

3 MY BABE (1955) from **His Best: The Chess 50th Anniversary Collection**
Walter's biggest hit, written by Willie Dixon.

4 TOO LATE (1956) from **His Best: The Chess 50th Anniversary Collection**
Another great song written for Walter by Dixon, who plays bass on a recording that also features Robert Lockwood on guitar.

5 IT AIN'T RIGHT (1956) from **His Best: The Chess 50th Anniversary Collection**
Covered a decade later by Eric Clapton on the one album he made with John Mayall's Bluesbreakers.

6 BOOM BOOM OUT GOES THE LIGHT (1955) from **His Best: The Chess 50th Anniversary Collection**
One of Walter's best-known compositions.

7 KEY TO THE HIGHWAY (1958) from **His Best: The Chess 50th Anniversary Collection**
A great vocal on a version of the Broonzy tune, backed by a stellar band including Muddy Waters and Otis Spann.

8 DEAD PRESIDENTS (1959) from **Willie Dixon: The Chess Box**
Blues harp at its grittiest, on yet another Willie Dixon composition.

Recruiting David and Louis Myers on guitars, and drummer **Fred Below** from the Four Aces, they became known as **Little Walter and the Jukes**. Their first recordings appeared on the Chess subsidiary **Checker** in 1952; early hits included "Can't Hold Out Much Longer", "Sad Hours", "Mean Old World", "Blues With A Feeling", "You're So Fine", "You Better Watch Yourself", "Tell Me Mama", "Boom Boom (Out Go The Lights)" and "Late Night", most of them displaying an astonishing originality.

Walter's best-known song, "My Babe", a Willie Dixon-inspired reworking of "This Train", gave him another R&B number one in 1955, and has been much covered ever since. His final hit came with a superb version of Big Bill Broonzy's "Key To The Highway" in 1958, with Otis Spann on piano and Muddy Waters on slide. He stayed with Chess until 1968, by which time he had recorded about hundred titles under his own name, while continuing to back the label's other big names on numerous other sides.

When Walter toured Britain in 1964, he thrilled audiences with his music, although some found his heavy drinking, quick temper and general belligerence off-putting. His end was tragic but perhaps all too inevitable; he died in February 1968 of a coronary thrombosis, the result of head injuries sustained in a street fight. He was just 37.

⊙ **Little Walter – His Best** Chess
A totally essential 20-track chronological selection of Little Walter's greatest solo recordings, cut between 1952 and 1960.

Robert Lockwood Jr.

b Turkey Scratch, Arkansas, March 27, 1915; d November 22, 2006

One of all too few pre-war country bluesmen to survive into the twenty-first century, **Robert Lockwood Jr.** learned the rudiments of blues guitar from his stepfather, **Robert Johnson**, even if you would scarcely have guessed

The steady rolling man: Robert Lockwood Jr.

it from his own unique style.

1915 was an historic year for the Delta blues. In addition to Lockwood – born in a farming hamlet 25 miles west of Helena, Arkansas – Muddy Waters, Willie Dixon, Little Walter, Memphis Slim, Johnny Shines and Honeyboy Edwards were all born within a hundred miles radius.

Lockwood's first musical lessons were on the family pump organ, but when Robert Johnson moved in with his mother Estella Coleman in the late 1920s, the legendary bluesman taught the boy to play guitar. By the age of fifteen, he was playing juke joints and street corners, sometimes with Johnson but also with **Johnny Shines** and **Sonny Boy "Rice Miller" Williamson**. Lockwood was 23 when Johnson died in 1938, and his own first recordings, made for Bluebird three years later in Chicago, emphasized his debt to his stepfather on sides such as "Take A Little Walk With Me" and "Little Boy Blue".

Also in 1941, Lockwood became one of the resident musicians along with Sonny Boy Williamson on the influential *King Biscuit Hour* radio show out of Helena. By the early 1950s, he had settled back in Chicago, where he became a session man for Chess records and others, backing the likes of Little Walter, Roosevelt Sykes, Sunnyland Slim and Eddie Boyd, in a guitar style that while still bearing the hallmark of Johnson's tuition was becoming much smoother and more urban. By the time Lockwood cut a classic series of guitar/piano duets with **Otis Spann** in 1960, little of Johnson's sound remained; his playing had moved in a sophisticated, jazzy direction influenced by the likes of Charlie Christian and T-Bone Walker.

Lockwood could have exploited his connections with Johnson to become one of the heroes of the folk-blues revival during the 1960s. Instead he moved to Cleveland, Ohio, in 1961, and spent the decade living quietly and playing local clubs. He re-emerged in the early 1970s to record the Delmark album *Steady Rollin' Man*, backed by Louis and Dave Myers and Fred Below, who as the **Aces** had once been **Little Walter**'s backing band. Further albums followed on Trix Records, while in the early 1980s he teamed up with another long-time friend and former Robert Johnson associate, **Johnny Shines**, to record three albums for Rounder. He also recorded for the French label Black and Blue.

Strangely, there were no further releases until 1998, when *I've Got To Find Myself A Woman* appeared on Verve. That was followed two years later by *Delta Crossroads* on Telarc. Well into the new century, Lockwood was still to be found leading an eight-piece band every Wednesday night at the Fat Fish Blues club in Cleveland until he died, aged 91.

⊙ **Steady Rolling Man** Delmark
Robert Lockwood Jr.'s debut album as a leader, recorded in 1970 when he was in his mid-fifties, and featuring the Myers brothers and Fred Below.

⊙ **Just The Blues** Bullseye Blues
A dozen tracks of potent jazz-tinged blues taken compiled from Lockwood's Rounder albums in the 1980s with Johnny Shines.

⊙ **Plays Robert And Robert** Evidence
On this 1982 album, cut in France, Robert Lockwood Jr. plays smooth and fluent versions of his stepfather's songs on a twelve-string guitar, plus a few of his own – hence the title.

⊙ **I've Got To Find Myself A Woman** Verve
The 1998 comeback, on a collection that defied Lockwood's 83 years and included songs by Robert

Johnson and Charles Brown, as well as his own "Little Boy Blue", written about his friend Sonny Boy Williamson.

John A. Lomax and Alan Lomax

Without the work of the father-and-son team of collectors and folklorists, **John A. Lomax** (b Goodman, Mississippi, Sept 23, 1875; d Jan 26, 1948) and **Alan Lomax** (b Austin, Texas, Jan 31, 1915; d 19 July, 2002), much of the early folk and blues heritage of American music might easily have been lost forever.

John Lomax began collecting cowboy and frontier ballads as early as 1910, and published his seminal *American Ballads And Folk Songs* in 1934. By then, the Library of Congress had made him head of its Archive of Folk Music and provided him with portable recording equipment. With his son Alan assisting him, he took to the road, and the pair made some three thousand recordings during the 1930s in their travels around the South. They began by recording **Leadbelly** in prison in Louisiana in 1933, and later helped to arrange his release, whereupon he went to work for John Lomax as his chauffeur. Other important field recordings included those with **Bukka White** at Parchman Farm in 1940, and with the then-unknown **Muddy Waters** at Stovall's Plantation in 1941 and 1942.

Having learned the ropes working with his father, Alan Lomax became assistant archivist at the Library of Congress in 1937, a post he held for five years, during which time he made some vital recordings on his own, including some with **Jelly Roll Morton**. Later on he made key recordings in the Mississippi and Louisiana state penitentiaries in 1947 and 1948, and undertook field trips far and wide outside the United States, recording folk songs in Haiti, the Bahamas, Great Britain, Italy and Spain. After living in Europe from 1950 until 1957, he returned to America and made further field recordings in the Southern states, assisted by the English folk singer **Shirley Collins**. Among those he found was the unrecorded 55-year-old **Mississippi Fred McDowell**, whom he discovered in 1959.

Alan's publications included *Mister Jelly Roll* (1949), a fictionalized biography of Morton; *The Rainbow Sign* (1950); *The Penguin Book Of American Folk Songs* (1961); and *The Land Where*

All are from the 2-CD collection, *The Alan Lomax Blues Songbook*

1 GOING DOWN THE RIVER (1959) Mississippi Fred McDowell
Also featuring McDowell's sister Fanny Davis on the kazoo.

2 STAGOLEE (1940) Lucious Curtis and Willie Ford
John Lomax found these two guitarists in Natchez; the song was based on a murder in St Louis in 1895.

3 WORRIED LIFE BLUES (1942) David Honeyboy Edwards
A version of the Big Maceo song, recorded in Clarksdale, where Edwards was at the time trying to pass himself off as Big Joe Williams.

4 PONY BLUES (1942) Son House
A slide guitar masterpiece based on Charley Patton's song.

5 TANGLE EYE BLUES (1948) Tangle Eye
A prison holler recorded on Parchman Farm. Tangle Eye's real name was Walter Jackson.

6 TROUBLE SO HARD (1937) Vera Ward Hall and Dock Reed
Recorded in Alabama, and famously sampled by Moby more than sixty years later.

7 LIFE IS LIKE THAT (1947) Memphis Slim
This New York super session featured Sonny Boy Williamson on harp and Big Bill Broonzy on bass.

8 KILL IT KID RAG (1940) Blind Willie McTell
The Lomaxes found McTell playing at a barbecue stand in Atlanta.

9 I BE'S TROUBLED (1941) Muddy Waters
This was recorded on Stovall's Plantation in Mississippi, though Waters cut the same song again in 1948, after his arrival in Chicago.

10 BLIND LEMON BLUES (1934)
A knife-blues recorded when Leadbelly was serving time in Angola penitentiary.

The Blues Began, his classic memoir of his search for the wellspring of American music "from the Brazos bottoms of Texas to the tidewater country of Virginia", which won a National Book Critics Circle Award in 1993.

⊙ **The Alan Lomax Blues Songbook** Rounder
A splendid double-CD introduction to the Lomaxes' field recordings, from Leadbelly to Muddy Waters.

Lonesome Sundown

b Donaldsville, Louisiana, Dec 12, 1928; d April 23, 1995

The extravagantly named **Lonesome Sundown** played a potent if somber form of Louisiana swamp blues that derived its inspiration as much from Muddy Waters and John Lee Hooker as from Clifton Chenier and the local zydeco sound.

Having taught himself piano while he was growing up, Cornelius Green took guitar lessons in the early 1950s. Although his chief influence was the new urban blues sound coming out of the northern cities, he joined **Clifton Chenier's** zydeco band in 1955, as part of a powerful two-guitar line-up with **Phillip Walker**. The record-

ings he made with Chenier for Specialty Records excited the interest of Louisiana producer **Jay Miller**, who signed him to **Excello Records** in 1956. As he did with many of his artists, Miller gave Cornelius Green a more evocative name; this time he surpassed himself when "Leave My Money Alone", his Excello debut, appeared as Lonesome Sundown.

Miller didn't record Sundown prolifically – there were just sixteen singles in nine years. But almost all were classics, including "My Home Is A Prison", "I'm A Mojo Man", "Lonesome Lonely Blues", "Hoo Doo Woman Blues", "I Stood By" and "I'm A Samplin' Man". On most of these sides, his dry, warm voice and gritty guitar playing were backed by the harmonica of **Lazy Lester** (or sometimes John Gradnigo), Lionel Prevost on tenor sax, and a succession of different pianists. Then in 1965, Sundown abruptly retired as a result of a religious conversion.

He didn't return to the studio until 1977, when he recorded the album *Been Gone Too Long* for Joliet. That was an excellent comeback, but after some live dates with his old friend Phillip Walker from Chenier's band, including a tour of Europe, he lapsed back into obscurity. In his later years he was not a well man and suffered two strokes, and he died in Louisiana in 1995.

⊙ **The Best Of The Excello Singles** Ace
A must-have collection of the excellent run of singles that Lonesome Sundown recorded with Jay Miller between 1956 and 1965.

⊙ **Been Gone Too Long** Hightone
The fine music on Lonesome Sundown's aptly titled 1977 comeback made his long absence all the more inexplicable, for he was only 49 at the time of recording and clearly still had much to offer.

Louisiana Red

b Bessemer, Alabama, March 23, 1936

Although during his early career, the guitarist, harmonica player and singer **Louisiana Red** was strongly influenced by Muddy Waters, Lightnin' Hopkins and Arthur "Big Boy" Crudup, he molded such influences into a style that was flamboyantly his own, characterized by his red-hot slide playing.

Born in Alabama, and not Mississippi as is often listed, Iverson Minter may well have derived his feel for the blues from a series of early tragedies. His mother having died of pneumonia a week after he was born, he was placed in an orphanage; while he was there, his father was the victim of a Ku Klux Klan lynching. At five he was sent to live with an aunt in Pittsburgh, and he began playing guitar at the age of eleven. Lying about his age, he joined the army in 1952 and served in Korea, then relocating to Chicago on his discharge in the mid-1950s. He jammed in the city's blues clubs with the likes of Muddy Waters and Little Walter, and recorded for the first time under the name **Playboy Fuller** on the self-released single "Gonna Play My Guitar". He also recorded for the Chess subsidiary Checker, releasing the single "Soon One Morning" as Rocky Fuller, and cutting several other sides that were not issued until the 1980s. In the late 1950s, he moved to Detroit, where he spent a couple of years playing with **John Lee Hooker**, before he moved once again, this time to New Jersey. He recorded his first sides as Louisiana Red in 1960 for the Atlas label, including "I Done Woke Up", backed by James Wayne and his Nighthawks.

The following year he was signed to Roulette by the veteran producer Henry Glover and recorded his debut album, *The Lowdown Back Porch Blues*. He recorded prolifically throughout the 1970s for Festival Records, Atco, Red Lightnin' and Blues Labor, and also appeared on albums by **Johnny Shines**, **Brownie McGhee** and **Roosevelt Sykes**. Then, in 1981, he left America to live in Germany, and spent several years recording and touring in Europe before making a comeback tour of the States in 1997. His most recent album, *No Turn On Red*, released on High Tone in 2005, included "September 11th Blues" about the terrorist attacks and a raunchy remake of "I Done Woke Up", which he had first recorded some 45 years earlier.

⊙ **The Lowdown Back Porch Blues** Sequel
Louisiana Red's debut album from 1962 featured plenty of his own unusually personal compositions, including "Red's Dream" and "I'm Louisiana Red", performed in a style that clearly owed much to the influence of Muddy Waters.

⊙ **Millennium Blues** Earwig
A fascinating 1999 recording that includes "Red's Vision", on which he reminisces about Muddy Waters and Lightnin' Hopkins, and "That Detroit Thing", which recalls his time in the Motor City with John Lee Hooker. There's also an acoustic segment with autobiographical songs about being raised in an orphanage and running away.

⊙ **A Different Shade Of Red: The Woodstock Sessions** Severn
Recorded in 2002, a fine if typically idiosyncratic electric blues collection of Louisiana Red's own compositions, recorded with former Band drummer Levon Helm in upstate New York. There's also an acoustic take on "Laundromat Blues", on which he unleashes some blistering slide.

M

Willie Mabon

b Hollywood, Tennessee, Oct 24, 1925; d April 19, 1986

The R&B hits that **Willie Mabon** recorded for Chess Records in Chicago during the 1950s were very different in style from the brash and assertive songs of Muddy Waters and Howlin' Wolf. But his salty, insinuating vocals and urbane piano style meant that for a while he was their equal in terms of commercial success, topping the R&B charts twice in 1952 and 1953, and until Chuck Berry came along, he held the distinction of having the biggest-selling record on the Chess label.

Mabon began playing the piano as a teenager, and moved first to Memphis in 1942 and then to Chicago a few years later. He initially sang and played piano in jazz clubs, but in the late 1940s formed the **Blues Rockers** with guitarist **Earl Dranes**. He first recorded in 1949, both for Apollo as Big Willie and for Aristocrat (the forerunner of Chess) as the Blues Rockers on "Times Are Getting Hard" / "Trouble In My Home". Around the same time, Mabon and his band took on Muddy Waters and his combo in a "Battle of the Blues" at Chicago's Ebony Lounge.

Mabon's next recording, the seminal "I Don't Know", was cut for Al Benson's Parrot Records in 1952 but was licensed to the new Chess label. Based on an older song by boogie-woogie pianist **Cripple Clarence Lofton**, it raced to the top of the R&B charts and spawned a host of covers and "answer" records. Signing to Chess, Mabon followed with another number one, "I'm Mad", and was almost as successful with "Poison Ivy". Further singles followed with "Come On Baby", "Seventh Son" (the first recorded version of the Willie Dixon classic) and "Knock On Wood", but they failed to sell so well, and by 1957 Mabon had switched to

the Federal label. He next moved to Formal, where he had minor hits in the early 1960s with "Just Got Some" and "I'm The Fixer", and then the USA label. Although he was largely overlooked by the blues revival of the 1960s, his polished piano and sax sound losing out to the more popular and fiery Chicago combination of guitar and harp, he was an influence on **Mose Allison** and the jazz-blues of British singer/keyboardist **Georgie Fame**.

Mabon moved to Paris, France, in 1972, and played the Montreux Jazz Festival the following year with a band that included **Mickey Baker** on guitar. He lived in Europe for the rest of his life, although he did return to the Windy City in 1979 to record the album *Chicago Blues Session* with an all-star band including Eddie Taylor and Hubert Sumlin on guitars. He continued to tour and make festival appearances until his death in 1986.

⊙ **Classics 1949–54** Classics
Twenty tracks from Willie Mabon's Chess heyday, including "I Don't Know", "I'm Mad" and "Poison Ivy", but not "Seventh Son", whose 1955 release falls outside the collection's chronological remit.

Lonnie Mack

b Harrison, Indiana, July 18, 1941

The roadhouse blues-rock of white guitarist **Lonnie Mack** has had a profound influence on most of modern rock's guitar heroes, from Eric Clapton to Stevie Ray Vaughan.

Mack grew up twenty miles west of Cincinnati, absorbing country music from family sing-alongs, blues from late-night black radio stations, and gospel from his local church. He learned to play guitar from his mother – he has been playing the same guitar, a Gibson Flying V serial number 7, since 1958 – and quit school in his teens to play in clubs and bars around Indiana, Kentucky and Ohio. He also began playing sessions in Cincinatti for labels such as King and Fraternity, recording with the likes of Hank Ballard, Freddie King and James Brown.

In 1963, in some spare studio time at the end of a session, Mack cut an instrumental version of Chuck Berry's "Memphis". He didn't even know that Fraternity had issued the track as a single until he heard it on the radio, and within weeks it was nestling in the top five of the pop charts. None of the follow-ups, which included "Wham!", "Where There's A Will There's A Way" and "Chicken

Pickin'", sold as well, although the album *The Wham Of That Memphis Man* was a fine showcase for his blues, R&B and gospel-drenched style.

When Fraternity Records went bankrupt in the late 1960s, Mack signed, somewhat surprisingly, to Elektra Records. At the time the label was home to such underground acts as Love, the Doors and Tim Buckley, and Elektra set about reinventing him for a rock audience, booking him into venues such as the Fillmore and getting him to play the guitar solo on "Roadhouse Blues" on the Doors' *Morrison Hotel* album. He recorded three solo albums for the label, but when Elektra was swallowed up by Warner Brothers, Mack walked out on his contract and returned to rural Indiana to play back-country bars and spend the rest of his time fishing.

He re-emerged in 1977 for a couple of albums on Capitol before he took another sabbatical, and then finally resurfaced in the mid-1980s, playing gigs with **Stevie Ray Vaughan**. **Alligator Records** offered him a new contract, and Vaughan co-produced the resulting 1985 album, *Strike Like Lightning*. When he toured in its support, Keith Richards, Ron Wood and Ry Cooder as well as Vaughan all joined him on stage, and his comeback year concluded spectacularly with a triumphant appearance at Carnegie Hall alongside label-mates Albert Collins and Roy Buchanan. After a second album for Alligator, Mack signed to Epic for the 1988 album *Lonnie's Roadhouses And Dancehalls*. He later returned to Alligator for a live album.

⊙ **Memphis Wham!** Ace
Lonnie Mack's 1963 debut, complemented by eight previously unreleased tracks. Frankly, you can hear why they were unreleased for so long – but the first half of the album remains a classic.

⊙ **Strike Like Lightning** Alligator
Co-producer Steve Ray Vaughan brings the best out of Lonnie Mack and his 1958 Flying V on this powerful 1985 comeback set.

Magic Sam

b Grenada County, Mississippi, Feb 14, 1937; d Dec 1, 1969

When he died at the age of 32, it seemed almost certain that the best of **Magic Sam** was still to come. However, he had already achieved much before his untimely demise, and in *West Side Soul* he left us one of the most coherent and exciting albums of modern urban blues ever to come out of Chicago.

Growing up in a Mississippi sharecropping family, Samuel Maghett was fascinated by the music he heard in the Delta, and made his first guitar from cigar boxes. By the time his family relocated to Chicago in 1950, he was already a proficient musician and he was soon playing guitar with the gospel group The Morning View Special and then **Homesick James's** band.

Encouraged by his uncle, the harpist **James "Shakey Jake" Harris**, he put his first band together in 1955 and began calling himself **Good Rocking Sam**. Like fellow young guitar tyros **Otis Rush** and **Buddy Guy**, with whom he played the clubs of Chicago, he combined the country blues he had heard growing up in the Delta with the electric sound of the first generation of great Chicago bluesmen to create a new and exciting twist on the blues. What became known as the West Side sound soon came to the ear of the ever-astute **Willie Dixon** at Chess Records. Despite his personal support, Dixon could not initially persuade Leonard and Philip Chess to give a break to Sam, Rush or Guy. So Dixon instead took all three to **Eli Toscano**, owner of the **Cobra** label, for whom Sam recorded his first session in 1957, backed by Dixon, pianist Little Brother Montgomery and drummer Billie Stepney. Toscano didn't like his Good Rocking name, and suggested Sad Sam as an alternative. As the guitarist was twenty years old and full of energy and optimism, he objected that Sad Sam sounded like a hopeless loser, and suggested **Magic Sam** instead.

Based on a riff borrowed from Ray Charles's "Lonely Avenue", Sam's first single "All Your Love" was a local hit with its minimalist guitar and high-pitched vocals. He followed with "21 Days In Jail", "Easy Baby" and "Call Me If You Need Me", which featured his uncle Shakey Jake. Then around 1960 it all went horribly wrong. Cobra went bust and while Otis Rush and Buddy Guy moved to Chess, Sam was drafted into the US army. After two months he deserted and returned to Chicago, where he briefly recorded for the Chief label. Inevitably the military police caught up with him and he was imprisoned for desertion. As a few decades earlier he would have been shot for such a crime, he counted his blessings. After a relatively short sentence and a dishonorable discharge, he returned to Chicago.

Although Sam recorded a few singles for different labels, only when Bob Koester signed him to Delmark Records in 1967 did he get his first chance to make an album. Backed by Ernest Johnson and Mack Thompson on bass, Odie Payne and his son alternating on drums, guitarists Otis Rush and Mighty Joe Young, and Swedish pianist Per Notini – credited as "Stockhom Sam", he was covering for Otis Spann who had been booked but failed to show up – he set about cutting *West Side Soul*. Despite a problem with the harmonica parts played by Sam's uncle Shakey Jake, which resulted in them being removed from the album, *West Side Soul* ranks among the very finest blues albums of the 1960s. Singing in a voice that contained echoes of both Otis Redding and Sam Cooke, Sam performed both his own compositions, like "I Need You So Bad" and the instrumental "Lookin' Good", and covers that included J.B. Lenoir's "Mama Talk To Your Daughter", a masterful rendition of Robert Johnson's "Sweet Home Chicago", and an exuberant take on Junior Parker's "I Feel So Good".

A companion album *Black Magic*, released a year later in 1968, was almost as good, and the following year Sam made the most famous live appearance of his career at the 1969 Ann Arbor Blues Festival. On a star-studded bill that boasted Muddy Waters, Howlin' Wolf, Mississippi Fred McDowell, Big Boy Crudup, Otis Rush, B.B. King, T-Bone Walker, Freddie King, Lightnin' Hopkins, Charlie Musselwhite, James Cotton, Clifton Chenier, Big Joe Williams, Roosevelt Sykes and Big Mama Thornton, Magic Sam – playing with a pick-up drummer when his own sticksman failed to show up – proceeded by all accounts to blow the lot of them off the stage. The festival made him the talk of the blues world and persuaded Stax Records to offer him a contract, but it was not to be. Just as he was about to ink the deal in December 1969, he suffered a fatal heart attack at the age of 32.

Sam's Ann Arbor festival performance was posthumously released as a live album, as was a brilliant earlier Chicago club recording from 1963, and he subsequently became a great influence on a new generation of bluesmen like **Robert Cray**. "Magic Sam had a different guitar sound," Willie Dixon wrote in his autobiography. "Most of the guys were playing the straight twelve bar blues thing, but the harmonies that he carried with the chords were a different thing altogether." Had he survived, who knows what he might have achieved.

⊙ **Magic Sam Live** Delmark
A double live set of Magic Sam at his very best, comprising one disc recorded in a Chicago club in 1963, and the second disc at the Ann Arbor Blues Festival in 1969.

⊙ **Easy Baby** Charly
A great collection of Magic Sam's early sides for Cobra and other labels.

⊙ **West Side Soul** Delmark
The album for which Magic Sam will forever be remembered is an essential presence in any blues collection worth the name.

Magic Slim

b Torrence, Mississippi, Aug 7, 1937

Standing well over six feet tall in his cowboy hat, readily identified by his slashing guitar style and booming voice, everything about **Magic Slim** is big, and he leads one of the busiest and best-loved blues bands currently working the circuit.

Born Morris Holt, he grew up singing in the local church choir. His first guitar was a "diddley-bow", a contraption that consisted of baling wire nailed to a wall, and was common all over the Delta in the prewar period. He also played the piano, but after losing the little finger on his right hand in a cotton gin accident, he found it difficult to play properly. The guitar was less of a problem, and by the late 1940s he was performing the blues at house parties at weekends, while working in the cotton fields during the week. While still a youth, he met **Magic Sam**, who gave him a few tips. "We used to sit up under the tree Sunday afternoons and play our little acoustic guitars," he recalls. "Magic Sam told me don't try to play like him, don't try to play like nobody. Get a sound of your own."

When Slim made his first trip to Chicago in 1955, Sam invited him to play bass in his band and gave him his nickname. But at eighteen, Slim's playing simply wasn't good enough to compete in a city full of great guitar players, and he soon returned to Mississippi with his tail between his legs. He spent the next few years in the Delta, practicing guitar and teaching his younger brothers, Nick and Douglas, to play bass and drums respectively. He didn't return to Chicago until the early 1960s, and he began his recording career with the single "Scufflin'" in 1966. The following year he formed his own band, the

Teardrops, with his younger brothers. By the mid-1970s, they had graduated from playing tiny joints on the South Side, such as Florence's where they had a famous residency, to touring Europe, where Slim found an appreciative audience for his boisterous, rough-and-tumble approach. His first album, *Born Under A Bad Sign*, appeared in 1977 on the French label MCM, and during the 1980s he released titles on Alligator, Rooster Blues, and the Austrian-based Wolf Records, by which time **John Primer** had joined his band.

Slim signed to Blind Pig Records in 1990 and released *Gravel Road*; its title track was one of the first tunes he had learned to play in Mississippi half a century earlier on the diddley-bow. Further albums followed on the label, including 1996's *Scufflin'*, named after his first single and released exactly thirty years on. *Black Tornado* appeared in 1998, *Snakebite* followed two years later, and then, probably best of all, *Blue Magic* in 2002. Yet there was always the nagging feeling that Slim's studio albums were no substitute for the excitement of his explosive live sets, a notion to which he responded in 2005 with the release of the in-concert CD and DVD, *Anything Can Happen*.

WESTMAN MUSIC

The real slim shady: hccus pocus from Magic Slim

⊙ **Grand Slam** Rooster Blues
A 1982 album that showcased Magic Slim's straight-ahead style, and betrayed the influence of Muddy Waters on the Teardrops' sound.

⊙ **Blue Magic** Blind Pig
Recording in Blind Pig's vintage Chicago warehouse in 2002, New York post-modern blues producer Poppa Chubby captured Slim's raw, rocking blues style better than anyone else has managed in the studio.

⊙ **Anything Can Happen** Blind Pig
Slashing guitar lines and gutbucket vocals, with all the excitement and energy of a Slim live show.

Johnny Mars

b Laurens, South Carolina, Dec 7, 1942

"Have harp, will travel" is **Johnny Mars'** motto, and there's no doubt the American-born, now London-based singer and harmonica player is one of the hardest-working modern bluesmen. Born into a South Carolina sharecropping family, Mars was given his first harmonica when he was nine. He moved all over the southeastern states with his family until 1958, when he went to live in New York with his married sister. He was soon gigging around the city, and joined the band Burning Bush, with whom he recorded for Mercury. During the early 1960s he met Magic Sam and the then-unknown Jimi Hendrix, both of whom he cites as major influences on his musical approach.

In 1967, Mars moved to San Francisco and formed **The Johnny Mars Band** with guitarist **Dan Kennedy**. They supported many of the big San

Malaco Records

founded in Jackson, Mississippi, 1962

One of the leading blues labels of recent decades, **Malaco** was originally formed by **Tommy Couch** and **Gerald "Wolf" Stephenson** as a booking agency for local and touring R&B acts around Mississippi.

It began its recording activities in the late 1960s when Couch, Stephenson and **Mitchell Malouf** built a studio in Jackson, conveniently situated halfway between Memphis and New Orleans. Based heavily on the Muscle Shoals model, they hired a house band to work on their records that included Jerry Puckett on guitar, Vernie Robbins on bass and the Chimneyville Brass, a loose group of the hottest local horn players. "There was nothing fancy about the studio," says Stephenson. "The main room was about twenty by thirty feet with a ten-foot ceiling, and I think the building itself was built in the 1940s. It had been a mechanic shop, a casket warehouse, a manufacturing facility for those little concrete statues you see in people's front yards, a tile distributor, a warehouse for empty Pepsi-Cola cases, but it had been empty for a while before we got there."

At first Malaco leased their masters to other labels, including such albums as Mississippi Fred McDowell's "I Do Not Play No Rock'n'Roll" which appeared on Capitol, and Paul Davis's "Mississippi River" which came out on Bang. Then in 1970, producer **Wardell Quezergue** arrived from New Orleans. Under the deal between them, Malaco supplied the studio and the house band, and Querzergue supplied the artists. These included **Jean Knight**, whose "Mr Big Stuff" was leased to Stax, and **King Floyd**, whose "Groove Me" appeared on Malaco's own imprint Chimneyville. Distributed by Atlantic, it crossed over to reach number six in the American pop charts.

During the 1970s, Malaco recorded sessions with the Pointer Sisters, James Carr, the Staple Singers and Rufus Thomas. However, by the middle of the decade the studio was on the point of going bust – as did Stax, further on up the road in Memphis. In the nick of time, **Dorothy Moore**'s massive hit with the country-soul ballad "Misty Blue" turned things around, and **Anita Ward**'s disco-flavored "Ring My Bell" soon followed it to the top of the charts. With its coffers replenished, Malaco set about building a formidable roster of blues, R&B, gospel and soul acts. Disco was sweeping all before it, but Malaco's response was the defiant advertising slogan: "The Last Soul Company". But there was plenty of blues on their agenda, too, and among those they signed up were **Little Milton**, **Johnny Taylor**, **Denise La Salle** and **Z.Z. Hill**, who had a massive crossover hit in 1982 with "Down Home Blues", all aimed at an enduring adult black audience with a particularly strong appeal to women.

By 1985, Malaco was prospering to such a degree that it was able to buy out the **Muscle Shoals** studios, which had been its initial inspiration. That same year the great **Bobby "Blue" Bland** signed to the label, while around the same time producer Tommy Couch Jr. joined the company and started the subsidiary imprint Waldoxy Records, to which he signed the likes of **Bobby Rush, Artie "Blues Boy" White** and others.

Today the Malaco Music Group comprises a dozen different labels, several recording studios, various music publishing companies and direct marketing and distribution divisions. Even so, the blues remains a core part of its operation after what the label's own website proudly describes as "more than thirty years of making black music for black people".

⊙ *Various Artists* **The Blues Is Alright Vols 1–4** Malaco
Prime blues and R&B cuts from the Malaco archives, with the likes of Bobby Bland and Little Milton on four individually available compilations. Those with a limited budget should probably go for volume one, which includes Z.Z. Hill's "Down Home Blues" as well as the great Little Milton track from which the series takes its name.

⊙ *Various Artists* **America's Most Wanted Vol One** Malaco
A collection of 21 more soul-tinged classics recorded at Malaco's Jackson, Mississippi, studios over the last thirty years.

Francisco groups of the day at venues such as the Fillmore. Mars' first visit to Europe in 1972 led to a record deal, and six years later he left America for good, relocating to West London, where he works regularly with Ray Fenwick, who produced his most acclaimed album, 1984's *Life On Mars*. In 1991 his harmonica was even featured on a record by the girl-group **Bananarama**, while he himself has recorded for several European labels, including Big Bear, JSP, Sundance, President and Lamborghini. In 1999 he recorded his first-ever American album, *Stateside*, produced by his old San Francisco friend, Dan Kennedy. He has also made an instructional video called *Play Rock & Blues Harp*, and runs seminars and workshops for Hohner Harmonicas.

⊙ **Life On Mars** BGO
A welcome reissue of Johnny Mars' best album, from 1984, which includes fine versions of such blues standards as "Don't Start Me Talking", "Born Under A Bad Sign" and "Back Door Man".

⊙ **Stateside** MM&K
On Mars' first American album, recorded in 1999, his wild playing goes a long way towards justifying the "Hendrix of the harmonica" tag that has sometimes been bestowed upon him.

John Mayall

b Macclesfield, Cheshire, Nov 29, 1933

John Mayall can rightly claim to be the father of the British blues. Alexis Korner and Cyril Davis among others preceded him as musical pioneers, while several of those employed, like Eric Clapton and Peter Green, went on to greater commercial success. But Mayall was the catalyst. Almost every significant British blues player passed through his band, and his influence was immeasurable.

Mayall's youthful experience could hardly have been further removed from that of sharecroppers in the Mississippi Delta; he was born into a middle-class family in Macclesfield in 1933. Quite why the blues struck such a chord with white boys growing up in the postwar suburbs of England has long been debated by musical historians and sociologists, but whatever the reason, there's no doubt that its resonance was profound. While Mayall's first exposure to African-American music came via his father's collection of jazz 78s, he also absorbed more local

styles, studying the "George Formby Teach Yourself Ukelele" program by correspondence course. By the time he formed his first group, the Powerhouse Four, at college in 1955, he had already fallen in love with the sound of the likes of Muddy Waters and John Lee Hooker. Three years, National Service with the army, including a tour of duty in Korea, interrupted his dreams of a musical career, but afforded him the opportunity to expand his knowledge of the blues via contact with black American servicemen and US armed forces radio.

Back in Britain, Mayall became a graphic designer for a Manchester firm by day, and played by night with his second band, the **Blues Syndicate**. He also showed an early flair for publicity when he persuaded the national press to run a story on the tree house in which he was living at the bottom of his parents' garden. Encouraged by **Alexis Korner**, whose **Blues Incorporated** group Mayall had supported at a gig at Manchester's Twisted Wheel club, he moved to London in January 1963. There he put together a new band, which he called the **Bluesbreakers**, and included bass player **John McVie**, later a founder member of Fleetwood Mac. He signed his first record deal in 1964, and released his debut album the following year – *John Mayall Plays John Mayall*, recorded live at the Klook's Kleek club in London's Hampstead. Other groups at the time, like the Rolling Stones, the Animals and the Yardbirds, drew from blues influences, but their blues were mixed with rock and pop flavors. Mayall's approach was more purist, offering an undiluted British take on the music of the Mississippi Delta and the clubs of Chicago's South Side. When a young guitarist called **Eric Clapton** joined Mayall in the summer of 1965, he found the band leader "very conventional and rather straight". However, Clapton, who had just left the Yardbirds in protest at their commercialism, relished the opportunity to play some pure blues, free of the pressure to deliver pop singles.

Clapton's presence ignited the group. Live audiences swelled dramatically, while the sole album he made with Mayall, 1966's *Bluesbreakers With Eric Clapton*, remains a landmark in British blues and gave Mayall his first top ten entry. For a while, Clapton also lodged with Mayall at his south London home, and he has since paid tribute to the amount he learned from having access to his unparalleled collection of blues records. Yet he soon proved to be an unreliable band member, quitting for example in 1965 while he disappeared to Greece for three months. He was temporarily replaced by **Peter Green**, but on his return asked for his old job back. Green was evicted to make way for him, but got his chance to become a permanent member when Clapton left for a second and final time in mid-1966, taking with him **Jack Bruce** (who had replaced McVie on bass) to form **Cream**.

As a guitarist Green's virtuosity was not far behind that of Clapton. Like his predecessor, he made just one studio album with the Bluesbreakers, 1967's *A Hard Road*, before he left in turn to form **Fleetwood Mac** with McVie and Mayall's drummer Mick Fleetwood. Mayall recruited a new set of musicians, including **Mick Taylor**, who later replaced Brian Jones in the Rolling Stones, and a brass section, and made *Crusade*, which gave him his third consecutive British top-ten album. With his former sidemen dominating the rock scene in bands like Cream and Fleetwood Mac, this was the point at which Mayall was dubbed "the father of the British blues". He exploited his high profile by releasing a total of four albums in less than twelve months – a predominantly solo set called *The Blues Alone*, the live albums *Diary Of A Band Volumes One And Two*, and *Bare Wires*. With the brass section playing a particularly prominent role, the latter proved his most commercially successful album, reaching number three in the British charts.

In early 1968, Mayall made his first tour of the United States, and supported Jimi Hendrix at the Fillmore West in San Francisco. He enjoyed the trip so much that by the end of the year, he had disbanded the Bluesbreakers and moved to America, buying a house in the Hollywood Hills. His first American-made album, *Blues From Laurel Canyon*, appeared in 1969, featuring a new band whose revolutionary line-up dispensed with a drummer. The album *Turning Point* followed later in the year and went gold. With the same group of musicians, Mayall made 1970's *Empty Rooms*, another British top-ten album, while a new line-up featuring virtuoso American musicians in guitarist Harvey Mandel, violinist Don "Sugarcane" Harris and bassist Larry Taylor recorded *USA Union* the same year.

By now, however, the British-led blues boom had all but run its course. As a new wave of heavier, "progressive" groups came to the fore, a reunion album featuring Clapton and other past Bluesbreakers called *Back To The Roots* provided

Mayall's final British chart entry in 1971. Arguably, the blues was never again so close to the rock mainstream. In an effort to broaden his audience, Mayall recorded the 1972 album *Jazz Blues Fusion*, with a band that included the jazz trumpeter Blue Mitchell. Three years later, he recruited a female vocalist to his band for the first time with the addition of Dee McKinnie for the album *New Year, New Band, New Company*. Neither was particularly inspired, and the decade ended disastrously when a fire destroyed his Laurel Canyon home in 1979, taking with it his priceless blues collection and meticulously kept personal diaries.

That was a bitter blow, and for a while Mayall stopped recording. But he steeled himself against the loss and began a new life by marrying the singer Maggie Parker. He reformed the Bluesbreakers in 1982 for successful tours of America and Australia, with a line-up that included old boys Mick Taylor and John McVie. Two years later he put together yet another entirely new Bluesbreakers line-up. Further albums followed for various labels, and the 1990s saw something of a critical revival, with such acclaimed releases as *A Sense Of Place* (his first major label release in many years, on Island in 1990), *Wake Up Call* (1992) and *Spinning Coin* (1995). By the end of the 1990s, Mayall's visits to Britain had become increasingly rare, but a seventieth birthday concert in Manchester in 2003, which featured many of his former sidemen, including Eric Clapton and Mick Taylor, generated considerable media interest and was the subject of a BBC television documentary and a DVD. "For me the well of the blues never runs dry," he observed in the film. "It's always an inspiration."

⊙ **Bluesbreakers With Eric Clapton** Decca
The seminal British blues album of its time features Eric Clapton at his very best, less pop than the Yardbirds and more focused than Cream.

⊙ **Turning Point** Decca
On this fascinating 1969 album, John Mayall abolished drums for more flowing, melodic jazz-blues grooves, with John Almond on flutes and sax.

⊙ **A Sense Of Place** Island
Mayall returned to form in 1990 with a spare production, decent original songs and well-chosen covers by Wilbert Harrison and J.J. Cale.

⊙ **London Blues 1964–69** Polydor
Two discs and forty well-chosen tracks from the days when the Bluesbreakers boasted such axemen as Eric

Clapton, Peter Green and Mick Taylor.

⊙ **Steppin' Out: An Introduction To John Mayall And The Bluesbreakers** Decca
A nicely presented and well-annotated 2001 compilation of seventeen key tracks from the British blues boom.

Percy Mayfield

b Minden, Louisiana, Aug 12, 1920; d Aug 11, 1984

The favorite songwriter of Ray Charles, **Percy Mayfield** was sometimes known as "the poet laureate of the blues". His much-covered compositions included "Hit The Road Jack" and the immortal blues ballad "Please Send Me Someone To Love", but he was also a subtle singer in his own right, in the laid-back West Coast style also associated with the likes of Charles Brown and Lowell Fulson.

Mayfield started out writing poetry before he turned his talent to songs, although when he first arrived in Los Angeles in 1942 he worked more prosaically as a dishwasher, short-order cook and taxi driver. Eventually he landed a spot singing with **George Como**'s band. Modeling himself on **Nat King Cole**, he became one of the so-called "sepia Sinatras" who dominated the West Coast postwar blues scene. In a crowded field, he came to feel that his best chance of success might be as a writer, and in 1947 he took the song "Two Years Of Torture" to Al Patrick's Supreme Records, suggesting that Jimmy Witherspoon might like to sing it. Instead, the label so liked his own mellow vocal on his demo that they suggested Mayfield recorded it himself, backed by saxophonist Maxwell Davis, guitarist Chuck Norris and Willard McDaniel on piano. It became a local hit and persuaded Art Rupe to sign him to the bigger **Specialty Records**, for whom Mayfield's first release was the regal "Please Send Me Someone To Love". That not only gave him a number one but has since become one of the most covered R&B songs of all time. "Lost Love", "Life Is Suicide", "What A Fool I Was", "Prayin' For Your Return", "Cry Baby" and "Big Question" all followed, and established Mayfield as an almost permanent presence on the R&B charts and as a songwriter capable of extraordinary precision and an evocative melancholy.

His run of hits was briefly halted when he was seriously injured in a car accident while return-ing to Los Angeles from a date in Las Vegas in September 1952. His face was permanently disfigured, and he returned home to Louisiana to recover, where he wrote the superb "Stranger In My Own Home Town" about his experience. Four months later he returned to the recording studio to cut "I Dare You Baby" and "River's Invitation", and he bravely defied his disfigurement to return to live performance a year after the crash.

When his Specialty contract expired in 1955, Mayfield signed to **Chess**, where he recorded songs such as "Are You Out There?" and "Double Dealing". The following year he switched to the Money label, and then Atco and Imperial, as it appeared that changed tastes in R&B were leaving his more introspective style on the sidelines.

Instead his fortunes took a dramatic upturn when **Ray Charles** recorded his "Hit The Road, Jack", and hired Mayfield as a full-time writer and performer on his own Tangerine label, distributed by ABC. Charles further recorded his "Hide Nor Hair", "At The Club", "Danger Zone" and "On The Other Hand, Baby". Mayfield also recorded two LPs for Tangerine, *My Jug And I* and *Bought Blues*, on which he was backed by Charles's band. He later moved to RCA Victor but by the mid-1970s had lapsed into obscurity. He was unfortunate that he had hit his creative peak before black music had become the sound of mainstream America, and he died the day before his 64th birthday in 1984.

⊙ **Poet Of The Blues** Specialty
Twenty-five classics of sublime melancholy from Percy Mayfield's early 1950s' heyday on Art Rupe's Specialty label, including "The River's Invitation", which was later covered by Aretha Franklin, and "Memory Pain", which John Lee Hooker reworked as "It Serves Me Right To Suffer".

⊙ **Tangerine And Atlantic Sides** Rhino
The best of Mayfield's recordings from the late 1950s and early 1960s, by which time his songwriting had taken on a deeper, post-crash introspection.

Tommy McClennan

b Yazoo City, Mississippi, April 8, 1908; d 1962

"He just play the blues. Straight blues," Honeyboy Edwards said of the physical, intense and raucous juke joint music of **Tommy McClennan**. "There wasn't nothin' betwixt nothin'. Just straight go."

McClennan's parents were sharecroppers on J.E. Sligh's plantation near Yazoo City, Mississippi. He taught himself to play guitar, influenced by local heroes Rubin Lacy, Charley Patton, Ishman Bracey and Tommy Johnson. Even in adulthood, he stood just 4 feet 10 inches tall, and weighed around 130 pounds, so he was hardly cut out for a life of hard labor. Even so, he was required to work in the cotton fields as a child, but at a young age he was soon spending his weekends playing on the streets of Greenwood for nickels and dimes, before he graduated to juke joints and dances, accompanied by the equally diminutive **Robert Petway**. They soon had a follower in **Honeyboy Edwards**, whose autobiography has filled in much of our knowledge about McClennan. Edwards graphically describes the sight of the "two midgets", and said that McClennan could never find a hat small enough for his head, so that his hat always hung down over his ears. He was also sickly, possibly due to tuberculosis, and his chronic alcoholism hardly helped. For all that, he could undeniably sing the blues.

By the mid-1930s, McClennan's reputation around the Delta had reached the ears of **Lester Melrose** of Bluebird Records, who first heard of him via Big Bill Broonzy. Melrose went in search of him and found him working on a plantation. After an initial altercation with the plantation owner resulted in the record-company scout being run off the land and fleeing for his life, he eventually got his man when he sent the money for McClennan to travel to Chicago for his first recording session in 1939.

Singing in a rough, urgent style that managed to disguise his minimal competency on the guitar ("he had a different style of playing," said Broonzy. "You just make the chords and change when you feel like changing"), McClennan delivered memorable versions of "Shake 'Em On Down" and "Bottle It Up And Go". His country ways didn't always go down well in Chicago; in his autobiography, Broonzy recalled that McClennan insisted on using the world "nigger" in "Bottle It Up And Go". At least one house party, this resulted in him being thrown through a window with his smashed guitar around his neck.

Nevertheless, McClennan recorded forty further songs in four more sessions for Melrose and Bluebird over the next two years. These included "Cotton Patch Blues"; "Cross Cut Saw Blues",

as later covered by Albert King; "Whisky Head Woman"; "New Highway 51", which was covered by Bob Dylan on his debut album; and "Deep Sea Blue", which reworked Petway's "Catfish Blues". His final sessions for the label took place in February 1942, and also found him assisting Petway on his "Boogie-woogie Woman".

After that, Melrose dispensed with his services, citing his unreliability and alcoholism, and McClennan disappeared from view into an alcoholic haze. There were unverified reports that he was still playing occasional club gigs in the mid-1950s, but it was many years before blues scholars even tracked down what had become of him. Once again, it was Honeyboy Edwards who provided the clues, recalling in his autobiography that he had run into McClennan again in 1962, destitute and living in a trailer. Edwards attempted to resurrect his career, but his alcoholism made it impossible, and he is understood to have died in a Chicago hospital later that year – alone, penniless and unable even to speak. The exact date of his death has never been verified, but the fact that he was just 54 and he hadn't recorded in twenty years tells its own story.

⊙ **The Bluebird Recordings 1939–1942** RCA
All 42 of the only recordings Tommy McClennan ever made, spread across two discs. Despite the years of sneering at the crudity of his guitar style, the likes of "You Can Mistreat Me Here", "Brown Skin Girl", "New Highway 51", and "It's Hard To Be Lonesome" are utterly unforgettable.

Jimmy McCracklin

b St Louis, Missouri, Aug 13, 1921

Best-known for his R&B hit "The Walk", Jimmy McCracklin has spent 60 years singing and playing the blues in his inimitably soulful style.

Born in St Louis in 1921 – even if he has often disputed the date, improbably claiming to be a full decade younger – McCracklin was introduced by his father at an early age to the veteran pianist **Walter Davis**, who gave him lessons. He was also briefly a professional boxer, but after serving in the US Navy during World War II he opted for a musical career. Upon his discharge, he headed for the West Coast, where he made his recording debut in 1945 on the Globe label with "Miss Mattie Left Me". On that occasion he was backed by J.D. Nicholson on piano, although on most of his subsequent recordings he took care of the piano duties himself.

McCracklin recorded further for various West Coast labels before signing to the Bihari brothers' **Modern** Records in 1948, when he formed his own band, the **Blues Blasters**, initially with Robert Kelton on guitar and later with Lafayette "Thing" Thomas. He was somehow involved in the recording of Roy Hawkins' original version of "The Thrill Is Gone", although his claim to have written the song that went on to become a hit for **B.B. King** has never been verified or accepted.

In the mid-1950s, McCracklin recorded briefly for the Swing Time and Peacock labels, and then returned to Modern before switching to Premium Records, for whom he cut "Get Back" with a thrilling big-band arrangement. By the time his huge hit "The Walk" appeared on Chess Records subsidiary Checker in 1958, he was already on his twelfth label. A novelty dance number reputedly written to show just how easy the rock'n'roll audience was to please, the song became a favorite on Dick Clark's influential TV show *American Bandstand* – McCracklin was the first blues artist ever to appear on the program – and the exposure helped to propel it into the US top ten. Follow-ups "Georgia Slop" and "The Wobble" were almost as much fun, but he had returned to a more direct blues style by the time of his next big hit, the gospel-blues "Just Got To Know" which appeared on Art-Tone Records in 1961. By1965 he'd switched labels once more to Imperial, where he enjoyed hits with "Every Night, Every Day" "Think", and "My Answer". The latter two were recorded in Houston with Bobby "Blue" Bland's horn section and musical director **Joe Scott**. McCracklin also penned "Tramp" for Lowell Fulson in 1967, which was an even bigger hit for **Otis Redding** and Carla Thomas, and he adapted easily to the soul era, recording two albums for Stax in the early 1970s.

McCracklin continued touring into the 1980s, although his recordings had by then slowed to a trickle. However, he came back strongly in the 1990s with the potent *My Story: A Taste Of The Blues* for Rounder's Bullseye Blues imprint.

⊙ **The Modern Recordings 1948–50** Ace
Twenty-five rocking, cracking early McCracklin tracks that have lost none of their power and conviction.

⊙ **The Walk: Jimmy McCracklin At His Best**

Razor & Tie
Twenty classic McCracklin sides including "Get Back", "Georgia Slop" and "The Wobble" as well as his perambulating signature tune.

⊙ **My Story: A Taste Of The Blues** Bullseye Blues
Jimmy McCracklin's classic sound was updated, but tastefully so, on this fine 1991 comeback album.

Mississippi Fred McDowell

b Rossville, Tennessee, Jan 12, 1904; d July 3, 1972

The blues revival of the 1960s rescued many Delta bluesmen from obscurity, but the discovery of **Mississippi Fred McDowell** was arguably its most dramatic and important achievement. While most of the blues pioneers who became heroes to a new generation had formerly been successful recording artists, with a stash of crackling old 78s to their name, McDowell was a totally unknown quantity. He had never been near a recording studio until **Alan Lomax** found him on his farm in 1959.

Despite the name by which he became known, McDowell wasn't actually born in Mississippi at all, but in Tennessee. His parents died when he was young, and having taught himself to play blues guitar aged fourteen, using a slide hollowed out of cattle bone, he made his way to Memphis during the 1920s. There he played on street corners for tips, and came under the influence of the likes of **Charley Patton**. However, he soon moved back to Como, Mississippi, where he farmed by day and played at parties, dances and fish fries on the weekend. His life followed this largely uneventful pattern for some thirty years until he was "discovered" by Lomax and his assistant **Shirley Collins**. She dramatically described their first encounter with him 45 years later in her book *America Over The Water*. "Towards dusk a slight figure in dungarees and carrying a guitar appeared out of the trees and walked into the clearing," she recalled. "He was a fifty-year-old farmer and he'd been picking cotton all day. Fred started to play bottleneck guitar, a shimmering and metallic sound. His singing was quiet but strong and with a heart-stopping intensity. By the time he'd finished his first blues, we knew we were in the presence of a great

Fred McDowell: a star at 60

White's "Shake 'Em On Down". One of McDowell's local nicknames was apparently "Shake 'Em", on account of the potency of his rendition of the song. According to Lomax, when he played back the tapes to McDowell, he could not hide his delight at finally being recorded and "stomped up and down on the porch, whooping and laughing".

When his excitement had subsided, McDowell happily settled back into his old pattern, picking cotton and playing for tips outside Stuckey's candy store in Como on the weekend. There he might have stayed until **Chris Strachwitz** of Arhoolie Records came looking for him again in 1964, recorded the albums *Fred McDowell, Volume 1*, and *Fred McDowell, Volume 2*, and also persuaded McDowell to become a professional musician for the first time in his life, at the age of sixty.

McDowell's emergence sent shock waves through the folk-blues world. How could this authentic backwoods bluesman, blessed with such a repertoire and such depth and emotional force, have been overlooked and remained unknown for so long? During the late 1920s and early 1930s, record company scouts had pored over the South and recorded many musicians with only a fraction of McDowell's towering talent. Somehow they had missed him, for he had been there in the hill country the entire time, working on his farm and playing on the weekend for tips. His versions of songs such

and extraordinary musician."

The recordings they made included blues and spirituals, several of them featuring McDowell's wife Annie Mae and his sister Fanny Davis on comb and paper. Titles included "61 Highway", "Diving Duck Blues", Blind Willie Johnson's "Keep Your Lamps Trimmed And Burning", "Jesus Gonna Make Up My Dying Bed", and, above all, Bukka

Playlist
Mississippi Fred McDowell

1 I'M GOING DOWN THE RIVER (1959) from **Fred McDowell: The First Recordings**
Ringing slide guitar work and a jumping beat from McDowell's legendary Lomax session in Como, Mississippi.

2 YOU GOTTA MOVE (1964) from **You Gotta Move**
As covered by the Rolling Stones on *Sticky Fingers*.

3 SHAKE EM ON DOWN (1959) from **Fred McDowell: The First Recordings**
McDowell recorded several versions of this song, but his first was perhaps the finest.

4 61 HIGHWAY BLUES (1959) from **Fred McDowell: The First Recordings**
Virtuoso bottleneck playing and a complex counterpoint with his right hand, on an old song first recorded by Will Batts in 1933.

5 KEEP YOUR LAMPS TRIMMED AND BURNING (1959) from **Fred McDowell: The First Recordings**

McDowell's playing was heavily influenced by Blind Willie Johnson, who wrote this tune.

6 YOU'RE GONNA BE SORRY (1959) from **Fred McDowell: The First Recordings**
Blues freestyling at its loosest, improvisational best.

7 WRITE ME A FEW LINES (1962) from **Mississippi Fred McDowell**
Recorded by Dick Spottswood at McDowell's home.

8 YOU AIN'T GONNA WORRY MY LIFE NO MORE (1969) from **I Do Not Play No Rock'n'Roll**
Also known as "Fred's Worried Life Blues", from the album recorded in London on which Fred finally plugged in and went electric.

9 THE TRAIN I RIDE (1969) from **I Do Not Play No Rock'n'Roll**
On which McDowell's strumming gets so frenzied that his electric guitar actually distorts during the climax.

as "Baby Please Don't Go", "Good Morning Little School Girl", and "Jesus Is On The Mainline" were all classics of the raw Delta blues style, delivered in an earthy voice and accompanied by slashing bottleneck guitar. Although he did play a little electric guitar, he refused to dilute or to update his sound to reflect changing times, and scorned the amplified rock influences of much modern blues, an attitude reflected in the title of his 1969 Capitol album, *I Do Not Play No Rock'n'Roll*. Despite this, he was a major influence on numerous rock artists, including Bonnie Raitt and the Rolling Stones, who recorded a haunting version of McDowell's "You Gotta Move" on their classic *Sticky Fingers* album.

McDowell was also much filmed in his final years, appearing in *The Blues Maker* (1968), the documentary *Fred McDowell* (1969), and *Roots Of American Music: Country And Urban Music* (1970). He continued touring almost until his death, appearing at the Newport Folk Festival and visiting Europe with the American Folk Blues Festival, and he was on tour when he was diagnosed with cancer in 1971. He died the following year aged 68, and was allegedly buried in a silver lamé suit that the Rolling Stones had bought him.

⊙ **The First Recordings** Rounder
Fourteen tracks of pure and unadulterated rural blues, captured by Alan Lomax on a portable reel-to-reel tape recorder in 1959.

⊙ **I Do Not Play No Rock'n'Roll** Varese
Mississippi Fred McDowell made these ragged but righteous recordings in 1969 just three years before his death.

⊙ **The Best Of Mississippi Fred McDowell** Arhoolie
An 18-track compilation drawn from the albums that Mississippi Fred McDowell recorded for Chris Strachwitz's label between 1964 and 1969, and featuring songs like "You Gotta Move", "Kokomo Blues", "Write Me A Few Of Your Lines", "Meet Down In Froggy Bottom" and "My Baby".

Brownie McGhee

b Knoxville, Tennessee, Nov 30, 1915; d Feb 16, 1966

While the singer and guitarist **Brownie McGhee** will always be best remembered for his long-running partnership with the harmonica player **Sonny Terry**, he also recorded widely as both solo act and sideman for others in a tougher, R&B-tinged style.

Walter Brown McGhee contracted polio as a small boy, which left him with an exaggerated limp. His father Duff McGhee taught him to play guitar, and his enforced immobility gave him plenty of time to practice, while his younger brother, Granville, also a talented guitarist, earned the nickname **Sticks** for pushing his stick-wielding sibling around in a cart.

McGhee also sang with the Golden Voices Gospel Quartet, and when he was 22, a local church organization paid for him to have an operation on his leg. That dramatically increased his mobility, and he enthusiastically took off as an itinerant musician, playing all over the Southeastern states. For a while he hooked up with washboard player George "Bull City Red" Washington, and he also befriended **Blind Boy Fuller**, who introduced him to the talent scout J.B. Long. Long recorded him for Okeh/Columbia in Chicago in 1940, in a two-day session that produced a dozen tracks. Much influenced by Fuller, some of McGhee's early sides were even issued under the name Blind Boy Fuller No. 2 and on his mentor's passing in 1941, he cut the tribute, "The Death Of Blind Boy Fuller". His third session for Okeh in 1941 paired him for the first time with Sonny Terry on "Workingman's Blues", although the two had met a couple of years earlier in South Carolina via their mutual acquaintance with Fuller.

By 1942, both men had relocated to New York, where they fell in with the Folkways crowd, which included Woody Guthrie, Pete Seeger, Leadbelly and Josh White. McGhee recorded prolifically in the 1940s both with and without Terry, playing acoustic country blues for a white folk audience and blues-tinged R&B for a black audience. He cut some particularly powerful R&B sides for Savoy, one of which, "My Fault", gave him a hit in 1948. McGhee also developed a secondary career as an actor, appearing on Broadway in Tennessee Williams' *Cat On A Hot Tin Roof* in the mid-1950s.

Yet it was as a Piedmont-style acoustic duo with Terry that the more profitable white market wanted to hear him, both on the American festival, club and coffee house circuit and in Europe, where the pair were among the first blues acts to tour in 1958. They also recorded a dozen or more acoustic albums for different folk labels, which many blues fans felt diluted their style, and it's certainly hard to escape the feeling that a certain blandness and repetition crept in as they attempted to please their international audiences. During over thirty years spent almost constantly in each other's company, the personal relationship between the two men deteriorated, until towards the end of their partnership they were barely on speaking terms, even appearing on stage separately in their final gigs.

After they split for good in the mid-1970s, Terry continued working while McGhee retired to the West Coast. He made a comeback to live work at the 1995 Chicago Blues Festival and the same year recorded the album *Brownie's Blues* for the Goldstar label, but he died the following year in Oakland, California at the age of eighty.

⊙ **The Complete Brownie McGhee** Columbia
A double album of Brownie McGhee's 1940–41 sides for Okeh, heavily influenced by Blind Boy Fuller and with some fascinating studio conversation between the songs.

⊙ **The Folkways Years 1945–59** Smithsonian Folkways
Ostensibly this album features Brownie McGhee's solo material for Mo Asch's pioneering label, but inevitably Terry crops up on a number of tracks.

⊙ **Midnight Special** Fantasy
Twenty tracks that McGhee recorded with Sonny Terry for a brace of Prestige/Bluesway albums in 1960.

Sticks McGhee

b Knoxville, Tennessee, March 23, 1918; d Aug 15, 1961

The younger brother of the more famous Brownie, Sticks McGhee cut some great boozy R&B tunes, the most memorable of which was his much-covered "Drinkin' Wine Spo-Dee-O-Dee".

Granville McGhee was born some two and a half years after his brother, and learned to play guitar by copying his older sibling. He was also required to push the polio-afflicted Brownie in a cart around the streets of Kingsport, which earning him the nickname Sticks. Brownie McGhee's physical disability spared him military service, but Sticks was called up to the US Army in 1942, and penned "Drinkin' Wine" in boot camp. After his discharge in 1946, he teamed up with his brother in New York and cut a version of the song for Mayo Williams' Harlem logo, with lyrics considerably cleaned up from those with which he had entertained his army buddies.

While the track initially failed to sell, a remake two years later, credited to "Stick McGhee & His Buddies" and featuring his brother on guitar and harmony vocal and "Big Chief" Ellis on piano, was a massive R&B hit. The song has since been covered by everyone from Jerry Lee Lewis to Kid Rock and the record enjoyed an added significance as the first major hit on Ahmet Ertegun's fledgling Atlantic label.

McGhee achieved another big hit on Atlantic with "Tennessee Waltz Blues" and a minor one with "Wee Wee Hours" before he moved to Essex and then to King Records, where he recorded a run of booze songs between 1953 and 1955 including "Whiskey Women And Loaded Dice", "Head Happy With Wine", "Jungle Juice" and "Double Crossin' Liquor". He later recorded for Savoy and Herald, and also backed Sonny Terry and Brownie McGhee on various recordings, before his death from lung cancer in 1961 at the age of 43.

⊙ **New York Blues** Ace
Pour yourself a stiff one and enjoy some of the best drinking songs ever recorded from Sticks McGhee's King years, including "Whiskey Women And Loaded Dice", "Head Happy With Wine", "Jungle Juice" and "Double Crossin' Liquor" – but not, sadly, "Spo-Dee-O-Dee".

⊙ **Classics 1947–51** Classics
Sticks' 1947 and 1949 versions of "Drinkin' Wine Spo-Dee-O-Dee", plus "Drank Up All The Wine Last Night" and seventeen others that surprisingly aren't about booze.

Jay "Hootie" McShann

b Muskogee, Oklahoma, Jan 12, 1916

On the occasion of his sixtieth birthday in 2005, Van Morrison was asked if he had any plans to retire. "I don't know why you're even asking me," he replied. "No one ever thinks of asking Jay McShann that question." At the time the veteran pianist and singer was 89 years old, and still going strong as one of the world's oldest surviving bluesmen.

James Columbus McShann was born in Oklahoma in 1916 – some sources claim 1909 – and taught himself piano as a child. He modeled his style on the jazz pianist **Earl Hines**, whom he heard on late-night radio broadcasts from Chicago's

Grand Terrace Ballroom, and began playing professionally in 1931, hobo-ing around Arkansas and Oklahoma until 1936, when he settled in Kansas City. There he fell under the boogie-woogie spell of Pete Johnson and Joe Turner, and formed first a small combo including Gus Johnson, Gene Ramey and the revolutionary talent of **Charlie Parker**, and then his own big band, the **Jay McShann Orchestra**. Walter Brown was on vocals, although McShann himself was also a more than effective blues shouter. He recorded first for Decca in 1941, before moving to Aladdin and then Mercury, playing a mixture of traditional Kansas City jazz and swinging blues tunes such as "Confessin' The Blues", "Hootie Blues", and "Ain't Nobody's Business", the latter featuring a new young singer called **Jimmy Witherspoon**.

By the 1950s, McShann had lapsed into obscurity. Although he continued playing locally around Kansas City and recorded a number of albums, not until the early 1970s did he return as a popular figure on the international festival circuit, playing the piano and singing the blues with renewed vigor. Indeed, approaching his seventies, he entered the most productive phase of his career, and kept up a rigorous recording and touring schedule for the next twenty years and more. He was the subject of the documentary film *Hootie Blues* in 1978, and his later albums have included solo outings, small group sessions and roaring big-band records, all keeping the classic and unique Kansas City blues sound alive.

In 1997, now well into his eighties, McShann signed to Stony Plain Records and recorded *Hootie's Jumpin' Blues* with Duke Robillard. That was followed by *Goin' To Kansas City* and then *Still Jumpin' The Blues*, featuring guest vocals from Maria Muldaur.

⊙ **Jumpin' The Blues** Proper
Fifty tracks on two CDs, representing the best of Jay McShann's R&B and jazz-blues with his 1940s orchestra.

⊙ **Hootie's Jumpin' Blues** Stony Plain
Rolling piano and bluesy vocals from the eighty-something-young McShann in 1997, and perfect accompaniment by guitarist/producer Duke Robillard and his band.

Blind Willie McTell

b Thompson, Georgia, May 5, 1901; d Aug 19, 1959

66 "Nobody can sing the blues like Blind Willie McTell," Bob Dylan sang in his heartfelt 1983 tribute to the Atlanta bluesman.

Although it's known that he was born in Georgia in 1901, considerable mystery surrounds McTell's precise name. William Samuel McTell is the most widely accepted version, but his tombstone says "Eddie McTier". One theory holds that he was born with the name McTier or McTear, but the family adopted McTell as a disguise, possibly because of their involvement in running an illegal whiskey still. It's also unclear whether he was born blind or lost his sight in early childhood. Raised in Statesboro, a few miles from Savannah, Willie learned to play the guitar from his mother and despite his lack of sight ran away in his early teens to play in touring carnivals, including the John Roberts Plantation Show. He later returned home and was sent to blind schools in New York and Macon, Georgia, where he learned to read both text and music in Braille. After hobo-ing around the East Coast for a couple of years and meeting up with **Blind Willie Johnson**, he was living in Atlanta by 1927, where he recorded his first four sides for Victor Records' field recording unit. A highly accomplished twelve-string guitarist – the instrument was favored by many of Atlanta bluesmen – blessed with a warm, ringing voice, he recorded for Victor again when they returned to the city the following year. This time they signed him to a four-year contract, although when other record companies came looking for him he skirted around that problem by the simple ruse of recording for different labels under different names. For Columbia he was Blind Sammie, Georgia Bill for Okeh, Red Hot Willie Glaze for Bluebird, and Blind Willie for Vocalion.

McTell's early sessions produced such classic sides as "Statesboro Blues", "Georgia Rag", "Broke Down Engine Blues", "Southern Can Is Mine" and "Mama Tain't Long Fo' Day", and he boasted an impressive repertoire that spanned blues, ragtime, gospel, dance tunes, pop and even country material. He married Ruth Kate Williams in 1934, and the following year the couple recorded several duets together of mostly religious material such as "Ain't It Good To Be A Christian". However, while he traveled, she stayed home, and spent 32 years working as a nurse at Fort Gordon. "He said 'baby, I was born a rambler'", she recalled in an interview in 1977. "'I'm gonna ramble until I die, but I'm preparing you to live after I'm gone.'"

In November 1940, **John** and **Alan Lomax** recorded and interviewed McTell for the Library of Congress in an Atlanta hotel room, after they found him playing for tips at a fast-food stand. The material offers a remarkable insight into the music and life of one of the true blues greats, although the sessions were not released until many years later as the Lomaxes were apparently not fans of his style. These were the only recordings he made between 1937 and 1948, although he still played for tips on Atlanta's Decatur Street and hobo-ed his way around the Southern and Southeastern states. He returned to the studio in 1949 when **Ahmet Ertegun**, who had just started Atlantic Records recorded fifteen sides with him, although only two of them, "Kill It, Kid" and a remake of "Broke Down Engine Blues", were released at the time under the name **Barrelhouse Sammy** (The Country Boy). Fortunately, the full tape was redis-covered in Atlantic's vaults in 1969.

In 1950 he recorded for Regal Records as **Pig'n'Whistle Red**, the name taken from a whites-only barbecue joint where he played requests for tips. He continued to play in juke joints and was a familiar sight playing on Atlanta street corners until the late 1950s, cutting his final session in 1956 when a local record store owner called Ed Rhodes recorded a varied selection of songs drawn from his thirty-year career and also taped him reminisc-ing about his life and times. The tapes were then forgotten in the store's attic for several years, and when they were rediscovered only one was salvage-able. That was subsequently released as *Blind Willie McTell's Last Session* on Prestige/Bluesville.

Around 1957, McTell gave up the blues and became a preacher. "He said he felt like he was com-ing to the end of his journey, he was coming back to God," his wife recalled twenty years later. He died of a cerebral hemorrhage in 1959 at the age of 58, which meant he did not live long enough to be rediscovered during the early 1960s folk-blues revival. But he left a legacy of wonderful songs, covered by Taj Mahal and the Allman Brothers among many others. It has often been said that McTell appealed to white audi-ences because he sounded like a white man trying to sound black. But the truth is that nobody – black or white – sang the blues like Blind Willie McTell.

Playlist
Blind Willie McTell

1 MAMA T'AINT LONG FO DAY (1927) from **The Definitive Blind Willie McTell**
The first of McTell's great slide guitar masterpieces.

2 STATESBORO BLUES (1928) from **The Definitive Blind Willie McTell**
Although Duane Allman and others subsequently made this a slide classic, oddly the bottleneck didn't feature on the original.

3 ATLANTA STRUT (1929) from **The Definitive Blind Willie McTell**
About a little girl who looked "like a lump of Lord have mercy".

4 TRAVELLIN' BLUES (1929) from **The Definitive Blind Willie McTell**
Supreme finger-picking finesse, originally released under the name "Blind Sammie".

5 GEORGIA RAG (1931) from **The Definitive Blind Willie McTell**
This time, accompanied by Curley Weaver, McTell was listed as "Georgia Bill".

6 DEATH ROOM BLUES (1933) from **The Definitive Blind Willie McTell**
"All my friends have forsake me, I haven't even got no home".

7 BROKE DOWN ENGINE BLUES (1931) from **The Definitive Blind Willie McTell**
McTell also recorded the song two years later in New York with Weaver and Buddy Moss, but this solo version is peer-less.

8 DYING CRAPSHOOTER'S BLUES (1940) from **The Complete Library Of Congress Recordings**
Gambling images and an unforgettable melody, recorded for the Lomaxes on a field trip to Atlanta.

9 OLD TIME RELIGION (1940) from **The Complete Library Of Congress Recordings**
One of McTell's most potent gospel sides, again recorded for John and Alan Lomax.

10 BLIND WILLIE MCTELL (1983) from **The Bootleg Series Vols 1–3** by BOB DYLAN
We just had to include this ultimate tribute.

⊙ **Complete Recorded Works Vol 1** Document
All Blind Willie McTell's early recordings from 1927–31, recorded for different labels under different names, and including such all-time classics as "Statesboro Blues" and "Broke down Engine Blues".

⊙ **Complete Library Of Congress Recordings** Document
The 1940 Lomax sessions in full. The interviews are almost as fascinating as the music, not least for the attitude of John Lomax – regarded as a liberal, but sounding distinctly racist.

⊙ **The Classic Years 1927–1940** JSP
A magnificent and comprehensive 4-disc box set that encompasses everything on the Document albums above plus much more, including the mid-1930s recordings McTell made with his wife.

⊙ **Atlanta Twelve String** Atlantic
The lost Atlantic tape from 1949, including remakes of "Broke Down Engine" and "Razor Blue" and the brilliant "Dying Crapshooter's Blues". To hear the prewar blues played in uncompromising fashion but recorded with the fidelity of modern equipment is a thrill indeed. For that reason it's many people's favorite McTell album.

⊙ **Last Session** OBC
Fifteen tracks that Blind Willie McTell recorded sitting on a high stool in the back of an Atlanta music store in 1956. Flawed yet fascinating – but not the place to start.

Lester Melrose

b Chicago, Dec14, 1891; d April, 1968

A key figure in recording the early bluesmen, **Lester Melrose** owned one of Chicago's first record stores with his brother Walter. He sold his share, however, when he met **Jelly Roll Morton** and became a record producer in 1923. Initially he was involved mostly with jazz, though one of his first blues recordings came with **Tampa Red** and **Georgia Tom** on "It's Tight Like That" for Vocalion in 1928.

During the 1930s, Melrose recorded most of the biggest names in Chicago, including **Big Bill Broonzy, Jazz Gillum,** Leroy Carr and Scrapper Blackwell, Sonny Boy "John Lee' Williamson, Memphis Minnie, Roosevelt Sykes, Lonnie Johnson, Big Joe Williams, Bukka White, Washboard Sam, Champion Jack Dupree, Big Boy Crudup, Victoria Spivey and Leroy Carr. He worked for most of

the main blues record companies simultaneously, including ARC, RCA Victor, Columbia and Okeh. He later calculated that between 1934 and 1951 he recorded "at least ninety percent of all rhythm and blues talent for RCA Victor and Columbia Records."

However, Melrose remains forever associated with **Bluebird**, which was created as a cheaper imprint of RCA Victor in January 1933. He became to Bluebird what Berry Gordy was to Motown or Sam Phillips to Sun. He decided who recorded, what they recorded, and how it was recorded, and especially favored small combos built around a tight coterie of musicians that included the likes of Tampa Red, Broonzy and Gillum. Although his recordings were acoustic, they were more city than country, and represent the first incarnation of a distinctive Chicago blues sound, known at the time as "the Bluebird beat". That his favored team all tended to play on each other's sessions added to the cohesiveness of the sound. With new additions like **Big Maceo**, Melrose continued to dominate Chicago blues until well into the 1940s when the new electric blues took over. The "Bluebird beat" was softer than the driving urban blues sound that superseded it, and tellingly held no place for the likes of Muddy Waters, who auditioned for Melrose but was rejected. Waters later dismissed Melrose's sound as "sweet jazz", though that didn't stop him recording an album of songs by Melrose's most significant artist, Big Bill Broonzy. In any case, the accusation wasn't entirely fair, as Melrose did also record such primitive and unadorned performers as **Bukka White**.

Many years later, Melrose recalled how he discovered his artists in an essay entitled "My Life In Recording", in a book edited by Chris Strachwitz and Pete Welding. "My record talent was obtained through just plain hard work," he wrote. "I used to visit clubs, taverns and booze joints in and around Chicago, also I used to travel all through the southern states in search of talent and sometimes I had very good luck. As I rule I had considerable trouble with plantation owners, as they were afraid I would be the cause of their help refusing to return." On one infamous occasion in 1939 when he was trying to sign **Tommy McClennan**, Melrose was run off a plantation and forced to leave his car behind. When his "talent" arrived from the Delta in Chicago, he paid Tampa Red to have them lodge in two rooms kept in his house specifically for the purpose.

As a white man, Melrose grew far richer from the blues than any of his artists, but in those different times, few ever seemed to have questioned the injustice. He regularly took songwriting credits and performance rights for himself, paying the artists only for the record session. Yet without him, the history of the Chicago blues would have been far poorer, and many of the great artists whose recordings are now legendary might never have entered a studio.

Memphis Jug Band

formed Memphis, Tennessee, in 1926 by Will Shade (b Memphis, Feb 5, 1898; d Sept 18, 1965)

Although the **Memphis Jug Band** was not the first such combo to emerge in the 1920s, it was easily the most historically important and popular group of the brief jug band craze, playing blues, rags, stomps, breakdowns, waltzes, vaudeville, hokum and minstrel songs and just about anything else its audience wanted to hear.

Formed by **Will Shade** (b Memphis, February 5, 1898; d September 18, 1965), who was sometimes known as Son Brimmer, after the grandmother who brought him up. The original line-up was basically a string band augmented by kazoo, washboard and jug. Key members included **Casey Bill Weldon** on guitar, **Ben Ramey** on kazoo, and **Charlie Polk** on jug but it was a loose and fluid combo and between 1926 and 1934, a host of other Memphis musicians played with them, including guitarist Charlie Burse, fiddlers Milton Robey and Charlie Pierce, vocalists Charlie Nickerson and Hattie Hart, pianist Jab Jones, guitarist Furry Lewis and mandolinist Vol Stevens.

The first jug bands probably came from Louisville, Kentucky, but the Memphis Jug Band were the brand leaders from the moment they first recorded for Victor Records in 1927. Over the next seven years, they recorded nearly sixty songs for Victor and then Columbia/Okeh in a freewheeling mix of styles delivered with a charm and humor that remains potent more than seventy years later. Among their best-known sides were "Stealin', Stealin'", "On The Road Again" (later covered by Canned Heat), and "K.C. Moan". They also

cut one session as the Picanninny Jug Band. After their last sides were recorded in 1934, the jug band style went into decline, but they continued playing around Memphis for several years to come. They also backed **Memphis Minnie**, who was married to Weldon for a time, and Shade's wife, Jenny Mae Clayton. Shade's career enjoyed a brief revival when he recorded with Burse and Cannon for the Folkways and Rounder labels in the early 1960s.

⊙ **The Best Of The Memphis Jug Band: Classic Recordings From The 1920s** Yazoo Twenty-three tracks which despite the title cover the years from 1928 until 1934. They include risqué songs about sex ("Memphis Yo Yo Blues") and drugs ("Cocaine Habit Blues"), plus such Memphis Jug Band classics as "On The Road Again", "K.C. Moan", "Memphis Shakedown", "He's In The Jailhouse Now", "Beale Street Mess Around" and "Insane Crazy Blues".

Memphis Minnie

b Algiers, Louisiana, June 3, 1897; d Aug 6, 1973

Memphis Minnie was the most important and successful female blues artist of her generation. She was also a fine guitar player; in fact, along with Rosetta Tharpe, she was one of the few women to shine on an instrument that at the time was regarded as essentially a male preserve.

Born Lizzie Douglas on a farm in Algiers, directly across the Mississippi River from the French Quarter of New Orleans, Minnie moved when she was seven to Walls in northern Mississippi. The following year she was given a guitar for her birthday. She swiftly became a child prodigy, playing local parties as "Kid" Douglas. By the age of thirteen, she had run away from home to play for tips on Beale Street in Memphis, and adopted the name by which she was known for the rest of her career. After touring the South with the Ringling Brothers circus, she was back in Memphis in the early 1920s, playing guitar with Willie Brown and in various jug bands. She lived at first with the guitarist **Casey Bill Weldon**, but subsequently married another musician, **Kansas Joe McCoy** – which is why she's sometimes listed as Memphis Minnie McCoy.

McCoy played guitar on Minnie's first recording session for Columbia Records in 1929, after a talent scout heard them playing together in a Beale Street barbershop and arranged for them to travel to the company's New York studios. That first session yielded a hit in "Bumble Bee" (later reworked by Muddy Waters as "Honey Bee"), and Minnie and McCoy remained musical partners for the next six years, forging a wonderful line in saucy backchat on numbers like "Can I Do It For You?" She also reprised "Bumble Bee" with the **Memphis Jug Band**, while **Bukka White** claimed that she sang back-up on his 1930 gospel recordings.

After Minnie and McCoy moved north to Chicago, she recorded prolifically and became a star of the Chicago club scene, hosting famous "Blue Monday" parties at Gatewood's Tavern. Tough and independent-minded, she cut a flamboyant figure, wearing bracelets made of silver dollars – an early form of bling, the effect of which on her Depression-era audience one can only imagine. Her break-up with Kansas Joe in 1935 has often been attributed to his jealousy that she was the more successful of the two, and the better guitarist. By 1939 she had married another guitarist, **Ernest Lawlars**, known as "Little Son Joe," with whom she recorded numerous sides for labels like Vocalion, Bluebird and Okeh. Among their most enduring recordings are "In My Girlish Days" and "Me And My Chauffeur Blues".

Minnie was a genuinely talented instrumentalist, In his autobiography, **Big Bill Broonzy** recalled her defeating both him and **Tampa Red** in a guitar contest, writing that she could "pick a guitar as good as any man" and "make a guitar cry, moan, talk and whistle the blues". In the mid-1930s she had already started augmenting the two-guitar format of her early recordings with piano, bass and occasionally trumpet, and in 1942, she became one of the first blues artists to take up the electric guitar. Adding a full rhythm section, she forged a bridge between the country blues and the electric urban blues for which Chicago would soon become famous.

The black writer **Langston Hughes**, who caught one of Minnie's performances around this time, memorably described the occasion in the *Chicago Defender*: "She beats out a good old steady down home rhythm on the strings – a rhythm so contagious that often it makes the crowd holler out loud. Then throughout the smoke and racket of the noisy Chicago bar float Louisiana bayous, muddy old swamps, Mississippi dust and sun, cotton fields, lonesome roads, train whistles in the night, mosquitoes at dawn and the Rural Free Delivery that never brings the right letter. All these things cry through the strings on Memphis Minnie's electric guitar."

During the late 1940s, Minnie ran a touring vaudeville company, and she lived briefly in Indianapolis and Detroit before returning to Chicago in the early 1950s. By then, the new sound emerging from Chess Records

A record company publicity photo of Memphis Minnie, 1930s

1 **BUMBLE BEE (1929)** from **The Essential Recordings Vol 1**
"He got the best old stinger any bumble bee that I ever seen".

2 **HOODOO LADY (1930)** from **Complete Recorded Works Vol 2**
"Boy, you better watch it 'cause she's tricky".

3 **DOWN IN THE ALLEY (1935)** from **Complete Recorded Works Vol 3**
"I met a man, asked me did I want to pally, yes, baby, let's go down in the alley".

4 **BUTCHER MAN (1933)** from **The Essential Recordings Vol 2**
"I'm going to tell everybody I've got the best butcher man in town, he can slice your ham, he can cut it from the fat on down".

5 **IN MY GIRLISH DAYS (1930)** from **The Essential Recordings Vol 1**
"Late hours at night, trying to play my hand, through my window, out stepped a man".

6 **MOANING THE BLUES (1934)** from **The Essential Recordings Vol 2**
"Oh, the blues got ways sometimes just like a natural man".

7 **GOOD GIRL BLUES (1930)** from **Complete Recorded Works Vol 3**
"I have been a good girl, going to church all of my days, but I'm going to learn to gamble so I can stay out late".

8 **ME AND MY CHAUFFEUR BLUES (1941)** from **The Essential Recordings Vol 1**
"I wants him to drive me, he drives so easy, I can't turn him down".

9 **WHEN THE LEVEE BREAKS (1929)** from **The Essential Recordings Vol 1**
"Oh cryin' won't help you, prayin' won't do no good, when the levee breaks".

10 **STINGING SNAKE BLUES (1934)** from **Complete Recorded Works Vol 4**
"I got a stinging snake, I love sometimes better than I do myself".

had rather overtaken her style, although she attempted to revive her popularity by recording a new version of "Me And My Chauffeur" for Chess in 1952. Not only changing musical tastes were against her; poor health prompted her to give up performing in 1958, whereupon she returned to Memphis. Shortly after Little Son Joe's death in 1961, she suffered a stroke that forced her to live most of the rest of her life in nursing homes. She died in 1973, aged 76.

⊙ **Bumble Bee** Indigo
A brilliant introduction to Memphis Minnie, starting with 1929's "When The Levee Breaks" and compiling her best sides through to 1941's "Me And My Chauffeur Blues".

⊙ **Memphis Minnie And Kansas Joe Vols 1–4** Document
These four separately available discs compile everything that Minnie recorded between 1929 and 1935.

⊙ **Hoodoo Lady** Columbia
Another worthwhile single-disc compilation, covering the years from 1933 until 1937.

Memphis Slim

b Memphis, Tennessee, Sept 3, 1915; d Feb 24, 1988

A prolific performer who combined his trademark thundering, barrelhouse, boogie-woogie piano with a more urbane and sophisticated vocal style, **Memphis Slim** effectively enjoyed two careers. The first saw him score a string of R&B hits in Chicago in 1950s. In the second, following a move to Paris in 1962, he became one of the most popular blues performers in Europe.

John "Peter" Chatman was the nephew of Sam and Bo Chatman of the **Mississippi Sheiks**. His early style was much influenced by **Roosevelt Sykes**, whose piano stool he took over at Beale Street's Midway Café in Memphis during the mid-1930s. He moved to Chicago at the end of the decade, and recorded his first sides in 1940 for Bluebird, including "Beer Drinking Woman" and "Diggin' My Potatoes", accompanied by **Washboard Sam**.

That same year, Slim became the regular pianist for **Big Bill Broonzy**, who encouraged him to be less imitative and to forge his own style. He left Broonzy in 1944 to form his own band, the seven-piece **House Rockers** featuring saxophonists Alex

Atkins and Ernest Cotton, and signed to Hy-Tone Records, who leased his recordings to King Records. He recorded "Lend Me Your Love" and "Rockin' The House" for Miracle in 1947, followed in 1948 by the R&B number one "Messin' Around (With The Blues)" and "Nobody Loves Me", which was later reworked by **B.B. King** as "Everyday I Have The Blues".

Slim cut the philosophical "Mother Earth" for Premium in 1951, and also recorded briefly for Chess and Mercury before signing to United Records in 1952. With Matt Murphy on guitar, he set about recording some of his finest sides, including "The Come Back" and "Sassy Mae". In 1959 he recorded the terrific *At The Gate Of Horn* album for Vee Jay, and followed it with prestigious appearances at New York's Carnegie Hall and the Newport Jazz Festival, before he relocated to Europe in 1962, styling himself " the ambassador of the blues". While he had fallen in love with the French capital while on tour with Willie Dixon, his distaste for the racism that was still rife back home was at least as important a factor in his decision. "I fought the shit a long time and then I got out of it," as he later explained.

Slim recorded and toured prolifically throughout the 1960s and 1970s, playing up to his self-appointed ambassadorial status by turning up to gigs in a Rolls Royce. He remained in Europe for the rest of his life and was given the honorific title Commandre d'Ordre des Artes et Lettres by the French government. Although many of the albums he recorded in Europe lacked the sharp focus of his earlier recordings, he recorded the potent *Together Again For The First Time* in 1985, a live album featuring his old friend Matt Murphy on guitar. It was not released until 1988, the year he died from kidney failure, aged 72.

⊙ **At The Gate Of Horn** Charly
Despite the misleading title – not only was it not recorded at Chicago's Gate Of Horn nightclub, it's not even a live album at all – this is a quite thrilling 1960 collection of re-recordings of Memphis Slim's greatest hits, backed by a stellar combo.

⊙ **The Folkways Years 1959–73** Smithsonian Folkways
Twenty-one fine tracks, featuring Memphis Slim solo as well as accompanied variously by Matt Murphy, Willie Dixon, Jazz Gillum and Pete Seeger, and complete with a 32-page booklet.

⊙ **Lonely Nights** Catfish
A compilation of tracks that Memphis Slim recorded in Paris between 1970 and 1976, with guests including Lowell Fulson and Carey Bell.

Amos Milburn

b Houston, Texas, April 1, 1923; d Jan 3, 1980

A magnificent purveyor of high-energy, rocking piano boogie during the immediate postwar era, **Amos Milburn** was a significant influence on such first-generation black rock'n'rollers as Fats Domino and Little Richard. But there was another side to his blues muse as well, for he also served up a potent side order in mellow, after-hours R&B ballads.

Milburn was born in Houston in 1923, and served in the US Navy, where he entertained his shipmates with imitations of Albert Ammons, Louis Jordan and Ivory Joe Hunter. He then signed to Eddie Mesner's Aladdin Records in 1946, and moved to the West Coast. Initial sides like "After Midnite" were mellow blues much in the style of Charles Brown, but his tumultuous boogie version of "Down The Road Apiece" was a pointer to what was to come. Calling his band the Aladdin Chicken Shakers, and teaming up with arranger and saxophonist **Maxwell Davis**, Milburn had by 1948 patented a full-tilt boogie style that was over the next few years to dominate the R&B charts. He kicked off a run of nineteen consecutive top ten R&B hits with "Chicken Shack Boogie", followed by the likes of "Hold Me Baby", "In The Middle Of The Night", "Empty Arms Blues" and "Real Pretty Mama Blues". Even better was to come in 1950, when Milburn added lyrics to an instrumental by Maxwell Davis called "Bristol Drive", and the song became "Bad Bad Whiskey". It went to number one, and the so-called "blues-in-a-bottle" song became his trademark; "Thinkin' and Drinkin'", "Let Me Go Home Whiskey", "One Scotch, One Bourbon, One Beer" and "Good Good Whiskey" followed in quick succession.

Even though he had been an influence on its birth, by the mid-1950s Milburn was rapidly being sidelined by the arrival of rock'n'roll. Although he revisited "Chicken Shack Boogie" on a blistering 1956 version that rocked even harder than his original recording, it seemed that nobody was paying much attention any more, and he left Aladdin in 1958. He briefly teamed up with Charles Brown for an album on Ace and even signed to Motown, which released the album *The Blues Boss* in 1963. He carried on playing clubs around Cleveland and Cincinatti until he retired to Houston on 1972. Johnny Otis brought him back to record an album for Blue Spectrum in the mid-1970s, but sadly the enfeebled Milburn had by then lost the capacity to play the piano following a series of strokes, and could only sing. He had a leg amputated in 1979 and died in early 1980 aged 56.

⊙ **The Best Of Amos Milburn – Down The Road Apiece** EMI
A brilliant double-album compilation of all Amos Milburn's Aladdin hits, including the classic booze songs.

⊙ **The Chicken Shack Boogie Man** Proper Records
Another fine and well-annotated collection, although it has to be said that all the Milburn compilations tend to replicate much of the same material.

J.D. Miller

b El Campo, Texas, 1923; d March 23, 1996

Like Lester Melrose, the name of the producer **Jay Miller** appears so regularly throughout this A-Z that he more than merits his own brief biography.

Miller initially started out as a musician, playing in country and Cajun bands around Lake Charles, Louisiana, during the late 1930s. After serving in World War II, he started to record Cajun artists like Lee Sonnier, Amidie Breaux, Doug Kerhsaw, Jimmie C. Newman and Nathan Abshire in southwest Louisiana in the late 1940s, on labels such as Feature, Fais Do-Do, Kajun and Cajun Classics. Working from his studios in Crowley, Louisiana – halfway between Lake Charles and Baton Rouge –he turned his attention to the blues by recording **Lightnin' Slim** in 1954. Over the next few years he built up a roster that included **Slim Harpo**, Lazy Lester and Silas Hogan, as well as white country acts such as Kitty Wells and Lefty Frizzell. While licensing many of his biggest acts to **Excello**, he also continued to release records on his own labels,

such as Zynn and Rocko. He died following quadruple bypass surgery in 1996.

Roy Milton

b Wynnewood, Oklahoma, July 21, 1907; d Sept 18, 1983

As drummer, singer and bandleader, **Roy Milton** followed the lead of Louis Jordan to become a significant and popular figure in the swinging world of postwar jump blues.

Milton's grandmother was a Chickasaw Indian, and young Roy was born and raised on an Oklahoma reservation before he moved to Tulsa. By the early 1930s, he was singing in the orchestra led by **Ernie Fields**. He moved to drums when the band's full-time drummer failed to show one night, having been arrested and thrown in jail. Some time around the mid-1930s, Milton moved to Los Angeles and formed a group called the **Solid Senders**, with whom he played local clubs throughout the war years. After releasing "Milton's Boogie" on his own label, he signed to the newlyformed Juke Box Records in 1945, and recorded "R.M. Blues", which became a major hit in 1946. With his original Solid Senders trio now expanded to a seven-piece that included saxophonists **Buddy Floyd** and **Jackie Kelso**, the singing bandleader followed with a string of potent R&B releases including "True Blues", "Camille's Boogie" (named after his pianist Camille Howard), "Red Light", "Sunny Side Of The Street", "Little Boy Blue", "Them There Eyes", "Thrill Me" and "My Blue Heaven".

By 1948 Juke Box had become Specialty Records. Milton and his Solid Senders scored further hits for the label with "Everything I Do Is Wrong", "Hop Skip And Jump" and "Information Blues" before Howard left to pursue a solo career. Milton then worked with different singers including Lil Greenwood and Mickey Champion, and won more chart success with "T-Town Twist" and "Gonna Leave You". His sales began to decline in the mid-1950s, and he left Specialty in 1955 for Dootone Records. Despite some terrific releases, including the instrumental "Succotash", the move failed to revive his career, and by the 1960s he was reduced to cutting remakes of his early hits such as "Red Light" and "Milton's Boogie". After a period out of the limelight, he toured with **Johnny Otis** and his Orchestra in the early 1970s, and resumed his recording career with albums for Kent and Otis's Blues Spectrum label. He also toured Europe, where he cut further albums for the French label Black & Blue, but his comeback was curtailed when he fell ill in 1982. He died the following year, aged 75.

⊙ **Roy Milton And His Solid Senders** Ace
A generous 25 jump blues sides that Roy Milton recorded between 1945 and 1955. Almost every one was a hit, from "Milton's Boogie" through to "T-Town Twist" via the magnificent "Hop Skip And Jump".

The Mississippi Sheiks

formed Jackson, Mississippi, c 1926

Named after Rudolph Valentino's movie *The Sheik*, the **Mississippi Sheiks** were a blues-playing string band, based around members of the Chatmon family, that blended blues, folk and country fiddle tunes.

The band formed in Jackson, the capital of Mississippi, in the mid-1920s, around a core personnel of guitarist **Walter Vinson** (sometimes spelt Vincson), who claimed he took up music because he "got tired of smellin' mule farts", and fiddler **Lonnie Chatmon**. The two were such close friends that for reasons best known to themselves, they called each other "Bruno", and everyone else "Doc". Regular additional members included **Bo Carter** (also known as Armenter Chatmon) and **Sam Chatmon**, who like Lonnie were the offspring of Ezell Chatmon, an uncle of Charley Patton, who had eleven sons by different "wives". On stage, the Sheiks' line-up could swell to a dozen strong, and it's said there were enough informal members that if they received two bookings for the same night, they would fulfill them both with different personnel.

Their first recording for Okeh in 1930 was "Sittin On Top Of The World", which was later recorded by Howlin' Wolf, Ray Charles and others. According to legend, Vinson started fooling around with the song one morning when playing on a street corner in Itta Bena, and by the time he'd finished writing it, he and Lonnie Chatmon had earned nineteen dollars in tips. The group's final recording came for the Bluebird label in 1935, but in the years between they cut more than seventy sides, toured throughout the South and appeared in both Chicago and New York. They also backed **Texas Alexander** on several sessions, and recorded further sides under other names such as the Mississippi Mud Steppers, the Down South Boys and the Carter Brothers. Unusually for the time, they were popular with both black and white audiences, due to the breadth of their repertoire, which ranged from waltzes and hokum songs full of outrageous double entendres to high-quality blues.

In the recording studio, the Sheiks tended to concentrate on blues. In addition to the much-covered "Sittin' On Top Of The World", their other memorable sides included "The World Is Going Wrong" and "I've Got Blood In My Eyes For You", both of which were covered by Bob Dylan on his 1993 album *World Gone Wrong*. In his liner notes, Dylan wrote a typically unconventional tribute: "A little known de facto group whom in their former glory must've been something to behold. Rebellion against routine seems to be their strong theme. All their songs are raw to the bone and are faultlessly made for the modern times (the new dark ages). Nothing effete about the Mississippi Sheiks."

Lonnie Chatmon did not live long after their final recordings in 1935, but Vinson recorded a few solo sides for Bluebird in Chicago in the 1940s, and even re-emerged to make further recordings under the Sheiks name in the 1960s, before his death in 1975.

⊙ **Stop And Listen** Yazoo
A wonderful collection of the Mississippi Sheiks' finest moments, from "Sittin' On Top Of The World" and "The World Is Going Wrong" to "Tell Me To Do Right" and "She's Crazy About Her Lovin'".

Little Brother Montgomery

b Kentwood, Louisiana, April 18, 1906; d Sept 6, 1985

The career of pianist **Little Brother Montgomery** straddled from the early country blues years to the electrified Chicago scene of the 1950s, and he was equally at home fronting blues bands and jazz groups.

Eurreal Wilford Montgomery was born across Lake Pontchartrain from the city of New Orleans, where he spent much of his childhood and where his father owned a honky-tonk. Growing up listening to pianists like **Jelly Roll Morton** at first hand, he was playing piano by the age of five, and copied everything he heard. By 1917 he'd stopped attending school, and had run away to perform in Louisiana's juke joints, lumber camps and barrelhouses. He played jazz in New Orleans with Clarence Desdunne and Buddy Petit, traveled with the guitarist **Big Joe Williams**, and by the late 1920s had landed in Chicago, where he played rent parties with the likes of **Blind Blake**.

Montgomery made his first recordings for Paramount in 1930, including "Vicksburg Blues" and "No Special Rider". He cut another eighteen sides for Bluebird in New Orleans in 1935 and 1936, although he spent much of the 1930s touring as leader of the Southland Troubadours jazz band. Around 1941 he settled in Chicago, where he lived for the rest of his life. Filling his busy diary with both blues and jazz engagements, he played with Kid Ory's Dixieland band at New York's Carnegie Hall in 1949, and appeared on Otis Rush and Magic Sam's first blues sides. He also played with **Buddy Guy**, when the guitarist accompanied him on "First Time I Met The Blues" for Chess in 1960.

That same year Montgomery made his first visit to Europe, and found a new audience. He recorded several blues albums during the 1960s for labels such as Bluesville, before setting up his own label in 1969, **FM**, which was named after his last initial and that of his second wife, Janet Floberg. Its first single release was a reprise of his classic "Vicksburg Blues", with a vocal by Jeanne Carroll. Despite his jazz leanings, Montgomery was one of the last of the classic barrelhouse pianists, and his recollections of his early years were a highlight of Giles Oakley's groundbreaking 1976 BBC TV series *The Devil's Music*. He continued working almost until his death in Chicago in 1985.

⊙ **1930–36** Document
Little Brother Montgomery's early Chicago sides as well as the more extensive Bluebird sessions in New Orleans half a dozen years later, totaling more than 25 tracks in one superb collection.

⊙ **Tasty Blues** OBC
A welcome reissue of an album that Little Brother Montgomery originally recorded for Prestige/Bluesville in 1960. Featuring bassist Julian Euell and guitarist Lafayette Thomas from Jimmy McCracklin's band, it includes strong versions of his seminal "Vicksburg Blues" and "No Special Rider".

⊙ **Goodbye Mr Blues** Delmark
These thirteen tracks, cut by Little Brother Montgomery with saxophonist Franz Jackson and the State Street Swingers in the 1940s, illustrate the jazz/blues crossover nature of his work, on such numbers as "South Rampart St. Parade", "Riverside Blues" and "Panama Rag".

⊙ **At Home** Earwig
Fourteen tracks recorded towards the end of his career, originally for his own label and showing what Montgomery sounded like when he was out to please no one but himself.

Whistlin' Alex Moore

b Dallas, Texas, Nov 22, 1899; d Jan 20, 1989

While his name might now make him sound like a mere novelty act, and he was certainly an eccentric, **Whistlin' Alex Moore** was also a masterful blues pianist whose career lasted half a century.

Born in the Freedmen's Town area of Dallas just weeks before the end of the nineteenth century, Alexander Herman Moore became the family breadwinner at an early age following the death of his father. While working to support his mother and two younger siblings, he learned first the harmonica and then the piano, asking to play at the houses of the white people to whom he delivered groceries. Having served in the US Army in World War I, he was by the 1920s peddling a unique style of piano that fused blues, ragtime and barrelhouse boogie at house parties and in bars around Dallas. It was around this time that he earned the nickname "Whistlin' Alex", on account of his unusual accompaniment to his piano playing.

In 1929, Moore cut half a dozen sides for Columbia in Chicago, and thereby became one of the first bluesmen to record. He recorded sporadically thereafter – for Decca in 1937, for the Dallas label Highway a decade later, and for RPM in 1951. But although he found plentiful night-time employment in supper clubs, dance lounges and a Dallas striptease bar called Pam's, he continued to work day jobs until he reached retirement age in 1965.

Moore benefited enormously from the folk-blues revival. He was rediscovered in 1960, when he was recorded by Chris Strachwitz and Paul Oliver for the Arhoolie label as well as for Oliver's

"Conversations With the Blues" project, performing again songs he'd recorded thirty years earlier such as "West Texas Woman" and "Blue Boomer Blues". On the sleeve of the Arhoolie album, Oliver wrote: "He is a true original, a folk blues singer who can sit at the piano and improvise endlessly piano themes and blues verses that are sometimes startling, sometimes comic, sometimes grim, and very often pure poetry."

Moore twice toured Europe with the American Folk Blues Festival, recording the album *Alex Moore In Europe* on the second occasion in 1969. A bachelor all his life, he explained his single status by declaring: "I always been married to my piano – my piano's my wife, my girlfriend, my lady, my bed." He made his final album for Rounder Records in 1988 and died aged 89 early the following year, suffering a heart attack as he was riding the bus home from a game of dominoes at the Martin Luther King Center in South Dallas.

⊙ **Complete Recorded Works 1929–51**
Document
Twenty-three tracks spanning 22 years hardly counts as prolific but there's some truly fine stuff here, including "Ice Pick Blues", "Blue Bloomer Blues" and a great two-part "Frankie And Johnny".

⊙ **From North Dallas To The East Side**
Arhoolie
Whistlin' Alex Moore recorded half these tracks in Dallas in 1960, while there's also a brace cut in Germany in 1968, and the rest date from 1947. All of which makes for an interesting contrast-and-compare exercise.

Gary Moore

b Belfast, Northern Ireland, April 4, 1952

One of a crop of highly talented Irish blues-rock guitarists that also included Rory Gallagher, **Gary Moore** made his name playing with rock bands **Skid Row** and **Thin Lizzy**. However, he didn't hit his peak until the early 1990s, with a series of solo albums that gave full rein to his power as a blues guitarist.

Seeing the likes of Jimi Hendrix, Fleetwood Mac and John Mayall's Bluesbreakers play in Belfast during the late 1960s gave Moore his first exposure to the blues. He then moved to Dublin, where he formed Skid Row, a power trio who signed to the

CBS label in 1970. After three albums, he embarked briefly on a solo career, then joined his friend Phil Lynott in Thin Lizzy.

By 1979 Moore was solo again, and enjoyed a top ten hit with the evocative "Parisienne Walkways", on which his tasteful, blues-soaked lead guitar was complemented by a Phil Lynott guest vocal. The subsequent album *Back On The Streets* was similarly well received. He explored his Celtic roots on *Wild Frontier* in 1987, but it was 1990's *Still Got The Blues* that announced a new-found musical maturity. The follow-up *After Hours* featured cameo appearances from blues greats Albert King, B.B. King and Albert Collins. That was followed by an album with Ginger Baker and Jack Bruce in the band BBM. Next, in 1995, came the excellent *Blues For Greeny*, an album of songs written by Peter Green and played on Green's old Gibson Les Paul, which the guitarist had gifted him many years earlier.

Back To The Blues came in 2001, recorded more or less live in the studio and mixing Moore originals with gritty covers of standards like "Stormy Monday". After a couple of experimental rock albums, he returned to his love of the blues yet again on 2004's *Power Of The Blues*. His rock-inflected style is not to everyone's taste, but that his love of the blues is genuine and deep-seated is indisputable.

⊙ **Still Got The Blues** Virgin
The 1990 album that marked Gary Moore's emergence as a blues guitarist of maturity and stature – and gave him the biggest seller of his career.

⊙ **Blues For Greeny** Virgin
On this 1995 release, Gary Moore used a set of Peter Green's compositions for Fleetwood Mac as a springboard for some blues guitar soloing of ferocious intensity.

⊙ **Best Of The Blues** Sanctuary
A double album compiling Gary Moore's more blues-oriented work, both live and in the studio, and featuring guest appearances by Albert King, B.B. King and Albert Collins.

Van Morrison

b Belfast, Northern Ireland, Aug 31, 1945

Among the most versatile and accomplished voices in contemporary music, **Van Morrison** might well on a typical album include elements of rock, pop, jazz, country and traditional Celtic music, but you can rest assured that blues and R&B will be in there serving as the foundation stones. Indeed, there are those who will tell you that Morrison is quite simply the finest white blues and R&B singer in the world today.

George Ivan Morrison grew up listening to his father's trad jazz records, but he really discovered the blues via the mid-1950s skiffle craze, with its covers of songs by the likes of Leadbelly. From there, he traced the music back to its roots, and a lifelong love affair began.

He learned to play guitar, saxophone and harmonica, and discovered an extraordinary voice which was perhaps only rivaled by Steve Winwood among British vocalists. After cutting his teeth in skiffle and Irish show bands he formed **Them**, a white R&B outfit in the style of such contemporaries as the Yardbirds, the Animals and the Rolling Stones, but with a grit and menace that few could match. Influenced by Ray Charles, Bobby Bland and the R&B shouters, Morrison was initially something of a blues purist. "Blues was my calling card," he said in 2005. "People tend to forget that I was discovered as a blues singer. It was nothing to do with rock music. To start with Them was a blues thing. When it stopped being that it started to go all wrong." Them enjoyed several pop hits, including a storming version of Big Joe Williams's "Baby Please Don't Go", "Here Comes The Night" and "Gloria", while Morrison's R&B roots were in evidence on such album tracks as "I Put A Spell On You", which boasted perhaps his finest early vocal performance.

By 1967, the group had split and Morrison had embarked on a solo career. Initially marketed as a romantic singer-songwriter he made the magical, flowing *Astral Weeks* in 1968, but then set off in a more R&B oriented direction. *Moondance* in 1968 straddled both camps, but his third album, 1970's *His Band And The Street Choir*, was a tough, R&B-tinged record of wonderful and original compositions. Around the same time he also formed the Caledonia Soul Orchestra, with whom he recorded one of the all-time great live albums, in 1974's *It's Too Late To Stop Now*. He then embarked on a musical journey of thrilling unpredictability, teaming up with Dr. John on 1977's *A Period Of Transition*, and embarking during the 1980s on a series of semi-mystical albums that explored the nature of transcendence, with titles such as *Inarticulate Speech Of The Heart* and *A Sense Of Wonder*.

Yet Morrison's blues were merely in abeyance, and they came to the fore again when he guested on the 1991 **John Lee Hooker** album *The Healer*. Six years later he produced an entire album for Hooker, with *Don't Look Back*. In the mid-1990s he dubbed his touring band Van Morrison's Soul and R&B Review, thereby symbolizing his return to the roots of the music that had first inspired him. A live album from this period, 1994's *A Night In San Francisco*, included guest appearances by Hooker and Junior Wells. 1996's *How Long Has This Been Going On* was a more jazz-inclined set, with sidemen including Georgie Fame and former James Brown saxophonist Pee Wee Ellis. The same year he recorded *Tell Me Something – The Songs Of Mose Allison*, an album that also featured contributions from Georgie Fame, Ben Sidran and Allison himself.

While recent albums have mixed many different styles, all have included healthy doses of blues and R&B. Highlights include 1999's *Back On Top*, 2002's under-rated *Down The Road* (the cover of which featured a picture of a record shop window displaying old vinyl LPs by many of Morrison's favorite blues and R&B artists), and 2005's *Magic Time*. He also sang duets on **Ray Charles**'s *Genius Loves Company* in 2003 and with **B.B. King** on his eightieth birthday album in 2005, and contributed songs to a brace of comeback albums by **Solomon Burke**. "I feel I'm part of a lineage that goes back to John Lee Hooker and Leadbelly and it's my duty to carry that lineage on," Morrison told this writer shortly before his sixtieth birthday in the summer of 2005. Long may he continue.

⊙ **The Story Of Them Featuring Van Morrison** Polydor
An amazingly consistent double album that compiles fifty glorious tracks, including the hits, Bob Dylan covers, "I Put A Spell On You" and blues covers such as "Stormy Monday", "Turn On Your Love Light" and "I Got A Woman".

⊙ **His Band And The Street Choir** Warners
Some Van Morrison fans were disappointed with this 1970 album, which followed in the wake of *Astral Weeks* and *Moondance*, because it was less singer-songwriter based and more R&B oriented – but that's exactly why we recommend it here.

⊙ **It's Too Late To Stop Now** Polydor
This outstanding 1974 live album features Van Morrison's Caledonia Soul Orchestra at their peak, on a set that includes great versions of several Van originals as well as potent covers of "I Believe To My Soul", Sonny Boy

Williamson's "Help Me" and "Take Your Hands Out Of My Pocket", "I Just Want To Make Love To You" and "Bring It On Home To Me".

⊙ **A Night In San Francisco** Polydor
No excuses are necessary for including a second in-concert album here, for Van Morrison is one of the world's great performers and his live sets tend to include more blues than his studio albums. Recorded in 1993, with guests including John Lee Hooker and Junior Wells.

⊙ **The Healing Game** Polydor
Really a joint album, recorded by Morrison and John Lee Hooker in 1997 and pure class all the way.

⊙ **Down The Road** Polydor
As with all Van Morrison's later albums, a vast array of styles is represented on this 2002 album. But the blues and R&B grooves are powerful, and he's singing better than ever.

Buddy Moss

b Jewel, Georgia, Jan 26, 1914; d Oct 19, 1984

Despite being overshadowed by more illustrious contemporaries during the 1930s, Buddy Moss was a guitarist of rare skill. A major figure in the rich history of the Piedmont blues, he was also a significant influence on **Blind Boy Fuller**.

The year of Eugene Moss's birth was for a long time given as 1906, but 1914 is now the widely accepted date. What's certain is that he was born one of the twelve children of sharecroppers, midway between Atlanta and Augusta in rural Georgia. His first instrument was the harmonica, and after the family moved to Augusta, he began playing at house parties and busking on the streets of Atlanta before he was in his teens. There he met **Curley Weaver** and **Barbecue Bob**, with whom he made his first recordings, as the **Georgia Cotton Pickers**, for Columbia in Atlanta in late 1930. Moss added harmonica to four sides, including "I'm On My Way Down Home" and "Diddle-Da-Diddle". Thanks to instruction from both Weaver and Barbecue Bob, he also swiftly became proficient on the guitar. When Bob died of pneumonia in 1931, Moss hooked up with **Blind Willie McTell** to performed as a duo at house parties and juke joints around Atlanta.

Moss's first solo recordings appeared in 1933, after he traveled to New York with Fred McMullen

and Curley Weaver for a four-day session for ARC, during which all three cut sides. Moss contributed eleven songs, including "Bye Bye Mama", "Daddy Don't Care" and "Red River Blues", which illustrated what a fine guitarist he had become, in a style influenced by both Barbecue Bob and Blind Blake. During the same sessions he also played harmonica on six sides recorded as the **Georgia Browns**, a group comprising Moss, Weaver, McMullen and the singer Ruth Willis. He returned to New York later in 1933 with Weaver and Blind Willie McTell, cutting another dozen tracks and accompanying both Weaver and McTell on their own recordings.

Another session in New York in 1934 produced "Some Lonesome Day" and "Dough Rollin' Papa" among other tunes. The following year he cut fifteen more sides, including "My Baby Won't Pay Me No Mind", with a new partner, **Josh White**, when he worked under the name "The Singing Christian". His career came to an abrupt halt later in 1935, when he was arrested for the murder of his wife and sentenced to a long prison term. However, he was paroled in 1941 on account of his good behavior and the testimony of James Baxter Long, Blind Boy Fuller's manager, who vouched for his future conduct. Moss moved to Elon College, North Carolina, where he lived in Long's home, working in the fields during the week and in Long's store on the weekends. Long also arranged for him to travel to New York to record for Okeh/Columbia with **Sonny Terry** and **Brownie McGhee**. Yet these were to prove his last recordings for a quarter of a century. For various reasons, not least the wartime ban on the use of shellac for 78rpm discs, he fell into obscurity. Although he continued to perform locally, he was forced to earn a living, working on a tobacco farm, as a truck driver and even as an elevator operator.

Moss's fortunes finally changed in 1964, when he saw his old partner Josh White perform in Atlanta. White introduced him to a blues promoter, who offered him the chance to perform again. A 1966 concert in Washington, D C, was recorded and later released on the Biograph label, and the same year he also played the Newport Folk Festival. He made other festival appearances throughout the 1970s and died in Atlanta in 1984 at the age of seventy.

⊙ **Complete Recordings Vols 1–3** Document
Everything Buddy Moss recorded solo and as an accompanist from 1930 until 1941, spread over three chronologically arranged discs.

⊙ **Atlanta Blues Legend** Biograph
Eleven songs that Biddy Moss recorded live on June 10, 1966, in Washington, D C, fleshed out on the CD reissue with another seven live tracks recorded elsewhere. Tracks include "Oh Lawdy Mama" and his covers of "Sitting On Top Of The World" and "Key To The Highway" (oddly called "I've Got To Keep To The Highway" on the sleeve).

Matt "Guitar" Murphy

b Sunflower, Mississippi, Dec 27, 1929

Best known for his appearance in the 1980 hit movie *The Blues Brothers*, **Matt "Guitar" Murphy** had by then been an ace blues guitarist for more than thirty years. He played with everyone from **Howlin' Wolf** to **Memphis Slim**, with whom he cut numerous sides of consistently high quality during the 1950s.

Murphy's family moved north from Mississippi to Memphis when he was a boy, and he learned to play blues guitar from an aunt's collection of 78s. By the time he was 21, he had backed Howlin' Wolf and played on early sides by Bobby Bland and Junior Parker (although not his "Mystery Train", which featured Murphy's brother **Floyd** instead). In 1952, he left Memphis for Chicago, to join Memphis Slim's House Rockers.

Murphy's jazzy blues licks can be heard on most of the recordings Slim subsequently made before he moved to Europe in 1962. After that, Murphy played sessions at Chess Records with Chuck Berry, Otis Rush, Sonny Boy Williamson and Etta James among others, and visited Europe with the American Folk Blues Festival in 1963. That tour also included Slim, Sonny Boy Williamson, Muddy Waters, Lonnie Johnson, Big Joe Williams, Victoria Spivey and Willie Dixon. Despite the heavyweight billing, his solo spot on "Matt's Guitar Boogie" still managed to be a nightly highlight of the show, and he also busied himself recording with Sonny Boy "Rice Miller" Williamson in Denmark during the trip.

For some reason Murphy then slipped back into obscurity for much of the rest of the 1960s, while he spent most of the 1970s playing with harpist **James Cotton**. Then in 1977 he was approached by John Belushi and Dan Akroyd, who cast him in *The Blues Brothers* as Aretha Franklin's guitarist husband. He also toured with the Blues Brothers Band and used his raised profile to form his own band in 1982. Forty years on from his first recordings with Bobby Bland and Junior Parker, he finally made his debut solo album in 1990 on Antone's, with brother Floyd on second guitar. Further albums followed on the Roesch label, including *The Blues Don't Bother Me* in 1996 and *Lucky Charm* in 2001.

⊙ **Way Down South** Texas Music Group
Matt "Guitar" Murphy's first solo album, recorded at the age of 61 in 1990, is bursting with tasty guitar licks, and brother Floyd lends sterling support.

Charlie Musselwhite

b Kosciusko, Mississippi, Jan 31, 1944

Probably the greatest white harmonica player of them all, **Charlie Musselwhite** has played and sung the blues for more than forty years, with a potent Delta authenticity married to a more contemporary rock'n'roll energy.

Born in the hill country of Mississippi, Musselwhite moved to Memphis with his family as a child. He arrived at just the right time; the city's music scene was exploding with the influences, both black and white, that were about to give birth to rock'n'roll. Musselwhite was friends at school with Johnny Cash's younger brother. He soon learned to play both harp and guitar, befriending such Memphis bluesmen as **Furry Lewis** and **Will Shade**, once of the Memphis Jug Band, from whom he absorbed as much blues lore as he could. Before long he was also making an illicit living running moonshine whiskey in the trunk of his Lincoln. In 1962, aged eighteen, he migrated north to Chicago and found an apartment in the basement of Delmark Records, where his roommate **Big Joe Williams** introduced him to such blues giants as Muddy Waters, Howlin' Wolf, John Lee Hooker and Big Walter Horton. The latter took Musselwhite under his wing and helped him hone his skills, and he made his recording debut with Horton on Vanguard's *Chicago! The Blues! Today!* series. Hooker also became a close personal friend, and some years later was best man at Musselwhite's wedding.

After several years sitting in with other bands, he formed his own combo in 1966, and his recorded debut as a bandleader followed with the 1967 Vanguard album *Stand Back! Here Comes Charlie*

The ace of harps: Charlie Musselwhite

RUF RECORDS

Germany in the 1980s, and another live set at the Cambridge folk festival for Mike Vernon's Blue Horizon label.

Following a personal battle with alcoholism, Musselwhite signed to Alligator in 1990 to stage a major comeback. His label debut, *Ace Of Harps*, found his fierce harmonica playing complemented with horns and jazz chording. Further Alligator albums featured guest appearances by John Lee Hooker and the Blind Boys Of Alabama. Particularly impressive was 1994's *In My Time*, released to mark his fiftieth birthday and conceived as a chronicle of his own musical history.

After leaving Alligator, he continued to tour and record prolifically. He turned up somewhat surprisingly on Peter Gabriel's global beat label, Real World, in 2004, with the album *Sanctuary*, which offered guest appearances by Ben Harper and his old friends the Blind Boys of Alabama. His harp playing is also much in demand for sessions, and he has played on albums by Bonnie Raitt, Tom Waits and even INXS among countless others.

⊙ **Stand Back! Here Comes Charlie Musselwhite's South Side Band** Vanguard
Musselwhite's 1967 debut as a bandleader featured the 21-year-old Harvey Mandel on guitar. File alongside the early Butterfield Blues Band albums as an example of white Chicago blues.

⊙ **Best Of The Vanguard Years** Vanguard
20-track compilation of the best tracks from the half-dozen albums Musselwhite's cut for Vanguard during the 1960s.

⊙ **The Ace Of Harps** Alligator
Charlie Musselwhite's 1990 comeback album dishes up plenty of raw blues with added touches of rock and funk, horns and jazz chording. Standouts include the acoustic "My Road Lies In Darkness", the blues boogie of "River Hip Mama" and the nine-minute tour-de-force "She May Be Your Woman".

⊙ **Deluxe Edition** Alligator
The highlights of Musselwhite's 1990s' albums for Alligator, collected on a single disc and with a terrific bonus track of an early-1960s home recording with his mentor, Memphis Jug Band man Will Shade.

Musselwhite's South Side Band. Its success enabled him to tour outside Chicago, and when he arrived in California, he decided to stay and immerse himself in the San Francisco music scene. His fusion of Memphis and Chicago-style blues and rock'n'roll energy made a firm favorite with rock audiences there, and a succession of fine guitar players, including **Harvey Mandel**, **Luther Tucker** and **Fenton Robinson**, passed through his bands. During the 1970s Musselwhite recorded a brace of albums for Arhoolie as well as an instructional harp record for Stefan Grossman's Kicking Mule label. By now a popular figure on the European festival circuit, he cut an album in

N-O

Tracy Nelson

b Madison, Wisconsin, Dec 27, 1944

Tracy Nelson has never been one to respect musical boundaries, and over her long career has sung folk, rock and country. Like Bonnie Raitt, however, her powerful voice has always sounded at its best when she's singing the blues.

As a teenager, Nelson immersed herself not in pop music but in the R&B beamed into her bedroom from the Nashville radio station WLAC. While studying at the University of Wisconsin, she caught the folk bug and began singing folk and blues at local coffee houses, and in a band called The Fabulous Imitations. She recorded her first album *Deep Are The Roots* for Prestige in Chicago in 1964. Produced by Sam Charters, it also featured harp-player **Charlie Musselwhite**, who showed her around Chicago's South Side and introduced her to Muddy Waters, Howlin' Wolf, Otis Spann and others.

Nelson moved to San Francisco in 1966, where the new psychedelic movement was taking shape, and formed **Mother Earth**. Taking its name from Memphis Slim's song, the band was a favorite at the Fillmore, regularly sharing the bill with the likes of Janis Joplin, the Grateful Dead and Jimi Hendrix. Their 1968 debut album was memorable for Nelson's composition "Down So Low", which became her signature song and was later covered by Etta James, Linda Ronstadt and Maria Muldaur among others. The second Mother Earth album, *Make A Joyful Noise*, was recorded in Nashville in 1969 as was the follow-up *Mother Earth Presents Tracy Nelson Country*. Produced by Elvis Presley's original Sun-era guitarist **Scotty Moore**, it included a fine version of Arthur "Big Boy" Crudup's "That's All Right Mama". As her website suggests,

the track could serve as a cipher for her career: "A blues song, made famous by a rock'n'roller, recorded on a country album by a folkie turned Fillmore goddess, produced by a rockabilly cat."

She launched her solo career in 1974 with an album that included her version of "It Takes A Lot To Laugh, It Takes A Train To Cry" (ranked by the *Rough Guide To Bob Dylan* among the best ten Dylan covers of all time), but from 1980 onwards she took an extended break from recording. She returned to the studio for Rounder in 1993 with *In The Here And Now*, her first straight blues record since her debut. She has followed it with several more albums of powerful blues-rock, as well as a collaboration with Marcia Ball and Irma Thomas on the 1998 album *Sing It!*

⊙ **In The Here And Now** Rounder
This 1993 album was Tracy Nelson's first release in thirteen years. Her powerful voice delivered songs such as Elmore James's "It Hurts Me Too", Percy Mayfield's "Please Send Me Someone To Love" and Willie Dixon's "Whatever I Am" with sassy bravura.

⊙ *Tracy Nelson, Marcia Ball and Irma Thomas* **Sing It** Rounder
Ball and Thomas make sterling contributions to this tripartite album by three great, gutsy, blues vocalists – but it's when Nelson sashays up to the microphone that the roof really gets blown off.

Robert Nighthawk

b Helena, Arkansas, Nov 30, 1909; d Nov 5, 1967

A slide guitarist with a fine fluid style and a strikingly mournful voice, **Robert Nighthawk** was the epitome of the itinerant bluesman. Spending much of his life rambling all over the South, he never seemed able to stay anywhere for very long, and as a result his recording sessions were sporadic. Even so, he was a major figure who was a powerful influence on the generation of great bluesmen who followed.

Robert Lee McCollum learned to play harmonica in 1924. Despite getting married in 1928 and having two children, he wasn't about to quit his rambling ways; one of his sons, Sam Carr, later claimed he was seven years old before he saw his father. He then didn't see him for another four years, although by 1944 he was playing bass in his father's band.

Some time around 1931, Nighthawk learned guitar from **Houston Stackhouse**, who may or may not have been his cousin but taught him a bunch of Tommy Johnson songs. The two men worked on a farm during the day and played together at dances and parties by night. By 1932, they had gone their separate ways as Nighthawk took to rambling further afield. On his travels he met Charley Patton, Will Shade, Jimmie Rodgers, Tommy Johnson, Son House and Robert Johnson, and **Muddy Waters** became a particular friend. Nighthawk provided the music at Muddy's first wedding in 1932, when the dancing and partying apparently got so frantic that the floor of his shack collapsed.

During those days Nighthawk also spent time in Memphis, where he met Sleepy John Estes, Yank Rachell, Memphis Slim, Big Bill Broonzy, Sonny Boy Williamson, Big Joe Williams and a young John Lee Hooker. Trouble with the law ("somethin' about a pistol", Stackhouse later recalled, although the darker truth appears to involve Nighthawk in a fatal shooting) caused his name to change to Robert Lee McCoy. Hightailing it to St Louis in 1935, he hooked up with Sonny Boy Williamson, Big Joe Williams and pianist Walter Davis. He made his first recordings for Bluebird in 1937, and cut 21 sides for the label in Chicago between 1937 and 1940, as well as four more for Decca and countless sessions backing Sonny Boy Williamson, Big Joe Williams, Sleepy John Estes and others. Among the names he recorded under were Robert Lee McCoy, Rambling Bob and Peetie's Boy, a reference to **Peetie Wheatstraw**, with whom he recorded and played around St Louis.

Nighthawk eventually moved to Chicago in 1940, doing sessions and playing around town. He even ran a record store from the basement of his brother's house, but he disappeared so regularly back to the Delta that nobody ever quite knew when he was going to be around. In the early 1940s he was back in Helena, Arkansas. It was around this time that he started to use the name Robert Nighthawk, taken from his 1937 side "Prowling Night Hawk". One of the first musicians to amplify his guitar, he also began to play slide, modeling his technique on **Tampa Red**, with whom he had often stayed in Chicago, and Eugene Powell (aka Sonny Boy Nelson).

In 1942, Nighthawk got himself a regular spot on KFFA radio in Helena, advertising Bright Star Flour, backed by guitarist Joe Willie Wilkins or Pinetop Perkins on piano, in competition with Sonny Boy Williamson's better-remembered *King Biscuit Hour*. Other regulars in Nighthawk's bands during the 1940s included **Earl Hooker** and a young **Ike Turner** on piano. However, such was Nighthawk's unpredictability that his band members would often wake up in the morning believing they were playing a gig that night, only to find the bandleader had taken off somewhere.

Nighthawk also broadcast on WROX out of Clarksdale on his trips down to the Delta, and married one of his several (and often simultaneous) wives there in 1947. In Clarksdale he played with **Dr. Ross**, his old friend **Houston Stackhouse**, and a singer called Ethel Mae. He cut several sides with Ethel Mae when he moved back up to Chicago and began recording for Aristocrat (soon to become Chess Records), on the recommendation of his Muddy Waters. Typically, his stay with Chess was a brief one, but it was long enough to lay down at least one all-time classic, in the shape of "Sweet Black Angel"/"Annie Lee", among the very first productions by **Willie Dixon**. He later recorded for United, but between returning to the South in 1952 and returning to Chicago in 1964 he spent no time in the studio.

During those years Nighthawk lived variously in Helena and the Mississippi towns of Friar's Point and Dundee, and played with a band that included his son Sam Carr and harmonica player Frank Frost. Jack Johnson joined the line-up on guitar in 1962, and they began performing as The Nighthawks. Back in Chicago a couple of years later, Nighthawk recorded for Chess, Decca and Testament and was even recorded live on Maxwell Street. Particularly memorable from this era are "Sorry My Angel" and "Someday", cut with a backing band that included **Buddy Guy** and **Walter "Shakey" Horton**. There is also some terrific footage of him playing in a Chicago club during this period.

Once again, however, Nighthawk didn't stay in Chicago long. Within a year or two, he was back in Helena. In 1967, after cutting his last sides playing in Houston Stackhouse's combo, he died of congestive heart failure.

⊙ **Robert Nighthawk: Prowling With The Nighthawk** (Document)
Twenty-six powerful sides that Nighthawk cut between 1937 and 1952 for the Bluebird, Decca, Aristocrat and United labels.

The Nighthawks

formed Washington, DC, 1972

With their energetic mix of blues, rock, soul, rockabilly and swing, the **Nighthawks** have been an institution on the live blues circuit for three decades and more, and earned themselves a reputation as one of the hardest working white blues bands around.

Founded by vocalist/harmonica player **Mark Wenner** and guitarist **Jimmy Thackery** in 1972, with Jan Zukowski on bass and Pete Ragusa on drums, they cut their teeth as the opening act or backing band for the likes of Muddy Waters, Otis Rush, Big Walter Horton and Elvin Bishop, and touring with Pinetop Perkins, John Hammond, Charlie Musselwhite and John Lee Hooker.

Though their early years saw them clock up an average of three hundred gigs per year, they also found time to cut some solidly workmanlike albums. *Open All Night* in 1976 portrayed them as Chicago blues traditionalists, while *Jacks And Kings*, three years later, included more original material as well guest appearances by Pinetop Perkins and Bob Margolin.

Thackery left the band in 1987 to pursue a solo career, but he proved hard to replace. During the late 1980s and early 1990s, the Nighthawks went through multiple line-up changes with the coming and going of Jimmy Hall on vocals/sax/harp, Mike Cowan on keyboards, Danny Morris on guitar/vocals and guitarist Jimmy Nalls. Pete Kanara's arrival on guitar in 1995 restored some stability, and he was still there a decade later alongside the other three founding members. This line-up has recorded such albums as 1996's *Pain & Paradise*, 1999's *Still Wild* and 2002's concert album *Live Tonight*. In recent years they say they have "cut down" on their touring schedule, although that term is relative, for they're still playing around two hundred dates a year.

⊙ **Ten Years Live** Varrick
A live tenth anniversary set released in 1983, featuring the Nighthawks' definitive storming bar-room blues.

⊙ **Open All Night** Genes
This 1976 album provides a decent representation of what the Nighthawks do best, including stirring covers of such blues standards as "Shake Your Money Maker", "Big Boss Man" and "Little By Little".

St Louis Jimmy Oden

b Nashville, Tennessee, June 26, 1903; d Dec 20, 1977

"Goin' Down Slow" has to be one of the most recorded of all blues songs, covered by such giants as Howlin' Wolf and B.B. King as well as by a host of white blues-rock bands. Even if everyone knows the song, however, far fewer know anything about its composer **St Louis Jimmy Oden**, who began recording in the 1930s and was still at in the 1960s.

James Burke Oden taught himself to play the piano as a child. Orphaned at the age of eight, he moved in 1917 to St Louis, where he worked in a barbershop and developed his skills as a blues singer. The first bluesman to befriend him and recognize his youthful talent was **Big Joe Williams**, but he made his first recordings with the pianist **Roosevelt Sykes** in Chicago in 1932. He moved there permanently the following year, and immediately earned the name St Louis Jimmy, although he was also known as Big Bloke, Poor Boy and Old Man Oden. He remained a fixture on the blues scene in the Windy City for the next forty years, recording prolifically. His most famous session came in 1941, when he cut "Goin' Down Slow" for Bluebird Records. Oden recorded a vast number of different versions of his best-known composition over the years, which despite its unappetizing subject matter ranks as one of the most enduring blues standards, covered by everyone from Howlin' Wolf to Eric Clapton, via B.B.King and the Allman Brothers. When Oden wrote, "I've had my fun if I never get well no more, all of my health is failing; Lord, I'm going down slow", he was talking about the debilitating effects of syphilis. Further sessions followed for Columbia, Bullet, Miracle and Aristocrat, for whom he cut "Florida Hurricane" in 1948 accompanied by pianist Sunnyland Slim and a young guitarist named **Muddy Waters**. The latter also cut versions of several Oden songs, including "Soon Forgotten" and "Take The Bitter With The Sweet". In later years Oden lived for a while in the basement of Waters' house, allegedly paying the rent by giving his friend a song or two.

Even after Oden entered a partnership with Joe Brown to form JOB Records in 1949, he continued to record for other labels. During the 1950s, he cut singles for Duke, with his old friend Roosevelt Sykes on piano, and remade "Goin' Down Slow" for Parrot in 1955. After a serious car crash in 1957, he decided to concentrate on writing rather than his own recording career, and penned songs for Little Walter, Otis Spann and others. However, in 1960 he was persuaded to record his debut album for Prestige's Bluesville subsidiary, backed by guitarist Jimmie Lee Robinson, pianist Robert Banks and a rocking New Orleans rhythm section. The ten original compositions, of course, included yet another version of "Goin' Down Slow". In the years before his death in Chicago, in 1977, he also recorded further sessions with Robert Lockwood and Otis Spann.

⊙ **Complete Works Vols One 1932–44**
Document
Twenty-five early tracks including the first of at least eight versions of "Goin' Down Slow" that St Louis Jimmy Oden cut in his long career.

⊙ **Complete Works Vol Two 1944–56**
Document
These two dozen Oden tracks include sides with Muddy Waters and Sunnyland Slim, as well as a couple more versions of "Goin' Down Slow".

Odetta

b Birmingham, Alabama, Dec 31, 1930

The voice of **Odetta** comes from the place where folk and blues meet, and it's pointless to argue about whether she belongs to one genre or the other. Like Leadbelly, whose songs she has spent a lifetime singing, she renders the distinction almost irrelevant.

Odetta Holmes Felicious Gorden didn't grow up singing folk or blues. Her first musical experiences were in church, while after the family had moved to Los Angeles in the mid-1930s, she received a classical training. In 1949 she landed a theatrical role in the LA production of *Finian's Rainbow*, while performing which she heard the blues harmonica of Sonny Terry. The following year she appeared in *Guys And Dolls* in San Francisco, and started to hang out with the city's folk music crowd, which centered on the Bohemian enclave of North Beach. As she launched on a new path as a folk-blues singer, accompanying herself on guitar, her early mentors included Paul Robeson, Pete Seeger and Harry Belafonte. In 1953, she traveled east to appear at New York's Blue Angel

club. On her debut album, *The Tin Angel*, which was released the following year, her voice betrayed her classical training, but its operatic tendencies lent a new and unusual emotional power to her folk-blues repertoire.

By the time Joan Baez and **Bob Dylan** appeared on the scene, Odetta was already a star of the burgeoning folk revival. Some time around 1959 or 1960, well before he arrived in Greenwich Village, Dylan heard one of her albums on the Tradition label – it must have been either *Odetta Sings Ballads And Blues* or *Odetta At The Gate Of Horn*. Many years later, he recalled the eureka moment in his autobiography: "Odetta was great. She was a deep singer, powerful strumming and a hammering-on style of playing. I learned almost every song on the record right there and then, even borrowing the hammering-on style." Although she was only in her thirties, Odetta was the grand dame of the folk revival. She was certainly one of its most prolific performers, releasing sixteen albums during the 1960s alone. These included a live set recorded at Carnegie Hall, 1962's *Odetta And The Blues*; a companion piece, *Odetta Sings The Blues*, which appeared six years later; and a collection on which she turned the tables with a collection of Dylan songs. She carried on touring regularly, but by 1985 had stopped recording. She made a comeback in 1999 with the album *Blues Everywhere I Go*, a tribute to the great early female blues singers, and followed three years later with *Looking' For A Home*, a collection of the songs of Leadbelly.

Odetta's repertoire encompasses folk, blues, spirituals, jazz, work hollers and civil rights songs to create a panoramic musical expression of the American experience. When David Letterman's *Late Show* returned to the airwaves from its New York TV studios a week after 9/11, the voice chosen to capture the blues of the traumatic event, and lend the necessary grace and dignity to the occasion, was that of the seventy-year-old Odetta.

⊙ **The Tradition Masters** Tradition
A double album of Odetta's 1950s' recordings, including great versions of "Gallows Tree", "Another Man Done Gone", "Muleskinner Blues" and "God's Gonna Cut You Down".

⊙ **Odetta: Best of the Vanguard Years**
Vanguard
A mixed bag of more than twenty 1960s' tracks, ranging from the great ("Nobody Knows You When You're Down And Out" and "House Of The Risin' Sun") to those you

Leadbelly fan, inspiration to Bob Dylan, civil rights supporter and damn good folk singer: Odetta

could probably do without ("If I Had A Hammer" and "He's Got The Whole World In His Hands").

⊙ **Blues Everywhere I Go** MC Records
Released in 1999, this was Odetta's first album in fifteen years. Her voice had lost some of its famous power, but she offered up pleasing versions of songs made famous by the female blues singers of the 1920s and 1930s, including such classics as "Homeless Blues" and "Rich Man Blues".

⊙ **Looking For A Home** MC Records
A 2002 collection of fifteen Leadbelly songs, including "Goodnight Irene", "In The Pines", "Jim Crow Blues", "Easy Rider" and "Midnight Special".

Johnny Otis

b Vallejo, California, Dec 28, 1921

As a drummer and bandleader, **Johnny Otis** has led a famous R&B revue for more than half a century. As if that weren't enough, as an all-round blues impresario, he has run his own record label and pursued parallel careers as

an author, disc jockey and educationalist.

Born to Greek-American parents, Johnny Veliotes grew up in a predominantly black neighborhood in Berkeley, where his father owned a grocery store, and identified readily with the black community around him. Having started his musical career in 1939 drumming with Count Otis Matthew's West Oakland House Rockers, he moved to Los Angeles four years later on the suggestion of Nat "King" Cole and Jimmy Witherspoon, to join Harlan Leonard's Kansas City Rockets. By 1945, Otis was leading his own band, and he had his first big hit that year with "Harlem Nocturne". After a run of further hits as a writer, performer and producer, including playing drums on **Charles Brown**'s first hit "Drifting Blues", he went on the road with his **California Rhythm & Blues Caravan**, which swiftly became one of the hottest musical attraction in black America. He also started a radio slot, which in turn led to the national weekly television series, *The Johnny Otis Show*, which ran for eight years. Among the many R&B singers Johnny Otis can claim to have discovered are Esther Phillips, Big Mama Thornton, Etta James, Sugar Pie DeSanto, Jackie Wilson and Little Willie John, while his production credits of the time include Thornton's original recording of "Hound Dog", Johnny Ace's "Pledging My Love" and Little Richard's earliest recordings. Highlights of his songwriting roll of honor include "Every Beat Of My Heart", "Roll With Me Henry" "So Fine", and "Willie And The Hand Jive". Setting up his own Blues Spectrum label, he recorded Big Joe Turner, Amos Milburn, Joe Liggins, Roy Milton, Eddie "Cleanhead" Vinson and Louis Jordan among others, while his own albums have continued to appear at sporadic intervals. His son **Shuggie Otis** is also a guitarist, who began recording as a teen prodigy in the late 1960s in a psychedelic blues-rock style much influenced by the likes of Jimi Hendrix.

⊙ Essential Recordings Cleopatra

This very brief 9-track compilation of recordings by Johnny Otis's own band nonetheless includes most of the tracks you'd want, such as "Harlem Nocturne" and "Willie And The Hand Jive".

P

Little Junior Parker

b Clarksdale, Mississippi, March 3, 1932; d Nov 18, 1971

Arguably the most underrated blues singer of his era, **Little Junior Parker** is best remembered for his early Sun recording of "Mystery Train", although he went on to record some potent soul-blues that his fans rate as highly as the work of the better-selling Bobby Bland.

Confusion surrounds the precise origins of Herman Parker, Jr. Some claim that he was born on the Arkansas side of the Mississippi River in 1927, but most accounts suggest he was born in Clarksdale, Mississippi, some five years later. What is undisputed is that he came of age musically on the fertile Memphis music scene of the 1940s. He learned his harmonica technique from **Sonny Boy Williamson** and played at an early age in **Howlin' Wolf**'s band, earning the name "Little Junior" on account of his extreme youth. During the late 1940s he played in the **Beale Streeters**, the legendary but unrecorded Memphis group that also included **Bobby Bland** and **B.B. King**, and formed his own band – the **Blue Flames**, with Auburn "Pat" Hare on guitar – in 1951.

Like so many Memphis bluesmen, Parker got his first recording opportunity courtesy of **Ike Turner**, who took him to Joe Bihari's Modern Records for his debut session in 1952. That produced the single "You're My Angel", on which Parker's velvet-smooth vocals were backed by Turner on piano and Matt Murphy on guitar.

The following year, Parker cut the boogie hit "Feelin' Good" for **Sun**, with Floyd Murphy, Matt's brother, on guitar. More hits followed for Sun, including "Love My Baby" and "Mystery Train". Recorded in autumn 1953, the latter was subse-

quently covered by Elvis Presley in 1955 as his final single for Sun, and has since been recorded by everyone from The Band to the Neville Brothers. "When I first heard that song, Little Junior Parker hadn't quite worked it out," producer Sam Phillips later recalled. "Back then it wasn't aeroplanes so much as trains, and when you went and put somebody on a train, it was like 'Oh man, I may never see them again'. We just messed around and it fell into that perfect groove."

Within months, however, Parker had left Sun for Don Robey's Houston-based **Duke Records**. Phillips sued, and Duke was ordered to pay Sun $17,500 – a huge sum, considering that a year later, RCA only paid Sun $35,000 for Presley's contract. Robey put Parker on the road with labelmate **Bobby Bland** as the Blues Consolidated Revue, and the show became one of the most popular attractions in the South with the two men as co-headliners. Yet for some reason, Parker's record sales failed to match Bland's success. His next big hit did not come until 1957, with "Next Time You See Me". An update of Roosevelt Sykes' "Driving Wheel" gave him another R&B hit in 1961, and was followed by "Annie Get Your Yo-Yo".

Parker adapted readily to the changing musical tastes of the 1960s, proving equally adept at down-home southern blues and soulful, punchy, horn-driven R&B. He stayed with Duke until 1966, when he moved on first to Mercury, then United Artists and Capitol, where he somewhat lost his way, recording covers of Beatles songs. The all-blues album *You Don't Have To Be Black To Love The Blues* suggested he still had much to offer, but sadly, he never got the chance to build upon its renewed promise. He died during surgery on a brain tumor in Chicago in 1971, at the age of just 39.

⊙ **Mystery Train** Rounder
Everything that Little Junior Parker recorded for Sun, plus additional tracks by Pat Hare and James Cotton – and a pic of the three of them with a youthful Elvis on the cover.

⊙ **Junior's Blues: The Duke Recordings Vol 1** MCA
These eighteen tracks prove just what a superbly soulful and underrated singer Little Junior Parker was, and feature brilliant arrangements by Joe Scott.

⊙ **Backtracking: The Duke Recordings Vol 2** MCA
More Parker greatness on mostly 1960s recordings, including R&B hits "Annie Get Your Yo-Yo" and "Man Or Mouse".

Charley Patton

b Bolton, Mississippi, May 1, 1891; d April 28, 1934

Perhaps only the hiss and crackle of many of his original recordings has prevented **Charley Patton** from receiving the same idolatry that surrounds Robert Johnson. For by any estimation, he ranks among the most significant and influential bluesmen of them all, and has a valid claim to be the true "king of the Delta blues".

Various dates have been advanced for Patton's birth, ranging between 1881 and 1891, but the latter is now generally accepted. Neither is there much agreement about the spelling of his name, which is often given as "Charley". What we know with some certainty is that some time towards the end of the nineteenth century, his sharecropping parents moved north to the Will Dockery Plantation, near Ruleville, which had opened for business in 1895. There the young Patton became fascinated by the playing of guitarist **Henry Sloan**, whom he followed around and soon copied. By his late teens he was by all accounts already a precociously fine performer and songwriter. Around 1910, he hooked up with guitarist **Willie Brown**, who later accompanied him on many of his recordings. In turn, he was soon exerting an influence on other guitarists, such as **Tommy Johnson**, who moved to the Ruleville vicinity around 1913 and added a version of Patton's "Pony Blues" to his repertoire.

Patton and Brown wandered all around the Delta, traveling north to Memphis and into Arkansas and Louisiana, playing plantation picnics and dances with various musicians, including members of the Chatmon family, to whom Patton was related. By 1926, a young **Robert Johnson** was following them around, eagerly picking up all the guitar tips he could. Despite his wanderings, Patton remained based on the plantations. He left Dockery's at the end of 1921 and moved to the Cottondale plantation, but was thrown off it by the owner only months later for beating his wife (one of several) in a drunken frenzy. He moved on again but by 1924 was back at Dockery's. Interestingly, when he died, by which time he was living on the Heathman-Dedham plantation near Indianola, his death certificate listed his occupation not as musician but "farmer".

Patton made his first recording in 1929, after he had written to Mississippi music store owner and part-time talent scout H.C. (Henry) Speir, asking if he could arrange for him to record. After traveling to Dockery's to hear him, Speir recommended him first to Victor, who rejected him, and then to Paramount. They invited him to travel 750 miles north to Richmond, Indiana, where he recorded fourteen sides in a single day on June 14, 1929, earning seven hundred dollars at fifty bucks a song. He was invited to record again three months later, this time at Paramount's new studio in Grafton, Wisconsin, where he cut 22 more sides, some with minimal accompaniment from fiddler **Henry Sims**. The tracks from both sessions bristle with an intensity that is huge and unforgettable, totally belying the fact that Patton was only five foot, five inches tall and weighed 135 pounds. It was said that his voice could carry five hundred yards without amplification and his gritty singing was an influence on **Howlin' Wolf**, who was just one of the many bluesmen who fell under his spell.

Those 1929 recordings, most of which were released as 78 singles, made Patton the biggest selling blues singer of his time, but his showmanship had already made him a Delta celebrity before he even entered a studio. "Charley Patton was a clowning man with a guitar," Sam Chatmon recalled. "He be in there putting his guitar all between his legs, carry it behind his head, lay down on the floor and never stopped picking". All this almost half a century before Jimi Hendrix, of course. Other accounts recall a dapper, raffish figure who enjoyed his fame and was a noted womanizer and drinker. "He was a nice guy but he just loved the bottle," Howlin' Wolf recalled. "Like all the rest of the musicians he was a great drinker. I did know him to play good and everybody liked him. He was a mixed-breed fellow, a light-skinned guy." Wolf suggested he looked like a Puerto Rican and many have suspected that he had some Mexican blood in him. Honeyboy Edwards reckoned: "Charlie always had a lot of women. Men didn't like him much because all the women was fools over him."

After his two 1929 sessions, Patton recorded again for Paramount the next year with **Willie Brown** and **Son House** accompanying him. However, the onset of the Depression meant that he didn't cut his fourth and final session until a couple of months before his death in 1934, when

Playlist
Charley Patton

All taken from *The Definitive Charley Patton*

1 MISSISSIPPI BOWEAVIL BLUES (1929)
"Bo weavil told the farmer that 'I 'tain't got ticket fare', sucks all the blossom and leave your hedges square."

2 DOWN THE DIRT ROAD BLUES (1929)
"My rider got somethin', she's tryin'a keep it hid."

3 PONY BLUES (1929)
"Took my baby, to meet the mornin' train, an' the blues come down, baby, like showers of rain."

4 A SPOONFUL BLUES (1929)
"In all a spoon', 'bout that spoon', the women goin' crazy, every day in their life 'bout a…'"

5 HIGH WATER EVERYWHERE (1929)
"Lord, the whole round country, man, is overflowed."

6 34 BLUES (1934)
"It may bring sorrow, Lord, and it may bring tears, oh, Lord, oh, Lord, let me see your brand new year."

7 PEA VINE BLUES (1929)
"I cried last night an' I, I ain't gonna cry anymore, 'cause the good book tells us you've got to reap just what you sow."

8 REVENUE MAN BLUES (1934)
"Come on, mama, let us, go to the edge of town, I know where there's a bird's nest, built down on the ground."

9 POOR ME (1934)
"You may go, you may stay, but she'll come back some sweet day, by and by, sweet mama, by and by."

10 HIGH SHERIFF BLUES (1934)
"Takes booze and blues, Lord, to carry me through But it did seem like years, in a jailhouse where there is no boo."

he traveled to New York and recorded around 25 sides for the American Record Company over three days. Several of the tracks also featured the singing of his last wife **Bertha Lee**, but only ten sides were ever released and the rest destroyed. By now, Patton's voice was a lesser instrument, as an assailant had attempted to cut his throat the previous year and damaged his vocal chords. It is unfortunate that the masters of his 1929 and 1930 recordings have not survived, for when Paramount went out of business, the metal masters were sold off as scrap to line chicken coops. Hence the Patton recordings we have are all taken from the original scratched and heavily played 78s, so that even modern digital noise-reduction processes have been unable to restore the original sound.

Nevertheless, he still left an extraordinary body of work, on songs such as "Where The Southern Crosses The Dog", "Down The Dirt Road Blues", "A Spoonful Blues", and the two-part "High Water Everywhere", his vivid account of the great Mississippi flood of 1927. Patton was a man of his times and also sang spirituals, ballads and songster pieces, as well as covering other hits of the day such as Sophie Tucker's "Some Of These Days". His songs describe a narrowly defined landscape of cotton towns, plantations, southern railway lines

and the local jail that you could almost call parochial. Yet even when singing about boll weevils and other such specific events and issues far removed from the experience of modern life, there's still a universality about the passions and emotions he conjures.

It's not so much Patton's repertoire as his sound that left an indelible mark on American music. His vaudeville-style vocal asides and phrasing, and his hoarse, ravaged voice influenced a generation of Delta bluesmen, while the propulsive beat and richly accented rhythmic sense of his guitar playing were equally widely copied, as was his slide technique, either played across his lap and fretted with a pocket knife, or upright with a bottleneck. He also added counter rhythms or emphasized certain beats by beating his guitar and stomping his feet. Many of the biggest names in the Delta blues, from Son House and Robert Johnson to John Lee Hooker and Howlin' Wolf, fell under his spell and they would have sounded very different without his influence.

Patton died from a chronic heart condition in 1934 in Indianola, Mississippi, when he was probably aged 42. His tombstone bears the legend: "The Voice Of The Delta – The Foremost Performer Of Early Mississippi Blues Whose Songs Became Cornerstones Of American Music."

⊙ **Screamin' And Hollerin' The Blues**
Revenant

The fifty-something recordings made by Patton between 1929 and 1934 are here stretched out to fill a seven-disc box set. Additions include recordings by his associates and others such as Tommy Johnson, Booker White and Howlin' Wolf who came within his orbit or under his influence, and an entire disc of interviews with those who knew him, such as Wolf and Pop Staples. The CDs are mounted on cardboard replicas of old 78s, slipped into replicas of the original paper sleeves, while the box includes sticker-reproductions of the original 78 labels and a book on Patton written by the late John Fahey, the moving spirit behind the project. Expect to pay around £90 ($130) for the whole package.

⊙ **The Voice Of The Delta: The Charley Patton Legacy** Indigo

If seven discs seem like too much of a good thing, this threee-disc set contains 56 tracks by Patton and a further twenty by the likes of Son House, Bertha Lee, Louise Johnson and Willie Brown.

⊙ **Charley Patton: Hang It On The Wall**
Complete Blues

And if even three discs are too many, this single-disc 20-track compilation contains most of what you need, including "Pony Blues", "High Water Everywhere" and "A Spoonful Blues".

Pinetop Perkins

b Belzoni, Mississippi, July 7, 1913

The pianist **Pinetop Perkins** was a sideman for many years, backing the likes of Sonny Boy Williamson, Robert Nighthawk and Muddy Waters. In due course, however, he became a star attraction in his own right, simply by outliving most of his contemporaries. He was still playing well into his nineties, as one of the last remaining links with the classic blues era.

Joe Willie Perkins began playing both piano and guitar in his teens, although his guitar skills were stunted after he suffered severed tendons in his left arm when he was stabbed by an angry chorus girl in Helena, Arkansas. Inspired by Clarence "Pinetop" Smith's "Pinetop's Boogie-woogie", he adopted his hero's name in lifelong tribute. Many later came to believe that Smith's tune was actually written by Perkins, but the simple arithmetic says otherwise: Smith died in 1929 when Perkins was still only fifteen.

In the 1940s, Perkins hooked up with **Robert Nighthawk**, playing on his radio show in Helena, before he switched to the rival *King Biscuit Hour* show fronted by **Sonny Boy (Rice Miller) Williamson**. However, he continued to play with Nighthawk, heading north to Chicago with the guitarist in 1949, when they cut several tracks for Aristocrat/Chess Records. He also toured and recorded with **Earl Hooker**, and cut some early sessions for Sam Phillips' Sun Records, including a version of "Pinetop's Boogie-woogie", although the track was not released until many years later.

Pinetop spent fifteen years playing around Chicago and St Louis before he was invited to replace Otis Spann in Muddy Waters' band in 1969. He stayed with Waters until 1980, appearing on several albums with him, and also played with other members of Waters' backing group, billed as the **Legendary Blues Band**, on a brace of albums on the Rounder label. It was only in the 1980s that he finally emerged as front man, recording for labels like Blind Pig, Black & Blue, Alligator, Earwig, Telarc and Shanachie. His 1992 album on the Antone's label, *Pinetop's Boogie-woogie*, found him backed by a stellar cast of fellow blues musicians including James Cotton and guitarists Matt "Guitar" Murphy, Jimmy Rogers, Hubert Sumlin and Luther Tucker. His 1998 release, *Legends*, again teamed him with Sumlin and found the pair blending a traditional Delta blues approach with a more modern electric blues-rock sound. In 2004, at the age of 91, he released the album *Ladies Man*.

⊙ **After Hours** Blind Pig

A 1988 release on which Perkins renders great versions of songs from the repertories of Muddy Waters, Memphis Slim and Robert Nighthawk, although the backing of Little Mike and the Tornadoes is not of similar quality.

⊙ **Legends** Telarc

Pinetop Perkins and guitarist Hubert Sumlin trade skills in 1998, on standards such as "Got My Mojo Working", "Rock Me Baby", "Hoochie Coochie Man", and "The Sky Is Crying".

⊙ **Live At Antone's** Texas Music Group

Pinetop Perkins as he should be heard, live in a tiny club, recorded in 1995 when he was in his 80s but sounding sixty years younger.

⊙ **Ladies Man** MC Records

At an astonishing 91 years old, Perkins teamed up in 2004 with a bunch of female singers including Ruth Brown, Susan Tedeschi and Angela Strehli, while Elvin Bishop added elegant slide.

Lucky Peterson

b Buffalo, New York, Dec 13, 1963

From a child prodigy novelty act to a blues veteran, **Lucky Peterson** has led an extraordinary career by any standards. His father James owned a blues venue called the Governor's Inn in Buffalo, and added curiosity value to the club's attractions by showcasing the young Judge Kenneth Peterson on organ and drums aged three years old. Jimmy Smith and Bill Doggett gave him keyboard lessons, and by the age of five he had even recorded his first single, "1,2,3,4", produced by none other than Willie Dixon. The stunt worked; before he was six years old Peterson had appeared on such prime-time American TV shows as Ed Sullivan and *The Tonight Show* with Johnny Carson.

With artists like Buddy Guy, Junior Wells, Muddy Waters and Koko Taylor regularly playing at the Governor's Inn, he had plenty of opportunity to learn the ways of the blues at first hand from its very finest exponents. In addition to organ, he

also mastered bass and piano, and was sitting in at a ridiculously young age with his father's band, backing artists such as Lightnin' Hopkins and Jimmy Reed.

Peterson continued playing at the Governor's Inn until he sat in with **Little Milton** one night in 1980, and was promptly asked to join his band on a permanent basis. Within months, he had become Milton's bandleader and was opening shows with his own 45-minute set. He stayed with Milton for three years and then joined **Bobby Bland**'s band. After cutting an album with his father, he recorded his adult solo debut in Paris in 1984 for the French label Isabel while on a "Young Blues Giants" tour of Europe.

When he returned to America, Peterson left Bland's touring band and relocated to Florida's Tampa Bay area to pursue a solo career. He became a regular session player for the Florida-based King Snake Records, whose repertoire appeared via Alligator, and released his own album on the senior label with 1989's *Lucky Strikes!* Further Alligator albums included 1990's *Triple Play*, which found

Young blues giant Lucky Peterson

him playing organ and lead guitar and singing the blues with a soulful, funky voice.

Since then he's expanded his musical horizons, moving to Verve for 1992's *I'm Ready*, which added contemporary rock and soul flavors to his blues stew. Further Verve albums followed, including 1996's rather fine Mahalia Jackson tribute, *Spirituals & Gospel*, recorded with Mavis Staples. He moved to Blue Thumb for a self-titled label debut in 1999, followed two years later by *Double Dealin'*. *Black Midnight Sun* appeared in 2003 with a strange production by Bill Laswell that strayed far beyond most definitions of the blues, even though it included material made famous by Muddy Waters and Howlin' Wolf.

⊙ **Triple Play** Alligator
Though reckoned by many to be Lucky Peterson's best, like all his releases, this 1990 album seems to divide listeners into those who think he's a journeyman and those who believe he's a new blues hero.

Kelly Joe Phelps

b Sumner, Washington, Oct 5, 1959

With his brooding and hypnotic style, Kelly Joe Phelps established himself during the 1990s as one of the finest acoustic country blues guitarists of his generation. On more recent albums he has developed into a broader-based contemporary singer-songwriter, but an aching blues melancholy remains at the emotional core of his music.

Raised in Washington but now resident in Portland, Oregon, Phelps learned folk songs from his father and began to play the drums and piano as a youth. His first musical enthusiasm was jazz, but during the mid-1980s he began listening to the acoustic blues of players such as Fred McDowell, Skip James, Blind Willie Johnson and Robert Pete Williams. After developing a following on the blues and folk club circuit and working as a guitar teacher for a decade, he released his debut album *Lead Me On* for the Burnside label in 1995. That revealed him as a magnificent acoustic slide player and a brilliant, moody singer, accompanied by stomp box percussion on superbly atmospheric versions of songs like "Hard Time Killin' Floor Blues", "Jesus Make Up My Dying Bed" and "Motherless Children", as well as six original compositions.

New country blues: Kelly Joe Phelps

By the time of the follow-up, 1997's *Roll Away The Stone*, Phelps had signed to Rykodisc. *Shine Eyed Mister Zen* followed in 1999 and found him expanding his songwriting skills, while 2001's *Sky Like A Broken Clock* moved further away from the blues, with little or no slide guitar, Phelps' fingerpicking accompanied by upright bass and drums. His fifth release, 2003's *Slingshot Professionals*, found him backed by a bigger band and richer arrangements. 2005's *Tap The Red Cane Whirlwind* was a live set that delighted his acoustic blues fans with mesmerizing versions of "Hard Time Killin' Floor Blues" and "I Am The Light Of The World".

⊙ **Lead Me On** Burnside
Kelly Joe Phelps' superb 1995 debut album featured great slide playing and haunting singing, with a blend of blues classics and original compositions.

⊙ **Roll Away The Stone** Rykodisc
Phelps' second album, released in 1997, built on the achievement of his debut and included a quite staggering version of "See That My Grave Is Kept Clean".

⊙ **Tap The Red Cane Whirlwind** Rykodisc
The live album Phelps' fans had long been urging him to make finally arrived in 2005. It didn't disappoint, with its stellar guitar playing and hypnotic moods.

Piano Red

**b Hampton, Georgia, Oct 19, 1911;
d July 25, 1985**

Over his long career, **Piano Red** also worked under the names **Willie Lee Perryman** and **Doctor Feelgood**, while as well as playing blues, he also turned his hand to boogie-woogie, R&B and even a little country and western.

Even though his older brother **Rufus** – who recorded as **Speckled Red** – was also a pianist, Willie Lee Perryman denied any fraternal influence, and instead cited Fats Waller as his inspiration. Like his brother, Willie was born albino and extremely nearsighted. He learned to play boogie-woogie and barrelhouse piano by ear. By the 1930s, he was traveling throughout Georgia, Alabama and Tennessee, playing under his birth name in honky-tonks and juke joints for black audiences but also performing in venues frequented by a white clientele. His first recording sessions were made in 1936 for Vocalion with the Atlanta-based blues guitarist **Blind Willie McTell**. The two men had traveled together under the name the **Dixie Jazz Hounds**, but the sides they recorded in tandem were never released, and sadly the masters were lost. However, Perryman gained something from the session; it was the talent scout who arranged it, W.L. Calaway, who gave him the name Piano Red. After that, he struggled to make a living as a musician. By the 1940s, he was working as an upholsterer and playing piano only on weekends. His luck took an upturn towards the end of the decade when he appeared on the Atlanta radio station WGST, which led to an invitation to record for RCA Victor.

His first session for RCA in 1950 produced the single "Rockin' With Red". Later covered by **Little Richard** as "She Knows How To Rock", it's often cited as a major influence on the birth of rock'n'roll. Other early RCA recordings included "Red's Boogie", "The Wrong Yo Yo", "Just Right Bounce" and "Laying The Boogie". His first full-length album, *Piano Red In Concert*, appeared on the RCA subsidiary Groove in 1956, and consisted of both studio sides and live tracks recorded at the Magnolia Ballroom, on Atlanta's West Side. When the Groove label was closed later that year, Red's contract reverted to the parent company, and he recorded several further sessions for RCA Victor,

including one in Nashville with Chet Atkins producing. After he was dropped by the label in 1958, he cut a session for Chess that produced the single "Get Up Mare", and then four singles for the Jax label.

He next turned up on Columbia's Okeh imprint in 1961 under the name **Doctor Feelgood and the Interns** with the raucous hit "Dr. Feelgood". Written by guitarist Curtis I. Smith, Perryman described the song as "about a doctor of love who only likes big womens". Its pop success persuaded him to adopt the name Dr. Feelgood for the next decade, dressing his band in white medical uniforms and changing the name of his Atlanta radio slot from the *Piano Red Show* to the *Dr. Feelgood Show*. In 1969 he stopped touring and began a residency at Muhlenbrink's Tavern in Atlanta. He performed at the venue six nights per week for the next ten years, until it closed in 1979. Reverting back to his Piano Red soubriquet in the early 1970s, he also recorded several further albums, including the excellent *Atlanta Bounce* for Arhoolie in 1972, and toured Europe several times before his death from cancer in 1985 at the age of 74.

⊙ **The Doctor Is In!** Bear Family

The ultimate box set, holding more than 120 tracks over four CDs, covers pretty much everything Piano Red ever recorded, from "Rockin' With Red" through to "Dr. Feelgood" and its B-side "Mister Moonlight", which found its way into the Beatles' early repertoire.

⊙ **Atlanta Bounce** Arhoolie

Twenty-one tracks of bouncing, rocking boogie piano, recorded in 1972, shortly after he had reverted back to the name Piano Red.

John Primer

b Camden, Mississippi, March 3, 1945

A sturdy upholder of the finest traditions of Chicago blues, guitarist **John Primer** paid his dues playing with such blues greats as Muddy Waters and Magic Slim. Not until the 1990s, however, did he cut his first solo album.

Primer sang in church as a boy, and listened at home to the likes of Muddy Waters and Elmore James, who inspired him to pick up a guitar at the age of nine. As soon as he turned eighteen he headed to Chicago to make his name as a blues guitarist. After a brief spell in a band called the Maintainers, he landed a job in the house band at Theresa's Lounge, one of the South Side's most important blues venues. He stayed for nine years, learning much from the band's other guitarist **Sammy Lawhorn**.

Only in 1979 did his career truly take off, when **Willie Dixon** invited him to join his Dixon's All-Stars. Primer stayed a year and then got the call to join **Muddy Waters**, playing in his final band until the great man's death in 1983. Primer immediately joined **Magic Slim**'s band the Teardrops, who made no secret of their debt to Waters. The guitarist fitted in perfectly and recorded for the Wolf label, both with Slim and with the Teardrops, and also on some solo sides for the label's voluminous Chicago Blues Session series.

Primer remained with Magic Slim for thirteen years. He finally released his first American solo album in 1993 with *Stuff You Got To Watch* on the Earwig label. Two years later he signed to Mike Vernon's Code Blue imprint and released the excellent *The Real Deal*, produced by Vernon with a backing band of harpist Billy Branch, pianist David Maxwell and bassist Johnny B. Gayden. *Keep On Lovin' The Blues* followed for the same label in 1997, and when Code Blue collapsed he moved to Telarc for 2000's *Knockin' At Your Door*.

⊙ **The Real Deal** Code Blue
A straight-ahead old-school Chicago blues album, on which John Primer is backed by a solid band for a set that combines his own compositions with songs by Willie Dixon, Walter Davis and Albert King.

Professor Longhair

b Bogalusa, Louisiana, Dec 19 1918; d Jan 30 1980

The unique blues, jazz, mambo, calypso, ragtime, zydeco fusion of **Professor Longhair**'s piano playing and his wild, cracked vocals were way too individual, and at times too plain weird, for him to sell records in large quantities. Yet "Fess", as he was affectionately known, is probably the most legendary of all New Orleans' R&B musicians and his influence on the city's finest, from Fats Domino to Dr. John by way of Allen Toussaint, was immense.

Henry Roeland Byrd began dancing for tips in the streets of the Crescent City during the 1930s. "The very first instrument I played was the bottom

of my feet, working out rhythms, tap dancing," he later recalled. "We used to dance all up and down Bourbon Street."

While working variously as a boxer, cook and professional gambler and card sharp, he learned guitar, drums and piano. His first paid gig as a musician came playing piano for his fellow members of the Civilian Conservation Corps. After service in the US Army during World War II, his professional break finally came in the late 1940s, when he sat in on piano at the Caldonia Club while Dave Bartholomew's band was taking a break. He went down so well that Bartholomew was fired. His replacement acquired a new name along with the gig – as all of his band wore their hair long they were instantly billed as Professor Longhair and the Four Hairs, "professor" being a traditional honorific title for piano players in Storyville.

Fess made his recording debut in 1949, cutting his signature tune "Mardi Gras In New Orleans" under the name **Professor Longhair and the Shuffling Hungarians** on the Star Talent label. He went on to record most of his best-known tunes during the early 1950s, including "Bald Head", "Tipitina", "Big Chief", "In The Night", "Go To The Mardi Gras" and "Ball the Wall". None apart from "Bald Head" was a hit outside New Orleans, but to the city's other musicians he was a heroic figure. His various performing names included Roy Byrd and his Blues Jumpers, Roy "Bald Head" Byrd, Roland Byrd, Professor Longhair and his Blues Scholars, and Professor Longhair and the Clippers; sometimes he changed for the hell of it, sometimes for contractual reasons.

By the 1960s, his lack of national sales meant that nobody was much interested in recording him. He took to hustling as a card player again and worked as a janitor in a record store, which is somewhat like Picasso turning house decorator. A famous appearance at the 1971 New Orleans Jazz & Heritage Festival heralded his comeback, he began recording again for Rounder Records, and his rediscovery turned him into a celebrity. He appeared in the documentary *Piano Players Rarely, If Ever, Play Together* with Allen Toussaint and Tuts Washington, headlined at the Montreux Jazz Festival in 1973, and in 1975 was flown by Paul and Linda McCartney to play a private party they were hosting on board the *Queen Mary*. The set he played was later released as an album.

In 1978, Fess recorded another fine live album at Tipitina's, the New Orleans nightclub named after one of his songs, while his final release, *Crawfish Fiesta*, which featured guest appearances by disciples such as **Dr. John**, was recorded for Alligator Records in 1979. It came out on January 30, 1980, the day he died at the age of 61.

⊙ **Fess: Anthology** Rhino
A double-album career retrospective that begins with "Mardi Gras In New Orleans" and "Bald Head" and ends in the 1970s with Fess's boogie-woogie collaboration with Allen Toussaint and Tuts Washington.

⊙ **Ball The Wall: Live At Tipitina's 1978** Night Train
Professor Longhair as he should be remembered: eighteen tracks recorded live in the Crescent City in the legendary club that took its name from one of his songs.

⊙ **Crawfish Fiesta** Alligator
A quarter of a century on, Alligator founder Bruce Iglauer still reckons this is one of the best records his label has ever released – and he's not far wrong.

Snooky Pryor

b Lambert, Mississippi, September 15, 1921; d November 10, 2006

Influenced by the great Sonny Boy "Rice Miller" Williamson, the harp player **Snooky Pryor** was a pioneer of the postwar Chicago blues sound and claims to have been the first player to amplify the harmonica.

Despite the objections of his father, a minister who thought the blues was the "devil's music", James Edward Pryor took up the harp as a boy after seeing Williamson play and swiftly became a highly proficient player. Stationed with the US Army at Fort Sheridan just outside Chicago in 1940, he spent his weekends playing on the city's famed Maxwell Street with the likes of Williamson and Homesick James. Back on base, he experimented with playing his harp through a powerful army PA. After his discharge in 1945, he threw himself wholeheartedly into the Chicago blues scene, dazzling audiences with the harp which he now regularly played through a primitive amp.

Pryor made his recording debut in 1948 with "Telephone Blues" on the Planet label, aided by

Moody Jones on guitar. The track is now considered one of the earliest postwar Chicago blues classics. In the 1950s he recorded for J.O.B., Parrot and Vee Jay, cutting such top-quality sides as "Someone To Love Me", "Snooky And Moody's Boogie", "Cryin' Shame" and "Judgment Day". He was also highly in demand as a session musician, playing on sides with **Sunnyland Slim**, **Floyd Jones** and **Homesick James**.

After releasing the novelty crossover attempt "Boogie Twist" in 1963, Pryor retired from music. Moving to Ullin, Illinois, he worked as a carpenter while he concentrated on raising his family. Once the children had grown up, he was coaxed back onto the road in the early 1970s, and toured Europe, where he also recorded. After that he seemed to disappear again into semi-retirement, but he re-emerged in 1989 with the album *Snooky*, on Blind Pig Records. Produced by guitarist Steve Freund, it announced to the world that the veteran harpist was alive and well, his chops still working. He also recorded for Antone's and Blind Pig, who hooked him up in 1991 with **Johnny Shines**, whom he'd worked with in the early 1950s in Chicago. Back then they had been part of one of the first full-on electrified blues combos, but forty years later, *Back To The Country* found them delightfully returning to the acoustic country blues of the Delta.

Shake My Hand followed in 1999. It saw Pryor return to the electric Chicago band sound, and included a remake of his "Telephone Blues" from half a century earlier. Despite his 78 years his vocals still sounded urgent, and his harp playing strong and evocative. *Double Shot*, a collaborative album with the guitarist **Mel Brown** followed a year later.

⊙ **Back To The Country** Blind Pig
Recorded with Johnny Shines in 1991, this is a fine collection of down-home country blues, including four Robert Johnson tunes.

⊙ **Shake My Hand** Blind Pig
On this 1999 album, once Snooky Pryor has sung and played the title track solo, a raw, rocking band joins him on such familiar material as "Work With Me Annie", "Pistol Packin' Mama" and his own classic "Telephone Blues". If the material is hardly original, his harp still sounds vigorous and his voice red-blooded.

R

Yank Rachell

b Brownsville, Tennessee, March 16, 1910; d April 9, 1997

James "Yank" Rachell was an unusual blues-man, in that although he also played the gui-tar, his main instrument was the mandolin, on which he was a self-taught and unique stylist.

The story of how Rachell came to take up the mandolin is a classic blues tale. On their Tennessee farm at the age of eight, he was given a young pig by his mother to raise for butchering. Soon afterwards, he heard a neighbor playing what he called a "tater-bug" on his front porch. He loved the sound so much that he asked if he could buy the instrument, which was in fact a round-backed mandolin. The price was named at five dollars, but the young Rachell, who had no money, traded his pig instead. His mother was furious. Many years later, he recalled her telling him: "Next fall when we're all eating pork, you can eat that mandolin." Instead, he taught himself to play it with extraordi-nary flair, and was soon making a far better living as a musician than he ever could from fattening livestock.

During the early 1920s, Rachell hooked up with the considerably older **Hambone Willie Newbern** – later to record the first version of "Rollin' And Tumblin'", in 1929 – and the two performed around Brownsville at house parties, picnics, medicine shows and fish fries. While doing so, Rachell also met **Sleepy John Estes**, who remained a lifelong friend. With **Hammie Nixon** on harmonica and jug, they played as a trio across Tennessee and the South. By the mid-1920s, they were in Memphis, busking on Beale Street. Rachell developed a con-siderable degree of showmanship, making up for the mandolin's musical limitations by such tricks as throwing the instrument in the air and strumming a chord as he caught it.

When the jug band craze took off in the late 1920s, Rachell, Estes and pianist Jab Jones formed the Three J's Jug Band. In 1929, they made their first recording for Victor with "Broken-Hearted, Ragged And Dirty Too". Further sides followed, including Rachell's own self-penned classic "Divin' Duck Blues", and the group also backed **Noah Lewis** on his Victor recordings. Rachell and Estes moved to Chicago early in the 1930s, where they recorded for Decca and Bluebird, but the mandolinist then returned to Brownsville, where he started a fam-ily and resumed farming. He continued to play at house parties and fish fries in Jackson where he met **John Lee "Sonny Boy" Williamson**. The two men recorded for Bluebird in Chicago in 1938 and guested on each other's records. In addition to the 24 sides he cut for Bluebird (on several of which, such as "38 Pistol Blues", he played guitar), Rachell also recorded over the next three years for Victor, Vocalion and Banner. Then the wartime restriction on the use of shellac brought his recording career to an abrupt halt.

Rachell subsequently moved to St Louis, and then in 1958 to Indianapolis, before re-emerging dur-ing the 1960s alongside his old friend Sleepy John. Estes had been rediscovered living in Brownsville, and his first response on coming out of retirement was to summon his old friends Rachell and Nixon once again. "I didn't have nothing else to do," as Rachell later put it; the trio played concerts and festivals in both America and Europe and recorded for the Blue Goose and Delmark labels.

Following Estes' death in 1977, Rachell recorded solo for Blind Pig, JSP and Wolf. He died in con-siderable poverty in 1997 at the age of 87. He never received his fair share of royalties, even though his songs, particularly "Divin' Duck Blues" and "She Caught The Katy (And Left Me A Mule To Ride)" were much covered by other artists. One of his final appearances was at a benefit concert which former Lovin' Spoonful singer John Sebastian helped to arrange for him two months before he died.

An amusing footnote: In the last interview Rachell gave before his death he was asked what was the "Katy" in the song that **Taj Mahal** had famously covered, and which was later included in the *Blues Brothers* film. It was all the result of a misunderstanding, he claimed; Taj had misheard the lyrics. "I didn't sing about no Katy," he insisted. "I sang 'my baby left town, left me a mule to ride, when the train left the station, the fool mule lay down and died.'"

⊙ **Brownsville Blues: His 23 Greatest Songs**
Wolf
It's Yank Rachell's show, though Estes and Nixon are in tow on many tracks. The title isn't strictly accurate, as "She Caught The Katy" isn't here, but just about everything else is.

⊙ **Yank Rachell** Random Chance
A reissue of Rachell's 1973 Blue Goose solo album, on which he revisits the songs he and Sleepy John sang way back when, including "Divin' Duck Blues".

Ma Rainey

b Columbus, Georgia, April 26, 1886; d Dec 22, 1939

Ma Rainey might not have been the first black woman to record a blues song; that distinction fell to Mamie Smith. Neither was she the biggest female blues singer of the 1920s, for her protégé Bessie Smith eventually surpassed her in fame. However, her earthy, powerful voice captured the essence of rural black southern life, and few would dispute her right to the title by which she has been known for more than eighty years, the "mother of the blues".

Born Gertrude Pridgett, she married **Will Rainey** in 1904. A comedy singer in a passing minstrel show, his party piece was apparently stuffing a saucer in his mouth. The couple toured as "Ma and Pa Rainey – Assassinators of the Blues" with the **Rabbit Foot Minstrels**, Silas Green's, Tolliver's Circus and other similar tent shows. She was almost certainly the first to sing blues in a minstrel act; she told the folklorist John Work that a girl had come to her tent when she was playing a small town in Missouri in 1902 and sung a strange and poignant song, which she promptly incorporated into her act and dubbed the "blues". She even insisted that she had invented the word.

A woman of generous temperament, Rainey fostered seven children and encouraged young singers, coaching the young **Bessie Smith** when she joined the Rabbit Foot Minstrels around 1914. She didn't record until 1923, by which time she had her own touring company and was widely popular across the South as "Madame Rainey". Paramount promoted her first record as being by the "mother of the blues – discovered at last". Despite her popularity, Rainey's studio career lasted just six years, but during that time she cut more than ninety sides for Paramount, including classics such as "Shave 'Em Dry Blues", "Walking Blues" and "See See Rider Blues", accompanied by the likes of Louis Armstrong, Lovie Austen, Buster Bailey, Georgia Tom Dorsey and Tampa Red, Coleman Hawkins, Kid Ory and Don Redmon. Poor recording quality

Playlist
Ma Rainey

1 BAD LUCK BLUES (1923) from **Don't Fish In My Sea**
"Lord, look where the time's done gone, hey Lord, there's something going all wrong."

2 DON'T FISH IN MY SEA (1926) from **Don't Fish In My Sea**
"If you don't like my ocean, don't fish in my sea, stay out of my valley, let my mountain be."

3 BLACK CAT HOOT OWL (1928) from **Don't Fish In My Sea**
"I feel my brain a-thumpin', I've got no time to lose, mama's superstitious, tryin' to overcome these blues."

4 YONDER COME THE BLUES (1925) from **Complete Recorded Works Vol 3**
"When I get a letter, it never brings good news, every time I see the mail, babe, yonder comes the blues."

5 SISSY BLUES (1926) from **Complete Recorded Works Vol 3**
"My man got a sissy, his name is Miss Kate, He shook that thing like jelly on a plate."

6 CHAIN GANG BLUES (1925) from **Complete Recorded Works Vol 3**
"Chains on my feet, padlock on my hand, it's all on account of stealing a woman's man."

7 BARREL HOUSE BLUES (1923) from **Complete Recorded Works Vol 1**
"Papa likes his sherry, mama likes her port, papa likes to shimmy, mama likes to sport."

sadly tends to make it difficult fully to evaluate her performances, but Rainey moaned and shouted in a rich contralto with a raw and earthy quality, and her larger-than-life personality is self-evident.

Famously ostentatious, Rainey liked to dress in expensive jewelry, a beaded headband, ostrich feathers and a black sequined dress. She'd emerge on stage bathed in blue light and blowing kisses from within a giant replica of a Victrola gramophone cabinet. She also always traveled with a suitcase full of fifty- and hundred-dollar bills, which perhaps made it unsurprising that her lyrics seldom portrayed women as downtrodden victims but as strong, independent and sexually liberated. She continued working as a blues singer until 1935 when she retired to Columbus, where she had been born. A good businesswoman, she had saved enough money to build and run two theaters in Georgia, although when she died of a heart attack in 1939 at the age of 53, her death certificate described her occupation as "housekeeping".

Some sixty years after her final recordings she was celebrated in the musical *Ma Rainey's Black Bottom*. Written by August Wilson, and named after a dance craze, it ran both on Broadway and in London's West End.

⊙ **Ma Rainey's Black Bottom** Yazoo
A good 14-track compilation released on the back of the success of the stage show of the same name, with Rainey's original recordings cleaned up as far as the wonders of modern digital technology allow.

⊙ **Complete Recorded Works Vols 1–4**
Document
Everything Ma Rainey ever recorded, on four discs. The most striking thing about listening all the way through to the 90-odd tracks in chronological order is how at the time blues and jazz had not yet gone their different ways and there was still little, if any, separation between the two.

Bonnie Raitt

b Los Angeles, Nov 8, 1949

Even if her later albums have straddled different genres, and at times strayed into anodyne "adult rock" territory, **Bonnie Raitt** remains at her best belting out the blues and playing slide guitar. She has also earned enormous respect through her role in setting up the Rhythm and Blues Foundation, established to channel money to ageing blues and R&B artists who never received proper royalties.

Bonnie was born into a musical family. Her father was the Broadway singer John Raitt, who starred in such shows as *Carousel*, *Oklahoma!* and *The Pajama Game*, while her mother was the pianist and singer Marge Goddard. Raised as a Quaker with a strong commitment to social activism, she started to play after receiving a Stella guitar as a Christmas present aged eight. Hearing the album *Blues At Newport 1963* when she was fourteen kindled her interest in blues and slide guitar, and when she left LA to study social relations and African studies at Harvard in the late 1960s, she spent her time playing blues and folk music in local coffee houses.

Before long Raitt was opening shows for the likes of **Sippie Wallace**, Mississippi Fred McDowell, Son House, Muddy Waters and John Lee Hooker. "It was an incredible gift for me to not only be friends with some of the greatest blues people who've ever lived, but to learn how they played, how they sang, how they lived their lives," she recalled later. Her debut album, *Bonnie Raitt*, appeared on Warner Brothers in 1971, and featured interpretations of classic blues by Robert Johnson and Sippie Wallace alongside tunes by contemporary songwriters.

A string of fine albums followed, featuring gritty doses of blues and R&B and her forceful bottleneck guitar style. In the 1980s, she released *The Glow*, *Green Light*, and *Nine Lives*, but she eventually parted company with Warner Brothers at the end of the decade, after more than fifteen years with the label. Although many suspected Raitt's career was in decline, after signing to EMI/Capitol in 1989 she went on to enjoy her greatest commercial success in her forties. *Nick Of Time*, her debut for the new label, went to number one in America and won a Grammy, while she was among those who assisted **John Lee Hooker**'s spectacular comeback on *The Healer*. *Luck Of The Draw*, released in 1991, sold seven million copies, while 1994's *Longing In Their Hearts* won another Grammy, not in the blues category to which she might once have been consigned but as best pop album.

That was followed in 1995 by the live album and film *Road Tested* – now available on DVD – which featured a guest appearance by **Charles Brown**. The following year came another Grammy for best rock instrumental performance for "SRV Shuffle", her

Blues belter and guitar gun-for-hire, Ms Bonnie Raitt

contribution to an all-star tribute album to **Stevie Ray Vaughan**. The decade also found her guesting on albums by Ruth Brown, Junior Wells, B.B. King, Charles Brown, Taj Mahal and Keb Mo.

Raitt has continued to release eclectic albums at regular intervals including 1998's *Fundamental*, 2002's *Silver Lining* and 2005's *Souls Alike*. She also duetted with **Ray Charles** on "Do I Ever Cross Your Mind?" on his final release, *Genius Loves Company*, while in 2003 she performed two songs in Martin Scorsese's acclaimed PBS television series, *The Blues*.

In 1988, she co-founded the Rhythm and Blues Foundation, which works to improve royalties and raise appreciation for a generation of R&B pioneers. Although her own music has moved away from pure blues, she continues to be a passionate advocate of the music. As she puts it, "the consolidation of the music business has made it difficult to encourage styles like the blues, which deserve to be celebrated as part of our most treasured national resources".

⊙ **Bonnie Raitt** Warners
Raitt's earthiest and most bluesy effort, from 1971, features assistance from Junior Wells and A.C. Reed on a set that includes splendid versions of Sippie Wallace's "Women Be Wise" and "Mighty Tight Woman".

⊙ **Give It Up** Warners
Raitt's second album, from 1972, mixes timeless country-blues with songs by up-and-coming young songwriters such as Jackson Browne, as well as her own "Love Me Like A Man", a showcase for her guitar technique.

⊙ **Takin' My Time** Warners
Another Raitt classic, this time from 1973, and including her tribute to Mississippi Fred McDowell plus a brilliant, blues-laden take on Randy Newman's "Guilty".

⊙ **Road Tested** EMI/Capitol
This double live album from 1995 does a good job of bridging Raitt's blues mama persona and her smoother rock style.

Jimmy Reed

b Dunleith, Mississippi, Sept 6, 1925; d Aug 29, 1976

With a simple but characterful style as instantly recognizable as that of John Lee Hooker or Muddy Waters, **Jimmy Reed** ranks among the true greats of postwar blues. He was much covered and blatantly copied, but his effortless, relaxed sound was never bettered by any of his imitators.

Born into a large sharecropping family, Mathis James Reed learned to play harmonica and guitar from **Eddie "Playboy" Taylor**, who was a couple of years older and also lived on Johnny Collier's plantation near Dunleith. That said, Reed never quite matched Taylor's proficiency on the guitar. After leaving school at fourteen, he worked in the fields and sang in the Pilgrim Rest Baptist Choir until he moved north to Chicago in 1943. The following year he was drafted into the Navy. On his discharge he returned briefly to Mississippi, where he married **Mary Lee Davis** ("Mama" Reed), then moved north again to Gary, Indiana, where he worked first in a meat-packing factory and then in a steel mill.

Away from his day job, Reed started gigging around both Gary and nearby Chicago, playing a single-stringed diddley-bow on the street with Willie Joe Duncan and in bars with the Gary Kings, alongside **John Brim** and **Albert King**. After failing an audition with Chess, he signed in 1953 for Chicago rival Vee Jay Records, apparently on a recommendation from King, who had just started making his own records for Parrot. At Vee Jay, he hooked up again with Taylor. Reed's first hit arrived in 1954, when he charted with "You Don't Have To Go". That song established the style from which he never wavered, characterized by slack-jawed vocals modeled on the little-known "Mushmouth" Robinson, accompanied by Taylor's insistent rhythm guitar and blasts of his own harp from the rack he wore around his neck.

After that, there was no stopping him. Reed went on to enjoy more hits than any other blues artist of the era, including "Ain't That Lovin' You Baby", "Shame Shame Shame", "You've Got Me Dizzy", "Bright Lights, Big City", "I'm Gonna Get My Baby", "Honest I Do", "Baby What You Want Me To Do" and "Big Boss Man". Most of the lyrics were written by his wife, "Mama" Reed, who in the studio also often whispered the words into his ear, for Reed never learned to read. Yet he delivered them with an effortless self-confidence over an irresistible boogie beat in his own distinctive take on the urban Chicago sound.

By the time Reed left Vee Jay in 1965, he had become a seminal influence on the British R&B boom, and the early sound in particular of the Rolling Stones, who covered "Honest I Do" on their debut album. However, by then he was far from well. He was always a heavy drinker, so when he fell ill in 1957, doctors assumed his fits were due to his rampant alcoholism. However, he was subsequently diagnosed as being epileptic. Touring Europe in the 1960s, he grew increasingly unreliable; he often appeared drunk on stage and frequently forgot his words. His manager Al Smith insisted that "Jimmy could put on almost as good a performance drunk as the average artists could sober", but it did not always seem that way to his audiences.

Reed's departure from Vee Jay also marked the end of his partnership with Taylor. He went on to record several albums for ABC-Bluesway during the late 1960s. After a couple of years off the road while he recuperated and attempted to reduce his drinking, he returned to active service in 1970 by touring with Clifton Chenier. He continued working until his death, recording in the 1970s for Bluesway, Roker, Blues On Blues and the Magic label, though little if any of his former seemingly effortless panache was apparent. He was on tour in Oakland, California, in August 1976 when he suffered an epileptic seizure and died in his sleep of respiratory failure, a week shy of his 51st birthday. The irony is that he had apparently finally overcome his drinking problem, and friends were hoping that after some distinctly lackluster years he was ready to make a major impact again.

⊙ **Bright Lights Big City** Charly
Justifiably subtitled "his greatest hits", as all of Jimmy Reed's charting singles bar "Take Out Some Insurance" are here.

Playlist
Jimmy Reed

1 BIG BOSS MAN (1960) from **The Sun Is Shining – The Master Of Down Home Blues**
Perhaps Reed's best-known song, this was in fact written by Willie Dixon, and later covered by the Grateful Dead.

2 BRIGHT LIGHTS, BIG CITY (1961) from **The Sun Is Shining – The Master Of Down Home Blues**
One of several Reed songs covered by the Rolling Stones. In their early days before the arrival of Charlie Watts, the band auditioned drummers by playing them Jimmy Reed records and announcing they wanted to sound like that…

3 SHAME SHAME SHAME (1963) from **The Sun Is Shining – The Master Of Down Home Blues**
"Well I tried to tell you baby but it make no sense, know you got me baby up against this fence".

4 ROCKIN' WITH REED (1953) from **Rockin' With Reed**
A song that became the title track of Reed's second album for Vee Jay six years later.

5 HONEST I DO (1957) from **I'm Jimmy Reed**
Reed's biggest crossover hit, and another one subsequently covered by the Rolling Stones.

6 BABY WHAT YOU WANT ME TO DO (1959) from **The Sun Is Shining – The Master Of Down Home Blues**
"You got me runnin', you got me hidin', you got me run, hide, hide, run, any way you wanna let it roll".

7 AIN'T THAT LOVIN' YOU BABY (1955) from **I'm Jimmy Reed**
"They may kill me baby, bury me like they do, my body might lie but my spirit gonna rise and come on home to you".

8 YOU DON'T HAVE TO GO (1953) from **I'm Jimmy Reed**
"Whoa baby, honey what's wrong wich' you?…"

9 TAKE OUT SOME INSURANCE (1959) from **Rockin' With Reed**
Sage advice from an improbable financial adviser.

⊙ **Blues Masters: The Very Best Of Jimmy Reed** Rhino
Seventeen great tracks that Jimmy Reed recorded for Vee Jay between 1953 and 1963.

⊙ **The Essential Boss Man: The Very Best Of The Vee-Jay Years, 1953–1966** Snapper
Three discs and 75 tracks in one of those few box sets that really can claim to be essential.

⊙ **I'm Jimmy Reed** Collectables
A nicely recreated CD edition of an album that first appeared on Vee Jay in 1958, and includes "Honest I Do" and "Ain't That Lovin' You Baby".

⊙ **The Masters** Eagle
Twenty of Jimmy Reed's classic Vee Jay recordings at a budget price, including most of his big hits.

Duke Robillard

b Woonsocket, Rhode Island, Oct 4, 1948

Best known as a founder member of **Roomful Of Blues** (who have their own entry in this book), **Duke Robillard** has since leaving the group in 1979 also pursued a successful solo career as both a performer and a producer.

Growing up in the unlikely blues pastures of Providence, Rhode Island, Robillard was as an aspiring young guitarist inspired by the recordings of Charley Patton, T-Bone Walker and Big Joe Turner, and traveled frequently to Boston to see top blues performers in action. He founded Roomful of Blues at nineteen years old, in 1967, and stayed a dozen years, leading the group through numerous line-up changes. After leaving the band, he played lead guitar with **Robert Gordon** before he joined the **Legendary Blues Band**.

In 1981 he put together **Duke Robillard & the Pleasure Kings**, who released three albums on Rounder Records, starting with their self-titled debut in 1984. At the same time he released a series of solo records, including 1988's blues-oriented *You Got Me*, as well as albums of jazz and swing.

In 1990 Robillard replaced Jimmie Vaughan in the **Fabulous Thunderbirds**, but he was soon alone again, signing with Point Blank/Virgin for 1994's *Temptation*. That was followed by *Duke's Blues* two years later, a fine homage to the classic blues sound of the 1950s. *Dangerous Place* came out on Virgin

in 1997, before he signed to Shanachie for 1999's *New Blues For Modern Man*, followed swiftly by *Conversations In Swing Guitar* and 2000's *Explorer*. Switching to Stony Plain in 2002, he proceeded to cut a prolific five albums in less than four years, including the all-blues set *Living With The Blues* and 2004's *Blue Mood*, a tribute to one of his earliest guitar heroes, T-Bone Walker.

Robillard has also recorded with or produced albums for Jimmy Witherspoon, John Hammond, Billy Boy Arnold, Pinetop Perkins, Snooky Pryor and Jay McShann, and worked with a vast array of other artists from Ruth Brown to Bob Dylan. He continues to tour relentlessly with the Duke Robillard Band, playing up to 250 dates a year.

⊙ **You Got Me** Rounder
Dr. John and Jimmie Vaughan help out on the best and most bluesy of Duke Robillard's Rounder albums, from 1998.

⊙ **Duke's Blues** Point Blank/Virgin
A fine mix of Robillard originals and classics from 1996, culminating with an amazing eleven-minute jam on Albert Collins'"Dyin' Flu".

⊙ **Living With The Blues** Stony Plain
This low-key but masterful 2002 set includes Robillard's renditions of blues classics by Freddie King and Tampa Red.

⊙ **Blue Mood** Stony Plain
A 12-track tribute to T-Bone on which Duke Robillard emulates both the fluidity of Walker's guitar playing and the husky power of his voice.

Fenton Robinson

b Greenwood, Mississippi, Sept 23, 1935; d Nov 25, 1997

With his mellow voice and jazz-oriented guitar playing, **Fenton Robinson** always epitomized elegance and grace, although there was no lack of emotion and passion in his blues, either.

Raised on a Mississippi plantation, Robinson built his first guitar from a cigar box and wire when he was eleven and taught himself to play by copying what he heard on radio shows like the *King Biscuit Hour*. He was particularly enamored of the style of **T-Bone Walker**, an influence that never left him.

Robinson got his first proper guitar, a Stella acoustic, in 1951, and took lessons in Memphis from **Charles McGowan**, whose band he ultimately joined after moving to the city in 1953. With McGowan he backed **Bobby Bland**, before moving to Little Rock, Arkansas, in 1954, and forming Fenton Robinson and the Castle Rockers. His first studio experience came with **Rosco Gordon** for Duke Records in 1956, while the following year he cut his debut as a bandleader with "Tennessee Woman" on Meteor Records, with a band that included his mentor McGowan. On a recommendation from Bland, he next moved to Don Robey's Duke Records. His many singles for the label, which often featured **James Booker** on piano, included his own composition "As The Years Go Passing By", which later became a hit for **Albert King**. Robinson and Booker also played on labelmate Larry Davis' "Texas Flood", later covered by Stevie Ray Vaughan.

Moving to Chicago in 1961, Robinson played sessions and clubs on the South Side. He only recorded sporadically, for labels like USA and Giant, until 1967, when he made the first recording, backed by members of B.B. King's touring band, of the song that was to become his calling card, "Somebody Loan Me A Dime". **Boz Scaggs** recorded a magnificent version of the song on his self-titled solo album two years later, with **Duane Allman** on lead guitar. Some claim this to be the finest solo Allman ever committed to tape, but there was an unseemly legal battle when Scaggs' name appeared on the writing credits.

Robinson's first album didn't appear until 1971, but it flopped and he took a gig with **Charlie Musselwhite**'s band. In 1974, he signed to Alligator Records, for whom he re-cut "Somebody Loan Me A Dime" as the title tune of his debut release. Then, just as his career finally appeared to be taking off, a past misdemeanor caught up with him, and he was convicted of involuntary manslaughter from a 1969 car accident. He served nine months of a longer prison sentence before being paroled for good behavior.

Back out of jail, Robinson released *I Hear Some Blues Downstairs* on Alligator in 1977, but didn't record again until 1984 for the Black Magic label in Holland. He continued playing festivals and clubs until his death from brain cancer in 1997.

⊙ **Somebody Loan Me A Dime** Alligator
Fenton Robinson's first album for Alligator, in 1974, stands as his finest hour, although you should check out the version of the title song on Boz Scaggs' debut.

⊙ **I Hear Some Blues Downstairs** Alligator
This 1977 album is not quite as good as its predecessor, but it's still a fine set, including versions of "Killing Floor", "Tell Me What's The Reason", Rosco Gordon's "Just A Little Bit" and T-Bone Walker's "West Side Baby" and "Tell Me What's The Reason", as well as a remake of Robinson's own "As The Years Go Passing By".

Jimmy Rogers

b Ruleville, Mississippi, June 3, 1924; d Dec 19, 1997

The guitarist **Jimmy Rogers** played a key role in the formation of Muddy Waters' great first band in Chicago in the 1940s. Despite being most famous as a sideman, however, he also recorded some exceptional blues records under his own name.

Taking the name Rogers from his stepfather, James A. Lane taught himself to play harmonica and guitar by listening to the records of Big Bill Broonzy, Memphis Minnie and Sonny Boy Williamson on radio station KFFA out of Helena, Arkansas, where he lived in the early 1940s. Moving to Memphis, he played with **Robert Lockwood Jr.** and **Robert Nighthawk**, then relocated to St Louis, where he teamed up with **Sunnyland Slim**. He arrived in Chicago in 1947, and immediately met **Muddy Waters**, with whom he seemed to develop an almost telepathic understanding. By introducing harp player **Little Walter** and pianist **Otis Spann** to Waters, Rogers played a key role in bringing together what many regard as the greatest Chicago blues band of all time.

The band proceeded to cut many of the classics that came to define the Chicago sound, including "Baby Please Don't Go", "Hoochie Coochie Man", "I Just Want To Make Love To You" and "I'm Ready". Such sides inevitably tended to overshadow Rogers' own records for Chess, often cut in time left over after Waters' sessions and featuring the same musicians, including Muddy himself, Little Walter, Spann, and either Willie Dixon or Big Crawford on bass. Nevertheless, Rogers made the R&B charts thirteen times under his own name, including "That's Alright", "Ludella", "Chicago Bound", "Walking By Myself", "Sloppy Drunk", "You're The One" and "The Last Time", most of which he wrote himself.

Rogers was also much in demand as a session guitarist, backing the likes of Howlin' Wolf, Sunnyland Slim and Sonny Boy Williamson after his stint with Waters and leading his own band around Chicago. Yet by the 1960s he was no longer able to make a living playing the blues, and bought a clothing store on Chicago's West Side. After the business was burned to the ground in a 1968 race riot, he finally returned to music and formed a new band with Johnny Littlejohn on second guitar and pianist Bob Riedy.

He signed to Leon Russell's Shelter label for the 1971 album *Gold Tailed Bird* and toured Europe in 1972 and 1973. Then he retired once more from music, this time to manage a Chicago apartment building, although he came back to play with Waters one last time on his 1977 album *I'm Ready*. This seemed to reignite his enthusiasm, for albums followed at sporadic intervals over the next fifteen years for labels like JSP, Blind Pig and Bedrock. The 1990s then produced a flurry of activity, partly inspired by the desire of some of the white musicians he had inspired decades earlier to see him receive his due before it was too late. He visited Britain in 1992 to play shows with both Eric Clapton and the Rolling Stones, and also headlined a Muddy Waters tribute tour. The album *Blue Bird*, released on the Analogue label, won him a W.C. Handy Award as best traditional blues recording, and featured a band that included his son, Jimmy D. Lane, on guitar, Johnnie Johnson on piano and Carey bell on harp.

Rogers' Indian summer was cut short when he died from cancer in late 1997 at the age of 73. *Blues, Blues, Blues*, his final album, which he had almost finished recording, was released posthumously on Atlantic, and featured guest appearances by Mick Jagger, Keith Richards, Eric Clapton, Taj Mahal, Jimmy Page, Robert Plant and Stephen Stills.

On its release, many of the guests paid generous tribute to him. Jagger said: "The first time I heard Jimmy was when I was buying my first blues records and listening to Muddy Waters and eventually I found out that Jimmy was the guitarist on these records that I loved," while Clapton simply called him "one of my all-time great guitar heroes".

⊙ **Complete Chess Recordings** Chess
More than fifty tracks over two discs from Jimmy Rogers' classic 1950s recordings, accompanied by Chicago's finest.

⊙ **Blues Blues Blues** Atlantic
For once all the superstar guests didn't hog the limelight on Jimmy Rogers' 1997 swansong – Clapton, Jagger and Richards were all simply there to encourage and assist on what was Rogers' show all the way.

Roy Rogers
b Vallejo, California, July 28, 1950

Best-known as the producer who masterminded John Lee Hooker's remarkable comeback on albums such as *The Healer* and *Mr Lucky*, **Roy Rogers** is also one of the finest blues slide guitar players of the modern era.

Born in California in 1950 and named after the king of the cowboys, Rogers began playing guitar aged twelve. Within a year, he was in a band playing Little Richard and Chuck Berry hits while dressed in gold lamé jackets. He discovered the blues when his older brother brought home Robert Johnson's *King Of The Delta Blues*, and slide guitar a few years later, when he heard Elmore James' "Dust My Broom". "From that minute I was into slide playing," he says.

By the time Rogers made his recording debut in 1976 on Waterhouse Records, as part of an acoustic duo with harp player **David Burgin**, he was a slide virtuoso. After the two split, Rogers formed the **Delta Rhythm Kings** in 1982, and played the American club circuit and toured Europe, before he joined **John Lee Hooker**'s Coast to Coast Blues Band. He stayed four years, and the two men established a close rapport. "I just can't say enough good things about Roy," Hooker said. "He plays so good. Some of the best slide I've heard, best blues I've heard. He gets real deep and funky, and he masters whatever he plays." Although he left Hooker's band in 1986, Rogers produced his 1989 star-studded comeback album *The Healer* as well as 1991's *Mr Lucky*, *Boom Boom* in 1992 and *Chill Out* in 1995.

Rogers' first solo album, *Chops Not Chaps*, had appeared in 1985, while he was still in Hooker's band. Originally released on his own label, it was later given wider distribution by Blind Pig. Hooker allowed his young protégé to promote the album as the support act on his shows. A second solo album, *Slidewinder*, came out on Blind Pig in 1987 and included duets with Hooker and New Orleans piano great **Allen Toussaint**. Further

Ride 'em cowboy: Roy Rogers

albums followed with 1989's *Blues On The Range* and a brace cut with harmonica virtuoso **Norton Buffalo**. Rogers recorded two albums for Liberty in the 1990s, then signed to Point Blank, the label for whom he'd produced Hooker, and released the sweaty, juke joint collection *Rhythm And Groove* in 1996. *Pleasure And Pain* was issued by Virgin two years later. His most recent album *Live! At the Sierra Nevada Brewery Big Room*, recorded with his band the Delta Rhythm Kings, appeared on his own label in 2004.

⊙ **Rhythm And Groove** Point Blank
This 1996 Roy Rogers album is a cooking collection of fine songs and stellar slide playing, although he's only a respectable rather than a great singer.

The Rolling Stones
formed London, 1962

No doubt some blues purists will object to the presence of the **Rolling Stones** in this book, and we'll keep things brief, for their story has been told enough times and only touches the blues at certain tangential points. However, the blues was an essential part of their origins and it would be churlish to leave them out, particularly when the likes of **Muddy Waters** were gener-

ous enough to thank the group for putting blues musicians back on the map in America, when they might otherwise have been forgotten.

When the band formed in 1962, the Rolling Stones were clearly inspired by blues and R&B every bit as much as by rock'n'roll. As a youth, **Mick Jagger** used to send off to Chess's mail order department in Chicago for records that were unavailable in Britain. **Keith Richards** was equally obsessed with the Chicago sounds of Chuck Berry and Jimmy Reed, while **Brian Jones** for a while called himself Elmo Lewis after a couple of his blues heroes – and, of course, the band's name itself was taken from a Muddy Waters song.

At their first recording session in February 1963, all the Stones really had in mind was to copy the Chess sound as accurately as they could, as they cut demos of songs by Waters, Reed and Bo Diddley. Their first single a few months later coupled Chuck Berry's "Come On" with Waters' "I Want To Be Loved", while their early live set consisted almost entirely of blues and R&B covers. As they moved from playing clubs to ballrooms, however, and began to respond to the success of the Beatles, the music began to change. Even so, they were still a full-on Chess tribute band when they cut their 1964 debut album, which included covers of Muddy Waters' "I Just Wanna Make Love To You", Jimmy Reed's "Honest I Do", Slim Harpo's "I'm A King Bee", and Rufus Thomas' "Walking The Dog". When they made their first visit to America later that year, one of their first stops was the Chess studio in Chicago. There they met Muddy Waters (although Keith Richards' story that he was up a ladder painting the walls can be discounted), Chuck Berry, Buddy Guy and Willie Dixon, who typically tried to sell them some of his songs. Over two days at Chess they also recorded fourteen songs, including covers of Irma Thomas' "Time Is On My Side" and the Valentinos' "It's All Over Now", which gave them their first number one single.

At a press conference at Heathrow on their return to Britain, Jagger expressed his shock at the lack of recognition in America for the Stones' blues heroes. "The kids had never heard of Muddy Waters," he complained. "They've got the greatest blues singer living among them and they don't even know." Waters never forget their support and thereafter always defended them when the Stones were under attack for "ripping off" black music.

Towards the end of 1964, the Stones released their most blues-drenched single of all. A fine version of Howlin' Wolf's 1961hit "Little Red Rooster", it featured Brian Jones making a decent stab at Hubert Sumlin's slide part. While it went to number one in Britain, manager Andrew Loog Oldham was determined to move the band away from their blues/R&B roots and push them in a more overtly commercial pop direction. He got his wish when after two years of relying heavily on covers for their hits, Jagger and Richards wrote the 1965 smash "(I Can't Get No) Satisfaction". From then on they wrote all of the Stones hits, and the pop element took over, until they returned to a bluesier, roots-rock sound on the 1968 album *Beggar's Banquet*.

After the troubled Jones had been replaced by former John Mayall's Bluesbreakers' guitarist **Mick Taylor**, the next few years found the band in their pomp as they forged a potent blues-rock sound. Largely based on Jagger–Richards compositions, it still included the occasional well-chosen cover, such as Robert Johnson's "Love In Vain", which appeared on *Let It Bleed* in 1969, and Mississippi Fred McDowell's "You Gotta Move", a stand-out on 1971's *Sticky Fingers*.

By the early 1970s the Stones were virtually unassailable as the greatest rock'n'roll band in the world, and despite assorted ups and downs that's a position they have sustained into the new millennium. Yet the band, and Richards in particular, have always been careful to continue to express an indebtedness to the blues and R&B, and blues performers have been regularly asked to support them on their gargantuan world tours. In recent years band members have also made guest appearances on albums by the likes of Hubert Sumlin, B.B. King, John Lee Hooker, Bo Diddley and Jimmy Rogers.

After an eight-year absence form the studio, the Stones returned in 2005 with the album *A Bigger Bang*, which included several blues-influenced tracks, including "The Back Of My Hand" and "Laugh I Nearly Died".

⊙ The Rolling Stones Decca

An essential artefact of the British R&B boom, the Stones' 1964 debut featured fabulous versions of songs such as "Route 66", "I Just Want To Make Love To You", "Honest I Do" and "I'm A King Bee".

⊙ Exile On Main Street Virgin

The Rolling Stones' 1972 masterpiece is permeated with dark and deep blues of a unique kind.

▣ Playlist
The Rolling Stones

1 LITTLE RED ROOSTER (1964) from **Rolling Stones Now**
"We thought just for a change we'd do a nice, straight blues on a single. What's wrong with that?" Mick Jagger, Nov 28, 1964.

2 I JUST WANNA MAKE LOVE TO YOU (1964) from **The Rolling Stones**
"They're my boys…" Muddy Waters in *Melody Maker*, May 23, 1964.

3 HONEST I DO (1964) from **The Rolling Stones**
Mick Jagger bought this Jimmy Reed single on import in the late 1950s.

4 TIME IS ON MY SIDE (DATE?) from **The Rolling Stones No 2**
They found the song on the B-side of an Irma Thomas single.

5 I CAN'T BE SATISFIED (1965) from **The Rolling Stones No 2**
Another Muddy Waters number, recorded during two days in the Chess studios in Chicago in June 1964, with some decent bottleneck guitar from Brian Jones.

6 THE LAST TIME (1965) from **Big Hits (High Tide & Green Grass)**
The composing credit may have said "Jagger-Richards", but it was based on a Staple Singers number.

7 LOVE IN VAIN (1969) from **Let It Bleed**
"Well I followed her to the stay-shun…" – Jagger's take on Robert Johnson is somewhat mannered, but there's some great slide guitar from Keith Richards.

8 YOU GOTTA MOVE (1971) from **Sticky Fingers**
They took this one from Mississippi Fred McDowell.

9 STOP BREAKING DOWN (1972) from **Exile On Main Street**
The Stones' second foray into the Robert Johnson songbook, from the album many regard as the high tide of their long career.

10 MANNISH BOY (1977) from **Love You Live**
Mick does Muddy, recorded live from an album that also included concert renditions of "Little Red Rooster" and "You Gotta Move".

Roomful Of Blues

formed Rhode Island in 1967

Is it a bar band, a college for musicians, or a brand and franchise? In its own way, **Roomful of Blues** is all of those and more. Over almost forty years, it has become an institution that transcends the ranks of the great musicians who have passed through it.

Founded in Westerly, Rhode Island, by guitarist **Duke Robillard** and pianist **Al Copley**, with drummer Fran Christina and bassist Larry Peduzzi on board as the rhythm section, RoB started out playing the club circuit as far afield as Boston. At first, they were oriented towards contemporary blues-rock, but Robillard changed their musical direction in 1970. Aided by a horn section featuring **Greg Piccolo**, Rich Lataille and Doug James, they began playing jump blues instead. By the mid-1970s, they were supporting established blues artists and even gigged with Count Basie. With the help of Doc Pomus they signed to Island, which released their self-titled debut album in 1977. After the release of a second album, 1979's *Let's Have A Party For Antilles*, Robillard left for a solo career and guitarist **Ronnie Earl** took over as bandleader.

Over the years the group has undergone numerous line-up changes. Female vocalist Lou Ann Barton spent a year with the group during the early 1980s, then Piccolo took over as singer for 1981's *Hot Little Mama*, released by Blue Flame. In addition to their own recordings they served as backing group for studio albums by **Eddie "Cleanhead" Vinson**, **Big Joe Turner** and **Earl King**; all three earned Grammy nominations.

RoB's 1984 Varrick album, *Dressed Up To Get Messed Up*, was their most successful to date. When Piccolo took an enforced break due to throat surgery, **Curtis Salgado** was brought in to front the group on 1987's *Live At Lupo's Heartbreak Hotel*, while founder member Copley also left, and was replaced on keyboards by Ron Levy.

Ronnie Earl too departed shortly afterwards, followed by Salgado when Piccolo returned, while the revolving door found guitarist Chris Vachon joining in 1990 and pianist Matt McCabe two years later. *Dance All Night*, the group's first album in seven years, appeared on Bullseye Blues in 1994. With **Sugar Ray Norcia** taking over vocal duties from Piccolo, further Bullseye albums followed

with 1995's *Turn It On! Turn It Up!* and *Under One Roof* in 1997. The line-up then underwent another major restructuring, to become a nine-piece fronted by vocalist **McKinley "Mac" Odom** for 1998's *There Goes The Neighborhood* and *Watch You When You Go* in 2001. The following year Odom was replaced by **Mark DuFresne**. Signing to Alligator Records in 2003, they released *That's Right!* that year, and *Standing Room Only* in 2005. They continue to tour with an ever-shifting line-up, while the horn section remains busy as a freelance unit.

⊙ **The Blues'll Make You Happy, Too** Rounder
A sturdy 14-track compilation covering Roomful of Blues' post-Robillard era, during the 1980s and 1990s.

⊙ **Standing Room Only** Alligator
Swing, jump and jive on a 2005 album from Roomful of Blues' latest eight-piece incarnation, led by guitarist Chris Vachon.

Doctor Ross

b Tunica, Mississippi, Oct 21, 1925; d May 28, 1993

The last of the great one-man blues bands, **Dr. Ross** played guitar and harp and sang in the tradition of Daddy Stovepipe, Jesse Fuller and Joe Hill Louis. His unique sound stemmed from the fact that he played guitar left-handed and upside down, and also played his harp "back to front".

Charles Isaiah Ross was born into a family that contained native American blood. He learned to play harmonica aged nine, and added guitar by the late 1930s, playing with a rhythmic, percussive strum reminiscent of **Barbecue Bob**. Having cut his teeth playing in juke joints, he landed a radio slot in Clarksdale, Mississippi, where he played with Willie Love. He was called up to the army in 1943 and trained as a paramedic, earning the nickname "Doctor". On his discharge in 1947, he found his way to Helena, Arkansas, and formed his Jump and Jive Band. He also appeared on the *King Biscuit Hour* radio show, developing the one-man band style for which he was to become famous. The early 1950s found him recording for Sam Phillips at **Sun**. Sides such as "Country Clown", "Chicago Breakdown" and "The Boogie Disease" showed him to be an original songwriter and a powerful singer, as well as showcasing clever interplay between his harmonica and guitar. However, he quit the label in 1954 and moved to Flint, Michigan, apparently concerned that his royalties were being used to promote Elvis Presley.

In Michigan, Ross worked for General Motors on the assembly line by day while continuing to play the blues by night, and releasing records on his own DIR label. The folk-blues revival of the early 1960s resuscitated his career, and he recorded for the Testament label and toured Europe in 1965 with the American Folk Blues Festival. While in London, he recorded the first album to appear on the Blue Horizon label. He returned several times to play in Europe, where he became more popular than at home, and made his last visit to Britain in 1991. He died two years later at the age of 67.

⊙ **Boogie Disease** Arhoolie
Twenty-plus tracks from Dr. Ross's early Memphis sessions between 1951 and 1954, both in one-man-band mode and with a down-home ensemble.

Otis Rush

b Philadelphia, Mississippi, April 29, 1934

Otis Rush has been singing the blues for half a century. Originally influenced by Muddy Waters, he swiftly developed a highly distinctive and powerful style notable for its dark, brooding emotional intensity. Something of a guitarist's guitarist, he exerted a considerable influence on a generation of British blues-rock players like Eric Clapton, Peter Green, Jeff Beck and Mick Taylor, as well as American instrumentalists from Mike Bloomfield to Johnny Winter.

One of seven children, Rush was born into a sharecropping family in East Mississippi in 1934, and learned to play the guitar aged eight by watching his older brothers. He played upside-down because he was left-handed but that didn't seem to hinder him, and he was soon playing in the local church, where his vocal ability was also evident early on. Determined not to work on a farm, he moved north to Chicago in 1949 at the tender age of fifteen, and worked in stockyards, steel mills and factories as well as driving a horse-drawn coal wagon. But by night he hung out in the blues clubs and came under the spell of **Muddy Waters**, who inspired him to follow in his footsteps. After months of hard practice

to get his chops into shape, Rush played his debut gigs as a solo guitarist and put his first band together in 1953, styling himself Little Otis.

He made an immediate impact in the clubs of the West Side, accompanying his impassioned soul-tinged vocals with aggressive, string-bending guitar playing. Not until 1955, however, when **Willie Dixon** signed him to Cobra Records, did he give up his succession of day jobs. The following year he had a major R&B hit with "I Can't Quit You Baby", which featured Walter Horton on harp and was later covered by **Led Zeppelin** on their debut album. He continued cutting such classics for Cobra as "Double Trouble", "Checking On My Baby" and "All Your Love" until the label folded in 1958, whereupon he signed to **Chess**, who had previously passed on him, feeling his style was too similar to Muddy Waters. For Chess he made the brilliant "So Many Roads, So Many Trains" in 1960, but for some reason the label still refused to make him a priority and he was allowed to leave for Duke, where he recorded 1962's excellent "Home Work".

The rest of the 1960s were not a happy time, and Rush was beset by contractual and personal difficulties. At the end of the decade, he recorded an album with **Mike Bloomfield** that also featured Duane Allman, and followed with albums on Mike Vernon's London-based Blue Horizon label and for Delmark back in Chicago. However, the Nick Gravenites-produced *Right Place Wrong Time*, recorded in 1971, remained unissued until Bullfrog put it out in 1976, and the lean years dragged on into the 1980s, when he eventually signed to Blind Pig and released the live album, *Tops*. During the 1990s, he released the excellent *Ain't Enough Comin' In* on Mercury, and 1998's *Any Place I'm Going* on House of Blues.

⊙ **Essential Collection: The Classic Cobra Recordings 1956–1958** Varese
Two dozen all-time Otis Rush classics, including "Double Trouble", "Checking On My Baby", "All Your Love", "Groaning The Blues" and, of course, "I Can't Quit You Baby".

⊙ **Right Place Wrong Time** Hightone
The 1971 album that inexplicably remained unreleased for five years. The closest Rush came during the 1970s to rivaling the intensity of his late 1950s sides for Cobra.

⊙ **Ain't Enough Comin' In** Mercury
Fat guitar solos and soulful vocals from Otis Rush at his sublime best in 1994, performing epic songs by the likes of Sam Cooke, Ray Charles, B.B. King and Albert King.

REDFERNS

Jimmy Rushing

b Oklahoma City, Oklahoma, Aug 26, 1902; d June 8, 1972

Although **Jimmy Rushing** sang with Count Basie's Orchestra for fifteen years, and also fronted his own group, even when backed by jazz instrumentation his voice was pure blues. Known as Mister Five-By-Five – an affectionate reference to his height and girth – he possessed a big tenor voice to match his size, which allowed him to dominate even the loudest, swingingest of big bands. But although he may have been a blues shouter, his phrasing and pitch were also supple and precise and his tone was rich and creamy.

The first instrument James Andrew Rushing learned was the violin. He also studied musical theory, took piano lessons, and sang in school and church choirs. On leaving school he moved to Los Angeles, where he worked a day job but sang at night in clubs and at parties, occasionally working with **Jelly Roll Morton**. He moved back to

Oklahoma City in 1926, and the following year joined **Walter Page's Blue Devils**, singing on the orchestra's 1929 Vocalion session in Kansas City.

Remaining in Kansas City, he joined **Bennie Moten's Orchestra**, with whom he made several recordings for Victor before signing on with **Count Basie**'s band in 1935. His first recording with Basie came the following year with "Boogie-woogie", and he appeared on dozens of sides with the band, including such classics as "Sent For You Yesterday", "Good Morning Blues" and "The Blues I Like To Hear". He also appeared with Basie at the first, legendary "From Spirituals to Swing" concert at New York's Carnegie Hall in 1938, as well as in several films featuring the band.

Not until 1950 did Rushing step out in front of his own band, recording prolifically with his own septet for Columbia, Okeh, King, Vanguard and Jazztone. During the ensuing decade he also sang with **Benny Goodman** and **Coleman Hawkins**, while in the 1960s he worked with jazz stars **Dave Brubeck** and **Thelonious Monk** and teamed up again with Goodman and Basie. He died of leukemia in New York City in 1972, at the age of 69.

⊙ **Jimmy Rushing With Count Basie And His Orchestra 1938–45** Giants of Jazz
Twenty tracks mixing blues and ballads, recorded with Basie for the Columbia and Brunswick labels.

⊙ **The Essential Jimmy Rushing** Vanguard
Classic swing-blues sides produced by John Hammond, including fine remakes of some of Rushing's best tunes with Basie, and featuring boogie-woogie king Pete Johnson plus the likes of Walter Page and Buddy Tate.

"Bitch With A Bad Attitude" and "How Can I Say I Miss You (When I Can't Get You To Leave)" with the occasional spirited cover from the archives of such 1920s blues divas as Bessie Smith, Ma Rainey, Memphis Minnie and Ida Cox. Their last album for Alligator was 2001's *Ain't Gonna Hush*.

In 1997, Rabson released her first solo album, *Music Makin' Mama*, also on Alligator. Her most recent release, 2005's *In A Family Way*, featured various members of her family. Adegbalola too put out a well-received solo album in 1999, *Bitter Sweet Blues*, which she followed with 2004's *Neo-Classic Blues*. Inspired by the glaring omission of blues-women from Martin Scorcese's PBS TV series *The Blues*, the album paid tribute to Ma Rainey, Bessie Smith, Alberta Hunter, Ida Cox, Lucille Bogan, Sippie Wallace and Victoria Spivey among others.

⊙ **The Uppity Blues Women** Alligator
Saffire's splendid 1990 debut album, on which tracks such as "Middle Aged Blues" and "Even Yuppies Get The Blues" happily live up to their spiky titles.

Saffire – The Uppity Blues Women

formed Virginia, 1984

With their bawdy, rollicking songs, the sassy acoustic trio **Saffire – The Uppity Blues Women** revive the tradition of the great female blues singers of the 1920s, while also adding topical touches of contemporary feminism.

Pianist **Ann Rabson** and guitarist/harmonica player **Gaye Adegbalola** originally formed the group in Fredericksburg, Virginia, in 1984. Pooling their resources with bassist **Earlene Lewis**, they recorded an album that they submitted as a finished entity to Alligator Records. Surprisingly, the label had never signed an all-acoustic act before, but Alligator president Bruce Iglauer fell in love with their songs and feisty personality, and their self-titled debut appeared on the label in 1990.

To Iglauer's considerable surprise, it became one of Alligator's biggest sellers, while Adegbalola won a Blues Music Award for song of the year for her raucous "Middle-Aged Blues Boogie", featuring the classic lines: "An old woman don't tell/an old woman don't yell/an old woman don't swell/and she's grateful as hell/I need a young, young man/to drive away my middle-aged blues." The album's success led to the group playing support slots with the likes of Koko Taylor, B.B. King, Ray Charles and Willie Dixon among others.

By the release of their third album in 1992, *Broadcasting*, Rabson and Adegbalola had been joined by multi-instrumentalist **Andra Faye McIntosh**. The group has been a trio ever since, recording a string of fine albums for Alligator, mixing stylishly inventive original songs such as

Son Seals

b Osceola, Arkansas, Aug 13, 1942; d Dec 2004

Among the greatest of the second generation of Chicago bluesmen, **Son Seals** emerged as a major voice with his debut album in 1973, writing most of his own material and playing guitar with a ferocious intensity matched by similarly fierce vocals.

Frank Seals was the youngest of thirteen children. In the back rooms of his father Jim's Arkansas juke joint, the Dipsy Doodle, he heard the likes of Sonny Boy Williamson, Albert King and Robert Nighthawk playing almost every night. Jim Seals, who played piano, trombone, guitar and drums, had toured with the Rabbit Foot Minstrels, and was also known as "Son", so when Frank first began playing he was initially known as "Little Son". "My father taught me everything from the start," he later recalled. "Tuning the guitar, fingering. Where I wanted to be riffing around all up and down the neck right away, he'd keep me on one chord for hours, until I could feel in it in my sleep. I'd get up the next morning, grab the guitar, and I'd be right on that chord."

At the age of thirteen, Seals was backing artists at the Dipsy Doodle on drums, while by the early

1960s he was leading his own band as a guitarist during the week in Little Rock, Arkansas. He joined **Earl Hooker**'s touring band on guitar in 1963, then got a gig drumming with **Albert King**, and played on his Stax album *Live Wire/Blues Power*. After the death of his father in 1971, Seals left Arkansas and moved to Chicago. There he jammed with the likes of Junior Wells, Hound Dog Taylor, James Cotton and Buddy Guy, and secured a residency at the Expressway Lounge on the South Side.

Seals' debut album, *The Son Seals Blues Band*, appeared on Alligator in 1973 and announced the arrival of a significant new blues artist. His second, 1977's *Midnight Son*, was even better, and led to regular tours of Europe. He continued recording for Alligator throughout the 1980s and 1990s before he moved to Telarc for a final album, *Lettin' Go*, but the last years of his life were marked by misfortune. In 1997 he was shot in the jaw by an ex-wife. Two years later his left leg was amputated below the knee as a result of diabetes.

He died of diabetes-related complications in December 2004 at the age of 58. "He played guitar like his life depended on it," Bruce Iglauer commented on the news of his death. "It was his sheer intensity. He didn't really play the guitar, he attacked it. And that's the way he approached his vocals, too. He didn't ask you to listen, he bullied you into it."

⊙ **The Son Seals Blues Band** Alligator
Son Seals' debut album from 1973 featuring original songs such as "Mother-In-Law Blues" and "Your Love Is Like A Cancer".

⊙ **Midnight Son** Alligator
His second album, released in 1977, is a tour-de-force of low-down growling vocals and hot guitar licks that brings to mind the great Albert Collins.

⊙ **Lettin' Go** Telarc
The jagged guitar riffs and uncompromising vocals of what sadly proved to be Seals' final album, released in 2000, suggested he still had much to offer.

Shakey Jake

b Earle, Arkansas, April 12, 1921; d March 2, 1990

Some say **Shakey Jake** was always a better gambler than he was musician. Indeed, he spent several years as a pro at the gaming tables, and took his name from the crapshooters' call "Shake 'em Jake". When not shooting craps, however, he blew a powerful blues harp, often in collaboration with his nephew **Magic Sam**.

James Harris moved to Chicago at age seven. He learned to play the harmonica after being inspired by seeing Sonny Boy Williamson, but didn't turn professional until he was in his mid-30s. He cut his first single in 1958 – "Call Me If You Need Me", backed by "Roll Your Moneymaker" – for the Artistic label, a subsidiary of Eli Toscano's Cobra Records. Produced by Willie Dixon and featuring Magic Sam and Syl Johnson on guitars, it was a powerful slice of raw Chicago blues, but Jake took a quite different path on his next recording, when Prestige's Bluesville label paired him with guitarist Bill Jennings and organist Jack McDuff for the 1960 jazz-blues fusion album *Good Times*.

A second album for the same label, *Mouth Harp Blues*, featured a quartet including guitarist Jimmie Lee Robinson from Little Walter's band. Jake continued playing with Magic Sam in Chicago until he moved in the late 1960s to Los Angeles, where he briefly ran a night club and recorded for the World Pacific label. He eventually returned to Arkansas, where he died in 1990, at the age of 68.

⊙ **Mouth Harp Blues** Original Blues Classics
A welcome CD reissue of Shakey Jake's second album, from 1960, a slab of jazzy blues featuring contributions from guitarist Jimmie Lee Robinson and R&B/ gospel organist Robert Banks.

Mem Shannon

b New Orleans, Dec 21, 1959

Having driven a cab in New Orleans for fifteen years, **Mem Shannon** emerged as one of a new breed of bluesmen during the 1990s, and the most exciting new talent to come out of the Crescent City in some time. Backed by his band, the Membership, he incorporates elements of funk, jazz and rock'n'roll into his music.

Shannon started out playing clarinet aged nine, before graduating to guitar during his teens. He discovered the blues via his father's record collection, and was further inspired by catching B.B. King in concert. After playing in a high school rock'n'roll band, he joined the Ebony Brothers Hot Band, playing bars around New Orleans, then linked up with covers band Free Enterprise. However, when his father died in 1981, he became the family bread-winner and took a job driving a cab, while playing guitar in a gospel group called the Dedicators. Not until 1990 did he begin to work on his own songs, in collaboration with **Peter Carter**, an old friend who had played bass in Free Enterprize, and with whom he formed a new band called The Membership. Many of the songs were about his experiences driving a cab, and in 1991, Shannon and his group won a talent contest that gave them a place on the bill at the New Orleans Jazz and Heritage Festival.

After a demo reached Joe Boyd, owner of Hannibal Records, Shannon's debut album, *A Cab Driver's Blues*, was released on the label in 1995. The songs were interspersed with snippets of conversation with passengers recorded in his cab. The album did well enough that he marked the next year's Jazz and Heritage Festival to announce that he was giving up driving his cab to become a full-time bluesman.

A second album followed in 1997, while when Hannibal Records folded Shannon moved to Shanachie for 1999's *Spend Some Time With Me*. That was followed two years later by *Memphis In The Morning*. By the time of 2005's *I'm From Phunkville* he'd moved to the Northern Blues label.

⊙ **A Cab Driver's Blues** Hannibal
The conversational snippets between Mem Shannon's autobiographical songs might have reduced his 1995 debut album to a set of novelty-value blues vignettes. But his writing is funny, witty, smart and honest enough to carry the day.

Kenny Wayne Shepherd

b Shreveport, Louisiana, June 12, 1977

I nfluenced as much by the likes of such modern bluesmen as Stevie Ray Vaughan and Robert Cray as the original pioneers, **Kenny Wayne Shepherd** exploded on to the blues scene as a teenage guitar slinger during the mid-1990s.

Shepherd began playing guitar aged seven, and was soon copying licks from his father's collection of Muddy Waters records. He played his first gigs with New Orleans bluesman Brian Lee at thirteen, and soon after formed his own band with lead vocalist **Corey Sterling**, signing to Irving

Azoff's Giant Records in 1993. Combining a surprising number of styles but rooted in the blues of Texas and Louisiana rather than Chicago, his debut album, *Ledbetter Heights*, was released in 1995. It sold more than five hundred thousand copies, becoming one of the best-selling blues records of the decade, while *Guitar World* magazine voted him third on a list of the planet's greatest guitarists after B.B. King and Eric Clapton.

By 1998's *Trouble Is*, Sterling had been replaced as vocalist by the more blues-oriented **Noah Hunt**. The album also featured guest appearances from James Cotton and Chris Layton of Double Trouble, and mixed Shepherd's original compositions with covers of songs by Jimi Hendrix and Bob Dylan. *Live On* followed a year later. His latest effort, 2004's *The Place You're In*, is essentially a rock record rather than a blues album, and finds Shepherd handling most of the lead vocals for the first time.

⊙ **Trouble Is** Warners
Probably the best of Kenny Wayne Shepherd's four albums to date, this 1998 offering blends authentic blues with a Southern rock sound, much in the style of Stevie Ray Vaughan.

Johnny Shines

b Memphis, Tennessee, April 25, 1915; d April 20, 1992

T he long career of guitarist and singer **Johnny Shines** more or less paralleled the development of the blues on either side of World War II. Having run with Robert Johnson as an itinerant Delta bluesman in the 1930s, he moved north to Chicago in the 1940s, recorded some classic urban blues in the 1950s, and was rediscovered during the 1960s blues revival.

John Ned Lee Shines Jr. learned guitar from his mother, and spent part of his youth living on Beale Street, where he was inspired by hearing the likes of Charley Patton, Lonnie Johnson and the young Howlin' Wolf. "They lived in a world of their own," he later recalled. "They sung like they were overcome with sadness, in a trance." He was soon taking his first steps towards joining that world, singing and playing on street corners for tips on Beale Street, but in 1932 when he was seventeen he moved to Arkansas to work as a sharecropper. Two years later, he met **Robert Johnson** and fell under his spell, abandoning farming to accompany the great bluesman on his wanderings around the South, playing bars and juke joints, and even traveling north across the Canadian border to Windsor, Ontario, where they appeared on a radio program together. Shines spent three years with Johnson before the two parted in Arkansas in 1937. He never saw him again; Johnson died the following year.

Shines continued to play around the South for a few years, then in 1941 migrated north, apparently with a grand if ill-conceived plan to make his way to Africa via Canada. He got no further than Chicago, where he found a job with a construction gang. He also immersed himself in the local blues scene and made his first recordings for Columbia in 1946, although they were not released until 1971. In 1950, he recorded a number of sides for Chess, some of which appeared under the name Shoe Shine Johnny, while in 1952 and 1953 he cut some top-class material for the JOB label, featuring **Big Walter Horton** on harmonica. They led to no commercial success, however, and he was reduced to session work.

Following a row with Musicians Union, Shines abandoned music in 1958, sold his guitar and amp, and went back to the construction business. Over the next few years his only connection with the blues was working as a freelance photographer at a Chicago blues club, and selling his pictures to the patrons. In 1964 he was tracked down by British blues researcher Mike Rowe, (who a decade later wrote the book *Chicago Breakdown*) on a tip from Willie Dixon. That led to Samuel Charters recording Shines in December 1965, with Walter Horton once again on harmonica, for the award-winning *Chicago/The Blues/Today!* Series on Vanguard Records. A re-energized Shine also recorded *Master Of The Modern Blues, Vol. 1* for Testament and *Last Night's Dream* for Blue Horizon. He visited Europe with Horton and Willie Dixon as part of the Chicago All-Stars, and started his own band,

Shines in the dark

continuing to record in the 1970s for various labels including Biograph, Advent and Tomato. When not touring he taught guitar in Tuscaloosa, Alabama, where he had relocated after the death of his daughter left him to bring up his grandchildren.

To many white blues fans, the main interest in Shines' work was the link he represented with the legend of Robert Johnson, and in his slashing slide guitar it was possible to hear the spirit of his old partner. He was interviewed repeatedly by those seeking his recollections of Johnson and resented it for a while, feeling that his own worth as a bluesman was being overshadowed. Eventually, however, he bowed to the inevitable and decided to make the most of the connection, covering Johnson's songs when he toured and recorded during the late 1970s with **Robert Lockwood Jr.**, Johnson's stepson.

A stroke in 1980 adversely affected Shines' guitar playing, but he continued to tour America and Europe. In 1990 he appeared in the documentary film *Searching For Robert Johnson* alongside Honeyboy Edwards, and had a late flurry of studio activity which led to the release of *Traditional*

Delta Blues and *Back To The Country*, a collaborative album with **Snooky Pryor**, both released in 1991. He died the following year in a Tuscaloosa hospital.

⊙ **Evening Shuffle** Westside
Fourteen potent songs that Johnny Shines recorded for the JOB label in 1952 and 1953; Big Walter Horton features on harp on some tracks.

⊙ **Heritage Of The Blues: Skull & Crossbones Blues** Hightone
A compilation culled principally from Johnny Shines' three albums for Testament in the 1960s, with a band including Horton, Otis Spann, Lee Jackson and Fred Below.

⊙ **Johnny Shines** Hightone
A reissue of a fine 1970 album that contains both traditional Delta-styled acoustic blues and hard-rocking Chicago-flavored numbers.

⊙ **Traditional Delta Blues** Biograph
A powerful 1991 album recorded when he was past his best as a guitarist but still a potent vocalist, offering nods to Robert Johnson on the likes of "Ramblin' Blues", "Milk Cow Blues" and "Dynaflow Blues".

Slim Harpo

b Lobdel, Louisiana, Jan 11, 1924; d Jan 31, 1970

Perhaps the most successful of all the Louisiana bluesmen, **Slim Harpo** sang and played guitar and harmonica in an infectious and accessible style, like a more down-home, laid-back version of Jimmy Reed. The writer Peter Guralnick reckoned his languid voice sounded as "if a black country and western singer or a white rhythm and blues singer were attempting to impersonate a member of the opposite genre", and his songs were widely covered, particularly by the British R&B bands in the early 1960s.

James Moore was born just outside of Baton Rouge in 1924. After his parents died when he was in his mid-teens, he dropped out of school to play harp in bars and juke joints, on street corners, and at rent parties and plantation picnics as Harmonica Slim. He also worked regularly with his brother-in-law **Lightnin' Slim**, who recommended him to **J.D. Miller**, who recorded and produced local blues artists in Crowley, Louisiana, for **Excello** Records. Having heard Moore back Lightnin' Slim on harmonica on 1955 sides like "Lightnin' Blues" and "I Can't Be Successful", Miller decided to record him on his own. However, a new name was required; another Harmonica Slim was already recording on the West Coast. Moore's wife Lovelle (who also co-wrote some of his songs) came up with Slim Harpo, and he was known by that name for the rest of his career.

His first single, "I'm A King Bee" backed with "'I've Got Love If You Want It", gave him a double-sided R&B hit in 1957. Further hits followed, including "Rainin' in My Heart", which crossed over to the pop charts in 1961; "I Love The Life I Live"; "Buzzin'"; "Little Queen Bee"; and "Shake Your Hips". The **Rolling Stones**' 1964 cover version of "I'm A King Bee" started a craze among British R&B groups to record his songs; the Kinks cut "I've Got Love If You Want It", Van Morrison and Them made "Don't Start Crying Now", and the Pretty

---

Playlist
Slim Harpo

1 I'M A KING BEE **(1957)** from **The Best Of Slim Harpo**
A classic sexual blues metaphor, that was just waiting for the Rolling Stones to cover it.

2 RAININ' IN MY HEART **(1961)** from **The Best Of Slim Harpo**
"Slim wrote a bunch of songs with his wife, Lovelle. Boy, I wish I had a wife like that, help me write songs…" An envious Bob Dylan introducing the track on XM Satellite Radio, May 2006.

3 BABY, SCRATCH MY BACK **(1966)** from **The Best Of Slim Harpo**
The song that took Slim into the pop charts under his own name.

4 SHAKE YOUR HIPS **(1966)** from **The Excello Singles Anthology**
Another train-like Harpo rhythm, later covered in pulsating fashion by the Stones on *Exile On Main Street*.

5 TIP ON IN **(1966)** from **The Best Of Slim Harpo**
"Let me see those fishnet hose" – possibly one of the lyrics Slim's wife didn't help him write.

Things did "Rainin' In My Heart". Such high-profile support helped Harpo to his biggest crossover hit in 1966, with "Baby, Scratch My Back". That was followed by "Tip On In" and "Tee-Ni-Nee-Ni-Nu".

Harpo reunited with Lightnin' Slim in 1967, and the pair toured together, playing mostly to white rock audiences. They were about to make a trip to Europe when Harpo suffered a heart attack in Baton Rouge and died in early 1970, at the age of 46. Two years later the Stones cut a version of his "Shake Your Hips" on *Exile On Main Street*.

⊙ **Best Of Slim Harpo** Hip-O-Records
Sixteen of Slim Harpo's best-known and most covered songs, from "I'm A King Bee" to "Baby Scratch My Back".

⊙ **The Excello Singles Anthology** Hip-O-Records
Holding 44 tracks, these two discs are perfect for anyone looking for a more extensive picture of Slim Harpo's career than that provided by the more limited "best of" above.

Bessie Smith

b Chattanooga, Tennessee, April 15, circa 1894; d Sept 26, 1937

K nown as the "Empress of the Blues", **Bessie Smith** boasted one of the greatest voices of the twentieth century, and her majestic delivery and indomitable spirit made her the first blues superstar. While she had her rivals, including Ma Rainey and Ida Cox, none matched her emotional intensity or the nobility of her rich contralto delivery.

The exact year of Smith's birth remains uncertain. It has been variously given as 1894, 1895, 1896, 1898 and 1900, but the earliest suggestion appears the most likely. One of seven children, she was orphaned aged eight, and was discovered by **Ma Rainey** when the older woman passed through Chattanooga around 1912. By then Bessie had already spent time singing on street corners for tips, but Rainey heard her signing with her brother Clarence in Moses Stokes' entertainment troupe. There has been much debate as to whether Rainey actually coached the young singer who was soon to eclipse her, or merely offered general encouragement, but there's no doubt she was

a major influence.

By 1913 Smith was to be found singing in a theater in Atlanta and she went on to sing with a number of other shows on the vaudeville circuit, including Charles P. Bailey's troupe and Pete Werley's Florida Cotton Blossoms. By 1920 she was a headline act in her own right. That was the year that Mamie Smith recorded "Crazy Blues", but Bessie had to wait another three years to make her recording debut. After she was rejected at auditions for a number of labels, Frank Walker signed her to Columbia and took her to New York where she cut "Down Hearted Blues", which had already been recorded by Alberta Hunter, and "Gulf Coast Blues". Released in the spring of 1923, it was the biggest seller of the year and made Bessie a national star virtually overnight.

During the 1920s, Smith toured the South as well as the major northern cities. Her dates were booked by TOBA – the acronym stood for the Theater Owners Booking Association, also known as "the Toby", but was jokingly said by musicians to stand for Tough On Black Artists (or Asses). It certainly wasn't that tough on Bessie Smith, how-

Despite what her powerful voice, and this photo, might suggest, Bessie Smith did not in fact possess two heads

ever. She was soon the highest paid black entertainer in America, earning two thousand dollars a week, a staggering sum at the time, and traveling between shows in her own railroad car. That was instructive of the set-up of the music industry at the time, in which record companies made their money from recordings and the artists from touring. In contrast to the riches she made from her shows, Columbia paid her just two hundred dollars per side for her recordings.

On her earliest sessions Smith was backed only by the pianist **Fletcher Henderson**, but she was later accompanied by the likes of **Louis Armstrong**, pianist James P. Johnson, trumpeters Joe Smith and Tommy Ladnier, guitarist Eddie Lang and trombonist Charlie Green. Following "Down Hearted Blues", her biggest hits included "Nobody Knows You When You're Down And Out", "Young Woman's Blues", "Empty Bed Blues", "A Good Man Is Hard To Find", "Careless Blues", and her definitive version of W.C. Handy's "St Louis Blues", featuring Armstrong's magnificent cornet. Her material ranged across various styles, from deep indigo melancholy to jaunty pop songs such as "Alexander's Ragtime Band".

But the rage for female blues signers was brief. Smith left behind some 160 recordings, but by 1930 male singers had taken command, and her recording career was all but over. While a victim of changing musical tastes, she was also an excessive drinker, downing gin by the tumbler full and hymning her favored tipple on songs such as "Gin House Blues" and "Me And My Gin". In 1929 she performed in the short movie *The St. Louis Blues*, which is the only footage of her that exists, while the same year she appeared in a Broadway musical called *Pansy*, which flopped badly.

Although Columbia dropped her in 1931, there was one final recording session for Okeh Records in 1933, when **John Hammond** put together a band including Coleman Hawkins, Benny Goodman and Jack Teargarden to accompany her. Smith appeared reluctant and complained "nobody wants to hear blues no more", and the four songs she recorded, all written by Coot Grant and Kid Sock Wilson and including "Gimme A Pigfoot" and "Take Me For A Buggy Ride", were in a swing style rather than pure blues. She sang superbly, but although the recordings were billed as her comeback, they led to no upturn in her declining popularity.

Smith's last few years were spent playing seedy Harlem theaters and touring the South, which had once been her empire. On September 27, 1937,

Hammond traveled to Mississippi to bring her back to New York, hoping to revive her career with another recording session and plans for a further film. That very day, she was in a car crash on the road between Clarksdale and Memphis. Her right arm was nearly severed and was immediately amputated, but she never recovered consciousness and died from loss of blood. She was 43. Hammond claimed in an article in *Down Beat* magazine that she died after being refused admission to a hospital because of her skin color. He later admitted his report was based on hearsay, and the claim has never been verified. Nonetheless, the rumor has persisted. It formed the subject of Edward Albee's 1959 play *The Death Of Bessie Smith*, while Alan Lomax repeated it in his 1993 book *The Land Where The Blues Began*.

Smith's impact on other singers was huge and Billie Holiday, Mahalia Jackson and Janis Joplin were among the many who claimed her as an influence. In 1970, when Joplin discovered that Smith's grave remained unmarked (despite a lavish funeral and ten thousand people filing past her coffin), she helped to pay for a headstone bearing the inscription: "The Greatest Blues Singer In The World Will Never Stop Singing."

⊙ **The Collection** Columbia
One of the best of the many single-disc Bessie Smith compilations on the market, featuring a wide-ranging selection from 1923's "Downhearted Blues" to her 1933 farewell session on songs such as "Gimme A Pigfoot" and "Do Your Duty".

⊙ **The Complete Recordings Vols 1–5**
Columbia
For those who want the whole caboodle, everything Bessie Smith recorded over five individually available 2-disc sets. The final volume in this five-volume collection contains various curiosities, including the *St Louis Blues* soundtrack and interviews with Smith's niece, Ruby Smith, who constructs a revealing image of her famous aunt.

Clara Smith

b Spartanburg, South Carolina, circa 1894; d Feb 2, 1935

Known as "the Queen of the Moaners", **Clara Smith** enjoyed brief but huge popularity in the 1920s. She was never a rival to her unrelated Columbia labelmate Bessie Smith, but

she recorded prolifically and the pair even cut a handful of duets together.

Little is known about Clara's early life. Even the given year of her birth, which makes her an exact contemporary of Bessie Smith, is guesswork. We do know, however, that by 1910 she was working the vaudeville circuit, and that years of touring all over the South built her a substantial following. By 1923, her fame had reached New York, where she opened the Clara Smith Theatrical Club in Harlem.

Smith recorded steadily for Columbia in New York, cutting 122 songs between 1923 and 1932 that were characterized by her melancholic but sensual voice. Several of her songs boasted risqué lyrics, including "Whip It To A Jelly", which contained the line "I wear my skirts up to my knees and whip that jelly with who I please," and most of her recordings used the same bunch of musicians as Bessie Smith, including **Louis Armstrong**, Charlie Green, Joe Smith and James P. Johnson. She also recorded duets with Smith and with Lonnie Johnson on guitar. She remained active, singing mostly in New York but occasionally touring as far as the West Coast, until she died suddenly and unexpectedly from a heart attack in 1935 at around forty years of age.

⊙ **The Essential Clara Smith** Classic Blues
Thirty-six tracks over two discs that prove Clara Smith was a major talent, and leave you wondering how much better she might be remembered had she not been eclipsed by her more famous Columbia namesake.

⊙ **Complete Recorded Works Vol 1–6**
Document
A valiant attempt to make up for the general neglect of Clara Smith by gathering together more than 120 tracks over six exhaustive CDs.

Mamie Smith

b Cincinnati, Ohio, May 26, 1883; d Sept 16, 1946

Although she was essentially a vaudeville singer, **Mamie Smith** secured herself a place in blues history in 1920 when she recorded "Crazy Blues", the first blues recording by an African-American singer.

Mamie Robinson toured with vaudeville and minstrel shows as a young woman, then moved to New York in 1913 to work as a cabaret singer. Five years later she appeared in Perry Bradford's musical, *Made In Harlem*. She also owed her recording debut to Bradford. Okeh Records was planning to record the white singer **Sophie Tucker** performing a pair of Bradford's songs in 1920. When Tucker fell ill, the composer persuaded Okeh not to cancel the session but to allow Mamie Smith to record instead. Backed by a white studio band, she cut "That Thing Called Love" and "You Can't Keep A Good Man Down". They sold well enough for her to be invited back for a further session in August 1920, when she recorded the Bradford-penned "Crazy Blues" and "It's Right Here For You, If You Don't Get It, 'Tain't No Fault of Mine", backed by her band the Jazz Hounds, comprising Johnny Dunn on cornet, Dope Andrews on trombone, Leroy Parker on violin and Willie "The Lion" Smith on piano. Those sides were the first recordings of vocal blues by an African-American singer and to the label's surprise, "Crazy Blues" became a huge seller in the black community, a market the record industry had not only previously neglected but had not even suspected existed. The success of Smith's record prompted the rush to sign a spate of further female blues singers such as **Ma Rainey** and **Bessie Smith**. Though swiftly eclipsed, Mamie continued to make successful recordings for Okeh throughout the 1920s and toured widely as Mamie Smith's Struttin' Along Review, billing herself as "The Queen of the Blues" and backed throughout by the Jazz Hounds.

Two years after appearing in the 1929 film, *Jail House Blues*, Smith retired from recording. She returned to films in 1939's *Paradise In Harlem*, but she never recorded again and was hospitalized with a long-term illness in 1944. She died two years later, at the age of 63.

⊙ **Crazy Blues: The Best Of Mamie Smith**
Columbia
A single disc collection, packed with 25 tracks and featuring the clearest remastering anyone has yet managed.

⊙ **Complete Recordings Vols 1–4** Document
The sound quality can make four discs of Mamie Smith seem like an endurance test, but completists will find it all here, including instrumentals by her backing musicians.

Otis Spann

b Jackson, Mississippi, March 21, 1930; d April 24, 1970

One of the finest pianists of the postwar blues era, **Otis Spann** was an integral part of the Chess sound in the 1950s. As well as playing in Muddy Waters' band for many years and recording with many of the label's other artists, including Howlin' Wolf, Little Walter and Bo Diddley, he also made powerful recordings under his own name.

The Mississippi-born Spann learned to play piano in his stepfather's church as a boy, taught by a local musician called Friday Ford. By 1944, he was playing in a local blues group in a style much influenced by the records of **Big Maceo**, who took Spann under his wing when he moved to Chicago sometime around 1946 or 1947. He later claimed to have already had careers as a footballer and a boxer by then, but he was much given to telling tall stories as a solo performer in later life, when he would regale audiences with picaresque tales of down-home life in Mississippi. Some had the whiff of exaggeration, some were just plain made up.

Spann began playing around Chicago, and had a regular gig in the house band at the Tick Tock club. That's probably where he was discovered by **Jimmy Rogers**, who recommended him to **Muddy Waters**, whose band he joined in 1952. He stayed with Waters for seventeen years, playing on many of his best recordings, including such classics as "Hoochie Coochie Man" and "I'm Ready". Alongside Lafayette Leake, he also became a Chess house pianist, accompanying **Bo Diddley** on his first session and playing on sides by the likes of Sonny Boy Williamson, Howlin' Wolf, Jimmy Rogers, Buddy Guy and Little Walter.

Recording under his own name, Spann made his debut in 1954 with "It Must Have Been The Devil", featuring B.B. King and Robert Lockwood on guitars, and the instrumental "Five Spot", allegedly recorded after an all-night party. Further Chess sessions with Willie Dixon and Robert Lockwood followed in 1956, but strangely the label didn't think much of Spann's powerful vocals and they went unreleased for many years. He continued playing with Waters, joining him on his first visit to Europe in 1958 and making a legendary appearance at the

Newport Jazz Festival two years later in a sensational performance that was captured for posterity on the Chess album, *Muddy Waters At Newport 1960*. That same year he cut a splendid album of his own for Candid with Robert Lockwood. He returned to Europe with Waters in 1963 as part of the American Folk Blues Festival, when he was recorded playing some superbly contemplative solo blues and singing in a broken, husky voice for Storyville Records in Copenhagen. Back again in Europe the following year, he teamed up with **Eric Clapton** to record two tracks, "Pretty Girls Everywhere" and "Stir Me Up".

When Spann returned to America, he continued to record with Waters, but he finally shed his sideman status and began recording prolifically under his own name, recording a string of albums for Prestige, Bluesway and Testament. In 1968 he recorded the album *The Biggest Thing Since Colossus* with guitarist Peter Green and other members of Fleetwood Mac, for Mike Vernon's Blue Horizon label.

During his last couple of years, Spann was not a well man. After appearing on Waters' album *Fathers And Sons*, he finally relinquished the piano stool in Waters' band to **Pinetop Perkins** in 1969. One of his very last performances was posthumously released as *Last Call: Live At Boston Tea Party, April 2, 1970*; by the time it was recorded, he was sick with cancer and too ill to sing, so his wife Lucille had to handle the vocals. Three weeks later he died in a Chicago hospital at the tragically young age of forty. Peter Malick, who played guitar in his final band and lived with Spann and his wife during the last year of his life, dubbed him "the Sweet Giant Of The Blues", a description with which no one has seen fit to argue.

⊙ **Otis Spann Is The Blues** Candid
Only Robert Lockwood's guitar backed Spann on his 1960 debut solo album, so he enjoyed plenty of space to indulge in the florid runs and two-handed rhythmic attack that characterized a style connecting Delta barrelhouse with modern Chicago.

⊙ **The Blues Is Where It's At** BGO
Spann's brilliant "live in the studio" recording from 1967 features members of Muddy Waters' band, and even Muddy himself on a couple of tracks.

⊙ **The Biggest Thing Since Colossus** Sony
This 1968 album may be immodestly titled, but it holds some fine playing from Spann and guitarist Peter Green.

⊙ **Last Call: Live At The Boston Tea Party, April 2, 1970** Mr Cat
Spann was dying of cancer when this live album was recorded; he couldn't sing, so his wife Lucille took the vocals. But he could still play, and his backing band led by guitarist Luther Johnson also did a fine job.

Speckled Red

b Monroe, Louisiana, Oct 23, 1892; d Jan 2, 1973

Playing in an endearingly earthy style reminiscent of Roosevelt Sykes and Little Brother Montgomery, pianist **Speckled Red** was a well-known figure on the Memphis blues scene during the 1930s.

Born in Louisiana but raised in Hampton, Georgia, Rufus Perryman was an albino, like his much younger brother **Piano Red** (Willie Perryman). He learned to play the organ in a local church. After his family moved to Atlanta when he was in his teens, he started performing barrelhouse piano at house parties and juke joints. He also toured with the Red Rose Minstrel Show, and lived in Detroit for a spell during the mid-1920s. By 1929, however, he was back in the South, cutting "The Dirty Dozens" at his first recording session for Brunswick in Memphis. Although the song, a kind of gangsta rap equivalent of its day, was a hit, a sequel, recorded at a second Brunswick session in 1930, flopped. The Depression years stopped Red recording again until 1938, when he cut some sides for Bluebird. In the early 1940s, he relocated to St Louis, where he spent the next decade and more playing in local clubs and bars.

Speckled Red recorded again in the mid-1950s for the Tone label and again for Folkways in 1960, but he didn't particularly benefit from the blues revival. He did, however, tour Europe, and in 1970 recorded music for the soundtrack of the film *Blues Like Showers Of Rain*. He died aged eighty in 1973.

⊙ **Complete Recorded Works 1929–1938** Document
Speckled Red was not exactly prolific; he recorded just 23 tracks in the decade when he was prominent on the Memphis scene. But they're all here, and if you want primitive barrelhouse blues or are thinking of throwing a rent party, it's the authentic article.

Victoria Spivey

b Houston, Texas, Oct 15, 1906 ; d Oct 3, 1976

Victoria Spivey was not only one of the earliest blues women, but she went on to become one of the most influential of them all, outlasting almost all of her contemporaries. By 1940, Bessie, Clara and Mamie Smith, not to mention Ma Rainey, were all dead. Like her friend Sippie Wallace, Spivey survived to be rediscovered in the blues boom of the 1960s, and she was even accompanied in the studio in 1962 by a young **Bob Dylan**, who later used a photograph of the event on the back of his 1970 album, *New Morning*.

By the time she was twelve, Spivey was playing piano in the Lincoln movie theater in Dallas, Texas, not to mention rough-and-tumble saloons and bordellos around Galveston and Houston, where she met **Blind Lemon Jefferson**. Inspired by **Sippie Wallace**, a local star who was eight years older and had come out of playing the same kind of dives, and also by the early recordings of **Ida Cox**, Spivey traveled north to St Louis in 1926, where she had heard Okeh Records had a field team looking for new recording acts. They were impressed enough to sign her, and her first release, "Black Snake Blues" backed with "Dirty Woman Blues", became a best-seller. Over the next two years she recorded regularly, cutting such superb sides as "TB Blues", "Dope Head Blues" and "Organ Grinder Blues", backed by musicians of the caliber of **Lonnie Johnson, Louis Armstrong**, King Oliver, Clarence Williams and Luis Russell. She also recorded with her younger sister Addie "Sweet Pease" Spivey (a third sister, Elton, recorded as "the Za Zu Girl").

By the early 1930s, tastes had changed, and most of the classic female blues singers were struggling to get heard. But Spivey continued recording and performing prolifically for Victor, Vocalion, Decca and Okeh. Perhaps her continued success was due to the fact that she relocated to New York City, which was less troubled by the Depression than most of the US, and where she worked in a number of African-American vaudeville shows such as the Hellzapoppin' Revue. She also toured and recorded with Louis Armstrong.

By the 1950s, Spivey had dropped out of music, and only sang in a church in Brooklyn. Encouraged by the blues revival, however, she came out of retirement in 1962 and formed her own label. She also persuaded other surviving classic female blues singers out of retirement, including Wallace and also **Alberta Hunter** and **Lucille Hegamin**, both of whom appeared on her *Songs We Taught Your Mother*. She toured Europe with the American Folk Blues Festival in 1963 and continued recording into the 1970s, dying in a New York hospital in 1976 two weeks short of her seventieth birthday.

⊙ **The Essential Victoria Spivey** Classic Blues Two discs and 36 delicious, innuendo-laden tracks, including "Steady Grind", "Organ Grinder Blues" and "Garter Snake Blues".

Houston Stackhouse

b Wesson, Mississippi, Sept 28, 1910; d Sept 23, 1980

Although **Houston Stackhouse** learned his blues from Tommy Johnson in the 1920s, was a friend of Robert Johnson, and taught Robert Nighhawk to play slide, it wasn't until the 1960s that he made his first recordings.

Houston Garth was born on the Randall Ford Plantation in Mississippi in 1910, but took the name Stackhouse from his stepfather during his teens. He learned to play his first instrument, the fiddle, from a musician on the plantation called Lace Powell, and also from his uncle, **Lonnie Chatmon** of the **Mississippi Sheiks**, and took up the harmonica and mandolin as well. During the mid-1920s he moved to Crystal Springs, Mississippi, where **Tommy Johnson** and his brothers taught him guitar. Soon he was playing with Johnson in clubs and juke joints. Then he moved to Hollandale, Mississippi, the home of his cousin, Robert Lee McCullum, later known as **Robert Nighthawk**. Stackhouse taught Nighthawk to play bottleneck guitar, and they performed together as a duo, with Houston on harmonica. He also met **Robert Johnson**, and played with him a number of times during 1936 and 1937. After Johnson's death, Stackhouse put together a string band known as The Mississippi Sheiks No. 2, featuring Carey "Ditty" Mason and Coochie Thomas, before he moved to Helena, Arkansas, in 1946, where he hooked up with Nighthawk once more, and took up electric guitar for the first time. From then on he played nothing else, except some harmonica. He performed with both Nighthawk and **Sonny Boy "Rice Miller" Williamson** on the radio shows *Mother's Best Flour Hour* and *King Biscuit Hour*. His radio work also brought him into contact with many of the great blues players, including Elmore James, Muddy Waters, Little Walter, Jimmy Rogers, Roosevelt Sykes and Earl Hooker.

Yet Stackhouse received no recording offers and was forced to take jobs outside music, working for the Chrysler Corporation in Helena until 1956, and then on a boat on the Mississippi River. He finally made his first recordings for the Flyright label in 1967. Albums followed on the Testament, Arhoolie, Matchbox and Adelphi labels, comprised mostly of covers of favorite songs by such old friends as Tommy Johnson, Elmore James and Robert Johnson. He became a regular fixture in local blues clubs, playing with "Ditty" Mason and "Peck" Curtis, until 1969 when Mason was killed after his car was hit by a train. After Curtis died the following year, Stackhouse left Helena for Memphis, where he shared a house with another former *King Biscuit* player, Joe Willie Wilkins.

Stackhouse toured Europe in 1970 and then retired back to Crystal Springs, making only occasional appearances before his death in 1980, five days short of his seventieth birthday.

⊙ **Masters Of Modern Blues** Testament
An album split fifty–fifty between tracks by Houston Stackhouse and his protégée Robert Nighthawk, Houston's sides were recorded in 1967, backed by Nighthawk and drummer James Curtis, and include a great cover of Tommy Johnson's "Cool Drink Of Water Blues".

Pops Staples

b Winona, Mississippi, Dec 28, 1914; d Dec 19, 2000

T he Staples Singers were one of America's leading gospel groups for more than forty years and also recorded some magnificent soul sides for Stax. But the group's patriarch, **Pops Staples**, had a solid grounding in the blues, and was taught to play guitar by none other than **Charley Patton**.

Growing up on Will Dockery's Delta plantation, Roebuck Staples watched Patton from an early age. When he was in his early teens, he persuaded the great bluesman to teach him to play, to the disap-

pointment of his deeply religious father who wanted him to confine his music-making to the local church. His words fell on deaf ears, and by his teens Roebuck was sneaking off at weekends to play blues at plantation picnics and on street corners for tips.

By 1935 he was married with a young family and moved to Chicago, where he worked various jobs while singing at weekends with gospel groups the Silver Trumpets and the Trumpet Jubilees. Concentrating on gospel rather than blues, he didn't touch a guitar for twelve years until he formed the **Staples Singers** with his children, Cleotha, Purvis, Yvonne and Mavis in 1952. He bought a cheap guitar to accompany them in a tremolo-heavy style and they began recording, first for the United label and then for Vee Jay. The story of gospel music lies outside the scope of this book, but suffice it to say that the Staples Singers transformed the genre by fusing spiritual music with versions of such secular songs as "Cotton Fields", Bob Dylan's "Blowin' In The Wind" and Woody Guthrie's "This Land Is Your Land". During the late 1960s the group moved to the Stax label, where they cut such inspirational soul records as "Respect Yourself", "I'll Take You There", and "If You're Ready (Come Go With Me)". Away from the family group, Staples also recorded a blues album in 1969, *Jammed Together*, with fellow guitarists **Albert King** and **Steve Cropper**. When gospel purists criticized his secular music, he replied by saying: "Ain't nobody want to go to heaven more than me, but we got to live down here too."

With the Staples Singers working less after Mavis left to pursue a solo career, he finally recorded his own debut solo album in 1992, at the age of 77, with *Peace To The Neighborhood*, which included guest spots from such admirers as **Bonnie Raitt** and **Ry Cooder**. That was followed three years later by *Father Father*, which won him a Grammy for best contemporary blues album. "Pops" died in 2000 at the age of 85.

⊙ **Jammed Together** Stax
This 1969 guitar summit, featuring Pops Staples with Albert King and Steve Cropper, might be a jam session, but there's no self-indulgent soloing, just sublime and controlled playing from the trio in their dramatically contrasting styles.

⊙ **Peace To The Neighborhood** Point Blank
Pops Staples' long-awaited 1992 solo debut was superb, featuring "I Shall Not Be Moved" and "Down In Mississippi" with Ry Cooder on slide guitar, and a magnificent version of the Staples' classic "This May Be The Last Time", as filched by the Rolling Stones.

⊙ **Father Father** Point Blank
On his 1995 follow-up, Staples' husky murmuring vocals and throbbing electric guitar deliver up thrilling versions of "Jesus Is Going To Make Up (My Dying Bed)", Bob Dylan's "You Gotta Serve Somebody" and Curtis Mayfield's "People Get Ready". Is it blues? Maybe not. But when it sounds as good as this, who cares?

Hubert Sumlin

b Greenwood, Mississippi, Nov 16, 1931

Hubert Sumlin cemented his place as a legendary figure in the blues by playing guitar for **Howlin' Wolf** for some twenty years. He has influenced everyone from Eric Clapton to Keith Richards, both of whom turned up to pay tribute on his most recent solo album, *About Them Shoes*.

One of thirteen children in a Mississippi sharecropping family, Sumlin moved to Arkansas as a boy. Like so many Delta bluesmen, he started out playing a "diddley-bow", consisting of baling wire that his brother nailed to a wall for him. He became so proficient plucking this twine that his mother spent an entire week's paycheck buying him a guitar. "I can still remember that day," he recalled in 2004. "My mom worked at a funeral parlor four miles away. She had to walk eight miles a day there and back to work. It was a Friday and I ran and met her. I loved that guitar, man. Played it all the time. I still have what's left of it."

When he was about ten, he stood on a pile of crates to peer at **Howlin' Wolf** through the window of a local juke joint. Transfixed by the music, he sneaked inside and sat on the edge of the stage. When the club owner tried to throw him out, Wolf insisted that he stayed, and afterwards saw him home. Within a couple of years Sumlin was playing in bars and at parties, and around 1950 he formed a band with harp player **James Cotton**, which recorded briefly for Sun Records. When Wolf heard them playing in Memphis, he invited him to join his band in Chicago. Sumlin wasn't Wolf's only guitar player in the 1950s; Willie Johnson and Jody Williams also cut some great sides with him. However, Hubert's playing was the deepest and most powerful.

Although he initially played with picks, he abandoned them at Wolf's suggestion in order to fin-

ger-pick his electric guitar. That gave him a more expressive tone, in which the human touch of flesh on steel perfectly echoed Wolf's roaring and moaning voice. By the 1960s, Sumlin was arguably the most important guitarist in Chicago. Among the classic sides on which he backed Wolf were "Shake For Me", "300 Pounds Of Joy", "Goin' Down Slow", "Little Red Rooster", "Backdoor Man", "Smokestack Lightnin'", "Sittin' On Top Of The World" and "Killing Floor". Sumlin left Wolf briefly to play with Muddy Waters for six months, and years later loved to tell the story of the two blues giants battling over his services. But Wolf won him back, and he played with him for the rest of his life.

After Wolf's death in 1976, his backing group continued under the leadership of sax/harp player **Eddie Shaw** as the **Wolf Gang**, featuring Sumlin, Detroit Junior on piano, Shorty Gilbert on bass and Chico Chism on drums. Sumlin left the band for a solo career in 1980, and made a series of albums for labels such as Black Top and Blind Pig on which the

The man who added howl to the Wolf: Hubert Sumlin

potency of his guitar playing could not quite cover his failings as a vocalist. He recorded *About Them Shoes* in 2000, but thanks to contractual difficulties it was not released until 2004, when it earned him the best reviews of his solo career.

By the time the record appeared, Sumlin had been diagnosed with lung cancer and suffered a heart attack and a stroke. However, after having one lung removed and quitting drinking and smoking, he tested cancer-free and resumed touring.

⊙ **About Them Shoes** Tone Cool
A star-studded album from 2000, on which Hubert Sumlin is helped out not only by Eric Clapton and Keith Richards, but also his old colleague James Cotton, on songs such as "I'm Ready", "Evil" and "Iodine In My Coffee".

Sunnyland Slim

**b Vance, Mississippi, Sept 5, 1907;
d March 17, 1995**

A seminal figure in Chicago blues, the big-voiced pianist **Sunnyland Slim** was both a prolific accompanist and a significant artist in his own right. His solo career began in 1947, and continued until his death almost half a century later.

The son of a Delta preacher, Albert Luandrew first learned to play an old pump organ, but by his teens was playing piano in juke joints around the Delta. By the late 1920s he had settled in Memphis, where he became a Beale Street regular, playing with the likes of **Little Brother Montgomery** and **Ma Rainey**, but he didn't get to record at that stage. Taking his name from one of his best-known compositions, "Sunnyland Train" – commemorating the line that ran from Memphis to St Louis – he moved to Chicago in 1939. There he sat in with musicians like Sonny Boy (John Lee) Williamson, Lonnie Johnson and Tampa Red from the old school, as well as rising stars like Muddy Waters and Little Walter.

Slim eventually cut his first solo sides for RCA Victor in 1947, but they were issued under the name **Doctor Clayton's Buddy**, a reference to the time he had spent accompanying the singer Doc Clayton, who had just died. Later that same year he did a session for Aristocrat, with two signifi-

cant results. The first was his own superb "Johnson Machine Gun Blues". The second was that this was the first time Leonard and Philip Chess met **Muddy Waters**, who was accompanying Slim on the session. While the Victor sides were rooted in the old prewar blues, the Aristocrat sessions helped usher in the new urban sound for which Chicago was about to become famous.

Although the Chess brothers signed Waters, they declined to record Slim further and he went on instead to work for a huge number of other Chicago-based labels. He cut singles for Hytone, Opera, Chance, Tempo-Tone, Mercury, Apollo, JOB, Regal, Vee Jay, Blue Lake, Club 51 and Cobra. He also played sessions for several other artists, including Robert Lockwood, J.B. Lenoir, Floyd James, Snooky Pryor and Otis Rush. His debut solo album, *Slim's Shout*, appeared on Prestige's Bluesville subsidiary in 1960, with **King Curtis** on sax, and contained definitive renditions of many of his best-known compositions, including "The Devil Is A Busy Man", "Shake It", "Brown Skin Woman" and "It's You Baby". His first tour of Europe came in 1964 with the American Folk Blues Festival while during that decade he recorded for Storyville, Blue Horizon, Delmark and other labels.

Slim continued to record and tour prolifically throughout the 1970s and into the 1980s, releasing several albums on his own Airway Records and also encouraging up-and-coming young blues players. Although he was increasingly frail in his final years and could not tour with the same vigor, he continued to work around the Windy City. He eventually died of kidney failure aged 87, after he developed internal complications following a bad fall on an icy pavement on his way home from a gig at a Chicago club in March 1995.

⊙ **Chicago Jump** Evidence
This strong 1980s set belies the fact Sunnyland Slim was in his late seventies at the time of the recording.

⊙ **Blues Masters: Sunnyland Slim** Storyville
A fine compilation of Slim's early 1960s material, including re-recordings of his 1950s classics such as "Johnson Machine Gun Blues".

⊙ **Midnight Jump** BGO
A CD reissue of a 1969 album on which Slim was produced by Mike Vernon, and joined by Walter "Sharkey" Horton, Johnny Shines and Willie Dixon.

Roosevelt Sykes

b Elmar, Arkansas, Jan 31, 1906;
d July 17, 1983

Over more than half a century playing the blues, the rotund, cigar-chomping **Roosevelt Sykes** became one of the most important and prolific blues pianists of them all. As the eminent blues historian Tony Russell observed: "Draw a diagram of blues piano history, and he will sit in the centre like a genial spider, the lines of his influence radiating in all directions."

Although Sykes was born in Arkansas, he lived as a child in St Louis. In 1921 he was back in his home state, applying the musical skills he had learned playing organ in church to performing barrelhouse piano in the juke joints and brothels of Helena. He returned to St Louis in the late 1920s, ready to make his reputation on a wider stage. By 1929, he was recording not only for Okeh Records, who released "Forty-Four Blues" the song that made his reputation, but for three other labels under the pseudonyms Dobby Bragg, Easy Papa Johnson and Willie Kelly. His energy was boundless as he played all over the Delta and up to Chicago, either solo or with other musicians, including **St Louis Jimmy Oden**, the writer of "Going Down Slow". His energies were not solely directed towards music; his reputation as a predatory, smooth-talking ladies man earned him the nickname "the Honeydripper".

After signing with Decca Records in 1935, Sykes recorded some seventy sides for the label, including "The Honeydripper" (with **Kokomo Arnold**), "Night Time Is The Right Time", "Driving Wheel" and "Soft And Mellow". He also acted as a talent scout for Decca. Then in 1941, he moved to Chicago, where he worked with the Jump Jackson Band and Memphis Minnie and formed a group called **The Honeydrippers**. Although he signed with United Records in 1951, by the mid-1950s he had left Chicago for New Orleans. There he recorded with **Dave Bartholomew** for Imperial, most notably on a rollicking version of Robert Johnson's "Sweet Home Chicago", and also cut albums for Folkways, Bluesville – including a great 1961 LP called *The Honeydripper* that featured King Curtis on sax – Delmark and Crown.

Sykes made his first visit to Britain in 1961 and performed with Chris Barber's jazz band. He returned to Europe several times, where he found an enthusiastic audience for his romping boogies and risqué songs such as "Dirty Mother For You", "Ice Cream Freezer" and "Peeping Tom". He continued working until his death in 1983, aged 77.

⊙ **Roosevelt Sykes 1931–41** Wolf
Classic sides from Sykes's heyday, including the original recording of "The Honeydripper".

⊙ **Blues By Roosevelt "The Honeydripper" Sykes** Folkways
An enjoyable compilation of Roosevelt Sykes's material from the early 1960s.

⊙ **The Original Honeydripper** Blind Pig
A live recording from the Blind Pig café in Michigan in 1977.

Taj Mahal

b New York City, May 17, 1942

No one over the last forty years has done more to keep the blues alive and relevant than **Taj Mahal**. As a singer, multi-instrumentalist, composer, producer, ethnomusicologist and collaborator, he has maintained a one-man musical crusade characterized by warmth, humor and soulfulness. Over the years he has ventured into Caribbean, Hawaiian, African and Cuban roots-based forms and incorporated elements of folk, jazz, zydeco, gospel, rock, pop, soul and R&B into his music. Yet somehow everything he has ever done has always remained firmly rooted in his love of the blues.

Henry St Claire Fredericks was born in Harlem during World War II, but grew up in Springfield, Massachusetts. The son of a jazz-pianist father of Caribbean descent, and a gospel-singing, schoolteacher mother, he was raised to be proud of his roots. At an early age, he learned to play piano, clarinet, trombone and harmonica. He added guitar in his early teens, playing with Lynnwood Perry, an accomplished picker from North Carolina, who moved in next door and taught the aspiring young musician both the Piedmont style of acoustic playing and the electric stylings of Muddy Waters, Jimmy Reed and the Chicago school.

Fredericks renamed himself Taj Mahal while attending the University of Massachusetts at Amherst as an agriculture student during the early 1960s, and claimed the idea came to him in a dream. In 1964 he moved to Los Angeles, where he formed the **Rising Sons** with **Ry Cooder** among others. At the Whiskey A Go Go on Sunset Strip, the group opened for such soul acts as Otis

Redding, the Temptations, and Martha and the Vandellas, but he also met and played with such blues legends as Howlin' Wolf, Muddy Waters, Junior Wells, Buddy Guy, Sleepy John Estes, Yank Rachel and Lightnin' Hopkins.

When the Rising Sons split up, Taj Mahal launched himself as a solo bluesman via a series of electrified country-blues albums that had a profound influence in both rock and blues circles, including *Taj Mahal* (1968) and *The Natch'l Blues* (1968). *Giant Step/De Old Folks At Home* followed in 1969, a double set comprising a traditional acoustic album and a second, more rock-oriented set.

During the 1970s, his musical canvas grew more adventurous as he wove other elements into his blues on albums such as *Happy To Be Just Like I Am* (1971), *Recycling The Blues And Other Related Stuff* (1972), *Mo' Roots* (1974), *Music Fuh Ya'* (1977), and *Evolution* (1978).

Taj Mahal's recorded output slowed up in the 1980s, although he continued to tour relentlessly

Renaissance bluesman: Taj Mahal

Playlist
Taj Mahal

1 **STATESBORO BLUES (1967)** from **Taj Mahal**
Taj does Willie McTell, on his debut solo album.

2 **SHE CAUGHT THE KATY AND LEFT ME A MULE TO RIDE (1968)** from **The Natch'l Blues**
A traditional song that proves blues poetry can be every bit as potent as Shakespeare, according to the singer himself.

3 **CORRINA (1968)** from **The Natch'l Blues**
An American folk-blues classic given an almost Caribbean flavor.

4 **GOING UP THE COUNTRY, PAINT MY MAIL BOX BLUE (1968)** from **The Natch'l Blues**
One of Taj's own compositions: "a true story – man, they're all true stories!"

5 **FISHIN' BLUES (1969)** from **De Old Folks At Home**
Henry Thomas's 1928 classic from the Harry Smith anthology, lovingly refashioned.

6 **YOU'RE GONNA NEED SOMEBODY ON YOUR BOND (1971)** from **The Real Thing**
Blind Willie Johnson updated, in a version on which Taj even manages to name-check Mavis Staples.

7 **HERE IN THE DARK (1995)** from **Phantom Blues**
Eric Clapton adds some stinging lead guitar.

8 **SENOR BLUES (1997)** from **Senor Blues**
A mellow take on the Horace Silver song.

9 **QUEEN BEE (1999)** from **Kulanjan**
Back to the African roots of the blues, on a collaboration with Malian kora player Toumani Diabaté.

10 **CRUISIN' (2000)** from **Shoutin' In Key**
Taj in his element, recorded live in 1998 with his excellent Phantom Blues Band.

from his new home in Hawaii. The 1990s, however, brought about a prolific regeneration with albums such as *Dancing The Blues* (1993), *Phantom Blues* (1996), *An Evening Of Acoustic Music* (1996) and the soul-tinged, Grammy-winning *Senor Blues* (1997). He also wrote the music for the theatrical production *Mule Bone*, staged at New York's Lincoln Center. At the same time, he launched a series of world music explorations, beginning with the aptly named *World Music* in 1993. Two years later he joined Indian classical musicians on *Mumtaz Mahal*, while *The Hula Blues* in 1998 was an Hawaiian album and 1999's *Kulanjan* paired him with the Malian kora player **Toumani Diabaté**.

Another Grammy-winning album came in 2000 with *Shoutin' In Key*, recorded with his Phantom Blues Band. In recent years he has toured with a smaller group, The Taj Mahal Trio, featuring Bill Rich on bass and Kester Smith, but he has also continued his world music collaboration, releasing an album recorded with the Cultural Music Club of Zanzibar in 2005. Yet he insists the blues is still the meat of all he does. "Everything else is flavor," he says.

⊙ **Taj Mahal** Sony
Taj Mahal's superb 1968 debut is a compendium of electrified country blues, including hard-hitting versions of "Dust My Broom", "Statesboro Blues" and "E Z Rider".

⊙ **Giant Steps/De Old Folks At Home** Sony
This is now a single 22-track CD, but on its original 1968 release it was a double vinyl album consisting of one LP of acoustic material such as "Fishing Blues" and "Stagger Lee" played on banjo, harmonica and guitar, and one of rocking electric tracks, including "Give Your Woman What She Wants" and "Good Morning Little Schoolgirl".

⊙ **The Natch'l Blues** Sony
A brilliantly diverse 1969 set ranging from the country blues of "She Caught The Katy" and "Going Up To The Country, Paint My Mailbox Blue" to the more soulful "You Don't Miss Your Water" and "Ain't That A Lotta Love".

⊙ **Phantom Blues** Private
There's something of a New Orleans flavor to this 1996 Taj Mahal album, thanks to such classics as Jesse Hill's "Ooh Poo Pah Doo" and Fats Domino's "Let The Four Winds Blow". Bonnie Raitt helps out on "I Need Your Loving", while Taj's one original, the tender, acoustic "Lovin' In My Baby's Eyes", is another highlight.

⊙ **Senor Blues** Private
Blues, jazz, rock and soul on an admirably versatile 1997 set that ranges from the wit of "You Rascal You" and "Mind Your Own Business" to the Otis Redding tribute "Mr Pitiful", via Horace Silver's jazzy title track.

⊙ **In Progress & In Motion 1965–1998** Sony
A superbly compiled 3-disc retrospective of Taj Mahal's long career, including plenty or rare and previously unreleased tracks to please collectors.

⊙ **The Essential Taj Mahal** Sony Legacy
This 2-disc, 36-track collection impressively covers not

only his Columbia material but later sides recorded for Warner Brothers, Private Music and Hannibal, all hand-picked by Taj himself.

Tampa Red

b Smithville, Georgia, Jan 8, 1904; d March 19, 1981

As a slide guitarist, **Tampa Red** wielded a bottleneck with sufficient virtuosity to earn him the soubriquet "the guitar wizard". But he also had a warm, attractive voice and was a fine songwriter. One of the true originals and innovators of the prewar blues, he recorded prolifically, cutting more than 300 solo sides, as well as backing other performers.

Hudson Woodbridge was raised in Tampa, Florida, by his grandmother's family, the Whittakers, whose name he adopted. Having spent a few years as an itinerant musician around the South, he arrived in Chicago in the mid-1920s, where he played on street corners and in small clubs. His big break came when he was hired to accompany **Ma Rainey**, through whom he met pianist **Georgia Tom Dorsey**. In 1928, the pair recorded "It's Tight Like That", a jaunty, hokum number with a lyric full of double entendres. Released on the Vocalion label, it became a national hit. As the **Hokum Boys**, the duo cut various follow-ups in similar vein, while Tampa Red also recorded as the Hokum Jug Band with **Frankie Jaxon**.

These early recordings display Tampa Red's stunning slide technique on a National steel guitar, which refined the earthier approach of most other contemporary slide players to create a purer, more deft sound. He was much in demand as a session player, and those whose recordings he graced included **Sonny Boy Williamson** (John Lee) and **Memphis Minnie**. His partnership with Georgia Tom ended in 1932 after they had cut "You Can't Get That Stuff No More". Prohibition ended the following year, and as the liquor followed again, blues clubs proliferated all over Chicago. Working sometimes as a trio and other times with his Chicago Five, Tampa Red became one of the city's hottest live acts.

In 1934, Red signed with Victor, for whom he recorded for the next twenty years. He was a cornerstone of the so-called "Bluebird beat", created by producer **Lester Melrose** and centered on the Victor subsidiary of that name. The home on 35th and State that Red shared with his wife and business partner Frances became a blues hub, as a lodging house, rehearsal space and informal booking agency for the blues musicians who arrived almost daily in the city from the Delta, often to record at the invitation of Melrose. "Tampa Red's house was a madhouse for old time musicians," **Willie Dixon** recalled in his autobiography. "Tampa Red's wife would be cooking chicken and we'd be having a ball."

By 1940 Red had made the transition to electric guitar, adopting a rhythmic approach that foreshadowed the postwar Chicago sound, and often recording with the pianist **Big Maceo**. He also recorded with the pianist Blind John Davis and Johnnie Jones. Among his best-known songs were "It Hurts Me Too", as covered by Elmore James, "Black Angel Blues", "Don't You Lie To Me" and "Love Me With A Feeling". Robert Nighthawk, Fats Domino and B. B. King also covered his compositions. The death of his wife in 1953 hit him hard; some say he never fully recovered from the blow. Always a heavy drinker, his alcoholism became acute. Although he was rediscovered by a new audience in 1959 and 1960, when he made a brace of albums for the Bluesville label, he eventually died destitute in Chicago in 1981 aged 77.

⊙ **The Guitar Wizard** Columbia
Seventeen tracks that were recorded between 1928 and 1934, mixing hokum and straight blues and including plenty of sides with Georgia Tom Dorsey on piano.

⊙ **It Hurts Me Too** Indigo
An excellent single-disc 23-track overview of Tampa Red's career, from 1928's "It's Tight Like That" with Georgia Tom to 1942's "She Wants To Sell My Monkey" with Big Maceo.

Eddie "Playboy" Taylor

b Benoit, Mississippi, Jan 29, 1923; d Dec 25, 1985

Listen to Jimmy Reed's records, and the sound of the guitar you hear will almost certainly be the work of **Eddie Taylor**.

Born and raised in the Delta, Taylor claimed to have seen Charley Patton, Son House and Robert Johnson play as a boy. By 1936, he was playing guitar himself. He also taught the basics of the instrument to **Jimmy Reed**, his boyhood friend on Johnny Collier's plantation. After a brief spell in Memphis, he arrived in Chicago in 1949, and hooked up with harpist **Snooky Pryor** and guitarist Floyd Jones. He also reunited with Reed, who had similarly traveled north to try his luck in the city's blues clubs. Initially it was Taylor who was the bandleader, but when he auditioned for Vee Jay in 1953, the label preferred Reed, and the roles were reversed. Taylor, who was a much better guitarist, played on most of Reed's big hits. such as "Ain't That Lovin' You Baby" and "Honest I Do". In 1955, he finally recorded for Vee Jay under his own name, cutting "Bad Boy" (with Reed on harmonica), "Ride 'Em On Down", "Big Town Playboy", "You'll Always Have A Home" and "I'm Gonna Love You". Brilliant sides, the lot of them. But when they failed to sell as well as Reed's records, Taylor went back to the role of sideman, not only with Reed but on records by John Lee Hooker, Elmore James and Sunnyland Slim.

Taylor's debut solo album eventually came in 1972, when he recorded *I Feel So Bad* for West Coast label Advent. That same year, he also toured Britain and recorded the album *Ready For Eddie* for the Birmingham-based label Big Bear. A reissue of his Vee Jay solo masters in 1981 rekindled interest in his early work, but he died in 1985, aged 62.

⊙ **Big Town Playboy** Charly
A fine compilation of seventeen tracks that Eddie Taylor recorded for Vee Jay & Vivid between 1955 and 1964, plus additional cuts that feature him accompanying Elmore James, John Lee Hooker, Floyd Jones and Jimmy Reed.

⊙ **I Feel So Bad** Hightone
Thanks to stellar guitar work and a great band, Eddie Taylor's 1975 debut album remains his best work.

⊙ **Ready For Eddie** Castle
This reissue of Taylor's 1975 album comes with the addition of previously unissued bonus tracks.

Hound Dog Taylor

b Natchez, Mississippi, April 12, 1915; d Dec 17, 1975

The good times always seemed to roll whenever **Hound Dog Taylor** played. The **HouseRockers** delivered their old-fashioned, foot-stomping, supercharged boogies with a hurricane of frenetic noise and minimum of sophistication, while Taylor's slashing, searing slide guitar tore the house down in a raw and rocking style that led critic Robert Christgau to dub the band "the Ramones of the blues."

Born into a sharecropping family in 1915, Theodore Roosevelt Taylor started out playing piano, and didn't take up the guitar until he was twenty. After working as a field hand by day and playing Delta juke joints and house parties by night, he moved north to Chicago in 1942, heeding a warning from the Ku Klux Klan, who objected to his affair with a white woman and burned a cross in his yard. In the Windy City he performed on Maxwell Street for tips, but was forced to work a factory job until the late 1950s, when he finally took the plunge and became a full-time musician. With a bottleneck style influenced by Elmore James, he recorded a couple of singles for local labels in the early 1960s. However, they went largely unnoticed outside of Chicago, while a session for Chess Records was not issued at the time and didn't see the light of day until the 1990s.

Taylor toured Europe with the American Folk Blues Festival in the mid-1960s, backing **Little Walter** and others, but not until his 1971 debut album – backed by his HouseRockers, who comprised second guitarist **Brewer Phillips** and drummer **Ted Harvey**, but no bassist – did he finally get a chance to show the world what he could do. Released on **Alligator Records**, which was set up by Delmark employee **Bruce Iglauer** specifically for that purpose, and recorded live in the studio over two evenings, it was an extraordinary record on which thirty years of pent-up raw energy seemed to tumble out of the grooves. Further albums followed on Alligator with 1974's *Natural Boogie* and the 1976 live outing *Beware Of The Dog*. Sadly, by the time of the latter's release Taylor had died from cancer at the age of sixty. At the time of his death he was facing a trial for attempted murder, having got into a drunken fight with Brewer Phillips one day in May 1975 and let off two bullets from a .22 rifle at him, hitting him once in the forearm and once in the leg. Phillips recovered and pressed charges, but visited his old friend on his deathbed in hospital and forgave him.

Taylor's success allowed the fledgling Alligator Records to survive and eventually thrive and in 1982 the label issued *Genuine Houserocking Music*, a collection of his unreleased studio tracks. He was also an influence on a generation of slide guitarists, including George Thorogood and Sonny Landreth. In 1998 Alligator honored his memory with a tribute album featuring Elvin Bishop, Luther Allison, Ronnie Earl, Son Seals and Alvin Youngblood Hart among others. A "Best Of" collection, *Deluxe Edition*, appeared the following year and in 2005 came *Release The Hound*, a collection of previously unreleased live and studio performances.

⊙ **Hound Dog Taylor And The HouseRockers**
Alligator
Taylor and his quintessential Chicago bar band went mad when finally let loose in a studio for the first time in 1971, with some furious no-frills boogie thrashing.

⊙ **Deluxe Edition** Alligator
A 15-track compilation of material recorded between 1971 and 1975, both in the studio and live, including a storming version of "Give Me Back My Wig".

Koko Taylor

b Memphis, Tennessee, Sept 28, 1935

T he voice of **Koko Taylor** is like an elemental force of nature. The closest thing Chicago ever produced to a female Howlin' Wolf, she's blues down to the marrow, and nobody can dispute her title as the current queen of the blues, a title to which she first laid claim some forty years

ago, with her bone-shivering version of "Wang Dang Doodle".

Raised on a farm near Memphis, but sadly orphaned by the age of eleven, Cora Walton earned the name Koko from her childhood love of chocolate. After her love of the blues was inspired from listening to B.B. King's radio show, she began singing with her brothers, who played home-made guitar and fife. However, she had little thought of becoming a professional blueswoman when she and her husband, Robert "Pops" Taylor, moved to Chicago to look for work in 1953. While she worked by day as a cleaner (a job she kept for twenty years), at night she frequented the blues clubs on the city's South Side, listening to the likes of Muddy Waters, Howlin' Wolf, Magic Sam, Buddy Guy and Junior Wells. With her husband's encouragement, she began sitting in with various bands. One night in 1962, she was approached by **Willie Dixon**, who told her there weren't enough female blues singers and offered to help get a recording contract. She released her first single, "Honky Tonk," on the USA label the following year, and in 1964 signed to **Chess**. Backed by Buddy Guy and Robert Nighthawk on guitars and Big Walter Horton on harp, her first session produced the great "I Got What It Takes", while her second release (on the label's Checker subsidiary) was her raucous version of "Wang Dang Doodle", written by Dixon and featuring Guy once again on guitar. Despite Taylor's protestations that "that ain't no song for a woman to sing", the sexually suggestive lyric was an integral part of its appeal, and one of the main reasons the single sold a million to become Chess's last big mainstream blues hit.

That success landed Taylor a berth on the 1967 American Folk Blues Festival tour of Europe. On her return she made a couple of albums for Chess, and gigged around Chicago with **Mighty Joe Young**. After parting from Chess she linked up briefly with Dixon's short-lived Yambo label, and formed her own band in 1972, the **Blues Machine**. She then signed to Alligator Records in 1975, by which time she had finally given up the cleaning jobs. Her first Alligator release, *I Got What It Takes*, was nominated for a Grammy, and she went on to record seven more albums for the label, with such appropriate titles as *The Earthshaker*, *Queen Of The Blues* and 1993's finale, *Force Of Nature*.

It was another seven years before Koko returned

with *Royal Blue*, which featured guest appearances from B.B. King, Kenny Wayne Shepherd, Johnnie Johnson and Keb Mo. During her years away from the studio, she continued to tour, opened her own blues club in Chicago, and remarried, after Pops Taylor had died following a road accident in 1988, in which she was also seriously injured.

Taylor has often spoken of the difficulties she has experienced making it as a woman in the male-dominated world of the blues. "It's tough being out here doing what I'm doing in what they call a man's world," she says. "It's not every woman that can hang in there and do what I'm doing."

⊙ **What It Takes** Chess
A brilliant anthology of Koko Taylor's Chess sides, featuring magnificent support from Buddy Guy among others.

⊙ **I Got What It Takes** Alligator
Backed on her 1975 Alligator debut by a rocking band led by Mighty Joe Young, Koko Taylor balanced blues standards such as "Mama He Treats Your Daughter Mean" and "Big Boss Man" with her own compositions such as "Voodoo Woman" and a surprise version of Webb Pierce's "Honky-Tonk Song".

⊙ **The Earthshaker** Alligator
Koko Taylor's second Alligator album, from 1978, includes a remake of "Wang Dang Doodle" and floor-shaking versions of "Let The Good Times Roll", "Spoonful", "Hey Bartender" and "You Can Have My Husband".

Sonny Terry

b Greensboro, North Carolina, Oct 24, 1911; d March 12, 1986

Sonny Terry was a giant of the blues, whose trademark "whooping" style made him one of the best-known and most influential harmonica players of all time. Together with his long-term partner the guitarist **Brownie McGhee** (see separate entry), he was among the first bluesmen to reach an international audience. They became blues missionaries, taking the music to those who had never heard it before.

Although sighted at birth, Saunders Terrell became blind by the age of sixteen as a result of two separate childhood accidents. As he could not work on the family farm, he turned to music for a living, after learning harp from his father. During the early 1930s, he was a familiar sight on the

streets of Raleigh, playing for tips. Then he met the guitarist **Blind Boy Fuller**, who in 1934 suggested Terry moved to Durham to accompany him. The two became a popular local attraction and traveled to New York in 1937 to record for the Vocalion label. The following year Terry performed in the first of John Hammond's legendary Spirituals to Swing concerts at New York's Carnegie Hall, taking the place of Fuller who was originally on the bill but missed the gig because he was in jail.

Terry met Brownie McGhee around the same time, but not until after Fuller died in 1941 did their partnership become permanent. Moving to New York, the duo became part of a Bohemian political circle that included **Leadbelly, Woody Guthrie** and **Pete Seeger**, whom Terry accompanied both on record and in concert. In 1946 he became part of the Broadway cast of the long-running production *Finian's Rainbow*, while he returned to Broadway in the mid-1950s when he and McGhee appeared in *Cat On A Hot Tin Roof*.

Terry cut a number of solo albums for Folkways, but he was at his most potent with McGhee, and they recorded prolifically for Folkways, Savoy, Fantasy and Old Town. By the late 1950s they were performing almost exclusively for white audiences, with a broad repertoire of blues, traditional folk tunes, rags and other material. They made the first of many visits to Britain in 1958, and during the 1960s were a major attraction at folk and blues festivals around the world. However, their appeal to white audiences and willingness to perform folk standards alongside blues material made them unfashionable with blues purists and deeply unfashionable in some quarters. The strain of spending most of their lives on the road together also began to tell. For the last few years of their partnership they barely spoke to each other off-stage, and often even appeared separately on it, before they split for good in the mid-1970s. Terry published an instructional harmonica manual in 1975, and shortly before his death, Johnny Winter helped to expose him to a younger blues audience by producing 1984's *Whoopin'*, which also featured Willie Dixon. He died in New York in 1986 aged 74.

⊙ **Absolutely The Best** Varese
There's a surprising lack of comprehensive, career-spanning Sonny & Brownie-compilations, which is an indication of how unfashionable they've become. But this is a decent effort, if on the short side at just fourteen tracks.

⊙ **Live At Sugar Hill** OBC
A great live recording from December 1961, recorded at the San Francisco club when Sonny Terry and Brownie McGhee were still actually speaking to each other.

⊙ **Sonny Terry: The Folkways Years, 1944–1963** Smithsonian Folkways
Seventeen songs culled from eight Sonny Terry solo albums, alongside previously unreleased Folkways recordings, spanning blues, gospel and folk harmonica styles.

⊙ **Whoopin'** Alligator
Not Sonny Terry's best, and you wouldn't expect it in 1984, when he was 72. But with Willie Dixon and Johnny Winter helping out, to quote an amazon.com contributor it's "a rocking little record", and definitely a high note for him to go out on.

Sister Rosetta Tharpe

b Cotton Plant, Arkansas, March 20, 1915; d Oct 9, 1973

She sang gospel and she sang jazz but she sure had the blues, too, and no account of the history of African-American music would be complete without reference to the contribution of **Rosetta Tharpe**.

Rosetta's mother, Katie Bell Nevin, was an evangelist in the Church of God in Christ who preached at revivalist tent meetings across the South. Her daughter was performing by the age of four as "Little Rosetta Nubin, the singing and guitar playing miracle". After the family moved to Chicago at the end of the 1920s, Rosetta began singing jazz and blues in private while performing gospel in public. In 1934 she married COGIC preacher Wilbur Thorpe (the name was later changed to Tharpe), and moved to New York, where she recorded with Lucky Millinder's orchestra. She appeared at John Hammond's From Spirituals To Swing concerts at Carnegie Hall in 1938 and 1939, and followed with appearances at nightclubs such as New York's Café Society with **Cab Calloway** and **Benny Goodman**. For a while she combined secular and spiritual in thrilling fashion, giving swing or boogie-woogie arrangements to gospel songs such as "This Train" and Thomas Dorsey's "Rock Me" and recording secular tunes such as 1942's "I Want A Tall Skinny Papa" with Millinder's band. In addition, she was an early pioneer of the electric guitar.

After World War II she recorded a series of gospel duets with **Marie Knight**, and cut further sides

in a jazz-blues vein. She toured Britain with Chris Barber's band but in later years restricted her live appearances to the gospel circuit. Her performing career was curtailed by a stroke in 1970, and she died three years later aged 58.

Needless, to say her unorthodox mix of gospel with blues and jazz styles was highly controversial and much criticized by some churchgoers. But she laid the ground for **Ray Charles** to fuse gospel and R&B, and pointed the way for the likes of Sam Cooke, the Staples Singers and Aretha Franklin to crossover from gospel into soul music.

⊙ **The Original Soul Sister** Proper
This fantastic 4-disc box features eighty-plus tracks, many of which demonstrate how Sister Rosetta Tharpe was one of the first artists fully to integrate blues and gospel music, and comes complete with a splendid forty-page illustrated booklet.

⊙ **The Gospel Of Blues** MCA/Universal
An excellent single-disc introduction to the way Rosetta Tharpe made gospel music swing, jump, stomp, wail and jive.

Henry Thomas

b Big Sandy, Texas, circa 1874; d unknown

Henry Thomas, also nicknamed Ragtime Texas, made a small but fascinating contribution to blues history. His handful of recordings provide something of a missing link between the blues and the rags, reels and minstrel songs that formed the repertoire of black music in the late nineteenth century.

Little is known about Thomas's life, but we do know that he was born to recently freed slaves in Texas in the mid-1870s and ran away with his guitar in his teens for the life of a hobo and street musician. He is believed to have performed at the 1893 Columbian Exhibition in Chicago and again at the World's Fair in St Louis in 1904, but we then lose sight of him until he made his first recordings for Vocalion in Chicago in 1927. By then he was in his fifties, making him one of the oldest of the early bluesmen who made it into a recording studio. At a number of sessions over the next two years, he cut a total of 23 sides in a rudimentary, old-fashioned style and booming voice. He also accompanied himself on a set of panpipes (cut from river reeds and sometimes known as quills), making him quite possibly the only bluesman ever to have played the instrument on disc.

Thomas's recorded legacy comprises less than two dozen sides, but it holds endless fascination. Although seven of his recordings are styled as "blues", they don't conform to an orthodox twelve-bar pattern, while the rest are square dance tunes and vaudeville numbers. However, the repertoire and style are believed to date back to Thomas's childhood, and thus represent a unique glimpse of what black secular music sounded like as the blues was taking shape and before the invention of recording technology. Some of his songs were his own compositions, but he was a human jukebox and other numbers were derived from popular ballads and ditties of the time. His material was widely revived in the 1960s. Bob Dylan reworked his "Honey Won't You Allow Me One More Chance"; the Grateful Dead adapted "Don't Ease Me In"; Taj Mahal covered "Fishing Blues"; and Canned Heat based their 1969 hit "Goin' Up The Country" on Thomas's "Bull Doze Blues", on the original of which he played the quills. His other recordings included "Cottonfield Blues", "Run, Molly, Run" (a variation on "Li'l Liza Jane"), the folk standard "John Henry" and "Railroadin' Some", on which he listed the stops on various Texas and Louisiana rail lines.

After his final session in 1929, Henry Thomas disappeared, although there are unconfirmed reports of him playing on Texas street corners as late as the 1950s. Besides the influence of his recorded legacy, blues scholars also believe that Thomas may have been among the traveling minstrels with whom **Blind Lemon Jefferson**, the first star of Texas blues, came into contact during his youth.

⊙ **Texas Worried Blues** Yazoo
All 23 of the known recordings that Henry Thomas made as Ragtime Texas, combining to make an indispensable piece of blues history.

Jesse Thomas

b Logansport, Louisiana, Feb 3, 1910; d Aug 13, 1995

Known sometimes as "Baby Face" or "Mule" and occasionally billed as "the Blues Troubadour", **Jesse Thomas** enjoyed an extraordinary blues career that spanned eight decades, from the 1920s to the 1990s.

Thomas's exact date of birth is uncertain, with suggested dates ranging between 1908 and 1911, but 1910 is believed to be the most likely. One of nine children, he grew up in a musical family on the Louisiana-Texas border. His father played the fiddle, while his older brother, **Willard Ramblin' Thomas** (1902–c1945) played slide guitar. When Jesse moved to Shreveport, he also got to know local blues musicians the **Black Ace** (Babe Turner) and **Oscar "Buddy" Woods**. Visiting his brother in Dallas in 1927, he saw **Lonnie Johnson** perform, and was impressed enough to abandon what had been his main instrument, the piano, in favor of the guitar. He also saw and heard Blind Lemon Jefferson and T-Bone Walker, and the following year moved to Dallas, working the streets of the Deep Ellum district alongside **Texas Alexander**.

Thomas appeared to have missed his opportunity to record when a local talent scout sent him to Chicago to audition for Paramount Records, who turned him down flat. However, he got another opportunity in 1929, when he cut four sides for Victor Records under the name **"Babyface" Thomas**, including "Down In Texas Blues" and "Blue Goose Blues". The latter was his signature tune, and celebrated the Blue Goose district of Shreveport where he had grown up.

He recorded again for Victor later the same year and backed the singer **Bessie Tucker**, before he moved to Oklahoma City, where he remained for the Depression years. In 1937, Thomas moved again, this time to Los Angeles, where a decade later he resumed his recording career. In the intervening years his music had changed dramatically. He'd been to college to study music theory and composition, and had absorbed jazz guitar styles and jump blues. All of these influences and experiences were brought to bear on some fine recordings accompanied by pianist **Lloyd Glenn**, such as "Another Fool Like Me" and "Double Do Love You". For a while he recorded prolifically, releasing sides on Swingtime, Modern, Specialty and Echo, but in 1957 he returned to Shreveport and went into semi-retirement, serving as a deacon in the local Baptist church.

Reappearing in the 1960s, however, Thomas became a popular festival attraction as something of an elder statesman of the blues. He also released occasional albums on his own Red River label, including 1979's *Down Behind Rise* and 1993's *Blues Moved In*. His final recording *Lookin' For That Woman* appeared on Black Top in 1995, the same year that he died in Shreveport after suffering a heart attack.

⊙ **Jesse Thomas 1948–58** Document
A fine collection of Thomas's Los Angeles recordings, bridging Texas and West Coast styles.

Rufus Thomas

b Cayce, Mississippi, March 26, 1917; d Dec 15, 2001

Among the most significant musicians ever to come out of Memphis, **Rufus Thomas** exerted a profound influence over the tapestry of blues, R&B, soul and rock'n'roll that makes up the city's musical heritage.

Thomas was born in a tiny hamlet on the Mississippi state line, but his family moved to Memphis, the city that remained his home for over eighty years, when he was two. By the 1930s, he was singing and doing a comedy turn in a traveling vaudeville show, the **Rabbit Foot Minstrels**, but he also performed in the clubs up and down Beale Street. In the 1940s he got a job hosting the amateur talent night at the Palace Theater, where he introduced young performers including B.B. King and Bobby "Blue" Bland. He also began presenting a two-hour show called *Hoot And Holler* for the black-run Memphis radio station WDIA, on which he gave early exposure to the likes of Rosco Gordon, Junior Parker and a youthful Elvis Presley.

In 1953, Thomas recorded "Bear Cat" for Sam Phillips' Sun Records as an answer song to Big Mama Thornton's "Hound Dog". That gave Phillips his first big hit, although of course Presley would later have a bigger hit with the song on RCA. Having been in at the birth of rock'n'roll, Thomas next helped launch soul as a major force, by becoming the first star on a new Memphis label called **Stax**, following the 1959 single "Cause I Love You", recorded with his daughter **Carla** (although the record initially appeared on Satellite). He stayed with Stax until its collapse in 1975, recording such memorable hits as "Walking The Dog", "Jump Back", "All Night Worker", "Do The Funky Chicken", "Push and Pull" and "The Breakdown". With their funky

mix of blues-soul, his songs were also recorded by the likes of Booker T & The MG's and King Curtis in Memphis, while British R&B groups who cut cover versions included the Rolling Stones, the Small Faces, the Spencer Davis Group and the Troggs.

Many of his releases by this stage were essentially novelty records, and he often cut a ridiculous figure dressed in hot pants and other outrageous garb; he claimed to be "the oldest teenager in the business", and even cut a rap record in the mid-1980s. By 1989, when he revisited his blues roots with *That Woman Is Poison* on the Alligator label, a semblance of decorum had returned. Another blues album followed in 1996 on Sequel, with *Blues Thang*. He remained a radio personality until his death and was also cast in a number of Hollywood movies, including *Mystery Train* (1989), *Great Balls Of Fire* (1989), *A Family Thing* (1996), and *Cookie's Fortune* (1999). After he died at the age of 84 in 2001, Memphis recognized his contribution to the city's music by naming a portion of Beale Street after him.

⊙ **Do The Funky Somethin': The Best Of Rufus Thomas** Atlantic
A good retrospective of Rufus Thomas's long career, from "Bear Cat" to "Do The Funky Chicken", via "Walking The Dog".

⊙ **The Funkiest Man Alive: The Stax Funk Sessions 1967–1975** Stax
An 18-track compilation of the best of the later years of Rufus Thomas's lengthy spell on Stax.

Tabby Thomas

b Baton Rouge, Louisiana, Jan 5, 1929

The owner of the famed Baton Rouge club Tabby's Blues Box, **Tabby Thomas** is also a fine singer in his own right, with a typical Louisiana swamp blues style.

Although he'd learned guitar and piano back home in Louisiana, Thomas first discovered that he could also sing while serving with the US Air Force in San Francisco. Entering a local talent contest, he not only won but defeated such fellow contestants as Etta James and Johnny Mathis. That led to his recording for a Hollywood label, but as soon as he was discharged he returned to try his luck in Louisiana. The local blues scene was dominated by the considerable figure of producer **Jay Miller**, who first recorded Thomas for Excello in 1954, although he had to wait until 1962 for his biggest local hit with "Hoodoo Party".

Thomas opened the Blues Box in 1981, and has run it ever since as a showcase for upcoming talent, and a home for such notable Louisiana bluesmen as Guitar Kelly, Silas Hogan, Henry Gray and his own son, **Chris Thomas King**. He continued to perform at the club himself until its closure at the end of 2004. Although a stroke left him unable to play an instrument he still sings and continues to present a blues show on local radio.

⊙ **Swamp Man Blues** Aim
An atmospheric 1999 album of Tabby Thomas delivering his characteristic swamp blues.

Big Mama Thornton

b Montgomery, Alabama, Dec 11, 1926; d July 25, 1984

Big Mama Thornton is one of those blues singers who remains doomed to be better known for the covers of her songs rather than her own recordings – in her case, Elvis Presley's appropriation of "Hound Dog" and Janis Joplin's borrowing of her "Ball And Chain".

One of seven children, Willie Mae Thornton grew up singing in the church where her father was a minister. She also taught herself to play drums and harmonica, and ran away at fourteen to sing with Sammy Green's Hot Harlem Revue, with whom she toured the South throughout the 1940s. Quitting in 1948, she settled in Houston, Texas, where she worked the bars and clubs. Soon after that she signed on for one of **Johnny Otis**'s package shows, which took her to New York to play the Apollo. Although on the first night she was the opening act, she went down so well that by the second show she had been promoted to headliner. Somewhere between those two shows she acquired the name Big Mama, a reference both to her swift rise up the bill and her six-foot, 350-pound physique.

It was after signing to **Don Robey**'s Peacock Records in 1951 that she cut the original version of "Hound Dog" in Los Angeles. Backed by a pared-down trio drawn from Johnny Otis's orchestra, consisting of Otis himself on drums, Peter Lewis playing some dirty guitar and Albert Winston on bass, Thornton turned in a growling, ferocious per-

formance on a song both she and Otis claimed to have written in the studio, although the courts subsequently determined that the credit belonged to the young writing team of Leiber and Stoller. Released as a single, with the celebratory "They Call Me Big Mama" on the B-side, it topped the charts and sold more than a million. She received a check for just five hundred dollars, the only payment she ever received for the recording in her entire career.

Thornton continued to record for Peacock until 1957, cutting fine sides including "Yes Baby" – a duet with **Johnny Ace**, who she was with when he accidentally blew his brains out playing Russian roulette in a Houston theater on Christmas Eve 1954 – "I Smell A Rat", "Stop Hoppin' On Me", "The Fish", the swinging "How Come" and "Just Like A Dog". However, she enjoyed no further hits. In the late 1950s, she moved to the San Francisco Bay area and recorded for various small labels on the West Coast. Her career took an upturn in 1965 when she joined the American Folk Blues Festival tour of Europe and signed to Arhoolie Records, who released the live album *Big Mama Thornton In Europe. Big Mama Thornton With The Chicago*

REDFERNS

Blues Band appeared in 1967, featuring guest appearances from Muddy Waters, James Cotton and Otis Spann, and was followed in 1968 by *Ball And Chain*, the title track of which was immediately covered by **Janis Joplin**.

During the 1970s Thornton made albums for Pentagram Records, Backbeat and various other labels, including Vanguard, which issued two live LPs recorded in front of prison audiences. One of her last appearances came at the 1983 Newport Jazz Festival, tapes from which were released by Buddha Records as *The Blues – A Real Summit Meeting*, featuring Thornton alongside Muddy Waters, B. B. King and Eddie "Cleanhead" Vinson. She died of a heart attack in Los Angeles in 1984, at the age of 57.

⊙ **Hound Dog: The Peacock Recordings**
MCA/Universal
The best of the recordings Big Mama Thornton made for Don Robey's label between 1952 and 1957, including, of course, "Hound Dog" and "They Call Me Big Mama".

⊙ **With The Muddy Waters Blues Band**
1966 Arhoolie
Big Mama Thornton recorded live in San Francisco, backed by Waters and Samuel Lawhorn on guitars, Otis Spann on piano and James Cotton on harmonica.

⊙ **Ball'N'Chain** Arhoolie
Sixteen classic studio sides recorded for Arhoolie in the 1960s, including "Little Red Rooster", "Bumble Bee", and a terrific "Wade In The Water", as well as the unforgettable title track.

George Thorogood

b Wilmington, Delaware, Dec 31, 1952

Inspired by the likes of Elmore James, Hound Dog Taylor (for whom he was a roadie) and Chuck Berry, **George Thorogood** earned a lot of success with his guitar-based blues-rock during the 1980s, even if his loud and sometimes formulaic riffs were probably more appreciated by rock audiences than by blues fans.

Thorogood decided to become a blues musician after seeing **John Hammond** in concert in 1970. Three years later, he assembled the **Destroyers** in Delaware, with a line-up of Michael Lenn on bass, Ron Smith on second guitar and Jeff Simon on drums. The group soon relocated to Boston, and were signed by Rounder Records. With Lenn

replaced by Billy Blough, their debut album *George Thorogood And The Destroyers* was released in early 1977, but their breakthrough came with the next year's follow-up, *Move It On Over*, which made the US Top 40 albums chart and went gold.

Bizarrely, Thorogood took a year off in 1980 to play baseball – he'd been a semi-pro in his teens – but he returned with the Destroyers to open several dates for the Rolling Stones on their 1981 American tour, and signed to EMI the following year. His label debut, *Bad To The Bone*, which featured a new addition to the Destroyers' line-up in saxophonist Hank Carter, became his biggest-selling album, driven by the success of the title track, which gave him a crossover hit single. A string of gold albums followed, including 1985's *Maverick*, by which time guitarist Steve Chrismar had joined the line-up.

Thorogood has continued touring ever since. Although by the 1990s he was playing smaller venues, he still records prolifically, and was heard most recently on 2003's *Ride 'Til I Die*.

⊙ **George Thorogood & The Destroyers** EMI
A two-disc, 30-track compilation of punk-rock thrashing meets Chicago blues.

Henry Townsend

b Shelby, Mississippi, Oct 27, 1909; d Sept 4, 2006

Influenced by Roosevelt Sykes and Lonnie Johnson, and one of the tiny handful of blues musicians who began playing in the 1920s who were still active into the new millennium, the guitarist and pianist **Henry Townsend** was a key figure in the development of St Louis as a blues center.

Townsend left his parents aged nine to live with grandparents in Cairo, Mississippi, where he learned to play guitar from a friend called David Perchfield. "We started playing standards, blues, and eventually we started playing tunes that David and myself wrote," Townsend later recalled. "We practiced anywhere people could stand for me to make my noises." By his early teens he'd left for St Louis where he befriended the son of a doctor – "the only black man in St Louis to own a Rolls Royce" – with whom he stayed. He was soon playing in speakeasies and at rent parties and fish fries, and sitting in with such musicians as Henry

Brown, Ike Rogers and **Pinetop Perkins**. He played in clubs that sold bootleg whiskey during Prohibition: "Sometimes they would be arrested, everybody in the club. Owner of the club would pay bail, then pay everyone double when they came back to work."

In 1929, Townsend made his first recordings for Columbia, traveling to Chicago to cut four sides featuring his open-tuned slide guitar, including "Long Ago", "Henry's Worried Blues" and "Mean Mistreater". Although he was paid three hundred dollars, a generous sum by the standards of the time, he had spent the lot before he got back to St Louis, and he declined Columbia's invitation to record a second session. Around 1931 he cut some sides for Paramount, and he also learned piano by playing along to **Roosevelt Sykes**' recordings. Throughout the 1930s he was a mainstay of the St Louis blues scene, touring with pianist **Walter Davis**, his on-off musical partner for twenty years, and playing sessions for Big Joe Williams, John Lee "Sonny Boy" Williamson and Robert Nighthawk. He also recorded another bunch of sides under his own name for Bluebird in the late 1930s, but although he was a highly original and inventive songwriter, they were to be his last as a headline artist until the 1960s. During the 1940s, he teamed up for a time with Roosevelt Sykes and added electric guitar to his arsenal, but by the 1950s, although he was still playing locally in St Louis clubs, he was largely forgotten. He re-emerged in his fifties with an album for Bluesville and went on to become a regular fixture at blues and folk festivals, cutting several albums for Adelphi before switching in the late 1970s to Nighthawk Records, for whom he recorded the excellent *Mule*. Townsend continued recording sporadically through the 1980s and into the 1990s, enjoying his position as a patriarch of St Louis blues and still making occasional live appearances into the new millennium. American public service television made a documentary film about his life in 1984.

⊙ **Henry's Worry Blues** Catfish
Seventeen sides from Henry Townsend's sessions between 1929 and 1938, supplemented with several tracks by J.D. Short and Joe Stone from the same era.

⊙ **Mule** Nighthawk Records
Returning to the studio some 51 years after his debut, Henry Townsend made this delightful comeback album of laid-back, after-hours blues in 1980.

Walter Trout

b Atlantic City, New Jersey, March 6, 1951

After years as a sideman with the likes of John Mayall & the Bluesbreakers and Canned Heat, the guitarist **Walter Trout** emerged from the shadows in his own right in 1989.

Somewhat surprisingly, it was not an early encounter with the blues but with the music of jazz great **Duke Ellington** that set Trout on his way to becoming a musician. He took up guitar, then got bitten by the rock bug as a teenager in the 1960s, and dis-

One free Radical: Walter Trout

covered the blues via cover versions. By the 1970s, he was considered an ace sideman, playing guitar behind the likes of John Lee Hooker, Big Mama Thornton and Joe Tex. Then in the 1980s he did a five-year stint in **Canned Heat**, replacing the late Bob Hite. He also served a further five years in **John Mayall's Bluesbreakers**, with whom he was playing when he was spotted in 1989 by a Danish concert promoter who offered to finance a solo tour.

Trout assembled his own band for the first time, and his debut album *Life In The Jungle* appeared on Provogue Records in 1990. That was followed by *Prisoner Of A Dream*, 1992's *Live (No More Fish Jokes)*, *Tellin' Stories* on Silvertone in 1994, a return to Provogue for *Breaking The Rules* and *Positively Beale Street*, and then a self-titled major label debut for A&M in 1998. Further albums have included *Live Trout*, recorded at the Tampa Blues Festival in March 2000, *Go The Distance* and *Relentless*.

After a five-year absence from the studio, he returned in 2006 with *Full Circle* which included guest appearances by John Mayall, Jeff Healey and Coco Montoya. Yet it is probably on the live circuit, where he regularly plays upwards of two hundred shows a year with his band the **Radicals**, that Trout's guitar-led blues-rock has made the biggest impact. "The blues shouldn't be a museum," he insists. "The music ought to constantly expand and be alive."

⊙ **Live Trout: Recorded At The Tampa Blues Fest March 2000** Ruf

Walter Trout's studio recordings tend to be workmanlike affairs, marred by a lack of truly memorable songs, but this double live album captures the over-the-top excitement of his blues-rock in a concert setting.

Tommy Tucker

b Springfield, Ohio, March 5, 1933; d Jan 22, 1982

Some performers will always be remembered for a single track. In the case of **Tommy Tucker**, that song was 1964's addictive twelve-bar blues "Hi-Heel Sneakers", with its wonderfully mysterious references to "wig hats on her head" and the need to wear boxing gloves "in case some fool might want to fight."

Robert Higginbotham began playing piano aged seven, and earned his first check as a professional

musician playing jazz in the 1940s with the **Bobby Woods Orchestra**. When doo-wop became the rage in the 1950s, Tucker and other members of the band became the **Cavaliers**, before he put together his own trio, the **Dusters**, along with guitarist Weldon Young and bassist Brenda Jones, to play R&B in bars around Dayton, Ohio. In 1961 Tucker and the Dusters relocated to Newark, New Jersey, and he released "Rock And Roll Machine" under the name Tee Tucker on Atco, who seemed to be grooming him as a singer in the Ray Charles mode. Young and Jones then went their own way (enjoying hits as the duo Dean & Jean), while after working briefly with experimental jazzman **Roland Kirk**, Tucker hooked up with R&B producer **Herb Abramson**. Together they recorded his composition "Hi-Heel Sneakers", with Young playing guitar on a track that this time was more Jimmy Reed than Ray Charles. Abramson, who had helped set up Atlantic Records but who was by now operating as an independent, leased it to Checker Records in 1964, and they watched it scale the pop charts. An album swiftly followed, which included the follow-up, "Long Tall Shorty", written by Don Covay in remarkably similar vein.

However, Tucker proved to be a one-hit wonder. Neither "Long Tall Shorty" nor further singles such as "Alimony" and "That's Life" bothered the charts. He traveled to Chicago in 1966 to record with producer Willie Dixon and harmonica player Big Walter Horton, but the resulting "I'm Shorty" again failed to set the world alight. In the 1970s, Tucker visited Europe as part of a "Blues Legends" package, and following an enthusiastic response, began recording again for the Red Lightnin' label. He was still active when he died of poisoning in 1982, at the age of 48. Both food poisoning and inhaling carbon tetrachloride from a hardwood floor treatment have been variously cited as the cause.

We couldn't find a decent compilation of Tucker's work currently available on CD, but "Hi-Heel Sneakers" is widely available on countless variousartist anthologies.

Ike Turner

b Clarksdale, Mississippi, Nov 5, 1931

Ike Turner's website boasts the strap line, "The Father of Rock'n'Roll". That's a reference to "Rocket 88", the number one hit he masterminded in 1951 under the name Jackie Brenston and the Delta Cats, which is widely acknowledged to be the first rock'n'roll record. However, Turner's career also intersects with the blues and R&B at a hundred different points – and that's without even mentioning his partnership with Tina.

Taught to play boogie-woogie piano by **Pinetop Perkins**, Turner tutored himself on guitar by playing along to blues records. He formed his first band the Top Hatters in school, and by the late 1940s they had become **Ike Turner's Kings of Rhythm**. Based in Memphis, Turner and his band worked Beale Street and Delta juke joints further afield, and he also played piano with **Robert Nighthawk** and **Sonny Boy Williamson**. Then in 1951, Turner and his band recorded a fast boogie he had written, called "Rocket 88", at Sam Phillips's Sun studio, with a lead vocal by saxophonist **Jackie Brenston**. Although the record might have been credited to Ike Turner and the Kings of Rhythm, instead the label read "Jackie Brenston and the Delta Cats". Dramatically different from the jazzy and sophisticated jump blues of the time, it was licensed to Chess and became an R&B number one hit. Not that Turner should worry too much about his lack of credit. He went on to become a top session guitarist, talent scout and producer throughout the 1950s, and then a major star in his own right in the 1960s. By contrast, Brenston sank into obscurity.

Turner was the lynchpin of the Memphis scene, organizing sessions for, and playing piano or guitar on sides by, Otis Rush, Junior Parker, Howlin' Wolf, B. B. King, Otis Rush, Rosco Gordon, Bobby "Blue" Bland and Johnny Ace among many others, and leasing the sides to a variety of labels including Chess, Modern and RPM Records. In 1956, he relocated to St Louis, where he reconstituted the Kings of Rhythm and became a top draw at local nightclubs. He also continued as a prolific producer and talent scout, organizing sessions for such R&B singers as Billy Gayles, Little Cooper and Anna Mae Bullock (b Brownsville, Tennessee, Nov 26, 1938). You may not have heard of the first two, but the world came to know Bullock under the rather more celebrated name of **Tina Turner**. He renamed the sixteen-year-old Bullock "Little Ann", and in 1958, by which time she'd given birth to a son by the group's sax player, she moved into Turner's house, and the pair married.

Their first recording as **Ike and Tina Turner** came in 1960, and Turner subsequently built the Ike and Tine Turner Revue around her, with a group of nine musicians and three backing singers called the Ikettes. Their R&B sound rapidly moved into mainstream soul and Phil Spector-produced pop, and Tina eventually walked out on her husband in 1975 after suffering years of mental and physical abuse. Ike retreated to his studio in Inglewood, California, and released a couple of solo albums, but his life was on the skids. His studio was destroyed by fire in 1982, and in 1990 he was sent to prison on drugs charges. He was still in jail when he and Tina were inducted into the Rock and Roll Hall of Fame the following year. Upon his release he wrote his autobiography, *Taking Back My Name*, which was published in 2001.

Some critics have argued that Ike created little memorable music in his long career, excepting his work with his wife and the freakish importance of "Rocket 88". That view has undoubtedly been exacerbated by the tarnishing of his reputation following the revelation of his abusive behavior towards Tina. He became an even greater object of scorn and ridicule when he was portrayed as a vicious womanizing Svengali in the 1993 biopic *What's Love Got To Do With It*. Yet whether or not he was a nice man should not detract from the vital role he played in the development of blues, R&B and rock'n'roll during the 1950s, and reissues of his work from that era testify to his innate musical intelligence.

⊙ **Rhythm Rockin' Blues** Ace
"Rocket 88" and twenty other 1950s tracks that Ike Turner recorded with his Kings of Rhythm.

Big Joe Turner

b Kansas City, Missouri, May 18, 1911; d Nov 24, 1985

The blues shouter **Big Joe Turner** revelled in the title "the Boss of the Blues". He was also a major influence on the birth of rock'n'roll, and jazz fans like to claim him as their own, too. Yet he appealed to all these different audiences without ever really much changing his style. Instead, his voice somehow seemed to work its magic on rock, blues and jazz fans all at the same time. Rock'n'roll, he said, "wasn't but a different name for the same music I been singing all my life".

Although Turner learned to sing in church, he developed an early love of more secular styles. In his early teens, he'd sneak into Kansas City clubs with a penciled-on moustache, wearing his father's hat to conceal the fact that he was underage. The Kansas City sound of the 1920s straddled both jazz and blues, and it gave the young Turner a foot in both camps. By the age of seventeen, he was working as a bartender at the Sunset Café, where **Pete Johnson** played piano. As well as serving the drinks, Turner was soon singing in an up-tempo swinging blues style over Johnson's boogie-woogie rhythms, in a partnership that was to last forty years. It was at the Sunset Café that he was heard in 1936 by **John Hammond**. In town to see Count Basie, Hammond was sufficiently impressed to take both Turner and Johnson to New York, where he arranged the duo a residency at the Famous Door club. Two years later they were back in the city at Hammond's behest to perform at his legendary 1938 Spirituals to Swing concert at Carnegie Hall, to appear on Benny Goodman's *Camel Caravan* radio show, and to record for Vocalion, for whom they cut "Roll 'Em Pete" and "Goin' Away Blues".

The Carnegie Hall appearance made the duo's reputation (as well as those of Johnson's fellow boogie-woogie pianists, **Albert Ammons** and **Meade Lux Lewis**). They were soon back at Café Society, and cut another Vocalion session with Hot Lips Page's band, when they laid down "Cherry Red" and "Café Society Blues", also featuring Ammons and Lewis.

In 1940 Turner signed to Decca, recording the superb "Piney Brown Blues" with Johnson and also cutting sides for the label backed by the likes of Freddie Slack Trio, Willie "The Lion" Smith and Art Tatum. During World War II, he relocated to Los Angeles, where he worked as part of **Duke Ellington**'s *Jump For Joy* revue, and he also toured with Meade Lux Lewis. Back in New York after the war, he carried on recording in a jump blues style, cutting eleven singles for National between 1945 and 1947. He next signed to Aladdin, recording a wonderful "Battle Of The Blues" session with **Wynonie Harris**, his chief rival as the most successful blues shouter of the era. By the end of the decade, however, Turner's star was in decline. Boogie-woogie and jump blues were on the way out, his vocal style (which had its roots in the days before amplification) was considered old-fashioned, and he appeared bound for oblivion.

Instead, the most successful period of his career was still to come. In 1951 he signed to the newly

formed Atlantic Records, where he enjoyed a spectacular run of success on the R&B charts starting with "Chain Of Love", backed by Van "Piano Man" Walls and His Orchestra. That was followed by "The Chill Is On", "Sweet Sixteen" and "Don't You Cry", written by Doc Pomus. In New Orleans in 1953, he recorded the self-penned classic "Honey Hush", which with its exhilarating sax solo gave him an R&B number one. Later that same year, "Shake, Rattle And Roll" provided another R&B number one. Subsequent cover versions by **Bill Haley** and the Comets and **Elvis Presley** helped Turner to become one of the few jazz and blues singers of his generation to find a new, white rock'n'roll audience, and he toured with Haley and with disc jockey Alan Freed's road show. He also appeared in the films *Harlem Rock And Roll* and *Shake, Rattle And Roll*, and enjoyed further hits with "Well All Right", "Flip, Flop And Fly", "Hide And Seek" and "Morning, Noon And Night", most of which featured **Elmore James** on guitar. In between his rock'n'roll tours he teamed up again with Pete Johnson in 1956 for the magnificent *The Boss Of The Blues* album, as well as live appearances together at the 1958 Newport Jazz Festival and in Europe. Next came the jazz-tinged 1959 album *Big Joe Rides Again*, with Jim Hall on guitar and Coleman Hawkins on sax. One of his final hits came with "Jump For Joy", featuring King Curtis.

As tastes changed and a new crop of soul stars came to the fore in the early 1960s, Turner was dropped after a dozen years with Atlantic, and fell back on playing jazz lounges in Los Angeles. He did, however, tour Europe again with the 1966 American Folk Blues Festival, and ended the decade singing with the Johnny Otis Show. Forays into the recording studio were now few and far between, but Turner enjoyed another revival in the 1970s when he signed to Norman Granz's Pablo Records, who recorded him with such old friends as Eddie "Cleanhead" Vinson, Pee Wee Crayton, Jay McShann and Jimmy Witherspoon. A stroke and diabetes severely knocked him back in the mid-1970s, although he continued performing and recording. As late as 1983 he was proving that he had not lost all of his old fire on an solid album produced by Doc Pomus, featuring **Roomful Of Blues** as his stalwart backing band. He died in 1985 at the age of 74, after what one blues historian, with no fear of contradiction, described as "a lifetime of hard living, hard drinking but above all hard singing".

⊙ **Greatest Hits** Atlantic
Twenty-one tracks from Big Joe Turner's 1950s Atlantic output chronicle how he became one of the few trad blues singers to enjoy increased sales in the rock'n'roll era.

Otha Turner

b Jackson, Mississippi, June 2, 1907; d Feb 26, 2003

Otha Turner was one of the last surviving links to the fife-and-drum tradition of the Mississippi hill country, which represented a direct link back to the work songs and field hollers of the nineteenth century.

Turner was born to sharecropping parents. His father abandoned the family shortly after he was born, leaving him to help his mother plow the fields and pick cotton from the earliest age. He began drumming in his teens and also taught himself how to make and play the hollow flute, known as a fife, which he fashioned from canes growing wild on his farm. He was soon playing the blues on the fife in the unique fife-and-drum style at plantation picnics. The style had formerly been widespread, and had its roots in a combination of early American colonial drumming and African influences.

For many years, Turner's **Rising Star Fife and Drum Corps**, which was made up of several generations of his immediate family, played in obscurity, and was seldom heard outside the Mississippi hill country, which also produced such blues musicians as **R.L. Burnside** and **Junior Kimbrough**. Eventually,

however, he raised enough money from his musical exploits to buy the farm near Como, Mississippi, on which he raised horses, hogs and cattle, and grew watermelon, corn and black-eyed peas, until the end of his life. The biggest event in his musical calendar was when his band played at the farm's annual Labor Day picnic.

First recorded for the Library of Congress in 1969, Turner in his later years became a popular attraction at blues festivals, attaining nationwide recognition via television appearances and the use of his music in the opening sequence of Martin Scorsese's film *Gangs Of New York*. His 1998 album *Everybody Hollerin' Goat* was named one of the essential blues albums of the decade by *Rolling Stone* magazine, and was followed in 2000 by *From Senegal To Senatobia*. Both appeared on Birdman Records and were produced by **Luther Dickinson** of the North Mississippi All Stars, on whose records he guested.

One of Turner's final performances came at Nashville's Ryman Auditorium in 2002, when he and his band re-created a rural Delta "picnic" on stage. By then they were the only Mississippi fife and drum band still in existence. He died in 2003 at the age of 95, and his daughter, Bernice Turner Pratcher, who also played in the family group, died later the same day.

⊙ **Everybody Hollerin' Goat** Birdman Records
With his Rising Star Fife and Drum Band, Otha Turner's debut album at the age of 90 is a fine testament to a dying tradition. This album includes no less than three versions of "Shimmy She Wobble", which may just be the best song title – ever.

V

Stevie Ray Vaughan

b Dallas, Texas, Oct 3, 1954; d Aug 27, 1990

It's astonishing how a single, charismatic figure can transform an entire musical genre, even one with as great a tradition and history as the blues. When **Stevie Ray Vaughan** arrived on the scene in the early 1980s, blues music was in the doldrums. From B.B. King to John Lee Hooker, plenty of the original pioneers were still around to remind us of past glories. But young artists with the vision to take the blues forward and point it at the new century that was hovering on the horizon were thin on the ground. Old blues hounds and young rock fans alike recognized Vaughan's forceful, imaginative playing as something special. Suddenly, it seemed, an entire generation of kids who were picking up guitars for the first time found something relevant in the blues again, arguably for the first time since the 1960s.

Young Stevie followed in the footsteps of his older brother **Jimmie Vaughan**, learning the blues from his collection of Albert King, Howlin' Wolf, Otis Rush and Lonnie Mack records and playing his secondhand guitars. After playing in a series of local school bands in Dallas, Stevie moved to Austin, Texas, in 1972, where his older brother had relocated a couple of years earlier. He joined first the Nightcrawlers and then the Cobras, before forming the **Triple Theatre Revue** with vocalist **Lou Ann Barton** in 1977. Two years later he formed **Double Trouble** (named after the Otis Rush song) with drummer Chris Layton and bassist Jackie Newhouse. The latter was soon replaced by Tommy Shannon from Johnny Winter's band, and the line-up was augmented by the addition of keyboardist Reese Wynans. An early fan was veteran Atlantic producer Jerry Wexler, whose good offices secured Vaughan a slot at the 1982 Montreux Jazz Festival. Although the jazz fans present booed his hard-edged blues-rock sound, **David Bowie**, who was also in the audience, was hugely impressed, and recruited him to play on his *Let's Dance* album.

Double Trouble's own 1983 debut *Texas Flood* was produced by **John Hammond,** still able to spot "the next big thing" after more than half a century in the business, and earned support in both blues and rock circles. It also made Vaughan a much sought-after session player, and he happily accepted invitations to play on records by many of his own heroes such as **James Brown** and **Lonnie Mack**. His distinctive, driving style, which found him playing simultaneous lead and rhythm parts, drew frequent comparisons with Jimi Hendrix.

Vaughan consolidated his success with the albums *Couldn't Stand The Weather* in 1984 and *Soul To Soul* the following year but drug abuse and alcoholism led to his collapse on tour in 1986, and he checked into a rehab center. On his emergence, he was not only cured but re-energized, playing with Bob Dylan and touring with Eric Clapton, and his recovery to rude health was further evident on 1989's superb Grammy-winning *In Step*. His comeback was cut tragically short, however, in the early morning of August 27, 1990, when he died in a helicopter crash near East Troy, Wisconsin, following a concert at the Alpine Valley Music Theatre, where he'd just blown a bunch of other guitarists off the stage, including Robert Cray, Buddy Guy and Eric Clapton (who gave up his seat on the helicopter to Vaughan).

Stevie Ray was just 35, and his premature death was all the more tragic for it was clear that his best days still lay ahead. It's a measure of his influence that if you visit his adopted home town of Austin, you will find an impressive, life-size bronze statue by the lake shore commemorating the city's most famous son – not George W. Bush, who once governed Texas from the city, but guitar-slinger extraordinaire Vaughan. Perhaps an even finer tribute came from B.B. King: "Most of us play a twelve-bar solo with two choruses and the rest is repetition. With Stevie Ray, the longer he played, the better."

A month after his death came the release of the duets album, *Family Style*, with his brother Jimmie, who inherited all his guitars and later wrote and

Playlist
Stevie Ray Vaughan

1 LOVE STRUCK BABY (1983) from **Texas Flood**
The opening track from the album that some claim saved the blues from extinction.

2 TEXAS FLOOD (1983) from **Texas Flood**
A slow blues jam around a tune written by Larry Davis, who first recorded the song for Duke in 1958 and was one of SRV's inspirations.

3 PRIDE AND JOY (1983) from **Texas Flood**
Classic up-tempo guitar blues, and one of the highlights of his debut album.

4 SCUTTLE BUTTIN' (1984) from **Couldn't Stand The Weather**
This furious instrumental opener to Stevie's second album merits inclusion for its title alone.

5 AIN'T GONE 'N' GIVE UP ON LOVE (1985) from **Soul To Soul**
Stevie's slow blues – and they don't get any more languid than this – were in many ways more impressive than his blues-rockers.

6 LOOK AT LITTLE SISTER (1985) from **Soul To Soul**
The other side of SRV, from the same album – pure rock'n'roll with its blues roots on parade.

7 THE HOUSE IS ROCKIN' (1989) from **In Step**
Stevie always opened his albums with a full-tilt boogie, and *In Step* was no exception

8 CROSSFIRE (1989) from **In Step**
A lot of guitar nuts reckon this track contains his best solo ever…

9 RIVIERA PARADISE (1989) from **In Step**
A compelling nine-minute instrumental that mixes blues, jazz and soul.

10 LIFE BY THE DROP (1991) from **The Sky Is Crying**
A rare acoustic recording from his posthumously released collection.

11 SIX STRINGS DOWN (1995) from **Strange Pleasure**
Brother Jimmy's moving eulogy to his younger sibling.

recorded a song about his brother called "Six Strings Down". B.B. King, Buddy Guy, Clapton, Cray and Bonnie Raitt joined Jimmie on a tribute album. Another posthumous Stevie Ray album, *The Sky Is Crying*, appeared in 1991, and was followed by further live recordings from his archives. While his blues-rock style is not to everyone's taste – indeed, his work has almost as many detractors as it has fans – there's no denying that he gave the blues scene a shot in the arm at a time when it was desperately needed.

⊙ **Texas Flood** Epic
Stevie Ray Vaughan's astonishingly assured 1983 debut, including such highlights as "Pride And Joy", "Love Struck Baby" and the title track.

⊙ **In Step** Epic
Fierce blues on Stevie Ray's 1988 comeback, which not only displays his stunning guitar playing but his emergence as a powerful songwriter.

⊙ **Family Style** Epic
Two ace blues guitar-slingers for the price of one from 1990, with Jimmie Vaughan matching his kid brother note for note.

⊙ **The Sky Is Crying** Epic
Lovingly assembled after Stevie Ray's death from tracks cut between 1984 and 1989, this may just be his finest album.

⊙ **A Tribute To Stevie Ray Vaughan** Epic
Star-studded tribute recorded live with the likes of B.B. King, Buddy Guy, Eric Clapton, Robert Cray, Dr. John, Bonnie Raitt and brother Jimmie.

Eddie "Cleanhead" Vinson

b Houston Texas, Dec 18, 1917; d July 2, 1988

Eddie Vinson never really wanted to be a blues shouter. His first love was playing alto saxophone in the style of Charlie Parker, which he did professionally for half a century. But after Big Bill Broonzy coached him to sing the blues, Vinson's Texan voice, with its trademark whooping falsetto, became a popular attraction with blues audiences in the 1940s and 1950s.

Vinson sang in the local Baptist church and took up alto saxophone as a child. During the early 1930s he began touring with Chester Boone's Territory Band whenever he could get time off school. He joined the band full-time in 1935 and stayed while Milton Larkins took over leadership. That enabled him to play alongside the likes of T-Bone Walker and Illinois Jacquet, who had spells with the band

REDFERNS

Clean head, dirty voice

he recorded several bop instrumentals and, more significantly, a series of raunchy jump-blues numbers including "Juice Head Baby", "Kidney Stew Blues", "Old Maid Boogie", "Some Women Do", "Oil Man Blues" and "Ever-Ready Blues".

In 1948 Vinson moved to King Records, whose roster at the time also included fellow jump-blues shouters Wynonie Harris and Roy Brown. There he cut "I'm Gonna Wind Your Clock", "I'm Weak But Willing" and "Somebody Done Stole My Cherry Red". He briefly rejoined Cootie Williams's band in the mid-1950s and in 1957 toured and recorded with Count Basie's Orchestra. His glory days as an R&B hit-maker and the popularity of the jump-blues shouters may have been over, but he continued to work steadily, appearing at jazz and blues festivals and recording for labels such as Black & Blue, Bluesway, Pablo, Muse and JSP.

during the late 1930s. He also became friends with **Big Bill Broonzy** and the pianist **Jay "Hootie" McShann**, both of whom encouraged him to sing the blues. However, Vinson was more interested at the time in the young alto player in McShann's band, **Charlie Parker**, whom he is said to have "kidnapped" for several days in order to prise tips on his technique out of him.

After leaving Larkins, Vinson joined **Cootie Williams**'s orchestra in New York in late 1941, and made his recording debut as a singer for Okeh Records the following year on the bluesy "When My Baby Left Me". He stayed with Williams until 1945, when he left to form his own big band. Signing to Mercury Records,

Miles Davis recorded his tunes, he made an album with **Cannonball Adderley** and toured Europe with his old friend McShann. Into the 1980s he recorded with Roomful of Blues, while and his final sessions took place in 1986 with Etta James for Muse. He died of a heart attack in Los Angeles in 1988 at the age of seventy.

⊙ **Kidney Stew Is Fine** Delmark
A superb 25-track introduction covering Eddie Vinson's 1940s recordings, with informative liner notes, photographs and discographies.

⊙ **Clean Head's Back In Town** Bethlehem
Classic Vinson, backed by Basie's men on a collection of cracking R&B and jump blues.

Joe Louis Walker

b San Francisco, Dec 25, 1949

It took **Joe Louis Walker** some time to emerge from the San Francisco blues scene, but by the beginning of the 1990s his crisp guitar work, gospel-influenced vocals and highly original songwriting had made him a highly respected name far beyond the Bay Area.

Walker grew up in a religious household in which gospel was the primary musical force, but which also boasted a collection of 78s by Amos Milburn, Howlin' Wolf and others. He was playing guitar by fourteen, and within a few years was proficient enough to open shows for the likes of Mississippi Fred McDowell, Muddy Waters, John Lee Hooker and Lightnin' Hopkins when they played the city's best-known blues haunt, the Matrix. By 1968 he was rooming in San Francisco's Haight-Ashbury district with **Mike Bloomfield**, who taught him to play slide and arranged him an audition with **Otis Rush**'s band in Chicago. He didn't get the gig, but almost thirty years later, Rush did guest on one of Walker's albums.

Back in Haight-Ashbury, it was the height of acid-rock and Walker got to jam with members of the city's leading psychedelic bands, including Steve Miller and the Grateful Dead. By the mid-1970s, drug abuse had sapped his talent and energy. In an effort to turn his life around, Walker joined a gospel group, the **Spiritual Corinthians**. He stayed with them for a decade, not returning to the blues until the mid-1980s when he formed his own band, the **Bosstalkers**. His debut album *Cold Is The Night* appeared on Hightone in 1986 and was followed by four more albums for the label, including two live sets recorded at Slim's, the San Francisco club owned by Boz Scaggs.

In 1993, Walker duetted with B.B. King on the latter's *Blues Summit* album, and also released his own album, *Blues Survivor*, on Verve. That was followed in 1994 by *JLW*, which teamed him with harp player **James Cotton** and the Tower of Power horn section. His next release, 1995's *Horns*, was co-produced by Steve Cropper and featured the Memphis Horns.

Great Guitars in 1997 lived up to its title and found Walker in stellar company on an album of duets. His final album for Verve, *Preacher And The President*, appeared in 1998 before a move to Blue Thumb for the stripped-down, part-acoustic *Silvertone Blues*, featuring his old friend Cotton and guitarist Alvin Youngblood Hart. Into the new millennium he has recorded for Telarc and Evidence; his most recent release was 2004's *New Direction* on Provogue Records.

⊙ **Cold Is The Night** Hightone
Joe Louis Walker's splendid 1986 debut was characterized by great guitar playing and adventurous songwriting.

⊙ **Live At Slim's Vols 1 & 2 Hightone**
So many modern bluesmen sound better on stage than in the studio, and Walker whips up a storm on two discs recorded live in San Francisco in 1990.

⊙ **Great Guitars** Polygram/Universal
Although this 1997 album features lots of celebrity friends, Walker stays in charge by writing or co-writing all but one of the songs himself, as Bonnie Raitt, Ike Turner, Taj Mahal, Buddy Guy, Matt Murphy, Steve Cropper, Scotty Moore and Gatemouth Brown parade their guitar skills.

T-Bone Walker

**b Linden, Texas, May 28, 1910;
d March 16, 1975**

T-Bone Walker created the electric blues guitar sound. He inspired B.B. King to plug in and every guitarist since owes him a debt either directly or indirectly, while his showmanship influenced everyone from Chuck Berry to Jimi Hendrix. Yet such accolades can sometimes obscure the potency of his own music, as urbane, sophisticated and mellow a take on the blues as can be heard anywhere.

Of mixed African-American and Cherokee descent, Aaron Thibeaux Walker was raised in the Oak Cliff district of Dallas, where his parents held open house to touring blues musicians.

This brought him into contact with the likes of legendary blues pioneers such as **Blind Lemon Jefferson**, and he acted as the blind musician's "lead boy" when he was in town, guiding him and helping collect money when Lemon would play for change in saloons and in the street. However, his own singing and blues style was influenced by the more urbane style of **Leroy Carr**. During the late 1920s he toured Texas first with a medicine show and then with Ida Cox's traveling revue, and made a one-off recording for Columbia in 1929 with "Wichita Falls Blues" and "Trinity River Blues", issued under the name Oak Cliff T-Bone.

In the years that followed, he moved to Oklahoma City, where around 1933 he worked as a street duet with **Charlie Christian**. That must have been a remarkable partnership; anyone who threw coins into their hat could have had no idea that one was about to become the founding genius of electric jazz guitar, while the other would hold a similar place in blues history. Both learned from a guitarist called **Chuck Richardson**, surely one of the great unsung heroes of American musical history. Moving to Los Angeles in 1934, Walker spent the rest of the decade playing jazz and big band swing, going on to record "T-Bone Blues" with Les Hite's Orchestra in the early 1940s, although ironically he was the featured singer and not the guitarist with the band.

Walker's distinctive electric guitar sound was not heard on disc until 1942, when he cut "Mean Old World" and "I Got A Break Baby" with Freddie Slack's band for Capitol Records. These contained some of the first amplified guitar solos ever heard in a blues context, yet the style already sounded sumptuously developed, as Walker answered his smoky vocal phrases with jazzy, single-note lead lines on the electric guitar. He went on to make a string of groundbreaking recordings that defined the sound of modern blues and changed the face of American popular music, reaching something of a peak on the sides he cut between 1946 and 1948 on Black & White Records, including 1947's classic "Stormy Monday Blues" (also known as "Call It Stormy Monday") and "T-Bone Shuffle", as well as such songs as "T-Bone Jumps Again" and "Description Blues". Coupled with the explosive stage act he had by now developed, which included such tricks as playing his guitar behind his head while doing the splits, it is hard to underestimate his impact. **B.B. King** rushed straight out to get an electric guitar after hearing "Stormy Monday", **John Lee Hooker** was equally influenced, and so was just about everyone else who had ever played a guitar.

For various reasons including a heavy touring schedule and trouble with the Musician's Union, Walker did not record again until 1950, when he signed a four-year deal with Imperial Records. He cut sides in New Orleans backed by Dave Bartholomew's band, and also recorded in Detroit with T.J. Fowler and in Los Angeles with his own more jazz-oriented combo, and a horn section

Playlist
T-Bone Walker

1 T-BONE BLUES (1940) from T-Bone Blues
A lovely slow, slow blues with a great T-Bone vocal and Hawaiian-style guitar from Frank Pasley.

2 MEAN OLD WORLD (1942) from T-Bone Blues
"I drink to keep from worryin' and I smile to keep from cryin'".

3 CALL IT STORMY MONDAY (1947) from T-Bone Blues
"Tuesday's just as bad. Wednesday's even worse; Thursday's awful sad. The eagle flies on Friday, Saturday I go out to play, Sunday I go to church where I kneel down and pray".

4 T-BONE SHUFFLE (1947) from T-Bone Blues
"There's nothing wrong with you that a good shuffle boogie won't cure".

5 MISFORTUNE BLUES (1948) from Midnight Blues: The Pioneer Of The Electric Blues Guitar
"Things sure do happen funny when you haven't got a cent".

6 STROLLING' WITH BONE (1952) from The Complete Imperial Recordings
A sophisticated instrumental that sums up how smart T-Bone's electric guitar playing had become.

7 PLAY ON LITTLE GIRL (1955) from T-Bone Blues
Swinging stuff, with Little Walter Jacobs on harp.

8 TWO BONES AND A PICK (1957) from T-Bone Blues
Dueling jazz-blues guitars with Barney Kessel.

9 WHY NOT (1955) from T-Bone Blues
Later covered as "Walkin' By Myself" by Jimmy Rogers, who cheekily credited it to himself.

arranged by Maxwell Davis. He moved to Atlantic Records in 1955, recording in Chicago with Junior Wells and in Los Angeles with Barney Kessel, culminating in the superb album *T-Bone Blues*, which eventually appeared in 1960.

Walker toured Europe with the American Folk Blues Festival in 1962, but the decade's blues revival didn't impinge too much on his life, although the album *Good Feelin'*, recorded in Paris proved he was still playing as incisively as ever and won him a Grammy in 1970. He suffered a stroke from which he never fully recovered in 1974, and died in Los Angeles the following year.

⊙ **The Complete Capitol/Black & White Recordings** EMI
Three discs and 75 classic T-Bone Walker tracks from the late 1940s, superbly annotated and attractively packaged. Essential.

⊙ **T-Bone Blues** Catifsh
A 25-track compilation of T-Bone's crucial 1950s recordings, from "Mean Old World" to "T-Bone Shuffle".

⊙ **The Complete Imperial Recordings 1950–54** EMI
Almost as vital as the Black & White package, featuring potent songs, superb arrangements, fine ensemble backing and memorable solos.

⊙ **T-Bone Blues** Atlantic
A single disc of T-Bone Walker's recordings from the mid- to late 1950s, which find him trading guitar leads with jazz virtuoso Barney Kessel.

Sippie Wallace

b Houston, Texas, Nov 1, 1898; d Nov 1, 1986

With her risqué lyrics and spirited, rough-cut vocals, **Sippie Wallace** was one of the early blues queens, even if her Texas roots always held her apart from the sophisticated urbanity of some of her more cosmopolitan sisters.

The daughter of a Baptist deacon, Beulah Thomas was raised in a musical family. She learned to sing and play piano in church, but it was her older brother George Thomas who introduced her to the blues. Away from church, she began singing with her younger brother Hersal on piano, but by her mid-teens she had left home to sing with touring tent shows. In 1915, she hooked

up with Hersal again and the pair relocated to New Orleans, where she married Matt Wallace and met jazz musicians such as **King Oliver** and **Louis Armstrong**. During the early 1920s she toured "the Toby" – named for the Theater Owners Booking Association, which booked black artists into black vaudeville theaters across the South – as "The Texas Nightingale", but by 1923 she had followed her brothers to Chicago. That same year, she began recording for Okeh Records. Her first sides "Shorty George" (written by her older brother) and "Up The Country Blues" sold well enough to establish as one of the earliest recording stars of the blues. Between 1923 and 1929 she recorded more than forty sides for Okeh, writing much of her material herself with her brothers providing the arrangements. Hersal died of food poisoning in 1926, but her records were also blessed by the presence of the cream of the musicians she got to know in New Orleans, including not only Oliver and Armstrong but **Clarence Williams**, **Sidney Bechet** and **Johnny Dodds**. Among the most enduring titles she cut at the time were "I'm A Mighty Tight Woman" and "Special Delivery Blues".

As the craze for female blues singers burned itself out, Wallace moved to Detroit and quit music in 1929. During the mid-1930s, she suffered a string of personal tragedies including the death of her husband and her brother George, and turned to religion for solace. For the next four decades, she sang and played the organ at the Leland Baptist Church in Detroit, only occasionally performing secular music, including a recording session with Jimmy Noone's Orchestra in 1937 and a further session in 1946. But it was not until 1966 that she seriously resumed her career, when she was coaxed out of retirement by another early blues queen, her fellow Texan **Victoria Spivey**. They recorded an album of duets together, which wasn't released until 1970, and Wallace also recorded the 1966 album *Sippie Wallace Sings The Blues* for Storyville, which featured Little Brother Montgomery and Roosevelt Sykes. That same year she toured Europe with the American Folk Blues Festival tour of Europe. A stroke in 1970 failed to stop her recording or performing, encouraged by **Bonnie Raitt**, who became her main cheerleader and recorded several of her songs, including "I'm A Mighty Tight Woman". With Raitt's help, Wallace landed a recording deal with Atlantic Records who released the Grammy-nominated album *Sippie* in 1983. That was Wallace's last recording before she died in 1986, a much-loved grand old dame of the blues.

⊙ **Complete Recorded Works Vols 1 & 2**
Document
Forty-seven Sippie Wallace tracks on two discs, volume one covering 1923–25 and volume two 1925–45.

⊙ **Mighty Tight Woman** Drive Archive
On the 1969 album that inspired Bonnie Raitt, Sippie Wallace's voice probably sounds better at seventy than it did three or four decades earlier.

Washboard Sam

b Walnut Ridge, Arkansas, July 15, 1910; d Nov 13, 1966

To call **Washboard Sam** the most popular blues performer on his instrument during the 1930s and 1940s is perhaps misleading. To be frank, outside of hokum and vaudeville acts there wasn't much competition; the washboard was considered a quaint and outdated instrument even in rural blues circles. Nonetheless, the hundreds of sides he recorded not only as a prolific sideman but also under his own name reveal him to have been a strong singer and accomplished and often witty lyricist.

Robert Brown is believed to have been the illegitimate son of Frank Broonzy, who also fathered **Big Bill Broonzy**. Raised on a farm, he moved to Memphis in the early 1920s, where he played his washboard with **Sleepy John Estes** and **Hammie Nixon** on street corners for tips. In 1932, he moved again, this time north to Chicago, where he hooked up with Broonzy and began supporting him on his Bluebird recordings. He also played with Bukka White, Memphis Slim, Tampa Red and Jazz Gillum, billed under various names including not only Washboard Sam but Ham Gravy and Shufflin' Sam.

Washboard Sam's own sides for Bluebird and Vocalion find him singing in a deep, resonant voice, often supported on guitar by Broonzy. For a while his recordings sold in huge numbers on hits such as "Mama Don't Allow" and "Diggin' Potatoes", but by the end of the 1940s, his popularity was in a tailspin as the electric blues made the washboard seem even more of a quaint anachronism. He recorded briefly for Chess Records in 1953 and then retired, although he was persuaded to return to the stage a decade later by Willie Dixon and Memphis Slim. He visited Europe in 1964 and the same year made his final recordings for Victoria Spivey's label. He died of heart disease in 1966, aged 56.

⊙ **The Essential Washboard Sam** Classic Blues
Two discs and 36 tracks, including "Mama Don't Allow", "Parchman Farm Blues", "Back Door", "Diggin' My Potatoes", "Soap And Water Blues" and "Bucket's Got A Hole In It". Victoria Spivey, Clara Smith and Texas Alexander also appear, but there's a singular lack of information in the packaging and even the limited track-listing is wrong in places.

Walter "Wolfman" Washington

b New Orleans, Louisiana, Dec 20, 1943

Among the most talented of the second generation of New Orleans bluesmen, **Walter "Wolfman" Washington** sings in a soaring, deep soul voice and accompanies himself on guitar with a funky, choked sound typical of the city's bluesmen.

By his late teens, Washington was playing in **Lee Dorsey**'s band, performing on Dorsey's hit single, "Ride Your Pony", before he joined **Irma Thomas**'s Tornados. He next moved on to the Lastie brothers' R&B outfit, A Taste of New Orleans, before forming his own band, the **Solar System**, in the 1970s. Even then he kept up his session work, beginning a twenty-year relationship backing the singer **Johnny Adams**. In New Orleans he played a weekly late-night residency at Dorothy's Medallion Lounge where he became a tourist attraction and he finally released his first solo album, *Leader Of The Pack*, on the local Hep' Me label in 1981. Six years later he signed to Rounder Records, recording *Wolf Tracks*, *Out Of The Dark* and *Wolf At The Door*. After a spell recording for Point Blank, Washington and his band, now known as the **Roadmasters**, went back to Rounder in 1997 and released *Funk Is In The House*, featuring a classic mix of blues, R&B and funk. *Blue Moon Risin'* followed in 1999 and *On The Prowl* a year later. Although he has been quiet on the recording front of late, he remains an energetic live performer.

⊙ **Funk Is In The House** Bullseye Blues/Rounder
Blues, R&B and funk from Walter "Wolfman" Washington
in 1997, an artist hitting his peak in his fifties.

Muddy Waters

b Rolling Fork, Mississippi, April 4, 1915; d April 30, 1983

The course of not only the blues but popular music over the last half century has been shaped by the sound that emerged in Chicago in the late 1940s and 1950s. And one name reigns supreme in that music as its prime mover, the original hoochie-coochie man, **Muddy Waters**.

McKinley Morganfield was born in Mississippi in 1915. After his mother died when he was three, he was raised on Stovall's Plantation near Clarksdale by his grandmother, who gave him his nickname because as a boy he was always playing in a nearby creek. From the age of nine he worked on a farm, and was drawn to the stark but expressive story-telling power of the blues. At thirteen he took up the harmonica, and he added guitar to his repertoire four years later, under the influence of the greatest of the early Delta bluesmen, Charley Patton, Tommy Johnson, Son House and Robert Johnson, whom he knew and heard playing on and around the plantation.

Within a year or so, Waters had mastered the jagged, intense sound of bottleneck style. Singing in a clipped but emotional vocal style, he honed his skills playing at rough-and-tumble country dances and plantation picnics, in juke joints, and at rent parties around the Delta, sometimes with fiddler **Henry "Son" Sims**, who had recorded with Patton. He was first recorded on the Stovall plantation in Mississippi Delta by **Alan Lomax** for the Library of Congress in 1941. Lomax was actually looking for Robert Johnson, and was unaware that he had died three years earlier. Instead, he found the great musician who would lead the blues into its next phase, although at this stage Waters was still very much the traditional acoustic Delta bluesman, as can be heard on tracks such as "Country Blues" and "Burr Clover Country Blues". Waters was paid twenty dollars and sent two copies of his first disc, which arrived with a letter from Lomax that read : "I think that you should keep in practice because I

feel sure that sometime you will get the break that you deserve."

Lomax returned to record him the following year on several sides with the Son Sims Four, and his support encouraged him to escape from the harsh struggle of life in the Delta and head north to Chicago. "Muddy was one of the first guys to drove a tractor at our plantation," Howard Stovall recalled later. "But he wasn't the most contented tractor driver in the world and he couldn't wait to get out of farming and into a life as an entertainer."

Waters moved to Chicago in 1943, and the country boy learned fast how to hustle in the big city. Befriended, as were so many musicians arriving in the city, by **Big Bill Broonzy**, he got his first break playing guitar behind **Sonny Boy "John Lee" Williamson**. In the clubs on the West and South sides, he soon switched from acoustic to electric guitar, and made a huge impact applying Delta bottleneck style to the amplified instrument. However, he was still working by day as a truck driver when he recorded "I Can't Be Satisfied" and "I Feel Like Going Home" for the Aristocrat label, shortly to become Chess Records, in 1948. These sides were followed by "Rolling And Tumblin'", "Rollin' Stone", and "Walking Blues". All featured Waters singing in a dark, majestic voice which coupled with his electric guitar playing gave the sound a new, exciting edge and compelling urgency.

Over the next few years, Waters defined the sound of modern blues on a series of records, the power of which has seldom been equaled and never surpassed. Vital, visceral and earthy, these are the bedrock of the electric blues and continue to resonate to this day with the same thrilling force they must have packed at the time. The music was still based in the traditional blues of his native Mississippi Delta. But Muddy rapidly broadened the base of his music to incorporate new urban sounds and textures. He also recorded with some remarkable musicians, as a trio with **Little Walter** on harmonica and **Big Crawford** on bass on such 1950–51 recordings as "Louisiana Blues" and "Long Distance Call", and with other brilliant players such as **Jimmy Rogers** on second guitar, **Otis Spann** on piano, drummer **Fred Bellow** and **Willie Dixon** on bass. This line-up created the template for the modern electric blues band, heard to brilliant effect on mid-1950s performances such as "I Just Want To Make Love To You", "Hoochie Coochie Man", "I'm Ready", "I've Got

My Mojo Working", "Mannish Boy" and "You Need Love", many of them written and often produced by Dixon. Others to play in Waters' various bands over the years included guitarists Buddy Guy, Earl Hooker, Pat Hare, Luther Tucker, Sammy Lawhorn, Luther Johnson and Buddy Guy, harmonica players Little Walter, Junior Wells and James Cotton, and pianists Pinetop Perkins and Memphis Slim. Many of his sidemen went on to form their own bands, spreading the Chicago blues gospel according to Waters yet further.

In 1958, Waters made his first visit to Britain, laying the seeds of another musical revolution that would produce the likes of the **Rolling Stones**, who took their name from one of his songs. The British R&B boom of the early 1960s was vital; back home, young black audiences were turning their back on Waters and other blues performers in favor of a new clutch of soul performers, who performed a new style of dance music that didn't emphasize its roots in the poverty and hardship of the Delta but exuded a new self-confident message that would later be summed-up in the phrase "say it loud, I'm black and I'm proud".

In 1959, Waters cut a great tribute album to one of his mentors, Big Bill Broonzy – *Muddy Waters Sings Big Bill* – but it fell on largely deaf ears out-side the new white folk-blues audience. The fol-lowing year he made a storming appearance at the Newport Folk Festival, captured on a live album. But when the Rolling Stones made their first visit to America in 1964, Mick Jagger complained that in Muddy Waters, young American music fans were privileged to have the greatest blues singer in the world in their midst, but they didn't even know who he was. By contrast, the previous year he had been treated as a legend when he toured Europe with the American Folk Blues Festival.

Eventually, Muddy's lionization by British rockers such as the Stones, Yardbirds and Eric Clapton led to a revival in his fortunes at home and he swapped the traditional chitlin' circuit of Southern bars, roadhouses and dance halls for rock audiences in college auditoriums and at festivals. Chess attempt-ed to cash in on the folk-blues revival by record-ing him once again as a rural rather than urban bluesman with the 1964 album *Muddy Waters Folk Singer*. Then a few years later, as bands like Cream and the Jimi Hendrix Experience forged a new style of heavy and progressive blues-rock, Chess moved in exactly the opposite direction, attempt-ing to update his sound on a series of records that have divided blues fans ever since. 1968's *Electric Mud*, which included a version of the Stones' "Let's

Playlist
Muddy Waters

1 COUNTRY BLUES NO 1 (1941) from **Martin Scorsese Presents Muddy Waters**
"Man, I can sing!" an excited Waters exclaimed after hear-ing Alan Lomax play back this first acoustic recording on Stovall's plantation.

2 BURYING GROUND BLUES (1946) from **Martin Scorsese Presents Muddy Waters**
Muddy's first Chicago recording with a band for Lester Melrose. It remained unissued for years.

3 I CAN'T BE SATISFIED (1948) from **The Chess Box**
With this single, the Chicago electric blues were born.

4 ROLLIN' STONE (1950) from **The Chess Box**
"I wish I was a catfish, swimmin' in a deep, blue sea, I would have all you good lookin women fishin', fishin' after me".

5 ROLLIN' AND TUMBLIN' (1950) from **The Chess Box**
" Well, ahh, mmm-hmmm, owww, oww ooo, aww, oww, oh Aaa, mmm-hmmm, oww, oh oh oh owww, oww ooo, aww, oww, oh…" – and oww ooo, everybody knew exactly what he meant.

6 (I'M) YOUR HOOCHIE COOCHIE MAN (1954) from **The Chess Box**
Another milestone – the first Willie Dixon song that Waters recorded.

7 I JUST WANT TO MAKE LOVE TO YOU (1954) from **The Chess Box**
Featuring Jimmy Rogers, Little Walter, Otis Spann, Willie Dixon and Fred Bellow – perhaps the greatest blues band ever.

8 MANNISH BOY (1955) from **The Chess Box**
"I'm a man, I'm a full grown man; man, I'm a natural born lovers man".

9 GOT MY MOJO WORKING (1956) from **The Chess Box**
"I'm going down to Louisiana to get me a mojo hand, I'm gonna have all you women right here at my command".

10 THE BLUES HAD A BABY AND THEY NAMED IT ROCK'N'ROLL (1976) from **Hard Again**
A blazing sunset late in the autumn of Muddy's career, pro-duced by Johnny Winter.

Spend The Night Together", was savaged at the time, and the politest description offered by any of the standard blues reference books is "misguided." Yet in recent years the album has been reclaimed as a lost classic that created a new style of psychedelic blues. The double 1969 set *Fathers And Sons* was better received, and included contributions from Paul Butterfield and Mike Bloomfield. *The London Sessions* in 1971, which featured the likes of Georgie Fame and Rory Gallagher, kept Waters in the public eye, as did an appearance in *The Last Waltz*, the film of the Band's farewell concert.

In 1977, Waters signed with Blue Sky Records, run by **Johnny Winter**, who produced four potent albums with him in the sunset of his career. The best of these were 1977's Grammy-winning *Hard Again* and the following year's *I'm Ready*. Waters also worked live with Winter in the early 1980s before he died peacefully in his sleep of heart failure at home in Westmont, Illinois, in 1983. He was 68, and his death felt like the passing of an era.

⊙ **The Complete Plantation Recordings** Chess
An hour's worth of rural, sharecropping Muddy Waters, recorded by Alan Lomax on the porch of his cabin on Stovall's Mississippi plantation in 1941 and 1942. Indispensable.

⊙ **The Best Of Muddy Waters** Chess
Waters' first album release from the late 1950s truly delivers exactly what it promises, in the shape of storming versions of "I Can't Be Satisfied", "Hoochie Coochie Man" and "I'm Ready" among others.

⊙ **The Chess Box** Chess
Three discs and 72 tracks covering the period from 1947 to 1972 – and you still want more of this music that shook the world.

⊙ **Muddy Waters At Newport** Chess
Acoustic Mud on a sublime 13-track live recording from the 1960 Newport Folk Festival.

⊙ **Muddy Water Folk Singer** Chess
This 1964 album may have been a cynical ploy for the 1960s white college folk-boom audience – but it still sounds great.

⊙ **Electric Mud** Chess
The controversial and notorious "psychedelic" album from 1968, all distorted fuzz-tone guitars, mixing new versions of his classic songs and such oddities as "Free Press News" and a cover of the Stones' "Let's Spend The Night Together".

⊙ **Hard Again** Sony
Dating from 1977, this is the first of the four Johnny

Winter-produced albums that were Muddy Waters' grand finale, hard and feral blues that find him still touched with genius.

Johnny "Guitar" Watson

b Houston, Texas, Feb 3, 1935; d May 17, 1996

Much influenced by his fellow Texans Clarence "Gatemouth" Brown and T-Bone Walker, **Johnny "Guitar" Watson** soon followed his heroes to Los Angeles, where he cut some great blues records and became the original "gangster of love". Yet his greatest success came in the 1970s when he reinvented himself as a pimp-styled soul man, playing funk and disco music.

By his early teens Watson was already a precocious musician, playing piano around Houston with future guitar greats **Albert Collins** and **Johnny Copeland**. In 1950, he upped sticks and moved to the West Coast, where he got his first break playing piano and singing with sax player Chuck Higgins' band on his 1952 cut, "Motorhead Baby". The following year he signed with Federal as Young John Watson, finally abandoning the piano for the guitar in 1954 on the brilliant instrumental "Space Guitar" and cutting several sides backed by **Amos Milburn**'s band. Moving to the Bihari Brothers' RPM label in 1955, he cut some tough blues sides including "Hot Little Mama", "Too Tired" and "Oh Baby", with horn arrangements by Maxwell Davis. His first hit for the label came in 1955 with his version of Earl King's "Those Lonely Lonely Nights". Two years later came the first version of his signature tune "Gangster of Love", later covered by the Steve Miller Band.

Further singles including "One Kiss" and "Johnny Guitar" followed on different labels before Watson hooked up with **Johnny Otis** at King for another version of "Gangster Of Love", which made the R&B charts in 1962. That was followed by the blues ballad "Cuttin' In", while in 1964 he signed to Chess Records, reverting to the piano for a jazz-tinged album. A tour of Britain in 1965 with **Larry Williams** earned him a lot of fans for both his music and his wild stage act, and he enjoyed a 1967 hit with Williams in the shape of "Mercy, Mercy, Mercy".

Several lean years ensued before Watson re-emerged in the mid-1970s on Fantasy as a newly-fashioned funkster in a white suit, surrounded by seductive-looking women. Moving to DJM, he released further albums in a funk and disco vein, including 1977's *A Real Mother For Ya* and *Gangster Of Love*, which included an updated version of the song he had first recorded twenty years earlier. He continued recording and touring until his death, enjoying occasional hits such as "Strike On Computers" in 1984. A decade later, the album *Bow Wow* earned him a Grammy nomination for best contemporary blues album, even though it was essentially another funk collection. Watson died of a heart attack while performing at the Yokohama Blues Cafe in Japan in 1996, at the age of 61.

⊙ **The Very Best Of Johnny Guitar Watson**
Rhino
18-track compilation of Johnny "Guitar" Watson's early R&B years, from the amazing "Space Guitar" to "Gangster Of Love".

⊙ **The Funk Anthology** Shout Factory
A 2-disc anthology that chronicles Johnny "Guitar" Watson's highly successful reinvention of himself during the 1970s and 1980s.

Curley Weaver

b Covington, Georgia, March 25, 1906; d Sept 20, 1960

The so-called "Georgia Guitar Wizard", **Curley Weaver**, ranks among the finest blues guitarists of the prewar era, often heard on record playing with such better-known bluesmen as Blind Willie McTell, Buddy Moss and Barbecue Bob.

Named James at birth and raised on a cotton plantation, Weaver had by the age of ten learned to play the guitar from his mother Savannah Shepard, who also taught the brothers, **Barbecue Bob** and **Charlie Lincoln**. He later picked up slide guitar from two local but never-recorded Georgia bluesmen, Nehemiah Smith and Blind Buddy Keith. By 1925 he had moved to Atlanta, where he busked on Decatur Street with harp player Eddie Mapp, and hooked up again with Barbecue Bob and his brother.

After Bob began recording for Columbia in 1927, he organized sessions for both Lincoln and

Weaver to record for the same label the following year. Curley cut "Sweet Petunia" and "No No Blues", and also gigged with Barbecue Bob as the **Georgia Cotton Pickers**. In 1930, he met harmonica player **Eugene "Buddy" Moss**, with whom he played for the next five years under the name the Georgia Browns. He further teamed up with **Blind Willie McTell**. Working together on and off over the ensuing twenty years, they forged perhaps the most important partnership in the Piedmont blues, Weaver's six-string matching McTell's twelve-string to create a wonderfully meshing guitar sound.

Indeed, whoever Weaver was accompanying, his playing was never less than dazzling, but he swiftly began to run out of partners. Barbecue Bob died of pneumonia in 1931, Mapp was also killed, and Moss was sent to prison in 1935. That left just McTell. The pair continued playing around Atlanta, recording together as late as 1950 for the Regal label. Weaver made a few more records but was troubled by the loss of his eyesight and died in 1962, thus missing out on the folk blues revival that might have lionized him.

⊙ **Georgia Guitar Wizard** Story Of The Blues
Sixteen tracks covering Curley Weaver's early recorded work from 1928 to 1935.

Katie Webster

b Houston, Texas, Jan 11, 1936; d Sept 5, 1999

With her sassy mix of swamp blues, R&B, boogie-woogie and gospel-soul, **Katie Webster** spent years pounding the piano on other people's records before she belatedly emerged in the 1980s as a blues queen in her own right.

Kathryn Jewel Thorne was born to deeply religious parents who believed the blues to be the devil's music. The family piano was kept under lock and key, and she was only allowed to play gospel and classical music under supervision. However, she listened to blues and R&B stations on a radio she kept hidden under the bedclothes. In her teens, when her parents left for California, she persuaded them to allow her to live with relatives in Louisiana, who proved far less rigid. Under this more relaxed regime, by the age of fifteen she was playing piano on sessions for the Louisiana labels, **Excello**, based in Crowley, and **Goldband**, in Lake Charles.

During the 1950s and early 1960s, Webster played on an estimated five-hundred-plus sides, with the likes of Guitar Junior (Lonnie Brooks), Slim Harpo, Lazy Lester, Lightnin' Slim, Clifton Chenier and countless others. She also recorded under her own name with the guitarist **Ashton Savoy** and toured with her band, the Uptighters. After **Otis Redding** caught them one night in 1964 at the Bamboo Club in Lake Charles, Louisiana, he invited her to join his touring band, and she stayed with him until his death. She can be heard on his *Live At The Whiskey A-Go-Go* album, and might easily have died in the plane crash that cost Redding his life in 1967, had she not been temporarily off the road because she was heavily pregnant.

Hit hard by Redding's death, Webster retired from music to concentrate on raising her family and looking after her ailing parents. Little more was heard of her until she re-emerged in the early 1980s to became a festival favorite, both in America and Europe, where she toured every year until her health declined. She recorded for several European labels and cut *You Know That's Right* in 1985 for Arhoolie, before decamping to Alligator. There she released three albums – 1988's *Swamp Boogie Queen*, which included guest spots from Bonnie Raitt and Robert Cray; *Two Fisted Mama!* the following year; and 1991's *No Foolin'*.

Katie Webster joined label mates Koko Taylor, Lonnie Brooks and Alvin Bishop on Alligator's Twentieth Anniversary tour in 1992, but the following year she suffered a stroke while on tour in Greece, losing some of the use of her left hand and most of her eyesight. While she was no longer able to tour, she continued to make selected festival appearances. She died in 1999 aged 63.

⊙ **Deluxe Edition** Alligator
A feast of belting swamp-infested blues and boogie, compiled from the best of Katie Webster's albums for Alligator.

⊙ **Two-Fisted Mama** Alligator
Power vocals, superb piano playing and great songwriting from Katie Webster in 1989, on tracks such as "Red Negligee" and "Pussycat Moan".

The hoodoo man: Junior Wells

Junior Wells

b Memphis, Tennessee, Dec 9, 1934; d Jan 15, 1998

A superb harmonica player, **Junior Wells** made his name playing in **Muddy Waters'** band, went on to form a highly effective partnership with Buddy Guy, and released some fine records under his own name, which incorporated soul and funk into Chicago-styled blues.

The son of sharecroppers, Amos Blakemore learned harmonica from his cousin **Little Junior Parker**. When his parents separated in 1946, the already wild and rebellious twelve-year-old moved with his mother to Chicago. Despite being under age, he was soon sneaking into blues clubs to jam; among those for whom he managed to play were

Tampa Red, Big Maceo and Sunnyland Slim. On one famous occasion his sister and her boyfriend took him to Sam's Ebony Lounge to see Muddy Waters playing with Little Walter Jacobs and Jimmy Rogers. "I went up to Muddy and told him I played harp," Wells later recalled of the incident. "Muddy said he'd let me try. Little Walter said, 'That little shrimp'. They stood me on a coke box to reach the mike and I made 45 dollars in tips."

Teaming up with Louis Myers on guitar and David Myers on bass, Wells formed a trio known variously as the Little Chicago Devils, the Deuces and then the Aces, whose number was boosted to four with the addition of drummer Fred Bellow. When Little Water left Waters' band in 1952 to tour under his own name, he took the rest of the Aces along with him, while the teenage Wells replaced him in Muddy's touring band. In 1953, he was called up to the US army, but that hardly seemed to interfere with his music career. He made his first recordings under his own name for the States label, allegedly while absent without leave, when he cut "Hoodoo Man", "Cut That Out", and two instrumentals, "Eagle Rock" and "Junior's Wail", with the Aces as his backing band, as well as "Lawdy! Lawdy!" with Waters moonlighting on guitar.

After his discharge, Wells's career continued to gather pace. During the late 1950s he recorded a series of classic sides for the Chief and Profile labels,

including "Lovey Dovey Lovely One", "I Could Cry", "Messin' With The Kid" (with **Earl Hooker** on guitar), "Come On In This House" and "Little By Little", on most of which his powerful vocals were given as much prominence as his harp playing. His long association with **Buddy Guy** began in 1965, when the guitarist appeared on Wells's debut album for Delmark, *Hoodoo Man Blues*. Produced by label owner Bob Koester, it is claimed to be one of the first studio albums specifically recorded as such by any Chicago bluesman – previous blues LPs had mostly been compilations of singles or occasionally live recordings. With Guy billed as "Friendly Chap" due to his contract with Chess, and backed by a rhythm section of Jack Myers on bass and Billy Warren on drums, the album was cut in just eight hours as Koester set out to capture the dynamics and energy of a live show. Back in the singles market, Wells enjoyed R&B hits in 1966 with the brass-driven "Up In Heah" and two years later with the funky "You're Tuff Enough". He also continued a productive working partnership with Guy on a series of further albums, and in 1970 the duo teamed up with pianist Junior Mance on the album *Buddy And The Juniors*. That same year they played support dates on the Rolling Stones' American tour. Although Wells had gone quiet on the recording front by the late 1970s, as Guy's fame eclipsed his own, he continued to play a residency at Theresa's club in Chicago. During the

Playlist
Junior Wells

1 HOODOO MAN (1953) from **The Various Artists Box Set Chicago Blues Classics Vol 3**
Harmonica blues as raw, rough and ready as you could want them.

2 LAWDY! LAWDY! (1953) from **The Various Artists Box Set Chicago Blues Classics Vol 3**
This gem, with Muddy Waters moonlighting on guitar, is surprisingly hard to find.

3 I COULD CRY (1957) from **Callin' All Blues**
Everyone knew he could blow. This was the track that announced he could sing, too.

4 LITTLE BY LITTLE (1960) from **Callin' All Blues**
"What you doing, baby, you know it ain't right, I wonder what you doing that it takes all night".

5 HOODOO MAN BLUES (1965) from **Hoodoo Man Blues**
The track that launched Wells's inspired partnership with Buddy Guy.

6 YOU'RE TUFF ENOUGH (1968) from **You're Tuff Enough: The Blue Rock Studio Recordings**
Blues-funk-rock par excellence.

7 MESSIN' WITH THE KID (1974) from **Drinkin' TNT And Smokin' Dynamite**
Written about his daughter and first recorded for Chief in 1960, but this live version, from the 1974 Montreux Jazz Fest with Buddy Guy, Pinetop Perkins and Bill Wyman, takes the prize.

8 GIVE ME ONE REASON (1996) from **Come On In This House**
Tracy Chapman's song turned into a blues scorcher by Wells's searing harp and vocal, and Sonny Landreth's scorching guitar.

1990s he participated in the blues harmonica summit album, *Harp Attack*, alongside James Cotton, Carey Bell and Billy Branch, and recorded a series of albums on Telarc, the best of which was 1996's *Come On In This House*, which won the annual W.C. Handy award for best traditional blues album. The following year he was diagnosed with cancer. He suffered a heart attack while undergoing treatment, which sent him into a coma from which he never recovered before his death in 1998.

⊙ **Hoodoo Man Blues** Delmark
Junior Wells's classic and never-bettered 1965 album with Buddy Guy, featuring such superbly swaggering numbers as "Snatch It Back And Hold It", "You Don't Love Me", "Chitlin' Con Carne" and the magnificent, declamatory title track.

⊙ **Best Of The Vanguard Years** Vanguard
Eighteen tracks from Junior Wells's 1960s' stay on Vanguard, including a splendid tribute to Sonny Boy "Rice Miller" Williamson and the topical "Vietcong Blues".

⊙ **Come On In This House** Telarc
Corey Harris, Alvin Youngblood Hart, Sonny Landreth, Derek Trucks, Tab Benoit and Bob Margolin help out on Junior Wells's fine 1996 album, the highlights of which include the title track and a brilliant if surprising cover of Tracy Chapman's "Give Me One Reason".

Peetie Wheatstraw

b Ripley, Tennessee, Dec 21, 1902; d Dec 21, 1941

The mysterious **Peetie Wheatstraw** wove a rich self-mythology as a hard-living, hard-loving bad man who operated under Satanic patronage. Calling himself "The Devil's Son-In-Law" or even the "High Sheriff of Hell", he played both guitar and piano, and was a hugely popular and influential figure, who recorded some 175 sides under his own name, as well as many more as an accompanist, between 1930 and his tragic end in 1941.

Born William Bunch in the same Tennessee town as **Sleepy John Estes**, he relocated with his family to Cotton Plant, Arkansas, soon after his birth. Little is known about his early years, but in 1927 he embarked upon the life of an itinerant musician. He traveled restlessly around the Deep South for a couple of years, before he pitched up in St Louis, Missouri, in 1929, now bearing the name of

Peetie Wheatstraw, appropriated from a character in African-American folklore. His blues were initially influenced by the guitar-piano duets of **Leroy Carr** and **Scrapper Blackwell**. Concentrating on the piano (although perversely the only surviving publicity picture of him shows him holding a guitar), he worked with a large number of talented guitarists, including Lonnie Johnson, Kokomo Arnold, Charley Jordan, Casey Bill Weldon, Bumble Bee Slim, Willie Fields and Charlie McCoy. He also played the guitar with Barrelhouse Buck on piano, but according to the St Louis bluesman Henry Townsend, his real preference was to accompany his moaning, half-mumbled and slurred vocals with his own stark solo piano.

In 1930 Wheatstraw traveled to Chicago to record his first sides, in a duet with a mysterious character known only as "Neckbones". A week later, accompanied by guitarist **Charley Jordan**, he recorded a further session for Vocalion, including "Four O'Clock In The Morning" and "Tennessee Peaches Blues". Underneath his name on the record's label was written " The Devil's Son-In-Law". Over the next decade he recorded prolifically, moving first to Bluebird for whom his first single in 1931 was "Devil's Son-In-Law", backed by another shameless piece of self-promotion about himself called simply "Peetie Wheastraw". In 1934 he shifted to Decca, where several of his sides, including "Deep Sea Lover" and "The First Shall Be Last" and "The Last Shall Be First", were credited only to "The High Sheriff From Hell".

Wheatstraw was also a fine songwriter, whose subject matter included loose women, alcohol, the supernatural, gambling, suicide and murder, as well as serious social comment. Almost all of his compositions included his signature statement, "Oh, well well." Several of Robert Johnson's songs including "Terraplane Blues", "Stones In My Passway", "I'm A Steady Rollin' Man", "Little Queen Of Spades" and "Milkcow Calf's Blues" drew on Wheatstraw's imagery. He also accompanied a number of other artists, including Kokomo Arnold and Bumble Bee Slim, while his own final recordings, such as "Gangster's Blues" and "Hearse Man Blues", found him experimenting in a more jazz-inspired framework, with pianist Lil Armstrong and trumpeter Jonah Jones.

His popularity was still at a peak when he met an unfortunate death in East St Louis in 1941. The car in which he was traveling attempted to shoot a crossing in front of an oncoming train – and failed to make it. Wheatstraw was just 39. The last song he ever recorded was called "Bring Me Flowers While I'm Living" and ended with the line: "If I don't go to heaven, ooh well well, I sure don't need no flowers in hell." Ralph Ellison later based a character in his novel, *Invisible Man*, on the Wheatstraw legend and the references in his songs to bootlegging, kidnapping and gunslinging, have led some to suggest that he was the first gangster rapper, half a century before his time.

⊙ **The Devil's Son-In-Law** Story of Blues
An excellent cross-selection of Peetie Wheatstraw's material, covering the years 1930 to 1941.

⊙ **The Essential Peetie Wheatstraw** Classic Blues
Another excellent introduction to the Wheatstraw oeuvre, spread over two discs and containing 36 tracks.

⊙ **Peetie Wheatstraw Complete Recordings Vols 1–7** Document
Probably for completists only, but you have to admire Document's style.

Bukka White

b Houston, Mississippi, Nov 12, 1906; d Feb 26, 1977

Bukka White led a battle-hardened life that landed him in Parchman Farm penitentiary on an assault charge, and his rural blues had a similarly tough earthiness. "I play so rough, I stomp 'em," he once claimed, and after his release from prison he wrote and recorded a set of the most intense songs to come out of the prewar blues experience, obsessed with prison, drink and death.

Born in the Mississippi hill country in 1906 – alternatively, some authorities suggest 1909 – **Booker T Washington White** learned to play guitar when he was nine. After moving to work on an uncle's farm near Clarksdale in the Delta, he had taken to hobo-ing around the South by his mid-teens. Singing and playing blues guitar, he was influenced by **Charley Patton** and George "Bullet" Williams, whose niece he later married. He lived for a time in St Louis, drifted back to Mississippi, and made his first recordings for the Victor label in Memphis in 1930. Only a handful of these fourteen sides, which mixed blues and spirituals, were

released. Among those were two gospel numbers credited to "the Singing Preacher" – and featuring Miss Minnie, believed to be Memphis Minnie – and "The Panama Limited" and "The New Frisco Train", both of which appeared under the name Washington White and featured his favorite trick of impersonating a train.

During the Depression years White drifted around the northern cities, had a spell as a baseball pitcher with the Birmingham Black Cats in the Negro Leagues, and fought a few bouts as a boxer. He didn't record again until 1937, when thanks to **Big Bill Broonzy** he traveled to Chicago for a session for Bluebird under the direction of **Lester Melrose**, at which he recorded "Pinebluff Arkansas" and the classic "Shake 'Em On Down". This was when he was first dubbed "Bukka", although whether that was a deliberate renaming or merely a misspelling on a record label isn't clear. At the time he was awaiting trial for shooting a man in the thigh during a brawl, in which White claimed to have been "ambushed." One story has it that he actually jumped bail to make the recording session, but was soon arrested and sent back to Mississippi, where he was sentenced to a three-year stretch in Parchman Farm.

In prison White was recorded by **John** and **Alan Lomax** for the Library of Congress under his prison nickname, Washington "Barrelhouse" White. When he emerged in late 1939, he was something of a celebrity, for while he was behind bars his "Shake 'Em On Down" had become a hit and had been covered by Broonzy. Melrose wasted no time in getting White back in the studio in Chicago for a further two-day session. That resulted in a dozen sides of magnificent, timeless country blues, notable for his powerful slide guitar and gruff, intense vocals, accompanied by Washboard Sam (whom Melrose apparently paid more for the session than he did White). Several of the songs appear to have been written while White was in prison, including "Parchman Farm Blues", "Good Gin Blues", "Bukka's Jitterbug Swing", "Aberdeen Mississippi Blues" and "Fixin' To Die Blues".

After that he settled in Memphis, where he played with Frank Stokes, shared his lodgings for a while with his young unknown cousin **B.B. King**, and worked in a factory. Then he disappeared from view, and when **Bob Dylan** covered his "Fixin' To Die Blues" on his 1961 debut album, most assumed that White was long dead. However, country blues enthusiasts John Fahey and Ed Denson suspected he might still be alive, and decided to find out. Their only clue being the title of Bukka's "Aberdeen Mississippi Blues", they mailed a letter to "Bukka White (Old Blues Singer), c/o General Delivery, Aberdeen, Mississippi." By chance, one of White's relatives was working in the Post Office and forwarded the letter to him in Memphis.

A meeting was arranged, and as a result White signed a recording contract with Chris Strachwitz's Arhoolie Records in 1963. Arhoolie subsequently released three albums of new material and reworked versions of his old 78s. Some blues purists claim that the new recordings showed that White's powers had deserted him, but that's a harsh judgment. While the 1960s' material may not have quite the intensity of the sessions recorded either side of his Parchman Farm years, it's still compelling, and White and his National steel remained a popular live attraction for another decade. He toured Europe in 1967 with the American Folk Blues Festival, and the following year sang at the Olympic Games in Mexico City. During the 1970s, he also made a few appearances with his cousin B.B. King. He died in Memphis in 1977, at the age of 70.

⊙ **The Complete Bukka White** Columbia
The title may be misleading, but you do get the fourteen sides from Bukka White's 1937 and 1940 recordings, the latter described by Greg Ward as "the last great country blues session ever recorded" before amplification took over.

⊙ **Sky Songs** Arhoolie
White still sounds compelling on this 1964 album, so titled by label owner Chris Strachwitz on account of his apparent ability to "pluck songs out of the sky".

Georgia White

b Sandersville, Georgia, March 9, 1903; d circa 1980

A prolific and highly popular artist during the late 1930s, **Georgia White** sang humorous and risqué blues songs in a barrelhouse boogie-woogie style, but she also had a more serious side and cut some moving slow blues numbers.

Little is known of White's early life and the accepted date for her birth, provided by her friend

Big Bill Broonzy, remains unverified. She seems to have moved to Chicago some time in the 1920s, and began working in nightclubs, making her first recording, "When You're Smiling, The Whole World Smiles With You" with clarinettist Jimmie Noone's Apex Club Orchestra, for the Vocalion label in 1930. She did not record again for another five years, although she may have worked for Decca as a house pianist. Then, between 1935 and 1941, she cut more than a hundred sides for the label. These include such mildly risqué numbers as "I'll Keep Sitting On It", "Take Me For A Buggy Ride", "Mama Knows What Papa Wants When Papa's Feeling Blue", "Hot Nuts" and her best-known song, "You Done Lost Your Good Thing Now". She also recorded under the alias Georgia Lawson.

Although White was a pianist herself, from her first sessions until the late 1930s, she was accompanied by **Richard M. Jones** on piano, and she recorded his "Trouble In Mind" and "Jazzin' Babies Blues". On her final few sessions, she was accompanied by **Lonnie Johnson** on guitar. During the 1940s, she formed an all-women band, played (but never recorded) with **Bumble Bee Slim**, and towards the end of the decade joined **Big Bill Broonzy** as the pianist in Big Bill's Laughing Trio. She was still singing around Chicago in the 1950s and gave her last known public performance in 1959, after which she disappeared from sight.

⊙ **Trouble In Mind** EPM
Twenty-five of Georgia White's best tracks recorded between 1935 and 1941, some with piano accompaniment and some with Lonnie Johnson on guitar.

Josh White

b Greenville, South Carolina, Feb 11, 1915; d Sept 5, 1969

For many years, blues purists have tended to disparage **Josh White**, accusing him of diluting his music for white audiences. He has been derided as an "entertainer" who somehow wasn't the "real deal" because he fashioned his style to suit whatever idiom was popular at the time, although the irony is that it has usually been white blues fans who have made such complaints. Certainly in later years he sang folk, popular and protest songs, often with little trace of the blues. But the harsh judgments made against him over the years seem somewhat unfair. A brave fight-er against injustice and racial prejudice, he was considered sufficiently subversive for the FBI to compile a 473-page dossier on him. He was also undeniably a major figure in African-American music for forty years. As Bill Wyman has observed, he "let people into the blues tent, enabling them to discover all sorts of performers who perhaps, in the eyes of the experts, offer a purer undiluted blues". Or as his biographer Elijah Wald put it, "Josh White's life is the history of black American music finding a white audience."

Born in South Carolina in 1915, White had an early grounding in church music, and learned his blues acting as a youthful guide or "lead boy" for blind street singers. He began recording in 1928, playing second guitar behind **Blind Joe Taggart**, and also recorded "Wang Wang Harmonica Blues" with the Carver Boys, a white old-time country group. But by the age of seventeen he was a star in the "race" market, and from 1932 onwards he recorded prolifically for ARC. Singing his blues in a mellifluous voice, he played guitar in the classic Piedmont style. Some sides were released under the name Pinewood Tom, while gospel songs such as "There's A Man Goin' Round Takin' Names" were credited to "Joshua White, the Singing Christian". He also played sessions for **Leroy Carr, Lucille Bogan** and many others.

Some time in the early 1930s White moved to New York, which is where the purist's criticisms begin. There he found a new and predominantly white audience, appearing alongside jazz figures like **Billie Holiday** at chic cabaret venues such as Café Society, sharing stages with Paul Robeson and Leadbelly, and performing for President Roosevelt. He also fell in with the radical political crowd around Woody Guthrie and became involved with the (predominantly white) folk scene. By now he was seldom singing blues but a diet of spirituals, work songs, folk tunes and traditional ballads. Pete Seeger even called him "Mr Folk Music", and he had a huge folk-pop hit with "One Meat Ball".

White was one of the first African-American performers to visit Britain, touring regularly from the early 1950s onwards, and he also starred on Broadway and in Hollywood films. A political activist who came under the scrutiny of Senator Joe McCarthy during the communist witch-hunt of the 1950s, he lost some support for admitting

he had been "a sucker for the Communists," but he maintained an outspoken stance on civil rights and sang on the famous 1963 March on Washington, where Martin Luther King made his "I have a dream" speech. He continued to record prolifically until his death in 1969, aged 54.

⊙ **The Essential Josh White** Classic Blues
Two discs and 36 tracks concentrating on White's more blues-oriented sides.

⊙ **Josh White Sings The Blues And Sings Vols I & 2** Collectables
A single-disc reissue of two albums from 1949 and 1950 (hence the strange title), combining the potent blues of "Motherless Children" and "St James Infirmary" with covers of songs such as "Miss Otis Regrets" and "Strange Fruit".

Rev. Robert Wilkins

b Hernando, Mississippi, Jan 16, 1896; d May 26, 1987

A versatile singer and guitarist who could play ragtime, blues, minstrel songs and gospel, the **Rev. Robert Wilkins** had two careers, first in the 1930s and then, after a thirty-year absence from the scene, in the 1960s when the Rolling Stones recorded his "Prodigal Son".

Born on a Mississippi farm some twenty miles south of Memphis, Wilkins was for most of his childhood named Robert Tim Oliver, after his step-father, who taught him guitar. He reassumed the name of his birth father in 1911, when he moved to Memphis to work. During World War One he served with the US army, and he became a pro-fessional musician after returning to Memphis in 1919. During the 1920s, he worked on Beale Street with the likes of Furry Lewis, Memphis Minnie and Son House, and also played in a jug band, making his first recording session in 1928 for the Victor label when he cut the droning, one-chord "Rolling Stone". The following year he cut his best-known side, "That's No Way To Get Along", for Brunswick in Memphis's Peabody Hotel. A couple more ses-sions followed before the Depression slowed record-ing opportunities, and for a while he worked for a medicine show. He returned to the studio in 1935, recording for Vocalion in Jackson, Mississippi, with Little Son Joe and Kid Spoons. Shortly afterwards he was playing a house party when a violent fight broke out. It is not recorded whether anyone was actually killed, but Wilkins was so distressed by what happened that he turned his back on the blues. Becoming a minister in the Church of God in Christ, he began playing gospel music.

Rediscovered by blues enthusiasts during the 1960s, Wilkins recorded the 1964 album *Memphis Gospel Singer*. Although he wouldn't play blues songs, he refashioned spiritual material with his old blues feel, and also restyled "That's No Way To Get Along" as a biblical narrative called "Prodigal Son". The song was heard by Mick Jagger and Keith Richards, who four years later covered it on the Rolling Stones album, *Beggar's Banquet*.

⊙ **The Original Rolling Stone** Yazoo
Early recordings from 1928 to 1935, including "I Do Blues", "Rollin' Stone", "Jailhouse Blues", "I'll Go With Her", and "That's No Way To Get Along", which Wilkins later reworked as "Prodigal Son".

Big Joe Williams

b Crawford, Mississippi, Oct 16, 1903; d Dec 17, 1982

Big Joe Williams was in many ways the epitome of the itinerant country blues singer. While he may have been footloose, cantankerous, not always reliable and prone to get in a fight, he was also a gifted songwriter, with a gruff, powerful voice and was a fine guitarist on his trademark, customized, ringing nine-string. He lived to become a much revered elder statesman of the blues, with a recording career that lasted over six decades.

Joe's father, "Red Bone" Williams, was part Cherokee, while his musical influence came from his mother's family, the Logans. He taught himself to play guitar on a home-made instrument, and took to the hobo life around 1918 when his stepfather threw him out. Living on his wits, he made his way around levee and lumber camps, saw mills, turpentine farms, juke joints and street corners from New Orleans to Chicago, playing anywhere he could and traveling with the likes of Little Brother Montgomery, harp player "Bullet" Williams and Honeyboy Edwards.

Known for a while as "Poor Joe", Williams developed a blues style that was strongly influenced by **Charley Patton**, playing in an open G tuning and slapping and beating his guitar to provide an accom-

Big Joe, with his custom guitar

panying rhythm, sometimes hitting the cheap instruments he favored so hard that they broke. It was on account of his constantly fiddling with cracked and fractured guitars and making them good again that he hit upon the idea of adding three extra strings to create a bigger, brighter ringing sound.

In 1930 Williams settled – in so far as he ever settled anywhere – in St Louis, after marrying the singer Bessie Mae Smith. He played in local bars and jukes with the likes of pianist Walter Davis and his cousin J.D. Short, who introduced him to producer **Lester Melrose**. By then he had already accompanied other artists in the studio, and may have made his recording debut as early as the 1920s, with Jed Davenport. He certainly appeared on record with the **Birmingham Jug Band** in 1930 for the Okeh label, but his first solo sides were cut when Melrose invited him to Chicago in 1935 to record for Bluebird. This session produced the first of several versions of his most famous song, "Baby, Please Don't Go". He carried on recording for Melrose for the next decade, cutting a string of great sides including "49 Highway" and "Crawling' King Snake".

During the 1930s Williams also performed and recorded with the likes of Robert Nighthawk, Peetie Wheatstraw and **Sonny Boy "John Lee" Williamson**, with whom he developed a productive partnership that ran from 1938 until Williamson's death a decade later. The 1950s found him sidelined, as first jump blues and then the electrified Chicago sound made his rural blues seem increasingly old-fashioned, although he still recorded for various labels including Trumpet and Vee Jay. But the folk-blues revival swept him back to prominence after he hooked up with Bob Koester, founder of Delmark Records, who released the album *Piney Woods Blues* in 1961. The following year the young Bob Dylan recorded with Williams and Victoria Spivey in New York, and Williams went on to cut albums for Folkways, Bluesville, Milestone and various other labels.

He continued playing festivals and blues clubs into his seventies, touring Europe several times and even Japan, making a new notch in his walking stick to mark every gig. He died in 1982 at the age of 79.

⊙ **Complete Recorded Big Joe Williams Vol 1 1935–41** Document
The original recordings of "Baby Please Don't Go", "Break 'Em On Down" and "Crawlin' King Snake" plus 21 others from Big Joe's early and wild hobo-ing days.

⊙ **Shake Your Boogie** Arhoolie
A dozen tracks that Big Joe Williams recorded in 1960, topped up with a dozen more cut in 1969, including the topical "The Death of Dr. Martin Luther King" and "Army Man In Vietnam".

⊙ **Blues On Highway 49** Delmark
Big Joe Williams's second album for Delmark was recorded in 1962, following the previous year's *Piney Woods Blues*, and was arguably an even more spirited collection than that splendid comeback.

⊙ **These Are My Blues** Testament
A strong 1965 live recording featuring 17 songs, mostly blues standards, both Williams's own and others.

Robert Pete Williams
b Zachary, Louisiana, March 14, 1914; d Dec 31, 1980

Recorded for the first time in 1958, when he was serving a life sentence for murder in the Louisiana state penitentiary, **Robert Pete Williams** had his own special brand of blues, uniquely eerie in its jagged rhythms, disorderly harmonies and stream-of-consciousness lyrics.

Born the son of sharecroppers near Baton Rouge, Williams was unschooled and worked as a farm laborer from when he was a boy. He began playing the blues when he was twenty on a home-made instrument fashioned from a cigar box and, by his own account, was strongly influenced by Blind Lemon Jefferson. At weekends he played at local dances, country suppers and fish fries all the way through from the 1930s until 1956, when he was convicted of murder and sent to Angola, the Louisiana state penitentiary. While in prison he was visited in 1958 by the folklorist **Harry Oster**, who recorded his somber and intense voice and understated guitar on songs such as "Prisoner's Talking Blues" and "Pardon Denied Again" for the Louisiana Folklore Society and Folk-Lyric labels.

Like Leadbelly more than two decades earlier, Williams in effect sang his way out of prison, for the recordings earned him "servitude parole" in 1959. This placed various requirements on him, including a ban on leaving the state of Louisiana until 1964, but he made further recordings for the Prestige-Bluesville label, As soon as the terms of his parole expired in 1964, he played the Newport Folk Festival and from then on became a festival favorite, visiting Europe twice. He died of heart disease at the end of 1980 at the age of 66. With his strongly African-accented sound, he left a legacy of some of the most unusual and unique blues ever recorded.

⊙ **Free Again** Original Blues Classics
These stories of Robert Pete Williams's life, set to music and recorded on his release from prison in 1959, have an eerie quality that was cited by Captain Beefheart as an influence.

⊙ **It's A Long Old Road** Aim
A welcome reissue of a 1966 album produced by John Fahey.

⊙ **Robert Pete Williams** Fat Possum
This reissue of a 1971 album features Robert Pete Williams's

tribute to Slim Harpo, as well as versions of "Freight Train Blues", "Got Me Way Down" and "Matchbox Blues".

Sonny Boy Williamson; "John Lee"

b Jackson, Tennessee, March 30, 1914; d June 1, 1948

As if blues history wasn't complicated enough, two completely unrelated musicians both performed and recorded as Sonny Boy Williamson. To add to the confusion, the younger of the two, John Lee, is widely known as **Sonny Boy Williamson I**. What's more straightforward, however, is his claim to have been the most important blues harmonica player of the prewar era, and a trailblazer who led the way for Little Walter and the harpists who shaped the new sound of Chicago after World War II.

John Lee Williamson's early years in Madison County, Tennessee, remain somewhat shady. He apparently learned to play the harmonica as a boy, and while in his teens he was in a gospel quartet called the Four Lambs. As a youth, he spent his summers away from Tennessee with an uncle in St Louis. Hobo-ing around the South in the 1930s, he met and worked with Sleepy John Estes, Homesick James, Yank Rachell and Billy Boy Arnold, who claimed to have taught him how to "choke" his harmonica. He landed in Chicago around 1935, staying with Tampa Red, and made his first recordings in 1937 for the **Bluebird** label. Backed by Big Joe Williams and Robert Nighthawk, the first song he recorded (but second to be released) was "Good Morning Little Schoolgirl", which has since become one of the most covered blues songs of all time. Over the next ten years, he cut more than 120 sides, including such classics as "Early In The Morning", "Better Cut That Out" and "I Been Dealin' With The Devil".

On all of them, he displays a harp-playing style that was second to none in terms of technique, but was also allied to great emotional power. On a technical level, he worked in a cross-note tuning, in which the key of the harmonica is a fourth above that of the music, so that the notes were drawn rather than blown, allowing a slurring and bending of the notes, allied to clever hand muting and tonguing and breath control effects.

Williamson was also a superb singer with a stammering style, and his other great technique was to blend voice and harp into one continuous call and response melodic line.

He died at the age 34 after being mugged on his way home from Chicago's Plantation Club one early morning in 1948. For long it was held that he had been attacked with an ice pick, but some scholars now dispute this. His final words were "Lord have mercy." Towards the end of his life he had started to work with a group featuring amplified guitar, and had he lived he would surely have rivaled Little Walter as one of the giants of the new Chicago sound.

⊙ **Shake The Boogie** Blue Boar
These twenty-five tracks, recorded between 1937 and 1947 and arranged chronologically, neatly demonstrate the difference between pre- and postwar Chicago blues styles as the sound is progressively beefed up with piano, bass, drums and electric guitar.

⊙ **Sugar Mama** Indigo
Two dozen of the first Sonny Boy Williamson's most seminal recordings at a budget price, including "Good Morning Little School Girl", "Blue Bird Blues", "Sloppy Drunk Blues" and "Decoration Blues".

Sonny Boy Williamson II; "Rice Miller"

b Glendora, Mississippi, Dec 5, 1899; d May 25, 1965

Although he claimed to be the original, and he was certainly the older of the two bluesmen to use the name, Rice Miller was actually **Sonny Boy Williamson II**. He borrowed the appellation sometime during the late 1930s or early 1940s, and used it until his death in 1965. The pilfered moniker may have deceived some, and helped him to find work. But in the end, he needed no such deception; he was a towering talent in his own right, and his achievements as a blues harpist and singer ultimately eclipsed those of the first Sonny Boy Williamson, whom he outlived by 17 years.

The date of his arrival in the world, which took place in Mississippi somewhere between Glendora and Tutwiler, is the subject of some controversy. For years it was believed that he was born in the last month of the nineteenth century, although his gravestone gives an earlier date of 1897. More recent research, however, has claimed that he was actually born as late as 1912. There has also been some confusion over Williamson's real name. He was allegedly the youngest of 21 children born to Millie Ford, and has often been referred to as Alex (or Aleck) Ford. It was long held that he was illegitimate and took his stepfather's name. Others now claim that his mother married a man named Miller in 1895 and he was born Alex Miller, acquiring the nickname "Rice" in his youth. Read the liner notes of the many Sonny Boy Williamson reissues, and it's hard to find two discs that tell the same story.

He took up harmonica at the age of five, which, depending on which date of birth you accept, may or may not have been around the same time that **W.C. Handy** heard the blues for the first time on the platform at nearby Tutwiler railway station. Miller began playing spirituals and was soon performing on street corners as "Little Boy Blue", then left home in his teens to hobo his way around Arkansas, Mississippi, Tennessee and Missouri, playing the usual circuit of levee camps, juke joints, house parties and picnics. He later claimed to have made his first recordings during the 1920s, but no evidence exists and he was a notoriously unreliable witness, which is a polite way of admitting that he was an inveterate liar. However, it's clear that on his travels he did meet and sometimes work with a number of the great early bluesmen, including Robert Johnson, Robert Lockwood Jr. Howlin' Wolf (whose half-sister he married), and Homesick James, who remembered him as Little Boy Blue, with a belt around his waist to hold all his harmonicas. During the 1930s he worked under many aliases (due, it seems, to a warrant for his arrest), including Willie Miller, W. M., Harmonica Blowin' Slim and Sonny Boy Miller. Some believe he may have started calling himself Sonny Boy Williamson as early as 1934, which was three years before his harp-playing rival had his first hits with songs such as "Good Morning Little School Girl" and "Bluebird Blues". Once his namesake became famous, however, Miller not only stuck with the name Williamson but started insisting he was "the one and only original Sonny Boy."

It's unclear whether his identity was known to Max Moore, owner of Interstate Grocer, the makers of King Biscuit flour, and the sponsors of the King Biscuit Hour radio show, which broadcast on KFFA radio out of Helena, Arkansas. In any case, in 1941 he was employed on the program as Sonny Boy Williamson. With the first Sonny Boy several hundred miles away in Chicago, the name may even have been the idea of Moore or the radio station owner, Sam Anderson, who hosted the show. Williamson performed daily on the fifteen-minute show for several years, and helped to make King Biscuit Hour the most influential radio show in blues history, broadcasting to a huge audience around Memphis (ten percent of the nation's black population was said to reside within a fifty-mile radius), and influencing a generation of soon-to-record blues artists including Muddy Waters, B.B. King and Howlin' Wolf. He also called his road band the King Biscuit Entertainers, whose number included pianist Willie Love (later **Pinetop Perkins**), drummer James "Peck" Curtis and guitarist Joe Willie Wilkins, and he advertised their gigs over the radio. It is claimed that both Sonny Boy Williamsons met during the early 1940s and Miller agreed to call himself "Sonny Boy Williams". If so, once his rival was back in Chicago he took no notice of their alleged pact, although he did use the shortened name for live work when he was in the Windy City in the early 1950s, presumably to placate Williamson's friends and family.

In the late 1940s, he hooked up again with **Elmore James**, with whom he had worked in the 1930s. For a time the pair lodged together in Belzoni, Mississippi, where they recorded a show from O.J. Turner's drugstore, sponsored by Talaho Syrup and broadcast on stations out of Yazoo City and Greenville, and later he played harp on James's classic recording of "Dust My Broom". In 1948, he took another radio job in West Memphis, hawking Hadacol Tonic on KWEM. Around this time he also helped the young B.B. King on his way. Double-booked one night to play shows in Clarksdale and West Memphis, he gave the latter gig to the upcoming guitarist.

Despite his radio success, it wasn't until 1951 that Williamson cut his first records for the Trumpet label in Jackson, Mississippi; owner Lillian McMurry apparently believed he was the same Sonny Boy who had cut "Good Morning Little Schoolgirl". He stayed with Trumpet until the label went bust in 1955, recording such classics as "Eyesight To The Blind", "Cross My Heart", "Nine Below Zero", "Mighty Long Time" and "West

Memphis Blues". By then he had moved north to Detroit, where he worked with Baby Boy Warren, and – with the original Sonny Boy Williamson having died seven years earlier – he also began working in Chicago, where he recorded for the Chess subsidiary, Checker Records.

Backed by a stellar Chess team including **Muddy Waters** and his band, Williamson made a spectacular start to his career with Checker with "Don't Start Me Talking". He stayed with Chess until he died, recording a string of classics including "Help Me", "All My Love In Vain", "One Way Out", "Your Funeral And My Trial", "Fattening Frogs For Snakes" and "Keep It To Yourself", delivered in a sly and knowing vocal style with the wit and timing of a master.

Williamson was an awkward and difficult man with a ready temper, and stories of knife fights with other musicians featured among the many unsavory tales about his behavior. But when he toured Europe with the American Folk Blues Festival in 1963, he was a sensation. Dressed more like a city gent than a Delta bluesman in a pin-stripe suit and bowler hat, he hypnotized audiences, snapping his fingers, clicking his tongue and generally dazzling with his charismatic showmanship and larger-than-life character. He was so popular he stayed on in Europe after the end of the tour and recorded with British blues musicians, including the Yardbirds, the Animals and the organist Brian Auger. He also recorded with Matt Murphy and Memphis Slim for the European-based Storyville label.

He returned to Arkansas in early 1965, telling everyone he had "come home to die". He resumed broadcasting on *King Biscuit Hour* and died in May the same year. He may only have been 52, but his appearance at the end of his life certainly suggested the 65 that has long been accepted.

⊙ **King Biscuit Time** Arhoolie
A misleading title, as this compilation is built around the best of the sides Sonny Boy Williamson recorded for Trumpet between 1951 and 1955. However, as a bonus there's a thirteen-minute broadcast from his last King Biscuit Show in May 1965, a fortnight before he died, which finds him covering "Stormy Monday" and plugging that night's show in Greenwood, Miss.

⊙ **The Essential Sonny Boy Williamson** Chess
Forty-five potent tracks over two discs covering Sonny Boy's work for Chess from 1955 until 1964, that distill the essence of his greatest period when he was in his pomp.

⊙ **Down And Out Blues** Chess
A fine collection of sides recorded between 1955 and 1958, from "Don't Start Me Talkin'" to "Wake Up Baby".

Johnny Winter

b Beaumont, Texas, Feb 23, 1944

Born cross-eyed and albino, **Johnny Winter** is one of the greatest American white bluesrockers. For a time he seemed to get lost in the trappings of rock stardom, but he went on to prove himself as a bluesman not only on some

---

Playlist
Sonny Boy Williamson II

1 KEEP IT TO YOURSELF (1953) from **Eyesight To The Blind**
"You have a husband, I have a wife, if you start to talkin', that's gonna mess up our life".

2 ONE WAY OUT (1961) from **His Best**
As famously covered by the Allman Brothers.

3 DON'T START ME TALKING (1955) from **His Best**
"Well, I'm goin' down to Rosie's, stop at Fannie Mae's, gonna tell Fannie what I heard, her boyfriend say".

4 EYESIGHT TO THE BLIND (1951) from **Eyesight To The Blind**
The original recording for Trumpet, later re-recorded for Chess as "Born Blind".

5 NINE BELOW ZERO (1951) from **Eyesight To The Blind**
Another Trumpet recording that was re-cut in quite different style for Chess a decade later.

6 HELP ME (1963) from **His Best**
"Bring my nightshirt, put on your morning gown, darlin' I know we stripped bare but I don't feel like lying down".

7 FATTENING FROGS FOR SNAKES (1957) from **His Best**
"Took me a long time, to find out my mistakes, but I bet you my bottom dollar, I'm not fattenin' no more frogs for snakes".

8 KEEP YOUR HANDS OUT OF MY POCKET (1958) from **His Best**
"Little girl if you don't stop ravish me, I will have to put the police on you".

roots-based albums of his own but producing the last great series of albums in Muddy Waters' long career, as well as collaborating with Sonny Terry.

Although John Dawson Winter was born in Texas in 1944, his father, who was at that time serving overseas with the US Army, had been a "boss" on Stovall's plantation near Leland, Mississippi. After the war he returned to Mississippi and worked as a cotton broker. When that enterprise went broke, the family moved to Texas, but they returned to Leland every summer. "I pretty much thought of myself as being from Mississippi till I was eleven or twelve," Winter later said.

He started learning the clarinet aged five, then switched first to the ukelele and subsequently the guitar, and formed his first band, Johnny and the Jammers, in 1959 with his younger brother **Edgar** (b Beaumont, Texas, Dec 28, 1946). After winning a radio talent contest, they recorded for a local label, and then passed through a succession of Texan R&B bands. Winter also backed visiting blues musicians when they toured Texas, but his solo break came with an album he recorded with John Turner on drums and Tommy Shannon on bass in 1969, which was released on Texan label Sonobeat as *The Progressive Blues Experiment*. After *Rolling Stone* praised the album, Winter was signed by Columbia. He went on to record a string of storming blues-rock albums that showcased his skills as a guitarist, although too often the hard rock element dominated, particularly after his group, **Johnny Winter Band**, was joined by ex-McCoys **Rick Derringer** on second guitar.

During the 1970s, Winter's problems with heroin addiction and related bouts of suicidal depression led to long lay-offs and some patchy albums. *Together*, recorded in 1976 with brother Edgar, was something of a revival, and he followed it by returning to his blues roots on the albums *Nothing But The Blues* in 1977 and *White Hot And Blue* the following year. He was joined on the former by **Muddy Waters** and his band, which marked the start of a fruitful collaboration. Winter toured and played festivals as a member of Waters' backing band, and produced four albums for the great man's final comeback, *Hard Again*, *I'm Ready*, *King Bee* and *Live Hard Again*, all of which were issued on Winter's own Blue Sky label between 1977 and 1981.

After Waters' death in 1983, he collaborated with

Sonny Terry on the last album of the harp player's long career, *Whoopin'*, for Alligator Records. He also signed to Alligator as a solo artist himself, recording a trio of blues-roots albums, all of which received Grammy nominations, culminating in 1987's *Third Degree*, which featured a guest appearance by Dr. John. He went on to record for Pointblank in the 1990s. With the dust now long settled on his rock star posturings of the late 1960s and early 1970s, he can be better appreciated.

⊙ **Johnny Winter** Columbia
Fiery blues playing, in both acoustic and electric mode, characterized Winter's 1969 major label debut.

⊙ **Nothin' But The Blues** Blue Sky
After the rockist years, Johnny Winter came back to the blues on this 1977 set, fronting Muddy Waters' band and with vocal assistance from Waters himself.

⊙ **Guitar Slinger** Alligator
A 1984 outing, drenched in the blues, which served to prove that Johnny Winter not only played the guitar like a demon, he could sing as well.

Jimmy Witherspoon

b Gurdon, Arkansas, Aug 8, 1923; d Sept 18, 1997

The deep baritone voice of **Jimmy Witherspoon** spanned blues, R&B and jazz, in a vocal style anchored in the big band tradition.

Witherspoon came from a musical family and learned to sing in church, but didn't become a professional singer until after his World War II service with the Merchant Marines. While in the Marines, he made his first live performance on an Armed Forces Radio broadcast in India with an American jazz group led by Teddy Weatherford, who urged him to take up singing as a career.

Suitably encouraged, when he returned to America in 1944 Witherspoon took over from Walter Brown in **Jay McShann**'s band. He toured with McShann for the next four years, developing his deep, booming style. By 1949, he was ready to branch out on his own, and he hit gold at the first attempt with "Ain't Nobody's Business". That was followed by a fine reworking of Leroy Carr's "In The Evening When The Sun Goes Down", and he had further hits with "No Rollin' Blues" and "Big Fine Girl". He continued to record throughout the 1950s for labels including Swingtime, Federal, Chess, RCA and Atlantic. Then, as his popularity with blues and R&B audiences waned, he switched with ease to a jazz-blues idiom, appearing at the 1959 Monterey Jazz Festival with Ben Webster, Roy Eldridge, Coleman Hawkins, Woody Herman and Earl Hines. The performance was captured on the superb album *Jimmy Witherspoon At Monterey*, and the following year he was back at the festival singing with Jon Hendricks.

During the 1960s, Witherspoon toured Europe with the Buck Clayton All Stars and sang with Count Basie. One of his strongest releases of all, straddling blues and jazz, came with *Evenin' Blues* in 1963, which featured **T-Bone Walker** on guitar and Clifford Scott on saxophone. Other notable albums during the decade included 1968's *The Blues Is Now* with Brother Jack McDuff, and 1969's *The Blues Singer*, on which he was accompanied by blues-rock musicians such as Canned Heat's Harvey Mandel, organist Barry Goldberg of Electric Flag and harpist Charlie Musselwhite. The following year, he recorded with Earl Hooker, Charles Brown and rock guitarist Joe Walsh, while in 1971 he sang on Eric Burdon's album *Guilty*. After a brief spell off the road in the early 1970s, during which time he served as a blues disc jockey in Los Angeles, he assembled a new touring band that included a then-unknown young guitarist called **Robben Ford**. Continuing to record for labels such as Blue Note and Fantasy, he also cut *Love Is A Five Letter Word* with British producer Mike Vernon. A bout of cancer temporarily stilled his voice, but he recovered and went on to make further albums, including 1986's *Midnight Lady Called The Blues*, written and produced by Dr. John and Doc Pomus. In the 1990s he returned to the blues on Mike Vernon's Indigo label with the emphatically titled *The Blues, The Whole Blues And Nothin' But The Blues*.

Although his voice had lost some of its power, Witherspoon's final years found him as active as ever on the world's stages, appearing on a 1993 live album with Van Morrison and released an in-concert recording with his former protégé Robben Ford. His final recording, *Spoon's Blues*, found him backed by Duke Robillard and his band, while his last appearance came at the House of Blues in Los Angeles in August 1997, when his son Lucky performed with his father's band for the first time. He died the following month at the age of 74.

⊙ **Jimmy Witherspoon Meets The Jazz Giants** Charly
"The finest album of jazz-blues singing you are ever likely to hear," reckons the writer Tony Russell and we're not about to disagree about the excellence of these live recordings from the 1959 Monterey Jazz Festival and a club date in LA two months later.

⊙ **Blowin' In From Kansas City** Ace
All the swinging jump-blues sides from Jimmy Witherspoon's early career in one convenient collection.

⊙ **Evenin' Blues** Original Blues Classics
A 1963 recording, with T-Bone Walker on guitar and Clifford Scott on sax, and first-rate vocals by Witherspoon on tracks such as "Money's Getting Cheaper" and "Grab Me A Freight".

Jimmy Yancey

**b Chicago, Illinois, Feb 20, 1898;
d Sept 17, 1951**

Jimmy Yancey worked most of his adult life as a groundkeeper for the Chicago White Sox baseball team. But although he didn't record until 1939, long before then his boogie-woogie piano playing had influenced other, younger pianists who went on to become better-known, including **Meade "Lux" Lewis** and **Albert Ammons**.

Born in the Windy City in 1898 (some sources claim 1894), Yancey began performing in vaudeville as a tap dancer and child singer from the age of six. By 1915 he was playing piano in Chicago clubs and at rent parties and writing his own songs. A "musician's musician", he was an influence on most of the other pianists playing around town, but by 1925 he had taken a job as a groundsman at the White Sox's Comiskey Park.

He continued to play in Chicago clubs, often accompanied by his wife Mama Yancey (b Estelle Harris, Cairo, Illinois, Jan 1, 1896; d April 19, 1986), who sang and played guitar. He remained virtually unknown outside Chicago until 1936, when Meade "Lux" Lewis recorded one of his tunes, "Yancey Special". Three years later, producer Dan Qualey signed him to his Solo Art label and recorded him playing "The Fives" and "Jimmy's Stuff".

He went on to record for Victor, Okeh and Bluebird, while in 1943 he made his first recording with Mama Yancey when they cut "Make Me A Pallet On The Floor". They appeared together at New York's Carnegie Hall in 1948 and recorded their final session for Atlantic in 1951, two months before Yancey's death.

Yancey had an attractive, unostentatious earthiness to his playing, and popularized a flexible, left-handed figure that became known as "the Yancey bass". Despite his musical fame, he worked as a groundsman until his death.

After that, Mama Yancey virtually retired from music, although she was coaxed back into the recording studio in 1961 for the album *South Side Blues* with Little Brother Montgomery and again for *Mama Yancey Sings* in 1965. Her final album, *Maybe I'll Cry*, was recorded when she was 87 years old in 1983, three years before her death.

⊙ **Jimmy Yancey Collected Recorded Works Vols 1–3** Document
Three volumes of everything they could find, ranging from the sublime to the forgettable. If you only want a single disc, volume one, which covers the 1939 and 1940 sessions and contains "The Fives" and "Jimmy's Stuff" is the one to go for, although if you want Mama Yancey's vocals, they're on volume three.

ZZ Top

formed Texas 1969 by Billy F. Gibbons, Dusty Hill, and Frank Beard

The beardy Texan blues-rock trio **ZZ Top** were formed in Houston at the end of the 1960s out of two other bands, Moving Sidewalks and American Blues. After a few false starts and various line-up changes, the trio that remains together to this day was in place by 1969, led by guitarist **Billy Gibbons (b Houston, Texas, Sept 16, 1949)**, who came from a well-to-do family and learned about blues and R&B from an African-American maid.

Various explanations of the band's name have been given over the years, including that it was an amalgamation of two brands of rolling-paper, called Zig-Zag and Top, and that it was intended as a tribute to R&B legend ZZ Hill. Whatever the truth, their first release, knowingly titled *ZZ Top's First Album*, displayed their indebtedness to the blues, although it was the trio's third album, 1973's *Tres Hombres*, that provided their breakthrough. It also included their first hit and signature tune, "La Grange", about a Texan whorehouse and based on a riff borrowed from John Lee Hooker's "Boogie Chillen".

After almost burning out in the mid-1970s, the group took a three-year break to recuperate from a grueling touring schedule. When they reassembled in 1979, Gibbons and Hill discovered that unbeknown to each other, both had grown the long beards that have been their trademark ever since.

Their comeback album *Deguello* included their cover of Elmore James's "Dust My Broom" and a rollicking version of Sam & Dave's R&B hit "I Thank You". But it was their 1983 release, *Eliminator*, that became the biggest seller of the group's career, shifting ten million copies. They've continued to release an album every few years ever since. To many their southern boogie style is monotonous and even robotic, but they've retained at least one foot in the blues and have become one of American music's most enduring attractions, both mainstream and maverick at the same time.

For their support of the blues, the band was given a piece of wood from Muddy Waters' shack in Clarksdale, Mississippi. They had it made into a guitar, named it the "Muddywood", and sent it on a tour to raise funds for the Delta Blues Museum.

⊙ **One Foot In The Blues** Warners
A 17-track compilation of ZZ Top's more blues-based material, covering their first album to 1990's Recycler, although oddly "La Grange" is missing.

Yazoo Records

founded in New York late 1960s by Nick Perls (1942–87)

Taking its name from Yazoo City deep in the Mississippi Delta, **Yazoo Records** was founded by the American blues enthusiast and scholar **Nick Perls** in the late 1960s to reissue classic blues material that had long been unavailable.

Perls' family were wealthy art gallery owners, so he was able to run Yazoo with a relaxed attitude. Specializing in out-of-print recordings from the 1920s, he set about releasing albums compiled from rare 78rpm recordings by the likes of Charley Patton, Blind Willie McTell, the Memphis Jug Band, Blind Blake and Blind Lemon Jefferson. In many instances, the Yazoo releases were the first time such material had been available in thirty or more years. A number of Yazoo's indispensable albums bore cover illustrations by the underground comic artist and blues enthusiast **Robert Crumb**, and the label also issued three boxed sets of card illustrations by Crumb, one each on blues, jazz and country artists.

A true collector, Perls once spent twenty thousand dollars buying a single collection of 78s, and had one of the largest private blues archives in America, but he was broad-minded enough to record a number of younger blues and jazz performers for Yazoo, including Larry Johnson, Jo-Ann Kelly, Woody Mann, Roger Hubbard and Roy Bookbinder.

A few months before he died from an AIDS-related illness in 1987, he sold Yazoo to New Jersey's Shanachie Records, run by **Richard Nevins**, a friend for two decades. True to its word, Shanachie has kept Yazoo's catalog in print to this date. "Yazoo's mission has been, and will continue to be, to make available as many classic performances of early rural American and ethnic music as we can and at the highest standards we possibly can," Shanachie's company profile states. "The goal is to broadly disseminate these wonderful performances, the likes of which will not be seen again, and to insure their preservation in excellent sound quality via these CDs, as in many cases only one to five copies of the original 78rpm recordings have survived."

Part Three

Bluesology

Bluesology

Ten great compilations to get you started

Collecting blues records can be a lifetime's mission, and recommendations are included at the end of every biography in the A–Z in this book. However, for those looking to make a more general start to a blues collection, here are ten samplers and compilations that offer an overview of different names, styles and eras in one convenient package.

⊙ **Sweet Home Chicago: A History Of Chicago Blues** Indigo
Seventy tracks from the world's blues capital across three discs, starting with the prewar sounds of Broonzy and Tampa Red, and continuing through the golden age of Muddy and Wolf on to more recent exponents such as Luther Allison and Carey Bell.

⊙ **Beginner's Guide To The Blues** Nascente
A themed, budget-priced 3-CD set compiled by the author of this book. Disc One contains country blues legends, disc two urban classics, and disc three more contemporary exponents of the genre.

⊙ **Martin Scorsese Presents The Blues: A Musical Journey** Universal/Hip-O Records
A 5-disc, 116-track box set compiled to tie-in with Scorsese's TV series of blues films, presenting a well-focused history of the blues from Mamie Smith's "Crazy Blues" to Keb Mo and Corey Harris. This is the most expensive set recommended here; Scorsese's name seems to command a premium, but the packaging is high quality.

⊙ **Century Of The Blues: The Definitive Country Blues Collection** Chrome Dreams
Exactly a hundred tracks on four discs chronicling the history of pre-war blues, mostly acoustic but ending with a handful of early electric guitar pioneers such as Lowell Fulson and T-Bone Walker.

⊙ **The Pre-war Blues Story** Best Of Blues
Two discs and 44 tracks, with an unbeatable line-up including Skip James, Charley Patton, Blind Lemon Jefferson, Son House, Leroy Carr, Memphis Minnie, Bessie Smith, Robert Johnson, Kokomo Arnold and 35 others.

⊙ **A Century Of Blues** EMI
Another 3-disc set, well chosen to display the diversity of the blues – from the early country bluesmen up to the blues-rock explosion of the 1960s.

⊙ **Hellhounds On Their Trail: A History Of Blues Guitar 1924–2001** Indigo
Three discs and 75 tracks, chronologically arranged and themed into "acoustic roots", "the blues goes electric" and "the rock era and beyond".

⊙ Roll And Tumble Blues: A History Of Slide Guitar Indigo

A companion volume to the above that concentrates on the history of slide and bottleneck from Sylvester Weaver and Blind Lemon Jefferson to Clapton, Page and Peter Green in the late 1960s, packing an astonishing 78 tracks onto three discs at a bargain price.

⊙ Simply Blues Union Square

Another nicely compiled box-set introduction, containing some of the biggest names in blues and, for once, mostly featuring their best-known tracks. To be honest, you probably could have got the sixty tracks onto three discs rather than four, but it's still a bargain at the price.

⊙ Blues Masters Volume One: Urban Blues Rhino Records

A superb 18-track starter-pack to jump blues and the great shouters, including Lowell Fulson, T-Bone Walker, Charles Brown, Jimmy Witherspoon, Pee Wee Crayton, Guitar Slim and others.

Blues books

Considering that many of the original bluesmen could neither read nor write, the blues has generated an enormous body of literature. The list presented here is neither comprehensive nor exclusive, but most, if not all of these volumes proved invaluable during the writing of this book.

All Music Guide To The Blues ed. Vladimir Bogdanov, Chris Woodstra & Stephen Thomas Erlewine Back Beat Books

This massive guide serves a somewhat different purpose to the *Rough Guide To The Blues* in that it is essentially a record guide rather than a history, reviewing and rating more than 7000 recordings from the 1920s Delta to the modern day, encompassing vinyl, tape and CD. The end of the book holds a series of useful essays about different blues styles, but it's the reviews that are its strong point.

Bessie Chris Albertson Yale University Press

Several biographies of Bessie Smith have appeared over the years, including a slim but very readable volume by the feminist writer Elaine Fienstein. But Albertson's work, first published in 1972 and revised and updated in 2004, is considered the definitive tome. Albertson won a Grammy in 1971 for "best sleeve notes" for the Bessie Smith compilation, *The World's Greatest Blues Singer*.

Big Bill Blues William Broonzy Da Capo Press

Written in the 1950s and based on a series of letters sent by Broonzy to Belgian fan Yannick Bruynoghe. Not all of the picaresque anecdotes and tall tales he recounts may be strictly true, but that doesn't detract from a delightful read. Above all, Broonzy's own voice comes through clear and strong, in stark contrast to the stilted style of so many other obviously ghosted musical autobiographies.

Billie Holiday Stuart Nicholson Weidenfeld & Nicolson

The best of a number of biographies of Lady Day. Nicholson covers not only the music but also her personal heartache, drug addiction, alcoholism and masochistic promiscuity, against the background of the racial prejudice and legal harassment she suffered all her life.

Bill Wyman's Blues Odyssey Bill Wyman Dorling Kindersley

It's presented in glossy coffee-table format and the use of Wyman's name is perhaps a bit of a cash-in, when one suspects much of the research was done by editor Pete Doggett. But don't let that deter you. Magnificently illustrated, the text is sharp, incisive and well-informed. Wyman is a genuine and committed blues enthusiast, and as a one-stop general introduction that covers all the bases in knowledgeable but accessible fashion, his *Blues Odyssey* is hard to beat.

Black Pearls: Blues Queens Of The 1920s Daphne Duval Harrison Rutgers University Press

Harrison examines the early "classic blues" scene of the 1920s, and the world of vaudeville from which most of its leading female stars came. Chapters on Sippie Wallace, Edith Wilson, Victoria Spivey and Alberta Hunter are all based on personal interviews conducted by the author are particularly insightful.

Blues: The British Connection Bob Brunning
Helter Skelter

The inside story of how the Rolling Stones, Eric Clapton, Fleetwood Mac, Rory Gallagher and others fell in love with the blues and then re-exported the music back to America is comprehensively told by the knowledgeable Brunning. To be honest, he's not the world's greatest writer, but he does have the huge advantage of actually having been there at the time, playing with Fleetwood Mac and various other British blues bands.

Blues Fell This Morning: Meaning In The Blues Paul Oliver Cambridge University Press

Oliver's classic study of the blues, first published in 1960, was a pioneering work that has hardly been affected by subsequent scholarship. Against the social and political background of African-American experience, he examines how blues lyrics have dealt with such topics as love, sex, gambling, the supernatural, travel, work, violence, punishment, disease and death. The book was most recently revised and updated in 1990.

The Blues From Robert Johnson To Robert Cray Tony Russell Carlton

Russell is the doyen of current British blues writers and this book is a fine and accessible basic guide. Forget the title and the publisher's desperation to get the magic words "Robert Johnson" onto the front cover, for he starts far further back than that and splits his history into "the nine ages of blues", beginning with the early years of the twentieth century. Well-organized sections cover key artists and seminal recordings, and he's refreshingly unafraid to express a critical judgment, sometimes provocatively so.

Blues Highway Richard Knight Trailblazer

English writer Richard Knight took a classic road trip through the cradle of the blues, exploring the area from New Orleans to Chicago via its main arteries of Highway 61, the Mississippi River and the Illinois Central Railroad. He offers a comprehensive guide to the region's blues landmarks and historical sites along the way, and also picks out the best bars, clubs and juke joints where the blues can still be heard.

Blues-Rock Explosion ed. Summer McStravick and John Roo Old Goat Publishing

Approaching the music from the rock end of the spectrum, the authors offer a splendidly detailed history of the memorable meeting of blues and rock during the 1960s. There's plenty about the British "blues invasion", but the book also fully covers US acts such as Paul Butterfield, Canned Heat and the Allman Brothers.

Blues Traveling: The Holy Sites Of Delta Blues Steve Cheseborough University Press of Mississippi

Much like Richard Knight in *Blues Highway*, Cheseborough guides us through the birthplaces and graves of the blues greats, visits the juke joints, gospel churches and other hallowed sites, and walks the dusty roads and levees of Mississippi. Not so much a travel guide as a pilgrimage.

Blues With A Feeling: The Little Walter Story Tony Glover, Scott Dirks & Ward Gaines Routledge

A meticulously researched account of the life of perhaps the greatest blues harmonica player of them all, based on contemporary accounts and press reports as well as interviews with surviving members of his family, friends, and fellow musicians. There's a detailed analysis of his recording career, and the authors paint a fascinating picture of the Chicago scene from the 1940s through the 1960s into the bargain.

Can't Be Satisfied: The Life And Times Of Muddy Waters Robert Gordon Jonathan Cape

With a forward by Keith Richards, Gordon digs deep into the story of the original Rolling Stone. Brilliantly researched and vividly written, his account crackles with an energy that reflects the excitement of Waters' own music and combines a fan's admiration with an historian's attention to detail. Unlike so many accounts of how Chess Records operated, neither does he flinch from exposing how Waters was robbed of his true reward by the label's "creative" book-keeping.

Chasin' That Devil Music: Searching For The Blues Gayle Dean Wardlow Back Beat Books

Focusing on the great Delta bluesmen of the 1920s and 1930s such as Charley Patton, Tommy Johnson, Son House and Blind Lemon Jefferson, Wardlow's splendidly illustrated volume is really a collection of essays but each hits the spot in its own way. Among the best is his account of a three-year hunt for the death certificate of Robert Johnson.

The Curious Listener's Guide To The Blues David Evans Pedigree Books

Sponsored by American National Public Radio, Evans – a music professor at the University of Memphis – offers an accessible tour around the performers, the songs, the styles and the recordings that have made the blues what it is today. In his early days, Evans was something of a purist who once complained that the white musicians who played with the old bluesmen in the 1960s were "contaminating" the music. These days he's relaxed enough to include Presley's version of "That's All Right" and performances by Cream and Canned Heat in his list of key blues tracks.

Deep Blues Robert Palmer Viking

One of the best accounts of the evolution of the Mississippi blues and its electrification in Chicago and other cities. There are plenty of great stories about the likes of Muddy Waters and Robert Lockwood Jr. and Palmer combines both enthusiasm and erudition to make it a hugely enjoyable read as well as an educative one.

The Devil's Music Giles Oakley Da Capo Press

In 1976 Oakley was commissioned by the BBC to make a television series about the history of the blues, and traveled all over the deep South with a film crew interviewing blues artists like Victoria Spivey, Little Brother Montgomery, Bukka White, Gus Cannon and others. Of course, it spawned a book as well, and a revived edition published in 1997 both showed that most of Oakley's judgments remain astute and brought the story upto-date. There's a certain BBC tone to his prose that today may come across as a little old-fashioned, but it's still a splendid and highly intelligent account.

Father Of The Blues W.C. Handy Da Capo Press

First published in 1941, Handy's autobiography reveals him to be a consummate storyteller. His account of his own musical life spans the birth of the blues, from his own beginnings as an entertainer playing in the minstrel bands of the late nineteenth century, through his now famous early encounter with the Delta blues in 1903 on a Tutwiler railroad platform, and on to his time as a songwriter and publisher in Memphis and later New York.

Hellhound On My Trail: The Life And Legend of Robert Johnson Stephen Calt Canongate

Five years in the writing, Calt's biography, published in 2006 on the seventieth anniversary of Johnson's first recordings, strips away the myth to look at the man and his music, based on years of research and hours of new interview material. He also explores the Delta culture that spawned Johnson, compares his work to that of his predecessors and contemporaries, and analyzes his guitar playing technique and songwriting.

I Am The Blues Willie Dixon Da Capo Books

An immodest but surely justifiable title for the autobiography of the man who ran the engine room at Chess Records for most of the label's existence. There's a homespun wisdom and deep common sense to his observations on the blues and life in general, while his account of his struggles to win back his copyrights and collect his rightful royalties offers a salutary lesson. Add plenty of rich stories about the likes of Muddy Waters and Howlin' Wolf, and you have a book every blues fan should read.

The Land Where The Blues Began Alan Lomax The New Press

As the title suggests, Lomax's book concentrates on chronicling his field trips around the Mississippi Delta. It's written in an impressionistic, almost novel-like style, and scholars claim that he's sometimes over careless with details. But he saw and recorded so much that the book is still an unparalleled treasure trove of blues lore and legend.

The Life And Legend Of Leadbelly Charlie Wolfe & Kip Lornell Harper Collins

A remarkable account of one of the most fascinating and complex figures in blues history. Wolfe and Lornell marshal the available source material about Leadbelly's often rambunctious life brilliantly, and supplement it with their own fresh research and interviews.

Rage To Survive: The Etta James Story Etta James & David Ritz De Capo Press

In one of the better ghosted blues autobiographies, James delivers a disarmingly honest portrayal of her chaotic childhood and the equally chaotic world of early rhythm and blues, not flinching when it comes to an account of her own dependency on drugs and bad men.

The Real Rhythm & Blues Hugh Gregory Blandford

Gregory takes as his subject the post-war R&B explosion, starting with Louis Jordan, but additionally examines the music's roots in blues and gospel. While his explorations extend as far as doo-wop, he also takes in all the significant post-war blues developments from Chess Records to Stevie Ray Vaughan and Robert Cray, with well-judged biographies of all the major artists.

Rollin' And Tumblin': The Post-War Blues Guitarists ed. Jas Obrecht Backbeat Books

Opening with a workmanlike history of blues guitar, *Rollin' and Tumblin'* goes on to feature interviews with some of the great electric guitar pioneers and practitioners of Chicago and Delta blues, including such names as Lightnin' Hopkins, T-Bone Walker, Elmore James, Jimmy Reed, John Lee Hooker and Freddie King. We can't honestly improve on the description of critic Dave Marsh who wrote: "This book's like a river of whisky and it made me feel like a diving duck."

Searching For Robert Johnson

Peter Guralnick Secker & Warburg

A slim volume – even the dust jacket admits it's really only an "extended essay" – but then Johnson's life was itself similarly brief. Nevertheless, Guralnick masterfully rounds up everything we can verifiably know of the truth behind the legend, the analysis of his music is insightful, and there's plenty of first-hand testimony from those who knew him, such as Robert Lockwood and Johnny Shines.

Souled American: How Black Music Transformed White Culture Kevin Phinney

Billboard Books

Phinney's book is not merely about the blues, but serves as an account of the century-long march of ghetto rhythms into the mainstream from ragtime and jazz through blues and soul to rap and hip-hop. An indispensable read for music fans and students of race and culture alike.

Spinning Blues Into Gold: The Chess Brothers And The Rise Of The Blues

Nadine Cohodas Aurum

Long regarded as the definitive history of Chess Records. While some say Cohodas tries too hard to be fair to Leonard and Philip Chess when it comes to the contentious issue of the allegations of exploitation and underpayment of royalties to their musicians, she nonetheless tells the story of Chicago's mightiest label with rare insight, and *Spinning Blues Into Gold* remains essential reading for all blues fans.

Story Of The Blues Paul Oliver

University Press Of New England

First published in 1969, Oliver's history of the blues has in some respects been superseded by subsequent scholarship, but it remains a seminal text as a general introduction by one of the most respected of all blues writers, and is particularly good on the geographical, economic and social factors that shaped the music.

The Story Of Chess Records

John Collis Bloomsbury

Collis's book may lack the detail of Cohodas' *Spinning Blues Into Gold*, but it's more attractively presented and his concentration on the key stories of Muddy Waters and Howlin' Wolf and then Chuck Berry and Bo Diddley lends the book greater focus. But there are frustrations, such as a lack of a discography, which should be fundamental to any history of a record label.

Strange Fruit: Billie Holiday, Cafe Society And An Early Cry For Civil Rights

David Margolick Harper Collins

A brilliant and unusual book that is, in effect, the biography of a song, but which additionally paints fascinating portraits of the singular woman who dared to sing about such a controversial subject as lynching, and of Abel Meeropol, the white Jewish schoolteacher and communist sympathizer who wrote it. Margolick also places Holiday's 1939 recording in its socio-political context, and rounds up the reactions of those who have since covered it.

Their Eyes Were Watching God

Zora Neale Hurston Harper Modern Classics

The only novel in this list, Hurston's book was first published in 1937. Based on her own field experiences, it tells the story of Janie Crawford, a young woman who abandons her secure but mundane life to take up with an itinerant blues musician. She depicts black life with great humanity and her characterization is rich and convincing. After some initial controversy, the book is now deservedly regarded as a classic of twentieth-century American fiction.

The World Don't Owe Me Nothing

David "Honeyboy" Edwards Independent Publishing Group

A wonderfully evocative story from one of the last of the great pre-war bluesmen, compiled over five years of extensive interviews. Edwards tells a thrillingly picaresque tale of hobo-ing, jail, gambling and singing the blues, tempered by his unflinching account of the brutality regularly meted out to him as a black man in the segregated world of the old South. Plenty of stories about those he traveled with, including Big Joe Williams, Robert Johnson and Muddy Waters, contribute further to an absorbing read.

Blues websites

Like most genres of music – indeed, like anything that inspires obsession or devotion – there are thousands of websites dedicated to the blues. Here is a selection of the most interesting.

Blues Festival Guide

www.bluesfestivalguide.com

An invaluable resource that maintains a full month-by-month directory of the literally hundreds of blues festivals that take place each year in America and around the rest of the world, which are far too numerous, and too ever-changing, to list them all in print.

Blues Foundation

wwww.blues.org

Established as a non-profit corporation in Memphis in 1980, the Blues Foundation has more than 135 affiliated organizations and membership in twenty countries, and serves as a hub for those promoting blues music around the world. Its website is a superb resource that reflects its key role in preserving the history of the blues through a Hall of Fame, Lifetime Achievement Awards and the annual Blues Music Awards, formerly known as the W.C. Handy Awards.

The Foundation also supports music education initiatives through a searchable database of blues educators and artists-in-residence, a bibliography, and a collection of blues-based curricula. The website claims to be "the first point of contact for anyone looking for information about the Blues", and it's no idle boast.

Blues Highway

www.theblueshighway.com

An all-purpose blues site with a chat room (called "Muddy's Canin", it requests "no fighting, no cussing, no spitting, no gambling, no sitting on the pool table, no exceptions"), blues radio listings and downloadable broadcasts, tributes to the blues greats, essays, news and a "blues mall" offering online shopping for discs and other blues-related items.

Blueslinks

www.blueslinks.nl

At the last count in January 2006, this Dutch-based site offered a mind-boggling 3826 different links to bands, clubs, festivals and a lot more around the world. Want to know where to hear live blues in Russia? Check the link to Moscow's Roadhouse Club. Or the name of Korea's top blues band? Try Bluefrog & Company.

BluesNet

www.bluesnet.hub.org

Another great site offering downloads, an "in the press" news service about the blues from around the world, and plenty of featured artists.

Blues World

www.bluesworld.com

A blues marketplace of links to record labels, festivals, books, magazines and just about anything else blues-related that money can possibly buy. If you're looking for a rare limited edition print of Robert Johnson by Robert Crumb, then this is just the place to find it and put in a bid.

Early Blues

www.earlyblues.com

This British-based educational website contains articles and essays and information about local and national blues artists. Early Blues also offers guitar lessons and blues history courses, both classroom and correspondence-based.

Rocking The Blues

www.rockingtheblues.com

Another British-based website with blues news, band info, where you can see the best live music and links to everything else blues-related.

Blues magazines

Well, there may be a million-and-one blues websites out there, but you can't surf the net while hoppin' a freight train or greasin' a skillet (one imagines). Here's a selection of the best blues mags.

Blues in Britain
A monthly title covering the contemporary British blues scene with news, interviews, profiles, live and CD reviews, plus a national gig guide.
Blues in Britain, 10 Messaline Avenue, London W3 6JX.
www.bluesinbritain.org, info@bluesinbritain.org, 020/8723-7376.

Blues Matters!
A British-based magazine that rejoices under the slogan "Blues Without The Blinkers", nicely designed and intelligently written with a fine balance between big names and supporting new and emerging blues talent. The title recently went full-color and currently publishes six issues per year.
Blues Matters! PO Box 18, Bridgend CF33 6YW.
www.bluesmatters.com, info@bluesmatters.com, 01656/743406.

Blues & Rhythm
Features, interviews and reviews from the world of blues, R&B and gospel, founded in 1984 and published ten times a year. Also maintains a good website and publishes a monthly top ten chart.
Blues & Rhythm, Tony Burke (editor), 82 Quenby Way, Bromham, Bedfordshire, MK43 8QP.
www.bluesandrhythm.co.uk, tonyburke@bluesandrhythm.co.uk, 0123/482-6158

Blues Revue
A glossy upmarket American title that's published ten times a year. Founded in 1991 it now claims to be "the world's largest print publication devoted to the full spectrum of the blues".
Blues Revue, Route 1, Box 75, Salem, WV 26426-9604, USA.
www.bluesrevue.com, info@bluesrevue.com, 304/782-1971.

Living Blues
America's oldest blues magazine, founded in Chicago in 1970, describes itself as "the magazine of the African-American blues tradition". That emphasis is reflected in its coverage – in 35 years it has never featured a white blues artist on its cover. Published six times a year.
Living Blues Magazine, P.O. Box 1848, 301 Hill Hall, University of Mississippi, MS 38677, USA.
www.livingblues.com.

The blues on screen: VHS & DVD

The development of DVD has led to an explosion in the availability of blues titles in recent years, and resulted in many hours of previously rare footage becoming widely available for the first time. This list is by no means exhaustive, but constitutes some of the more interesting releases that landed on our doormat while writing this book.

Bill Wyman's Blues Odyssey: A Journey To Music's Heart And Soul Catfish Entertainment
The former Rolling Stone pays personal tribute to the music and musicians that inspired him. Live footage is interspersed with interviews with the likes of B.B. King, the late Sam Phillips, Buddy Guy and the children of Charley Patton and Muddy Waters, all linked by Wyman's enthusiastic commentary.

Blues Legends: Memphis Slim & Sonny Boy Williamson Live In Europe Hip-O Records
Terrific live performances from Memphis Slim and Sonny Boy "Rice Miller" Williamson, filmed in Europe between 1962 and 1965, plus three bonus numbers by Otis Spann.

Martin Scorsese Presents The Blues Snapper
Available individually or in a 7-disc box set, this series of films made for American television under the overall direction of Martin Scorsese takes the viewer on a cultural odyssey from Africa to the Mississippi Delta, Memphis and Chicago, and includes a front-row seat to performances by the likes of Ali Farka Touré, B.B. King, Ray Charles and Eric Clapton, plus archive footage of the early bluesmen. In addition to Scorsese's own film, the individual directors and titles of the seven films are Wim Wenders – *The Soul Of A Man*; Richard Pearce – *The Road To Memphis*; Charles Burnett – *Warming By The Devil's Fire*; Marc Levin – *Godfathers & Sons*; Mike Figgis – *Red, White & Blues*; Clint Eastwood – *Piano Blues*.

Deep Blues Shout Factory
Made by filmmaker Robert Mugge in 1990 with a somewhat irritating commentary by rock star Dave Stewart and writer Robert Palmer, *Deep Blues* is nevertheless a splendid voyage around the music of Mississippi and Memphis. The raw, elemental blues of the late R.L. Burnside and Junior Kimbrough from the Mississippi hill country is particularly impressive.

Blues Masters: The Essential History Of The Blues Rhino
The list of those whose performances are captured in this 103-minute film tells its own story and justifies the title – Son House, Leadbelly, Bessie Smith, B.B. King, Billie Holiday, Muddy Waters, Buddy Guy, Big Joe Turner, Mamie Smith, Jimmy Rushing, Ethel Waters with Count Basie, Big Bill Broonzy, Ida Cox, Jimmy Witherspoon and Big Joe Williams.

The Search For Robert Johnson Sony
John Hammond, Jr. explores the life and times of the legendary bluesman in this appealing film, traveling through the small towns of the Mississippi Delta and interviewing several of Robert Johnson's contemporaries and acquaintances, including Johnny Shines. He also performs Johnson's music in various Delta settings, including at the inevitable crossroads.

B.B. King: Live In Africa Geneon
King in his prime, playing before a crowd of fifty thousand people in Kinshasa, Zaire, in 1974, at a concert staged to coincide with the classic George Foreman/Muhammad Ali "rumble in the jungle" world heavyweight championship fight. Songs include "I Believe In My Soul", "Why I Sing The Blues", "Ain't Nobody Home", "Sweet Sixteen", "The Thrill Is Gone" and "Guess Who".

John Lee Hooker: Come And See About Me: The Definitive DVD Eagle Vision
A trawl through the archive footage of the great man's career, beginning with three performances from the 1960s, but with a heavy bias in favor of his comeback of the late 1980s and early 1990s, including duets with Eric Clapton, Ry Cooder, Van Morrison, Bonnie Raitt and Carlos Santana.

Muddy Waters: Messin' With The Blues DTS
Filmed at the Montreux Jazz Festival in 1974, Muddy is joined in a nine-track performance by Junior Wells, Buddy Guy and Pinetop Perkins.

American Roots Music Universal
A four-hour, four-episode television history of American roots music on two discs, narrated by Kris Kristofferson and covering not only blues but also country, gospel, folk, bluegrass. Cajun, tejano and Native American styles. Among the blues performers featured are Muddy Waters and B.B. King.

The American Folk Blues Festival 1962–69, Vols One To Three Hip-O Records
Thee individually available DVDs filmed on the famous annual AFB festival tours of Europe, with an all-star line-up that includes Sonny Boy Williamson, Willie Dixon, Lightnin' Hopkins, Victoria Spivey, T-Bone Walker, Howlin' Wolf, Big Mama Thornton, Otis Rush, Lonnie Johnson, Muddy Waters, Mississippi Fred McDowell, Big Joe Turner, Skip James and a host of others. As unmissable today as they were at the time.

The Howlin' Wolf Story: The Secret History Of Rock'n'Roll Bluebird
Director Don McGlynn's compelling portrait of the late, great Chester Burnett, including interviews with the likes of Hubert Sumlin and Billy Boy Arnold and plenty of never-before-seen footage. Savor in particular the shot of a youthful Mick Jagger gazing up at the great man with a look of awe on his face.

You See Me Laughin': The Last Of The Hill Country Bluesmen Fat Possum
This great documentary features juke-joint performers R.L. Burnside, Junior Kimbrough, Cedell Davis and T-Model Ford, plus somewhat gratuitous interviews with the likes of Iggy Pop and Bono.

Festival! Eagle Vision

Dylan and Baez get star billing on the packaging of Murray Lerner's film shot at the Newport Folk Festival between 1963 and 1966. But blues aficionados will cherish it for the footage of Son House, Mississippi John Hurt, Howlin' Wolf and the Butterfield Blues Band.

Devil Got My Woman: Blues At Newport 1966 Vestapol

By the 1966 Newport Festival Bob Dylan had long gone, leaving the stage to the likes of Son House, Bukka White, Howlin' Wolf and Skip James. Director Alan Lomax hit on the great idea of re-creating a traditional southern juke joint, stocked the bar, and let nature take its course, capturing on camera not only some scintillating performances but such wonderful scenes as that of a drunk Son House dancing with Bukka White. Hugely recommended.

Lightnin' Hopkins 1960–79 Vestapol

A compendium of archive footage of Hopkins, beginning with German filmmaker Dietrich Wavzyn's 1960 film of Lightnin' on his Houston home turf, followed by further film from 1967 and 1970 performances, and an Austin City Limits TV show from 1979 which finds him playing with a Stratocaster and a wah-wah pedal.

Legends Of Bottleneck Blues Guitar
Vestapol

Historic footage of some classic Delta bottleneck blues guitarists filmed after their rediscovery in the 1960s, including Son House, Johnny Shines, Fred McDowell, Jesse Fuller, Furry Lewis and Mance Lipscomb. They're all great, but Son House is sensational.

Legends Of Country Blues Guitar Vol. 1
Vestapol

Performances filmed between 1965 and 1970 and drawn from a wide variety of sources, featuring Big Bill Broonzy, Mississippi John Hurt, Son House, Mance Lipscomb, Rev. Gary Davis, Robert Pete Williams, Josh White and Brownie McGhee. There's no commentary or contextualizing – just the music of some of the greatest blues musicians who ever lived.

Index

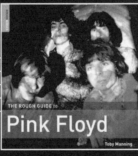